The History of Civilization

Edited by C. K. OGDEN, M.A.

Race and History

The History of Civilization

In the Section of this Series devoted to PRE-HISTORY *and* ANTIQUITY *are included the following volumes :—*

I. *Introduction and Pre-History*

*SOCIAL ORGANIZATION	W. H. R. Rivers
THE EARTH BEFORE HISTORY	E. Perrier
PREHISTORIC MAN	J. de Morgan
LANGUAGE : A LINGUISTIC INTRODUCTION TO HISTORY .	J. Vendryes
A GEOGRAPHICAL INTRODUCTION TO HISTORY . . .	L. Febvre
RACE AND HISTORY	E. Pittard
FROM TRIBE TO EMPIRE	A. Moret
*WOMAN'S PLACE IN SIMPLE SOCIETIES	J. L. Myres
*CYCLES IN HISTORY	J. L. Myres
*THE DIFFUSION OF CULTURE	G. Elliot Smith
*THE MIGRATION OF SYMBOLS	D. A. Mackenzie
*THE DAWN OF EUROPEAN CIVILIZATION	V. G. Childe

II. *The Early Empires*

THE NILE AND EGYPTIAN CIVILIZATION	A. Moret
*COLOUR SYMBOLISM OF ANCIENT EGYPT	D. A. Mackenzie
MESOPOTAMIA	L. Delaporte
THE ÆGEAN CIVILIZATION	G. Glotz

* An asterisk indicates that the volume does not form part of the French collection " L'Evolution de l'Humanité " (of which the present work is No. 5 of the First Section), published under the direction of M. Henri Berr, Editor of the " Revue de Synthêse Historique ".

A full list of the SERIES *will be found at the end of this volume.*

Race and History

An Ethnological Introduction to History

By

EUGÈNE PITTARD

Professor of Anthropology at the University of Geneva

NEW YORK

ALFRED A. KNOPF

1926

Translated by

V. C. C. COLLUM

Fellow of the Royal Anthropological Institute of Great Britain and Ireland

PRINTED IN GREAT BRITAIN BY HEADLEY BROTHERS,
18, DEVONSHIRE STREET, E.C.2 ; AND ASHFORD, KENT.

CONTENTS

PART III

THE RACES OF ASIA

PART IV

THE RACES OF AFRICA

academic authors which still permits them to use to-day the word Race *in an absolutely false sense when they are dealing with human groupings. . . . It must be fully understood that* Race, *representing the continuity of a physical type, stands for an essentially natural grouping, which can have nothing, and in general has nothing in common with the people, the nationality the language, or the customs corresponding to groupings that are purely artificial, in no way anthropological, and due entirely to history, whose actual products they are. Thus there is no Breton* Race, *but there is a Breton* People ; *no French* Race, *but a French* Nation ; *no Aryan* Race, *but Aryan Languages* ; no *Latin* Race, *but a Latin* Civilization."[1]

Here then is a sound doctrine whose rule Professor Pittard rigorously applies in the present volume. He tells us that "anthropological realities[2] have frequently been obscured by the mirages of ethnographic, linguistic and historical facts" (*p.* 54). *Beneath the "manufactured" race he seeks the anthropological "reality": before all else we have to deal with the more important of the somatic characters differentiating human groupings : build and height, colour of hair and eyes, craniological and facial form.*

The cephalic index—or the relation between the length and breadth of the skull—would appear to correspond to that distinctively racial feature most resistant to other influences, and which, being hereditary, is only modified by heredity—that is to say, by a crossing of races.[3] This establishes a radical difference between the human beings who have succeeded one another upon this earth and who have made history. Is this difference a difference in origin, or must we admit monogenism? It is an open

[1] Les Hommes Fossiles, *p.* 320. *On the nebulousness of the idea of* race, *and on the confusion of race with language and civilization, see J. de Morgan,* Prehistoric Man, *pp.* 6-7, 21, 83 ; *J. Vendryes,* Language, *pp.* 235, 304 *ff* ; *A. Moret,* From Tribe to Empire ; *A. Jardé,* The Formation of the Greek People ; *cf. L. Febvre's* le developpement des Langues et l'Histoire, *in* Rev. de Synth. Hist., *vol. xxvii* (1913), *p.* 52.

[2] *It is also advisable to limit the sense of the word* anthropology. *See* la Synthèse en Histoire, *p.* 79.

[3] *We must mention researches, however, which are still in progress relative to the chemical composition of the blood of human "races."*

question—perhaps one that can never be settled. Let us say at once that this difference is of little moment historically. The cephalic index, " though a fundamental character in any racial classification, has neither psychological nor social significance " : it is the brain within the unchanging braincase that is subject to modification.[1]

The colour of the skin, which for long has been considered as furnishing a means of distinguishing between different races of humanity, constitutes but a secondary character from the anthropological viewpoint ; but from the point of view of history it is of more importance than the cephalic index. The action of similar conditions of geographical environment, such as heat, humidity, altitude, neighbourhood of the sea, and food, which in the beginning[2] *was of capital importance in regard to human morphology and which differentiated white, black and yellow men, was exercised on the brain both directly and through the medium of social conditions. Thus there exist inner differentiations corresponding with those that are exterior. But, we repeat, the brain undergoes change : there are certain influences which operate on it alone. Human group psychology, though* corresponding *to this or that physical character, is not* linked *with it. Ultimately colour may be but an expression of obsolete conditions : the outward expression persists in vain : new conditions have produced their inward effect.*

The influence on Man's physical nature of his external environment, real and incontestable though it be, is above all Ante-Historic, *and has become progressively less.*[3] *In proportion as this factor continues to act on Man's physical nature it complicates the racial factor : it works in opposition to its original purpose. In proportion, too, as heredity assimilates*

[1] *See Cornejo, in* Sociologie générale, *Vol. I., p.* 358 ; *cf. pp.* 372 *ff.*

[2] *See Perrier,* The Earth before History, *pp.* 87, 194 ; *Febvre,* A Geographical Introduction to History, *p. viii ; M. Boule, op. cit, p.* 321 ; *de Morgan,* Les premières civilisations, *p.* 10.

[3] *See Febvre,* A Geographical Introduction to History, *pp. ix* and 100 *and Pittard, pp.* 15, 17, *where he says : " I do not wish to give the impression that under no circumstances do I believe in the influence of environment " : nevertheless, he also says : " Man, more than any other species, is in possession of the fullest means of escape, not from his environment—in which he is obliged to live—but from its reactions."*

divers elements—where new combinations are effected by the union of individuals, or, to an even greater extent, by the mingling of races—it becomes the agent of modification as much as of conservation. This contingency itself, by multiplying differences, tends to efface the great primitive distinctions. Indeed, one may say that the racial factor is constantly stultifying itself, constantly being neutralized by the very agents that produced it—environment and heredity.

Here we come face to face with that question of migration which has already crossed our path[1], *but which was deliberately reserved for consideration in this volume.*

*
* *

Certain portions of Professor Pittard's book invite us to draw indispensable distinctions in the matter of these displacements of population and their due part in history.

As we read certain passages it would almost seem that our author does not attach to such movements the importance attributed to them by others. According to him, we have been prone to believe too readily that " conquest has been necessarily followed by ethnic transformation " (p. 11). " And the actual invasions ? . . . What could have been their anthropological influences on the regions invaded ? I think that certain among them have been greatly exaggerated." (p. 12). And again he says elsewhere that in the peopling of Europe " these populations, arriving one after the other, must have caused profound ethnical perturbations among the older inhabitants. These disturbances must not be exaggerated : but neither must they be minimised." (*p.* 79).[2]

Obviously there is nothing absolute about this thesis. Though many of the invaders did not succeed in leaving any considerable ethnical imprint, Pittard does not deny that " in certain peculiarly favoured instances " such invasions were able to play the part

[1] *See Febvre,* A Geographical Introduction to History, *Foreword, p. xv.*

[2] *Cf. what de Morgan says,* Prehistoric Man, *p.* 74, *of migrations, " to which formerly perhaps too much importance was given, but which to-day seem to be too much denied."*

of modifying agencies. (*p.* 13). *He tells us that " the primitive races became mixed from the time that the wanderings of humanity over the continents became intensive. Up till the Mesolithic Western Europe knew only Dolichocephals—of different types, it is true. The arrival of the first Brachycephals profoundly disturbed this relative unity. From that day forward—and the mingling increases progressively as time goes on—it is impossible to speak of pure races as regards Europe."* (*p.* 17; *cf. p.* 85).

The perusal of this book invites and also aids towards the achievement of greater precision in the study of such phenomena as migration, conquest, colonization *and* emigration, *and will be of assistance in any search for such correlation as may exist between these phenomena and* nomadism.

Migration *is a basic phenomenon which has played a capital rôle both in pre-history and proto-history. It is the transplantation en masse of human groups that have not yet sent their roots deep into the soil. " . . . . a phenomenon not easily to be explained in terms of the principles dominating the spirit and society of our times. A modern being who pictures to himself these strung-out hordes winding over the mountains and across river fords, may borrow here and there some point of comparison from his own experience, but his thoughts soon turn to the beasts of the field and the birds of the air—to the flight of swallows, cranes or wild duck, to the herds of bison that once ranged the savannahs of the Mississippi, or those dense flocks of pigeons that darkened the skies in the North American States. This outward analogy covers certain profound resemblances, and reveals to us something of the massiveness and formlessness of the epoch. Even if we suppose that the initial impetus was an ordered one based on lucid concepts, we have to own that it was propagated by the simple play of a concrete vision and movement. A few would start moving; others would follow them—and then everybody would go. The reason, for many, being merely that " one was going." " One "—so vague and yet so comprehensive, really meaning nobody in particular—expresses with sufficient nicety the collective unity of such a group whose will prevails with each member because it is the will of all.*[1]

If we wish to understand this "initial impetus" we shall find it has both natural and psychological causes.

The physical history of the globe, from our present point of view, has had repercussions on which de Morgan has insisted with reason. He says: "The more primitive Man is, the less easy does he find it to escape from the laws of nature."[2] *He explains the primitive exoduses in part by cataclysms such as the increasing extent of the ice, floods—or their antithesis, drought. "Avesta shows us the Aryans fleeing before the machinations of the Evil Principle which ever causes to freeze and thus renders uninhabitable the lands Ahuramazda created for them. This ancient tradition indicates, in a manner impossible to mistake, the cause of the entire Aryan migration."*[3]

If physical causes, with their echoes in the animal and vegetable kingdoms, have driven away vast crowds of human beings, causes of the same order have operated to attract and retain them, as, for instance, the advantages of certain regions, or of the coast—at all events until the time when hardy groups of wanderers opened up the sea routes. It has been said of Europe in general, and particularly of Western Europe, that it constituted a cul-de-sac in which masses of immigrants succeeded or were heaped up upon each other.[4] *Professor Pittard, in different terms, speaks of it as a "vast Cosmopolis" where, from neolithic times, "races have mingled together, one superposed on top of another, in an inextricable tangle" (pp.* 74, 77, *and* 85).

This phenomenon of migration, however, has also an inner cause whose consequence varies according to time and the nature of men: this is a complex activating spring made up of the desire for change, the hope of betterment, the longing for adventure,

[1] *Ouvre.* Les formes littéraires de la Pensée grecque, *p.* 9.

[2] Des origines des Sémites et de celles des Indo-Européens, *in* Rev. de Synth. hist., *Vol. XXXIV, p.* 26.

[3] Les civilisations primitives, *p.* 163; *cf. pp.* 128, 152, 252, 313, 444. *See also* Prehistoric Man, *pp.* 5, 19, 287, 288 ff., *and art. quoted, pp.* 5, 16, 23.

[4] *On the* Migratory Routes, *see J. de Morgan, and L. Febvre, op. cit., and J. Brunhes and C. Vallaux,* La Géographie de l'Histoire, *Notes to pp.* 243-253.

the attraction of the unknown—unrest *in its etymological sense, which, if it entails mishaps, at the same time is the very spur to progress. Ratzel's "space hunger" is meaningless except as a tendency to be—and to be more at large and more at liberty. What we divine for prehistory, history itself actually demonstrates to us in those periods of feverish exaltation when whole human groups, with material ends or ideals in view, tear themselves up by the roots—temporarily, at all events—or fling themselves into some quest of the Golden Fleece, search for a Holy Land or even a New World.*[1]

Thus we see in the early days of humanity perpetual movement under the pressure of external and inner forces—movement of which no-one has given a better idea than de Morgan. One perceives dimly—to use the terminology which again and again flows from the pen of the historian—reservoirs of humanity whose flood-gates are opened, a periodic tide whose waves are dissipated in creaming foam—waters agitated by ripples and eddies.

The more attractive the regions were over which these human floods flowed, the more the different races were mingled in strife and in lending each other mutual aid, and the more freely psychic and social characters were communicated from one to another, thus giving to different peoples of composite formation characters quite foreign to the original features of their ethnic components. Ethnic purity—of a relative order—is preserved only in the most ungrateful and retired regions (as in the most humble classes among the "submerged tenth"—les pauvres diables) as Pittard calls them, with whom any alliance is undesirable). And this mingling of races appears as a factor of development, of enrichment—in such manner that isolated groups, like families whose grandeur keeps them apart from the rest, become impoverished and degenerate. France—an "ethnical synthesis"—perhaps owes her "multiform genius" (p. 134) *to her "anthropological wealth."*

In proportion as these groups become more sedentary and send their roots deeper into the soil that provides the most favourable environment, so does invasion *play its part in history.*

[1] *See Moret,* From Tribe to Empire ; *Brunhes and Vallaux, op. cit. p.* 249.

It is the phenomenon according to which a people, which has remained more or less migratory, precipitates itself, either en masse or in bands, by land or by sea, on to a people which has become rooted in the soil. The invader does not turn this people out ; no longer does the invading host drive before it the people it attacks as in the epoch of unstable populations ; it takes its place, smaller or larger as the case may be, among them ; it either disturbs or assimilates to some degree the existing civilization ; it infuses into them a certain amount of its blood. Protohistory shows us this clearly enough, especially in the East, as in Mesopotamia, Egypt, Crete and Greece, where we see sudden irruptions of barbarian hordes dislocating nascent empires.[1]

Conquest, Colonization[2] *and* Emigration *are attenuated forms of invasion and of migration and constitute the different modes of action of a sedentary group on another group—generally sedentary itself. Political ambition, economic hunger, overpopulation, political and religious persecution may establish a violent or a pacific contact between different groups and cause more or less profound repercussions in their social and psychic life, and even in their ethnic constitution. Brunhes, following Haddon, distinguishes among the movements of peoples those modifying the character of the race, in that they exert their force en masse* (Racial drift) *; and those modifying its civilization only* (Cultural drift) *in that the newcomers only infiltrate and become diluted in the earlier population of the region*[3] *; still, even infiltration is not without its " racial " influence.*[4]

As for Nomadism, *it is the survival of the primitive condition of migration into a stage in which sedentariness predominates. " Owing to scarcity of water and an infertile soil—perhaps even owing to the traditional custom of living on the resources furnished by their flocks, an easier mode of existence than living*

[1] *See* Prehistoric Man (*Conclusion*), From Tribe to Empire, Chaldæo-Assyrian Civilization, The Ægean Civilization, *and* The Formation of the Greek People.

[2] *We mean* political *conquest or annexation.*

[3] *Brunhes and Vallaux, op. cit.*, p. 229 ; *Haddon's* The Wanderings of Peoples.

[4] *For Greek colonization see Jardé,* Formation of the Greek People.

by agriculture—the Arab (of the Arabian peninsular) has preserved the methods of our earliest ancestors who wandered over the world in the wake of the most suitable habitat, seeking those physical conditions most favourable to life. Thousands of years have gone by . . . the Arab remains a nomad."[1]

Doubtless something of the spirit of adventure born of a life of adventure still clings to nomadism. An Egyptian text says of the Asiatic that he " can never remain long in the same place; his legs are always on the move."[2] *The nomad, gradually pressed back by sedentary populations, adopts the steppe and the desert for his domain. The desert and the sea, having certain characters in common,*[3] *share in a like attraction. Cahun, in his excellent* Introduction à l'Histoire de l'Asie, *tells how the Turks and Mongols found intoxication in wild gallops over the Puszla, the green moorland " dappled with flowers." Nevertheless he is of opinion that " one does not live in the desert when one can live anywhere else " and that " once the nomad comes into contact with sedentary folk he cannot do without them " ; many nomads, in fact, are vanquished men—exiles. When it is not a question of Hobson's choice, nomadism often appears to be the " way of life " that corresponds to a definite self-interest. It may be that the nomad finds resources in his pastoral life superior to those of his sedentary neighbour—especially when he complements them by adding to them those of his neighbour. The nomad is a land pirate, a corsair who, by his daring raids, takes from rich and peaceable sedentary men such resources as he lacks himself ; or he is the broker—or both at once. There is in him something of the mariner." " Throughout history the ancient peoples of the East, the nomads, have lived . . . on the borders of the sedentary folk, constituting an element of disturbance and perpetual insecurity, but also a virile source of new blood for the city populations. If they have persisted in this elementary way of life up to our own day, surviving the great empires, the very*

[1] *P. J. André,* l'Islam et les races, *I, p.* 5. *See also Moret,* From Tribe to Empire.

[2] *Moret.*

[3] *See Febvre,* A Geographical Introduction to History.

duration of this survival proves that they are a necessary element in the conditions of life Nature offers to the oriental peoples."[1]

The nomad, an effective agent in the relation between human groups, has the mobility of all fecundating germs.[2] *Though there may be epochs and zones of privileged movement, movement is always and everywhere going on. And this movement which carries human elements with it does not come to an end with migration. The various phenomena we have just passed in review constitute a perpetual stirring and mixing together of humanity.*[3] *One cannot deny the considerable influence which this mixing together—added to transformation of environment and changes of locality—exercises on race. To use Paul Lacombe's phraseology—war, and peace likewise, fighting and mutual aid, have " thoroughly mixed together the human paste."*[4] *The result is not merely a mingling of blood but, and perhaps to an even greater extent, a psychical modification.*

Even when there is no mingling of their blood, human groups in contact with one another imitate each other, and this is naturally more marked when such mingling does take place. The imitation of fashion (" imitation-mode "), to use the expression of Tarde, acts contrary to the imitation of custom (" l'imitation-coutume"), works against heredity, and moulds and diversifies the intellectual and moral type.

In such a contact between groups the social organization becomes modified not only by the psychic transformation of individuals but by action of a different nature—the new needs which may result from the density and the fresh distribution of the component parts in a composite group. That social organization is in large measure the function of the demographic nature of the group is one of the principles of the Durkheimian sociology that we should be most ready to adopt. Other things being equal (since other factors intervene), like demographical conditions tend to create like social institutions. Thus readaptations of society

[1] *Moret. See also Febvre*, pp. 329 *ff*.

[2] *Cornejo, op. cit., I., p.* 308.

[3] *See Brunhes and Vallaux, op. cit. pp.* 202-207.

[4] La psychologie des individus et des sociétés chez Taine, historien des littératures, *p.* 126.

are produced, either independently of racial action or even in opposition to it.

There is another element, however, which has its part in this elimination of the racial factor—the progress of the mind. As we said in the Foreword to A Geographical Introduction to History, *"There is an inner environment where a special causality holds sway: thanks to logical causality, humanity escapes more and more from blind determinism—from the mechanical causality of the external environment" (p. xv.). As they free themselves from their environment—Febvre made this clear in striking fashion—men escape from the chrysalis of race. The form of the head loses all relation to its content during the course of evolution: humanity becomes more and more "humanized" and men are assimilated by logical progress and pure thought in proportion as these intervene, triumph over the urge of instinct, and preside over social transformations and civilized life.*[1]

When we come to examine into the matter, the racial factor is even less consistent than the factor of environment. Environment is modified but slowly and relatively, above all under the action of human groups—in historic times. The possibilities it offers to the life of a society may sleep, grow drowsy, awake, or re-awake quite suddenly. Race effaces itself irrevocably, in all but exceptional cases of atavism. Doubtless there are—to quote a celebrated phrase—more of the dead than of the living; but the dead exert less influence by their blood than by the institutions and ideas they have left behind them: and this influence is limited as little spatially as in terms of time. It might well be said that history makes the race to a far greater degree than race makes history; but such a formula would be somewhat equivocal for it would lend to the word "race" a double meaning. One ought rather to say that the anthropological *race disintegrates and multiplies into historic races or* ethnic groups, *and that these ethnic groups mingle together and become transformed into* Peoples *and* Nations. *Nations actually interpenetrate one another even while they are making war upon one another; they accomplish*

[1] *On the social factor see Foreword to* A Geographical Introduction to History, *and on the logical factor see Foreword to* Greek Thought and the Scientific Spirit.

in common the work of civilization and tend to become unified as Society. Humanity makes—or remakes—itself; physical unity, if it ever existed, has been gradually replaced by psychical unity and the unity of resemblance has been replaced by the unity of consciousness.

Such then is the meaning of evolution in so far as it concerns race, and such is the hypothesis to be verified in the present series.

*

* *

In fine, Ethnology—*which is specially concerned with the anthropological characters of ethnic families*[1]*—should be placed in between* Prehistoric Anthropology (*to which the chapters of this book dealing with preliminary considerations are largely dedicated*), *and* Collective Ethnology *or the psychological study of given historical groups, both ancient peoples and modern nations* (*all to be dealt with methodically in successive volumes of this series*) ; *ethnology, then, fills three parts in four of the present volume.*

*Professor Eugène Pittard has been good enough to deal with the subject that was to have been treated by J. Deniker. The learned librarian of the Muséum de Paris, author of a work that has long been a classic—*Les Races et les Peuples de la Terre*—although he had meditated since* 1912 *the writing of the book I asked him to undertake, died in* 1918 *without having made sufficient progress with the work to enable another to make use of of the notes and rough drafts he left. Professor Pittard was peculiarly well placed to take over such a work, and he has followed it up with masterly devotion and with that keen and infectious enthusiasm of his for nice problems that yet are of the very greatest import and interest.*

The plan he has adopted is at once prudent and highly attractive. He certainly gives definite indications and enunciates hypotheses in so far as concerns ethnic pre-history in his general considerations ; but the major portion of his book is dedicated to a review of human groupings which play or have played their

[1] *See* La Synthèse en Histoire, *pp.* 78 *ff. Ethnology must be distinguished from ethnography, which is descriptive and not comparative and which, further, makes great use of archæological data.*

part in the full light of history. And these groupings, with which history has provided him, he analyses, proceeding from the complex to find, or at all events to glimpse, the relatively simple. He examines "country by country, such ethnological adventures as have befallen it."[1] *He has chosen the West as his jumping-off point—since he is bound to proceed along some definite line of exposition—and takes the reader thence across the continents. Here we shall no longer find the traditional division into Aryans, Semites, and Mongols—which is not entirely an anthropological one. Still, when we have followed Professor Pittard in his world-course by way of the peoples thereof, we shall have gathered a number of items of information which will mutually shed light one upon another and in their entirety will illumine to its farthest depths the mysterious past of our species.*[2]

Professor Pittard's book is more than a work of erudition: it is both a fine book and a good book. I congratulate myself on having stimulated its production, not merely because of all that it contains, but also on account of the spirit in which it has been conceived and carried out—the very spirit that inspires our series. If I am not mistaken, it was Claude Bernard who said of the scholar that he must both "possess faith and be a sceptic." Such, precisely, is the intellectual attitude of Professor Pittard.

He is a sceptic:—in other words, he is not easily convinced, is in no hurry to accept seductive theories or simplist hypotheses. He will have no share in "helping to build up the romance of prehistory" (p. 83). On the very threshold of his book he declares: "Many a time we shall have to cry 'Beware' to the imagination" (p. 9). "Let us be wise and reserve judgment" (p. 72); we must not fear to "be honest and say that we do not know" (p. 27). Classifications and genealogies have a provisory character, a "changing physiognomy"; the property of science is ceaselessly to undo that new progress may be made."[3]

He is a sceptic—yet he has a robust faith. He neither questions achieved results nor depreciates them. He even finds

[1] *Page* 78; *cf.* p. 74, *note* (1).

[2] *See pp.* 9 *and* 27.

[3] Page 88; *cf. pp.* 17, 19, 29, 40, 46, 54, 62, 65, 129.

them "encouraging" when he plumbs the full depth of our ignorance in the nineteenth century. "How far we have come during the last fifty years! Where once there seemed to be nothing but disorder and lack of precision, order has gradually been established and we are approaching clarity. Every day more light penetrates to the obscurest depths of our knowledge" (p. 470).[1] *He sets up an enthralling program of problems which have every chance of being solved by loyal collaboration between anthropologists. He has confidence in the future, provided always that the points at issue are treated by men within whose jurisdiction they come; there are some upon which none but the ethnologist has the authority to pronounce. Provided, too, that the necessary research is carried out methodically and with devotion—for up till now the body of anthropological evidence is small and has been gathered in haphazard fashion. We should ponder the many passages in which he calls for fresh excavation, indicates the fields yet to be explored,*[2] *or protests against the vandalism of archæologists who, seeking archæological objects only, have thrown aside or destroyed human remains.*[3] *These passages should be compared with those in which J. de Morgan sets before researchers the splendid scientific adventures that yet remain to be undertaken.*[4]

We cannot repeat too often that from the point of view of synthesis the study of Man's distant past has an attraction and promises a harvest of quite a different kind from that to be expected from the study of many of the texts of the Middle Ages or of modern times, which can only add a few fresh details to the history of personalities and events already comparatively well known. The synthetic mind has this virtue, that is discriminates between what is useful and what is superfluous, between the essential and the accessory, and that it directs the worker towards tasks that are both urgent and fruitful. Let us say, then, with Professor Pittard:

1 *Cf. pp.* 27, 93, 219, 387.

2 *See e.g. pp.* 292, 298, 313, 323, 332, 361, 386, 387, 392, 397, 401, 410, 431, 451, 460, *and the Conclusion.*

3 "*Archæologists alone have destroyed more bone fragments than either natural agencies or field labourers*" (p. 117); *cf. pp.* 77, 86, 101, 295, 304, 316.

4 *See also the eloquent appeals of Marcellin Boule in* Les Hommes Fossiles, *Note, p.* 175.

"Our liveliest wish is that this volume may contribute to a demonstration of the great interest of anthropological research in quarters where such interest does not yet exist, and that it may give fresh impetus to it where it has begun to languish"[1] (*p*. 470).

HENRI BERR.

[1] "*Anthropological study, in a manner of speaking, is a French science. A considerable volume of enquiries was undertaken under the inspiration of Broca and his students. Unfortunately such researches have been almost entirely abandoned at the present time in France.*" (*p*. 130.)

Our [illegible] that this [illegible] is a [illegible] of the great [illegible] in [illegible] does not [illegible] that it is the [illegible] has begun to [illegible].

RACE AND HISTORY

AUTHOR'S PREFACE

MAY not a [illegible] with [illegible] who [illegible] or [illegible] what [illegible]

For example, by [illegible] he can provide [illegible] as I [illegible] to do [illegible] the task of [illegible] and [illegible]. May not some [illegible] be more [illegible] difficult to put together than others, and may not their raw material be less [illegible] and well [illegible] — coming almost ready-made, as it does, from the [illegible] — at a disadvantage in his efforts to [illegible] it to his purpose.

Certain subjects are abundantly provided with [illegible]. By [illegible] I mean general works in which [illegible] problems [illegible] have been [illegible] that [illegible] or [illegible] the ground has been worked over again and again, whereas others are still virgin and so far as [illegible] is concerned. These differences in the condition of [illegible] even the most [illegible] to men at the same moment.

Certain subjects are like a [illegible] whose [illegible] alleys are bordered with [illegible] and set off by [illegible]. There [illegible] complacently [illegible] the [illegible] impression of the [illegible] and attention of [illegible].

Others, again, are [illegible] where the [illegible] man has scarcely [illegible]. I think [illegible]

RACE AND HISTORY

AUTHOR'S PREFACE

MAY not a scrupulous author's preliminary explanations as to the work he sets before his readers be essential, or at all events useful, when circumstances demand such explanation?

For example, by such means he can provide an excuse—as I intend to do here—for the lack of accord between his intentions and their accomplishment. May not some books be more technically difficult to put together than others, and may not their raw material be less fashioned, less well prepared? —Coming almost rough-hewn, as it does, from the quarry, the labourer using it is at a disadvantage in his efforts to mould it to his purpose.

Certain subjects are abundantly provided with literature. By literature I mean general works in which the inherent problems of such subjects have been approached from different angles: to put it differently, for such subjects the ground has been worked over again and again, whereas others are still virgin soil so far as documentation is concerned. These differences in the condition of affairs are natural: all objects, even the most attractive, have not proved of equal interest to men at the same moment.

Certain subjects are like a French garden whose straight alleys are bordered with harmoniously grouped clumps of foliage and set off by elegant pieces of statuary. There one may take one's pleasure at ease. As one's regard passes complacently over the well-kept lawns there is a general impression of the garden's venerable age, and of the daily care and attention of generations of gardeners.

Others, again, are like wild woodland where the hand of man has scarcely been felt; a thicket where there is no lack of growth but in which shrubs and plants of varying hardiness and fragrance are overrun with brambles in which the feet are continually being caught.

I have only been able, by parting the branches here and there, to let a little light penetrate into that tangled forest of applied Anthropology, in which there are but a few tentative lanes roughly cleared. It must not be thought that I have been able to do more: this work is but the first stage of the clearing process.

Even viewed thus, the collaboration of all anthropologists would be desirable for the making of such a book. It is impossible for one man authoritatively to deal with the enormous mass of documentation that has been gathered but which has not yet been adequately classified or discussed: a knowledge of each locality considered would be required in order to review it critically. It is inconceivable that one man could use, day after day, all that is written in every language on every people—unless he were to dissemble by appearing to be acquainted with it all.

This book cannot, then, be other than an outline. One must not throw dust in the eyes of the reader with regard to a subject of such delicacy, to which Morality and Sociology, along with History, are obliged to come for information—otherwise they would be but dead letters. Nor must one be in too great a hurry to be positive. There are many who "bluff" in the field of science to-day and display tinsel for gold. Even the cultivated public is too easily taken in. It is attracted, like the lark, by the dazzling reflection in a mirror. It is too ready to accept the echo rather than the authoritative voice.

All I have attempted to do is to set out facts—a few facts. But, as I have been unable to set out everything, I ask the indulgence of those confrères whose work I have not been able to mention. It is not that I do not recognize at its full value the importance of their researches and the merit of their conclusions, but simply that it was impossible for me to say everything within the limits of a single volume: hence any injustices—for which I beg to be excused! Even the choice of the ethnic groups or nations about which I should speak has necessarily been somewhat arbitrary. What criterion was I to take for guide? I have not attempted to deal with the ethnology of the United States because then I should have had to deal also with all the youthful American republics, whose history, though so engaging, was yet made only by immigrants of yesterday. In so far as possible I have dealt with countries possessing the most venerable history; that is why, in the two Americas, I have only dealt with the Incas and the Aztecs, because they are among the oldest Americans and because, during a certain time, American civilization centred in them and each of them set their seal indelibly on an epoch.

On the other hand it seemed to me imperative to say something about the Polynesian races although they have little part in History. I have been prevented by the force of circumstances from devoting more than a few short pages to such peoples as the Chinese and Japanese, whose importance is tremendous from every point of view.

Only rarely have I gone beyond what the facts themselves show. Sometimes, by a phrase, I have indicated my opinion —or by a point of interrogation I have shown where I disagree. Several volumes would have been necessary had I followed and argued with certain authors step by step.

But why labour the point further? In a word, I simply ask that my good intentions be recognized.

I have used the word race in its common acceptance, without pedantic scientific Byzantinism, as meaning simply a collection of like individuals of the same blood sprung from the same stock. In a book such as this I do not wish to enter into a discussion as to the particular sense in which one should understand the expressions genus, species, race and variety. I know well that for the monogenist the question is not without importance. But, in the pages which follow, such a discussion would serve no useful purpose.

The following definition of race, by Boule,[1] admirably suits this volume: "By race we should understand the continuity of a physical type, expressing affinities of blood, representing an essentially natural grouping, which can have nothing, and in general has nothing in common with the people, the nationality, the language, or the customs corresponding to groupings that are purely artificial, in no way

[1] *Les Hommes Fossiles*, p. 322.

anthropological, and arising entirely from history, whose actual products they are."

Anthropology has a word to say in many of the general questions envisaged by this great work on the *Evolution of Humanity*.[1] I have only been able to approach in a very modest way a few of those questions with which our studies are primarily engaged, while leaving to others, in whose domain they fall, the task of discussing their historical or sociological bearings.

In short, I simply place before the cultivated public evidence, difficult for it to procure, which will perhaps give a clearer view of certain human adventures, and which may also, perhaps, assist towards the better envisaging of the future.

My ambition goes no farther.

[1] *l'Evolution de l'Humanite*, the French series, of which this is Vol. V, incorporated into *The History of Civilization*.

PART I

GENERAL CONSIDERATIONS

CHAPTER I

Race and History

RACE and History! Does not the juxtaposition of these two words contain an entire program—suggest, in advance, a problem solved? They suppose, do they not, that race alone, without any extraneous factor, may have determined the course of History?

The question of the relation existing between the two is of importance. Is it possible seriously and scientifically to establish the relation of cause and effect between the human race on the one hand, or certain human races considered specifically as possessing particular innate characters, acting as though by destiny—and, on the other, the events of History such as have been unfolded during the course of the ages?

It is an old, old question. Historians and publicists have sought to discover such a relation—sometimes it has seemed to arise quite naturally—and to discover, too, a clearly defined mechanism, as they have gazed upon the multiform and variegated picture of the universal adventures of mankind—a picture that is very often deceptive. Faced with the more striking of these effects they have attempted to single out from among those human caprices born of the complex which we call race, the particular modifying force of the social phenomena observed.

Are we not stimulated to the imagining of such hypotheses by the spectacle of the great vanished civilizations, and of the decadence that succeeded such glories, where yet no intervention of natural causes can be regarded as the responsible factor?

Camille Jullian, in his preface to Dottin's *Les Anciens Peuples de l'Europe*,[1] wrote: ". . . for the question of

[1] **LX**, p. xi.

race, in whatever fashion one resolves it, is *the most important of all questions in the history of peoples.* [My italics.] One might almost say that we only recount this history in order to give an answer to the racial question."

If I understand the author's thought aright, history, as he envisages it, ultimately leads to the knowledge of whether a certain people belongs to the conquering race—with whom conquest, so to speak, is a natural act—and certain other peoples to the conquered race—these peoples being predestined to occupy this position of inferiority—conquering and conquered being understood here in the social as well as the military sense.

There have been great nations and great civilizations side by side with undistinguished and mediocre civilizations in every period of history. Can we say that one and the other are the simple results of racial composition?

Do there exist ethnic groups in the world—we are not here concerned with their spatial diversity—that we can separate into strong races and weak races, and of whom the first are destined to take the direction of events? Is it obligatory that the " course of the ages " should be regulated by them? On the other hand, if these strong races were able greatly to create and to maintain their lead for so long, what plausible explanation exists to account for their weakness, decadence and inevitable downfall? Why did Chaldea, Persia, Egypt, Greece and Rome, after shedding their effulgence over the world, finally fade away? To evoke some mysterious rhythm of destiny going from greatness to decrepitude, and leave it at that, without any effort to penetrate further, seems inadequate by way of an explanation.

Can it be that the stronger races allowed themselves to be infiltrated and encroached upon by elements of the weaker races and that in this way they lessened their power?—that the effects of war slowed down their birthrate of the fit, and, thus exhausted, that they let it be made good, from generation to generation, by the weaker races? So that, as the more virile types diminished with the passage of time, they were succeeded by other types, in increasing numbers, of less and less capacity? Is instability of civilization a simple function of ethnic instability—of the ebb and flow of the component racial elements to be observed in a single nation?

Is it possible to discern differences in intrinsic worth between human races?—for the sake of simplicity, we speak here of races of the same colour. Is it possible, further, to appreciate these differences ?

It is fifty years now since Gobineau gave philosophic form to such speculations. One knows with what ardour he maintained the co-existence at one and the same time of superior and inferior races, and with what warmth he defended the importance of racial purity in the creation and maintainence of the highest forms of civilization. The racial determinism of History was never in doubt for him. What did he say of the Carthaginians in connection with the battle of Zama ?—that if Rome had been defeated instead of being victorious the fate of the world would have been nowise changed, for the simple reason that the " Phœnician stock " was inferior to that from which Scipio's soldiers were sprung, and that the reciprocal relations between the two nations —the one inevitably dominating the other—would soon have been restored.

The following lines seem to me to be thoroughly representative of the doctrine of this brilliant writer :[1]

" ' All men ', say the defenders of human equality, ' are provided with an equal intellectual equipment, similar in nature, in worth ' "—anthropologists do not say that—" ' and in capacity.' These may not be their exact words, but that, at all events, is their meaning. Thus the Huron's cerebellum contains in the germ a mind in every respect similar to that of an Englishman or a Frenchman ! Why, then, did he never discover, during all these centuries, printing or steam ? If this Huron is the equal of our compatriots I might legitimately ask him how it comes about that neither a Cæsar nor a Charlemagne has been produced from among the warriors of his tribe, and by what inexplicable negligence his singers and his sorcerers have failed to become Homers and Hippocrates. The usual method of getting out of the difficulty is to bring to the fore the sovereign influence of environment. According to this doctrine an island can never know the social marvels that a continent may produce ; the north can never be as the south ; forest does not permit of the developments favoured by the open plain. *Que sais-je !* The humidity of a marsh will stimulate the growth of a civilization that the dryness of the Sahara would infallibly suffocate. However ingenious these

[1] **LXXXIV**, p. 36.

little hypotheses may be, facts are all against them. Despite wind, rain, cold, heat, drought and fertility, barbarism and civilization have flourished in turn, the world over, and on the same soil. The dull-witted *fellah* is dried up by the same sun that scorched the powerful priest of Memphis; the learned Berlin professor teaches beneath the same inclement skies that once saw the wretchedness of the uncivilized Finn."

One would need a particularly extensive knowledge of each chapter of universal History and of every detail composing it, to be able to argue these matters with Gobineau, even from the historical point of view alone. And to argue them more profoundly it would be necessary, despite his opinion, to appeal to that much-abused environment—to geography, geology, climate, enthnography, anthropology, etc. Human History is closely linked with natural History, a connection that was thoroughly well understood by the editor of the *Revue de Synthèse historique* when he inaugurated the series *l'Evolution de l'Humanité*. Sociology must be appealed to: human life is socially such a complex! Does our individual physiology and psychology—so singularly changeable—play no part in the existence of the society to which we belong? It is said that desire rules the world. But desire is a physiological state. It is not always identical in quality, or even quantity, with all men. Why?

So many questions come crowding together at the point of the pen. It will be realized that it is impossible to refer to them all, despite the interest they present. Nevertheless, the task that devolves upon us here is bound to be of some assistance in the attempt to throw light on such questions. It is a task that will be carried out, philosophically, in an altogether different manner from that of Gobineau. In his day they talked of race without knowing much about races: anthropological analysis was only just beginning to be outlined. And fundamental errors, prolonged to infinity—and still being taught to-day, alas!—inevitably fell from the pens of writers. Our studies, here, are objective. They have not been entered upon with a view of any particular demonstration. We seek neither to destroy nor to build up a theory. Our enquiry is a disinterested one, both morally and intellectually. In the following pages an ethnologist will set forth, or rather, will endeavour to set forth, so far as present research goes, an ethnic presentment of each State, spatially first, and then, where possible, in terms of time. Readers who wish to establish relations of causality between races, of which they thus catch a glimpse, and historical events, must do so for themselves. However, it may happen that the ethnologist charged with the writing of this volume will underline, from time to time, any facts that appear to him to be of such a nature as to establish a relation between race and History.

Anthropological studies of the quality of those here utilised are exposed to many dangers and run the gauntlet of many a cause for error. They run no risk so long as they are concerned with the single analysis of the morphological characters of a human group ; the results arrived at are not questioned. It is when the synthetic spirit desires to take in hand the evidence collected that misunderstandings may arise. Many a time, in the course of this work, we shall have to cry ‘ Beware ’ to the imagination. It had been well for the peace of mind of all of us if, in an endeavour to avoid calamities, anthropologists had been able to send this warning cry across the world fifty years sooner !

Our errors of ratiocination are infinite. And one asks oneself what can be done to weed out these many tares from the field of our labours. The worst and most frequent error encumbering our literature, and an error that therefore interferes with the progress of scientific achievement, is undoubtedly the constant confusion occurring, in comparisons, between convergent characters and inherited characters. Why, driven by a single desire for logic, this strenuous effort to establish a genetic link between two facts that are more or less similar, or between two more or less identical findings ? For the last thirty years comparative ethnography has been poisoned by pseudo-ethnographers who never cease covering paper with ink. Anthropologists, happily, have in general been less prolific of error. And if some among them, publicists of vivid imagination rather than laboratory students, have attempted to establish filiation between human groups similar in appearance, the harm done is not so great but that it can be rectified. Because a certain group happens to be dolichocephalic and of small stature, that is no reason why it must inevitably be related to other groups possessing these general morphological characters. Has it not been claimed, largely on the strength of such characters, that the Eskimo are undeniably the descendents of the Magdalenians of France!

Travellers in a hurry to write their accounts of their travels and anxious at any cost to provide "something new" have also disturbed the even course of our knowledge of human races. Insufficiently equipped with scientific knowledge and devoid of judgment, they have sometimes arrived at the most unexpected approximations. And since for a long time any control has been wanting, the path of knowledge has been obstructed by inexact definitions: more or less mutilated place-names permitting of certain linguistic parallels have served as the point of departure for attempts at establishing the most improbable ethnic relationships. Was there not an attempt to derive from the Caucasus those populations who brought bronze[1] to the West, simply on the strength of a linguistic resemblance in the words representing tin? In order to lend added authority to this derivation, people even went so far as to describe the mines which furnished this precious metal. Whereas it happens that tin is not found in those parts.

How much time is lost in weeding out the field cultivated thus negligently by labourers, too many of whom are unworthy!

Even our classifications, intended merely to render more clear that which seems confused, sometimes conduce to error because, in setting them up, we too easily forget their frailty, and because, at the same time, thanks to our obvious desire to simplify things, we are apt to recognize in them a higher value than that of a momentary expedient. Sometimes we confound these classifications with the eternal realities. Yet, as Cuvier said, "classification embraces only a relation of immediate contiguity; it can but place a being between two others, and is constantly found to be at fault. The true method is to see each being among all the others; to show all the ramifications by which it is linked, in a greater or lesser degree, with that vast network which constitutes organized Nature; it is this method alone which gives us a large and true conception of that Nature that is worthy of it and of its author.

[1] LXIII, p. 22.

But ten or even twenty of such connecting lines do not suffice to explain all these innumerable relationships."

That conquest has been necessarily followed by ethnic transformation is a notion that certain historians have too readily promulgated, and, thanks to them, alas! it has become a current proposition. Many other folk—among them some whom one would never expect—have assisted towards establishing this error. Certain among the vanquished, flattered at the notion that their ancestors were the victims of such and such conquerors, made famous by History, have been too ready to acquiesce in the belief that they had been thereby modified anthropoligically. Do not simple folk believe that, thanks to Roman victories, Rome peopled all the conquered districts with her soldiers ?[1] Do we not at this day see politicians and writers decorating their respective countries with similar false labels, either out of sheer love of a grandiose period, or from motives that go deeper—motives that are Roman.

See what has happened in Roumania, where the humblest shepherd, because he speaks a language derived from Latin, or because he remembers that his forbears were vanquished by Rome (it was no easy victory, either, and he would have good grounds for pride in the splendid resistance put up by the Dacians) imagines to himself that the purest blood of Trajan flows through his veins! The other so-called Latin races take a leaf out of the Roumanian shepherd's book when they vaunt with a somewhat naive vanity their characteristic language and its unexpressed and flattering suggestion—or the suggestion that is supposed to be so flattering. They picture to themselves one knows not what direct relationship to the Cæsars. Yet is this so desirable an honour ? Without a moment's hesitation I would prefer to call myself a descendent of the Dacians, or Celts, or Gauls. It is, at the least, just as honourable ; and, moreover, it conforms more nearly to the truth.

Conquest, to leave an ethnic imprint, must be followed by colonization. And here, too, let us understand one another.

[1] That is to say, in this connection, men belonging to her ethnic group.

The Greek colonization in Asia Minor and Italy was not carried out by men of " Greek race." Demographical statistics alone show that it was not possible. The same applies for Carthage and the Arabs. It is essential that these platitudes, which may lead to such hopeless confusion, should be rooted out of our textbooks. And if I am insistent, it is because one is constantly coming across such inaccuracies in one's reading, constantly hearing them repeated in conversation.

Further, does such present-day colonization as we may be able to instance bring to the conquered country human elements that come from the conquering people alone? We know well that this is not the case. What we can here observe for ourselves should prove a salutary warning to us when we are discussing the past. Certain parts of Algeria and Tunisia contain many more Spaniards, Italians and Maltese than Frenchmen. Has it not often been said: France conquers that others may colonize? The chances of war have sometimes given vast territories to quite small human groups. The conqueror could not occupy it all with his own unaided strength. He could not, however potent and eugenic his birthrate, give it his racial physiognomy. He contented himself with sending administrators out to it and establishing garrisons which were frequently composed of mercenaries of highly varied races, and often even of natives of the occupied country. Because the language of the conqueror was imposed on the vanquished, that is not to say that the conqueror himself modified in any way whatever the ethnic character of the conquered.

And the actual invasions? Invasions such as we usually picture them to ourselves—veritable movements of a whole people trekking en masse with no hope of return? What could have been their anthropological influences on the regions invaded? I think that certain among them have been greatly exaggerated. In the first place these invasions were not accomplished by means of the vast hordes which writers, employing literary artifices intended to strike the imagination, apparently indicate to us. Such hordes would have hopelessly hindered the rapidity of movement of the fighting men, a condition essential to conquest. They would have been an encumbrance to those forming the active invading party. Then conquest itself ceaselessly decimates the conquering forces by death in battle and also by diseases of which it is the cause. How much, ethnically speaking, would remain of an invading body—which we will suppose to have been of homogeneous race when it set forth—at the end of a certain period ?

An example taken at random will suffice, in regard to invading groups, to convince anyone of the semi-impossibility of their leaving behind anywhere any considerable anthropological souvenir or of their imposing any ethnic imprint. Something I have been reading, à propos the Iberian peninsular, makes me think of the Visigoths. Let us juxtapose certain dates and certain facts in this connection. The Emperor Valens authorized the Visigoths, in 376, to establish themselves on the right bank of the Danube. Two years after this they are already plundering the Balkan peninsular, fighting the Romans at Hadrianople, and advancing on Constantinople. Theodosius repulses them, but they continue to devastate Thrace, Macedonia and Illyria. How many of these Visigoths, warring in such wise, remained at the end of some years ? The facts are positive—for us they are demonstrative : types of the Germanic race which one might attribute to the presence of these Visigoths are rare in the Balkan peninsular.

In 410 the Visigoths sacked Rome. In 412 they were between the Loire and the Pyrenees : in 415 in Spain. Thirty-nine years have passed since their establishment on the right bank of the Danube. Are we here dealing with a single invasion ? The men who were twenty-five when they set out would now be sixty-five—if they had survived so much adventuring. What racial influence will they be able to exercise on Spain ? Will it even be perceptible ? In any case it could be but slight.

And when Roderic, their last king, was vanquished by the Arabs in 711, to what ethnic family, I ask, did the armies belong which the conquerers from Africa had to overcome ? Were they still composed of Visigoths ? That is scarcely credible. We shall see, when we come to study Spain, that it is sufficiently difficult to discover any groups among the population of that country which could be anthropologically linked up with the Visigoths : men of Germanic type are rare in Iberia. Then, it is always possible that the Visigoths did not belong to the Germanic race !

What has been said of the Visigoths could quite well be extended to other invasions. However, I would not obstinately deny that these, in certain peculiarly favoured cases, have succeeded in playing the modifying rôle that they are believed to have played. There are examples to the contrary.

For a very long period—from proto-historic times at the least—the purest of ethnic groups have allowed themselves to be penetrated by foreign blood. Ethnic cohesion was menaced from the day that privileged individuals came to possess territory up till then common to all : from the day that personal wealth became possible. Once the social laws ceased to forbid and strictly to guard against exogamy, those who had possessions sought to increase them by making alliances from among those around them. Those who became chiefs, nobles and aristocrats endeavoured in marriage to extend their patrimony. And the last thing that they worried about was the foreign blood that they introduced into their clan. That is why, in every race—in the least modified races, those in which the principal groups have remained outside the great streams of human circulation—it is the " submerged tenth " who possess the highest degree of ethnic nobility.

The abuse of the influence of physical environment as the principal determinant of variations in Man reveals to us another attempt at facile explanation in the application of the law of minimum effort. What has not been solemnly put down to it ? With what assurance has it been sought to convince us that environment is everything, that men are eminently plastic beings, submitting without protest to every sort of influence ! No single character could resist the moulding hand of environment, that all-powerful sculptor who, just as education renders our intellect and moral character rigid, petrifies as with a glaze our different morphologies. Has not the influence of " environment " been invoked to explain the anatomical variety seen in Jews, thenceforward acquired by very reason of such influence ? Does not the morphological Americanization of various European immigrants in America, call, on certain points, for all reserve on our part ? What mechanism other than hybridization could environment employ to mould the cranial character of the new Americans ? No one is able to tell us.

I am well aware of one definite fact in America : the average height of the American, in certain parts, is greater than that of the Europeans from whom they are sprung.

Here, however, we can make out the explanation—mesological, but one in which economic and social environment alone come into play. That which I have given reposes, in large measure, on the agricultural use of machinery, so widespread in America and still so little known on this side of the Atlantic. We know that our European rural populations begin their heavy manual work very early. Carrying burdens on the back or on the head, and carting loads in wheelbarrows, lead to profound skeletal modifications when the subject is still actively growing, such as: compression of the vertebral bodies; diminution in the degree of obliquity of the neck of the femur; an increased antero-posterior curvature of the shaft of the femur, etc. Thus may be partly accounted for the smaller stature of rural and mountain populations, recognized almost everywhere, in comparison with that of urban populations of the same ethnic group, though other factors may be added, such as fewer hours of sleep—that is to say, shorter periods in which the body reclines extended, a position which considerably favours height development. Such rough daily toil, and the daily repetition of such heavy work, is generally spared to American children and adolescents.

Sitting on the seat of a plough, a reaper or a machine-rake, or driving a binder does not necessitate the same quality or quantity of effort as is required of our rural labourers.

In any case it is enough that a certain percentage of Americans benefit by those superior conditions for the result of them to be appreciable in statistics and for the general average of height to be influenced.

I do not wish to give the impression, however, that under no circumstances do I believe in the influence of environment. Whether one is a monogenist or a polygenist it must be recognized that a certain number of morphological facts and special anatomical characters embarrass us not a little to account for their origin. These influences, however, have been so much exaggerated, and their intervention is so convenient when it is desired to get over a difficulty of interpretation, that it is necessary to stress the facts in a contrary sense even if only to warn the younger generation against this lazy fashion of not thinking things out for themselves. Man, more than any other species, is in possession of the fullest means of escape—not from his environment—in which he is obliged to live—but from its reactions. For him many biological problems do not arise in the same way as for his humbler brethren. This difference gives him an immense advantage in nature. And we should never lose sight of this greater freedom of his from constraint. To insist on likening Man to an organism—no matter what—whose experimental environment we can circumscribe at will and watch minutely is not far short of deception. Human biology is a complex of a different sort from that of a yeast, an ear of wheat, or a protozoon, or even from that of the higher mammals that come nearest to us.

None the less we do see certain modifications—are they likely to last ?—within the bounds of those ethnical groups that can be easily and properly observed. For instance, height appears to be increasing sensibly in a given race and for both sexes among urban groups of similar economical conditions. This phenomenon will make itself seriously felt in the next statistics of European stature. And I see no valid explanation of it. The facile argument of better diet is always made to do duty. I do not believe in it for a moment. Furthermore, I hold that this increase in stature is a " biological mistake " ; it is not favourable to those who suffer it. Hence it should not be used as a sociological argument and as though this increase had been due to more favourable economic factors. Some time ago I attempted to explain it by the easier survival of urban populations who are much better off for medical care than rural folk far from a town.[1]

Then height is not the only factor to be faced. An increase in mean brachycephaly has been reported in many parts, of the municipality of London, for instance. Long ago I reported this transformation for the departments of Savoy.[2] Similar examples in Poland and elsewhere are known. For the moment the only explanation of this biological phenomenon that I can see is that there is a greater concentration of brachycephalic types in these places. A higher brachycephaly in a smaller number of individuals would lead to the same result. No other mechanism of brachycephalization appears to be acceptable for the time bring in the known conditions of the regions under consideration.[3]

[1] CC.

[2] CXCVIII.

[3] For possible mesological reactions resulting in morphological modifications in the American people, see the works of Boas and his school. This anthropologist firmly believes in the influence of environment, an opinion with which I am not in agreement.

Hence the transformation which certain ethnic groups—or fractions thereof—undergo, are phenomena of extremely nice interpretation, and I think the greatest caution is indicated for biologists—and, spatially, for anthropologists particularly—in all that touches the mesological explanations that may be given. As for those whose competence does not lie within the disciplines of the natural sciences, they would do well to abstain from interpretation in this domain.

To-day the researches of Anthropology are prosecuted in every direction: everywhere their findings deserve to be considered with attention. The Universities, especially in America, are fully alive to what is being done. Historians, geographers, sociologists, even the naturalists themselves, cannot get on without the result of our labours, and cannot ignore what we have to say in these matters. If they neglect to listen, they would be as physicians undertaking to cure disease before ever they had set eyes on a sick man. Would it not be well, first of all, to make acquaintance with Man before arguing about his works, their origin, and condition, possible variations and promising or unfavourable future? For Man was their creator, Man lived in them and modified them, and still lives in them and transforms them daily.

The degree of ethnical purity of a human race is first and foremost a function of its geographical isolation. An unmixed stock is assured to a human group by the very difficulty it experiences in leaving its natural environment or, and this comes to the same thing, the difficulty any other group experiences in approaching it. A palæolithic group marooned on an island by some geographical hazard such as the sinking of a continent, in the days before navigation was invented, would show, even to-day, its old-time morphological characters. Primitive races became mixed from the time that the wanderings of humanity over the continents became intensive. Up till the Mesolithic, Western Europe knew only Dolicocephals—of different types, it is true. The arrival of the first Brachycephals profoundly disturbed this relative unity. From that day forward—and the mingling increases progressively as time goes on—it is impossible to speak of pure races as regards Europe.

And, naturally, it is less so than ever to-day—even if we take the Lapps and Samoyeds, who would seem to be better protected, by their geographical position, from admixture, than others. The Lapps are much intermarried with Scandinavians and the Samoyeds with Russians.

Certain groups, however, have undergone relatively less transformation than others. The isolation of high valleys, great poverty (bad economic conditions have never attracted strangers from without), religious fanaticism and extreme conservatism in the matter of ancestral customs, all conduce to a fierce hostility to anything new ; still other reasons may explain the comparative lack of mixed blood in certain districts. In such conditions of ethnical preservation we have the chance of finding a considerable percentage of individuals of the same type. Many European countries can still show smaller or larger groups of this kind to-day, relatively well preserved. We can count on a similar percentage in still another set of circumstances, as when the primitive " human kingdom " finds itself situated far from the beaten track—Scandinavia, for example—and when, in addition, the conditions of existence offered by this " kingdom " are very poor. Consequently its more favoured neighbours did not seek to fall upon it. If a high birthrate increased its population unduly, portions of it would swarm from the hive and settle elsewhere ; the groups that remained behind, being almost undisturbed by foreign elements, were able, like an untroubled spring, to maintain their primitive purity. The anthropological map of Scandinavia is of almost uniform tint.[1] Furthermore, all the other reasons for preservation already indicated—or some of them—can add their quota to this geographical cause for homogeneity.

Degrees of ethnic purity are perceptible to Anthropology alone—that is to say, they are appreciable only by detailed analyses based on exact methods. No traveller's description—unless the traveller be a specialist—can be taken into serious consideration. Those written by close observers may put us on the right track to be followed, callipers and camera in hand ; but with the best will in the world we must not put greater

[1] With reservations, however, which will appear further on.

credence in them—no more, in fact, than in the majority of published drawings of human types. When one comes to study any given population, and to go through the documentation furnished by travellers who have been to these parts, one is almost always struck by the disparity in the descriptions. And, when attempted comparisons have been added, they are generally useless.

This is because most travellers pay far more attention to the expression of a face, to gestures and costume, or, often enough, to the desire to make the type conform to the requirements of some intellectual theory, than they do to objective morphological observations which entail the taking of a great deal of trouble. Ah ! this imagination ! said Pascal. Are we not sufficiently burdened by " Roman types " (what, exactly, is a Roman type, ethnologically !), by " Arab types " (or " Saracens " according to the locality), etc. ! It is enough for some invasion to have taken place somewhere for people to think that they have discovered—or rather, to wish to discover—precious anthropological traces of the invaders in the population invaded. And sometimes, unintentionally, and in perfect good faith, the facts are strained. It is enough for a philologically Germanic group to have occupied a certain territory in the past for people to think they can pick out in that territory's population the authentic Germanic type—even though, very often, this type does not so much as exist, the group in question having been Germanic only in speech. Every day, in our reading, we come across instances of a similar confusion, and that is why we emphasize the point so strongly.

Then what are we to say of the political labels substituted for ethnic characters ? Some have been deliberately created for definite ends, such as the assimilation of different races by a conqueror. Russia can furnish us with a number of examples, and the former Austria-Hungary as well. For other such labels we must not postulate such dark designs. They have been naively fabricated from the spoken language, and from history, and so on. An anthropologist, *a priori*, however, has to beware of both. Hints of this sort may provide him with a frame. But he himself will paint the picture.

Anthropologists themselves must sometimes be in doubt over their own work—facile ethnic approximations and unproven parallelisms. Labels have been lightly bestowed in these domains, also, and have singularly complicated research. The mistakes we have made—and still make, alas !—have generally been with regard to former populations. For some it has been enough, in any prehistoric or proto-historic period, that ethnographic resemblances should be noted between human groups, widely separated, geographically, for such groups at once to have their relationship established. Nothing is less proven, in a large number of cases, than such common descent. Because their implements are much the same, or even identical, and their methods of sepulture similar, that is not to say that the populations who used these tools or who practised these funerary rites are necessarily sprung from the same ethnic stock.

And if ethnographical approximations necessarily imply blood relationship, do ethnographical differences equally postulate ethnical contrasts ? We know quite well that this is not so. None the less it is the case that parallel series of ethnographic observations made at different points are of the highest interest. They should never be neglected. We ourselves shall employ this method over and over again. It has frequently furnished the key to difficult interpretations, and, deprived of it, many problems would still be most obscure. But it is a method to be used with caution, since results obtained in this way are merely potentialities, after all, not proofs.

A while back we spoke of variations in the cephalic index. In certain circles a great deal has been made of the differences established—or thought to have been established—in the same canton or district between the cephalic index of the governing classes and that of the rest of the population. This finding, which is of little value and would appear to be nothing more than the assertion of a curious anatomical phenomenon, becomes, in the hands of certain people, a forcible political and social argument. Such evidence can be put in the same category with the Gobinist theory of the social superiority of the tall Dolichocephals. We all know what a fuss was made about the peoples who possessed the double characters of tall stature and a low cephalic index associated with fair-headedness and blue eyes.

The cities of Central and Western Europe in which political and social life is mainly elaborated, attract the Dolichocephals to themselves by some wondrous power of selection—that is to say, those to whom the most brilliant of destinies is assured, the Dolichocephals whose ancestors (according to certain publicists with a smattering of anthropology) were the makers of History. Is this not, in a more modest way, but with a potency that is permanent and ever increasing, to credit our cities with a social phenomenon attributed to certain privileged States ?

Is it not amazing to read, in a book that elsewhere contains interesting pages, sentences such as these : " Even for the expert it is suggestive to find that a man's destiny has depended on two or three millimetres more or less in the length or breadth of his skull ; it is a statement that strikes one as sufficiently extraordinary, but it is one to which the facts are constantly bringing us back."[1]

I do not want to be drawn into a discussion of the relation, claimed to be that of cause and effect, between the human type spatially described as *Homo europæus,* and the political or social success of a country or a group of which this type is supposed to be the author. This *Homo,* one may be sure, is no other than the Nordic or Germanic type of most of the present-day classifications ! Many pages would be required for such a controversy. But I must beg my readers to believe that there is no lack of arguments to set up against such assimilations.

To do it properly and go into the question objectively one would have to take those famous books of Gobineau and the recent works of such of his emulators as Ammon, Lapouge, Chamberlain, etc., and lay bare their contents, chapter by chapter. One would soon find objections springing up at every turn. The most indulgent reader would demand proof when confronted with certain statements—but proofs are never forthcoming. That is to say, proofs that really are proofs. One would find in these works assertions of this sort (taken at random) : " . . . in fact, the dominant class of the feudal period belonged almost exclusively to *Homo europæus.*"[2] Or : " When one studies portrait collections from the Renaissance up to the eighteenth century, one is struck by the complete

[1] **CXXXII**, p. 400.
[2] *Ibid*, p. 246.

predominance of long heads dominating long, narrow faces with thin aquiline noses."[1] Admitting that these portraits represent such a type, are they really to be considered anthropological documents? What man of science would dare to trust to them? Or again: "Look down from above on to any present-day political meeting or gathering of men of influence, the brachycephals will easily be in a majority. The fair heads that once dominated have become rare."[2]

What a number of criticisms are challenged by these two or three sentences gathered from among a hundred others! Criticisms of method even more than of "facts". That a considerable, even a large portion of the French governing class of feudal times was of northern race we will willingly believe. One may even go further and say that it is obvious—unless History lies. But who is to point out to us the relative number of northern types in the whole nation—that is to say, in the loaf of which those types were to become the leaven? Who is to demonstrate to us the real strength of their influence? I do not see how relations of such gravity are to be established on such fragile and imperfect "evidence."

How is it possible to establish a definite relation—one that is called definite—between that part of the then French population which we are supposing to be of northern race—and of which we have no real morphological description—and political events of which it was perhaps the testimony or the collaborator rather than the animating principle? The invaders, become conquerors, took to themselves all the best places. They at once became a military aristocracy, typical of the feudal world. This has always happened, and no doubt always will happen whatever the ethnic group to which the conquerors belong. It was not because they possessed the particular ethnic complex we know to have been theirs, nor by virtue of any racial determinism that the men of northern race, by right of might, took first place, but simply because they were conquerors.

Is it to be thought for a moment that, had the Germans won the great war, the Bavarian and Austrian Brachycephals would not have insisted on getting a few of the best places in the vanquished country? Would they not have become the equivalent of the barons and feudal lords? And anyone

[1] **CXXXII**, p. 248.
[2] *Ibid*, p. 252.

describing such a " European Society " as for the moment we are supposing, would give a diametrically opposite picture of it from that of de Lapouge. When William the Conqueror landed in England did he not, directly he had won his victory, and simply because he was the victor, distribute all the profitable posts to his captains and soldiers without bothering himself for an instant as to what race they belonged ? From that day the feudal presentment of England—which was largely dolichocephal—became disparate. Why, in a work of which, we repeat, certain chapters delight us by their wit, have recourse to such principles of causality as these, easy enough to put on paper, but impossible to demonstrate with the evidence at our disposal ?

The supposed laws of " dolichocephalic concentration " and " urban elimination " likewise lay themselves open to a number of criticisms. To say that an urban existence operates selectively in favour of the dolichoid elements and destroys or eliminates the brachycephals,[1] is to put forward an effective formula calculated to impress the masses, but I can see nowhere the demonstration that would induce one to believe in this " law." And that other formula known as the " law of stratification "[2] which is rendered thus in its deceptive brevity : " The cephalic index progressively diminishes and the proportion of dolichocephals progessively increases as we go from the lower to the upper classes of a given locality." There it is ! But in what way, and in how many towns have these characteristics been observed ? We are not told.

However, here is the possible explanation : everyone, I imagine, agrees in accepting town influence—an extraordinarily vague term—as a contributory factor to the increase of mean height (which, as we have said, is a deplorable result, considerably diminishing the stamina of individuals). I believe I have shown that this increase in height has for direct consequence an increase in dolichocephaly[3] owing to the relatively greater development of the antero-posterio diameter of the skull in proportion as the height increases. The transversal diameter grows less rapidly. Thus dolichocephaly is increased quite naturally. We have to deal, then, with a law of morphological correlation and nothing more.

[1] **CXXXIII**, p. 432.
[2] *Ibid*, p. 433.
[3] **CXCVII**, p. 279.

But why pursue it further! Is it any exaggeration to say that for the moment there is no occasion to accept the laws enunciated, at least in this authoritative form? Our documents of comparative morphology are far too insufficient for us to be able to adopt any other attitude than that of expectation and caution. Scientific doubt was never more necessary than here because such suppositions, in the hands of enthusiasts, may lead to unjustifiable social upsets. In such matters cautiousness is simply a question of honesty.

Over and above all this, these despized Brachycephals, these representatives of the inferior race *Homo alpinus*, would seem to have invented and propagated two things of capital importance to the progress of civilization. In effect, it is to them that we probably owe the culture of cereals and animal domestication, and that is by no means a small contribution. It might even be found to outweigh a certain number of raids and massacres. Did not these inventions, indeed, have a larger part in determining social progress, and for a longer period, and was not their influence of wider extent than all the warlike disturbances of the Northerners put together?

And if, further, we were to go beyond the ethnic limits of present-day Europe, should we not find civilizations which appear to be the exclusive possession of Brachycephals whom we might find to be related to our *Homo alpinus*? We say, advisedly, "which appear to be," because we can never be sure of the determinant, certain and indisputable rôle of this or that group in a heterogeneous mass, in such complex events as those of which History is made up. For example, there are many Brachycephals—brachycephalic Aryans—among those divers peoples who have left behind them traces of great civilizations and whom we call the Aryans. The present increase in brachycephaly (if, indeed, it is everywhere demonstrable, which the insufficiency of the evidence at our disposal makes it impossible for us to know) might just as well give rise to comments of a much more favourable nature than those so generously—and so lightly—bestowed on it. Might not a sociologist claim that the wonderful flowering of knowledge at the end of the last century and the beginning of the twentieth correspond exactly with the decrease, on one hand, of the disturbing dolichocephalic elements, and, on the other, with the increase, established for certain parts of the European population, in individuals having short, broad heads?

We will not press it, because we might easily be led into going too far.

*
* *

Which continent, in the present state of our knowledge, contains the oldest traces of Man? In other words, and to take up, for the moment, the position of monogenism, what part of the world saw the genesis of the first human pair?

It is impossible to answer such a question; and the reader will see better how impossible it is the further he proceeds with the present volume. Were we to take as a basis the mere technique of the oldest known implements, more than one continent might claim the honour of having been the cradle of Humanity.

But there is another and insurmountable obstacle to any such decision and this lies in giving any parallel chronology for different continents to human phenomena and to those geological phenomena which surrounded and dominated them. No expert, we believe, who studies human origins would dare to assert that Indian Chellean implements, for example, are contemporaneous with the Chellean implements of Europe or of Africa. They are identical in form, but is the date at which they were made the same? In which of the three continents was this industry started? Are we to admit, by a polygenism that embraces the whole of Eur-Asia and Africa, and even America, that men everywhere spontaneously invented the Chellean "coup de poing"?

Such hypotheses, based on an examination of the implements which demonstrate the existence of Man, are largely the hypotheses of prehistorians. What, however, have the palæontologists got to say on the matter—for they can go much further back into the "course of the ages"?—palæontologists who have specialized in the study of the higher mammals, seeking among them the phylum to which, in the theory of evolution, the genus *Homo* belonged? In general, they are extremely reserved. They will tell you that the first thing to be done is to find out the places in which the evolution of the Primates could best have been accomplished. The chief fact which Palæontology seems to have established is, in the words of Marcellin Boule, that "from the very primitive stages, lemurian and platyrrhine, the evolution of the group potentially containing the human branch was pursued neither in North America, whence all the Primates appear to have disappeared since the upper Eocene, nor in South America, where the Platyrrhine branch reigned alone. It is therefore in the old continent that our cradle must be sought. Humanity is a product of the Old World."[1]

There are fanatics among those who have attempted to solve this problem—to the comprehension of which one can never bring too great a preliminary reserve. There are those who still believe that "everything came from Asia." The persistence of ancient philological theories which, by the simplicity of their means, so greatly attracted our predecessors? Perhaps! It must always be remembered that the discovery of *Pithecanthropus erectus*, and the fact that there was a remarkable evolution of Primates in southern Asia, and that ancient palæolithic implements are known there, militates in favour of this continent. And Africa? Why should the cradle of mankind not be there? Peringuey's hypotheses in this connection are very attractive. It is possible that chance has particularly favoured research in Asia, while the work done in Africa has not proved very profitable—as yet.[2] And what about those continents sunk beneath the waters at the end of the Tertiary and of which we shall never know anything? And Europe?

Need we add that the mere fact that in any given part of the world there has been discovered a wealth of evolutionary simian forms in no way proves for certain that these forms must have gone on evolving in that district until they arrived at Man. It may quite well be that Man, by one of those mutations to which naturalists impute so much importance to-day, derives from a still unknown collateral branch and from a group of monkeys inferior to the Primates; and even in some locality where Simiae must have been rare, as in Europe—where all traces of them so far discovered would occupy but little room in a glass case.

[1] **XXI**, p. 454.

[2] Africa becomes more and more promising. The recent discovery by Dart of a skull which he considers intermediate between Ape and Man (*Australopithecus Africanus*) and which he considers may represent a new group, which he calls *Homo-Simiadæ*, may substantiate our hopes. Further description and discussion must, however, be awaited. In the meantime see the description in *Nature*, 7th February, 1925.

Even to-day, an attitude of doubt is the wisest. If an answer must be given to the question put, we shall have to be honest and say that we do not know.

From this negative reply it must not be inferred, however, that everything appertaining to the origin of Man is completely unknown. It is true that we do not know where humanity first appeared, nor under what form it appeared, yet, all the same, we can definitely state of Quaternary man that in the beginning the form of his anatomical complex was not identical with that which Man possesses to-day. And, further, we can make out, far back in the past, and with surprising detail, the material manifestations of the stages through which Humanity passed. After all, these are magnificent acquisitions to our knowledge of which the first part of the second half of the nineteenth century was entirely ignorant.

CHAPTER II

Classification of the Races of Mankind

i

A FEW WORDS ON THE EVOLUTION OF INDUSTRIES AND THE CLASSIFICATION OF THE PREHISTORIC PERIOD

LET us make ourselves quite clear at the outset. What follows in this chapter applies to Europe, but not necessarily to other continents. It is possible that some day certain parallels may be established between the stages of prehistoric evolution in Europe and those of other parts of the world, but they cannot be established yet. This reservation should always be borne in mind when we pass from one continent to another. Certain populations to-day are still practically in the stone age, and others have only recently passed out of it. The neolithic stage lasted much longer in Western Asia than it did in Europe. The Scandinavian and the Mediterranean Bronze ages are not synchronous.

Having made these remarks, let us remember that Man probably existed at the end of the Tertiary era, in the Pliocene at least. It has been claimed on several occasions that the remains of human skeletons have been discovered in various tertiary layers, but not one of these finds has been substantiated. I will say nothing, here, about eoliths, because a paragraph has been devoted to these flints in one of the volumes of this collection,[1] but I think I ought to mention, since the discovery has quite recently been confirmed, the finding of flints in tertiary strata at Ipswich, Suffolk, which specialists of such renown at the Abbé Breuil, Dr. Capitan, and Burkitt among others[2] consider to have been intentionally flaked. If

[1] **CLXIII**, p. 35.

[2] Reid Moir has already published a considerable number of memoirs describing his discoveries, among the more recent, see **CLXI**. Since this chapter was written an international commission has been to Ipswich. It published a report of its investigations in **XXXIII**, p. 53.

these Ipswich flints are really implements we shall have to put back the age of Humanity considerably.

It is quite a long time since Reid Moir, the discoverer of these sensational objects, first found such flints. Scientific men remained sceptical with some reason, because, only too often, discoveries of a similar nature, claimed to have been made, have had to be set aside after careful discussion—as at Thenay, Otta, Puy Courny, etc. This time it really seems that there is something to be excited about. The Red Crag, in which the English writer found the implements in question, belongs to the Upper Pliocene, and is situated in a layer that is earlier than the first glacial period (Günzian). If these two conditions, the Pliocene stratum and the indubitable human flaking of the flints[1] are proven, the existence of tertiary Man will have been established. It will only remain to hope that human bones—or prehuman—may be found in the same geological beds. Their absence, however, will not substract from our certainty. Have we not had to wait three quarters of a century for a few miserable portions of a skeleton dating from the Chellean and Acheulean, although we had all the implements belonging to these periods ?

On the other hand, nothing in our palæontological conceptions is opposed to the putting of the historic origins of Man so far back in the past. I would even say that, given the point which Man had reached in the early Quaternary, all our reasoning leads us to suppose that he must be older than the Quaternary ; unless we are to postulate that a double mutation, morphological and industrial, was accomplished at the same time. But let us leave aside this question which is not finally settled (we must not imitate our—sometimes illustrious—predecessors who, in the course of a congress, and without having seen a single element of the matter in debate, confirmed the existence of Anthropopithecus, merely by a *jeu d'esprit*) and briefly recall the stages to-day established as representing the succession of human industries. If we refer to de Morgan's *Prehistoric Man* for the details, the following short table will suffice :

[1] Personally I am unable to give an opinion : I have not seen the specimens, but only photographs of them, which is not enough. But experts of great authority have pronounced for them, among them the Abbé Breuil and Burkitt (who had been present) at the Liége Congress (1921), Osborne (in *Natural History*, 1921), Capitan, who has just published a memoir on the matter—**XXXII**, p. 126, and others as well.

Classification of Prehistoric Periods

PALÆOLITHIC (Age of worked stone)	Chellean (Chelles, Seine-et-Marne). Acheulean (Saint-Acheul, Somme). Moustierian (Grotte du Moustier, Dordogne). Aurignacian (Grotte d'Aurignac, Haute-Garonne). Solutrean (Solutré, near Mâcon). Magdalenian (Grotte de la Madeleine, Dordogne).
TRANSITION PHASE :	Azilian (Grotte du Mas d'Azil, Ariège).
NEOLITHIC	or Polished Stone Age.
COPPER AGE (?)	
BRONZE AGE	
IRON AGE	

The Palæolithic belongs to the pleistocene period of the geologists. The holocene period begins from the Neolithic, which, like the Palæolithic, has been sub-divided. It was in the Neolithic that the lake dwellings, so numerous in Switzerland, were constructed. Let us remember that they continued to exist during the bronze age.

ii

THE CLASSIFICATION OF HUMAN RACES

The further we go back into the past the scarcer becomes our morphological human documentation. It is only a few years since the time when we had not a single bone fragment earlier than the Moustierian. Two finds belonging to the Chellean period have come to supply us with somewhat niggardly information about the human types of this distant epoch. We shall speak of them, and give the necessary details, later. Moustierian human remains are more abundant ; and those of the Reindeer age more so still. Further, from now on, we shall be able to form a fairly correct idea of the human palæolithic types.

Skeletons of the neolithic period are numerous. Let us at once note this interesting fact concerning them : whereas the European Palæolithic knew only dolichocephalic populations, the Neolithic knew many that were brachycephalic. These will make their appearance even from the Azilian.

In the bronze and iron ages different ethnic types will succeed one another in the same district. A number of human aggregations are now on the move. It seems that certain industrial changes go hand in hand with these changes in population. Thus, in England, the neolithic Dolichocephals buried in the long barrows do not maintain their racial purity ; Brachycephals succeed them in the bronze age.

Nevertheless, it must not be assumed from this that every modification in a civilization is always and everywhere marked by some new ethnic contribution.

Just as, for example, in the Middle Ages, the European populations came by fresh elements of civilization through the "Arabs" without ethnically being "Arabized" in the smallest degree, so the prehistoric populations modified their civilization without the intervention of any new populations to bring such changes about.

In current—even in scientific—speech, the word *race* has been singularly twisted out of its proper signification. Race must not be confounded with language or nationality. There exists no such thing as a "Latin Race," a "Germanic Race" or a "Slavonic Race". Let us always keep before us the aphorism : race is a zoological, language a social fact. Men of the same race may have changed their tongue in the course of their history—there is no lack of examples—without thereby modifying in any way whatsoever their anatomical characteristics. If we are to accept this confusion, due to language as a unifying agency, the philological charts will present us with some of those extraordinary ethnic relationships that the textbooks indicate as really existing. The same tint will do for Bavarians and Prussians in Germany, for Normans and Mediterraneans in France, and for Venetians and Calabrians in Italy, and so on, and Heaven knows these groups differ the one from the other !

Comparative morphology is the point of departure for any natural classification and must serve when we wish to establish sub-divisions in the genus *Homo* as naturally as it does for the genus *Equus* or *Elephas*.

It would be beside the point to indicate, in a book intended for a non-specialist public, all the somatological characters employed by anthropologists in establishing this classification. We will point out the principal ones only, those which can easily be understood by any cultivated reader.

It was realized long ago that for a rational classification acceptable to all, morphological characters alone must be taken into consideration.

Did not Hippocrates write : " Those who are wont to hear the nature of Man spoken of to persons who desire to know it by means foreign to medicine will find nothing in this book to satisfy them."[1] And Herodotus, that great descriptive writer, did he not in his day make use of this method when he established a classification of Ethiopians in the army of Xerxes, to wit, Orientals with straight hair, and Orientals with frizzy hair ? A similar classification, based on hirsute characters, was to have a considerable success with Haeckel twenty-two centuries later.

Scylax, at about the same time as Herodotus, describing a periplus of the Mediterranean, states that among the brown people of Africa the inhabitants of the Gulf of Gabes region are fair and tall, thus early associating two characteristics.

Thus the chief descriptive characters—those which at once strike the attention (they did not in those days yet make use of anthropometric data)—height, the colour of the skin, the form and colour of the hair, were early employed.

We know that the Egyptians in their pictorial representations discriminated between the chief human races that came under their notice. Champollion has made known the paintings of the royal tombs of Bibân el Moluk and the ethnic types there distinguished.

The great maritime discoveries and the great continental journeys brought observers face to face with new types which had to be classified and whose presence was singularly to upset the old moral order. At the end of the thirteenth century Marco Polo, arriving at the Hindu-Kush, pointed out the presence of Sia-Push or Blond Kaffirs. The discovery of America, and in the sixteenth century, that of the oceanic islands, placed us in contact with a variety of human types on whose existence the philosophers of old were far from counting and the theologians less so. The doctrine of original unity

[1] Hippocrates made some very interesting anthropological observations on the Macrocephals. C. p. 59.

established of old by St. Augustine and accepted throughout the Christian world, in appearance at least—the Inquisition looked after those who were recalcitrant—received a severe shock. And in spite of a papal decree declaring that the Indians discovered by Columbus were descended from Adam and Eve—like the inhabitants of Europe—the notion of a plurality of races slowly made progress.

Confronted with these diversities of colour and form, recorded one after the other, it became essential to attempt a classification. First of all the dichotomic method was employed (by the Englishman, Bradley), the colour of the skin representing the leading distinction. We had thus the Whites, Blacks and Intermediates, these groups being subdivided according to the beard and hair. Abyssinians were straight-haired Blacks; Negroes were woolly-haired Blacks. Something had been accomplished. Linnæus, coming afterwards, carried these subdivisions much further, employing new descriptive characters. He even added to these zoological diagnoses others—which raise a smile to-day—that were ethnographical and social. Thus it came about that tabular classifications were gradually set up to keep pace with discoveries and increasingly accurate observations. Soon a distinction came to be made between main and secondary races. Thus Geoffroy Saint-Hilaire, in 1860, recognized four main races, namely Caucasian, Mongolian, Ethiopian and Hottentot, subdivided into thirteen secondary races. A few years later Huxley enumerated five—Negroid, Australoid, Mongoloid, Zanthochroic and Melanocroic, with fourteen secondary races. In 1879 Haeckel attempted a classification based on hair type, as follows: Lophokomoi (woolly haired, like "pepper corns"); Eriokomoi (woolly haired, closely embedded); Euthykomoi (straight haired); Euplokomoi (curly haired).

All these were the essays of naturalists, men whose profession consisted, among other things, in discovering some means of finding their way amid the diversity of species, and of classifying animals—which cannot be grouped according to their different languages! In 1887 de Quatrefages set up three primitive stems—Negro, Yellow and White, subdivided into numerous branches.

The considerable differences revealed between these essays at classification[1] when one comes to compare them, and the

[1] **LXXIX**, p. 125; **CXVII**; **CCLV**, p. 502; **CCIX**.

variation in the point of view to be observed in the same author in measure as he ponders the problem, suffice to indicate how difficult such problems are.

It is to be noted that each time the proposed new classification contains a larger number of secondary races. This is because modern work has confronted us with many more complexities than we had imagined to exist. And we are not at the end of our troubles. Yet all the time I feel that many of these present complexities are apparent only and that wider investigation, while authorizing readjustments and a new regrouping,[1] will enable us to reduce them.

We see that up till that time it was the same descriptive characters that had been almost exclusively employed. But description is not the final stage of science. Did not William Thompson (Lord Kelvin) say that knowledge resulted from measurement more than anything else, and that the end of science was to find, by numbers, what relations were established between phenomena? In effect, do not measurements have this cardinal virtue, that they eliminate, *ipso facto*, all errors arising from our feelings, from our own poor qualities as observers, and from the fragile nature of our testimony? Callipers, footrules, measuring and photographic apparatus are without preconceived ideas. Our lack of objectivity and the difficulty we experience in disregarding the personal factor as represented by ourselves, when dealing with Man, have caused a considerable slowing-down in the progress of Anthropology.

None the less, we must not forget that anthropologists were the first among biologists to attempt to put their observations into figures, that is to say to remove these observations from all cause of subjective error. Morphometry reinforced descriptive morphology, and to craniology was added craniometry.

The oldest mensurations go back sufficiently far. If we mistake not, it was the Belgian Spigel, when he was professor at Padua somewhere about the year 1625, who first made cranial mensurations. Later, the Frenchman, Daubenton, and especially the Dutchman, Camper, should figure among the first craniometrists. It was Camper who invented the projection method.

Thenceforward the means of investigation by measurement have multiplied rapidly. Each generation perfects them further

[1] **CXCV**, p. 564.

and the technique constantly becomes more strict. It is impossible here not to mention François Paul Broca, one of the men who gave to Anthropology its most powerful momentum, the repercussions of which have been felt throughout the world, though by rights we ought to recall many other names as well. With an admirable understanding of what was required, incomparable patience, and extraordinary technical mastery, he studied, accepted or reformed the means in use and invented new ways of research. And when various Congresses had the task of internationally standardizing the measurements to be made both on the living subject and the skeleton (Monaco, 1906, Geneva, 1912),[1] Broca's work was the basis of all the deliberations.

Craniometric and anthropometric technique scientifically ordered have raised the plane of classification one degree. To-day we can base our classification on an ensemble of exact (since they are obtained by measurement) morphological characters which should be added to descriptive information. In 1889[2] and then again in 1900[3] Deniker attempted a classification of human races based solely on their physical characters (colour of skin, nature of hair, stature, form of the head, nose, etc.). Under "six heads" established according to the nature of the hair, Deniker set out twenty-nine races (or sub-races). It is impossible to go into details here, and readers interested in the question would do well to refer to the table drawn up by this author, always bearing in mind that this table cannot represent the exact grouping of human races according to their real racial affinities.

Deniker brings in the colour of the hair along with its form, and also the colour of the eyes. The first subdivision of the "six heads" is according to the colour of the skin; and after that other measurable (and, occasionally, descriptive) characters come in.

This simple statement shows that it is necessary to know what are the methods followed. We shall set them out in a very few words:[4]

[1] **CLXXXV**, p. 377; **LXVII**, p. 484.

[2] **LVI**, p. 320.

[3] **LVII**, p. 339. (Eng. trans., p. 285.)

[4] For methods of classifying human races and for the distribution of ethnic types see R. Dixon's *The Racial History of Man*, New York and London, 1923.

Colour of the skin.—Broca[1] provided a scale for the colour of the skin, which anthropologists not working in laboratories were constrained to simplify. Later on, when it becomes necessary to pursue the study of details within the boundaries of these large and well defined groups, perhaps we may have to return to the thirty-four shades of Broca. But " in the field " at a time when it is not always easy to examine men (sometimes even it is dangerous) we can only keep what is indispensable, and one willingly uses the scale of six principal shades put into service by the English. Deniker[2] accepts and calls them to mind : pale white, florid or rosy (Scandinavians, North Germans, English, etc.) ; brownish white (Mediterraneans) ; yellowish white or wheaten-colour (Chinese) ; olive-yellow (South American Indians, Indonesians, Polynesians) ; the dark yellow-brown of the Malays, for example ; the copper colour of the Bejas and Fulahs, etc. ; the chocolate brown of the Australians ; very dark brown ; and black.

Hair.—This character, we have seen above, has had a number of classifiers. To simplify matters we can reduce to four the principal varieties of hair : (1) straight hair (American Indians, Chinese) ; (2) crisp or woolly hair (Negroes, together with the tufted variety of the Melanesians, and the " pepper corn " variety of the Hottentots and Bushmen) ; (3) wavy hair (very common among Europeans) ; (4) frizzy hair. In this latter type the hair twists up in spirals (certain Nilotic peoples, Australians, etc.).[3]

Colour of Eyes and Hair.—The pigment of the iris membrane is contained in two layers. When granulations are found in the pigmentary membrane alone, the eye looks blue or grey. When the granulations accumulate in the median layer as well, the iris is of varying shades of brown. Three fundamental shades have been suggested for eyes : light (blue or grey) ; dark (light brown ranging to dark brown) ; intermediate (green, yellow grey, etc.). Dark irides are the most common in Man. Blue and grey eyes are now known only among Europeans and—a fact of great importance—among certain

[1] **XXVI.**
[2] **LVII**, p. 43. (p. 47 of English translation).
[3] The differing aspect of the hair is explained by the different manner in which it is embedded and by the different form revealed by transverse section. For example, straight or wavy hair is circular in section, whereas the " pepper corn " variety is elliptical.

Central and Western Asiatic peoples. Even in Europe the two fundamental types are well represented, with a geographical distribution fairly sharply limited to north and south. Nevertheless, in the Balkan peninsular which, *a priori*, should contain only men with dark irides, light irides—particularly grey ones—are common.

With regard to hair colour, five principal shades may be indicated : black, brown, chestnut, blond and red. Red-haired races, however, do not exist ; this colour in individual. In any diagnosis of north European types one would nearly always have to write—fair hair and blue eyes.

The blue-eyed races constitute for Anthropology (in Asia especially)—and perhaps in History—a problem of the highest degree of interest. Are the individuals possessing these characters in their proper home ? Or are they the descendants of immigrants coming from a country where that character is the rule ? Many ethnologists—pan-Germans, if one may say so—have imagined that in these populations they can recognise the great-great-grandchildren of prehistoric Kimri. This is possible. We shall have something to say about this hypothesis.

Height.—Spatially this is an extremely variable character. There exist very tall and very small races. It is probable that these are phenomena which have never changed. It is vain to try to make us believe that tall races derive from races that were originally small—unless some sudden mutation is invoked.

Considered as an average, height, like other morphological characters, is thus hereditary. Small races have always been small. True, we must not deny certain fluctuations in height in every ethnic group.—But these are modifications which have little effect on averages. Perhaps we may now be witnessing a regular increase in height in countries where there is intense urban life—we have already alluded to it. But any populations which have not yet reached this stage of social life—among so-called uncivilized populations in particular—we see no such phenomenon. This increase in stature has been invoked in numberless discussions on human geography and sociology, and also on general biology. No acceptable conclusion for its explanation has been formulated.

The Akkas of the Mombutu country of Central Africa (1 metre 38), and the Negritos of the Philippines (1 metre 46), and of the Andamans (1 metre 48) are among those human groups having the smallest stature. We shall see that there are no populations of very small stature in Europe or America. The smallest Europeans are the Lapps (1 metre 529); the smallest Americans are perhaps the Caribs, then the Fuegians and the Eskimo (1 metre 57). But these are big men by comparison with the Akkas. Asia is the continent of small stature in so far as many portions of her territory are concerned, but there are also a few districts where the height is very great. In India as in furthest Siberia, in Indo-China and among the Japanese are to be found many human groups whose height is no more than 1 metre 57. The average height of Asia is certainly less than the average of the other continents.

Among the tallest of human groups the Scots must be given first place. Until our inquiries are prosecuted further they remain the tallest men in the world—(Galloway Scots, 1 metre 79), with, perhaps, the Pila-Pila of West Africa (a small series). Northern Europe is the domain of very great stature—Livonians, Norwegians and Swedes; so is one part of south-east Europe—Bosnians, Herzegovinians, Montenegrins and many Albanians. Oceania is also a region of tall stature, and so is North America (Indians and "Yankees"). Men of great height are also spread over wide territories in Africa.

The following shows the nomenclature of stature:

Small	less than 1 metre 60.
Height below the average ..	1 m. 60 to 1 m. 649.
Height above the average ..	1 m. 65 to 1 m. 699.
Very tall	1 m. 70 and over.

In order to furnish exact information height should be measured from full grown adults. Maturity is not reached at the same time in all peoples, nor, in the same population, among all social groups. Height diminishes with old age. Equally, it is absolutely essential to consider the height of each sex separately. We know that the woman is smaller (about 9 to 12 cms) than the man of her own ethnic group.

The Cephalic Index.—The study of crania was one of the earliest to which anthropologists devoted themselves; this was because the skull holds that noble organ, the brain, on which depends all our associative life. A very large proportion of all anthropometric work is given up to craniometry. We shall not here attempt to give the results of these special studies, several of which, however, can be used for the classification of human races. We shall deal with one among them only, that which enables us to represent, *grosso modo*, the shape of the cranial ovoid—the cephalic index, worked out by the Swede, Retzius, in 1845.

This index is the relation the maximum width of the skull bears to its greatest length, this being taken as 100.

The perception that Man's cranial ovoid is not always of the same shape is no new thing. Without going back so far as Hippocrates' description of the Macrocephals, we know that Vésale remarked that " the head of the Genoese, the Greeks and the Turks suggests a globe, whereas that of the Belgians is oblong "—which, as a matter of fact, is only relatively true.

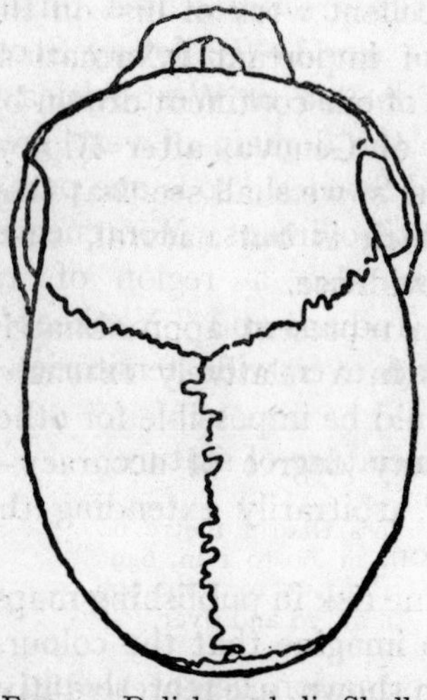

FIG. 1. Dolichocephalic Skull.

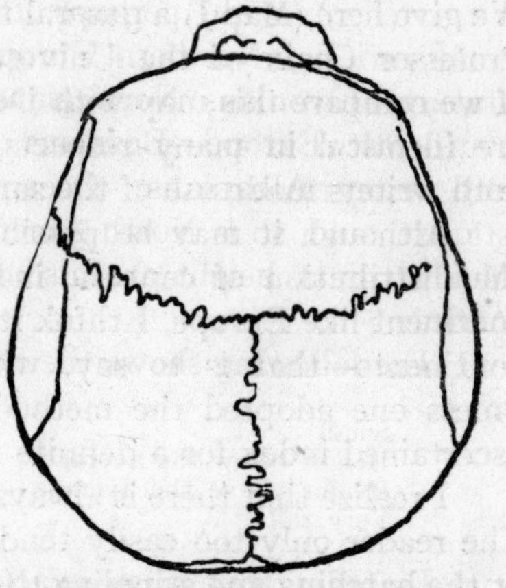

FIG. 2. Brachycephalic skull.

Short, broad skulls are brachycephalic (fig. 2) and long and relatively narrow skulls are dolichocephalic (fig. 1). The two figures here compared show the difference clearly. These characters of brachycephaly and dolichocephaly are hereditary, and lend to a human group a clear cut ethnical physiognomy. Scandinavians, Eskimo, Papuans, and most Negroes are dolichocephalic; Lapps, Bavarians, Auvergnats, Tunguses and Armenians are brachycephalic.

The following is the nomenclature of the cephalic index (cranial index) as set forth by Broca; we give in a second column the classification Deniker employed for the living subject :

	Skeleton (Broca).	Living Subject (Deniker).[1]
Hyperdolichocephalic	—	Under 75.9.
Dolichocephalic	Under 75.	76-77.
Sub-dolichocephalic	75.01-77.77.	78-79.
Mesaticephalic	77.78-80.	80-81.
Sub-brachycephalic	80.01-83.33.	82-83.
Brachycephalic	83.34 and over.	84-85.
Hyperbrachycephalic	—	86 and over.

We do not yet know the exact geographical distribution of the cephalic index throughout the world.

For Europe, the best known region in this regard, we have Deniker's map which can still be used. About the same time Ripley's maps appeared in that excellent work of his[2] on the races of Europe, which was full of important information. We give here (Map I) a general map of our continent drawn by Professor Chaix of the University of Geneva, after Ripley. If we compare this map with Deniker's, we shall see that they are identical in many respects, which is but natural, since both writers made use of the same evidence.

Although it may be possible to represent approximately the distribution of cephalic indices in a relatively extensive continent like Europe, I think it would be impossible for other continents—that is to say, with any degree of accuracy—unless one adopted the method of arbitrarily extending the ascertained index for a definite region.

I realize that there is always some risk in publishing maps. The reader only too easily tends to imagine that the colours, or the hatching and stippling therein shown, are representative of certainties. For instance, in Ripley's map, the large black patch of the middle portion of the Balkan peninsular and the horizontal hatching above and below it show results arrived at by this method of extension. My studies in the Balkan peninsular have modified this too simplist arrangement which, moreover, for certain parts, is actually inaccurate. I call attention to this in passing merely to show how short-lived is the representative value of ethnological maps, at all events up till the present.

[1] **LV**, p. 4.
[2] **CCXX.**

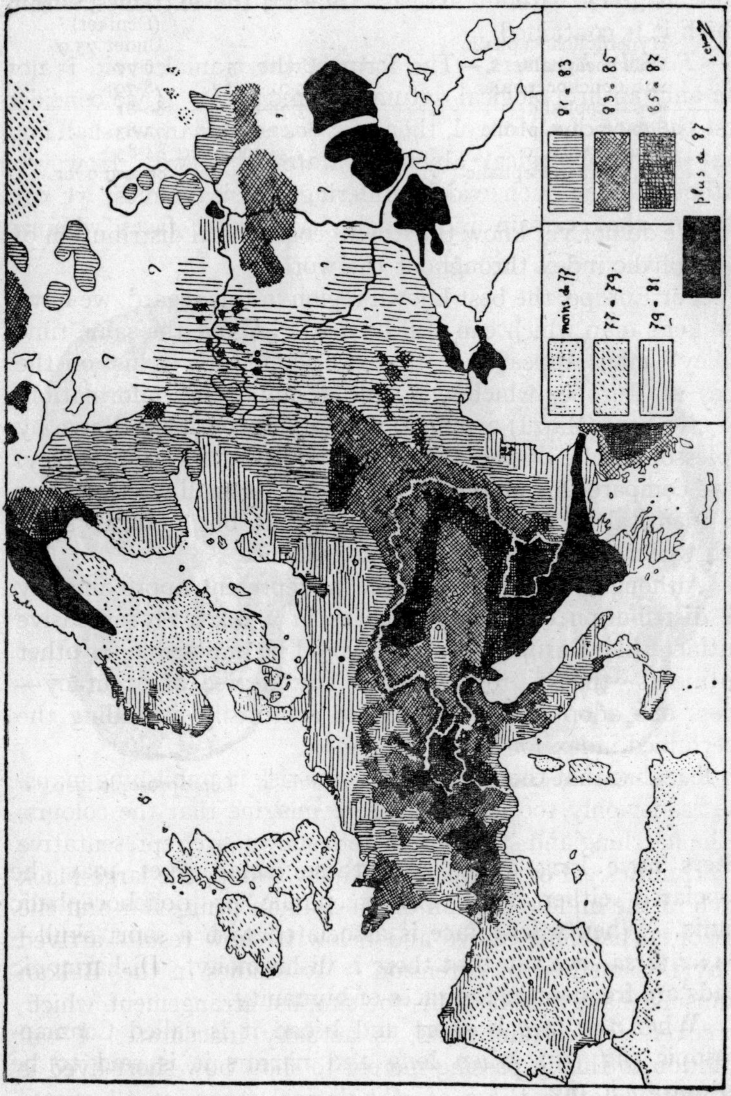

MAP I. Approximate distribution of cephalic indices (after Ripley).

Finally, such maps can represent only a rendering of the mean indices. And it is a matter of common knowledge how greatly one has to beware of such averages when the mean alone is given without at least showing the extremes within which it is contained.

Facial Characters.—The form of the cranial ovoid is not the only anthropological datum to remember. If we consider first the face of a Mongol, then of a Scandinavian, we shall find that a morphological abyss separates the two. However, without taking such widely differing physiognomies, we can observe that certain individuals have short faces whereas

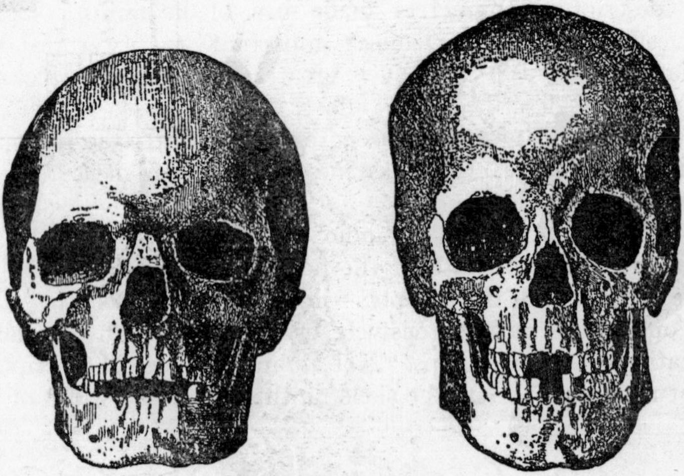

FIG. 3. Chamaeprosopic face. FIG. 4. Leptoprosopic face. (After Kollmann-Bale).

others have long ones. And these facial types may be associated either with brachycephalic or dolichocephalic crania. When a long face is associated with a short skull—or *vice versa*—we say that there is disharmony. Disharmonic heads are frequent in the races of humanity.

When the face is short and broad it is called Chamaeprosopic (fig. 3); when long and narrow it is said to be leptoprosopic (fig. 4).

The general oval of the face is a character of which travellers have always taken note. But such observations, without measurements, are largely useless owing to their lack of precision. Need we add that in the general technique of anthropometry, there is an index of the principal dimensions of the face just as for the skull? Two special facial characters will detain us for a moment—that relating to the nose and that of prognathism.

Every schoolboy knows what a difference there is between the nose of a Negro or an Australian, and that of a European or a Sioux Indian. Not a history book but mentions the Bourbon nose and the prognathism of the Hapsburgs. Has it not even been sought to use certain of these characters as signs of degeneracy and of inferiority in an evolutionary sense?[1]

The shape of the nose takes a foremost place in the list of descriptive characters made use of in anthropological investigations. It is most important to ascertain this character. But it is of even greater importance to measure the organ described. In effect, certain noses which are platyrrhine in appearance because of their width (the Kalmuks, for instance) are classed as mesorrhine when measurements come to be made.

That is why the nasal index should always be found.[2] It consists in the breadth of the nose—measured by straddling the nostrils with the callipers—in relation to its length. This is one of the most extensively used characters in the classification of human groups. Not an anthropological description but mentions it. On the skeleton the length and width of the

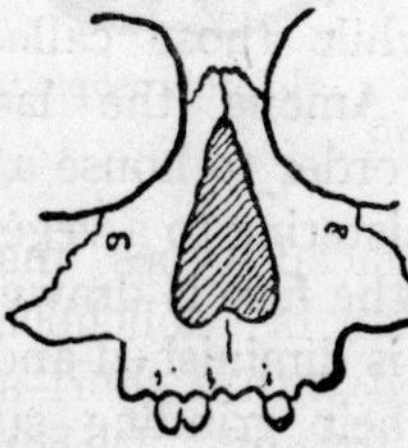

FIG. 5.
Leptorrhine nasal opening.

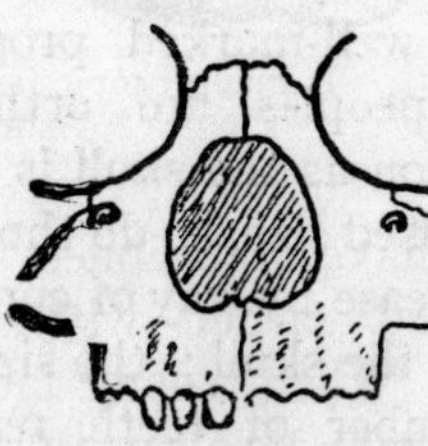

FIG. 6.
Platyrrine nasal opening.

nasal opening is measured, which may present shapes and dimensions that differ greatly (fig. 5 and 6); the index is found from the same relation as that given above.

[1] LXXV.

[2] XXVII, p. 172.

Below is the nomenclature of this index, both for the living subject and the skeleton :

	Nasal Index.	
	Skeleton (Broca).	Living Subject (Deneker).
Leptorrhinians	under 47.9.	Under 70.
Mesorrhinians	48-52.9.	70-84.9.
Platyrrhinians	from 53.	85-99.9
Ultra platyrrhinians	—	over 100.

The Asiatics of Asia Minor (Armenians, Kurds, Turks and Caucasians), Europeans in general, and Arabs are leptorrhinian ; a large number of yellow men and North American Indians are mesorrhinian.

Among the most platyrrhinian populations are the Negroes and Australians.

Prognathism.—A projecting facial angle is thus called. Anthropoid apes, even if they sometimes closely approach Man by certain characters, are very far removed from him by others. For instance the face in the ape is beyond comparison larger and more prominent than in Man. It is a muzzle. Prehistoric Man, particularly the Neanderthal type, has an enormously large face—very much larger, in relation to the cranium, than to-day—and a sort of muzzle.

Without going into too many details, let us say that prognathism may be maxillary and dental, or maxillary only, or dental only. What are known as lower peoples show a more or less well-marked prognathism ; while those called the higher peoples are orthognathous. Among the last, in proportion as the skull is developed in order to house a brain of increased size, so do those organs ministering to a vegetative life decrease by way of compensation ; the face is drawn back beneath the skull ; the size of the jaws is diminished and even the number of teeth reduced and their grinding surface lessened.[1]

The observation of prognathism goes back very far, but the measures taken to express it were but slowly acquired. Formerly, when artists wanted to represent Negroes they painted them as black Whites. Albrecht Dürer was the exception. It was after having remarked this arbitrary morphology of the painters with their Negroes " faits de chic "

[1] **CLI**, p. 17 ; **CXCIX**.

that Pierre Camper sought a precise method of representing the different types of face and invented the facial angle.

Few techniques have been so much studied, upset and revised. This was because a philosophic idea was connected with the knowledge of the facial angle.

Even to-day one sees angle values quoted on many occasions where they are quite out of place, and exaggerated significance attached to them. Morphologists do not ask so much of them. But for them, likewise, prognathism remains a problem for whose solution contradictory means are continually being proposed. Some years ago Paul Rivet authoritatively took up the study of this technique whose utilization is of genuine importance to the classification of human groups.[1]

Many other observable and mensurable characters—both in the skeleton and the living subject—are invoked by anthropologists, such as the related size of the different segments making up stature (there are macroskeletal and brachyskeletal races); the size of the brain and the pattern of its convolutions; the shape of the eye (for instance, the Mongoloid as compared with the European eye), etc. Readers who wish to pursue a knowledge of these details further will find them in the anthropological textbooks.

It is quite certain that the classifications of to-day will not for ever continue to exist in their present form. Their changing physiognomy is not the result of fashion—science knows no fluctuations of this sort—but the consequence of the never-ceasing progress accomplished by naturalists.

[1] CCXXI, p. 35 and 175.

CHAPTER III

Race and Language

As we have already remarked, race has too often been confused with language. Unfortunately, even to-day we hear of "the Latin," "the Germanic" or "the Slavonic" races in current speech, in any number of textbooks and in journalistic parlance. I do not doubt that the authors of these textbooks know perfectly well that such "races" do not exist. They say it is merely a method of making clear to their pupils certain distributions of population speaking languages of common origin. Conceded. But has not this method the grave disadvantage of engraving more deeply an existing error on the minds of a number of people? Would it not be wise to abandon it? Do we not daily see political writers and journalists speaking with a naïve—and dangerous—assurance of these so-called races, as though they could by a word give to all the people of a State who speak one language an identical anthropological physiognomy? Even historians occasionally permit themselves to slip into the use of such definitions without analysing them. Their guilt is even greater.

Most modern linguists associate themselves with anthropologists in deploring such errors.[1] They are long-lived, however, and it will take the combined forces of all to eliminate them from habitual usage.

Systematic anthropology is sufficiently advanced to-day for us to be able to form a general idea (general and no more, we must have the honesty to admit) of the principal races of the earth. This done, let a map showing the distribution of languages be given to an ethnologist, and ask him if he can exactly superpose it on the map of the distribution of races!

[1] "The truth is that language and race are two entirely distinct notions between which one must not for a single instant admit even the shadow of a likeness; no anthropological argument, under the smallest pretext, should contain a single word of linguistics, nor should any linguistic argument contain a single word of anthropology. When this essential separation has been resolved upon both sciences may be made to progress. Till then we shall only be wasting paper and ink."—From a letter to Salomon Reinach from Havet, *l'Anthropologie*, 1900, p. 483.

There are in the world diverse races—highly diverse, even—who speak the same tongue. There are also men of the same race who speak different languages. I will not give the two easy instance of those Negroes who, in the French or English colonies, express themselves in French or English and thus should figure, by linguistic-racial right, the first in the ranks of the Latin " races " and the second in those of the Germanic " races " ; this would be a little too obvious. But how many populations, among the natives of South America, gradually forget their original language to accept Spanish in its place ? Have not the Votiaks and Permiaks of Northeast Russia, who are of Ugrian race, become Russianized in speech ?

In the north of Western Asia and in Persia, do not people of the same race in the zoological sense speak different languages ? Has not a similar phenomenon occurred in the Balkan peninsular and in many other places besides ?

How many changes shall we not see if we go back even a short way into the past ! It is only necessary to open an atlas and slightly to recall one's history. When the Normans first touched at the coasts of the old Frankish empire they undoubtedly spoke a Scandinavian language, and the Franks themselves a German dialect. It is possible that some among them primitively came of the same race : the tall stature of this Northeastern portion of France and its frequent dolichocephaly alone would bring this to mind.

The most remarkable modern instance of this superposition of language on race and of the apparent absorption of the second by the first is provided by the United States. Throughout this vast territory, 120 million people coming from all parts of the world and belonging to numerous races have managed to become merged into a new type—the " Yankee ". The principal human substratum of the great Republic has been supplied by the tall dolichocephalic blond race (the Nordic race) ; the small sub-brachychephalic blond race (Eastern race—Russians) ; the tall sub-dolichocephalic brunet race (the Atlanto-Mediterranean race). The census of 1910 further distinguished those who had been born abroad, that is to say, the most recent human stratum. Somewhere near 4 or 5 million people belonged to the first of the three races given above ; nearly 2 millions to the second, and about the same number to the third. Although the representatives of these races largely mingle in marriage, and thereby disturb the primitive ethnic physiognomy, it is still the case that a certain number among the rest, drawn to consanguinity, may preserve more or less intact the characters of the race to which they themselves belong. But they all speak English. This great human mass, extraordinarily composite as regards race, is *one* as regards language. And in this enumeration of the mingling of these races quoted above we have designedly left out ethnic groups which are still more disparate, like certain natives (Cherokees and others), and the Negroes, who could also, either directly or as half-breeds, be given the same linguistic label.

This example will suffice.

Pangermanism, panslavism, panturanianism " are formulæ born of the minds of intellectuals and politicians; they are not realities springing spontaneously from a consciousness of ethnic community between different peoples . . . ;" " races " are grouped, regrouped, carved up and occasionally manufactured on the map of Europe (and on the map of other parts of the world) according to the will of political necessity or opportunity.[1]

History is especially concerned with these questions. Racial hatred, veritable zoological antipathies, have been sedulously fostered and fanned into flame by the intellectuals, many of whom must have been well aware of the lie they were inculcating. And of how many wars have these racial hatreds not been the occasion during the course of centuries! Have not such arguments been used at various tumes to induce peoples to engage in crusades for the " salvation of the race " ? —to " inflame the masses " who, apart from a few excited little groups, are rarely attracted towards the hazards of war. How many books have been written with such titles, redoubtable in their brevity, as " Racial Conflict " ![2] " From that century in which people have talked the most of universal brotherhood and racial equality will date and does date a violent antagonism between fraternal groups of the human family. The mass of men are sincere. They take up new ideas and new impulses in all good faith. They do not lightly relinquish them. By this

[1] **XXVIII**, p. 642.

[2] Such, in particular, was the title of a book by Gumplovicz (*Les Luttes des Races*); though this author does not use the term *race* in its full zoological implication (**LXXXVII**).

talk of race to which they have lent ear they have been trained, as races, to detest one another; and hate is even more difficult to unlearn than love "[1].

Pangermanism and panslavism may be linguistic formulæ in which political desires are enwrapped; they are not expressions of race. German-speaking people belong to many races. There is at least as much difference between a Pomeranian from the Baltic coast and a Bavarian from the Ammer massif as there is between a horse and a zebra. As for panslavism, it incorporates individuals who differ in another way as regards race. We shall see here, without quitting European soil, representatives of the Lapponic race, those of the tall dolichocephalic (Nordic) race; of the east European race (a large number of Russians); of the Ugrian race (Votiaks, for instance), and of the Turki-Tatar (Crimean Tatars) and Mongolian (Kalmuks) races. How many races, even languages and how many sociological states, squeezed into one single, redoubtable word! For us who are ethnologists it is interesting to note that these imperialistic notions were born before the great anthropological researches were undertaken. And, noting this, we are constrained to say, further, that it is partly the fault of the intellectuals that so many ills have come upon the world. The Universities (and should they not open wide their windows to truth?), had they welcomed more readily than they have done (we except North America) the teaching of Anthropology, would have played the noble part of pacifists which devolves upon them. Many imperialist notions are the result of the mistaken generalizations of linguists maintained and prolonged by geographers and historians, and made use of by politicians. Ethnographic and anthropological studies conduce as naturally as water runs downhill to a reasoning that runs counter to imperialism. It would be very difficult, impossible indeed, to be at one and the same time an anthropologist and a political consolidator after the manner of a Russian Czar. Had systematic anthropological research preceded philological research it is possible that a certain number of political events, whose happening can never be too deeply regretted from the standpoint of world justice and world peace, would never have been set going. For we know what success may attend a phrase or a formula, what a power

[1] **XXVIII**, p. 644.

of suggestion it may carry and how hard it may hit, the ease with which, by force of repetition and by taking advantage of the law of least effort, it can be made to penetrate among the masses of the people. The tale of History is strewn with such formulæ of which the lack of any knowledge of anthropology permitted clever politicians to make use.

Let us drive home the gist of this paragraph by an examination of the Latin races. In Europe seven countries speak languages derived from Latin—France, Walloon Belgium, French Switzerland, Italy, Spain, Portugal, and, to the east of the continent, Roumania. To these we must add a few small groups in German territory—Rhoetians, etc. This ensemble, which is not very considerable in extent, comprises at the least representatives of the following races[1] :—Nordic (Belgium-France) ; Atlanto-Mediterranean (Iberian peninsular, France, Italy) ; Ibero-Insular (Iberian peninsular, France, Italy) Cevenole (Italy, Switzerland, France, Iberian peninsular—northern part).

These racial differences are not supported on mere imperceptible nuances. They are perfectly clear-cut, visible to all eyes, even to those least aware. If we were to put, on the podium of a classroom, an authentic Norman (big, blond, dolichocephalic, clear-complexioned), an authentic Cevenole (medium height, brachycephalic, brunet), and an authentic Mediterranean (small, brunet, dolichochephalic), the audience would not hesitate a moment in picking out the disparities, just as, for example, in a natural history museum they would pick out similar disparities between the three sorts of *Lepus* :—*alpinus*, *timidus*, and *cuniculus*. We may add, too, that the differences in the genus *Homo* are much wider.

What is the origin of these diverse races ? Are they the produce of physical surroundings which in so clear-cut a fashion have modified one single race ? Where shall we find them at home from the earliest times ? History explains their presence in part, for some thousands of years. Many of these races appeared during the invasion epoch, which we can place as far back as the beginning of the Mesolithic. The Pleistocene renders intelligible the presence of others. France—since for the moment we are taking this country as an example—has never ceased to be populated from the early Quaternary.

[1] Deniker's classification.

During thousands of years these peoples spoke on this soil languages of which we know nothing, except that they are believed to be " derived from the primitive Indo-European language ". In order to be able to say with certainty that such a language was the earliest that men used in Western Europe we should have to demonstrate that the earliest French prehistory is later than the earliest prehistory of the localities of which this Indo-European language was the expression. Does such proof exist ? Who, for instance, has proved that the Indian Chellean is anterior to the French Chellean ?

We said above that languages in the course of history have changed masters in singular fashion. But those who thus spoke them, by accepting a new idiom owing to the force of circumstances did not therefore modify their physical characters nor change the colour of their skin and hair any more than their anatomical structure. A colony of Scandinavians, supposing they were to emigrate to North America and become isolated in the midst of other groups, would continue, provided they married among themselves, to conserve their tall stature, their dolichocephaly and their light eyes, although they lost they own language—and, because the acquisition of a new language is indispensable—substituted English for it. The same would happen in the case of a colony of Cevenoles or Auvergnats who, maintaining themselves in the same conditions of ethnic isolation, would in no way modify their brachycephaly, their medium height or their brown hair by the act of accepting a new speech.

It is possible to note a number of linguistic superpositions in the same place and in a very short space of time. Quadrilingual Switzerland provides proof of it. The canton of Le Valais, undoubtedly Celtic, has become, in the course of a history which is certainly not very long, first Roman, then Germanic, and now, in part, has returned to a Latin tongue. The Roman portions of the primitive Swiss cantons would have been Germanized from about the beginning of the fith century. This Germanic superposition took a long time to make itself manifest. For Central Switzerland it appears to have been achieved towards the middle of the ninth century.[1]

Alemannic, concentrated on the northern slope of the Bernese Alps, did not all at once get through the cols leading

[1] **CCXCVIII**, p. 98 ; **XXX**, p. 101 ; **CXCVI**.

into the valley of the Rhone. This immigration of a language would appear to have been well established in the region of the upper course of the Valaisian Rhone in the ninth century according to some, and probably much later according to others who do not give it as definitely established in the Rhodanian basin until the beginning of the twelfth century.

Although it has been overlaid with three or four linguistic strata, this region of central Europe has none the less preserved its anthropological characters. In the outlying lateral valleys of the Valais, and even in many parts of the great Rhone valley, the population has remained ethnically pure, at least up to the time of the establishment of the great Alpine roads and railways. Few European territories exhibit a similar percentage of like types—of individuals in whom the same morphological characters are to be found. Thus, reposing in a single cemetery or ossuary, and offering us a homogeneous picture of anatomical characters, there are representatives of the same ethnic group on whom were imposed diverse linguistic labels.

I do not wish to give the impression that contemporary linguists themselves accord any racial value to linguistic expressions. If such an idea existed long ago, it is no longer current. A note at the beginning of this paragraph has already made that clear. Max Müller long ago wrote: " By solidarizing and mixing up the science of language and the science of ethnology, both have been grievously injured." The classification of races should be altogether independent of that of languages, and the researches made with a view of these classifications should *a priori* be absolutely free from any linguistic entanglements. It is Meillet who says: " One speaks readily of Romance peoples, of the Slav race, of an Aryan type—all so many expressions devoid of precise meaning. Either they add nothing at all to the idea of the relationship of languages, or they add what is erroneous." It is a matter of everyday experience that no link necessarily exists between a language and the " race " of those who speak it.[1]

Vendryes confirms this attitude in the book he contributes to this historical synthesis[2] where he says: " Whatever be the rôle played by changes in race in the transformations of language, the essential bonds between these two concepts

[1] **CLIV**, p. 81;
[2] **CCLXIV**, p. 235.

cannot be established. We must not confound hereditary ethnical characteristics with institutions such as languages, religion, and culture, which are eminently transmissible, and can be borrowed and exchanged. Glancing over the linguistic map of modern Europe, we see that under the uniformity of the same language very mixed races may be concealed." An anthropologist would not speak otherwise, and this scientific entente between the two disciplines should be emphasized. Nevertheless it would be peurile on the part of anthropologists not to accord full attention to linguistic facts. Philologists should exhibit the same attitude in face of the facts of anthropology.

CHAPTER IV

Primitive Human Races

We shall not deal in this book with hypotheses relating to Tertiary man. We know that up till now no universally accepted discovery (though we have to bear in mind the Ipswich finds) allows us to assert his existence in this geological period. Nor shall we deal with the occasionally somewhat lively arguments which have arisen between South American anthropologists—chiefly of the Argentine Republic—and those of Europe on the subject of the presumptive pliocene—or even earlier—origin of American autochthones. We shall not leave Eur-Asian and Eur-African soil, because it is both in this great continental land mass that the more important pages of History have been written and the earliest indisputable human remains found.

The present populations of these continents are the descendants—it could not be otherwise—of the populations which occupied Europe, Asia and Africa in our most distant past. But have these various and so clearly discernible types all got distinct genealogical trees? Or are they but the branches and offshoots of some primitive trunk whose subsequent development baffles us? And are these genealogical trees still rooted in the same places in which they first began to grow?

At every page we come up against the fact that anthropological research is far from being as advanced as we could wish. Furthermore it has been unfortunately subordinated, in the mind of many intellectuals, to philological research which, as we have seen, introduced so many erroneous notions into this subject of Man's origins. Nevertheless, despite this double deficit, ethnologists have already shown us this important fact, namely that the extreme diversity of types which we believe to exist—sometimes they cause us to hesitate to attack the problem of origins—may be summed up in a less complex presentment. In the ethnic domain, too, we are often deceived by appearances. Anthropological realities have frequently been obscured by the mirages of ethnographic, linguistic and historical facts. Fewer human races exist—the word *race* has been so freely used—than one might at first imagine. Anthropology cannot yet indicate their exact number because its investigations are neither sufficient in number nor sufficiently precise. It readily admits the insufficiency of its conclusions. The list of races so far tabled must often be considered to have a merely conventional value, and in any case to represent but a temporary phase of our knowledge.

Ethnogenic anthropological research leads to a dual result ; it establishes the morphological characters of the living populations scattered over the earth's surface in such fashion as to permit of their being grouped according to their natural affinities, and it makes known to us the characters of vanished populations at all periods of History—and History, as we conceive it, begins with human life. Once this dual knowledge is solidly based, we can attempt to establish the descent of present day from primitive races.

Fossil Man—he belongs to several epochs—is the name given to the men who were the contemporaries of extinct species of animals, themselves fossils, such as the woolly Rhinoceros, the Mammoth, the cave Bear and Lion, and the great-horned Deer, to take but two or three examples familiar to all. The fossil men dug up in quaternary strata are thus the earliest human ancestors of contemporary populations. We can compare their morphological—their racial—characters with the same characters observed in living populations, and endeavour to find out whether—even at this distance of time—there exists any bond of relationship between these groups.

The sum total of finds relating to fossil Man is still inconsiderable. It has been much increased in the last decades, but it still lags far behind what is required. Nevertheless, during the last fifteen years or so we have been confronted with some singularly impressive facts.

Chellean Man

Of the Chellean period—the earliest chapter of our history—we possess but a few skeletal fragments, and the interpretation which has been given of them makes us wish ardently for further discoveries. Two human races evidently lived on European soil at that time, *Homo heidelbergensis* whose extraordinarily uncouth characters we can imagine; and another race, up till now known as *Eoanthropus dawsoni* (or *Homo dawsoni*), the morphological characters of whose skull would seem to indicate a more highly evolved race.

But what scanty osteological documents these are! Of Heidelberg Man only a lower jaw has been found, in 1907, near the little village of Mauer, about 10 kilometres southeast of Heidelberg, under a layer of loess and gravel, at a depth of 24 metres.[1] The fauna encountered at the same level is particularly archaic if we look upon it as pleistocene. That is why many writers have considered the Mauer jaw to belong to the Pliocene. French palæontologists, Boule in particular, approximating the Mauer beds to those of the North of France, consider that this skeletal fragment may be attributed to the Chellean period. However that may be, the Mauer jaw is to-day perhaps the most venerable human relic known; but that relic alone does not permit us to reconstitute with certainty the complete portrait of this *Homo heidelbergensis*. It has been said that the Mauer jaw prescribes with sufficient exactitude its pithecoid and its human characters and that thus we have in it an ideal form intermediate between the Apes and Man. It would seem wise to reserve judgment. Despite all the laws of correlation as we know them, it is best to wait before setting this specimen on his feet as one of our ancestors. We repeat, he must have been singularly brutelike in build, and if we wish at once to attempt to trace the descendants of this primitive race, in all probability we should look in the direction of *Homo neanderthalensis*.

The second oldest representative of our kind is to be found among the documents contributed by English soil to human palæontology. This is the Piltdown skull. These fragments, as venerable, and more interesting because more complete than the Mauer jaw, were brought to the knowledge of anthropologists in 1912 through a communication to the Geological Society of London. Shown by Charles Dawson and Smith Woodward it caused, as might be expected, a sensation in the learned world. Piltdown lies on the course of the Ouse, to the north of Newhaven in Sussex. Successive finds of bone fragments in a gravel bed permitted, first of all, the reconstruction of almost a complete skull. Such a restoration,

[1] CCXXXVII; XXII.

difficult to accomplish, is always open to criticism in certain respects. Nevertheless we have before us sufficient anatomical elements to give us a picture of the morphological aspect of this distant forbear of ours, or at all events of his cephalic aspect.

The stratification of the gravel beds containing these human remains testifies to an old alluvial formation earlier than the last scooping out of the Ouse valley, the animal fossils of this layer dating the Piltdown skull at about the same period as the Mauer jaw. Maybe it is even older ? Maybe the Piltdown stratum is more recent and only Acheulean ?

The incomplete jaw, discovered beside some cranial fragments, has been the subject of lively controversy. Some attribute it to the skull of *Eoanthropus,* while others, diametrically opposed to this view—and they also bring cogent reasons in support of their opinion—consider that the jaw is that of a Chimpanzee.[1]

If we now have to envisage the destinies of these two primitive races, we should picture to ourselves the possibility of the Heidelberg race having given birth to the Piltdown race, and the Piltdown race of the type with progressive characters which we meet with in Aurignacian times. This last race—which undoubtedly led to the creation of at least one modern dolichocephalic type—we should call by a composite name—Cro-Magnon-Laugerie-Chancelade—if we were monogenist. We shall have to explain these nominal approximations which appear to be disharmonic.

If we are to admit that the Piltdown line has come down to our day, may we believe that the same thing has happened in regard to the Heidelberg-Neanderthal line ? The answer is much more difficult. Many anthropologists admit that the Neanderthaloid characters sometimes met with in certain individuals in Europe in periods later than the Palæolithic, and even in present day populations, should be regarded as atavisms showing reversion to this ancient race. Others, led unhesitatingly by Marcellin Boule, consider that *Homo neanderthalensis* became extinct at the close of the Moustierian period.[2]

It is a fact that, so far, the skeletons dug up in strata belonging to the Reindeer age to not possess the characters

[1] This jaw, it would seem, is more and more coming to be regarded as human.

[2] XXII, p. 242.

afferent to the Neanderthal type. If representatives of this inferior race continued to move about on European soil, why do we not find a single specimen among those in the gallery of upper Palæolithic man?

The upper Pleistocene, or Reindeer age, comprises the Aurignacian, Solutrean and Magdalenian periods. In view of the stratigraphic uncertainties of some of the early excavations it would appear to be wiser—I am not alone in holding this opinion—to group the skeletons of these three periods together, and to present the human races of this epoch as though there had been no subdivision of the civilization of this portion of the Palæolithic. Authorities are not agreed as to the number of human races at that time. Some count four—Cro-Magnon, Grimaldi, Laugerie, Chancelade. (And we must also mention, if only to keep it in memory, the *Homo aurignacensis* type created by Klaatsch from a skeleton found at Combe-Capelle.) Other writers only count three, making one type of the Laugerie and Chancelade races. It is this latter definition that we certainly ought to accept.

Moustierian Man

The middle Pleistocene or Neanderthal race of Man, which we have said can be considered as being descended from the Heidelberg race, shows itself with singularly homogeneous morphological characters during the course of the Moustierian age, whether we take the Gibraltar Man or those of la Chapelle-aux-Saints, Spy, or Neanderthal. Confronted with this relative abundance and with such homogeneity, we ask ourselves what can have become of the descendants of Piltdown Man, with his characters more nearly approaching those of *Homo sapiens*, during these times. Why have we not found their remains?

Is the Moustierian civilization specifically the work of *Homo neanderthalensis*? We might well think so, considering the industries and the skeletons so far discovered, which, in every station in Belgium, Germany, France and Croatia are the same.

Everyone knows the excellent monograph by Boule on the Fossil Man of la Chapelle-aux-Saints, at the close of which this savant brought together all the discoveries relating to the human type of the Moustierian epoch. After having recalled those finds coming from the same horizon, Boule gave a complete diagnosis of this particular race. Those who wish to make acquaintance with it in detail will find what they want in his book. We shall content ourselves here with summing up the principal features while recalling that the exceptional morphological brutality of this human type for long led people to suppose that the remains discovered could only be pathological.[1]

The head of this fossil man was extraordinarily rugged. The skull is elongated and at the same time flattened (platybasia); the posterior region, instead of being rounded, is depressed and projecting. The forehead is receding and has enormous superciliary arches which in some ways recall the visor-like skull of *Pithecanthropus erectus*. The face is large and projecting, forming a kind of muzzle, whereas in present-day Europeans the face is almost entirely dominated by the cranium. Enormous round orbits, a deep depression separating the nasal bones from those of the forehead, a powerful lower jaw, and the absence of a chin, complete, as so many inferior characters, the general aspect of the bony skeleton of the head.

What strikes the least observant from the outset, when the cranium is examined in profile, is the upsetting of that proportion to which we are accustomed between the size of the face and the size of the head. Roughly speaking, the highest races may be characterised as having a large cranium and a small face. Such a picture presents itself as natural to our minds, because, in the complex of the head, the face in great part represents the lower functions of vegetative existence, whereas the cranium, which houses the brain, represents the higher functions of our associative life. This image really represents a genuine evolution: we see in the higher races a continual decrease of the face, jaws, and even the teeth, in proportion as we achieve our cerebral ascent.

Even if, in the Neanderthal race, the brain-case is large, the face itself is enormous. This powerful face must have lent an aspect of bestiality to Moustierian Man to which no living race—not even the Australians—can approach. Furthermore, the large cranium of *Homo neanderthalensis* did not hold such a highly convolute brain as those of present day Europeans. It is much less highly organized. Was this, perhaps, why the

[1] **XXIII** and **XXII**, p. 185.

Moustierian race did not survive? Did it find itself unadaptable in face of the new (?) conditions imposed on Man's existance towards the close of Moustierian and the beginning of Aurignacian times?

This exceptionally powerful head was carried on a body that was likewise exceptionally powerful and whose skeleton preserved a fairly large number of pithecoid souvenirs. The vertebral column was short and massive and the cervical vertebrae resembled in many a detail those of the chimpanzee. Both the cervical and lumbar curvatures appear to have been less pronounced than in present day man, to whom they permit, with the help of various organs, the complete biped position. The thoracic cavity was supplied with powerful ribs. The massive arms must have been unusually powerful. Maybe complete extension of the forearm was impossible. This Neanderthal race must have had short legs and bowed femurs with very large extremities. The tibia was also short, with the head in-curved behind (retroversion). The articular surface of the knee was thus not horizontal but sloped in a downward and backward direction. Therefore an absolutely vertical stance of thigh and leg was impossible, and the posture of the men of those times—or at all events of the race we are now describing—must have been one of semi-flexion.

The stature of *Homo neanderthalensis* was less than that of present day human races. The height of males would have been somewhere about 1 metre 55. As for the height of the females, it would seem to have already shown that sex difference of from 9 to 12 cms—varying with the ethnic group—which we see to-day.

Just now, when speaking of the bony skeleton of the head, we saw that the cranium of the Chapelle-aux-Saints man was particularly large, and that the brain represented a considerable mass. It must not be thought that this was the case with all the individuals of this group. The capacity of the Chapelle-aux-Saints cranium has been estimated at 1600 cubic cms; but the other representatives of this race have furnished quite low figures—1408 cubic cms in the Neanderthal, and 1300 in the Gibraltar skull, and so on.

This Moustierian race is differently labelled by different writers:—*Homo neanderthalensis*, *Homo spyensis*, *Homo mousteriensis*, *Homo krapinensis*, *Homo breladensis*, etc.; each writer describing it having added the name of the station in which he found the human skeleton or skeletons to that of the genus Homo, so that we have Neanderthal Man, Spy Man, le Moustier Man, and so forth. Others have called him *Homo primigenius*, or *Homo antiquus*—dangerous appelations, especially the first. We should bear in mind the unfortunate mistake relating to *Elephas primigenius*. We feel that all anthropologists would do well to rally to the view expressed by Boule (who could likewise have bestowed a new specific name in the Chapelle-aux-Saints man) that all the human types of this group whose morphology he has so well described, should bear the common label of *Homo neanderthalensis*.

Upper Palæolithic Man

It is obvious that the decline of the Moustierian civilization, even if it did coincide exactly with the disappearance of the race of *Homo neanderthalensis*, does not imply that mankind died out and then revived by a sort of spontaneous generation directly the new civilizations began to be elaborated. Only a few years past we should have been greatly embarrassed to account for the presence from the earliest phase of the Reindeer age of a human race differing so greatly from that of Neanderthal that it would seem impossible that one should be descended from the other—unless we postulate the intervention of an inexplicable evolution. The Piltdown discovery sheds a little more light on our perplexity although it is not yet complete day. It authorizes us to postulate two human races existing contemporaneously on European soil at the beginning of the Palæolithic, at any rate from Chellean times. As has been said already, the Moustierian period has yielded no representatives of this more highly evolved race that was to come to full maturity in the upper Palæolithic. Is it not certain that one day we shall find them ?[1]

The civilization of this tripartite period, which has been called the Reindeer age, is very different from that of the preceding periods. Side by side with a more elaborate panoply of flint implements—which would appear to indicate a necessary response to more varied needs than had hitherto existed—we find an intensive utilization of elephant tusks and of horn and bone. Spear points, polishers, harpoons, needles, etc., are fabricated from these materials of which no profit has been made in preceding ages. But what very largely differentiates

[1] See Note at end of Chapter, p. 78. (Translator.)

the new from the old civilization is the development of a hitherto unknown expression of human thought. The plastic arts make their appearance.

At first, in the Aurignacian period, these consisted in hesitant and crudely executed sculptures and gravings, which, to boot, are extremely rare. Then, when we get to Magdalenian times—was material existence more assured, perhaps ?—we see an efflorescence of magnificent and, in some ways, unsurpassable art. It is manifested in all manner of techniques —sculpture, graving, painting, modelling. Everyone knows the wealth and variety of these works of art in reindeer horn, ivory and bone, and on stone, which have been yielded by all the Magdalenian centres of Europe. Known to all, to-day, are those impressive frescoes, so largely conceived, painted on the walls of the caves of Altamira, Font de Gaume and elsewhere.

To what race belonged these ingenious craftsmen, these incomparable artists whose hands were guided by so clear a vision of the synthetic form that they were never at a loss for a single detail ?—whose skill was so amazing that their first strokes, with nothing added, gave a perfect picture of the living animal and its action ?—a picture so truthful that there is never the smallest doubt as to the zoological quality of the species represented ?

Are we to include these artists among the original peoples of Europe ? Or are they, according to the old philological doctrines, Asiatic immigrants who have appeared by one knows not what mysterious routes that are easy to point out only in the study and on a map ?

We can claim, without fear, these men of the upper Palæolithic as the ancestors of at least one or two of our existing races. If, when faced with the reconstructed Neanderthal Man, we feel some repugnance owing to its bestiality in considering the type as belonging to our genealogical tree, we shall feel no such repugnance when confronted with *Homo sapiens* of the close of quaternary times. We shall be quite willing to recognize that we are descended from this man whose biped posture is more perfect, and whose forehead, looked at from the front, is full of nobility ; whose face no longer shows the prognathism which gave to *Homo neanderthalensis* so brutal an expression. The architecture of the Man of Cro-Magnon and the Man of Laugerie-Chancelade is one that is obviously highly developed.

These new races remain quite "in the air" so far as any relation to the human races of the ancient Quaternary goes. We may, however, suppose that one of them at least is linked up with the Piltdown race, but this is nothing but a hypothesis. Our discoveries so far do not authorize us to go further. Let us, moreover, remember that Piltdown is represented only by some cranial fragments. When we come to consider the descendants of these races, we are in less uncertainty, for we see them come down to our own day and we can point them out.

The stature of this pleistocene group is not homogeneous. One of these races is very tall, whereas the other is probably below the average height.

The tall skeletons were yielded by the Cro-Magnon (Dordogne) and Baoussé-Roussé (Italy) stations. The old man of Cro-Magnon must have been very tall (1 metre 82). His companions were not quite so tall (Hamy gives an average height of 1 metre 78). The five adult skeletons of Baoussé-Roussé measured by Verneau range in height from 1 metre 79 to 1 metre 94 (average 1 metre 87). These are extraordinary figures.

No existing European population can show an average like this, since it exceeded 1 metre 82. No population in the world even, because the greatest average height is that of the Galloway Scots, and perhaps the Pila-Pila of West Africa, and their average does not go beyond 1 metre 79. Will this extraordinarily great stature of the biggest men of the Reindeer age be maintained without alteration in our anthropological tables ? Or will new discoveries lower the figure as it stands to-day ? It would be strange if our finds to date had yielded us exceptional types only.

The less tall race is represented by a certain number of skeletons, among which the best known are those of Laugerie and Chancelade, both in the Dordogne. The average height of this population was probably less than the mean height of present day Europeans, because so far we have only been able to give it 1 metre 62 to 1 metre 63. Such a difference between this and the Cro-Magnon race requires that, for the moment at least, we should consider the two separately. Their portraits, rapidly sketched in, may be given as follows :

Cro-Magnon race : individually very tall, with powerful muscles, having bowed femurs with pilaster, and laterally flattened (platycnemic) tibias ; dolichocephalic skull and short, broad face ; quadrilateral orbits ; long, narrow nasal opening (leptorrhiny) ; powerful jaw and prominent chin. The face is prognathous but much less so than in *Homo neanderthalensis*.

Laugerie-Chancelade race : individually small, but vigorously muscled ; powerful femurs with pilaster, and platycnemic and slightly retroverted tibias ; large feet ; very long and powerful arms. The dolichocephalic skull and the wide, high face constitute a harmonious type (which our Cro-Magnon Man is not) ; the orbits are large, the nose leptorrhine ; the powerful lower jaw shows a prominent chin. The face is not prognathous.

These two strongly-built, muscular races were not made for brute conflict alone. Their cerebral development is remarkable. A well-modelled cranium houses a highly organized brain. These races possess all that is needful both for conquering nature and for maintaining the position won, for they have strength at the disposition of intelligence. It would seem that both of them, as de Quatrefages said of the Cro-Magnon race, " are in every respect armed for the struggle against the difficulties and dangers of wild life."

Scarcely had these fossil races been brought to light before it was attempted to show what group—or groups—might be considered to be their descendants. The small Dolichocephals—the Laugerie-Chancelade race—were at once approximated to the Eskimo. Certain resemblances in their morphological characters, such as dolichocephaly and hypsicephaly, a leptoprosopic face, the sagittal crest, and small stature ; together with certain ethnographic comparisons—artistic representations in particular—seemed to promise well for this line of investigation. At the time of the final melting of the glaciers the Magdalenians would have followed the reindeer herds in their great trek northwards. Thus, for this race, the climatic environment would have remained the same, and the relation between the fauna (the reindeer in especial) and Man would have been preserved. The present day Eskimo, who have developed little since the close of the upper Palæolithic, have retained an art which is highly reminiscent of that of their Magdalenian (?) ancestors, and their morphology has remained very much like that of their quaternary forbears !

Hamy appears to support this point of view in his *Précis de Paléontologie humaine*. Speaking of the Eskimo, he writes : " Both by their manners and customs and the material of their industry and art, the present day Hyperboreans would appear to be closely related to the quaternary troglodytes of our country. We have already said that they do not differ greatly from the latter in their anatomy. In the circumpolar regions they still keep in being the Reindeer age of France, Belgium and Switzerland with its zoological, ethnographical and other characteristics."[1] This opinion, which Hamy has doubtless abandoned, has been by turns accepted and contested. Even to-day, though it finds resolute detractors among American anthropologists, it meets with support from English anthropologists like Sollas and Boyd Dawkins, and from French ones like Hervé.

Similarities certainly exist between the zoological and ethnographical characters of Eskimo and Magdalenians. But is it absolutely essential that a common origin should be invoked to explain them ? Now that the earth is beginning to be explored, do we not witness some singular approximations—they are apparent only—between populations widely separated geographically ? Can we not admit that these characters, thus placed in parallel, are merely convergent and not derivative ? I know well that conclusions such as I have here expressed lead to the admission of a singularly widely distributed polygenism ; but in objectively welcoming such an alternative, at all events for the moment, are we not facing reality, facing all the results of modern work ?

If we are to believe that the Eskimo are descended from the men of Laugerie-Chancelade, are we to think that *all* the men of this quaternary race became Hyperboreans ? Must we believe that when the glaciers finally retreated, *all* the Magdalenians, marching as one man towards their hyperborean destiny, went north ? Such an hypothesis could only have any verisimilitude if the small people had constituted but one little group all obeying a single will. Palæ-ethnological discoveries are not yet sufficient in number for eastern and northern Europe, any more than they are for Asia, for us to be able to come to any conclusion, no matter what, in regard to this question.

So far as I am concerned, I am quite ready to believe that at least a part of the Mediterranean populations can claim the men of Laugerie-Chancelade as ancestors. Such a

[1] **XCI**, p. 366.

supposition, it is obvious, leads to the belief that the Magdalenian population, instead of emigrating to the North, remained, after the climatic and geographical changes, in the same places in which we previously found them.

What was the fate of the Cro-Magnon race ?

Like the men of the Laugerie-Chancelade race, they probably remained on during the Mesolithic, in the same places in which they had sojourned since Aurignacian times. We have every right to think that a part of those populations which we shall see in the Neolithic belong to this stock. Anthropologists of the quality of Broca, de Quatrefages, Hamy, Collignon and Verneau have not been afraid to see the descendants of this race in certain populations of France, Spain and Africa :—the south-west of France, the Dordogne, the Landes and the Basque districts being thus peopled by men of Cro-Magnon type. But to find the best representatives of this race we must go and seek them on the other side of the Mediterranean, in North Africa and on the sea-coast of the African North-West. On one hand the Berbers, and on the other the Guanches would seem to present the closest morphological affinity with this ancient stock. May such affinity also be sought, perhaps, among certain representatives of the populations of Northern Europe ? The association of great height with dolichocephaly but without the concomitant leptoprosopy leads us to such an hypothesis. Able minds have considered that this northern race and a part, at least, of the Berber race, are but two branches of the same anthropological tree, separated since prehistoric times.

To sum up, we can establish the presence—the survival, one might say—of two races in Europe (we shall speak of a third directly) when palæolithic times were drawing towards their close—the tall Cro-Magnon race and the small Laugerie-Chancelade race. Both of them were dolichocephalic. One of them would really appear to descend from the Piltdown race. But which ? The comparative size of the skull, which, in other circumstances, might be used, will not here suffice. We must wait for fresh finds in lower Palæolithic centres. Of the two races which lived during the same epoch—or which preceded the two races mentioned above—one is considered to be extinct—*Homo neanderthalensis*. The offshoot from the genealogical tree representing this race would appear to have withered towards the close of the Moustierian.

We have not yet spoken of a fourth race which would appear to have been but sparsely represented in Europe and whose geographical origin it would seem that we should seek on the other side of the Mediterranean on the soil of that venerable African continent which was so propitious to the development of the human species.

The Grimaldi Race

Canon de Villeneuve, who was charged by the Prince of Monaco with the systematic excavation of the famous caves of Baoussé-Roussé, found two extraordinary skeletons on June 3rd, 1901, in the Grotte des Enfants, one of the caves excavated in this little limestone massif. They lay at a depth of 8 metres 50 in a deposit belonging to the Moustierian period. These two skeletons, buried together, were described by Professor Verneau of the Muséum de Paris, as negroid. He gave the name of the Grimaldi race to the human type to which they belonged,[1] and it is by this name, or as Negroids, that these skeletons are known among anthropologists.

At what Palæolithic horizon should we place them ? Do they really belong to the Moustierian period, as, at first sight, the floor level in which they were discovered would seem to show ? The Abbé de Villeneuve indicates that these Negroid skeletons were in a trench, about 75 cms. deep, dug in the Moustierian deposit, but that in reality they belonged to a more recent epoch—that which chronologically lies immediately above the Moustierian, that is to say, they belonged to the Aurignacian civilization. We must thus consider the Grimaldi Negroids to be Aurignacians who had been interred in a Moustierian stratum.

When Verneau's first memoir[2] appeared it caused great surprise in anthropological circles. What could be the meaning of the presence on European soil of individuals whose morphology differed so greatly from that of the fossil men hitherto discovered ? Was it a question of exceptional characters, of some sort of morphological abnormality ? Or were they confronted with the problem of an African race having penetrated at such a very remote date to the European coast ? Verneau cautiously kept an open mind on the question.

[1] The Italian commune in which the massif of Baoussé-Roués is situated is called Grimaldi.

[2] **CCLXVI.**

He concluded his memoir thus: "One fact remains, namely, that earlier than the Cro-Magnon race [Reindeer age] and later than the Spy race [*Homo neanderthalensis*], another ethnic element was represented in our regions and that this element showed negroid characters. If I have been able to demonstrate thus much I shall have reached the goal at which I aimed in writing this short note."[1] Fortunate discoveries were soon to throw light on the matter.

A few years earlier Piette and Salomon Reinach had described some steatite statuettes found precisely in this same Grimaldi region and in this identical massif of Baoussé-Roussé. They had been discovered by Julien in one of the caves—la Barma Grande. This collection consists of five female statuettes, remarkable among other things for the full development of the breasts and buttocks. Two among them, at least, are undeniably steatopygous. And steatopygy is an African peculiarity. One must admit that this encounter in one and the same place with negroid skeletons and steatopygous statuettes becomes a fact of the deepest interest. And the interest in this direction is not yet exhausted

Eight years after the finding of the negroid skeletons Szombathy published the photograph of a figurine discovered in the Aurignacian centre at Willendorf (Lower Austria), in beds of loess that are rich in palæolithic floors. This statuette, carved from a bit of oolitic limestone, is 11 cms. in height. It represents a nude woman in whom the sub-gluteal region is extraordinarily developed. Enormous breasts, a protruding abdomen, and fat buttocks recall the similar characteristics seen in elderly Bushmen women. The hair is represented in little tufts.

In 1912 Dr. Lalanne found several bas-reliefs, of great value in the elucidation of this question,[2] in the magnificent Laussel (Dordogne) beds. Two of these represent females; the other represents a young man. Without going into irrelevant details, let us say that the female figures are characterized by a pronounced steatopygy and voluminous breasts. These sculptures are thus approximated in their general morphology to the Willendorf woman and the Grimaldi

[1] **CCLXVI.** The parentheses in this quotation are not Verneau's. I have interpolated them for the better guidance of non-anthropological readers.

[2] **CXXXI, p. 129.**

figurines. The young man, on the contrary, is slim and lean. In 1922 Dr. R. de St. Périer had the good fortune to dig up a new steatopygous statuette of a woman in ivory in an Aurignarian stratum in the Grotte des Rideaux at Lespugue in the Haute Garonne, measuring 147mm. in height, and of which some excellent photographs have appeared in *Anthropologie.*[1]

It is impossible not to collate these figurations of Grimaldi, Willendorf and Laussel[2] with the discovery of negroid skeletons at Baoussé-Roussé. The one discovery illuminates the other, and they mutually explain and complement one another. And from these documents alone we are driven to think that during the Palæolithic—at all events during the Aurignacian stage of it—there were representatives, on European soil, of a population whose morphological characters could not but belong to a steatopygous race. The realism of these statuettes and bas-reliefs indicates that the artists who produced them had their models before them. Such forms are not invented, and are certainly not invented at several different places in Europe at the same time. and with such precision in the concomitant characters. Further, we may add this piece of ethnic information: steatopygy, where it does exist, is limited to females. The youth of Laussel is not steatopygous. This difference in the way in which the sexes are represented show clearly that these sculptures are not conventional but are more or less faithful portraits of human types then extant, which the sculptors copied.[3]

A number of questions, whose importance for primitive History leap to the eyes, now present themselves. The first of these is: In what part of the world do we find populations at once negroid and steatopygous?

It is not difficult to give the answer. Such persons are known only in Africa. Are we to conclude, then, that during

[1] R. de St. Périer, "Statuette de femme stéatopyge découverte à Lespugue (Haute Garonne)," *l'Anthropologie*, 1922, p. 361.

[2] They have also been found at Brassempouy (Landes).

[3] Professor Verneau, quoted on p. 68, with regard to negroid characters in European skeletons, remains, in his latest utterance on the question of the origin of the Grimaldi type, unconvinced that it was African: "I would like to believe it, but . . . up to date, the type has not been discovered in Africa except at an epoch more recent than that in which our Baoussé-Roussé specimens lived."—"La race de Neanderthal et la race de Grimaldi: leur role dans l'Humanité," *Journal of the Roy. Anthr. Inst.*, London, Vol. liv, 1924, p. 228. [Translator's Note.]

the Aurignacian period, at least, there was immigration into Europe from Africa? But we must know whether there was in prehistoric Africa a palæolithic civilization which might have been at that time related to our own. And we must also find out what road could have been followed by these Africans, who had not yet invented navigation. Fifteen years ago we could not even have thought of answering such questions on the earliest human migrations. To-day we have the means of formulating hypotheses which appear to be very attractive.

With every day that passes it becomes more clear that Africa was in possession of palæolithic and neolithic civilizations identical with our own. Everywhere in that vast continent a number of finds have been made which have provided prehistorians with plenty of comparative material. The ancient and middle Pleistocene of Africa had its Chellean, Acheulean and Moustierian lithic forms[1] just like Europe. And the implements characteristic of our Reindeer age civilization are also generally found in Africa. It is impossible however, at the present moment, to establish an indisputable chronological parallelism between the two continents.

Southern Africa would appear to have been one vast centre of palæolithic civilization. But is it the earliest centre, taking Eur-Africa into consideration as a whole? From the Cape Colony to the Mediterranean shores one meets with a long train of stone implements of all the lithic ages, sometimes in prodigal profusion.

The wide Sahara, to-day almost impassable, did not present so bare an aspect in the Pleistocene, nor did it constitute such an obstacle. The African climate was less arid, and the fauna, now banished to that great triangle comprehended between the Sudan and Table Mountain, was then distributed over the entire continent. The inhabitants of the country now known as Morocco, Algeria and Tunisia knew the elephant, the rhinoceros and the giraffe.

Can we use this resemblance—which sometimes becomes identity—between the stone industries of Africa[2] and Europe as an argument in favour of a unique Eur-African race in pleistocene times? The time has not yet arrived when we can positively assert it, but the chances in favour of such an

[1] See more especially the important finds of Reygasse, **CCXVII**.

[2] The stratigraphy of palæolithic Africa is far from being known. Few of the African stations are stratified.

approximation become less dubious with every day that passes.[1]

Steatopygy, an unusual characteristic, is particularly marked in the Hottentot and Bushmen people and, to a less degree, in some of the East Africa groups. Further, it is the Hottentots whose hair presents that curious feature which anthropologists call " pepper corn " hair. The Willendorf woman, who is both steatopygous and represented with " pepper corn " hair, thus associates the characters peculiar to Hottentots, and the Aurignacian sculptors, let us repeat, could not have invented such a type, having these two characters.

It is generally known that the Hottentots and Bushmen who to-day have been pressed back into limited areas, once occupied large tracts of Africa. Their geographical territory extented, at the least, from 15° S. lattitude to the Cape of Good Hope. In former times they populated the southern district of Lake Nyassa. Pushed back from the north by the Bantu and from the south by the Whites, and stamped out by these two invaders, they survive merely as a few nomadic families wandering in Namaqualand and the Kalahari district. The purest representative of this primitive race, whose extinction, alas ! seems imminent, is the Bosjesman or " bushman ". The Hottentots are much more mixed with their neighbours, the Bantu, several of whose morphological characters they have acquired by crossbreeding. Finally, do not let us forget that the Hottentots and Bushmen are yellow-skinned. This weak pigmentation might explain—if explanation be called for—the gradual passing of the yellow to the white type in prehistoric times.

If, thus, we accept the relationship—based on morphological and ethnographical characters—of at any rate a portion of the European with the African Aurignacians, the only question that still arises is as to which of them are the ancestors of the others.

Many reasons appear to militate in favour of the African lithic civilization being the older, among others that a portion of the holocene fauna of North Africa is fossil whereas in Europe it is not. *Bubalus antiquus*, so ably represented by

[1] We can also call to our aid arguments drawn from the rock gravings of North Africa and the paintings discovered on the cave walls in South Africa.

prehistoric Africans in their rock engravings, is extinct. Flamand found drawings of Bubalus and of men using polished stone axes on the same panel.

There still remains the problem of communications between the two continents. We know that in the early Pleistocene Europe and Africa were continuous with Asia. The Mediterranean was of much smaller extent than now because its secondary waters had not yet been formed. Man was the contemporary of many of the subsidences which resulted in the present geography of southern Europe. There was no obstacle to the passage of the Africans of those early palæolithic times. Their way lay open without a break, notably across the wide Tuniso-Sicilian land bridge.[1]

The centre of the African Aurignacian civilization may be sought in the Great Lakes region, a little to the north of the district which was still inhabited by the Hottentots and Bushmen during recent centuries. Thence this civilization would have proceeded on the one hand in the direction of South Africa, where wall paintings resembling the French ones are found in certain caves; and on the other towards the Mediterranean coast. The Getulian implements, like the Petit Poucet pebbles, mark the route taken by these migrations in both directions. Thus the European Aurignacian and the African Getulian would be simply two geographical aspects of an identical culture. And the Negroids (and steatopygous people) of Europe would thus represent the types—the only types so far discovered—of the African hordes that passed across to our continent, perhaps towards the end of the mid-Quaternary?

Obviously we cannot legitimately regard the problem as solved. But the importance of these modern finds enabling us to get somewhere near an explanation of our origin can be well understood. Let us be wise and reserve judgment. We must not allow our eagerness to discover a new link in the chain uniting past with present to lead us too hastily to

[1] It has been readily admitted that the continents were separated before the Aurignacian period. Maybe these interruptions to continuous passage are later than is commonly supposed. Or possibly the Aurignacians are simply the descendants of those who passed across earlier still? The Gibraltar land-bridge was cut in the Pliocene. Is it possible that it was temporarily re-established later on?

establish genealogies which we may be obliged to abandon to-morrow !

*
* *

We have seen the Neanderthal race disappear (?) in the Moustierian period. What can have been the cause of this extinction ? It has been sought in the general simplicity of its cerebral convolutions in which are seated the sensory motor territories of the associative centre. This associative centre in which impressions are concentrated and interpreted is not apparent in the lower mammals, whereas it is greatly developed in Monkeys and attains its maximum in Man.

Every textbook indicates the part played by the anterior portion of the frontal lobes in intellectual activity. The gradual development of these frontal lobes by slow evolution or by sudden mutations may be regarded as one of the greatest gains of human kind. It is thanks to this transformation that humanity has been able to survive, develop, and become master of the organic world. The following quotation from the Belgian anthropologist, Houzé, well brings out the importance of this achievement. "In the progress of the cerebral hemispheres up through the geological periods, it is the frontal lobe, the seat of the most complicated associations and the most accurately adjusted mental combinations, that has grown larger. In Man it has acquired such pre-eminence that it has rendered defensive adaptation unnecessary (*Homo nudus et inermis*). The frontal lobe itself has become the most redoubtable weapon for both attack and defence." Was *Homo neanderthalensis* deficient, by comparison with other men, in his cerebral equipment, for the struggle for existence ? And—if it has ever been absolutely and definitively demonstrated—was his extinction due to an unequal struggle against other and more highly organized men, such as those whose presence has been revealed to us by the post-Moustierian Palæolithic ? Or had this species, like other animal species who have now disappeared, reached the extreme limits of its " vital possibilities " ?

Are certain human races, like powerful civilizations which, after having known periods of magnificence they were unable to survive, have vanished forever—are these human races doomed to become extinct after having reached, as it were, the natural term of their career—doomed by (this is obviously but a manner of speaking) a complete incapacity to perpetuate themselves? It will be realized that we must content ourselves with simply asking these questions. Discussions of this kind are outside our prescribed scope.

The Human Races from Mesolithic Times.

Although the skeletons (still very few) recovered from various palæolithic horizons have thrown a good deal of light on our ethnic history during those times, directly we come to the neolithic period difficulties of a more serious nature begin. Europe—the one continent about which we have any certain knowledge in regard to its successive populations—becomes peopled more densely and in greater variety. Genuine migrations have now begun, and races have become mixed, one superposed on top of another, in an inextricable tangle.[1]

One ethnic fact of considerable importance intervened before the beginning of the Neolithic even, during the intermediate Azilian period, and that was the appearance of a brachycephalic population. Such a morphological type had been hitherto unknown in our continent.[2] Whence came this new race? Have the inadequate excavations of the Palæolithic not yet shown it to us? Or did this new Man, really unknown to the chipped stone age of Europe, come from a neighbouring continent? If so, Asia naturally suggests itself because of its large brachycephalic bloc, and also on account of its geographical proximity.

[1] The impossibility of seeing this problem whole, like some general problem, obliges us to refer the reader to the different chapters in which are examined the anthropological events of which each country has been the theatre.

[2] Recent discoveries of human skeletons at Solutré have shaken the foundations of the ethnogeny that has been built up for the Palæolithic. Excavations at this celebrated site have been resumed since 1922 by MM. Déperet, Mayet and Fabian Arcelin (son of Adrien Arcelin, one of the discoverers of Solutré). Up to date five new skeletons have been dug out of *Aurignacian* strata. Palæolithic skulls have hitherto been long ones. Brachycephaly, it was thought, appeared only in the Mesolithic. But Solutré has now furnished several skulls of mesaticephalic, one of sub-brachycephalic form. It will be necessary to revert to these highly important discoveries which will probably force us to revize former judgments on the skeletons previously found at Solutré and to construct quite other hypotheses as to the origin of the peoples of the polished stone age. It is impossible to over-emphasize the importance of these discoveries. See the Bulletins of the local Association for the advancement of human palæontology and prehistory, published at Lyon since 1923; Proceedings of the Academie des Sciences, *Revue Anthrop.*, Paris.

The neolithic civilization as a whole differs greatly in its main lines from the palæolithic civilizations. And so it was at once imagined that this new civilization was brought in by this brachycephalic race and that it appeared first to the east.

The comparative chronology of prehistoric times in Egypt, in Western Asia and Europe, would seem to confirm this eastern origin for the profound double modification of the human race itself and its manner of living.

It is unnecessary for us to recall here the characteristics of the Neolithic or those of the curious and very important Azilian period preceding it, for readers have only to refer to de Morgan's *Prehistoric Man* in this series to become acquainted with details such as the change in the climate, and also in the fauna, many of whose representatives become extinct while others migrate either to northern latitudes (Reindeer, Gluttons, Lemmings), or to high altitudes (Wild Goat, Chamois, Marmot, etc.) ; the profound economic, social and religious revolution and the ethnic modifications which ensued. These transformations are so great that early anthropologists could see no other explanation than that of an invasion. It is true that in the time of Broca, who delivered such a fine address on this subject, Piette's work on the Azilian phase had not yet appeared.

Even before the Neolithic, and in this intermediate Azilian period, as we have said, the ancient ethnic characteristics of Europe were profoundly modified. The Bavarian station of Ofnet shows us a brachycephalic element added to those dolichocephalic types which, up till then, had provided the entire Palæolithic population. Until this station was discovered in 1907-8 the earliest recorded appearance of brachycephaly was during the polished stone age. Of twenty-one measurable crania (thirty-three were recovered from the Ofnet cave) eight are brachycephalic—and extremely brachycephalic at that, according to Schlitz's text[1]—five are dolichocephalic, and eight mesaticephalic. One could never have anticipated such a mixture.

Here is already an anthropological picture in miniature, an epitome, of what the population of the continent of Europe was to be from that time forward. A fresh chapter of universal history opens. And in this corner of the world it is written

[1] **CCXXXVI**, p. 33. The description of the crania is on p. 241.

by a race or races rather different from those which, up till now, have succeeded one another in Europe from Chellean times. And if we say races, it is because not only the Brachycephals and Mesaticephals of Ofnet are new items in our inventory of Humanity, but the Dolichocephals of this station themselves appear to be different from the old Dolichocephals of the Palæolithic, whether those of Laugerie-Chancelade or those of Cro-Magnon. In fact the Ofnet Dolichocephals have a leptoprosopic face associated with a long head. They are not disharmonic. Unfortunately we have only the bones of the head; the rest of the body would be necessary for a definitive determination.[1]

It is probable that, when we come to discover skeletons in the earliest Danish Neolithic, anterior even to the oldest kitchen-middens, like the horizons excavated, for instance, at Maglemose and Svaerdborg,[2] we shall find that they are similar to the dolichocephalic type at Ofnet, because these evidently represent the oldest stock of that race which to-day still forms the main element of the population in all those States on the borders of the Baltic and the North Sea. From the Neolithic proper onwards we shall meet with this northern race, at any rate in Scandinavia and Denmark. There are certainly a few representatives of the brachycephalic type associated with it, but as a whole the Scandinavian population is already what our anthropological analyses show it to be to-day.

We have still, however, to explain the presence during the course of this intermediate period of a "Mongoloid type" of Brachycephals mixed with the dolichocephalic population in the Southwest of Europe, at Mugem. Does any relationship exist between these ancient Portuguese and these ancient Bavarians who lived approximately at the same period? If

[1] The importance of this Ofnet discovery from the point of view of European happenings, has not yet been sufficiently realized. As a matter of fact we shall see that from the time that the earliest pages of written history appear, northern and central Europe are already under the dominion of at least two of the types met with in the Bavarian station, namely the Dolichocephals of the northern race and the Brachycephals of the type of *Homo alpinus* (a name that is open to argument), who are to become the representatives of the Celtic race of the anthropologists of the middle of the 19th century. And these types will simply be the descendants of the men who, having already mingled their destinies towards the close of the Magdalenian, established the famous collective burial place. Future finds will probably do nothing to modify our views on this point.

[2] **CCXXIX**; **CXXII**. (The earliest Scandinavian stone age is in question.)

such does exist, and if, on the other hand, the Ofnet men can be shown to be related to the Asiatic Brachycephals, how are we to interpret the Mugem finds, at such a distance from Bavaria? Thus will the last word have been said à propos the date at which the first Brachycephals appeared in Europe?

To sum up, at the moment when the Mesolithic dawn is breaking, we shall find in our continent—Europe alone is envisaged owing to the present state of our discoveries—only the ancestors of the present dolichocephalic populations of Mediterranean type and the descendants of the Cro-Magnon type. But very shortly afterwards we shall witness the arrival of two other races whose destinies will be among the most resounding the world has known.

Thus the "Azilian-Tardenoisian" period (like intermediate forms in palæontology) would appear to be one of those most worthy of the attention of anthropologists. It is this period which holds the secret of our history, because it was during this time that the new men appeared in Europe who profoundly transformed the ancient civilization by bringing about the substitution of agriculture, animal domestication and stock-raising for the former hunting and fishing existence. By the care we bring to our excavations we may both extract the minute details of the social life—in the modern sense of the word—of these first sedentary Europeans, and also, perhaps, discover their ethnic origin.

We shall find representatives of the brachycephalic type superposed very closely on those of the Palæolithic in many parts of Europe, but we do not yet know how they came to be where we find them. The routes they followed should be indicated by their interments, since men have ever lavished care on their dead, but these sepultures, alas! have largely disappeared since the Azilian period. Nevertheless, all chance is not quite lost of gathering up the threads ignorantly broken by those who went before us. The Metal age will show us even more of the movement of peoples than the preceding ages.

Many of the routes across Europe were traced out by their Neolithic predecessors. The new civilization will advance especially along those routes which brought the Brachycephals of the polished stone age and even the advance guard of the Nordics to all parts, more or less, of the continent, and also along those further highways which are constantly being discovered and are not always quite what one would have imagined. We shall get a closer knowledge of those who brought these civilizations when we come to examine, country by country, such ethnological adventures as have befallen each of them.

Was each civilization, as it arose, in the hands of one particular race? Nothing is less certain. The successive penetration of copper, bronze and iron was by commercial highways, and no particular human type would appear to have been the sole propagator responsible. On the other hand, it is evident that, especially in the iron age, a considerable expansion of the Nordic race took place very nearly all over Europe. To what determining influences was this expansion due?

This prolific and warlike race will at once begin those adventurous travels which are to lead it very far from its point of departure. It will appear almost everywhere, and almost everywhere will leave traces of its passage in the form of colonies of varying density of population. Several among them will have a great destiny.

It will penetrate through Spain as far as North Africa, and by way of the Balkan peninsular as far as Asia Minor. Maybe we shall find traces of it much further afield, among the mountains which border the north of Eastern Turkestan?

To-day the greater part of these contingents—in some districts they are almost homogeneous—will be found grouped from the west of the Channel to the north of Scandinavia.

Thus we arrive at the threshold of historic times.*

* *Translator's Note* (see p. 61.) The discovery of a skull in a Moustierian level in Palestine by Turville-Petre, described at the meeting of the British Association at Southampton (1925) "throws a welcome light on these problems" in the words of Sir Arthur Keith, who examined the fragment, and who has pronounced the opinion that the Galilean man represents a peculiar variety of the Neanderthal species, "one that makes an approach in several respects to man of the modern type". *The Times*, Sir Arthur Keith's description of "The Galilee Skull". August 14th, 1925.

PART II

THE RACES OF EUROPE

CHAPTER I

An Attempted General Classification

WE do not yet know exactly when the first Europeans appeared. Theoretically, there is nothing in the way of this having happened in the Tertiary era. Man, geologically of great antiquity, may have sprung from an offshoot that was not borne on the anthropoid branch, and may have evolved earlier than did this branch, in the Miocene. This miocene member of the Human family may have become a real Man in the Pliocene. But these are but intellectual concepts. Not a single human trace has been discovered in the Miocene; not a bone fragment in the Pliocene.

Man appears in the early Quaternary already well differentiated from his hypothetical ancestral stock and in possession of all his own specific characters, and for details in regard to the prehistoric European races we must turn to the chapter in which fossil Man and his successors were discussed. We must not forget, however, that Europe is the continent which so far has yielded the earliest human relics. Both their chronological authenticity and their ethnological place can be vouched for on the strength of the many discussions and verifications that have taken place.

The present population of central and western Europe is in part descended from these prehistoric peoples, and in part from those who later on in the course of history migrated from the northern and eastern portions of the continent. These peoples came, perhaps, from western Asia—some of them certainly did so.

At first it would seem that these populations, arriving one after the other, must have caused profound ethnical perturbations among the older inhabitants. These disturbances must not be exaggerated: but neither must they be minimized. If we consider only the time of the great invasions, what do we see?—hordes, having different names, coming one after the other, like avalanches in spring; but was their ethnic origin so diverse? There are the Germanic folk and the Huns, two races!

Other men in the more distant part preceded these invading hordes. Their adventures and their names are forgotten. No doubt many of them belonged to the northern race, at all events a part of the neolithic and bronze age Dolichocephals. This being the case, the newcomers no more changed the ethnic physiognomy of the country in which their predecessors were established, than the invaders who made Rome tremble.

The problem of these invasions must also be looked at from another and important side. Did these moving hordes, who have been indiscriminately called Germanic peoples, incontestably belong to a Germanic race? An affirmative answer to this question has been too hastily given, and people —historians especially—have been in too much of a hurry to believe that such an affirmative should be based on philology or chroniclers' tales alone. I would wish to illustrate by an example the kind of mistake that can thus be made. The Alemanni, that confederation of "Germanic" peoples who once dwelt on both banks of the Rhine and ended by establishing themselves in Alsace, Swabia, and Switzerland, are considered to be the authentic German type—and those who dare to think otherwise are very bold persons indeed. Have they not given their name to a large proportion of these Germans? Let us investigate this matter.

If the Allemanni were really of Germanic race they should have possessed the well-known morphological and descriptive characteristics of this race—tall stature, dolichocephaly, light eyes and fair hair. In the three countries just indicated the populations in whose veins runs the Alemannic blood, supposing the Alemanni to be Germanic in race, ought to have retained the above physical features, and a rapid anthropological enquiry should suffice to indicate them. We will undertake such an enquiry, limiting it to a district, designedly circumscribed, in the Swiss Alpine massif, namely the Valais. In this region intermixture in modern times has been less easy than elsewhere, because communication with it is difficult. In order to simplify matters we will confine our enquiry to the cranial characters alone, which, moreover, will be quite sufficient.

The ancient sepultures of Germany have yielded numerous skeletons permitting the definite establishment of the physical type of the early Germans so far as their head-form goes, and this was remarkable for its dolichocephaly. This character has been preserved in the heart of the present population of a part of the Reich, as we shall see later. These ancient groups have pushed their way into certain parts of Germany where the majority of the people are not "Germanic," but are brunet and brachycephalic—the Celtic type of Broca. For instance, in north Bavaria Ranke found a fairly imposing proportion of the Germanic type—21 per cent. Equally high percentages (Hölder's) are to be met with in Württemberg, in the Grand Duchy of Baden, etc.

The ancestors of the present Germanic-type population of South Germany are to be found in the Row Grave sepultures (*Reihengräber*), which in general followed on after the Iron age mounds. The average cephalic index of these Germans is consistently low: 71.3 (Ecker), 72 (Hölder), etc. The height-breadth index varies from 95 to 109 and the height-length from 69 to 78. These skulls, further, are leptorrhinian and leptoprosopic.[1]

Such peoples of Germanic race as established themselves in the upper Rhône valley must have been—outside a few hypothetical groups—Burgundians, and, later, Alemanni. Are they, as they ought to be, related to the Kymric type of Broca? In so far as concerns the first of these "Germanic" peoples, the answer is positive. We know that dolichochephaly and tall stature prevailed among them. The Burgundian skeletons so far studied plainly authorize us, in every case, to class them in the Nordic, Kymric, or Germanic group.[2]

A similar conclusion is not possible in the case of the Alemanni.

If we admit what the historians teach, that is to say that an Alemannic invasion overran the eastern Valais between the ninth and twelfth centuries, these invaders should have given their own ethnic expression to this geographical district. Further, we know that no other important colonization has

[1] **XCV**, p. 65.

[2] In France and Switzerland the Burgundian sepultures have always yielded dolichocephalic types.

taken place since this Alemannic movement. Between the twelfth and fourteenth centuries a few Italian families came over the passes, but their ethnic influence has not been of a transformative order. Thus the anthropological characters of the Alemannic "Germanic" group ought to have been perpetuated up to our own days in the central and eastern Valaisian population with but slender chances of modifying crosses.

Among the skulls contained in the ossuaries of this Swiss canton, many date back hundreds of years and some may go back to the twelfth century. They represent the ancestral type infinitely better even than the present population. They stand a far better chance than contemporary skulls of representing the race, the authentic ethnic physiognomy, of the population of the end of the Middle Ages, because they are much nearer to that period. Yet every Valaisian ossuary has yielded a considerable proportion of brachycephalic and a very small number of dolichocephalic skulls. The conclusion forced on us is this: either the Alemanni really belonged—anthropologically and philologically—to the Kymric, Germanic group, in which case they merely introduced their language in the district under consideration, the population on which they imposed it belonging to quite a different anthropological type (Broca's Celtic type). Or else the Alemanni who brought their German tongue into the Valais were not a branch of the main Germanic tree—from the anthropological viewpoint, that is—belonging to the tall, dolichocephalic, long-faced group, *Homo europæus*. They merely bore its linguistic and political label.

According to the latter hypothesis (which seems to us the more likely one) we can picture these Alemanni (Celtic group[1]) come originally from one knows not whence, being included among the contingents of the northern race at the very earliest period of history. By the first centuries of our era they were mingled with them, speaking the same language and following the same political fortunes. Once arrived in

[1] To avoid confusion it should be realized that the author uses 'Celts' and 'Celtic' throughout the book for the type commonly described in English usage as 'Alpine'. The 'Celts' of English usage, i.e., the Celtic-speaking peoples, will be found to figure under the name of 'Germans', which name the author does not, as is usual in English, restrict to German-speaking peoples, but extends to all the northern types commonly spoken of in English as 'Nordic'.—[Translator's Note.]

different parts of central Europe, they stayed there. They constitute a portion of the great brachycephalic division, the remainder being constituted by the prehistoric Brachycephals of the neolithic period and bronze ages—of which the Bavarians, the Alpine Swiss, the Tyrolese, the North Italians, a portion of the French people, and still others as well, to-day form a part.

Finally, nothing prevents us from supposing that the Alemanni were but a fraction of this great brachycephalic group of unknown origin—it has been called Ural-Altaic (?)—which appeared in Europe from the Neolithic onwards. These primitive Brachycephals, as we might call them, would not all at the same time have invaded the Alpine massif. A certain proportion of them would have remained outside the districts which the Roman historians were to know later on. Many centuries afterwards, a fraction of this primitive mass of people coming to occupy the soil of Germany would have borne the name of Alemanni.

Europe possessed a brachycephalic population imposing in numbers at the polished stone period, after the Mesolithic. Newcomers, they lived side by side with a dolichocephalic population in the western portion of the continent. Hervé attempted to trace the route followed by these round-headed Neolithics by the proportion of brachycephalic types in the burials of central and western Europe. It would appear that they came from the east via the Danube valley and the Hungarian plains and so reached the Alpine massif. Then they apparently divided into two streams, one passing to the north and the other to the south of the massif. The northern group peopled Switzerland and South Germany—notably Bavaria ; the southern group installed itself in the Tyrol, North Italy, eastern France (the Alps, Cevennes and the central Massif). It appears more and more likely that it was by the mountain passes and not by the river country that the Brachycephals penetrated into the principal Alpine valleys.

Must it be admitted, as has been thought—though I do not want to help build up the romance of prehistory !—that, having been at first limited to the mountain massifs of central Europe, the neolithic Brachycephals then burst with fury on the dolichocephalic population of France ? Why imagine any such "cataclysms"? It is perfectly possible that their entrance into France was effected peacefully and pacifically. Perhaps these people, whose civilization was so different from that of those who had hitherto occupied France, were favorably received because they brought new elements into their everyday lives. It is an established fact that from this time forward a singular change came over the ethnic physiognomy of the country that was to become Gaul, and certain aspects of this transformation leave us speculating.

The British Isles would appear to have remained longer in their "splendid isolation." Peopled from the Chellean period, England continued to be inhabited by dolichocephalic people without a break up till the bronze age. The long barrow sepultures of the neolithic period contain dolichocephalic types only. In Thurnam's well-known series the indices range from 63 to 77. Were these neolithic Dolichocephals descended from the older palæolithic Dolichocephals of the same region, who had adopted a new civilization? Or did they belong to the company of European neolithic Dolichocephals?

It would seem that the bronze age, in England, was brought in by a population of different type. In the round barrows Thurnam found a large majority of brachycephalic types (the indices range from 74 to 89). And nothing is more interesting than to note the contrast between the two series.[1] This contrast resembles that observable for France if the palæolithic series of skulls is placed alongside a series of modern skulls from the central Plateau.

In the case of England it is obvious that the new chapter of history written in the bronze age was the work of an individual race. Here we can invoke the relation between race and history. Still, to make quite sure, we must await those results which further and more careful excavations cannot fail to yield.[2]

What stands out with complete certainty from these few remarks above is that the anthropological map of Europe was a thing of streaks and patches even before the proto-historic period. Certain districts have retained their primitive Dolichocephals; others have been penetrated by a few rare

[1] **CCLV**, p. 385; **X**.

[2] See note 2 on p. 194 of the Chapter on the British Isles. [Translator's Note.]

brachycephalic elements (Spain and Portugal), while neighbouring territories contain, side by side, imposing contingents of both races; finally, still others present a homogeneous brachycephalic front, with a few timid forerunners of Dolichocephals beginning to appear. The hour of the ethnic invasions has really begun, and the mingling and cross-breeding of races will quickly follow.

To a superficial observer Europe must look like a vast ethnic Cosmopolis in which it is impossible, from our point of view, to distinguish anything at all. Such a conception is inaccurate. Doubtless we might seek in vain to pick out with any certainty ethnic groups in an urban population. But do we not fairly easily discover in them the presence of certain individual types? Were we to place together all the Auvergnats dwelling in Paris, or all the Scandinavians, or English, should we not be constituting little classes of human beings whose physical characters would stand out in clear contrast? And such a sorting out, without pushing it to extreme limits, could be carried further than these two or three groups. Are not Corsican born "Parisians," come of old Corsican families, very different from "Parisians" born in Normandy of old Norman families?

Naturally, if we were to take the whole of France instead of Paris this building up of ethnic groups would be both easier and more striking in its results. Certain Alsatian valleys have shown such a high percentage of brachycephalic types that the particular ethnic quality of these valleys is clearly manifest. Naturally the race did not remain absolutely pure even here, but it has preserved its early physiognomy with sufficient sharpness to enable us to place a colour or a sign representative of it on a map. Other instances are not hard to find, such as the central Massif, and Corsica, whose physiognomies are very different; each shows well-marked ethnic features of its own.

Elsewhere than in France it is easy enough to establish similar facts. In the old German empire Brandenburg is dolichocephalic, and Bavaria brachycephalic. Southern Italy, from the latitude of Rome, is entirely dolichocephalic, and North Italy, bordering France, is entirely brachycephalic from Switzerland to the Tyrol.

And if we have chosen to pay more attention to these three States than to other parts of Europe, it is because these States are among those which appear to offer the greatest difficulty in arriving at such results. Have not these territories always been battlefields ? Large masses of men come from all quarters in every epoch have traversed them, jostled each other upon them, or peaceably settled there.

A priori, these regions would thus appear to contain a greater mixture of human elements than any others. If, therefore, we have managed to sort out from among these populations, which we know to be mixed, the races which have successively composed them, a similar task would seem to be much less difficult for other European States which have escaped, chiefly for geographical reasons, such invasions and such occasions for ethnic impurity—Scandinavia, for example.

*
* *

The anthropological analysis of Europe has been begun, but is very far from having been completed. Widespread investigations have been undertaken in different lands—in France, Italy, Spain, Scandinavia, etc. Elsewhere, however, such investigation has hardly been started, and for very wide regions we are even without any research at all.

In Deniker's map showing the approximate distribution of the races of Europe[1] a large area of central and western Europe remains blank, namely nearly the whole of Russia, the Balkan peninsular, North Germany, etc.

During the twenty years that have gone by since this map was first published a good deal of work has been done which will permit to-day of our tinting these blank areas in several places. Still, taken as a whole, Europe is far from being anthropologically known even now. Further, it must not be imagined that even the coloured or hatched portions indicating the present state of our knowledge give any final expression of their character. Far from this being so, there remain yet many local investigations to be undertaken which should yield precious data, and the data of many early investigations need rearrangement. Nevertheless, we have obtained some general idea—we must not ask more—on the subject of the races peopling Europe. Future work may modify some of our present

[1] **LVIII**, p. 384. (English Translation, p. 327).

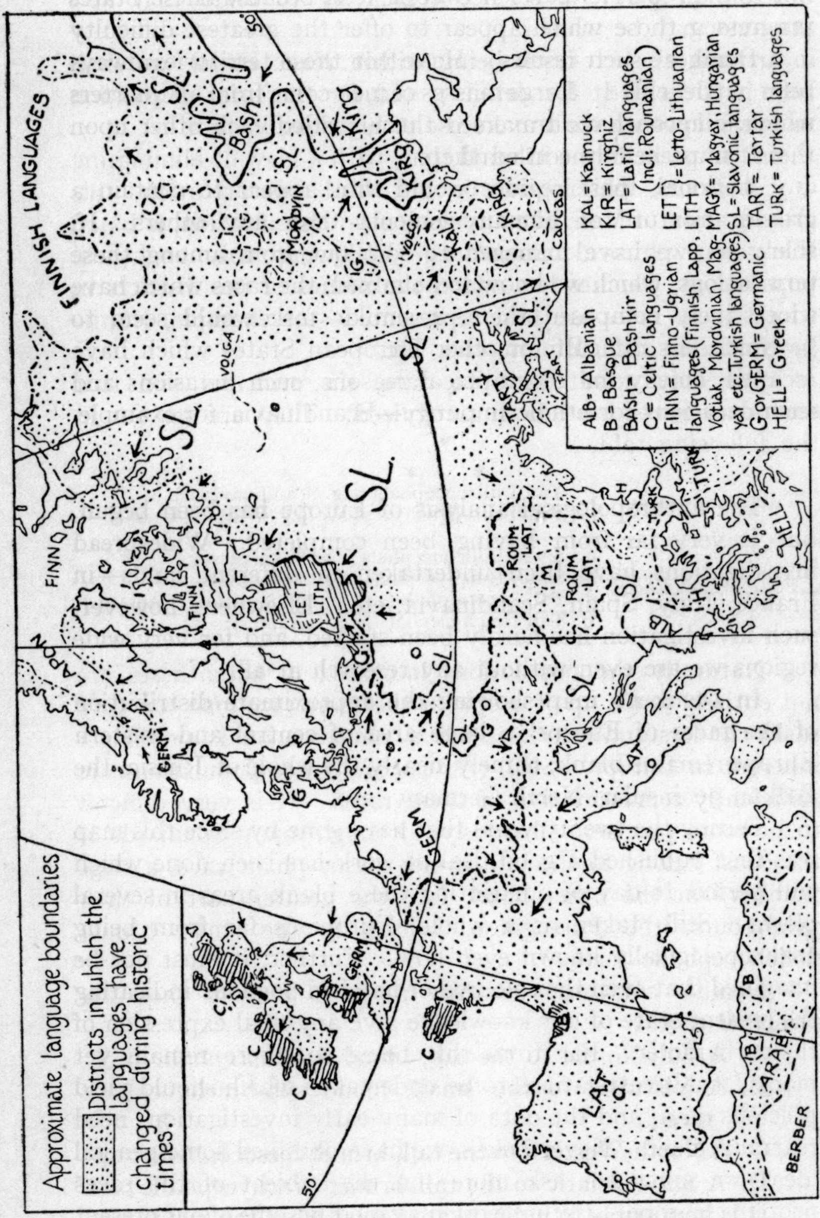

(Map after Emile Chaix).

Map II. Approximate boundaries of the languages of Europe.

conceptions, more especially in particular cases. But is it not the property of science ceaselessly to undo that new progress may be made ?

Deniker's text-book being within reach of all, we shall refer readers to it for details ; and for the brief exposition which follows we shall make use of his classification.

It must be borne in mind that, with a view of eliminating any national, philological or historical interpretation, this classification of Man, like any zoological classification, is based solely on physical characters. Following this zoological terminology Deniker has added the names of the districts in which these races are best represented—for example, Nordic (=Northern) race, Dinaric race, etc.

We may admit that, to date, six principal and four secondary races have been recognized. They are set out in the following table :

Two Blond Races	Tall Dolichocephals (e.g. Scandinavians). Small sub-Brachycephals (e.g. White Russians).
Four Brunet Races	Small Dolichocephals (e.g. Portuguese). Small Brachycephals (e.g. Auvergnats) Tall Mesocephals (e.g. certain maritime Spaniards). Tall Brachycephals (e.g. Bosnians).

Naturally the populations indicated in parentheses are not entirely made up of people of the same race (one can very easily understand why). Such a phenomenon is no longer inherent in Europe. Still, *grosso modo,* these populations are sufficiently representative of these races. It is very difficult to be more precise. Obviously, although many Spaniards of the coast belong to the tall brunet mesocephalic race, a large number, on the other hand, like the greater part of their neighbours, the Portuguese, belong to the small brunet dolichocephalic race.

Deniker attaches secondary races to four of these six principal races :

A. A Sub-Nordic to the tall, blond dolichocephalic race ;

B. A Vistulan to the small, blond sub-brachycephalic race ;

C. A North-Western to the tall, brunet mesocephalic race ;

D. A Sub-Adriatic to the tall, brunet brachycephalic race.

It is impossible to indicate at present what the future may have to say to these sub-divisions. My own impression is that a fresh grouping of the same " human documents " would yield other results for certain territories. I can only give an impression, but it is not lightly put forward; I have become aware of it after having had many thousands of measurements from Eastern Europe through my hands.

Let us glance rapidly at the present races of Europe as Deniker gives them[1]:

I. Tall, blond dolichocephalic race. Great stature, averaging 1 metre 72 to 1 metre 73; fair wavy hair; eyes generally blue; clear skin; long face; straight nose; dolichocephalic head (index 76 to 79).

It is also called the Nordic, Germanic, or Kymric (Broca) race, and it is zoologically named *Homo europæus*. The name Germanic, and even more so Nordic, indicates its geographical distribution. It is found in the northern part of Europe, but it has not penetrated to any extent into Russian territory. It is domiciled entirely to the north of 50° N. lat., and on the east—on either side of the Gulf of Finland—it does not pass beyond 30° E. long. Scandinavians,[2] Finns, Russians (old empire), Germans, Danes, Dutch, English, Belgians and Northern French (we give populations according to the name of the State to which they belong) are the main populations belonging to this race, with the addition, in various localities, of "strays" or scattered members.

To this main race Deniker attaches a secondary one, still blond and tall, but in which the head is less dolichocephalic (is it so in reality, or is this merely the effect of averages?). He calls it the sub-Nordic race. It appears to differ from the other in more than its less elongated skull by having straight hair (instead of wavy), and a frequently retroussé nose (instead of a straight one). Its domain, also, is that which has just been described.

II. Small, blond sub-brachycephalic race. Height: 1 metre 63 to 1 metre 64; straight ash-coloured or flaxen hair; blue or grey eyes; skull moderately short (cephalic index 82 to 83 on the living subject).

It is probable that a large number of Western and Central Russians belong to this race. Because its distribution is almost entirely in the east of Europe Deniker calls it Eastern. Has this race perhaps filtered in all along the Baltic among the representatives of the Nordic race? Deniker attaches to it

[1] **LVII**, p. 386. (English translation, p. 326 ff.)
[2] We do not say *the* Scandinavians, or *the* Finns, etc.

a secondary race whose stature is a little less and whose skull is not so round (Vistulan race). It chiefly inhabits the southern portion of the domain occupied by the main race.

III. Small, brunet dolichocephalic (or Ibero-Insular) race. Low stature: 1 metre 61 to 1 metre 62; black hair; very dark eyes; bronzed skin; nose ordinarily straight. The mean cephalic index lies between 73 and 76 in the living subject. Its geographical domain is the central and western part of the European Mediterranean area, principally Southern Italy and the Isles (Sicily, Sardinia, Corsica, the Balearic Islands), and the Iberian peninsular. It is the *Homo meridionalis* of Lapouge. It has penetrated here and there into the western portion of France. This type is as sharply delimitated as that of the Nordic race. It must be well known to all who have travelled on the Mediterranean coast.

IV. Small, brunet highly brachycephalic race. This is the old Celtic race of the anthropologists—the word "Celtic" being used in a purely conventional sense. Height: 1 metre 63 to 1 metre 64. Dark hair, brown or black; brown eyes. Its marked brachycephaly is shown by a cephalic index of 85 to 87 on the living subject.

The mountainous parts of central Europe, a portion of the Apennines (northern part of Italy) and the west of France are peopled by representatives of this race, which appears in small scattered islands from the central French massif to the Eastern Carpathians and Bukovina. Maybe the Roumanian mountain folk belong to this ethnic group? We shall refer to these again when dealing with the Balkan peninsular.

I can now advance my own opinion as to this race. I believe it to be descended from the race which appeared in central Europe during the Mesolithic, but especially in neolithic times. Maybe its ancestors were the builders of the Swiss lake dwellings?

V. Tall, brunet mesocephalic race (Littoral or Atlanto-Mediterranean race). Height above the average (1 metre 66). Very dark hair; brown eyes. Cephalic index 79 to 80 in the living subject, indicating sub-brachycephaly and even mesaticephaly. This race would appear to be distributed more especially along the Mediterranean coasts of Spain, France, and Italy, mingled in part with the Ibero-Insular race. We also find it on the Atlantic coasts, south of the Bay of Biscay, and in the Atlantic district of France lying between the mouths

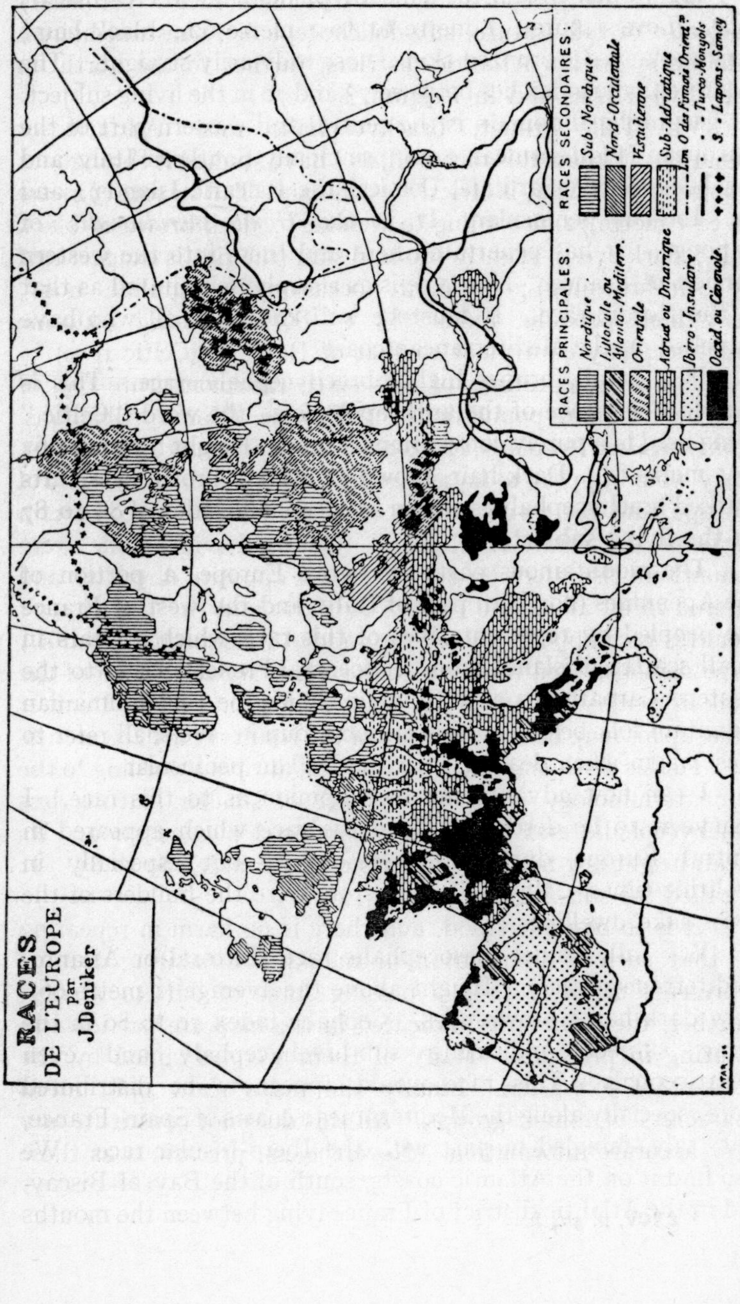

MAP III. Distribution of European Races according to Deniker.

of the Gironde and the Loire. But it is very little known. It is thought that it does not penetrate further than 250 kilometres into the interior.

Maybe we should attach to this main race a secondary one, also of tall stature, sub-dolichocephalic, chestnut-haired, inhabiting certain Atlantic districts, further to the north, in the British Isles and in Belgium ?

VI. Tall, brunet, brachycephalic race (Adriatic or Dinaric). I know this race well, as I have studied it throughout a large area of what is strictly its domain. Tall stature (1 metre 68 to 1 metre 72, according to Deniker) ; dark brown or black hair ; dark eyes ; slightly bronzed skin (the tint is exaggerated by sun-browning) ; straight, occasionally aquiline nose ; very high cephalic index (85 to 86) indicating extreme brachycephaly equivalent to that of Race IV (Celtic race).

The representatives of this sixth race constitute one of the handsomest populations of Europe (North Albanians, Montenegrins, Bosnians, Herzegovinians and many Dalmatians. They would appear to have penetrated to North Italy, central Europe, and the Swiss canton of Grisons ? Maybe to certain parts of the south of Russia ? Unless, having come from somewhere else, they progressed in the opposite direction and filtered in all along the eastern Adriatic and the Ionian sea ! For this race appears to have expanded its habitat—I think I have demonstrated this[1]—over the whole western slope of the Balkan peninsular as far as Cape Matapan. When Deniker drew up his map he was unaware of the results of my researches.

To this sixth main race is attached, always according to the same terminology, a secondary race of smaller stature, less brachycephalic and with less pronounced pigmentation. Its mean height is 1 metre 66 and its cephalic index 82 to 85. It is called the sub-Adriatic race.

It is to be understood, and there is no harm in repeating it, that such a distribution of mankind inhabiting Europe represents no more than a passing stage of our knowledge. Further, the boundaries indicated in the map are particularly wanting in precision. Many of them were obtained by the method of extension. Finally the maps show only mean characters of ethnic groups. All this does not constitute any very accurate information. Nevertheless, precarious as these

[1] CXCV, p. 564 ff.

results may be, they are distinctly encouraging. Where we imagined all to be chaos they have shown us that a pattern exists, and that there is even a possibility of classification.

I think we may legitimately conclude that the fact that we can envisage the existence of these six races marks a great advance on the knowledge of the preceding generation. It matters little whether they continue to be six or whether they increase or diminish in number. What has been actually achieved is the recognition of the fact that there are in Europe diverse races differing sufficiently one from the other to admit of classification. Furthermore—and this fact may prove of considerable interest—they are otherwise grouped than within the political boundaries of States.

We have seen that certain countries number fewer races within their borders than others—Portugal, Scandinavia and Denmark, for example. They were better protected than their neighbours from ethnic invasion. In neolithic times the Pyrenees would seem to have constituted a sufficiently serious obstacle to the further penetration of certain groups. In northern Europe the representatives of Race IV did not reach Denmark or Scandinavia, just as, in the Mediterranean, though it lay so close to their principal habitat, they failed to reach the Isles.

We are in the habit of thinking of European lands according to their political distribution. The mind prefers to follow the beaten path. This is why, as we go from west to east, we shall take an analytical look at each of these States, briefly indicating its ethnic destinies during the course of past History, and the main lines of its present anthropological physiognomy.

CHAPTER II

The Iberian Peninsular

If the prehistoric relations existing between Europe and Africa were indeed those suggested—and this, I think, is demonstrated more clearly every day—a considerable part was played by the Iberian peninsular in the primitive history of the continent. Not that the Peninsular has yielded us anything so interesting as the steatopygous statuettes of France, Italy and Austria, or the negroid skeletons of Baoussé-Roussé. But then the excavation done in Spain and Portugal, hardly outlined till the last few years, is as nothing compared with the work done in the southwest of France, for instance, taking only that south of a line drawn from Lyon to la Rochelle. No comparison can be made between the two districts in this respect. In thirty years time, judging from what is now being undertaken, the scientific possessions of the Iberian peninsular may be on a very large scale indeed.[1]

It is already quite certain that the Iberian peninsular was populated from the very earliest times. Without going back to the Otta flints of Portugal, which were claimed to be Tertiary, and at the time of the discovery were considered by some prehistorians as having been worked by the unskilful hands of *Anthropithecus riberoii*, we know that the old palæolithic civilizations were represented in the Peninsular.

[1] Among the most meritorious efforts of the last few years we may cite those of the *Societad de estudios vascos* which has taken as its mission the study of northwest Spain. Aranzadi and his collaborators have already published a good many Notes on the prehistory and anthropology of this region, among the most recent: *Exploracion de . . . dolmenes de la Sierra de Ataun-Borunda*, and other places. *L'Anthropologie physique* has also benefited by the same sympathy and goodwill. And men like Bosh y Gimpera and his collaborators have devoted to it their youthful strength and vigour. We should also mention workers such as Don José M. de Barandiaran and Don Enrique de Eguren along with Aranzadi. These publications hail from San Sebastian. See also, for further data concerning the anthropology and prehistory of the Iberian peninsular: *O Archeologo Portuguěs*, Lisbon; and the journal of the *Societad espanola de Antropologia e etnografia y prehistoria* Madrid (1921 and onwards); the *Butlleti de l'Associacio catalana d'antropologia, etnologia i prehistoria*, Barcelona (1923 and onwards).

Both Portugal and Spain have furnished Chellean "coups de poing".

In this connection it may be recalled that Spain was one of the first countries in which the Chellean industry was noted in the alluvia. As far back as 1850 flints, more or less in fragments, were collected from the Manzanares gravel. But in 1862 Louis Lartet obtained a characteristic "coup de poing", found by a workman, from the San Isidro quarries. This discovery, coming very shortly after the great discussion relating to the French flints found by Boucher de Perthes, caused the excitement one would expect. Since then a number of other tools of the same epoch have been collected in Spanish territory.[1]

The Torralba station, excavated by the Marquis of Cerralbo,[2] would appear to go still further back in pleistocene times.

Here, on the slope of the Sierra Ministra, at a height of 1112 metres (on the railway line from Madrid to Saragossa) are deposits of marl which have slipped into and silted up to a depth of two metres the basin of an ancient lake formed at the foot of the slope, from which elephants, rhinoceroses, horses, stags and oxen came to drink.

These deposits consist of a kind of magma into which are liberally mixed the bones of fossil species and human implements. Everything is *in situ*. Not a bone or a tool has been rolled. Elephant tusks are particularly plentiful and some among them are very fine. The discoverer attributed them in part to *Elephas meridionalis*. The other bones have been identified as those of *Rhinoceros etruscus*, *Elephas antiquus*, and Sténon's horse. Admitting the correctness of the identification, this would mean that the last animals of the Pliocene were associated with the oldest animals of the Quaternary. As for the implements they consist of two kinds —natural stones that have been used by Man, and genuine tools, the last very much worn, and rarely of flint. They are made from very hard limestone, chalcedony and quartzite. The Marquis of Cerralbo attributed the establishment of these ancient Spanish hunters on the flanks of the Sierra Ministra to a pre-Chellean period. Other writers make the period not quite so remote.

[1] **CLXVI**, p. 80.
[2] **XXXVII**, p. 277.

The strict Chellean is certainly very widely distributed in Spain. But it has been notified in sporadic instances only. In the last few years Iberian anthropologists have made a list of the earlier discoveries, and Joaquim Fontes has begun a series of notes designed to clear up the important subject of Portuguese prehistory.

The Portuguese palæolithic civilization, as a whole, is still little known. It is not so many years since we were restricted to the two Chellean "coups de poing" mentioned by Cartailhac[1] as the main early human manifestations which we could quote when speaking of the west of the Peninsular. However, Cardoso has since then notified the result of his researches in the valley of the Alcantara, where he believes he has discovered palæolithic implements of a transition Acheulean or Chelleo-Moustierian period; and fifteen years earlier Frederico de Vasconcellos showed some rudely worked quartzites attributable to the Chellean.

The young Portuguese savants of the present day have laid upon themselves the task, than which none could be more noble, of resuscitating the earliest pages of the history of their land. And we have witnessed the appearance of a series of extremely interesting memoirs both on the prehistoric archæology and the anthropology of Portugal. The early finds of Carlos Ribeiro have been examined afresh and the palæolithic objects discovered and collected by Choffat, which this great geologist never had time to describe, have likewise had monographs consecrated to them.

Up to the present not a single skeleton which could be dated with certainty as palæolithic has been discovered in Portugal,[2] but the neolithic period—still too little known—

[1] **XXXIV**, p. 29.

[2] In the Lisbon Geological Museum there are the remains of a skeleton found when a trench for the drainage of water was opened in the Valle do Arceiro, near Villa Nova da Rainha, at a depth of 3 metres 70. "At this level the soil consists of a very ancient formation, probably quaternary, according to Ribeiro." The remains consist of a skull, very incomplete, part of a lower jaw, and some pieces of long bones. They were unaccompanied by any implement which could have dated them. The cephalic index of the cranial vault would be about 80.11. This would somewhat resemble the Furfooz skull. See Francisco de Paula e Oliveira, chapter on "Anthropologie" in the above quoted volume by Cartailhac: also the papers by Joaquim Fontes in the Bulletin of the Portuguese Society of Natural Sciences, **LXXII**.

which has left considerable deposits in certain places, has yielded skeletons to which we must devote a few words.

The Portuguese kitchen-middens were recognized for the first time in 1865 by F. A. Pereira da Costa.[1] They are numerous in the lower Tagus valley, particularly in the neighbourhood of Lisbon. Oliveira has notified them in the valley of the Mira (to the north of the Tagus), on the right bank of this stream, notably in the neighbourhood of Villa Nova de Milfontes. Carlos Ribeiro and Paula e Oliveira excavated a part of these deposits corresponding, says Cartailhac, " like those of Denmark and other lands, to a special civilization less advanced and probably earlier than that of the neolithic stations and sepultures."

One of these mounds has become famous owing to the studies devoted to it—the one known as the Mugem mound, more explicitly the Cabeço d'Arruda, situated close to the Tagus, on the left bank at the bottom of the marshy Mugem valley. It is a mound some 100 metres long by 60 wide, rising about 7 metres above the level of the natural soil, composed of pliocene sands emerging five metres above the marsh. It is an imposing mass which must have once been even larger. It is composed of a vast quantity of shells, generally broken, of dried mud, and sand. Mammalian bones (*Bos*, *Cervus*, *Equus*, etc.) and fish bones are met with in this deposit. These bones are " isolated, broken, sometimes burned, and not gnawed, which proves the absence of the domestic dog." There are also worked flints, broken and burned pebbles, cinders and charcoal, and, finally, human skeletons.

The shells " are nearly all of *Lutraria compressa*. There are also *Tapes* and a few small specimens of *Cardium*, and *Ostrea*, *Buccinum*, *Nucula*, *Pecten* and *Solen*. Living specimens are now only found in the clay of the salt beds of the Tagus and Sado, in places very remote from Mugem and at a much lower level." " It is not admissible that a group of men settled here went so far to seek a meagre food-supply. Evidently in their day the Tagus was wider and the sea water went up at least as far as Mugem. This takes us back to a very distant period, probably anterior to the last up-rising of the Portuguese littoral ".[2]

[1] **CLXXXVII.**
[2] **XXXIV**, p. 52, 53.

Worked flints are scarce and of poor quality, made from minute flakes with a bevelled edge, and a chipped and very sharp point—arrow heads or harpoon heads, similar to the small geometrically shaped flints studied by A. de Mortillet, and to those which already existed in the Magdalenian deposits (Grotte de Serinya, for instance) ; and a few bone objects. The lower intact layers of the mounds yield no traces of pottery or polished stone—only the upper portions. It is towards the base of the deposits, of which they occupy nearly half the width, that the human skeletons were found.

The Cabeço d'Arruda furnished about eighty, of various ages and of both sexes. It is a rich necropolis. The bodies, rarely laid out straight, seem to have been placed in the crouched position. The fragments of bones recovered had not been disjointed. No grave-goods accompanied them.

The antiquity of these skeletons should be put down as belonging to the earliest Neolithic—to judge from Cartailhac's remark on the subject of the physical geography of the district. If these burials are anterior to the last uprising of the Portuguese littoral, that would bring us very near to the Pleistocene. And from this time forward, says Hervé,[1] "the study of the Mugem skeletons will no doubt permit us, in view of the more than probable continuity of the population from one period to another, to gain some idea of the last of the quaternary races in the Hispano-Portuguese peninsular, where they have hitherto been known only from their industry."

The skeletons from the Mugem kitchen-midden (they are assembled in the Lisbon Geological Museum)[2] show two quite distinct types, one dolichocephalic, the other brachycephalic, or sub-brachycephalic. And we must underline without delay the interest of this first fact. We already know that Palæolithic man was dolichocephalic. If, of these two types met with at Mugem, the Brachycephals have to be considered the earliest people to arrive on the bank of the Tagus at the beginning of the kitchen-midden period, then this result will singularly modify our ideas as to the succession of ethnic types in Europe.

The dolichocephalic skulls are all alike : their individual variations are but slight. They are thick skulls of poor encephalic capacity. The photographs given by F. de Paula e

[1] XCIV, p. 265.
[2] XXXIV, p. 320.

Oliveira in Cartailhac's book[1] show morphological harmony—long skulls and leptoprosopic faces, and leptorrhine nasal openings. Those skulls belonging to this first group which could be measured gave a cephalic index ranging from 71.1 to 75.5 (mean index, 73.8). The face is long, as we said, but prognathous.

The long bones have enabled the height to be calculated, and this would have been between 1 metre 56 and 1 metre 57. The women, naturally smaller, would scarcely have reached a height of 1 metre 44. These people were therefore very small. Nevertheless the kitchen-middens of Moita de Sebastiao yielded taller male skeletons—1 metre 63.

This race, small and dolichocephalic, also presents the character of having a very short arm in relation to the forearm and of having femora with pilasters and frequently platycnemic tibiae.

At the Lisbon Congress[2] de Quatrefages approximated this Mugem race to the palæolithic skeletons then known. He showed that although these Portuguese skeletons approximated to the la Vézère troglodytes in certain of their characters, in others they differed from them, notably in stature and by the fact that the troglodyte skulls are disharmonic. He therefore proposed a special group for them—the Mugem race.

Hervé,[3] however, was opposed to this conclusion. For him the Mugem race could perfectly well be approximated to the Magdalenians of Laugerie-Chancelade. They differed from this type in having pronounced eyebrow ridges, by their prognathism, and their mesorrhine nasal characters. But these could be explained by the presence, side by side with the Mugem race, of a population descended from the earliest Neanderthaloid occupants of the district and by an intimate contact between them.

The second type of this mesolithic period, as we have said, is brachycephalic. Only a small number of skulls of this kind were met with, but the presence of the race is indubitable. The exact cephalic indices are difficult to give, because the skulls in question have been posthumously deformed. But it is certain that there were in the Cabeço d'Arruda individuals of extreme brachycephaly and also sub-brachycephals. The

1 **CLXXXVI**, p. 291.
2 Discussion, **CLXXXVI**.
3 **XCIV**, p. 268.

face of these individuals is broad, flattened and very prognathous; the very large malar bones project in front. The first to describe these skeletons (de Paula e Oliveira), struck by these characters, thought himself justified in writing: "I would call attention to the fact that this globular skull and broad prognathous face recalls the cranial type of certain races belonging to the Mongolian group." For the present, however, we must not adventure into such a genealogy. The observation applies to a mere morphological approximation.

Thus, buried in the Mugem shellheap, we have two perfectly distinct races. And, since these representatives were laid to earth side by side, we have every reason to believe that these two races, living simultaneously in the south of Portugal, were not in enmity one to the other.

The dolichocephalic type is likely to be the earlier of the two on Iberian territory. It is extremely probable that this type represents the indigenous race, that which may have descended from the small Dolichocephals of the Magdalenian period, such as we have come to know them in the palæolithic sepultures of the Dordogne. Are we sure of the feasibility of such a descent as from north to south? Human relations between Spain, Portugal and France in quaternary times may not, perhaps, have followed the road we imagine. Discoveries made in Africa, and certain finds in Europe, should prompt us to be cautious. We must still curb our imagination. All the same, the Mugem burials bring us face to face with a fact of importance for the primitive history of European races. We must say still a few more words on the subject.

When we study the chronological succession of the races of Europe, it seems to us to be difficult to place the arrival in western Europe of the first brachycephalic emigrants further back than the true Neolithic.[1] Ofnet, a mesolithic station in which there are Brachycephals, is sufficiently far off. Yet here, towards the extreme boundary of western Europe, we have established that round-headed people existed at a certainly very early period. The Portuguese kitchen-middens are considered to be earlier than the Danish ones.[2] The

[1] Quite recent research (1923-24) has revealed round-headed palæolithic skulls of the Ofnet type at Solutré and at Aveline's Hole in the Mendips. See **CXXIII** (p. 142, 1925 edition). (Translator's Note.)

[2] We shall see, however, in the chapter dealing with Denmark, that the experts of that country have discovered prehistoric horizons which can be considered as even earlier (the Maglemose peat, Svaerdborg).

scraper-blade, so common in the Danish shell mounds, is not found here; pottery is absent in the deep layers, and the dog, the first animal domesticated by the North European tribes, is missing at Mugem.

If these Portuguese deposits are really anterior to those of the North European coasts, whence came the Brachycephals buried in them? I do not wish to build up premature theories. But it is impossible not to call attention to the fact that, on the other side of the Straits of Gibraltar, there have also been dug up equally brachycephalic skulls from neolithic strata in North Africa. I know well that all is by no means clear in regard to these neolithic brachycephalic Africans (up till now they would appear to come from dolmen burials); but we must not forget the prognathism of the Mugem skulls. In general the Swiss neolithic Brachycephals, the probable builders of the lake dwellings, do not present this character and they have been found on one of the highways leading to the Southwest of Europe from the habitat of the Nordics or neolithic Eastern folk. Have we then already the right to conclude that at Mugem we have the remains of an African migration bringing brachycephalic types for the first time on southern European soil? I do not think we have that right yet. But it is obvious that we must attentively consider the discoveries of human skeletons which will be made in the old Neolithic of North Africa and in the Neolithic of the Iberian peninsular.

The Mugem kitchen-middens, in natural succession to the Magdalenian, will thus lead us, without any transition, to the Neolithic period properly so-called.

The people of the polished stone age in the Iberian peninsular seem to have lived chiefly out in the open, which the climate permitted—building themselves huts which were sometimes grouped together in villages. More rarely, it would seem, they occupied caves and rock-shelters. And in spite of the fact that a large number of these huts have disappeared owing to their exposed situation, scientific explorers occasionally come across them. In the southeast of Spain Henri and Louis Siret have notified a fairly large number. They consisted of habitations hollowed out in the ground and surrounded by stones, over which were raised walls and roofs of branches.

Humble homes, such as the folk of the polished stone age built throughout Europe, they sheltered a humble existence. In these pits dug in the ground, some few yards in area, we find cinders and charcoal and their simple goods. These Neolithics of Iberia buried their dead in natural caves—they are numerous in Portugal—in artificial caves and in the megalithic monuments known as dolmens. Dolmens are called *antas* in Portugal, where Cartailhac has noted a large number, and *arcas* in Spain, where they appear to be relatively more rare,[1] although in the southern provinces, in Andalusia for example, they are frequent, and sometimes of considerable size (e.g., the *allée couverte* of la Cueva de Mengal). In the southeast of Spain the neolithic burials have been well studied by the two Sirets. They are not of uniform type. One or more skeletons are to be found in polygonal spaces of from 1 metre 50 to 2 metres 50 in diameter enclosed by stones set on the ground. Or sometimes it is a rectangular vault 1 metre 80 long by 1 metre 50 wide, and 60 cms deep, formed of slabs of stone ; or a cist burial such as is frequently found in Europe in this period. This variety in the manner of burying the dead must not, however, be taken to mean that it represents the ethnographic expression of different races. Louis Siret says of the study of these funerary monuments that it " shows that of all these contemporary systems of construction . . . suitable local conditions alone are responsible for the method chosen. Taken in their entirety, they reveal a remarkable unity of idea and are characteristic of a single and even a very long period."

The quality of the grave goods lends support to this conclusion. Whether such objects have been collected from natural or artificial caves, or from megalithic monuments, they present a genuine uniformity. Though these grave goods are alike among themselves they differ from those of the rest of Europe for the same epoch in having certain characteristics of their own, and L. Siret considered that the neolithic civilization of Iberia came from the eastern Mediterranean.[2] We know that many prehistorians support this opinion.

[1] It used to be thought that there were practically no megalithic monuments in the north of Spain, and the country was divided into two zones—the western dolmen zone, running all along the Atlantic and to the south ; and the rest of the country. But now, as we have seen, the young Spanish archæological schools are discovering them every day in the north.

[2] CCXLIII, pp. 5 and 402.

We are now faced with the question—was the new industry introduced by isolated traders who, by their contributions of merchandise and travellers' tales gradually modified the existing civilization, or was this overthrown by the arrival of fresh human hordes—by an invasion ? The reply can only be given after a study of the human remains themselves.

Unfortunately a large number of these have disappeared. In the Peninsular more than perhaps anywhere else skeletons have been destroyed. Hervé gives some lamentable details.[1] The remains of the neolithic folk of Iberia have been scattered by the hundred. Nevertheless, with what was saved from this vandalism we can attempt, after a fashion, to trace the ethnic physiognomy of the early population of Spain and Portugal.

In Portugal the Neolithic is represented as at Mugem, by two types, Dolichocephals and Brachycephals. The dolichocephalic type is still in the majority as it was in the mesolithic period. A few details are essential.

The brachycephalic skulls (they nearly all come from caves in the neighbourhood of the Tagus) have been described by Paula e Oliveira as bearing a manifest resemblance to those of Mugem. He says that they are " remarkable particularly for their bi-parietal breadth which is in contrast to the narrowness of the anterior region. We can establish for all of them the same characteristics to which Broca called attention in the Brachycephals of Orrouy[2] ". This approximation has been emphasized by French anthropologists. As for the dolichocephalic type, it has not altered, but it is more refined than it was. A greater encephalic development is manifest ; the eyebrow bosses have disappeared and the prognathism is less. Certain morphological influences which might have been attributed to the older race of Neanderthaloid type have vanished. And while anthropologists have scruples about approximating the mesolithic Dolichocephals of Mugem to the French Magdalenian Dolichocephals, ancestors of the leptoprosopic and orthognathous Baumes-Chaudes Dolichocephals of the neolithic period, this approximation to the Iberian Neolithic man appears to them to be obvious.

Thus there were two human types living on either side of the Pyrenees in the polished stone period. The dolichocephalic

[1] **XCIV**, p. 272.
[2] **CLXXXVI**.

race is the older, and may go back at least to Magdalenian times.

Do we find this double ethnic physiognomy in Spain as well as in Portugal ?

Spain has furnished us with skeletal documents in the shape of remains far older than anything discovered in the territory of her western neighbour.

The skull known as the Gibraltar skull, extracted in 1848 from the ossiferous breccia of the Forbes Quarry cavern and described by Busk, and also by Huxley, who drew attention to the simian form of the dental arch, is to-day considered to date from the middle Pleistocene. The fauna with which it was contemporary represents a southern facies of that epoch, and both are fossilized to the same degree. Boule does not hesitate to place the Gibraltar skull among the list of Moustierian skulls of the type of *Homo neanderthalensis* with which Busk had aforetime rightly compared it.[1]

During the upper Palæolithic (the Reindeer age) large numbers of men wandered over Spanish ground. In the French Magdalenian age they left on the walls of many caverns and on rocks in the open gravings and paintings which have been made known to us with all the details we could wish in the scientific reviews and in special works. To what race did those admirable artists belong who painted the cavern roofs of Altamira (province of Santander), the astounding and life-like scenes of combat of the Minateda frieze, and many others as well ?[2] It is very difficult at this time of day to answer such a question. Human skeletons of the Reindeer age, of unchallengeable authenticity, are still to find in Spain. Not that finds have not been notified, here and there[3] ; but these are still doubtful and inadequate.

By comparison with what French ethnology of Magdalenian neolithic times has shown, we may legitimately consider that the Spanish Magdalenians belonged to the same dolichocephalic type as the French Magdalenians.

We have a few Spanish skeletons of the polished stone age. First of all those coming from the Gibraltar caves which served for so long as habitations and burial places. Numberless

[1] **XXI**, p. 180.
[2] **XXIII**.
[3] **CXCII**, p. 278.

human bone fragments were obtained from these caves, in layers which contained neolithic grave goods. Busk described them, and, later, Broca.[1] The majority consist of dolichocephalic skulls characterized by protruberant occipital bosses which have earned for the type the description of " crânes à chignon ". The Baumes-Chaudes type exhibits this same morphological quality. The face is orthognathous.

The femurs of these neolithic troglodytes show the bony pilaster of which we have already spoken, and the tibias are platycnemic.

All these skeletal characters resemble those which we have noted as existing in the neolithic dolichocephalic people of Portugal. We may be permitted to suppose that at that prehistoric period the whole of the southern portion of the Peninsular was inhabited by men of the same race. And just as in Portugal these Dolichocephals had, side by side with them, a minority of Brachycephals, so was it also in Gibraltar.

This is not the place in which to recall all the discoveries of polished stone age skeletons in the Iberian peninsular. I will simply say that what we have observed in the case of Gibraltar appears to be true of the whole country. The dolichocephaly of the Iberian Neolithics in general is highly accentuated (frequently indices are 72 to 74), and Verneau has insisted on the many features possessed by these skulls recalling those of the Vézère crania.

This similarity of the population on either side of the Pyrenees makes us think that the primitive neolithic peoples of Spain and Portugal were related to the French population of the same period—always with the reservation that we made above in connection with the African Brachycephals. But whence came the Neanderthaloid types of the middle Quaternary of which the Gibraltar skull is a representative and of which the mesolithic Dolichocephals of Mugem seem to have retained many morphological souvenirs ?

Before we can attempt to trace any sort of filiation it is essential that we should know what are the physical features of the existing population of the Iberian peninsular.

* * *

Spain by no means takes a back seat among the European States which have set ethnological enquiries on foot. When

[1] **XXIV**, 1869, p. 146 and 148.

we think of the somatic anthropology of the Peninsular two names stand out first and foremost and with them two lengthy and detailed works. To put them in their chronological order, they are Aranzadi and his study of 494 Spanish crania[1]; and Oloriz and his examination of 8,368 living Spaniards.[2] Thanks to them we have a good idea of the general morphological character of Spanish skulls. Later their observations were carried a good deal further by A. de Hoyos Sainz who published a series of 3,500 living Spanish crania.[3] Few countries can show efforts comparable with these in self-study, and our confrères from the other side of the Pyrenees are to be congratulated on their enterprise. Hoyos' last memoir confirms the indications relating to the geographical distribution of hyman types sketched out by the preceding work.

One piece of information stands out from these important researches. Spain, taken as a whole, is a remarkably dolichocephalic region. This gives it a clear-cut physiognomy among European States.[4] The most usual cephalic index among Spaniards is 77. Three-fifths of the population have an index lying between 75 and 79.9, and few of the ethnic groups of Europe can show such marked homogeneity in this respect.

Oloriz, " making ten different combinations of the distribution of the mean cephalic index, from the most frequent index, and by provinces and districts," has constituted eleven geographical regions which correspond fairly closely with the Spanish provinces. Following Deniker's example[5] we will make use of them in order to illustrate the ethnic physiognomy of the kingdom.

The large promontory of Galicia (not counting, in the north, the province of Lugo), with several mountain chains running across it, constitutes the Galician region in which the average indices, taken by provinces, range from 78.4 to 79, and is clearly a sub-dolichocephalic area.

Further east, the great slope of the Cantabrian mountains, facing the Atlantic (northern Galicia, Asturias, and littoral

[1] **VII.**

[2] **CLXXXII.** Deniker made extensive use of these two studies in his memoir on the European cephalic index.

[3] **CXIII**, p. 447.

[4] There are exceptions to this general dolichocephaly, and one even finds centres of hyper-brachycephaly (in the province of Alicante, for example).

[5] **LV**, p. 19.

of Old Castile) forms the Cantabrian region. Here the cephalic index is slightly higher. And—a point to be remembered—it is that part of this territory lying between Galicia and the province of Santander which possesses the most mesocephalic heads, as though some influence due to a rather brachycephalic population had been at work in this spot.

The Basque and Navarra region, composed of the three Basque provinces (Vizcay, Alava and Guipuzcoa) and of Navarra, repeats the physiognomy of the Galician region (mean index of 78.8). The least dolichocephalic portion of this region is the province of Alava, facing the Ebro basin, of which the town of Vitoria is the most important urban centre.

In contrast with the Galician promontory, the Catalan region, on the Mediterranean, is even rather more dolichocephalic (index of 78.1). It is interesting to note that the littoral provinces, in spite of their probably greater accessibility to "foreigners," retain their ethnic character, and that this is even accentuated as we go towards the south, in the province of Tarragona, where the head once more takes on its most usual aspect in Spain (index of 77.6).

The extensive region of Leon and Old Castile, dominated on three sides by mountain chains whose streams drain into the Douro and thence into the Atlantic, is also remarkably homogeneous. And yet the road lies well open to the exterior. The average indices range from 77.2 to 78.1. The last figure is due to Salamanca and Segovia, both of which lie to the south, at the foot of the Sierras, whose backbone forms that almost transversal ridge across the map of Spain which at once strikes the eye.

Both the Aragon and the Valencia regions, especially the second, show individuals of even more marked dolichocephaly. The lowest cephalic index of all the Spanish zones is that of the Valencia region, in which Castellon and Alicante show sharply dolichocephalic. All the indices of the Aragon canton are 77. It is only the fractions that differ.

In the eighth or Lower Castile region, comprising nearly the whole of New Castile, Estramadura and the north of Murcia, the cephalic character of the inhabitants undergoes a sudden change, both units of the index rising by comparison with the foregoing regions. And these territories which depart furthest from the habitual dolichocephaly of the rest of Spain are those containing the cities of Madrid and Toledo. Even if this should be because the population of Madrid includes many "foreigners," can we say the same for Toledo?

Upper Andalusia constitutes the ninth region (provinces of Almeria, Grenada, Jaen, Cordoba and Murcia), where the cephalic indices are all expressed by the figure 77 and a fraction, except for Murcia which is sub-dolichocephalic, with 78.

The tenth region, Lower Andalusia, raises the index for all its provinces, with 78.5 for Sevilla, and 79.5 for Cadiz; all are sub-dolichocephalic.

As for the Balearic Isles, they also contain Dolichocephals. Thus, in recapitulating the result of these observations we get a picture of Spain, as a whole, as a country of long-headed people. And if we set aside a portion of the Cantabrian region and the Basque country, we perceive, with Deniker, that a line drawn from Corunna to Murcia will divide the kingdom into two parts, the one to the northeast dolichocephalic, and that to the southwest sub-dolichocephalic.

Oloriz, taking all the indices which he arrived at, has arranged them orographically, whereby he obtains a curious result whose general physiognomy only we shall here indicate. The inhabitants of the low countries are much less dolichocephalic than those of the highlands. On the plateaux, from a height upwards of 1000 metres, the people have a very low cephalic index (77.49). As we go lower in the geographical scale from 1000 to 500 metres, we find sub-dolichocephalic folk—78.20. And when we get down to sea level the index actually departs slightly from dolichocephaly—78.45.

How should these facts be interpreted? Are these changes merely the arithmetical result of a different arrangement of the various districts? Does height increase with altitude in Spain? And is this diminution in dolichocephaly in the lowlands due to that law of anatomical correlation according to which the tallest men are also the longest-headed?[1]

We must emphasize the almost complete absence of Brachycephals in Spanish territory, which, throughout history, was overrun by numberless invaders. Save for one corner—the Galician-Cantabrian coast, corresponding with Oloriz's second region—there is no Spanish group of any size (we do not say there are no individuals) touched by brachycephaly.[2] The most numerous mesaticephalic groups are in the south-

[1] CXCVII.

[2] See an earlier note on p. 106.

southwest between Cadiz and Huelva, in the country watered by the lower Guadalquivir and the Rio Tinto. It would not appear that we can lay this ethnic modification at the door of the copper mines of this district, with their many workmen, because Cadiz has a slightly higher index than Huelva. It is true that the Cadiz district includes the port of the same name, and that maritime towns usually contain all kinds of men.

Another mesocephalic island lies to the west of Barcelona, and consists of Lerida (Balaguer district in the Pyrenean foothills). We still see a remarkable uniformity in the cranial morphology of extensive districts. Thus the whole of Aragon, part of Old Castile, and certain neighbouring regions (seventeen groups of districts) have indices which remain constant between 76.5 and 77.9.

A general study of height has been carried out by the same authors (Oloriz, Aranzadi and Hoyos). The stature of Spaniards, relatively low throughout the kingdom, does not, however, show complete uniformity. This mean height, taken from Oloriz, figures as 1 metre 635. Hoyos and Aranzadi make it even less.

Nowhere does the height go above the mean. All the same, here and there it shows regions where there is a certain disparity in both sexes.

If we follow Deniker and draw a line from San Sebastian to the Portuguese frontier at a point between Badajoz and Huelva, we find the smallest stature to west of it. Galicia, Asturias, northern Leon, and nearly the whole of Old Castile belong to this small stature group, which, as a rule, drops below 1 metre 63. In the south of the province of Leon the Salamanca region brings it up again to 1 metre 64. A little further to the north Burgos brings it up still more—to 1 metre 65.

To the east of this line, the littoral zone of Catalonia and Valencia shows the tallest men in Spain, with a height reaching 1 metre 67. Maybe the early anthropologists would have seen in this the influence of the nearness of the Mediterranean. And this greater height is again and again prolonged towards the interior.

Have we here a different race from that which inhabits the rest of Spain? Deniker is firmly convinced of it. Having established that the cephalic index of this population, chiefly a coastal one, was more dolichocephalic than anywhere else in Spain, he created an Atlanto-Mediterranean race in which these two main characters are associated, the rest of the kingdom being inhabited by the Ibero-Insular race.

The representatives of this Atlanto-Mediterranean race have not filtered very far into the rest of the country, and by the time we get to Aragon and New Castile we already find again, even in this district of the tallest men, the smaller people we have seen in the west.

Certain exceptional features in Spanish ethnology would seem to be capable of explanation by the historian. Should we not find traces somewhere of the Arab-Berber influence, seeing that these people occupied the territory for so long? May not eight centuries of domination have left some ethnic imprint? It is very difficult to answer this question with any degree of certainty at present, because such a reply could only be based on accurate research which has not yet been undertaken. Nevertheless, we can say this much, that the Granada and Sevilla districts, in which the "Arab" influence survived longest, do show some of the tallest statures in Spain. Are we to conclude in favour of a racial souvenir of this early occupation?

It has likewise been put down to Berber influence that a stature above the general Spanish height is to be seen in the "Maragates", wandering pedlars established on the skirts of the Leon mountains. These people, studied by Aragon,[1] and having a height of 1 metre 65—therefore taller than other Spaniards—are dolichocephalic like their compatriots in the surrounding districts.

The earliest inhabitants noticed by ancient authors are Iberians and Celts; then come Phœnicians, Greeks, Carthaginians, and Romans. In 410 the invasions began, bringing Vandals, Swabians (Suevi), Alans, and especially Visigoths. These were to be pushed back by the "Arabs," who reigned as masters for many centuries, and they were to retain only the little kindgom of the Asturias.

What were the most important anthropological characters of these invaders—of these Visigoths or Western Goths, whom we are taught to regard as coming from Scandinavia? What appears to be obvious is that either we must find in their

[1] IV, p. 321.

descendants the general Germanic type to which the Goths belonged, or else these Goths were Goths only in name! And Spain cannot show any population that has preserved the Germanic type. The races occupying the kingdom are dolichocephalic, it is true, but they are small, brunet, and dark-eyed. We cannot therefore speak of an anthropological influence due to the Visigoths.[1]

Must we then go back further still to earlier historic populations to find the ancestral image of the present inhabitants of Spain? We think that it would be quite in vain to prosecute our investigations among the Romans, and equally so among the Carthaginians, Greeks or Phœnicians. Must we then consider the Iberians as the parent stock of these small, brunet, dolichocephalic people? A claim has been made to explain the small stature of Northern Spaniards by a Celtic influence! I do not know what to make of such an idea. It seems to me to be quite mistaken.

Let us, however, go further back into the past, and we shall find the proto-historic and prehistoric populations of which we have already spoken.

It will be recalled that the Mugem burials in Portugal and those of various places in Spain revealed human types of small stature that were dolichocephalic, and which could be related by their general characters to the earlier Laugerie-Chancelade race. But we also found brachycephalic types. Does the greater part of the Spanish population derive from this prehistoric dolichocephalic type? Or must we completely abandon any filiation to palæolithic and neolithic people and have recourse to an "Arab-Berber" peopling of the country?

We know from the work both of Chantre and Bertholon that "Arabs"—ethnic complex that they are—include groups of varying stature, some in any case quite small, which might be approximated to the Spaniards, and that they also are brunet and dolichocephalic. Their dolichocephaly, however, is even greater than that of the Spaniards. In any case we should have to find out whether this cranial form indicated by mean characters does not manifest itself under another aspect when we come to examine its representatives individually. *A priori* it might indeed seem singular that this lengthy "Arab" occupation should have left no important imprint in the

[1] See chapter on General Considerations.

country. Thus it would be possible to imagine that at the time of the invasion or invasions—for there were several—the various contingents of " Arab " invaders, by some extraordinary chance, were more especially made up of individuals belonging to ethnic groups that were not so tall as their congeners.

On the other hand, it is quite certain that the human type christened 'Celtic' by anthropologists—people of medium height, brachycephalic and brunet—did not play a part of any importance in the make up of the Spanish nation. It may be that a few individuals of the type filtered into the northwest of Spain.

As for Portugal, ethnologically it differs in no way from Spain. The peninsular constitutes a solid whole the main lines of whose historic and ethnic destiny have been identical.

The same invasions overran both Spain and Portugal. Are we not told, in this connection, that of all the invaders of the fifth century, the Swabians (Suevi) only remained in Portugal? But the Suevi are also people of Germanic race. What, then, are we to think of an emigration of German peoples, having the clear-cut anthropological characters of this group, which should occupy a country for two hundred years and yet not leave in it a single trace of their physical type?

Perhaps the Suevi were not of Germanic race? No more than were the Goths, the Vandals and the Alans. Here, too, the problem becomes tantalizing. Were the Suevi but a clan bearing a Germanic name and speaking a Germanic tongue, yet composed of men of another race? If this, however, were the case, whence came these people of small stature so clearly dolichocephalic and with skin, eyes and hair so differently pigmented from that of the northern peoples, who were to form these great " Germanic " contingents? Here, as in Spain, we can but turn our eyes to those two groups—the prehistoric peoples and the " Arabs ".

We are familiar with some of the remains of Portuguese prehistoric men. They were analysed at the beginning of this chapter devoted to the prehistory of the Iberian peninsular. And we know that they may be related to the Laugerie-Chancelade race. And are we to think that these people multiplied to such an extent as to account, single-handed, for the present population? Yet why should the Iberian peninsular be an exception to a prodigious increase in birthrate which certainly explains the growth of populations in the world as a whole? Primitive human groups at the outset were certainly made up of numerically small collections of people. They did not increase by the aid of contributions come from one knows not whence.

Anthropological documentation in regard to the living population of Portugal shows us that the country is inhabited almost throughout by small Dolichocephals. Some hundreds of measured crania from different parts of Portugal supply indices ranging from 74.5 to 77.6. The last figure is yielded by a female series, and in dolichocephalic groups the dolichocephaly of the women is always less than that of the men.

The geographical distribution of the cranial form of the Portuguese shows that although Portugal as a whole is dolichocephalic, there are yet certain details to be taken into consideration in this almost uniform region. Thus the most dolichocephalic district is that of Tras os Montes (index of 74.5) and the least dolichocephalic is that of Minho (index of 78 on the living). And yet these two provinces, both north of the Douro, touch. The second is maritime, whereas the first is included within the prolongation of the Asturias mountains. Another province having a relatively high index is Algarve (index of 77.3) at the extreme south of Portugal.

Have the mountainous regions been the better able to preserve their initial dolichocephalic types? One might think so when it is seen that together with the province of Tras os Montes that of Beira Alta, equally hilly, since the western continuation of the Sierra de Gata runs into it and the Serra da Estrella crosses it, shows the lowest index (74.6 on the living).

The mean height in Portugal is comprised within the near neighbourhood of 1 metre 640. It varies little from one province to another. The minimum height seems to be met with in the province of Minho, where we also find the least amount of dolichocephaly. It is to be noted that the cities of Coimbra and Lisbon show a smaller stature than that furnished by the country as a whole. This observation is of a nature to upset our conceptions relating to urban influence in increasing height.

When we examine the map of Portugal we find a good deal that is not easy to explain. Certain regions stand out abruptly from the rest of the country by a fairly sharp rise in the height of their inhabitants. Vizeu, in the northwest of the Serra da Estrella, is an example, and so also are the centre of the province of Alemtejo and the two districts of Evora and Beja. In the province of Beira Alta the Vizeu district appears to possess the tallest stature for the whole of Portugal (1 metre 67). Yet on the other side of the Serra da Estrella the Guarda district, still in the same province, shows the low stature of 1 metre 64! The same is true of the province of Alemtejo, where there is a district of small stature in the north side by side with two districts showing greater height.

The anthropologist Medes Correa,[1] my distinguished confrère, does not appear to believe that the Portuguese of to-day can be considered, as a whole, to be the descendants of the Mugem prehistoric people. Such morphological survivals as still existed towards the close of the Neolithic among the then inhabitants of Portugal would have dwindled more and more in proportion as we come down to our own epoch.

The historians will have something to say, I imagine, after reading the above few indications. Maybe they will give reasons to explain the exceptional facts we have established, such as the creation of those ethnic islands which are considered to have been revealed in various parts of the Peninsular. Perhaps the facts of the anthropology of Iberia will furnish them with arguments or suggestions.

Collaboration between Anthropology and History would seem essential in Iberia. Heretofore certain problems have seemed insoluble because one of the unknown factors could not be expressed in any fashion or by any symbol. It is quite a different matter to-day.

[1] CLVII.

CHAPTER III

FRANCE

FRANCE, of all European countries—hence of the whole world up till the present—has furnished anthropologists with the largest number of skeletal remains dating from the Palæolithic, just as she has also furnished to prehistorians the largest number of human settlements of the same period. Her implements of the various sub-divisions of the Pleistocene are to be seen in the cases of every museum in the world. Palæolithic dwelling places positively abound in France, and they are very far from being known in their entirety.

This is due to the favoured circumstances and situation which France has enjoyed and occupied from the earliest days, the glaciers of the Ice Age having failed to penetrate very far into her territory.

At a time when the great Russian glacier submerged all northern Europe, and England was only habitable south of the Thames, while Switzerland was simply a mass of continental ice comparable to Greenland to-day, a considerable area of France was still ice-free. Animal life, pressed back on all sides by the morainic offensive, found its way to these favoured lands.

There were great troops and herds of the various quaternary species on French territory, proof of which is manifold if we mention the extraordinary number of certain of the large carnivores. Never, perhaps, had Man of the pre-cultivation period had such plentiful sources of food at his disposal.

Need we refer, merely by way of example, in post-glacial times, to the incomprehensible accumulations of horses' bones at Solutré ?

Although the oldest palæolithic civilization (Chellean and Acheulean) is lavishly represented in France, there have not yet been met with any skeletal remains—leaving out of account, of course, the Moulin-Quignon jaw—belonging to those epochs of the remote past. It is from Germany (Mauer) and England

(Piltdown) that these important, though rare, documents have come. But directly we come to Moustierian times we find skeletons in abundance in French ground.

From 1859 onwards human bones began to be collected, beginning with the jaw from Arcy-sur-Cure (Yonne). Then in 1883 part of a jaw was found at Marcilly (Eure); the Gourdan fragments and the Malarnaud (Ariège) jaw in 1889; and also jaws at Isturitz (Basses Pyrénées) in 1895, and in several of the caverns of the Ariège (l'Estelas, Aubert) and the Aude (Sallelès-Cabardès). Ten years later Favraud found three more pieces of human jawbones in the Charente (in the middle course of the Petit Puy). In 1908 there was the great discovery of the Chapelle-aux-Saints by Bardon and J. and A. Bouyssonie. The skeleton, almost complete, was the subject of a fine monograph by Boule. In 1909 Hauser discovered the le Moustier skeleton and Capitan and Peyrony, in the same year, excavated the first of the la Ferrassie (Dordogne) skeletons, and a fruitful harvest is still being yielded by this station. In 1911 H. Martin found the la Quina skeleton.

These discoveries extended over a wide area, ranging from the Basses Pyrénées and the Ariège as far as the Eure. In other words, the Moustierians were distributed over the whole of France.

We do not know what fate befell these Neanderthal people. Some anthropologists have indicated a certain survival of Neanderthaloid characters in skulls belonging to post-Moustierian periods and even in times reaching to our own day. But Boule, who has made a special study of this race, does not believe in such a survival. In his opinion the Neanderthal race has been extinct in Europe—or let us be more exact and say, in France—since the close of the Moustierian period.[1] And how has this come about? Was it by migration to distant lands? As we cannot find its descendants in any part of the world, we must envisage the dying out of this group. But in those far-off days there was not the same reason for Man's struggle to supplant Man as there is to-day. Then what can have been the true cause of this disappearance? The reply has been given that they lacked the power of adaptation. Possibly. But power of adaptation to what? It must be admitted that serious objections can be raised against this last hypothesis.

[1] **XXI**, p. 245.

Boule does recognize the possibility of hybridization, and that an infusion of Neanderthaloid blood into other human groups belonging to the *Homo sapiens* branch, or to one of them, may have taken place. But since we cannot to-day find any direct descendants of Neanderthal man this infusion could have been incidental only and without any sequel.

The human races of the upper Pleistocene are very different. A race of finer and different type succeeded in the Reindeer Age to these people of brute-like anatomy who made their cutters and hand-points under the Moustierian skies. These are the Laugerie-Chancelade and Cro-Magnon races whose main characteristics we have already given. Men of these races seem to have been distributed all over France. And though they seem to have been more thickly settled in the southwest (various stations) and the southeast (Grimaldi, near the French frontier), the chances of hunting and other adventures drew them much further to the north (les Hoteaux, department of the Ain). And here, it should be understood, we are speaking only of the skeletons that have been found, and not of the industries that have been noted, which are much more widely distributed. These also mark the presence of these races pretty well all over the territory of ancient Gaul.

Thus, when quaternary times were drawing to a close, the human races established on French soil could already claim to be multiple in origin.

*

* *

The neolithic period has left numerous osseous relics in France. Unfortunately many of these are gone, and the authors of this regrettable loss were archæologists of the bad old days, specimens of whom still exist, sad to relate. Cartailhac has said[1]: "We ought to have maps giving the distribution and the density of all the ancient races of France. But the thousands of burials which are known have served no purpose. Archæologists alone have destroyed more bone fragments than either natural agencies or field labourers. It is amazing how very few bones in good condition and of certain provenance are to be found in the Muséum[2] and the Musée Broca, in public or in private collections."

[1] **XXXV**, p. 331.
[2] i.e. the Paris Museum of Natural History. (Translator's Note.)

But before beginning to study the neolithic population it is essential to ask ourselves what was the fate of the French population of the upper Quaternary. Here I may mention a hypothesis which no longer finds favour to-day, namely the northward migration of the Magdalenians in the track of the reindeer. It was supposed that when climatic changes induced the reindeer to depart to those northern regions he occupies to-day, the hunters who could not do without this game followed him thither. Groups of people belonging to the Laugerie-Chancelade race, in particular, would thus have emigrated to the northwest and passed thence into North America before the land bridge between the two continents was broken. According to this hypotheses, the Eskimo would be the descendants of the people who inhabited France in the Magdalenian age. They are said to have " preserved the same head-form, harpoons and throwing sticks, the same gentle and pacific manners, together with the artistic sentiment and indifference towards the dead which characterized the French Magdalenians ".[1]

It is unnecessary to add that these are simply deductions made from ethnographic and morphological concordances—insufficient, to boot. And in this, as in many another case, concordance does not necessarily mean descent. There are sufficiently wide differences between the general osteology of the Eskimo and the Magdalenians. And it would also be necessary to demonstrate that the passage from northwest Europe to North America existed at precisely *that moment.*

Even if the migration of herds of reindeer drew after them a certain number of hunters, it is probable, nevertheless, that many of them stayed where they were and continued to inhabit the caverns and rock shelters. Further, although the reindeer had gone, there still remained immense herds of other wild animals in France. We have proof of this in the fact that in mesolithic times deer took the place of reindeer in the diet of the people, just as deerhorn replaced reindeer-horn in the manufacture of harpoons.

Thus the Laugerie-Chancelade race continued to inhabit France, accepting those fundamental modifications in the facts of civilization which were to supervene during the passage from the Palæolithic to the Mesolithic and Neolithic. Perhaps it

[1] **CLXV**, p. 326.

was even to be responsible for them. Soon this race was to appear in our terminology under the name of Baumes-Chaudes, but this is merely a change of label.

The Baumes-Chaudes are caverns in the Lozère which served as ossuaries in the neolithic period. They were discovered by Dr. Prunières. Gabriel de Mortillet described them thus: "The Lozère Tarn flows through deep and narrow gorges whose precipitous walls rise to a height of several hundred metres. It is in the rock walls of one of these gorges, near the village of Saint-Georges de Lévejac, situated on the *causse*, that these caverns open, some two-thirds of the way up, below the escarpment. The two principal caverns, situated on a terrace, are joined together by a sort of rock shelter. The entrances of both consist of light, dry chambers containing the refuse of habitation. The northernmost cavern narrows at a depth of 35 metres and becomes dark and damp, and the soil is covered with stalagmites containing numerous human bones. They are so firmly welded together that it is difficult to extract them. Prunières, however, was able to establish that these bones, dated by potsherds, are like those found in the southern cavern. This dark, damp portion of the cavern ends in a deep well.

The southernmost cavern contains a human ossuary 25 metres long by an average 4 metres wide, and 50 centimetres in depth. The bones of 300 individuals of various ages and different sex were jumbled together anyhow in this space. The skulls alone appear to have been grouped together or placed with care at certain points."[1]

When the discoverer laid his first study of this ossuary before the Société d'anthropologie de Paris, he stated that there was not a single brachycephalic, nor even a mesaticephalic skull out of 60 complete specimens. All these individuals whose bodies had been piled up in these natural burial places were dolichocephalic in type. One could not ask for greater ethnic purity.

Hervé described this race as follows:—"Occipital dolichocephaly; mean cephalic index, 72.6; frontal region moderately broad; large cranial capacity; horizontal circumference of skull, 543 mm in the men and 533 in the women; simple sutures; orthognathous face; mean nasal index, 42.7

[1] **CLXV**, p. 313.

mean orbital index, 83.6; thickened *linia aspera* of femur; tibiæ, in most cases, flattened; fibulæ channelled to a varying extent; ulna occasionally in-curved at distal end. The mean length (423 cms) of 15 Baumes-Chaudes femurs yields a height of 1 metre 61."

Finds similar to those of the Baumes-Chaudes, though not yielding so many crania, have been made in several other places in France, as in the Lozère, Aveyron, and departments of the Gard, Vaucluse, Bouches-du-Rhône and Ariège. In these caves and dolmens the race had remained everywhere more or less pure. Here and there one just begins to note morphological disturbance, more especially in the dolmen burials. These monuments, belonging to a later epoch, more often yield new types than the sepulchral caves—generally mesaticephalic, sometimes sub-brachycephalic. This is proof that a population characterized by this ethnic quality had begun to penetrate France. Still, it is possible to state positively that a portion of the country—the southern regions, or in general, the territory south of 46°, save only the eastern Alpine region—was of an almost uniform anthropological character up till the close of—especially up to the middle of—the neolithic period. This relative purity of human type by its very geographical localization would seem to indicate that those whom it characterized were descendants of the upper Palæolithic people who likewise inhabited this southern territory.

Further north, in the department of Saône-et-Loire, we come to the celebrated prehistoric Crot-du-Charnier at Solutré. There has been much discussion as to the age of the skeletons formerly recovered from it. De Ferry and Adrien Arcelin on the one hand, de Quatrefages and Hamy on the other, have accepted them as representing Palæolithic man. The Abbé Ducrost maintained that they could not date from an epoch earlier than the polished stone age. Broca, with the habitual caution which gives such authority to his work, described the Solutré crania under the title of "prehistoric series" in order not to compromise the solution of the archæological question. The human race as found in this eponymous station—which gives its name to the Solutrean period—is no longer homogeneous. The cephalic index varies widely, from 68.3—extreme dolichocephaly—to 88.2—extreme brachycephaly. What a difference there is here from the series obtained in the south of

France! Here the foreign penetration is tremendous. It is the first invasion from the East.[1]

Nowhere else on the territory of ancient Gaul has there been such a mixture. Dolichocephals are in a proportion only of 38.8 per cent., whilst Brachycephals (and sub-Brachycephals) are almost as numerous—33.3 per cent. It was thus a mixed population which dwelt in the shelter of the Roche de Solutré.[2] And this piebald population was not merely made up of two elements living side by side; it was already freely crossed if we are to judge by the proportion of mesaticephals (27 per cent.) mingled with the two principal morphological types.

The Solutré Dolichocephals are of the same race as the Magdalenian Dolichocephals who inhabited the south of France. Broca at once recognized this. The study of the long bones and the crania tend to establish, he said, "a certain affinity between the Solutré population of the dolichocephalic race to which the troglodytes of Périgord and la Lozère belonged."

On the eastern confines of France the Belfort region has showed, notably in the Cravanches cavern, the survival of this same early troglodyte type to a considerable extent. However, the presence of two mesaticephalic skulls side by side with a dolichocephalic series brings proof that cross-breeding had begun.

All prehistorians—I would also like to be able to say all historians—are familiar with the excavations of the Baron de Baye in the valley of the Petit Morin (Marne) and the fine discoveries which he made in many of the sepulchral caves. More than a thousand burials were found and the finder of these relics was able to bring together an admirable collection of human skeletons. Broca began the study of them, and so did Quatrefages. These neolithic people of the Champagne district were of two races, in proportions that varied considerably. The Dolichocephals still represent a definite majority (50 per cent.); whereas the Brachycephals have become nearly twice as frequent (27.3 per cent.). But the proportion of mesaticephalic individuals (22.7 per cent.) shows that intermarriage between the two principal races had been going

[1] Obviously the series of Solutré skeletons yielded by the earlier excavations should be closely re-examined.

[2] The discoveries made in 1922-24 suggest that this was so even in Aurignacian times—though up to now only in this one locality in France. See the note on p. 74.

on for a long time.[1] The dolichocephalic palæolithic race also survives here, as it did in the stations of the same epoch which we have already briefly enumerated. Its characteristics are visible here not only in the type of the skull but in that of other parts of the skeleton. De Quatrefages pictures a fairly large number of fossil races as existing. He found most of them—five out of six—in the de Baye collection,[2] the Canstadt race alone not putting in an appearance. But, as we know, to-day this multiplicity of fossil races no longer gains the credence it did in the time of the illustrious author of *Crania ethnica*.

These ethnic mixtures, chiefly revealed in the neolithic sepultures of eastern France and the Champagne, we shall find again in varying proportions in the departments of Seine-et-Oise and Seine-et-Marne, and, farther away still, in the Breton peninsular. The Armorican burials of the neolithic period show an immense majority of dolichocephalic skulls, " amongst which are some rare mesaticephalic, and a few still more rare brachycephalic examples, revealing only a very slight intermixture."

And what has just been demonstrated for a few departments may doubtless be extended to the whole of France. In the neolithic period the descendants of the Magdalenian cave-dwellers still constituted the majority of the French population. In some parts—the southern departments—they even made up practically the entire population.

Analyses of the ages that followed will show brachycephalic majorities in departments which had been inhabited only by Dolichocephals for thousands of years. In regions such as the Central Plateau and Brittany the races dwelling there will be completely modified in kind by one ethnic replacement after another. To-day certain districts would need to be searched diligently before any descendants of the Magdalenian cave-dwellers, that very substratum of the French population and true native stock, could be found among their inhabitants.

In anthropological literature this ethnic group, to-day widespread in Europe, especially in its central and western regions, bears a variety of names. It is the Celtic race of

[1] The above percentages are calculated on the Broca series. Probably the proportion of Dolichocephals should be increased. Two crania deposited in the Museum at Lyon are dolichocephalic. But the facts already established remain unaltered. **XXV**, p. 28.

[2] **CCVI**, p. 107.

Broca—the term "Celtic" being used as an arbitrary ethnological convention—the Ligurian, Celto-Ligurian, or Rheto-Ligurian race, or, for some, *Homo alpinus*. In France, during the neolithic period, it is called the Grenelle race, and also the neolithic brachycephalic race.

The origin of these Brachycephals is unknown. We have every reason to think that they came from Asia, probably via the shores of the Black Sea and the Danube valley. And, in spite of the instinctive repugnance that may be felt in regard to oriental mirages, I think it is difficult in the present state of our knowledge to envisage any other origin. In these circumstances we must follow the geographer Schrader's thought, when he writes: "To-day it is a commonplace to say that Europe is a mere peninsular of Asia—the most delicate, the most refined, the best balanced, but nothing more. Europe is the child of Asia.

Whatever the ethnographic origin of the population of Europe may be, it is practically certain that a large proportion of it grew up and multiplied in Europe itself, although we are bound to admit in all geographical probability that an Asiatic tide flowed into and modified it time and time again."[1]

If, however, these neolithic Brachycephals did indeed come from Asia it is very improbable that they ever belonged to one of the yellow races. On their arrival in Europe they already possessed the characters which we know them to have to-day—in localities where very little intermixture has taken place. Naturally the area of characterization of this race has been sought in Asia. Heirs of ancient tradition, dominated by classical memories and by an apparent geographical determinism, we have given them—how could it be otherwise? —a name that is sufficiently vague: we call them Ural-Altaics.

And in face of these successive irruptions the Dolichocephals of Baumes-Chaudes, abandoning the ground where their ancestors had dwelt for thousands of years, apparently withdrew to the west and south of France, where we find their descendants to-day. Does not the Ibero-Aquitaine type carry on the type of the neolithic Dolichocephals, who themselves, as we know, carried on the Magdalenian Dolichocephal type? Have we not seen representatives of this very race in the Hispanic peninsular, at Mugem? This retreat hypothesis has been accepted by all French anthropologists.

[1] CCXXXVIII, p. 105.

Have we not seen that the sepultures containing the least homogeneous types, and that the lowest percentages of Baumes-Chaudes Dolichocephals are those, to the east, in the Alpine region (Isère) ; to the northeast, in the departments close to Alsace-Lorraine and Belgium ? It was through these two districts that the brachycephalic stream flowed into France.

The ethnic physiognomy of France during the bronze age is less well known. One cause of this relative lack of knowledge arises from the fact that during this period new religious notions led to the burning of the dead. Those to whom hitherto a most careful burial had been given, since every part of the body had to be preserved intact, were henceforward to be reduced to dust in pursuance of a new philosophical idea. Did the living by this means hope to secure for themselves freedom from the haunting presence of the ghosts of the dead ? Did they think that by committing the body to the flames they could liberate the soul from its fleshly tabernacle ? It can well be imagined, in the face of this change in ritual, how chagrined are the anthropologists at no longer finding, for quite a long time, such abundant scientific " material " as in the preceding periods. Henceforward, and until we are better documented, such knowledge of the peopling of a certain part of France as we shall get will be based on comparison with neighbouring regions and on such facts as we can gain from those people whom we find *in situ* in subsequent periods. By these indirect methods we shall once more be able to follow the thread which the rite of incineration if it has not broken has at least worn singularly thin as regards certain areas.

Not that we are entirely without French skeletons of the bronze age[1] ; but their number is very small by comparison

[1] Many people still believe, on the word of certain archæologists that, as Alexandre Bertrand taught, bronze age burials are absent in Gaul (*a*). Yet one has but to open Déchelette, who completely cleared up this question, to be convinced to the contrary (*b*). Inhumation continued to be the custom throughout Europe during the first half of the bronze age. In France inhumation prevailed only in Bronze Age iv. Though we must always remember that Armorica was the exception—as it frequently is in the history of France—maybe on account of its race ? Even by the end of the Neolithic the Breton dolmens often cover charred human remains, more often, indeed, in some districts, than they cover skeletons. And we may emphasize this ethnographic fact—of real importance for the history of France—that while the inhumation rite still continued to be current usage in Europe as a whole and in Western Asia, Armorica constituted an island where religious ideas particular to itself imposed burning. Travelling east in space, to find a similar ritual imposition we should have to go as far afield as India. In anterior Asia, the Caucasus, Armenia, Persia, Anatolia, etc., incineration is rare.

(*a*) **XV**, p. 195. (*b*) **LI**, p. 134 ff.

with that of the neolithic epoch. Maybe this poverty may also result from the fact that archæologists who discovered burials by inhumation belonging to the bronze age were so obnubilated by the metal objects they found that they paid less attention to preserving the human bones than they did even with burials of neolithic times!

What road did bronze take across France? Does the introduction of this new civilization correspond to modifications of the ethnic physiognomy of ancient Gaul?

The importance of such a query can well be understood. If the introduction of bronze merely meant that fresh knowledge was spread, each one learning the new process from his neighbours; or even if its introduction had come about by its being carried across the country by itinerant traders, the ethnic results would be very different from what they would be if the new invention had been brought in by a new people. In either of the first two cases we should not have to envisage stratification or ethnic intermixture. In our own day the introduction of telegraphs, telephones and electric light into the most remote Alpine villages has in no way altered the anthropological characters of the inhabitants among whom these new facts of civilization have been introduced.

Recent discoveries and a more rational, and above all, a more comparative use of the documentation collected, are modifying the ideas with which we were inculcated on the subject of the routes by which copper and bronze penetrated into Gaul. Bronze appears more and more likely to be a discovery of the Orientals. But the birthplace of these earliest metallurgists is still unknown to us. Mesopotamia? The valley of the Nile? Western Asia? So far as Europe is concerned it would appear that the Ægean region has been, if not a centre of creation, at least—and with certainty—a point whence the new products were diffused to the west and north.[1] Two main routes went from this centre to France—one along the shores of the Mediterranean (Sicily and the Iberian peninsular) and the Atlantic; while the Balkan peninsular route was via the Danube. This last route led northeast, as far as the Baltic. Western France was reached by the first current, whereas the second, after having penetrated Switzerland, passed to eastern France. This last current flowed faster, it would seem, than the other. Savoy and

[1] LXVI, p. 222.

Provence used copper earlier than the people of Armorica or of the Ile-de-France.

If these hypotheses, relating to the penetration of the earliest metals into France, such as we have presented them, are to be accepted, we shall then have to conclude that the bronze age did not lead to profound modifications—due to the new civilization—in the ethnic characters of the existing population. And this is exactly what would seem to have happened. I say *seem*, because, as we have indicated, there is unfortunately very little actual evidence relating to the French " race " of those days to go on.

In England, on the contrary, this was one of the principal periods when ethnic change did take place. Was it, perhaps, the isolated position of the British Isles which led to this delay ?

According to statistics collected by Salmon and which may be extended to apply to the whole of France until we have more ample information, it appears that there were still 57·7 per cent. of Dolichocephals to only 22 per cent. of Brachycephals in the neolithic burials. It is highly probable that the proportion of Brachycephals had increased considerably at the bronze age, together with, as would be only natural, the numbers of Mesaticephals. At the same time, it must be born in mind, with regard to these intermediate forms, that the Brachycephals may already have been more or less cross-bred by the time they arrived in France, and that we know nothing of the localities in which such early crosses may have taken place or with what races they had been effected.

Many ethnologists have held the view that these new arrivals were of somewhat different race from those who had brought the polished stone civilization. A more marked round-headedness and a cerebral capacity that was perhaps a little greater led them to this supposition, and they labelled these people Neobrachycephals. I think that there is reason to reserve judgment yet awhile in regard to this belief in another race.

Thus the French population presents a heterogeneous ethnic aspect at the moment when History is about to write its annals. It is composed in the first place of the descendants of palæolithic and neolithic Dolichocephals (genealogy: Chellean—Cro-Magnon—Laugerie-Baumes-Chaudes) ; of descendants of the tall northern Dolichocephals ; and finally of descendants of the Brachycephals (Proto- and Neo-Brachycephals ?) of the polished stone and bronze ages.[1]

What part is each of these two main ethnic groups to play from this time forward in the destinies of France ? Is their respective influence to be proportionate to their numbers ? Or is one of them to gain the ascendancy owing to exceptional innate qualities ? Who can inform us with certainty as to these important points ?

We know that certain sociologists believe themselves to be justified in stating that the dolichocephalic group—the descendants of the neolithic Dolichocephals of northern origin —was the one which achieved great things while the poor Brachycephals remained humbly in the background. This hypothesis—it has been singularly to the taste of imperialists of all shades, particularly of German writers—has already been subjected to a rapid examination in the General Introduction. It would be profitless to return to it.

*
* *

Historic times will bring us face to face with a variety of ethnological facts, the details of whose influence are even to-day very little known. There will be a succession of peoples, some coming from the northeast from identical geographical areas—though they themselves bear various names ; others collecting from every point of the horizon. The list of these peoples is a long one. And even if we eliminate tribal names and retain only those of the larger groups, it is still lengthy. In it we shall read, among others, such names as Iberians, Ligurians, Aquitani and Basques, Celts, Phœnicians and Carthaginians, and Saracens. Of these first hordes, the Ibero-Ligurians and the Celts are those which have been retained chiefly by those who concern themselves with the origin of the French people.

Then comes the Roman conquest. What ethnogenic action did it have ? For my part I am of opinion that it had practically none.

But a further contingent—singularly disturbing—appears on the horizon. It is composed of the "Germanic" races :— the Galli, Cimbrians, Belgae, Suevi, Alemanni, Visigoths, Burgundians, Lombards, Franks, Saxons, and Nordmanns

[1] These Brachycephals are people of middle height and cannot be related to the tall Brachycephals represented by the Dinaric race.

(Normans). These groups in differing proportions enter into the composition of the French people. Has not one among them given its name to France? It is mainly to these turbulent hordes that the Gobineau school turns for illustration of the more glorious chapters of European history, and in this instance of French history. In their eyes the other ethnic groups have not played a comparable rôle!

Maybe a few Alans have persisted in the neighbourhood of Valence and to the east of the Rhône?—and in the Orleans district, and in Armorica? Is the Sèvre-Nantaise cephalic deformity attributable to the Theiphals? As for the Gypsies who, since the fifteenth century, have penetrated to some extent into every part of France, they are held in too little esteem for them to have been able to mix their blood to any appreciable extent with that of French people.

Though the list of peoples, more or less complete, the long and variegated enumeration of tribes and clans who have penetrated to French soil may disturb the historian, it leaves the anthropologist quite calm. It must not be forgotten that many of these names have no racial equation. Many of these peoples have a common ethnic origin, and, therefore, like morphological characters. Many have sprung from the same stock as the neolithic Dolichocephals and the Brachycephals of the same epoch—both of whom came from the Northeast or the East—and as these two types who pursued their destinies in the bronze age. One must be on one's guard against the notion that "somewhere" in Asia or in eastern Europe there existed so many centres in which these people first appear (Agassiz called them cradles of humanity), from out of which flowed ethnic rivers, like streams of clear water—but of differing quality one from another; a Ligurian, a Celtic, a Gallic, a Norman stream, and so on. Many of these streams, which bore different names, carried waters which were anthropologically one and the same.

It is quite certain that many of the Dolichocephals and Brachycephals who figured in the historic invasions joined, on French soil, the descendants of their common ancestors. These people, sprung from an identical primitive stock, often regarded one another as enemies; and there were times when one of them would be the conquerors and the others their victims. Both were too far removed from their first origin to have retained even the memory of their community of race.

If we follow the course of History a little further back it would be profitless, I think, to seek what share the first Phœnician and Greek colonies had in the make-up of the French nation. They were but merchants, birds of passage, and always few in number. There is no doubt whatever that their influence was absolutely nil.

As for the Ligurians—we must agree as to the anthropological value to be given to this term—it is possible that they played an important rôle in the ethnogeny of France. At one time a great deal was published on the subject of the Ligurian skull. Usually there is agreement in including it in the Celtic group of Celto-Ligurians, Rhetians, Rheto-Ligurians, etc. These Ligurians would thus have rejoined, on French territory, one of their advance guards, the neolithic Brachycephals.

The Iberians would possibly have exerted a powerful influence. They are credited with having peopled a part of the Atlantic shore, the Basque region. They would have extended over an area from the Pyrenees to the islands of the Italian Mediterranean all along the coast of the Golfe du Lion. In our present day classification there exists an Ibero-Insular race, representing the type *Homo meridionalis*. As we have seen it is characterized by small stature and a dolichocephalic head. The Portuguese, Spaniards, French of the Midi, and South Italians belong to it. But can it be stated, without causing us to raise our eyebrows, that this race is the living presentment of the Iberians of History? If we want to place this ethnic group as regards its prehistoric origin it would seem that we must seek for the link in the direction of the Dolichocephals of the Laugerie-Chancelade type.

As for the Celts, they are, like the Aryans, merely a conventional term for anthropologists. After endless argument that has gone on for nearly fifty years and traces of which may be found in the Proceedings of anthropological societies all over Europe, notably in those of the Société de Paris, it has ended in agreement being reached that the French Celtic type —as conceived by anthropologists—should be regarded as the brachycephalic type to be found in the Central Plateau, Morvan, etc. It is just as well that they went no further, for nothing is less clear than the descriptions of the Celts given by the authors of antiquity. From the point of view of their earliest origin the Celts must be approximated to the Ligurians.

They would thus constitute the two main branches of the brachycephalic tree which made its appearance during the neolithic period.

Celtae and Galli are one and the same for many contemporary writers. For anthropologists the Galli belong to the tall, dolichocephalic and blond Kymric group. These descriptive qualities are indicated by all the authors of antiquity. Diodorus Siculus and Ammianus Marcellinus have left us portraits that agree in this regard. So also has Titus Livy in so far as concerns the Galatæ of Italy and Asia Minor. Was it not Strabo who assimilated the men of Gallic race to the Germans in respect of their physical characters? The Galatæ and other Germanic peoples of different names who invaded French soil belonged to the tall race of neolithic Dolichocephals. Not all of them, however—as we saw in the case of the Alans. The "Germanic race", in so far as part of it is concerned, appears to have consisted of an ethnic aggregation.

Hence the peoples who most actively participated in the invasions can be placed in three main ethnic groups, all three of which already had representatives in France in the various prehistoric periods. The Ligurians and Celts belonged to the neolithic brachycephalic group; the Ibero-Insular people (the Iberians of history) belonged to the small dolichocephalic race called Laugerie-Chancelade; and the Galatæ and the greater part of the other "Germanic" peoples belonged to the race of neolithic Dolichocephals. But it must be remembered that this general view of the matter is by no means a definite certainty. Anthropological study of the French population is not yet sufficiently advanced—although more so, perhaps, than in the case of other European populations—to warrant us in doing more than put it forward as an opinion.

*

* *

And now, what are the present anthropological characters of the French population?

We have just said that France is among the countries whose ethnology is the best known.

This is because anthropological study, in a manner of speaking, is a French science. A considerable volume of investigations was undertaken under the inspiration of Broca and his students.[1] Unfortunately such researches have been

[1] XLVIII.

almost entirely abandoned at the present time in France. It is certain that in the social turmoil in which we live, social problems of extreme importance for the future of the races of Europe must invite our scientific intervention—such as the study of genealogical descents, and of ethnic crosses, etc. But that does not alter the fact that the anthropological analysis of a country remains the basis of all subsequent study, from whatever view-point. Eugenics without an anthropological basis can only work in the dark.

In the first place we will look at the distribution of cranial forms in French territory.

At the outset we shall see a great escarpment of Brachycephals from the department of Meurthe-et-Moselle as far as the department of Haute-Garonne. The Vosges, Jura, part of the Alps, the French Central Plateau—to keep within the general lines of their habitat—are peopled by men of this type. A large number of them have associated with a brachycephalic head a low stature, brown hair, and eyes that are generally dark. This is the human group which is considered by the " Gobinists " to represent the lowest quality of the French population !—Featureless *eilotes* living side by side with aristocratic dolichocephalic populations of " Germanic " origin who have ever inspired the more brilliant periods of history !

For modern ethnologists this small, brunet, brachycephalic race is the Cevenole or Western race of Deniker, the Celtic race of Broca (or Ligurian, Rhetian, or Celto-Ligurian, etc., of which we spoke awhile back). Fertile, hard-working, thrifty, enemy of risk, it overflows French territory at many points, notably in the direction of Switzerland, the north of Italy and Belgium. Later on we shall meet with it again in those countries which in prehistoric times formed the stages on the road leading to France—as Bavaria, the Tyrol, etc. It is the type of the *Homo alpinus* of Lapouge,

To north and south of this great mass of brachycephaly (these are necessarily but generalizations) France contains very different human types.

To the north, there are first small Brachycephals arrested at the base of the Breton promontory, and in many of its districts. But in this wide area of French territory the population is principally mesaticephalic. With this head-form goes a taller stature in the people of this region than is to be found in the Brachycephals of the central provinces. These morphological indications lead us to think that the French people of these parts can claim a dual origin. They would be the result of a cross between tall Dolichocephals and small Brachycephals. This hypothesis would seem to be confirmed by the presence among them of a great many individuals having dolichocephalic or sub-dolichocephalic heads representing in all likelihood the remains of a population that departed less from the initial type.

Are these people, particularly those in the northeast of the Republic, the least modified descendants of the Gaulish tribes? It is possible. But it is not certain, because we do not really know whether the Germanic invasions recorded by History were accomplished by contingents sufficiently large to people a wide area. When we speak of tall French Dolichocephals the prehistoric populations which possessed both these characters must not be forgotten. The historians of the invasions have made hay of events which took place in epochs with which they are not concerned. I am aware that these neolithic Dolichocephals—we have said so before—may have sprung from the same stock as that which was later on to provide the Germanic peoples. Thus both of them would belong to the same race.

Keeping always to the north of the great brachycephalic strip, we shall find sub-dolichocephalic and mesaticephalic contingents to the south of the Loire and to the west of this river within the loop it describes in running from south to north.

Thus, to the north of the great brachycephalic massif, France is inhabited by a population that is mainly dolichocephalic and cross-bred. Once more, this is but a rough outline, a simplist picture which a detailed anthropological investigation perhaps would modify in many places.

On the other side of this brachycephalic massif we shall find a mixed population in which mesaticephalic elements predominate. In this population, more or less cross-bred or more or less intermixed—the two things are not at all the same, but means are lacking to enable us to discern details—we shall meet with numerous representatives of the race known as Mediterranean. We know its general characteristics:—a dolichocephalic head, height slightly below the average, dark hair and eyes. It will be recalled how very different are these Dolichocephals from those inhabiting the north of France. There is almost as much difference between these northern and Mediterranean populations as there is between a horse and a zebra—both of which belong to the genus *Equus*.

Maybe there exist also in France a certain number of representatives of the Dinaric or Adriatic race, or rather, of the sub-Adriatic race of Deniker ? They are believed to have been noted to the northeast of the brachycephalic bloc. Possibly a part of the Jura is peopled by men of this race ? On the Swiss slope of the Jurassic chain, in the canton of Vaud, for instance, one meets with a tall, brachycephalic and brunet population which might be related to this Adriatic race. Deniker's map gives representatives of this ethnic group all along the course of the Loire.

This rapid survey shows us that France is far from possessing anthropological unity. She is much better off as regards unity of language which she possesses almost completely. There is a far greater number of different races inhabiting French territory than is the case with the Iberian peninsular which we studied previously.

To sum up. The French population is an ethnic complex. Around a palæolithic nucleus, itself made up of different anatomical elements, various human types, come from different regions, have successively aggregated from neolithic times onwards. Nevertheless, it is not to be thought that the multiplicity of groups mentioned in History represents an equal multiplicity of races. If these groups had remained strictly separate it would be easy enough to perceive it. But juxtaposition, intermixture, and cross-breeding have increased the apparent complexity.

France presents itself to ethnologists as a synthesis of Europe : it would appear to include more ethnic types even than Italy.

In what way are we to explain such an afflux of races to French territory ? Evidently by the geographical consideration that its exceptionally favourable situation renders it suitable to be peopled by human beings, and that special facilities exist for its penetration in almost every direction, but notably on its eastern borders. Yet, all the same, we must not allow ourselves to be dominated by the fact of these easy communications, because we know that the prehistoric people thought little of crossing the Alpine passes. And, elsewhere, other lands, relatively as much favoured as France in regard to facilities for communications, never experienced analogous human occupation.

Maybe it is to this anthropological wealth that France owes her multiform genius. Each of these races has contributed its personal qualities to the common stock ; for it is obvious that they have not all exactly the same "human values ". The diverse proportions of these multiple contributions may perhaps serve to explain the variations of French history. The North and the Midi have not always acted in the same manner ; has not Brittany sometimes been a dissident region ?

This ethnic synthesis which would seem to be unique in the elements used—because it appears in very different guise from that of the United States, for instance—gives to France a special place in the sum total of European peoples.

CHAPTER IV

ITALY

A LAND of history and warfare, Italy, like Northern France, has been a battleground for opposing armies, and her soil has been trodden and retrodden not only by representatives of every European race but by Saracens as well. She has been assailed from all sides, by land and by sea, by those who came out of Europe and those who came out of Africa.

At first sight the result of these varied assaults would appear to be an inextricable mingling of peoples, an almost unbelievable ethnic patchwork. Nothing of the kind has happened, however—so true is it that a conqueror (when he belongs to a different ethnic type) but rarely gives his physical characters to the people he invades. Italy thus shows us how cautious we should be in envisaging in the morphological modification of a people influences due to warlike expeditions. Neither is it the first time in the course of this volume that we have come across facts of the same order.

Just as the Balkan peninsular was once upon a time joined to Asia Minor, and constituted, with the land now sunk beneath the Ægean, a compact mass of a geographical type very different from what it is to-day, so did Italy throw out a wide area of land towards Africa, in the direction of Tunisia and Tripoli. At that period the Adriatic was not a wide gulf as it is to-day ; its shores were not indented further north than the Bocche di Cattaro. On the other side of the peninsular as it exists to-day, the Ligurian Alps linked up Corsica and Sardinia with the body of Italy, and this wide promontory took the form, on the map, of a huge pendant suspended from southern Europe. The waters of the Po and the Adige very likely carried their sands down a thalweg which ran between the heights of the Apennines on the right, and the barren ridges of the Dinaric Alps on the left.

Italy experienced little of the glacial phenomena of the Quaternary. Her geographical situation left her practically beyond the reach of the great event which had so much influence on the dispersion of flora, fauna and mankind. North of her present territory where the ice invasion was at its most puissant the great alpine continental ice barrier dominated the whole of the plain of the Po with its glaciers and moraines. To the west this barrier left open only a narrow strip of the Mediterranean littoral for the passage of Palæolithic man, as the mountain ranges came down towards the sea. It was along this strip that the Baoussé-Roussé people came, and it was here, too, that later on, the Via Aurelia was to pass.

To the east, along the edges of the plains of Lombardy and Venetia, communications were established by the mountains of Istria—we know that mountain masses were no obstacle to population—and beyond the Karst plateau the way lay open to the plains of the Save and the Danube. Thus Italy was in no way isolated from the European world.

The long Apennine range was free from any but a few small local glaciers on its highest summits, and these faced across to those which lay on the other side of what is now the Tyrrhenian Sea, in the higher Corsican valleys.

Thus Palæolithic man had free passage into the Peninsular from whichever way he came. In the Chellean also men overran the favoured lands of Italy; they camped on the terraces along the banks of rivers where their implements, otherwise somewhat rare, have been found. They established themselves in caverns and rock shelters, and several of these have become famous to science—those of the Baoussé-Roussé massif in particular.

The Peninsular appears to have been widely inhabited both in the neolithic epoch and in the bronze age. The lacustrine stations of Upper Italy (Lakes Varese, Garda, Varano, etc.) and the *terramare*, both by their relative abundance and the wealth of archæological objects found, mark the density of the population.

Up till the first discoveries of human skeletons in the Baoussé-Roussé caves, Italy had scarcely furnished any evidence of a sort to inform us as to what human races had peopled the country in primitive times. In the heroic age of Anthropology finds of bone fragments in Italian territory were notified which seemed to point to the existence of Tertiary man. The Savona skeleton, dug out of the pliocene marl, and which Issel supposed to be contemporaneous with it, and the skeleton of Castenedolo near Brescia, which Ragazzoni also discovered in pliocene strata when he was looking for fossils, are to-day no longer considered to date from that far off epoch. And until we come to strata belonging to the Reindeer age no authentic human remains permit us to picture to ourselves the morphological characters of the Italians of palæolithic times.

The Baoussé-Roussé caves are situated in the commune of Ventimiglia, a short distance from the French frontier. They are hollowed out in the nummulitic limestone. They face seawards, and the Via Aurelia passes below them. These caves have been known for a long time, and Horace Bénédict de Saussure visited them in 1786. This spot, so far, has furnished from a very restricted area a larger number of complete skeletons, dating from the Pleistocene, than any other region in Europe. In 1872 Rivière discovered human remains there for the first time—the celebrated Homme de Menton. In 1901 Prince Albert I of Monaco began to excavate anew. Between these two dates the contractors who were exploiting the massif by quarrying stone for building purposes had also made several finds. To-day we have sixteen palæolithic skeletons all obtained from this one small archæological district. Among them must be mentioned the famous Negroids described by Verneau. All details relating to these discoveries will be found in Marcellin Boule's book, already freely quoted in our earlier chapters, to which the reader is referred.[1]

Italy, inhabited as it was from the beginning of the Palæolithic, must have had its general anthropological characters fixed from the bronze age—at least as regards the actual peninsular. It is possible, however, that the great invasions will be found to modify this primitive state in certain districts particularly affected by these migrations. We will endeavour to find out if this is so.

Thanks to numerous local investigations we are beginning to know the anthropological characters of the Italians. We can represent the general physiognomy of Italy to ourselves in its main lines—but its main lines only, for here, as elsewhere, details are still to seek on many points. Nevertheless, the Peninsular is one of the countries in which such investigation has been pushed farthest.

[1] See also Prof. Verneau's 1924 Huxley Memorial Lecture delivered before the Roy. Anthr. Inst. of Great Britain and Ireland, *Journal*, vol. liv., 1925, *La race de Néanderthal, et la race de Grimaldi ; leur rôle dans l'Humanité.* (Translator's Note.)

Among the savants who have principally contributed to the anthropological knowledge of Italy we must place first and foremost Ridolfo Livi, whose fine works will long remain a mine of precious information.[1]

When we examine simultaneously the charts of height and of the cephalic index, we see that the Peninsular is divided —it must be understood that this is a schematic image—into two nearly equal parts. This division approximately follows an oblique line which cuts the Italian boot at the level of Ancona and thence goes along the mid-course of the Tiber to Rome. The southern part of the Tuscan Apennines and the Sibilline mountains would seem to enclose brachycephalic and brunet individuals related to the Celtic race, whereas the south of the Peninsular, Corsica and Sardina are all peopled by men of the Ibero-Insular race.

The orographic map of Italy comes very near to explaining the best part of the anthropological map of the country; human geography would here seem to have scored its point. The vast plains of the Po and the Adige, thanks to the fertility of the soil and the easy communications they offered, arrested the brachycephalic inhabitants—probably of two different races—who, after having peopled the lower portions of the Pennine Alps, spread throughout the territory of Emilia. But the northern buttresses of the Ligurian and Tuscan mountains, owing to their low altitude, are easy barriers to cross. After which one comes to valleys leading by way of the Arno and the Tiber to the Tyrrhenian shore. And all along the Italian coast there is free passage way. Thus, masters of the plain, assured of communications with the two seas, and held there by those favoured skies that were less ardent than the southern heavens beyond Umbria, the Italian Brachycephals and sub-Brachycephals might well be contained within this definite geographical domain. And it was here, in this part of the Peninsular, bounded by the upper Tiber and the Po, that Italy's noblest destinies were shaped. It was here that, later on, Lucca and Florence, Pisa and Bologna, Sienna and Perugia were to build up their resplendent civilizations.

It was not the Italian Dolichocephals inhabiting the south of the peninsular who played the decisive part in the intellectual greatness of Italy. There are various reasons, probably independent of race, explanatory of this relative lack

[1] CXLIII, Part I and II.

of initiative. And for what remains of Italy's history of the later centuries one may well ask of the Piedmontese Brachycephals if, as regards the Peninsular, it was not principally in their ranks that military valour was fostered and, later still, loyal devotion to the cause of Italian unity? Were not Cavour and Garibaldi Brachycephals of Northern Italy?

In this regard it becomes necessary to remark—for we may appear to be supporting the arguments of Gobineau—that there would not seem to be much connection between the high civilization of old-time Italy and the presence, in those very places where this civilization shone most brilliantly, of a population belonging to the Germanic type, as there ought to be according to the unadulterated doctrine. The facts merit thorough and unprejudiced study, and we shall come back to them later.

The mean height of Italians (about 1 metre 64) is almost the same as that of their French neighbours. And, as in their case, the mean is obtained from the association of heterogeneous human elements. Venezia, for example, contains men whose height is considerable (1 metre 66 at least). And as all this northeast region is peopled by markedly pigmented Brachycephals, we can now admit that there is here some survival either of a Dinaric racial influence, or of fairly strong contingents of the race itself. We may call to mind that the Dalmatians, Bosnians, Herzegovinians, Montenegrins and Northern Albanians are its best representatives.

Those regions having the lowest stature are Basilicata (1 metre 58 to 1 metre 59) and Sardinia. And for this island it is mainly the eastern portion that forms the centre of very low stature. In order to find in Europe human groups—of a certain numerical size—comparable in smallness of stature we must go to the north of the continent, to the Lapps, the Voguls, and, in the east of Russia, to certain small groups of Tatars from the Volga. But we must not jump to the conclusion that these small statures establish any sort of relationship between these different peoples!

These islands of very small people in Italy represent a problem about which I imagine History will have a word to say. Perhaps, even, History alone can solve it? In any case I do not think, by way of explaining such small statures, that there is any occasion to bring in the influence of a geographical environment to lower or retard the development of the average height of any given ethnic group whose origin is still difficult to understand. As is known, I am not by any means a partisan of such mesological influences on Man.

Further, it will be useful to note that a few steps beyond southern Italy, on the other side of the Adriatic, we no longer find districts characterized by such small stature. It was not from this side that the small men came. Nor is it towards the Greek colonies which settled in the south of Italy that we must look. The result would be deceptive. We have already said why.

For the rest, and it is now, above all, that the problem becomes interesting, these human groups of small stature in Basilicata and eastern Sardinia must not be supposed to have a common origin. The quality of their cephalic index is too different to let us suppose it for an instant; the first is mesaticephalic, the second hyperdolichocephalic. It would not seem that this is a statistical illusion resulting from mixed examples which falsify the averages. It is therefore impossible to envisage, in the recent past, a common parent stock for these two populations.

Examining the Peninsular as a whole, we note that in a general way height diminishes as we go from north to south. In Upper Italy, in those alluvial lands through which the Po runs, and in the mountain buttresses which run from Istria towards the French frontier, height diminishes as we go from east to west: the Venetians are bigger than the Piedmontese.

South of the Ancona-Rome line the South Italian zone of small stature likewise shows a lack of uniformity—the men of the Adriatic shore are smaller than those of the Mediterranean. In this connection I would instance immediately an interesting phenomenon which my studies in Albania made palpable, namely that the Albanian colonies of South Italy which arrived in this country after Scander-Beg's adventure do not present the same morphological and descriptive characteristics as do the majority of Albanians in Albania. This is a problem we shall meet again when we come to study the Balkan peninsular.[1] But we can be quite certain, from now onwards, that the Albanian colonists of small stature in Italy are not Albanians who have degenerated as a result of a change in geographical environment.

[1] **CXCIV**, p. 267.

We mentioned just now two islands of small stature. And now here are two of tall stature; and of a stature that is notably greater than the average for Italy.

First of all there is the Udine island. It forms a southern prolongation of that escarpment of the Dinaric race which appears to go across Europe from the eastern Balkans to Belgium. Then there is the Lucca-Massa island. Collected in the valleys of Monte-Cimone and the rocky promontories that descend towards the Arno, these men, the tallest in Italy, have extended their habitat by sending out peaks all along the coast—from the Ligurian and also the Tuscan Apennines. We shall come across these tall people again when we speak of the head-form of the Italians.

The mean cephalic index of Italy (taken on a study of 300,000 individuals) is 81.7. It indicates mesaticephaly. But this piece of information by itself is of no use to us, it throws no light on anything. Of what use is an index obtained by the adding together of 300,000 characters which we already know to be disparate? It gives us to understand, however, that there has been either an extraordinary amount of cross-breeding between extreme types, or else that there must be two types of heads side by side whose mean furnished this intermediate picture.

The second hypothesis corresponds with the actuality. South of the ideal Ancona-Rome line there is a dolichocephalic population, or a population approaching this type; to the north of this line there is a brachycephalic population. And now, thanks to the character of stature, already known, we begin to have some accurate idea of the races of Italy, and it will be possible to establish some relation between History and Anthropology.

The cephalic index of the Piedmontese is 85.9, whereas that of the Calabrians is 78.4. The Venetians are recorded as 85.2, and the Sardinians as 77.5 on the general table of indices. The dolichocephalic mass in the south presents even lower indices. In the heel of the Italian boot, in Apulia, the mean cephalic index does not reach 77. It is the same in the rocky prolongation which ends at Reggio. It would seem that these two promontories are like culs-de-sac into which have collected together those men who are at once the smallest and the most dolichocephalic of the Peninsular.

These few observations show how inaccurate an anthropological picture of Italy the Italian mean cephalic index, if used simply as such, would give ; and of what little practical use it is to us as evidence from the view point taken up in this book.

The southern regions have been occupied by, among other invaders, Visigoths and Normans. Yet it is not the anatomical characters of these groups that are expressed in the present population of these provinces. Such an observation should serve as still another example to strengthen what we have already said many times over, namely that conquerors do not often give to the conquered country their own ethnic imprint.[1]

To the north of the Ancona-Rome line we shall also be able to distinguish a disparate island in the sea of brachycephaly. This is the Lucca-Massa region already mentioned in connection with Italian stature as having a height greater than that of the mean for northern Italy. This group of tall stature is dolichocephalic. In addition, it is, geographically, sufficiently sharply circumscribed. This fact accentuates still more the interest which this population has for us. Do not the people of Lucca claim that their city was founded by Lydians ? And do not the legends of Lydia tell us that one of their tribes, the Tyrrhians, emigrated into Italy ? Fancies, doubtless ! It would seem, all the same, that a serious investigation ought to be undertaken in this district. Do these tall Dolichocephals perhaps represent a relic of the great invasions ? This in itself merits that they should be profoundly studied.

Outside this curious anomaly, northern Italy—we are keeping always to general facts—forms a brachycephalic bloc. All the men of Venezia, and those of the two banks of the Po, and of Emilia, considered from this point of view constitute a sufficiently coherent anthropological entity.

The conclusions—rapid and provisory as they are—to be drawn from the above facts may be expressed in the following fashion :—Italian territory, inhabited at every period of history by peoples bearing different names, and some of whom were of different ethnic origin (these peoples coming to superpose themselves on the prehistoric races) is to-day inhabited by the representatives of three main races :—

[1] See General Considerations.

(1) The Adriatic or Dinaric race, tall, brachycephalic and brunet, inhabited the northeast. In order to get there it would have come along the Karst plateau and established itself in the first place in the Udine and Belluno region (that is, if its earliest legitimate habitat is to be indicated as in the Balkan peninsular). Then, following the coasts, and crossing the arms of the Adige and the Po, it flowed along the coast, keeping contact with the sea. Towards the interior of the country it would appear to have stopped at the foot of all the mountain chains. It came to a halt in front of the obstacle of the Ligurian and Tuscan Apennines. The gulf of Venice and Trieste, then, separated—up till the war—men of a common ethnic origin.

(2) The Western or Cevenole race, brunet, brachycephalic and small, installed itself to the west of the Dinaric people. Its domain is bounded in the north by the Swiss mountain buttresses, in the west by the French Alpine groups; in the south by the Ligurian Apennines. But these representatives of *Homo alpinus* do not seem to constitute such a homogeneous bloc as their neighbours to the east. It would appear to be very probable that this race is formed, in large part, of the descendants of the polished stone and bronze age populations, or of those who constructed their palafittes on the lakes of Switzerland and upper Italy.

(3) The Ibero-Insular race—the *Homo meridionalis* of certain authors—is distributed in the south of Italy; it would appear to be the more pure as we advance towards the rough country of Basilicata and Calabria. This ethnic type—small, dark-haired, dolichocephalic—also peoples the Italian islands.

To these three main races we must add that interesting but, as regards its origin, enigmatic group of the Ligurian Apennines and the littoral of the Riviera di Levante characterized by tall stature and dolichocephaly. Ought we to connect it, zoologically, with the Atlanto-Mediterranean race of Deniker—which, with breaks, inhabits the country extending from the French coast almost to the mouth of the Tiber? Have we here survivals of a Nordic type? Or should we rather credit, historically, the idea that they are a remnant of the Germanic bands of Radegast rather than that they constitute a residue of hypothetical Lydians?

Thus the people of Italy no more than the other

populations we have so far studied can seek their ethnic origin in a single human cradle.

Here and there heterogeneous groups exist in the Peninsular, manifesting their differences from the principal body by the use of another language, such as the Vaudois of Piedmont who speak French, the German-speaking people of the provinces of Verona and Vicenza, the Albanians, Greeks, and the Dalmatians (Slavs) of the Abruzzi. The great war added to the contingents of many of these linguistic—and sometimes anthropological—groups, notably in the Tyrol. To what anthropological sub-divisions do these people belong ?

I have already said what is to be thought of those Albanians of Italy who only distantly resemble, by their physical characters, the majority of the Albanians of Albania.

As for the Slavs of the Abruzzi who recognize as their ancestors Dalmatians who came from the other side of the Adriatic, I think that it would be difficult to imagine that they really are men of the Yugo-Slav " race." They are very far from presenting the characters of the Dinaric race to which they would thus have to be related.

The inhabitants of the large Italian islands of the Mediterranean—Sardinia and Sicily, which are regions peopled at a very ancient date—belong, in general, to the Ibero-Insular race, with varying degrees of purity. The numerous invasions of which these places have been the theatre may have played a part in a modern modification of the initial type. But it is impossible to be sure under what decisive ethnic influences nor in what measure these modifications took place. There are those who say that as you pass along the streets of Palermo you can recognize, in the people you meet, representatives of every race that ever came from Sicily. Let us leave them to their pastime.

CHAPTER V

SWITZERLAND

WHEN ethnological questions are under discussion a glance at the map of Europe will at once suggest that Switzerland, owing to its central position, ought to provide samples of all the European races. Has it not been said in this connection that it is the turning-plate of Europe?

Nevertheless, nothing could be farther from the truth. A country's geographical position is not the only factor in its attraction and retention of mankind; its own internal conditions, and the difficulty or facility with which it can be inhabited all count. It is not enough that man can penetrate to it; he must be able to stay there.

The general architecture of Switzerland presents to its inhabitants three main regions which have become classic in the textbooks—the Jura, the Plateau, and the Alps. The Alpine massif naturally holds the least mixed races, firstly because life there is hard, and many people, not finding it to their taste, went away again after entering it. Further, because many of its valleys are culs-de-sac having no communication with the outside, so that races having gone into them and found that they could live there have remained permanently. Finally, because the earliest inhabitants who settled on this poor land monopolized its resources to the full and there was no room left for new arrivals.

Almost throughout the Palæolithic Switzerland was practically inaccessible. It was largely covered by glaciers. On this continental ice, which from the central massifs spread out in all directions, a few groups of hunters pursued their game, notably the cave bear. The Moustierian station of Wildkirchli (the Sântis massif) was probably nothing more than a halting-place, and the same would probably apply to the station of Cotencher in the Neuchâtel Jura. The highest known station in Europe is Drachenloch at an altitude of 2,445 metres. It would likewise seem to have been but a temporary camp of the Swiss Moustierians. The discoverer, Bächler (excavations of 1917 to 1923) appears to have come upon a kind of hunters' den and a sanctuary in which *Ursus spelœus* was the object of special rites.[1]

In the post glacial epoch, when the ice was gradually melting, the northern and western periphery of Switzerland was occupied by several Magdalenian and Azilian stations.

No skeletal remains of the palæolithic epoch have been found in Switzerland, with the exception of a few fragments devoid of interest. But we can imagine that the Moustierian hunters who roamed over prehistoric Helvetia, and the Magdalenian hunters who established themselves in the country later on, belonged to the same races as those which were wandering over the neighbouring country, notably in France, at that time.

In the neolithic period Switzerland was thickly populated. As in other lands the Neolithic folk used caves as habitations. but in the main they established themselves on the lakes.

The Swiss lake dwellings have done inestimable service to science. Thanks to the discoveries made in a large number of the lakes and peat bogs of Switzerland the polished stone age civilization has had a flood of light thrown upon it. This is because the objects of the period were preserved both by carbonization (the lake cities were destroyed by fire) and by being deposited in the heart of the imputrescible peat of which the "fumier lacustre" is composed.

The Lake folk constructed their houses on piles in all those lakes whose shores sloped gradually.[2] Hundreds of thousands of these piles were driven into the mud to support the little low houses in which, for several thousands of years, Central European civilization, with varying local facies, was to evolve up to the close of the bronze age.

The neolithic skeletons so far found in Switzerland are not a great many but the list increases with every year. They

[1] Emile Bächler: *Das Drachenloch ob Vättis im Taminatale* 2445 *m.* etc. St. Gallen, 1921.

[2] Vouga is now of opinion that at least some of the lake dwellings were not built actually on the water (Lake Neuchâtel is in question), but above highwater mark "on the marshy ground from which the water had recently retreated." This hypothesis supposes a considerable alteration in the level of the Swiss lakes. The genuine lake cities, according to Vouga, only date from the bronze age. See *Le Globe*, the organ of the Geneva Geographical Society, 1923, p. 13; and "Les stations lacustres du lac de Neuchâtel," *l'Anthropologie*, Paris, 1923, p. 49.

are found in tombs (often crouched, in stone cists); but are also met with in the mud of the lakes, among the débris of the palafittes, between the piles.

The analysis of all these crania would seem to demonstrate that during the neolithic period, and, perhaps, for the first time, Switzerland saw the arrival of bands of Brachycephals on her territory. Very likely they came in through the eastern and southern Alpine passes—especially the eastern—and they got as far as the Plateau. It was these Brachycephals, apparently, who constructed the lake dwellings, a material manifestation hitherto unknown in the western world. They brought with them the cultivation of cereals and the domestication of animals (dogs, oxen, sheep, goats and pigs—horses were not domesticated until the bronze age); they instituted navigation. One may say that they brought about the greatest of all social revolutions.

The skeletal remains found in the lake dwellings enable us to picture to ourselves the succession of human events which happened at the time.

Into this country, which appears to have been so sparsely inhabited by Palæolithic people that practically not an anatomical trace of them has come down to us, flowed a brachycephalic wave, probably of Asiatic origin and identical with the people we came to know when studying France, which spread widely to almost every part of the country, though the larger contingents concentrated on the lakes. And it is among the débris of the platforms of these lake dwellings that we chiefly find their remains.

What, in the face of the flood of invaders, became of those descendants of the palæolithic Dolichocephals who must have continued to roam Switzerland, even if in the form of very small troops of hunters? Did they return to the west? Or were they mingled with the invaders? What apparently does emerge as the result of our finds is that towards the middle of the neolithic period new Dolichocephals came and mingled with the Lake brachycephalic people. Where did they come from? Were they part of the advance guard of the dolichocephalic Nordic people who invaded France at about this epoch? Or can they claim as their ancestors, also as in France, the Magdalenian Palæolithic people of the Laugerie-Chancelade type? We are not yet in a position to have any knowledge on the subject.

The Dolichocephals appear to be more numerous at about the time when the bronze age was succeeding the polished stone age. Is this the result of a fresh migration? These later Dolichocephals of the second edition appear to belong to the race which, in France, is predominant in the dolmen burials. Hamy called them neolithic Dolichocephals. A northern origin has been attributed to them, and, as a type, their homologies are sought in the German Row-grave (*Reihengräber*) burials.

Towards the close of the bronze age the Neo-Brachycephals (see the chapter on France) appear to become preponderant, they have a higher cephalic index and a greater cranial capacity than their predecessors. In the nomenclature of His and Rütimeyer this race is represented by the type called Disentis.[1]

Nevertheless I have pointed out more than once that we are not justified in assuming any such synthesis[2] as definitive. I have emphasized the fact that the human evidence obtained from the Lake dwellings has not hitherto been collected stratigraphically.[3] The succession referred to has been established from discoveries made in stations of different epochs and it has been assumed that this spatial view could be transposed accurately in terms of time. I recognize the legitimacy of this contention. And yet, when one has had considerable personal experience of excavation work one remains sceptical of such procedure, and convinced that a demonstration based on strict stratigraphic examination would merit greater confidence.

However, only a few days before I came to write these lines a skull was found *in situ* in a well defined level of a horizon belonging to the earliest Lake Neolithic in the now high and dry neolithic station of Auvernier (Lake Neuchâtel). And this skull, which should have been brachycephalic according to the above theory, is dolichocephalic. Is this the first crack to appear in this ethnogenic construction? I do not know. But it seems to me to be necessary to call attention to this discovery by very reason of the success, so far justified, which has attended the above described synthesis.[4] However

[1] **CI.**
[2] **XCVI**, p. 137.
[3] **CXCIII.**
[4] **CXCIII.**

that may be, it was the Brachycephals of the neolithic period and the bronze age who gave to the majority of the present Swiss population its ethnic expression.

During the iron age Dolichocephals are still numerous in Switzerland; certainly fresh contingents of this type had arrived. We cannot exactly be sure what percentage they account for in the population of the time. They would seem to be preponderant on the Plateau. A few large cemeteries of this region and epoch—such as Münsingen, for example—contain this human type almost exclusively, with mesaticephalic individuals alongside them.

At the dawn of the prehistoric period Switzerland was inhabited by a mixed population—Brachycephals who would appear to be definitely grouped in the Alpine massif, and Dolichocephals on the Plateau.

Before going further we must say something about a human group whose influence on Swiss ethnogeny is inconsiderable, but which we must not, however, pass by in silence—we mean the Pygmies.

During the neolithic period there were scattered at several points on Swiss territory a population of very low stature. These were not degenerate individuals whose development had been arrested. They were normal people, and this particular race has been noted, also, in other lands.

The discovery of pygmy skeletons was made in several cantons, in Géronde (Valais), Mooseedorf (Berne), Schweizersbild and Dachsenbühl (Schaffhausen) and Chamblandes (Vaud). In these burials the skeletons belong to both sexes. Their number is not yet sufficient to have enabled us to work out acceptable mean heights.

Very low stature (we are speaking of adults) has been met with, for example 1 metre 33 in a woman of the Ergolz Marshes (Bâle-Campagne). In the Schweizersbild station (in the neolithic part of this station) Kollmann found a mean of 1 metre 424 (the lowest stature was 1 metre 35 and the tallest 1 metre 50) in three adults. At Chamblandes Schenk obtained by reconstruction a height of 1 metre 356 (minimum height) from an adult woman, etc.

How did these Pygmies come to be in Switzerland in those days? Whence could they have come? In 1894 Studer and Bannwarth arrived at the conclusion that the mesocephalic Pygmies of Chamblandes came from the shores of the

Mediterranean. They based their assumption on the débris of sea shell used as ornament found with the skeletons. But the interpretation of such an origin, very doubtful in this elementary form, at once aroused controversy.

The presence of Pygmies in Europe in the neolithic epoch raises considerable problems. It goes down to the very origin of the European population. We may recall that in the Preface to this book the question came up of the probable peopling of Europe by Africa during the middle Pleistocene. Although it is true that Pygmies exist elsewhere than in Africa, it is nevertheless in this continent that important contingents are to be found. The arrival in Europe of small steatopygous people in Aurignacian times or earlier is practically recognized. We do not want to indulge in hypotheses that are too precarious, but neither can we forget this adventure, in which, by comparison, we may seek an explanation.

Finally, skeletons, having more or less accentuated Negroid characters, of different epochs have been found at many points in Europe. We must recall the celebrated discovery at Baoussé-Roussé of the Grimaldi race described by Verneau.[1]

In 1903 Hervé notified two skulls with Negroid characters.[2] One belonged to the neolithic period and came from the Pointe de Conguel (Brittany) dolmen ; the other, probably of the Gaulish period, was found in the Toul-Bras (Brittany) islet. In Switzerland Schenk[3] met with similar skulls having a Negroid aspect, in the neolithic burial of Chamblandes. These individuals are to be approximated to the men of the Grimaldi race by their facial skeleton, the form of the pelvis, and the proportions of bones and limbs. In my turn I notified skulls with more or less definite Negroid characters, for a later date, in the valley of the valaisian Rhône.[4]

Anthropological data for both the historic and contemporary periods are still few and far between. A general investigation which would elicit definitively the Swiss ethnic characters is badly needed. We have called for it for a long time past. It should completely cover both the human

[1] **CCLXVI**, p. 561.
[2] **XCVII.**
[3] **CCXXXIII.**
[4] I am well aware that these particular characters may be interpreted otherwise than as a survival.

remains deposited in collections and ossuaries, and the living population studied at first hand district by district. So many hypotheses, probably quite unfounded, have been enunciated in respect of certain groups whose ethnographical characteristics were in one way or another exceptional! The canton of Valais has especially been the subject of such suppositions as that the Val d'Anniviers was peopled by the Huns, or that the Saracens peopled other valleys, notably the Saas, or that the Suevi were responsible for the population, etc. It is high time that we should get at the truth of the matter. An anthropological investigation confined within the bounds of these historical claims is most desirable, circumscribed though the field may be.

Even the precise distribution of the forms of the cephalic index for Switzerland is still unknown. In 1867 His and Rütimeyer (*Crania Helvetica*) established four cranial types for Switzerland after a study of 100 crania of "historic times" and some 150 modern skulls. These types were: the Sion type (of pre-Roman times); the Hochberg type (from Roman times to the fifth century A.D.); the Bel-Air type (from the fifth century Burgundian and Alemannic epoch to the ninth century); the Disentis type (of the Middle Ages and the present day). The mean index of the first is 77.2; of the second 70.2; of the third 73.8; and of the fourth 86.5. One can readily understand the historical conclusions that might be drawn from such a succession of types: the sub-Dolichocephals inhabited Switzerland before the arrival of the Romans, and this population was submerged by the Barbarian invaders—who must have belonged to the Germanic races if we are to judge of them by their very low cephalic index. But, from the ninth century onwards all this dolichocephalic population was to be effaced and replaced by Brachycephals of the Disentis type.

I hasten to say that this is not the picture we draw to-day of the ethnogenic events in Switzerland. Numerous discoveries have come to modify the conceptions of His and Rütimeyer, notably all those connected with the prehistoric period. It is impossible, for example, to admit that there were no descendents of the Lake Brachycephals in Switzerland in "pre-Roman" times.

The Burgundian and Alemannic period has provided the most important osteological data. We may take it that the following approximate distribution of ethnic elements was true of that time: Dolichocephals 40 per cent.; Mesaticephals 28 per cent.; Brachycephals 32 per cent. The relatively high percentage of Dolichocephals clearly indicates a Kymric influence for this epoch. Those Swiss areas which were historically Burgundian would seem to have partially preserved this type. Otherwise, how could it happen that in areas clearly brachycephalic to-day, the Brachycephals have increased the early dolichocephalic elements?

Taking Switzerland as a whole we are justified in thinking that brachycephaly gradually diminishes as we go from east to west. The Grisons are decidedly brachycephalic, and the same applies to central Switzerland and to the Valais. Brachycephaly becomes less in the canton of Vaud, and is least well represented in Geneva. Thus I found an index of only 80.6 for the living in this canton. Furthermore, there seems to be evidence that between the Middle Ages and the present day dolichocephaly has slightly increased, probably following the same route.

These variations explain themselves as regards the large towns of the Plateau, where intermixture is easily accomplished. But it is difficult to admit that the variations in the past were not due to historical phenomena. Herein lie some interesting problems to solve.

Among the ethnico-historical hypotheses to which Switzerland has given rise I will quote one by way of an example: the canton of Valais which I have carefully studied throughout its extent and in all its valleys, is one of the most distinctively brachycephalic regions in Europe. Only in one portion of this area does this character of relative purity cease to exist, and this is an island practically contained between the little towns of Sion and Sierre. This Sion-Sierre island holds a population whose percentage of round-heads is the lowest for the canton. Yet the ossuaries preserved within the bounds of this island—some of which certainly date from the Middle Ages, exhibit a remarkable proportion of long skulls. And if we go still further back into the past we shall see that iron age burials furnished dolichocephalic crania.

We may thus admit that a dolichocephalic population of the Kymric type penetrated into the Valais in proto-historic times and that it never came out again. Its historical descendants have maintained the existence of the original type. Even to-day, despite intermixture, which is naturally easier than in those times, this original type has partially persisted. During the Middle Ages the history of the Valais was a turbulent one. And many of its men—Cardinal Matthieu Schinner, for example—played a considerable part in world History. It would be interesting to know by whom, ethnically speaking, these enterprises were suggested and carried out.

Once more we repeat, a study of Switzerland as a whole is imperative. Its results would doubtless throw light on many of the dark places of proto-historic anthropology and European history. And I take advantage of the opportunity thus offered of calling the attention of my confrères of eastern Switzerland to the question of discovering whether the Adriatic race penetrated to the Grisons, this being of undeniable general interest. Does it, or does it not exist in certain valleys of this canton ? One of my students has undertaken this study, and it is not yet finished. All those countries grouped round about Switzerland expect from this State that it will prosecute its anthropological researches to the utmost.

One further point : we have said that Switzerland, from the neolithic period onwards, was peopled by men from the east. The route of this immigration appears to have been the same as that followed in the bronze age. Objects dating from these two periods, notably the last, have been found along many of the Alpine passes. In this regard it must be remembered that in prehistoric times the Alps would not appear to have been inaccessible or difficult of passage to the people who crossed them. They became so later ; one might even say, to exaggerate a little, that from historic times until the day of Horace Bénédict de Saussure, the Alpine region outside the passes was the *terra incognita* of central Europe.

Throughout the Middle Ages the mystery which enveloped them certainly contributed to their preservation from ethnic intermixture. When one sees the proportion of one physical type attaining to 90 out of every 100 for the entire series—as in the Valais, for instance—one would be much embarrassed to supply an explanation if one did not believe in such a conservation.

In the remote valleys, many other anthropological problems have arisen as a result of their very isolation. There is the problem of consanguineous marriages, for instance, which merits attack, since its social importance has been recognised and bitterly discussed times without number. Our space, however, is strictly limited. And in any case this problem does not quite lie within the scope of this book.

CHAPTER VI

GERMANY

GERMANY is not so well known in the details of her ethnic characterization as she should be, despite the large number of her anthropologists of worth and the very important work published in the country.

Yet it was quite a long time ago that a Commission was appointed to undertake a vast anthropological investigation throughout the German Empire. Here and there, in isolated papers, we find a few traces of this analysis. It has been said that if more extended publication has not taken place, and if Germany has not given these anthropological maps to the world it was due to the veto of the late Emperor (??) who did not wish it to be known that the Empire was not anthropologically homogeneous!

But let us pass over what, maybe, is no more than legend. Historical facts alone would lead us to suppose that Germany could not have been peopled throughout by men of one race. Without going too far back into the past, did not the conquests of the nineteenth century add to the Empire portions of neighbouring States whose population at first sight could hardly appear to belong to the same stock as the Germans themselves—such as the Lorrainers of France, the Poles, and the Danes of Schleswig.

In early times aggregations of all sorts took place—as, for example, in the days of the invasions—of whose ethnogenic consequence we know nothing. Human groups of whom we know no more than their names appeared one after another in the same spot. Was each new group of the same origin as its predecessors? And their successors in turn, were they different? Those names by which they were known and which have been handed down to us by the chroniclers—were they nothing but distinctive titles like the names of different troops of the same regiment? Or did they represent something more—the memory of a different parent stock?

Germany, or at all events the western and southern part of her territory, was inhabited by mankind from a very early period.

To the southeast of Heidelberg, in a part of the primitive course of the Neckar, the Mauer quarry has yielded one of the most ancient fragments of human remains that exist. It has been alluded to already in the first pages of this book.

The lower jaw here discovered is unfortunately the only portion recovered of this little evolved race known as *Homo heidelbergensis*, from which, in all probability, Neanderthal man, found also in German ground, is to descend in the Moustierian. The stations of Taubach and Ehringsdorf, near Weimar, also date, like the Mauer jaw, from the Chellean.

The south and west of Germany were inhabited continuously throughout every phase of the Palæolithic. And during the last thirty years German museums have been enriched by numerous finds, made in almost every region outside the bounds of the early Scandinavian glaciers. More recently still Reindeer age burials have been revealed in the Magdalenian levels at Obercassel, near Bonn, from which two skeletons (a man and a woman) coloured red, and in a good state of preservation, have been dug up. Both are distinctly dolichocephalic, like all Europeans of this period.

The Ofnet station in Bavaria has shown that South Germany in the mesolithic period, by the addition of a brachycephalic type, already possessed representatives of at least two very divergent human races.

From the neolithic period onwards skeletal remains become abundant. Germany was peopled at that time principally by Dolichocephals, and throughout the proto-historic period and the early centuries of our era they seem to maintain remarkable cohesion, principally in the northern region. The row-grave burials (*Reihengräber*) which, though there were many earlier, date mainly from the fourth to the eighth century, contain very tall long-headed people. This dolichocephalic type is still numerous in Germany to-day, particularly in the northern area.

We have seen that Brachycephals appear in the curious Ofnet sepulture. There is nothing astonishing, therefore, in the fact that throughout the course of the neolithic period we find their representatives associated with dolichocephalic types: this phenomenon, moreover, is common to all Europe at that time. These Brachycephals, however, did not at first arrive in large numbers. All the German statistics show that the dolichocephalic type was the more numerous during the polished stone age.

In the bronze age the Dolichocephals were still in a real majority and their physical type testifies to a remarkable homogeneity in most localities.

In the Hallstatt period of the iron age the population is much more dolichocephalic than in the La Tène period which followed it.

Thus, when we come to the threshold of historic times we shall see that Germany possessed representatives of many races; one among them is preponderant from the Neolithic onwards—the tall, dolichocephalic type of the row-graves which, by some authors, has been called *Homo nordicus*, and is the Kymric type of Broca.

Only a few years ago Schliz attempted to synthesize[1], in a few pictures, the successive ethnic physiognomies of Germany; and in some very welcome phototypes he grouped, according to epochs, the human types met with in each epoch. Such work has naturally but a relative value for those who would go deeper, but it nevertheless gives a sufficiently good idea of the ethnological happenings during the course of prehistory and proto-history.

The German type, by virtue of a sort of psychological mirage, has been personified by the public. Roughly speaking, its presentment is that of a tall long-headed, florid-complexioned man with fair hair and light eyes—the great blond Dolichocephal whom the Gobinists made the fashion, and for whom a noble destiny was laid claim to by reason of his very race.

These morphological characters exist in abundance among the people of the northern regions of the country. But there are also millions of Germans who belong to no such type. To be convinced of this and to realize the racial heterogeneity of Germany one has only to cross the country from the Swiss frontier at Stettin or from Dantzig, for example. The passage through Württemberg and Bavaria and arrival in Pomerania or East Prussia would bring one into contact with at least two principal ethnic types that are very different from one another—the brunet Brachycephal and the blond Dolichocephal. It

[1] CCXXXV, p. 202 ff.

would even be sufficient to take a walk in the streets of a large city like Berlin, an anthropological microcosm of the whole Reich, to obtain a vision of the same nature. Germany is populated partly by people who belong to the Germanic race of the ethnologist and partly by people belonging to other races. We shall soon make their acquaintance.

Then we know, further, that the Germanic race—the Nordic race—is far from being completely confined to the political territory of the Reich. It everywhere overflows the bounds of the old Empire, and at different periods troops of its representatives have filtered into many regions far removed from those boundaries. The Barbarian invasions have left remnants of this race almost everywhere in Europe and even in Asia. We shall come across them later on.

The European area north of the Danube was very imperfectly known to the Græco-Roman world. The ancient geographers even believed that the greater part of the northern territories of our continent were half desert. Did they not give this curious pretext for their ignorance, that "the Thracians assert that the country beyond the Ister is full of bees which prevent further penetration" (Herodotus). Many centuries after Herodotus, geographical knowledge as touching Germany was no further advanced. That is precisely why it has been possible to say that the Germans made their appearance very late in History.

Nevertheless the amber route by which amber came from the Baltic (it did not come only from there, as has been commonly believed) had been found long before, and the civilization of proto-historic times at the least had placed the peoples of North and South freely in communication by the agency of through-trade. It thus seems strange that the writers of the Græco-Roman epoch should be so ill-informed.

Though they knew so little of Germany, the authors of antiquity none the less gave descriptions of the Germans. Herodotus himself noted the presence of the Budini of the Caspian with their ruddy hair and blue eyes. In the second century Perseus, the king of Macedonia, took into his pay 10,000 Barbarians who "according to Polybius, Livy and Plutarch were Galatae and Bastarnae, Getae according to Appian, and in any case Germans."[1]

[1] **XCV**, p. 65.

And if history mentions with some hesitation the presence of Gauls in Italy in 222, under the name of Gaesatae, it is quite definite in saying that the great invasion of the Cimbri and Teutoni in the years 113 to 101 was Germanic. Cimbri, that is to say, that Plutarch says were regarded " as of Germanic race because of their large proportions and the blue colour of their eyes " ; Cimbri, who differed in no way from the Galatae, as Cæsar later on also observes. The Roman general emphasizes the fact that the Belgæ were Germans attracted from the other side of the Rhine by the fatness of the land. And does he not mention, in this connection, several Germanic tribes established in Limbourg and Luxembourg, in the south of what is now Belgium ? The Suevi of Ariovistus whom Cæsar also fought against, were a German group, at least in name ! And others as well.

At that time the degree of civilization arrived at by the Germans appears to have been inferior to that of their southern neighbours. If they did not let Græco-Roman culture penetrate among them so rapidly as other peoples had done, we should be grateful to them from an ethnographic point of view, because we are thus the better able to realize what was personal, peculiar to themselves and autochthonous in the Germanic civilization in those days, such as it is revealed to us in the burials. Furthermore, no matter what may be said on the subject, we should also be grateful to them—I speak here for those who think that " liberty is the greatest good of all "—for having so valiantly struggled to preserve their liberty. Roman imperialism, glutted with conquest (it exhausted itself thereby)—which certain Germans in the nineteenth and twentieth century, steeped in the most complete classicism, were to attempt to revive—is not such a noble moral or political attitude that we are bound to admire it.

Have historians really got to the bottom of the reasons which led to the linguistic separation of these two main branches of the great Kymric racial tree—the Germanic and the Galatic ? The almost constant divergences which were to manifest themselves right through European history between the Gauls and the Germans may be said to date from that moment. It must be understood that in this connection ' Gauls ' are not synonymous with ' Frenchmen '—these last being composite of many other races. But it cannot be denied that a fairly large number of present-day Frenchmen, more especially in the north and the east, are authentic descendants—like a fairly large number of Belgians, Swiss, etc.—of the people who created this schism in the Kymric group. We shall find that ethnic consanguinity exists between these various contingents despite differences of manners and tongue, and on this point research only confirms what the historians of antiquity have told us.

There is one point, however, on which too much insistence cannot be laid—did all these groups who accomplished the invasions, or all the peoples established at that time on the left bank of the Rhine, really represent human elements of homogeneous race? The old historians, we know, described the physical appearance of the Germans—their tall stature, fair hair and blue eyes. Did they copy these descriptions from one another? That I cannot tell, but the description itself remains. In any case, were not these chroniclers—these men who themselves were doubtless brunet and of medium height—struck by the characters the genuine Kymri presented, which were so very different from their own? And maybe they were so obnubilated by these great differences that they omitted to tell us whether there were, within the ranks of the Germanic peoples whom they described so complaisantly, men belonging to other races than those they depicted.

There is good reason to think that the invaders who attacked the fertile lands of the west and the south were not solely tall, fair, blue-eyed men. Let us not forget Ofnet. Nor that from the Mesolithic onwards we have observed representatives of many ethnic groups on what is German ground to-day.

Why should not Brachycephals of the Bavarian type, for instance, have participated in greater or lesser numbers in the irruptions, in the ranks of the other "Germans", contributing to their success, and sharing in the gains? Such a collaboration would explain many ethnological facts.

Since the prehistoric period many Germans have gone forth beyond the bounds of old Germany at divers epochs. In Gaul the Burgundians and Franks formed veritable colonies; the Burgundian influence is manifest in many localities in France.

What evidence is there enabling us to establish a connection between the inhabitants of old Germany—pre-historic Germany, even—and the Germans of to-day ? Does anything authorize us to assert that the inhabitants of Germany are German in race ? (We know that some of them are not.)

There is the testimony of the texts in the descriptions left by those who actually saw these invading hordes, or who, accompanying the Roman forces, fought against them in Germany itself. Then we have evidence of greater demonstrative worth in the contents of the early graves. It is easy enough to reconstruct the ethnic physiognomy of the ancient Germans, and we can then compare it with that of the present inhabitants of Germany.

Can we consider the description Tacitus gives as a synthesis of all the observations made during his times and in the times before him ? The diagnosis is always the same—great stature, reddish hair, blue eyes, and fierceness. (The last, no doubt, in their quality as an enemy.)

Roman writers have also mentioned the late puberty of the Germans, which is certainly an ethnic peculiarity of the Kymric group. There is a sufficiently great contrast in this respect between the young girls of North Germany and those of central and western France. If the existing statistics are correct there is as much as a year's difference between them. And has it not been remarked that young French girls who are tall and have blue eyes arrive at puberty later than the others ? I have before me results of investigations varying from 14 years and 3½ months (southeast France) to 16 years and 1 month (Hanover). All these indications are in agreement.

In those districts which the early historians assigned to Germanic tribes the existing population almost everywhere presents types reminiscent of the descriptions of classic writers —though the majorities naturally vary with the social, economic and political phenomena exemplified. Great stature, fair hair and light eyes are faithfully reproduced. Tacitus would say : " These are they ! I recognize them ! " Modern anthropologists have added to these the characteristic of dolichocephaly of which the Roman writers were ignorant. According to Hölder it would even appear that pigmentation decreases as dolichocephaly becomes more pronounced.

This Kymric tint with which the whole of North Germany is shaded and which deepens in the west, has left its trail in distinctly German districts of non-Germanic race, such as Bavaria. To the north of this country, where dwelt the

Hermunduri tribes, one finds that, among the existing brachycephalic and brunet population, at least 20 per cent. are of Germanic type, survivals, no doubt, of the irruption period. And everywhere throughout Germany it is the case that a low cephalic index, blue eyes and fair hair are associated with the morphological character of tall stature.

We briefly indicated at the beginning of this chapter what has been the succession of ethnic types in Germany. It is necessary that we should go into greater detail and quote figures. We shall mainly appeal to the skeletons found in the row-graves, because these cemeteries, which are sometimes of great extent, have supplied a wealth of osteological material; and because they represent many centuries in time, stretching as they do from the iron age (it has even been asserted that some of them go back to neolithic times) to the introduction of Christianity; and finally, because spatially they are to be found scattered all over the Reich, to east, west and south.

The general conclusion arrived at respecting them, whether the signature be Echer's, von Hölder's, Virchow's or Kollmann's is identical. The Reihengräber crania (we are speaking synthetically) are dolichocephalic, sometimes even pronouncedly so, since the mean indices of Echer and von Hölder respectively are 71.3 and 72. To this dolichocephaly is added remarkable height of vault. A long and relatively narrow face goes with this long skull. The Basel anthropologist, Kollman, calls them leptoprosopic dolichocephals on account of the association of these two characters. The nasal aperture is narrow and the orbital cavity rather shallow.

The row-grave cemeteries of those regions of Germany to-day characterized by their brachycephaly show relatively high percentages of Dolichocephals. Thus there has been ethnic superposition in these localities. In Bavaria, for instance, a country of round-heads, one again sees Dolichocephals in a majority of over 30 per cent., whereas at the same period Brachycephals only accounted for half this figure. The presence of more than 50 per cent. of Mesaticephals would seem to indicate that at some time there was a considerable intermixture of peoples in this region. To the west, in Württemberg, the earliest row-graves contain only 2 per cent. of Brachycephals. And it was later, only, thanks to growing intimacy of contact with the population of the south-east, that the number of Brachycephals increased. Thus primitive

Germany, south as much as north, clearly belonged to the Nordic race so far as the shape of its skulls is concerned.

Do its other morphological characters confirm this testimony?

We have not yet sufficient evidence as regards height either with reference to the prehistoric people or those of the later Middle Ages. Von Hölder gives the Reihengräber Dolichocephals a mean height of 1 metre 86 (women, 1 metre 69). Such figures, however, appear to be very high. Lehmann-Nitsche, computing by Manouvrier's method, and using, it is true, data coming from southern Bavaria, finds a somewhat lower mean height of 1 metre 683, nevertheless 3 cms greater than the European mean.

I would draw attention, however, by way of advancing an explanation of this figure so different from that of von Hölder's, to the fact that the Allach row-graves (Munich neighbourhood) on whose skeletons Lehmann-Nitsche's observations were made, contain 18 per cent. of brachycephalic and 48.5 per cent. of mesocephalic individuals. These individuals are shorter than the Dolichocephals.

Has the present-day population of Germany preserved the physiognomy we have just indicated, or has it replaced it by some other, and, if so, what other? We have but one means of finding out—by having recourse to modern anthropological investigation.[1]

We have already mentioned the poverty of these results—that is to say, of the published results. Nevertheless we can gain a general view of the country, notably of its southern portions, and so make the necessary comparisons with the ancient population.

In North Germany the height is certainly great. Its mean must exceed 1 metre 69. Meisner,[2] in his investigation of Schleswig and the neighbouring districts—he leaves out all stature lower than 1 metre 55 and greater than 1 metre 85—obtained a mean of 1 metre 692. This figure would doubtless have been exceeded if the investigator had included in his statistics men whose height exceeded 1 metre 85, which, as one knows, must have been fairly numerous in a group of tall men.

Meisner included along with Schleswig-Holstein a few

[1] **CCXL**, No. 9.
[2] **CLV**, p. 235.

small districts belonging to Hanover, Oldenburg and the free cities of Hamburg, Lübeck and Bremen, with their adjacent territory. He ascertained that the population of Holstein was not so tall as that of Schleswig, which, at first sight, would seem to be explained by the presence in the last-named of populous cities, lying close together, such as Hamburg-Altona and Lübeck, and the influence of such towns, distinctly exemplified by Lübeck and Bremen, in raising the height average. But we are left in perplexity when we find that the city and district of Hamburg, in which more than 90 per cent. of the total is represented by the urban population, shows a lower stature. Must we here bring into consideration the maritime character of the city—with its lower degree of stability in the population as a whole than that of inland towns? But then—is one sure about this lower degree of stability? And what about the two positive instances of Lübeck and Bremen?

Thus we see that even this single morphological factor of height brings us up against difficult problems, the elucidation of which would be assisted by wider demographic investigation, and detailed observation of regional history.

In connection with these difficult problems there is another result from Meisner's investigation[1] which should be pointed out. In the Schleswig-Holstein isthmus he noted that height is greater in the islands than on the coasts, and on the coasts than in the interior, and that it is greater on the western coast than on the eastern. Thus the Frisians of the islands and the west coast would be taller than the Danes of the interior. But Danes are also tall. Are there then, among these landsmen, and going under the name of Danes, remnants of early infiltration by another race and of early colonization of which all memory may have been lost? It does not seem at all unlikely when we realize that for Meisner the "tall folk" of Schleswig-Holstein are also blond, with a long face (the leptoprosopy of the Germanic race) and narrow nose; whereas the "small folk" are brunet, with a broad face and relatively short, wide nose.

And this brachycephalic brunet race of medium height, such as it is to be found in South Germany and in many other regions of Europe, did it push forward an advance guard—or leave a remainder—in this locality during some early passage? We must refer to the historians.

[1] **CLV**, p. 101.

We can picture to ourselves the whole of North Germany—though the extension is, perhaps, stretching a point, since our information does not cover the whole area—as presenting the general characteristics in regard to height which have been ascertained for Schleswig-Holstein. It goes without saying that here and there there are exceptions—along the course of the Elbe in particular, it would seem. In the statistics for several thousand recruits from the Grand Duchy of Mecklenburg[1]—they were not full grown—we get a mean of 1 metre 68.

It would seem that stature diminishes as one goes eastward. In explanation of such a phenonemon the neighbourhood of Poles, who are notably smaller than men of Germanic race, may be put forward. Hanover and Oldenburg, on the contrary, probably possess the greatest stature of the whole of North Germany.

The following observation, which confirms the facts of history, has also been made, namely that there are taller men in the maritime provinces than in the interior of the country. We realize here a manifestly Scandinavian influence—a northern race that has remained more pure. As for the course of the Elbe, it has always served as a road for ethnic groups following the river, either going up or down this open valley. Later we shall come across souvenirs of their passage.

The rest of Germany brings us face to face with morphological problems whose interpretation can be supplied by History alone. One might say that in this regard Germany can teach us a great deal.

In the first place let us note that in the west, in the Rhenish country of which Coblenz may be said to be the centre, stature does not reach the figure of the various North German districts, though slightly above the European mean (1 metre 666). Let us, however, proceed towards Thuringia and the kingdom of Saxony. The mean stature in the old principality of Schwarzburg-Sondershausen lies somewhere about 1 metre 68. A little further south, in the territory round about Erfurt, maybe it is a little higher. If we cross the Thuringian mountains we shall see the height of the inhabitants of Saxe-Meiningen becoming less—1 metre 66. This gradual diminution to be observed as one goes from north to south we shall also remark as we progress from west to east.

[1] **CLVI**, p. 317.

How are these data to be interpreted? Were we to ask sociologists knowing nothing of the figures what they thought of this problem, they would say that Thuringia, where economic conditions are unfavorable, ought to be an area of small stature. And this is just what it is not. Other areas, far more favoured economically, have a smaller stature even than Thuringia.

Were we to interrogate a theorist who believes in the influence of environment he would endeavour to establish some relation between the western more mountainous regions and the eastern areas of lower altitude. But it would be easy to point out to him that he also was wrong. And the results of observations like these lead us to protest once again against too readily expressed assertions on the part of these two disciplines when, in a given area, they come across variations in stature. It is much to be desired that both of them would take a course of instruction in anthropology. With greater familiarity in handling such evidence they would offer better attempts at its interpretation.

Going still further east, the old kingdom of Saxony[1] exhibits one of the lowest mean statures of Germany. Do all the Saxons of this part of the Reich reach the European mean? There are grounds for doubting it, when we see the neighbourhood of Bautzen and of Zwickau reaching 1 metre 64 with difficulty, and even remaining below it. As regards these industrial regions it has been sought to fix responsibility for this low stature on work in the mines and factories. I do not think this explanation is valid. It would be more legitimate to seek an acceptable explanation in the undeniable ethnic influence due to the Wends of former days and to the Poles of to-day, who have filtered into and across Silesia. A portion of both these infiltrations would have been Germanized; but another portion would have contributed its own morphological qualities to the cross. Large cities like Leipzig and Dresden have a greater stature than the mean for the surrounding country districts, as is usual in urban agglomerations.

Nevertheless, in Saxony as a whole there exist regions where the height is greater. Definite evidence of this is to be found in the work of Mackeprang,[2] who found a mean height of 1 metre 655 yielded by 100,000 soldiers.

[1] **LIII**, p. 76.
[2] **LIII**, p. 80. and 293.

Continuing in an eastward direction we shall see this characteristic picture of a diminishing stature as furnished by east Saxony accentuated more and more as we come to Silesia and the former German territories of the Warthe and the Vistula which were returned to the Poles after the great war. The Polish influence of small stature is felt everywhere, even in the area of West and East Prussia. Though the northern portion of these provinces may be inhabited by men of Nordic race the interior contains numerous individuals of Polish race who at once lower the mean height.

Let us now enter the three southern States—the old Grand Duchy of Baden, Württemberg, and Bavaria.

When we roughly examine the old Duchy of Baden[1] we perceive that the southern part of the country contains statures notably lower than in the north and northeast. For the country as a whole one might be correct in indicating 1 metre 66 as the height of the men of Baden, but if the country is cut in two at the level of the town of Lahr, we see that the inhabitants north of this line are taller than their congeners who dwell south of it. A Kymric influence manifests itself almost all along the German Rhine from Strasbourg onwards. Certainly the banks of this river are not exclusively peopled by individuals of this race, but it has left enough of its blood to keep alive a morphological memory of the true Germans.

I think the above main features can be extended to Württemberg where the mean height is also somewhere round about 1 metre 66. Between the two States extend the low hills of the Black Forest (the Feldberg is 1493 metres high) pushing especially into the old Grand Duchy of Baden, and this region is for both districts the zone of lowest stature (attaining scarcely to 1 mètre 65). Why does this massif, where the influence of physical environment can hardly be adduced, shelter the smallest men? Are we to credit that it is an ancient refuge chosen by the people of "Celtic" brachycephalic type—a type of lower stature than the northern Dolichocephals? Such would be a very bold assertion.

As for the Bavarians, their mean height scarcely goes beyond 1 metre 65 (the European mean). But looked at thus the information has no signification. If, however, we subdivide Bavaria according to districts, summary though the method

[1] I, p. 80.

may be, we secure data of some interest for History. In the former kingdom of King Ludwig we see two areas of greater stature, the north and the south of the country. The districts watered by the Danube hold the smallest men, and here, too, the proportion of small statures is the greatest. Struck by these general facts the Bavarian anthropologist, Ranke,[1] readily attributed them to differing conditions of existence, because, he said, " in these hilly regions I see different groups (we will not add ethnic)—Swabian, Alemannic and Bavarian, presenting the same proportion of tall stature, and because, in the Danube plains, these same groups also show the maximum number of individuals of low stature." This was because Ranke was still dominated by the linguistic idea, and because, for him, these three labels represented three ethnic groups.

We should readily envisage a different hypothesis: we have seen that numerous representatives of the Germanic race penetrated here from the north of Bavaria and from beyond the Thuringian forest. Moreover, throughout the course of History, we are familiar with the expansive powers of this race. The low heights which dominate the course of the Main in the north could prove no obstacle to their spread.

So far as southern Bavaria is concerned, we will refer to the map published by Deniker giving the mean statures of Europe.[2] We shall there see the Diniaric race thrusting out spearheads to the north-west from the Balkan peninsular, where its strongest contingents are to be found. We have already seen a similar penetration in this direction by the tall Brachycephals in North Italy, in Venetia, and we have probably also identified them in Switzerland in the Grisons. The Tyrolean passes appear to have been crossed by the prehistoric peoples. The Inn valley would have provided them with a turning-off place to be followed westwards by some of them into Switzerland and by others northwards into Bavaria.

Thus the Bavarian ethnic problem, looked at from the point of view of history, becomes one of the most interesting there is. We cannot yet comprehend it in its entirety because ethnological investigation has not yet been carried far enough; but we can already get some idea of its main lines.

To sum up, Germany presents a heterogeneous aspect even if we consider only the stature of her people. There are

[1] **CCXI**, p. 1.
[2] **LIII**, p. 83.

at least two principal races in the country. The Germanic race is far from monopolizing German territory. Though North Germany, especially the northern seaboard, may legitimately be considered a Kymric domain, the same cannot be said for the south, nor for the central area into which the Germanic race has merely filtered.

It would seem that two human streams concurrently occupied what is now Germany: to the north the stream above-mentioned, to the south a tall brachycephalic stream. To the centre a Polish (Vistulan sub-race) spearhead has been thrust, at least as far as the heart of the kingdom of Saxony. Between these main streams there were doubtless cross-currents, water-meets and eddies. Those tribes of Germanic race which in Cæsar's day dwelt along the Rhine have left numerous descendants in those parts.

But these are merely a few broad strokes of a huge fresco. We must go seek further data.

We have seen that in her most distant past Germany was populated by dolichocephalic people. We have seen that the row-graves (Reihengräber) contain this human type almost exclusively. We must now find out whether the living population of Germany still everywhere continues to manifest this cranial morphology or whether other races have been superposed on the early one. If the answer is in the affirmative we must ask ourselves where and how these changes have been effected, and to what extent they have been operative.

We will take up the cephalic description of Germany in the same order as that in which we have studied stature.

North Germany is the domain of the long-heads. Practically everywhere where callipers have been used they have brought out this character. Certainly it is less definite as a character than in the days when Germany buried her dead in the row-grave cemeteries. Ethnic intermixture has taken place since those days and has raised the cephalic index. It is now round about 79. But there is no more doubt about the mean dolichocephaly or sub-dolichocephaly of the inhabitants than about their light eyes and fair hair. From Friesland to East Prussia the majority of the people exhibit either long-headedness or, by the sub-dolichocephalic form of the head, a very lively reminiscence of long-headedness. In

Schleswig-Holstein the proportion of Brachycephals does not appear to exceed one fourth of the people, though there is ground for believing that greater facilities for intermixture exist in such areas than elsewhere.[1] The nearer we come to Denmark the larger becomes the proportion of Dolichocephals. Schleswig is definitely more dolichocephalic than Holstein. Danish influence thus maintained itself in this province, now rightly returned to its former masters.

Pursuing our investigation further east, we find the same general characteristics in East Germany. A cephalic index of 79 would also seem to be the most common mean.[2] And the cranial form associates itself with stature in such a way as to assure a certain homogeneity among the people of the seaboard.

A sketch of Central Germany[3]—our present knowledge does not allow us to give more—will bring us up against interesting facts. The Rhenish district, where our study of stature showed us definite intermixture of races with a considerable survival of the Kymric type, will show us a cephalic index in which the influence of Brachycephals is nevertheless manifest. It will be less so, however, than in Nassau and the old Grand Duchy of Hesse, where the indices rise to brachycephaly (84.) The Saxon States likewise merit attention. In the former Duchies of Saxe-Coburg and Saxe-Meiningen the cephalic indices are also brachycephalic (84). But the round-headedness at once diminishes when we pass the Thuringian forest and penetrate into the former Duchies of Saxe-Gotha (index of 82) and Saxe-Weimar (index of 81.5). We have already remarked much the same thing when we were trying to find out the height characters of this region, namely that this low chain of hills, although it did not really separate two ethnic groups, at all events served more or less as a line of delimitation between them. South of the Thuringian forest the people are smaller and more brachycephalic than north of it, where Germanic influence to some extent persists.

Going further east, though our knowledge is still indefinite, the former kingdom of Saxony appears to be a sub-brachycephalic area. We can write down the same observations here in regard to cranial form as we made in connection with

1 **LV**, p. 52.
2 **CXLII**, p. 188, and 1878, p. 1.
3 **LV**, p. 52.

stature in the matter of the "Slav" influence of the Vistulan sub-race.

South Germany (the three States of Baden, Württemberg, and Bavaria) exhibit cephalic indices very different from those manifested in the northern parts of the Reich. From 79, the figure for the country lying along the Baltic and North Sea, there is a jump to 84.85, and even 87.5 in certain ossuaries of Upper Bavaria. One could not have a better illustration of the disparity existing between North and South Germans, and one realizes in face of this evidence what good reason they had to fear the publication of anthropological maps who wished to make people believe in the ethnic unity of the Empire.

In the old Grand Duchy of Baden[1] the cephalic indices taken by regions go from sub-brachycephaly (83) to the most definite brachycephaly (85.5) in the Black Forest zone.

Summing up the numerous indications furnished by Ammon, his predecessors and successors,[2] one may say that as a whole the Baden district is sub-brachycephalic but contains definitely brachycephalic islands notably in the centre and the mountainous south. The district of Wolfach, east of Lahr and Offenburg, is even hyperbrachycephalic (index of 86). When we descend the slopes of the Black Forest and advance in the direction of the Neckar, that is to day towards the frontiers of Hesse, the indices become lower. Thus the Karlsruhe district shows an index of 83.3; Heidelberg, 83.1; and Mannheim about 82, because we are now gradually approaching the territory in which individuals of Germanic race are in the majority.

In Württemberg the mean cephalic index is somewhat lower than in the old Grand Duchy of Baden, since it lies between 82 and 83. The Rauhe Alb chain which diagonally runs across Württemberg bounds a zone to the north where long-heads are much more frequent than to the south. It is not the dolichocephaly or the sub-dolichocephaly of the genuine German type. But the frequent mesaticephaly seen in different localities of this area shows that the Germanic race has left some souvenir of its presence. In the south, on the contrary, whether in the eastern extensions of the Black Forest or close to the Swiss frontier, brachycephalic types are far the most numerous.

[1] **I.**
[2] **LV**, p. 55.

As for Bavaria, it is definitely brachycephalic. An even sheet of brachycephaly extends, as it were, north and south over very nearly the whole of the country. As regards cranial morphology, the Bavarians constitute, if one may say so, a special group in Germany. If Ranke[1] was correct in his view, this State represents in the south of the Reich as clear cut an ethnic bloc as certain districts of North Germany do for the dolichocephalic type. To this must be added, as yet another character differentiating the Bavarians, that the proportion of brunets among them is at the lowest between 17 and 30 per cent.

In the centre of Bavaria the country dipping to the river on either side of the Danube does not contain equally short-headed people. It would seem that we might hold responsible for this attenuation of a morphological character common to the rest of the country the facility of passage which this valley affords. Although there is no ground for considering every river valley as a migration route, nevertheless we must not refuse to recognize that certain valleys do bear this character.

The reader who has waded through this long classification, whose dryness we have sought to veil, and who has followed on the map the ethnic distribution we have attempted to point out, will be able to draw his own conclusions. He will be able to form a picture of the ethnic physiognomy of Germany both in the past and the present.

He will have seen that present-day Germany can no more boast of containing a pure race within its frontiers than most of the other European States. We have discovered the presence of at least two main races within its territory; we described them as we went along and there is no need to remind readers of their morphological characters.

Looking at the problem in a general way, what most impresses itself on us is that the population of North Germany must be classed with the other northern peoples of Europe distributed from the British Isles to Finland. Together with these the population of North Germany constitutes, so far as any European race can be so constituted in our days, that certainly very coherent group which we call the Nordic race, and which Ripley called the Teutonic, and Broca the Kymric race. We know that Ammon, Lapouge and others have made

[1] CCX.

of this category the type of *Homo europæus.* These people speak Low-German (platt-deutsch, nieder-deutsch).

As regards South Germany, it is peopled by quite another type. With moderate stature this race in certain cases associates a very definitely brachycephalic cranium (Bavaria); and in others sub-brachycephaly (Württemberg, Baden), and hair which in a large proportion of cases is brown or chestnut.

To what races, to-day more or less determinate, can we attribute this South German population? It is hard to say. It is very probable that we can put the Bavarians—those among them, in the main, who dwell in the south of Bavaria and to the north of the Danube valley—in the Cevenole or Western race. To the west of this compact mass, fairly well defined, the mountainous region of Württemberg and the Grand Duchy of Baden—the frontier zone of the Black Forest—would also appear to be populated by people belonging to the same race. The other inhabitants of South Germany—the Nordics excepted—may be grouped into a secondary race, sub-brachycephalic, of medium height, and with chestnut hair, which Deniker, *faute de mieux*, created as a pendant to his principal races.

Besides these, there exist in the country situated to the east of Central Germany numerous representatives of the secondary Vistulan race, to which a large number of the Poles belong. Finally, we are not overbold in adding that an advance guard of the Dinaric race penetrated to South Germany.

Although we have found it possible to establish this racial differentiation, which the future, perhaps, may modify, it is impossible, on the contrary, to compute the numerical strength of each race. The statistics allow of no such adjunction.

CHAPTER VII

BELGIUM

AT a time when the ice had spread farthest over North Europe, forbidding all human settlement in those regions, nearly the whole of Belgium enjoyed the same advantages as a large part of France in that it was outside the sphere of this geological phenomenon. The Scandinavian continental ice with its massive alluvial deposits, came to a halt almost on the present frontier between Belgium and Holland. The terminal moraines extend no further than the level of Antwerp. South of this line the rich lands which have caused Belgium to be one of the most thickly populated countries in the world were habitable.

The palæolithic people established themselves in Belgium as well as in France. Hunters of the race of *Homo neanderthalensis* ranged over the Belgian valleys and installed themselves in caves and beneath the overhanging shelter of rocks. They have left behind them abundant traces of their industry and some few of their own skeletal form. Belgium, as a matter of fact, has furnished science with several of the most celebrated of such human remains, such as the la Naulette jaw, and the Spy fragments, which have provided food for anthropological discussion for many a long day.

It is certain that Man's destiny in palæolithic Belgium was the same—with certain reservations—as in France. The Spy hunters who, in the province of Namur, gave burial to their dead, belonged, maybe, to the same bands as those who at this period, roamed over France. In any case they were of the same race. We have no indubitable human remains of the upper Palæolithic coming from Belgium. But the discoveries made in Gaulish territory, and the recent finds at Obercassel near Bonn[1] (R. bank of the Rhine), which associate themselves with archæological finds made in Belgium itself,

[1] For account of this discovery see *Der diluviale Menschenfund von Obercassel bei Bonn*, by Verworm, R. Bonnet and G. Steinmann, Wiesbaden, 1919. (Translator's Note.)

encourage us to believe that one day we shall find Reindeer-age hunters in Belgium. It would be extraordinary if the men of the upper Palæolithic, who ranged over France and western Germany at a very short distance from Belgian territory, had not buried some of their people there.

Thus Belgium is presented to us as an extension of France from the point of view of its racial destinies in the most distant past. The same ethnological phenomena are revealed in both these neighbouring lands.

When the northern regions which were to subside beneath the waters had disappeared, the climate became gradually modified, perhaps a little more rapidly in maritime districts than in the interior of the continent. This stage of physical geography coincided with the commencement of the neolithic period. The new civilization introducing polished stone implements appears to have penetrated into Belgium as a result of trading rather than of warlike invasion. The successors of the palæolithic Dolichocephals received and adopted the social modifications which were thus brought to them without the personal intervention of those responsible for them. Later, the folk of this new civilization themselves arrived in Belgium. The series of Belgian crania dating from the beginning of the Neolithic would seem to persuade us that events came to pass in this way. Many among these skulls have been exhaustively studied, notably by Fraipont[1] and Houzé.

By what routes did the neolithic Brachycephals penetrate into Belgium ?

It is extremely likely—we are here following the hypotheses of Hervé—that this race, probably Asiatic, came along the valley of the Danube. Its northern contingent, which was to give to Bavaria its ethnic characteristics, continued thence north of the Alpine massif. But did it then cross the Rhine, where it flows through the plains to the north of the Westerwald and the Sieben Gebirge, where the Obercassel interments mark an earlier human stage ? Or did it come through the passes and cross the Rhine higher up in its course ? From this left bank the way to Belgium would have been easier. Nothing enables us to say which was the more likely route of the two.

Belgian writers admit that the Brachycephals penetrated into the country along the course of the Meuse, and therefore

[1] **LXXIII**, p. 311.

by the Franco-Swiss route. On this point Houzé is most categorical. And whereas it had been supposed that Belgium became at one time a centre of brachycephaly whence groups of these people went forth in various directions, Houzé said: "The Belgian area was a centre of immigration, not of emigration. It has served as a route over which a large number of historical invasions have passed, but never has its exiguous territory permitted of its constituting for any people a centre sufficiently important to serve as the base for invasion of neighbouring regions".[1]

Another interesting fact worthy of attention is that a certain number of the neolithic constructors of lake dwellings who established themselves on most of the Swiss lakes, both Italian and French, also established themselves in the Belgian low country.

All those phases of prehistory which followed the Neolithic were abundantly represented in Belgium, and the collections in the museums of that country are among the richest in existence.

Belgian archæologists are of opinion that, as regards the introduction of metals, bronze and iron were brought in in two different ways. Whereas the bronze age appears to have resulted from commercial importations—as in the neolithic period—the iron age was inaugurated as a result of conquest. Invading warriors, the prelude to the Germanic invasions, brought the new civilization.

At the time of the historic invasions the Belgæ, often mentioned as valiant soldiers by early writers—did not Cæsar single them out for praise in this respect?—would seem to have followed the Galatæ in their advance to France. They even established themselves well to the fore in ancient Gaul, either under their own name or under that of related tribes. There is a whole literature of the subject whose detailed perusal does not concern us.

Before we say anything about the anthropological conditions of historic Belgium, let us note that the conquering Belgæ did not establish themselves in any very great numbers on Belgian soil. The accounts left by the annalists, if we can credit them at all, give us proof of it. Dion Cassius wrote that the Belgæ, near the Rhine, were a "mixed race", and Ptolemy when he speaks of Belgic Gaul, seems to imply the presence

[1] CIX, p. 97.

of an anthropological mixture in this country, since he calls it Belgic Celto-Galatia.

These terms were political denominations for the ancient writers. All we know of the Belgæ[1] of this period, that is of those whose tribal names have been preserved—the Menapii, Nervii, Tungri, etc.—leads us to think of them as of Germanic race. They were tall, with remarkably fair skins, fair or reddish hair and blue eyes.[2]

Excavation, both in the Flemish and Walloon provinces of Belgium, has revealed the physical characters of the invaders. The many studies of Frankish cemeteries by Houzé have enabled anthropologists to reconstruct the stature —always considerable—and to indicate the cranial characters —generally dolichocephalic—of these ancient Germans. In respect of this index Houzé has even made the important observation[3] that the Franks of the early invasions show a higher degree of dolichocephaly than their immediate successors who were cross-bred owing to intermixture with the Brachycephals of the polished stone age. The Franks are leptorrhinians. With a view of avoiding sterile discussions between historians and anthropologists Houzé proposed to give to this type a geographical definition and to call it the Hallstatt type, in memory of the station of this name where so many graves were found containing individuals identical with those studied in Belgium.[4]

To what degree has this Germanic race persisted in the Belgium of our day? We shall see directly. But we shall realize from now on that it was unable to displace the peoples descended from the quaternary Dolichocephals and the polished stone age Brachycephals which it found on Belgian soil. Is not the prime interest of a warrior people to preserve the sedentary population among whom it establishes itself, and, if possible, to get on with them? Otherwise, how is the warrior people itself to live? In those far off times pillage would not have provided much in the way of property for an

[1] Numerous discussions of this subject will be found in the Brussels *Bull. de la Soc. d'Anthropologie*.

[2] See also, for a summary of these discussions in English, Rice Holmes' *Cæsar's Conquest of Gaul*, 2nd edition, 1911, the parts on the Celtæ and the Belgæ in Section II of Appendix, "The Ethnology of Gaul", pp. 257-343, especially p. 322 ff. (Translator's Note.)

[3] **CVIII**, p. 28.

[4] **CV**, p. 15.

invader. Hence it would seem to be obvious, without knowing anything as yet of the anthropological characteristics of Belgium, that we ought to find in that country a good many descendants of the neolithic Brachycephals, varying fairly extensively in numbers according to locality.

We know that Belgium is linguistically divided into two main zones, the northern provinces speaking Flemish and the southern Walloon.

We shall observe here, in contradistinction to what usually happens elsewhere when we try to fit race into the geographical framework of language, that there is a certain relation subsisting between the two. The Flemish zone is more dolichocephalic than the Walloon, and, at the same time, there is a larger proportion of Dolichocephals (we are no longer speaking of a mean character) throughout the Flemish zone.

Taking the cephalic indices only into consideration the difference is also sharply defined. I have before me the figures of two series which are not of much importance numerically, but are still sufficiently indicatory: the cephalic index of the Flemings (there are included men of different Flemish provinces) is 78.8, and that of the Walloons is 83.3. According to the terminology, the first of these expresses sub-dolichocephaly, and the second sub-brachycephaly. Obviously these are not clear-cut characters such as would be exhibited by populations of pure race, but they are nevertheless valuable indications. Intermixture has taken place in both directions. The Brachycephals of Latin tongue have attenuated the characters of the German Dolichocephals, and *vice versa*; but the primitive ethnic colours are to be found in each of these groups. Let us add to these characters of the cephalic index the important observation that fair people are more numerous in the Flemish and brunets in the Walloon zone.

In order to bring out this quality of the physical types of Belgium I cannot do better than quote Houzé, as follows: "The Flemings descended from the Germans are blond and blue-eyed, with the occipital protuberance highly accentuated, and a long face; they are sub-dolichocephalic in the more Germanized provinces, such as Limburg, the province of Antwerp, and the north of Brabant; they are mesaticephalic in the two Flanders owing to the fusion with the Celtic element; this mesaticephaly corresponds to a greater proportion of brunets than in the other Flemish districts.

"The Walloons, descendants of the Celts, have dark hair and eyes, scarcely any occipital protuberance, highly developed superciliary ridges, and a broad face harmonizing with the sub-brachycephaly which sharply distinguishes them from the Flemings. They have remained sub-brachycephalic in the hilly districts, in the Ardennes and in the south of Brabant; they have become mesaticephalic in the province of Liége—the first to bear the brunt of all the Germanic invasions—in the province of Namur, where the Meuse has always excited the envy of invaders, and in Hainaut, which the dolichocephalic current has always crossed to spread out towards the south."[1]

This is a generalized image at which we must look more in detail.

The French brachycephalic bloc is prolonged quite definitely into the southeast of the Belgian country. A glance at the cephalic index chart drawn up by Deniker[2] is sufficient to convince anyone of this. The Argonne hills and the Lorraine plateau are areas peopled by Brachycephals. These areas, prolonged towards the Forest of the Ardennes, retain their characters more or less intact. The Grand Duchy of Luxembourg at the foot of the Lorraine mountains is a geographical compartment inhabited by people having, short, broad heads. The Meuse corridor, which during the polished stone age would have served as a way for the Brachycephals to advance towards the northwest, continued to serve as a channel during the proto-historic and historic periods. People of the same race would have come to augment the earlier contingents.—That is to say, if we suppose that the neolithic flood was of greater volume, numerically, than one would suspect at first sight. Thus Belgium would have maintained itself, in this district, in a sort of ethnical *statu quo ante*, increasing its population only by a high birthrate.

The hills of Artois did not, like the southwestern country, facilitate the confinement of the Brachycephals to one locality. Between the Ardennes and the sea the way lies open. Furthermore, the people of this part of the country are of another type it is a mesaticephalic type, that is to say, it is the result of

[1] **CX**, p. 20; **CXII**, p. 397;
[2] **LV**, p. 37.

cross-breeding. And this characteristic is prolonged southwards to beyond the Somme as far as the Marne. These territorial delimitations within which so many different human ingredients have been stirred up and mixed throughout the ages—for here we are in the everlasting highway of European migration—these districts reflect ethnically the historical events of which they have been the theatre. It is here that the descendants of the neolithic Brachycephals have been in unceasing contact with the dolichocephalic immigrants coming from the north and west. Their successors have continued to keep this " Watch on the Rhine."

This rough and ready distribution, based on data yielded by the cephalic index, does not work out precisely in the same way when stature is employed for its demonstration.[1] Still, although we find variation in certain points, the general facts are confirmed.

Save in one locality, situated to the north of Valenciennes at the extremity of the Ardennes hills, where stature is low, the height of the Belgians is classed in anthropological parlance as medium. As a whole it is about a centimetre greater than that of Frenchmen (Flemish influence), and about a centimetre lower than that of Dutchmen (Walloon influence). This looks like confirmation, as regards the Belgian population as a whole, of what we have just said about the territorial boundaries between the two main European races. By their stature Belgians, as a whole, are no longer Northerners ; but they are not yet quite the same as their French neighbours. They still share, either as a mixed or as a cross-bred population, in the characters of the races responsible for their existence.

It is in territorial delimitations such as these that the value of an accurate distinction between the various human elements would lie. They would quite surely result in revealing the primitive types and in enabling a reconstruction of the features of the original races to be effected.

The linguistic dividing line in Belgium is just as characteristic of human stature as it was of cephalic index.

The Flemish zone contains taller men than the Walloon. The mean stature of the Flemings is 1 metre 661 ; of the

[1] LIII, p. 46.

Walloons 1 metre 648. Furthermore, the proportion of tall individuals is greater in the Flemish zone. Thus it is legitimate to conclude that a certain number of individuals from the Walloon zone passed over into the area of their northern neighbours and thereby diminished the mean height of those neighbours. Here, too, such a discrimination as that of which we spoke just now would put these facts in their proper light.

Belgian authorities have remarked this watering down in the Flemish provinces of the characteristics representative of the Germanic race. Limburg contains the tallest population of all Belgium. Going west from this province we note that height diminishes: "from Limburg to west Flanders the Germans have lost in ethnic influence what they have gained in territorial expansion."[1]

The map showing the present state of stature in Belgium is extremely instructive. In it one sees that if the greatest stature is to be found in Limburg (1 metre 666), the lowest is to be found in Hainaut (1 metre 640), the province in which we remarked the influence of the neighbouring French people.

In this map the province of Brabant well illustrates the contact of the two races in question. Stature, greater than in the Walloon country, is yet less than in the Flemish districts. This is due to the fact that in this mixed zone two arrondissements are Flemish and only one Walloon.

The fact that the Belgian Brachycephals are taller than the French Brachycephals may be explained in the same fashion. It is evident that the Belgian population characterized by a round head-form is of the same origin—since its other characters are concomitant—as the French brachycephalic population. Its greater average height would seem to be due to the infiltration of people of Germanic origin whom we call Flemings to-day. For I do not think there is any ground for bringing in the arrival in that country of immigrants of Asiatic race by way of explanation of this greater height of the Belgian Brachycephals.

These taller Brachycephals and these Dolichocephals whose stature is lower than one would have supposed *a priori*, would clearly appear to express ethnic intermixture. With regard to the quality of these variations, it would seem also that the neolithic Brachycephals and their descendants must

[1] **CXI**, p. 278.

have constituted a sufficiently coherent mass before the arrival of the Germans.

This is what Houzé, also, thought when he wrote the following: " Pre-Germanic Belgium was inhabited by the descendants of the Neanderthal, Cro-Magnon, and Furfooz races. The brachycephalic element must have predominated, because, despite their successive invasions, the tall dolichocephalic Germans have been more or less absorbed. Their influence has made itself felt chiefly in the Belgian Low country, in the Flemish zone. Mid and upper Belgium, although strongly impregnated with German blood, has been better able to resist the immigrants.

The proportions of the various groups of height will change year by year as a result of a more and more intimate intermixture of our populations who are divided by language, cephalic index, the colour of the hair and eyes, stature, and other physical and moral characters already mentioned."

We alluded just now to the Adriatic—or sub-Adriatic—race whose presence it is believed has been demonstrated in some parts of Belgium. In passing I ask myself whether this secondary race of Deniker's is such in appearance only? Is it not a product of the mistake made in making too wide a use of mean characters? I am well aware that there is nothing to prevent the Adriatic race from filtering from the Dinaric region through Croatia, Carinthia and South Germany as far as Lorraine and Belgium; but I do not think such penetration has yet been completely demonstrated. Then, do we know under what conditions the Adriatic race was confined within those areas in which we find it at its most homogeneous and in its greatest concentration? Whence did it come in the beginning? From the north or the east?

According to the present state of our knowledge the Belgian people of the present day appear to be composed in the main of two races. The Nordic (or Germanic) race established itself in the northern part of the country, and the Celtic race in the southern part. Neither the one nor the other is pure. Inhabiting territory where communications were open, they were easily penetrated. The principal result of this juxtaposition and cross-breeding has been diminution in stature and attenuation of dolichocephaly on the one hand, and a slight increase of stature and a diminution of brachycephaly on the other.

Maybe there also exist, notably in the southeastern districts of Belgium, attenuated representatives of the Adriatic race ?

Political opinion has often been highly divergent between the Walloons and Flemings in Belgium. During the great war—and even afterwards—these divergences sometimes took on a separationist complexion.

Is this to say that we must see therein a racial influence—something like the imperative voice of ethnic necessity ? I think, rather, that the history of these latter centuries will explain without any other aid the differences between these " états d'âme."

But the retort may be made that we have also to explain why some peoples accept, or refuse to accept, certain primary destinies out of which their entire future flows. I admit that my difficulty is that I can reply with nothing beyond mere words.

CHAPTER VIII

THE BRITISH ISLES

GREAT BRITAIN and Ireland have not always enjoyed a "splendid isolation". In the early Quaternary, when Europe was finding its geological equilibrium, there was a land bridge between the south of England and the north of France. On its width authorities do not agree. According to some it was relatively narrow, bounded on east and west by constricted gulfs, while others hold that there was a land connection eastwards as far as the Low Countries and westwards as far as Brittany. This was low-lying land in whose thalweg the existing Thames and Rhine waters flowed northeast and those of the Seine west. Thus the geographical aspect of this area was very different from what it is to-day. The St. George's Channel then formed a huge lake, narrow and with an indented shore like a fiord, spreading its waters to the southeast; and the north of Ireland was joined to Scotland. The existing geography is the result of successive land subsidences.[1]

Southern England has been inhabited from very early times. One of the most ancient of all human remains (the Piltdown skull) was found here. Though there is not one of them left in Scotland to-day, the Scottish glaciers long covered the whole of the British Isles with a continuous sheet of ice, with the exception of that part of the country south of the Thames and the mouth of the Severn. Slightly to the north of this line, however, the summits of the Pennine range emerged like lost islands in the immensity of the ice sheet, and pushed a headland out to the sea to the east. At the foot of the ice barrier *Elephas* and the whole procession of quaternary mammals roamed in search of pasture. Palæolithic hunters pursued them, and have left us their implements.

Whence came these palæolithic people? Was it perhaps from France? In any case from regions in those days joined to the south of England.

[1] **LXXVIII**, p. 316 and map.

England, however, would seem to have been inhabited earlier even than this. As I write these lines the special journals announce and comment on fresh discoveries by Reid Moir in the pliocene formations near Ipswich.[1] It looks more and more certain that the implements found in the Red Crag of the upper Pliocene have been deliberately flaked. Hence these finds once more raise the burning question of Tertiary man. Even though it may be answered affirmatively as regard artefacts, we may possibly have to wait a long time before we discover the remains of their fabricator. Yet who knows! Chance is a most gallant worker! Moreover, it is not so long since we came into possession of our few bone fragments of Chellean man, and we have more chances than our predecessors had of making rapid progress in discovery.

In proportion as the glaciers disappeared, with an increasing amelioration of the climate, Man pushed further into the lands freed from the ice. Thus, from Quaternary times onwards England gradually became populated further and further to the north. Civilizations identical with those flourishing on the neighbouring ice-free continent, in France, blossomed also on English soil. The Chellean folk flaked their hand axes (coups de poing) in England, and the Moustierian people their cutters and points. Traces of this industry are found both in the alluvium and in caves. The genealogy of the English industries is recorded stratigraphically in exactly the same manner for the same periods as it is on the Continent.

Furthermore, the crania found in England (the Piltdown skull must be considered as a case apart) exhibit the same ethnic features as those found in neighbouring regions on the Continent. They are representative both of the inferior brutal type (*Homo neanderthalensis*) and the more highly evolved and noble type (Laugerie-Chancelade).

Had the Ipswich skeleton been recognized by science as a discovery whose stratigraphic origin was beyond doubt, England would have possessed the most ancient human remains in Europe, but, as is known, Reid Moir loyally admitted that

[1] **CLXI.** Reid Moir has carried his researches further. In February, 1925, he showed further flints, which he believes to be intentionally flaked, to the Royal Anthropological Institute. These have not been accepted by all prehistorians.

he had been mistaken with regard to the general chronological date to be attributed to this skeleton.[1]

Nevertheless England has contributed to Anthropology one of the earliest and most valuable human remains that our history could have—the Piltdown skull of which mention has been made already and whose philosophical importance is considerable. A certain number of authorities still consider that the Galley Hill cranium which was found in 1888 in the middle of the pleistcene gravel of Northfleet, in Kent,[2] belongs to the Chellean. If this discovery is to be considered authentic in regard to its chronology it would prove that the *Homo sapiens* type goes back to a very distant epoch. Moreover, is this not made plain by the remains of *Eoanthropus dawsoni*? But too much doubt still hangs over the Galley Hill specimen to let us consider it here as demonstrative. Boule, who saw the cranium in the British Museum, definitely reserves judgment.[3]

Human remains belonging to the Moustierian race are, so far, rare in England. In 1884 there was found in a clay pocket in the Bury St Edmunds chalk in Suffolk a few fragments of jawbones and skulls "barely in a sufficient state of preservation to allow of them being classed as of Neanderthal type."[4]

In 1911[5] Marett discovered a few human molars in association with bones of *Rhinoceros tichorhinus* and Moustierian implements in the St. Brelade cave in Jersey.[6]

Human remains belonging to the later period of the Palæolithic are likewise extremely rare in England, though the earliest discovery of a pleistocene skeleton (not counting

[1] **CLXI**, p. 194.

[2] **CXXIII**, p. 178 (a chapter is devoted to this discovery) and p. 143 (This reference is to the 1915 edition. In the 1925 edition Sir Arthur Keith (p. xiii of Preface to 2nd edition) admits that his faith in the antiquity of Galley Hill man has been shaken considerably.) (Translator's Note.)

[3] **XXI**, p. 181.

[4] The provenance of this quotation is not given. Sir Arthur Keith says, on p. 246 of the new edition of **CXXIII**, "the Bury St. Edmunds skull is such a fragmentary document that one may well hesitate in forming any certain conclusion as to the type of person it represents." (Translator's Note.)

[5] The actual discovery was made in 1910. (Translator's Note.)

[6] **CLI** and **CXXIII**, p. 183 (2nd edition.)

the Cannstadt skull found in Württemberg—whose chronological position is doubtful) was made here—the famous Red Lady of Paviland dug up in 1823 by Buckland in the Paviland cave in Wales, and now in the Oxford Museum. The description was due to the fact that the bones were coloured red by iron oxide. The skeleton dates from the Aurignacian period and presents the Cro-Magnon racial characters.[1]

Up to date the discoveries made in England have in no way contradicted the testimony of France as regard human types or upset the palæolithic genealogy established.

Although the generations of Man at the close of the Pleistocene followed one another in the British Isles in the same order of culture and ethnic type as on the continent, England, nevertheless, was to be isolated from the rest of Europe for a certain period. When the polished stone civilization appeared on the scene the then dolichocephalic folk of England were not invaded by Brachycephals as were the dolichocephalic folk of France of the same period. The sea, which at that time had for long cut off from each other these two portions of the continent, temporarily saved the British Isles from this invasion. The English folk of the time accepted the new civilization, but the men responsible for it remained without, or if they got into the country they only came in, so to speak, in minute doses.

We have seen that the skeletons in the long barrows had a dolichocephalic cranium and a leptoprosopic face. They belonged to the group of neolithic Dolichocephals described in the chapter on France. It is only in the bronze age that any notable quantity of Brachycephals are to be found in England.

The round barrows contain quite a different kind of skeleton from the long barrows. Thurnam demonstrates[2] that 65 skeletons found in the long barrows all gave relatively very low cephalic indices (from 63 to 77), the mean being 71. This figure shows a very high degree of dolichocephaly. Seventy crania from the round barrows, on the contrary, yielded no index lower than 74; the most highly brachycephalic individuals reached 89. The mean cephalic index of this

[1] **CCXLVI**, p. 1; **CXXIII**, p. 67 (2nd edition); **XXI**, p. 261. (See also Prof. Sollas's Huxley Memorial Lecture, *Journ.* Roy. Anthrop. Inst., 1913, vol. xliii, p. 1.)

[2] **CCLV**, p. 385.

series is 81. Placing these two groups side by side, in two columns, one sees that the figures of the 2nd column begin where the others leave off. The picture is that of a genuine succession of foreign elements. And if the round barrows contain a certain number of dolichocephalic skeletons the explanation is simple—the Brachycephals newly arrived on English territory did not exterminate the earlier population (maybe, moreover, they came in peace). There was no reason why they should exterminate them ; they simply mixed with the older population. The bronze age tombs present the earliest image of that anthropologically composite group, in which Dolichocephals predominate, which was thenceforward to become the English people. Moreover, these Brachycephals were never, at any period of history or in any part of the British Isles, to become sufficiently numerous to impose themselves ethnically on the population. Even to-day the ethnic physiognomy of England, considered as a whole, is distinctly dolichocephalic.

During the great war the journalists of Western Europe who visited the British front all reported the impression made on them by the physique of the troops, their generally tall stature and their air of good health. Without being anthropologists they realized that they saw before them a distinct race having special features such as height, pigmentation, etc. This is proof of the fact that even to-day certain regions have been less ethnically contaminated than others.

*

* *

What are the present anthropological characteristics of the inhabitants of the British Isles ?

Quite a constellation of anthropologists whose work goes back to an early date (and here we must mention Beddoe), have studied England, so that we are enabled to grasp in its main lines the ethnic physiognomy of her people.

The first fact to emerge from a glance at the population as a whole is that the English must be classed as belonging to the Nordic (or Germanic) race on account of their tall stature, their dolichocephaly and their fair hair. But perfect ethnic harmony does not exist everywhere throughout the United Kingdom and the above characters are not always concomitant as they ought to be, racially, for a precise diagnosis of the type.

In his chart of the cephalic index Ripley[1] does not cite any mean index higher than 80.4 (in the west of Ireland) ; and the lowest figure (76 and odd fractions) is met with both in Ireland and in Scotland and England. In Deniker's map[2] a large part of the British Isles remains blank. Such areas as are coloured are dolichocephalic and sub-dolichocephalic (Scotland, England, Wales and Ireland). One small area in the west of Ireland remains apart. It lies in the peninsular dominated by the Mayo mountains in a Gaelic speaking district, where the percentage of dark-haired individuals is very high.

Reading over again the work of Beddoe and examining Ripley's and Deniker's maps, one realizes the urgent necessity for those regional investigations which we never cease to call for in all lands, and which are here needed for a knowledge of the descriptive anthropology of the British Isles. When, for example, one places the distribution of hair colour side by side with the distribution of dolichocephalic indices and of stature, one is very much struck by certain correspondences. And the anthropological maps, which sometimes are based only on two or three thousand observed cases, are really inadequate. Frequently, moreover, they lead to serious errors on the part of writers who do not possess the qualifications necessary for a critical appreciation of such data.

The blond regions of the British Isles are mainly in the north and east of England, and after these come the south and north of Scotland. But in between these two last blond zones there are districts in Argyll and Inverness where dark-haired people are numerous, whereas in no part of England are there so many dark-haired folk except Cornwall. There are very few fair individuals in Ireland, it would seem, and it is somewhat surprising for more than one reason to find such a large proportion of dark-haired people in Ulster. One would not expect it there, knowing that in Ulster there are so many English immigrants. And at the same time one is surprised to note that Ulster, relatively so rich in pigmentation, seems to contain a population of rather tall men. I think that we are here confronted with an insufficient differentiation of these different characters and we should only risk premature conclusions were we to try to discriminate further. Are we faced with the results of cross-breeding where one of the

[1] CCXX, p. 300.
[2] LV.

progenitors supplied the tall stature and dolichocephaly and the other the dark hair ?

Stature merits more detailed study, district by district, throughout the whole of the British Isles, than it has hitherto received. It would be sure to reveal interesting facts about the early population settled in Albion from pre-historic times. Certain areas are inhabited by people whose mean height presents notable variations even within circumscribed districts, and this may be a hint of originally heterogeneous ethnic elements. We must not lose sight of the arrival of the brachycephalic type at least with the introduction of bronze. What has become of that element in the population of the British Isles as a whole ? Did they remain concentrated in certain localities ? Or did they mix their blood with that of other types ?

In any case, such as they are, the data relative to English stature do yield information of lively interest.

The first point is that Scotland appears to possess the tallest men in the world. The Scottish Highlanders—especially one group of them—are the tallest men in existence. They are taller than the Patagonians, who for long figured at the top of the anthropological lists. They are taller than the tallest men in Africa (the Fulani, probably)[1], or in North America (probably the Cheyenne and Mohave Indians), taller than any of the Polynesians.

Moreover, tall men are common to almost the whole of Scotland. Their mean height is greater than 1 metre 72. To equal this figure in Europe we must go to the Livonians of Courland, and to the European population of Norway. In one locality, Galloway, in the southwest, the Scots stature even reaches 1 metre 78. Stature decreases with regularity as we go north from this district. It decreases suddenly in the west, in Lanark (1 metre 73) ; and this is interesting because across on the other side of the water Ireland constitutes a centre of lower stature. Irish influence might have been felt on the west side of Scotland. And such a modification, coming from such a source, would indicate human emigration from Ireland into Scotland at some undetermined date which ought to be discovered.

[1] Recent observations on the people of Dahomey would seem to indicate that there are very tall individuals in West Africa : the average of the Pila-Pila (a little group which, perhaps, was a picked one) measured by Gironcourt was 1 metre 87. **CCLXVII**, p. 538.

However, in spite of the diminished height in the west the stature of the Scots none the less remains extraordinarily great by comparison with the world's mean. These tall men were always formidable fighters: the Romans were unable to penetrate their mountain fastnesses.

To what can we ascribe this great stature? This is the kind of phenomenon that must embarrass those who put everything down to the influence of environment.

In England there is a decrease in stature as we go from north southwards, due to the influence, in the north, of the tall stature of the Scots, notably those, so near the border, in the hills of Galloway. On the east coast the stature is great, as also in the Cornish peninsular. And as regards Cornwall, the superposition of the map for height on that of the chart for hair and eye colour, with a view of arriving at an ethnic diagnosis, likewise gives food for thought.

In the English midlands the average height of the people only reaches 1 metre 68. This is a low figure by comparison with that for Scotland, but it is high in relation to the rest of Europe, and calls for certain observations. Here we are among the most industrial centres of the country, in an area where the manufacturing towns are most thickly concentrated. We have already called attention to the fact that stature is usually higher in those rural districts surrounding urban centres. Do the English towns form an exception to this rule? Beddoe, in his investigations, noted that the height of industrial workers in England appears to be below that of the country people. But, as I have already remarked, the further our anthropological investigations advance the more do we note the reality of this increased height in large urban centres.

What, then, are we to think of this lower stature in the midlands and south of England?

Is it due, in part at all events, to some as yet unrevealed ethnic factor? It is an open question—all the more so in that it would appear that the ethnic influence of those human groups whose historical arrival in the British Isles is known to us, has persisted quite distinctly.

In general the tall stature zones correspond with the districts in which the Scandinavians formerly settled. The lower stature of the present population (is it really lower, or is this a deceptive appearance due to the means?) in those parts where the Angles and Saxons got a footing would suggest that the invaders were smaller people. In a general way, too, the people of localities having Celtic names are of smaller stature.[1]

Nevertheless we repeat that all these facts call for confirmation by more careful investigations than those which yielded the results of which we now make use, investigations as strictly detailed as those Houzé demanded for Belgium when he proposed that each commune should be analysed separately.

Wales is inhabited by smaller men than those of the rest of the British Isles. Do these people not claim a different origin, and do they not speak another language ? All the same, we must remain sceptical as regards such a correspondence. The harmony is too facile ! Was Wales always and entirely a land so set apart that ethnically it could never have been contaminated.

As for Ireland, it is in much the same case as England in regard to the stature of its inhabitants. The littoral is almost everywhere peopled by tall men, whereas in the interior one finds smaller people. One fact indicated by Taylor merits notice.[2] The shore regions characterized by tall stature are precisely those in which traces of Scandinavian place-names are to be found. Thus we see in Ireland something of the nature noted in England—the persistence of the population which came formerly from Norway.

Speaking of Ireland, we must not omit to mention one further little fact. The locality in which the lowest stature has so far been noted by anthropologists is exactly that in which, in connection with the cephalic index, we have drawn attention to the presence of individuals with brachycephalic heads—the western peninsular dominated by the Mayo mountains.

[1] We must also envisage the influence of Brythons. It is believed that the first Brythons arrived in England during the Hallstatt period (formerly their arrival was considered to be between 500 and 300 B.C., during the first La Tène period). The new hypothesis is based on the discovery of earlier pottery coming from Celtic or Celticized lands and found for the first time at Hengistbury Head to the west of Southampton (*Report of the Society of Antiquaries of London*, No. iii, 1915). This ceramic (keeled or globular vases recalling those of the Pyrenean tumuli dating from the close of the Hallstatt period) carries on the bronze age ceramics of Bavaria and would represent the arrival in Aquitania of Celts who had come from thence (**CXV**, p. 268). Might we not suppose that these importers of Celtic pottery had arrived still earlier in England, and could we not attribute to them the brachycephaly of the round barrows ? I merely put the question.

[2] **LIII**, p. 60.

This area serves to demonstrate at one and the same time the solid basis for our ideas about morphological characters being hereditary, and also the necessity to make more exact investigations so that regional analysis can everywhere be effected. This confined district, facing the Atlantic, possesses at once the lowest stature and by its mean character the nearest approach to brachycephaly in the whole of the British Isles. Over and above this, dark hair is common in the locality. The attention of historians and linguists ought to be drawn to this fact of ethnological geography—this probable relic of a forgotten group.

If we sum up what the distribution of the cephalic index reveals in the four political divisions of the British Isles, we shall note the remarkable uniformity of the mean index. Looked at thus, England, Scotland, Wales and Ireland are peopled by Dolichocephals and sub-Dolichocephals. The Scots would appear to have the longest heads (index of 77.8), and the Welsh the shortest (index of 78.8). But the geographical masses to which we apply these mean indices are, as we know, more apparent than real. English writers have recently shown the presence of numerous Brachycephals in Ireland, and, what is much more interesting because less expected, of Mesaticephals and sub-Brachycephals at many points in the north of Scotland and in England.

Evidently the British, despite their island isolation, do not represent—or no longer represent—a pure race. Moreover, historical events seen in the light of Anthropology would suggest this conclusion. It is only necessary to recall the characteristics of the dolichocephalic races of the old and new stone ages, and to call to mind the brachycephalic population which succeeded them in the bronze age, and in all likelihood, in the iron age. Both types have left descendants. A certain number of these, confined within geographical bounds not conducive to intermixture, have been able to preserve their ancestral characters; the rest have been crossed. We shall note, however, that in both cases the product is nearly always tall. This character has survived ethnic mixture, and has dominated it. This is a fact which ethnologists and eugenists should underline.

The British Isles, by their very insularity, pose a certain number of problems to anthropologists in which historians may find arguments. Is it not asserted that nothing is known of the population which inhabited these islands before Cæsar landed in England? We are told that Celts and Gaels and Iberians lived in Ireland and that at a later date the Scots invaded Caledonia. Did they not give their name to Scotland? But who were the ancestors of these Scots? Where did they come from before they settled down in Ireland? Were they not the descendants of the Scandinavians, of those hardy navigators who landed, in many periods, in the British Isles?[1]

We noted above how great is the stature of the Scots. This people, furthermore, is largely dolichocephalic. Did the primitive inhabitants of Ireland possess these same characters? But these morphological characters would not seem to square with those we imagine ought to be represented by the Celts, the Gaels and the Iberians. Ireland, then, was already an ethnic complex! How did this come about? One of two things must have happened: either the Scots, arriving in Scotland, found there a population exhibiting the characters still possessed by the Scottish people and did not in any way modify them, or else the Scots were of the same "ethnic colour" as the Caledonians whom they invaded. Or we may suppose again that the Scots were of different race from the Caledonians, but that they were more or less absorbed by them.

As for the Angles, Picts, Saxons, Danes and Normans, whose invasions of the British Isles followed one upon the other, they would all appear to have belonged to the Germanic race. Thus the British Isles would have known two main dolichocephalic stocks, the prehistoric people (up to and including the Neolithic folk), and the Kymric invaders. The brachycephalic stock of the bronze age whose presence we note in continental Europe, notably in the Swiss Lake dwellings, might have been the one that provided the British brachycephalic races; it would have been the first cause of cross-breeding. Should we perhaps consider it, according to the new ideas, to be an advance guard of the Brythons of the Hallstatt period?[2]

[1] We said further back that those coastal regions in Ireland in which the tallest people are to be found (Taylor) are those which show traces of Scandinavian place-names.

[2] Round-headed individuals of the same type as those found at Ofnet and recently at Solutré, of Aurignacian age, were excavated in 1922 by the Speleological Society of Bristol University from Aveline's Hole and described by Prof. E. Fawcett and Sir A. Keith in Nos. 1, 2 and 4 of the published *Proceedings*, vol. i. 1919-20, 1920-21, and 1923-24. Thus people having an index of 80 were living in the West of England somewhere between 8,000 and 10,000 B.C. (Translator's Note.)

By a proposition in the opposite sense, the British Isles give us some information as to the anthropological characters of the peoples mentioned above—Angles, Picts, etc., about whom we know nothing certain. Judging by the present ethnic physiognomy of the British Isles, it would seem probable that these peoples belonged to the tall, fresh-complexioned race of Dolichocephals. They were Nordic groups.[1] A description of the present-day English would serve as a morphological description of these old invaders, whose characters are known to us only from accounts whose greatest virtue lies no more in their precision than in their authenticity.

The Angles, a people of ancient Germany, contrary to many of the tribes of that country, really belonged to the race bearing that name.

[1] In the Preface to the 2nd edition (1925) of **CXXIII**, p. vii, Sir Arthur Keith says :—" In England during the last ten years many things have happened which alter our outlook on ancient man. To the list of crania of Palæolithic Englishman I have had to add three found in a cave in the Mendips by the enthusiastic members of the Speleological Society of Bristol University, and one from Baker's Hole on the Thames, near Gravesend, entrusted to me for examination by Mr. Martin A. C. Hinton. These bear out the conclusion reached in the last edition that men with long, narrow heads lived in England long before the dawn of the Neolithic period." These discoveries are respectively described on pp. 140 ff. and 162 ff. (Translator's Note.)

CHAPTER IX

HOLLAND

THE Low Countries, like the British Isles north of the Thames, and like the other northern countries, cannot contribute data to the earliest European archæology. To be convinced of the impossibility of their so doing one has only to recall the great glacial expansion which covered northern Europe with an ice sheet up to about the level of Antwerp. The localities which would have been the most favourable for human occupation were Dutch Limburg and the hilly country dominating it, beyond Maastricht, whose rich flint quarries were exploited by the neolithic people and in which area the Campignian industry left so many souvenirs. Holland will not add to the list of prehistoric skeletons yielded by European excavation any such data as were supplied to human Palæontology by her more favoured neighbour, Belgium. But the modern Anthropology of Holland will contribute some very interesting information.

Only a few years ago Holland was considered to belong entirely to the Nordic group. The language spoken by its inhabitants certainly helped to suggest this attribution. The men of the Low Countries were grouped together with the Germans of the west in order arbitrarily—as we shall see—to extend the habitat of the tall blond Dolichocephals of the continent.

To-day we see matters in a somewhat different light. And although many Dutch folk certainly belong to the Nordic race, they have close beside them in their own territory a fairly large proportion of fellow citizens who do not resemble them physically in the least. A large part of southwest Holland is peopled by Brachycephals, frequently brunets, and these roundheads who occupy a part of the Dutch territory are not immigrants of yesterday. Fifty years ago Sasse picked out ultra-brachycephalic specimens with a cephalic index of 85.6, from among crania in the Zeeland tumuli

(Zuid-Beveland island). Further, throughout this southwest portion of the country, in which inundations have been so frequent and so destructive, and in which the human work of defence against them has been so marvellous, the flooded towns whose cemeteries have been discovered, notably several cities submerged in the sixteenth century, also yielded, as we shall see, a large number of obvious Brachycephals. Thus it is certain that when the Romans first came to know the Batavi—we will give this name to all the Dutch for the moment—they were not exclusively composed of those tall, blue-eyed men who so greatly astonished the Legionaries. There were already among them, in numbers impossible to picture from our modern statistics, men of the Celtic race—Brachycephals with dark hair and eyes.

For all those who are interested not only in events, but in their causes, and for all those who seek to link the men themselves with historic events, it would be of the greatest interest to know which of these two human groups was on Dutch soil first. The anthropologists of the country are not in agreement on this point, and two different camps of ethnologists have asserted, with equal authority, the priority of the group whose defenders they have constituted themselves.

This question of history will answer itself when more numerous discoveries of ancient burials have been made, and have been described with the necessary method. But, we repeat, except in Dutch Limburg, there is little chance of meeting with human remains earlier than the Neolithic.

We shall have to settle one controversial matter at once—the question of the survival of the Neanderthaloid type in the Zuider Zee region. We know that among the dolichocephalic Frisian crania a form was met with which, by its relative platycephaly, its prominent superciliary arches, and its flattened forehead, recalls—though not very closely—the classic type of the Neanderthal race. Thus *Batavus genuinus* of Blumenbach, studied by Huxley, and mentioned by de Quartrefages and Hamy in their *Crania ethnica,* need not detain us long. These, spatially, were exceptional characters, more or less exaggerated in one direction or another, such as are to be found in every craniological series. It would only be to exaggerate its importance to consider this type as the survival, in one small corner of Holland, of the ancient Moustierian human type.[1]

Let us take a rapid glance at Holland's anthropological inventory. In general the men of the Low Countries are notably above the average height (1 metre 675 to 1 metre 68). But such a datum gives no information as to whether the Dutch race is homogeneous or otherwise, and even completely disguises the ethnic realities of the country. It falsifies the synthetic picture that we have to build up. It is only when we come to examine individual specimens that we find that about one-third of the inhabitants exceed 1 metre 70 ; which leads us to think that there must be a certain number of Dutchmen of small and medium stature. But are these scattered among the general mass of the population, or are they to be found in special areas ?

The distribution of stature according to provinces at once throws light on the question. In fact, even when it is merely indicated by the inadequate method of averaging, we shall see that stature increases as we go from south northwards. In general, those Dutchmen dwelling nearest to Belgium are smaller than their fellow citizens of the northern provinces. Thus the men of North Brabant are much smaller (1 metre 65) than those of Friesland (1 metre 69). We need go no further to realize the ethnic duality of Holland. The three southern provinces of the Low Countries—Zeeland, North Brabant and Limburg—exhibit the three lowest statures of the whole kingdom. Limburg, however, contiguous to Germany, contains a large proportion of individuals of Germanic race. Of the above three provinces, it has the least low stature (1 metre 668).

Thus, height alone, a single element among racial distinctions, permits us to assert that Holland does not contain a pure race, but that two races at least are to be met with in its territory. We have already noted this phenomenon in Belgium, but there it was more apparent because it was still marked by a difference in language.

[1] I nevertheless recall that Virchow gave to a few crania from the islands of Urk and Marken, in the Zuider Zee, a genealogical significance when he set down the early Frisians as belonging, not to the Germanic but to a much more primitive Neanderthaloid type !

Following Bolk[1] we may at once name these two races—one is Kymric, the other Celtic. At what period did they respectively establish themselves ? And under what conditions are they met with ? Which of them, among the tribes whose names the Romans preserved, belonged to the Kymric and which to the Celtic race ?

The solution of the last point, which would be of some interest to historians, should not be impossible if the tribes mentioned by the Roman chroniclers have stayed where they were then located. As a fact, anthropological studies are sufficiently far advanced in Holland (though this is not to say they are complete—far from it) to enable us to superpose the map giving the anthropological characters of the present-day population on that of the distribution of the ancient tribes of Cæsar's day.

The statistics of height by themselves will allow of our finding the point of contact of the two principal races. This lies in the boundary zone stretching along the northwest of Belgium and southwest of Holland, and lying in the present-day Belgian areas of the province of Antwerp and the Flanders, and the present-day Dutch areas of North Brabant and Zeeland.

This last district still exhibits a lively image of this juxtaposition of races. The whole of the western portion is inhabited by men notably taller (1 metre 678) than in the eastern portion (1 metre 654). The maritime zone—we shall adduce proof thereof, later on—really seems to hold men of the Kymric race : coasts, maybe, occupied by Scandinavian pirates ? The landward zone, which in the map looks like a geographical portion of Belgium, and contains the little town of Axel, exhibits a stature that is even remarkably low (1 metre 625), the lowest for the whole of Holland—though the mean is obtained from insufficient numbers. Later on we shall see whether other morphological characters are associated with height in such a way as to mark the existence in this locality of a special ethnic group.

The island of Walcheren is a kind of ethnic synthesis, in miniature, of the two races in question. Its western portion contains tall men, far exceeding the Dutch average (Kymric race). The eastern portion, on the contrary, is inhabited by

[1] XVIII.

the smallest people in the kingdom (Celtic race). Their height is that of the inhabitants of mainland Zeeland.

Dutch pigmentation and the Dutch cephalic index as a whole afford a striking demonstration of the general fact that there are two principal races, clearly differentiated, in the southern Low Countries.

The whole of the northern part of the country and all those districts lying along the Zuider Zee are inhabited by longer-headed people than those of the south. Nevertheless the northern provinces do not exhibit such extreme dolichocephaly as is seen in Scandinavia among the North Norwegians and the Swedes. The mean index for North Holland is slightly higher than among these people. Admixture with the Celtic race? Yet, as a whole, they are at least sub-dolichocephalic. Thus Friesland has a mean index of 79.7; Groningen province 79.8; South Holland 79; and Gelderland 79. North Brabant itself should yield an index of 79. All this betokens sub-dolichocephaly. The province of North Holland appears to be mesocephalic. In all likelihood it owes this character to the city of Amsterdam, which groups together representatives of both the main races and whose cephalic index is the highest in Holland (not counting the southwest of the kingdom), namely 80.7.

With regard to the general dolichocephaly (or sub-dolichocephaly) of the north of Holland, we must add that the crania disinterred from the early tumuli and studied by Sasse and by Folmer showed indices of a far higher degree of dolichocephaly than those of the present-day.[1] One may say that in the course of her history Holland has become brachycephalized. This in no way prejudices the question as to which of the two races first inhabited the country.

A word as to the pigmentation of the Dutch.

Eye colour has been the subject of a long and minute investigation by Bolk on nearly 500,000 persons. In order to eliminate foreign ethnic factors the Jews were not included in this analysis.[2]

It is impossible to enter into all the details here, but Bolk's map[3] makes the certainty of the existence of these two human

[1] **CCXXX**; **LXXI**; **LV**, p. 39; **CLIII**, p. 5.

[2] They would not have materially altered the results of the investigation.

[3] **XVIII**, p. 579.

groups jump to the eyes—in the north a light-eyed area, in the south an area in which the people have dark eyes.

Now we are in a position to associate light coloured eyes with dolichocephaly and tall stature in order to assert the existence of the Germanic type in the northern provinces, and there is every chance of finding similar associations of a different set of characters revealing the presence of the Celtic race in the southern area. In the interests of accuracy, however, we must make a comment on the subject of Bolk's map. His investigation, important as it was, is not beyond criticism. It was carried out, as a matter of fact, in the schools. and we know how pigmentation may change during life. Fortunately the very large numbers on which the Dutch writer's investigation was based give his results a good chance of being accurate. However—that still remains to be seen!

Travellers and writers who have noted the relative frequency of dark hair and eyes in the south of Holland have at once put this pigmentary wealth down to Spanish influence dating from the time of Charles V. The Dutch have legitimately protested against such an explanation. Modern anthropological investigations have supplied them with much more demonstrative reasons for not believing in such intermixture, only too easy to invent on the strength of historical events. The brown eyes and hair of the southern provinces of Holland are far older than the Spanish period.[1] One may consider it, without much fear of going wrong, to be prehistoric and as dating here, as in Belgium, from the neolithic invasions.

We must now consider the southwest of the Netherlands separately—that region in which, as we already know, we shall realize better than anywhere else the coming into contact of the two principal races of Western Europe. In this confined area there are facts of a nature to encourage our researches, and results which should inspire confidence in anthropological endeavour.

We have already mentioned that the Dutch anthropologist Sasse, when describing the crania found in the ancient tumuli at Nieuwland (Zuid-Beveland island), make known their extreme brachycephaly—85.6. Was this something exceptional—a brachycephalic island completely isolated,

[1] One ought to be able, further, to associate with these the dolicho cephaly of the Spaniards, their stature, etc.

spatially and temporally, in the midst of a quite different ethnic world ?

We know that the whole of southwest Holland is land reclaimed from the sea. The alluvia of the Rhine-Schelde delta, at the mercy of river and sea, are of an incredible instability. The lands comprised between these two divagating river mouths have only been created by dint of prodigious courage, patience under adversity, and the most arduous toil. It has been said that Egypt is the gift of the Nile, Holland the gift of the Rhine. The comparison is inaccurate. In the Low Countries human toil alone is responsible. Certain portions of Holland are the result of the greatest defence against the elements the world has ever seen. And in spite of their gigantic labour and their dykes, the Dutch are often vanquished by the ocean. During the last five centuries many a town has been swallowed up by the sea.

Occasionally we find the contents of the cemeteries washed up by the tide ; thus we are enabled to find out what the early population of Zeeland was like. Crania from the town of Saaftingen, submerged in 1540, were extreme in their brachycephaly (cephalic index of 86.8) ; those from the cemetery of Colijnsplaat even more so (88.2). Sasse's results do not, therefore, stand alone. They are extended spatially and go back with perfect precision into the past. Nevertheless, the skeletons washed up by the tide from the town of Reymerswaal, swallowed up in 1631, were much less brachycephalic (82.4). We are here on the boundary of the ethnic island.

The town of Domburg, on the northern shore of the island of Walcheren has been the subject of special study. The place where the cemetery was situated was called Woonplaats der Gothen in the early maps, in spite of the fact that the Goths are supposed never to have lived in the island. The skulls from this cemetery used to be attributed to the Normans who in former days made frequent incursions within the island borders ; but there is no proof whatever that such a theory is justified. It was based entirely on the differences noted between the types found in this graveyard and the present-day population, of which some explanation was naturally attempted. The majority of the crania of ancient Domburg are dolichocephalic. The tables giving the measurements made by de Man and Sasse indicated no more than 12 per cent. of subbrachycephals.

It has been said that the name Zeeland means *hat Zeeuwen land*—the land of the Suevi. But at what period did these Suevi, who for long had been raiding, take the place of the Menapii who occupied the delta of the rivers in Cæsar's day? Saint Eloi, who converted the Suevi in the seventh century, makes no further mention of the Menapii who "directly according to the inhabitants are called, in Latin, by the name of *Zeelandi*. But are these the same Suevi as those who, according to Tacitus, pillaged the Usipetes coming from the British Isles in the year 83? Or are they those Suevi who, as early as the time of Augustus, were settled on the left bank of the Rhine, or those who, in the time of Honorius (395-423) came to establish themselves in these regions by the permission of the inhabitants after having been driven out of their own country by the Ostrogoths? These last were attacked in the fifth century by the Frisians, but they remained in Zeeland until 881, when they were almost annihilated by Godfried the Dane."[1]

On the authority especially of the cephalic characters revealed by the skeletons found at Domburg, de Man came to the conclusion that this old cemetery "held the bodies of early Suevi, Anglo-Saxons, Normans and Zeelanders up till 920; and that the population that afterwards inhabited Walcheren for long retained the dolichocephalic type", but that, gradually, the Brachycephals coming probably from the south of Holland and the north of Brabant, modified this primitive type.[2] According to this writer the present-day brachycephalic population is foreign to the locality, and represents immigrants who settled here chiefly from the tenth century onwards.

When he grouped these early cemeteries chronologically de Man noted that the earlier they were the higher the proportion of dolichocephalic types they contained. Thus old Domburg, already mentioned, contained 70 per cent. of crania whose cephalic index was below 76. The pre-fifteenth century cemetery of Goes held 62 per cent.; that of Bagÿnehof 59 per cent. (the date of the interments here probably ranged from 1271 to 1723); whilst that of the port of Vlissingen (Flushing) in use from 1600 to 1812, contained no more than 33 per cent. of the dolichocephalic type.

[1] **CXX**, p. 144.
[2] **CXLVII**.

The Belgian anthropologist Jacques is of exactly the contrary opinion to de Man as regards the early origin of the Zeelanders. He thinks that the Brachycephals represent the primitive human element. According to him the ethnic evidence is in agreement with the historic evidence in permitting the conclusion that "the population inhabiting the islands after the period of the Saxon, Frisian and Norman invasions is that which has continued to keep and which still keeps to-day traces of the primitive brachycephaly." [1] He notes that the present-day neighbouring population has a much lower cephalic index than that of the early population; and, therefore, one must admit that the Brachycephals of Zeeland have remained in the localities where they are still to be seen to-day from the very earliest times.

On the strength of this I am not far from accepting Jacques' hypothesis, especially after what we have found in Belgium.

In Cæsar's time Holland was known as the island of the Batavi, and he made a treaty with this people for the conquest of Belgic Gaul. Two other peoples also appear as groups of sufficient importance to hold the attention of historians—the Frisians, whose name was to take the place of that of the Batavi, and the Bructeri. These last occupied the banks of the Ems, having Frisians on the north, Batavi on the west, and Usipetes on the south. It would seem almost certain that these tribes were made up of men of Kymric race. History, which considers that they are related to the Germanic tribes, is here in agreement with Ethnology.

If I am asked what I think about the Brachycephals of southwest Holland, I refer the reader to the chapter on the anthropology of Germany. It will be remembered that inhabitants with round heads have been known in that country from the Mesolithic, evidenced by the collective interments of Ofnet. These Brachycephals still occupy a large part of the south and centre of Germany. They crossed the Rhine in large numbers at different periods.

It is possible that we find in Zeeland a remnant of this race which sojourned on the west of the Rhine and was driven by the pressure of invasions from the east to the territory between the Rhine and the Schelde in Brabant. They

[1] **CXX**, p. 149.

constructed mounds of earth—*terpen*—to protect themselves against river floods and the ravages of the sea in this land of rivers and great marshes. These intrepid barbarians whose descendants dwelt, according to the Latin historians, on "floating lands" would have developed into those formidable antagonists of the allied forces of ocean and river who so magnificently created maritime southwest Holland. Perhaps, too, these prehistoric Brachycephals, in choosing to cross the Rhine like some of the early Belgians at its southernmost portion, then followed the corridor of the Meuse?

The anthropology of the Low Countries is far from having said its last word. Here is a single instance, to end up with. Bolk has noted a well preserved blond type, which he does not class as belonging to the Nordic race, in the most northerly part of North Holland, in Friesland and Drenthe. These blond people have blue eyes, but their stature is smaller than that characteristic of *Homo europaeus*, and their skulls incline towards brachycephaly. Further, the face is broad and short. What are we to think of this type?

There still lies many a good day's work ahead of our Dutch colleagues who would know in every detail the ethnic elements of their country.

CHAPTER X

SCANDINAVIA

CIVILIZATION is much younger in the north of Europe than in the central and southern portions of the continent. We know the reason for this difference: the frontal expansion of the Scottish and Scandinavian glaciers united was so great that a large part of northern Europe was submerged.

Until quite recently it was usual to make the history of the Scandinavian peoples open during the kitchen-midden period (polished stone age).[1] During the last few years it has become evident, as the result of accurately studied discoveries, that we must place it somewhat further back in the past.

In Denmark, as long ago as 1900, the Mellerup finds in the to-day well-known Maglemose peat, in the west of Zealand island, showed Sarauw[2] that Scandinavian prehistory went further back than the period of the shell mounds, and this by virtue of the double revelation of stratigraphy and the nature of the objects recovered. Quite recently excavations in the Svaerdborg peat have confirmed this view. Thus a new page of early history is added to the ancient past of the Nordic peoples. This period is known as the "oldest stone age" with the mental reservation that the expression applies only to Scandinavian lands.[3]

It was under the peat at no great depth that the Danish archæologists made their discoveries, at the edge of a bed of mud lying immediately below the peat deposit. The archæological horizon is a shallow one. It is rich in flint and contains a large number of animal bones.

These prehistoric accumulations appear to be of considerable extent, but at present we cannot postulate a sedentary condition for these people: no permanent settlements have

[1] Sophus Müller's *Nordische Altertumskunde* will suffice in general. **CLXVII.**

[2] **CCXXIX.**

[3] **CXXII.**

been revealed. Were these men simply hunters who sojourned temporarily in lands rich in game?

The débris of animal bones, recovered in large quantities, and indicating long occupation, have enabled the fauna of the period to be reconstructed. The list includes the species usually met with in the polished stone age. The Danish archæologists have emphasised the frequency with which Elk, European Bison and Beaver occur in these deposits. The dog is already domesticated. This discovery places the earliest domestication of animals somewhat further back than was thought.

One feature of the earliest Scandinavian civilization must be noted—the exceptional frequency of implements of bone and deerhorn. In this connection we will quote F. Johansen: "Implements of bone and deerhorn are more numerous and more varied in this than in any subsequent period of our prehistory. No other feature contributes more to bestow on the earliest phase of our civilization that special character which strikes us at first sight."[1]

Whence came this people whose bone and horn implements were already so rich in variety of form—hatchets of different kinds, hammers and clubs, picks and mattocks, spear points both straight-edged and barbed, etc.? From what parts did they come? What was the ethnic origin of these men who do not appear to have known the use of pottery, and to what physical type did they belong?

Unfortunately human remains from this particular archæological horizon are practically non-existent.

Bound up with this primitive population is the whole problem of the peopling of Scandinavia, and, perhaps, of the Baltic lands to the east as well. Doubtless this occupation of the Danish peninsular by Man was effected from the south in a northerly direction. It was probably accomplished by the tall dolichocephalic race which to this day peoples the Scandinavian countries. We shall come to know it better in the periods immediately following this earliest stone age.

Denmark also had its Reindeer age. But it is not synchronous with that of Western Europe. In the north the archæological horizon containing the remains of this ruminant is more recent. In their northward migration after the first

[1] **CXXII**, p. 289.

melting of the quaternary ice the reindeer herds stopped for a long time in the Danish prairies and woods, and Man certainly hunted them in this region. Danish archæologists thus admit a still more ancient human phase in Denmark than that which we have just discussed, despite the fact that its existence has not been conclusively demonstrated. "We may consider it as an accepted fact," says Johansen[1] "that our earliest stone age was not inaugurated by the Svaerdborg-Mullerup civilization." In fact, was there not found in 1904, in the environs of Viborg, the cut upper extremity of a reindeer antler? And should not this find be added to the discoveries of three picks, also of reindeer horn, in Vejleby (the Horn district of Zealand), in Norre Lyngby (Vendsyssel) and in the Odense Canal?

This early stage of civilization appears still to be in the air, for to-day we can neither link it up with the Magdalenian civilization of Western Europe, nor bring it intimately into contact with the Danish "earliest stone age" civilization. Although it still appears as sporadic in Denmark, it is nevertheless already spatially linked with similar finds in Brandenburg. As for the civilization which came after it (that of Svaerdborg-Mullerup), according to Sarauw we can follow it, with variants, through North Germany and Belgium as far as northern France, whence it disappeared perhaps at the close of the Palæolithic. From North Germany it is diffused as far afield as Russia.

Though it is impossible for the moment to be sure where the birthplace of this civilization was (it was probably Western Europe) it would seem certain that it was introduced into Denmark from the south at a time when Zealand was still a part of the German mainland. From Zealand it would have sent out ramifications in all directions into Denmark and as far as central Sweden and southern Norway.

When it comes to placing the Svaerdborg-Mullerup civilization in time, Scandinavian archæologists consider that its most likely chronological horizon is that in which the European Azilian phase is seen. It was not the exclusive apanage of the three countries since it expanded along the Baltic littoral and extended even into Esthonia.

Sophus Müller could say that "neither invention nor creative effort was to be found among the Scandinavians of

[1] CXXII, p. 347.

the stone age." Such an assertion seems unjust in the face of the existence of those flint-knappers who were such admirable workmen in stone. Does not the same writer, speaking of those elements transmitted via the south of Europe to the northern regions, himself say that " imitation " is hardly the right word to use in describing the relation of this northern civilization to that of the lands of the South ? It is better to speak of " adoption, assimilation, and participation. The foreign contribution was so completely absorbed and so thoroughly nationalized that it is often difficult to determine its provenance and to determine the itinerary followed ".[1]

Is there not a certain amount of " invention and creative effort " in the " nationalization " of an invention ? The Scandinavians, having for the fabrication of their axe-heads, only materials like flint and hard rocks that were very hard to work, yet produced marvels of workmanship, copied in shape it is true from similar objects coming from the South.

This technical skill going hand in hand with a remarkable decorative sense will find a further and truly magnificent development in the bronze age. And, without entering into the question of origin and filiation, which have been treated by Scandinavian and other writers, we must recognize the exceptional brilliance from more than one point of view of the Scandinavian bronze age as a " mysterious phenomenon." It goes without saying that a number of different theories, geographical and economic, have been propounded to explain this problem. One finds a certain difficulty in understanding the former. The latter, marked by an abundant exploitation of the amber of the Jutland coast, and the export of this precious resin to southern lands, is worth more, for are not works of art everywhere and always a function of wealth ? But why again drag in here a theory of ethnic superpositions—like some watered down edition of the theory of cataclysms—namely, the replacement of a primitive by another population ?

Such a supposition appears the less legitimate when we call to mind that important phase of civilization represented by the fine northern stone culture. Are we then to admit that with each new culture a new people arrives on the scene ? It is a ridiculous notion. I have seen the white metal articles of daily use among the poorer folk of Europe introduced into

[1] **CLXVII**, p. 65.

an oasis in Southern Tunisia; they came, alas! as substitutes for the beautiful native articles which our ethnographical museums of to-day diligently seek to collect. I can certify that this transformation in household ware has not been accompanied by any anthropological transformation!

Do our European export houses which have established branches everywhere in Africa, and which are bringing about so complete a transformation of the ethnographic character of the country, do they send forth along with their merchandise "ethnic wares" destined to submerge the Dark Continent?

As regards Scandinavia, we shall see that there is no need whatever to appeal to the hypothesis of an ethnic superposition such as Sophus Müller pictures. Human races did not succeed each other in Scandinavia as the eminent archæologist too readily believed.

In any case would there not be something rather bizarre in admitting such ideas from the point of view of the archæological arguments alone? Has not the mediocrity of the bronze age in Western Europe been compared with "the plenitude and decorative richness of the same civilization in Scandinavia"? And does not this single fact in itself destroy the notion of ethnic substitution above envisaged? Why should the human group which, when it was confined to a certain degree of south latitude, was so mediocre an artisan and so poor an artist, suddenly supply such admirable workmen as the Scandinavians proved themselves, when it arrived in the North?

Furthermore, the anthropological study of the human remains recovered in the northern countries and dating from the stone age to proto-historic times will throw conclusive light on the matter of this controversy, and shortly we shall enter upon it.

But we may draw attention at once to the following facts. In the first place collections of similar articles, with the same purity of form and decorative beauty, have been left by the bronze age in all these Scandinavian countries, including the Danish islands, and this archæological picture may be enlarged so as to include North Germany as regards a good number of these articles. Secondly, the whole of the geographical area thus archæologically defined belongs to the same human group.

Moreover, the present physiognomy of this general area appears to be a continuation without break of what it was in the stone and bronze ages. The anthropological picture of those days has undergone no alteration. The artists of the Scandinavian bronze age were the descendants of those incomparable flint workers who went before them, and their descendants were successively to adopt, from one generation to another, the iron civilization and those that followed it. For even if " one almost sees with regret the southron influence suddenly interrupting the fine independent evolution of the Scandinavian countries by the introduction into them of the Celtic iron civilization " we must not—let us repeat it once again—think that it was an ethnic wave which came to submerge the early civilization. It was a sociological phenomenon of which the autochthones were the witnesses and in which they were also the actors. My own impression—the state of our knowledge is not yet sufficiently advanced to enable one to assert it as fact—is that few regions of Europe can show such ethnic continuity across time and in the same locale. But do not let us anticipate.

Sophus Müller would seem to have recognized this ethnic unity by implication when he wrote, in regard to the bronze age : " The special culture of the Scandinavian North was brought in and maintained by a special nationality, or at least, by groups of closely related peoples." The " brought in " is the only thing about which we do not agree.

Would not the definite archæological retardation noted for each period in Scandinavia also furnish proof in support of the ethnic immutability of these northern lands ? And, finally, was any morphological transformation in the Scandinavian peoples observed to follow the victory at Alesia which threw open northern Europe to the Romans ? Roman civilization penetrated by the highway of commerce as far as southern Norway and central Sweden without bringing about any disturbance of race in these countries.

Scandinavian anthropological collections representing the early times in those countries contain important evidence. This evidence comes from the stone and bronze ages and also from the iron age. We owe our most complete knowledge of these human remains to the fine work G. Retzius wrote[1] on the Swedish crania. This study may well serve as a synthetic picture of the Scandinavian peoples during the course of those

[1] CCXV.

three civilizations. It offers the best basis for any comparison with the living population.

Cranial forms in these three periods occur in the proportions—(which might just as well be extended to take in all these northern countries)—set out below.

In the stone age the population is definitely dolichocephalic. Adding Dolichocephals and sub-Dolichocephals together we get a percentage of 67. Brachycephalic types, on the contrary, are scarce (6 per cent.). The population of this period is already cross-bred (26 per cent. are mesaticephalic in type). Furthermore, the majority of the Dolichocephals of the Scandinavian stone age are leptoprosopes.

In the bronze age the dolichocephalic element has increased to a percentage of 75. In the iron age it accounts for 87 per cent. A few sub-Brachycephals exist alongside of them—10 per cent. in the bronze age, and 12 per cent. in the iron age. And all these skulls are in the majority leptoprosopic.

Do not these results lead to the conclusion, first, that an indubitably dolichocephalic population lived in the earliest inhabited Scandinavian territory? The men who fashioned the beautiful flint daggers belonged to the long-headed race. And second, that this ethnic type persisted and increased naturally during the periods that followed, up to the dawn of historic times? And does this not absolutely contradict the archæological theory which would like to make out that with each new civilization that appeared in Scandinavia there was substituted for the preceding population (what became of it?) a fresh one bringing in the latest culture?

The ethnic physiognomy of Scandinavia has scarcely changed during these long prehistoric periods, unless in so far as with each stage it would appear to have become a little more dolichocephalic. And let us remember that this physiognomy is little different from that of other European countries in the same periods.

We observe, for example, as in France, the simultaneous presence during the stone age of Brachycephals and Dolichocephals. But, whereas in certain parts of Central and Western Europe the brachycephalic majorities, in measure as history unfolds, impose profound ethnic transformations calculated to explain many a social modification and many a political upset, this does not seem to have occurred in Scandinavia.

The neolithic Dolichocephals of northern origin, as Hamy

calls them, after having peopled Jutland and the islands (these at the time being but extensions of the mainland) advanced into southern Scandinavia: this movement is shown in Montelius' map of the stone age burials of Sweden, which gives their frequency according to locality. Once settled in Scandinavia these Dolichocephals never came out again.

What does the anthropological analysis of the present day population show us?

In the first place that the men of the three northern States belong to the category of tall people—they are somewhat smaller in Denmark than in Sweden and Norway. And this in itself marks the more complete isolation of Scandinavia properly so-called, where human infiltration is less easy than in Denmark. Furthermore, it is confirmation of the ideas we put forward on the subject of the relative purity of the northern race in Scandinavia, which are in opposition to those of certain archæologists.

In Denmark, where a fairly large number of investigations have been made[1] and where such work is in full swing, the average height must exceed 1 metre 69. There is very little variation throughout the country. Jutland has taller people than the islands, except for the island of Bornholm, which lies topographically in Swedish waters and whose population, maybe, has been more specifically Swedish. The islands show a stature somewhere about 1 metre 68.

Jutland provides a phenomenon already noted in Schleswig-Holstein, namely that the people of the western are somewhat taller than those of the eastern coast. We know that this cannot be due to any mesological influence—but that historic facts must certainly be invoked to account for it. The city of Copenhagen possesses the highest stature (1 metre 699) of the entire kingdom.

As for Sweden, height statistics were collected fifty years ago. In 1902 G. Retzius, with the collaboration of Fürst, brought out a good volume full of results[2] which may be considered definitive. A large number of maps, graphs and tables give us precise information on the geographical distribution of height, pigmentation, cephalic indices, etc. It is a work of the very first importance for all who would seek information on the ethnic physiognomy of Sweden. The mean

[1] **CXLVI**; **LIII**, p. 72.
[2] **CCXVI.**

stature of the country slightly exceeds 1 metre 71. And if we desire to have proof that this tall stature in Sweden is not a mere matter of arithmetic, do we not find it in this single fact that there are more than 60 per cent. of individuals whose height is greater than 1 metre 70? No matter where one turns in Sweden, tall men are always to be found. Few countries present such spatial uniformity, a fresh proof in support of our contention in regard to the racial unity of Scandinavia at all periods of history. One region alone shows stature below 1 metre 70, and that is Lapland, in the north, where it is probable that Lapp blood (small men) may have been introduced, and, perhaps, a little more Finnish blood than there is in other provinces.

In two or three regions in Sweden there are very tall men, as for instance the provinces of Hälsingland and Härjedalen in the central part of the kingdom, a small piece of coast territory to the west of lake Vener, and the island of Gotland. All exceed 1 metre 72. Physical environment counts for nothing in this height distribution. One finds very tall men equally along the sea shore and in the zones lying at an elevation of between 500 and 1000 metres. The "racial" factor alone is responsible and it is vain to attempt complicated explanations; the small stature of Lapland is a further proof of what we here put forward.

This single indication permits us to suppose that the people who first entered Scandinavia were tall and have remained so ever since.

The Norwegians are also tall men. The general mean, as in Sweden, should exceed 1 metre 71. And, as in Sweden, the only diminution we see, spatially, is in the northern territory of Finmark, still peopled in part by Lapps, Finns and half-breeds of the two peoples. Their stature (1 metre 67 to 1 metre 68) is even smaller than in Lapland. With this exception, Norwegian stature is everywhere great, particularly in the north and in the south-west where the mean would doubtless be 1 metre 72, whereas it is lower in the southern prefectures. Perhaps the Lofoten Islands are peopled by the tallest men in Norway, or even of all the north of Europe?

Certain curious observations have been made in connection with the stature of Norwegians. The question has been asked whether the seaboard, the country inland, and the land lying between the two, show differences in the height of the inhabitants. The answer approximately given—we shall say why it is only approximate, later—is that the seamen and coast dwellers are not quite so tall as the inland folk. The tallest of all are those who dwell beside the fjords, and who occupy the regions lying between the genuine interior and the ocean seaboard.

For the moment I do not see what interpretation can be given to these data. We must not allow our imagination to run away with us and put it down to environment alone!

Can we discover with certainty any foreign influences in this geographically isolated peninsular, so much better protected by its difficulty of approach than most European countries?

There is but one way to find out—to assess according to circumscribed regions the results yielded by the different anthropological investigations. This is what Arbo[1] attempted, for stature first, by means of 100,000 recruits of twenty-one years of age, examined with great care, throughout Norway. This exact method at once showed results. First of all two islands of great stature appeared, one in the north at about the level of North Trondhjem, and the other in the south, in that tumbled region whose deep valleys are filled by the waters of the Hardanger fjord. And this island is extended towards the south, without actually reaching the coast, as far as the vicinity of Kristiansand.

But if we follow the west coast, we find the investigation shows that from a little south of Trondhjem fjord the people are smaller, and we shall go on finding these smaller folk until we come to the southern frontier.

It becomes apparent, then, without going into further detail, that the racial unity of Norway has been disturbed in places. We do not as yet exactly understand the meaning of these exceptional facts, or their veritable cause. We are aware of them, and that is always something, for we can then allow other disciplines to take the place of ours and to go further. Finnish colonies have been notified in the west of Norway. Is it the case that these colonies are composed of people whose name agrees with their ethnic quality?

[1] VII. All Arbo's works have appeared in a Scandinavian language. Some of them contain resumés in German or French. That which here concerns us appeared in the Norwegian review *Ymer* (Stockholm), with a French resumé entitled "Y a-t-il eu des immigrations successives dans la péninsule Scandinave?"

Thus the examination of Scandinavian stature alone raises many queries in the course of our investigation. Do we find the same thing happens in regard to cranial form?

All our knowledge of Denmark in this respect goes to show that it is peopled in the majority by Dolichocephals. But there is not complete homogeneity throughout the country. Islands of dolichocephaly less marked than that of Jutland appear in certain localities. It is the same in Schleswig, where the decrease of dolichocephaly is even more noticeable. In this locality we come nearer to the round-headed folk who peopled Central Germany from the time of the polished stone age. Their descendants, mixed with Dolichocephals, have not, however, completely effaced their old-time characters.

We may say that Sweden is nowadays pretty well known as regards its anthropological characteristics, as we found was the case when dealing with stature. This is because Anders Retzius' native land owed it to itself to show the importance of such research and to extend it as far as possible. The Swedish State was among the first in Europe to institute extensive anthropological investigations, and to-day we are able to point to maps in which the ethnic data of each province are set out with a considerable likelihood of finality. They supply us with some interesting information.

Let us go back to the fine work of Gustave Retzius and Fürst.

Considered as a whole Sweden is dolichocephalic. Its provincial cephalic indices vary little from one province to another—from 74.8 in Södermanland (south of lake Mälaren) to 77.5 in Lapland, where we at once become aware of the brachycephalic influence of the Lapps. The midland region, which stretches from south of the Great Lakes territory to beyond 64° north lat. constitutes an almost continuous dolichocephalic bloc that does not exceed a cephalic index of 76. Only the district of Uppland, north of Stockholm, and Hälsingland, more to the north still, break this homogeneity by indices a little less dolichocephalic. To north and south of this almost compact bloc, the heads become less long in proportion as we go farther away from it. This change is easy to explain in the north of Sweden. On one hand the highly brachycephalic Lapps, and on the other the western Finns, generally mesocephalic, have each exerted an influence.

But it is difficult to make out why the indices seem to grow higher in proportion as we advance towards Scania. This province, opposite Danish Zealand, has a cephalic index (77) almost as high as that of Lapland. There would seem to be but one explanation. We know that the Danes are less dolichocephalic than the Swedes and that the people of Zealand are less so than those of Jutland. The same influence tending to bring about a diminution in dolichocephaly has made its effect felt on both sides of the Sound. It has gone over from the island to the mainland. But this action cannot be localised in these two neighbouring districts. It comes from much further off, in the south, and has made itself felt gradually as it comes nearer and nearer. We believe that the very road it has followed can be traced, but we still lack details to enable us to state exactly what were the ethnic origins of those who took this road. Perhaps it was an eastern contingent of those Brachycephals who went to people the British Isles in the bronze age?

Taken as a whole, Norway is also a dolichocephalic land. But this characteristic cannot be graphically rendered by one uniform tint. And the cephalic index will show localization just as stature did. If we are to envisage the Norwegian population as a whole it must be considered as being sub-dolichocephalic. Against this general background, however, we see genuine dolichocephaly standing out in a parallel running from north to south, as Deniker was able to illustrate on his map, which we may fruitfully examine despite a few more recent investigations by Arbo, the great describer of Norway.

These dolichocephalic areas make three long trails on the map. The more central of the three, situated "nearer to Sweden than Norway, extends from Trondhjem in the north to Kragerö on the southeast coast." It includes, from north to south, "the district of Trondhjem, upper Gudbrandsdal with the Lom valley; the high valley of Valdres (not very pronounced dolichocephaly); the district of Kröderen, with the valleys of Sigdal and Numedal, fairly high; and finally the districts of Laurvik and Skien, by which the dolichocephals reached the Norwegian coast at a single point only, between Skien fjord and the town of Kragerö."[1] A few dolichocephalic islands situated in the province of Telemarken join this central

[1] LV, p. 48.

dolichocephalic strip to another one situated more to the west and constituted by the neighbouring district of Hardanger fjord (60° north lat.) to the north; the district of Bykle (the upper valley of the Otter) to the centre; and by the island of Exen Grinden between the high valleys of Kwinn and Mandal to the south. As for the eastern strip, it is formed by the middle and lower valley of Österdal, the Solör district and the island of Tydalen (southeast of Trondhjem) more to the north.

One of the most interesting results revealed by the most modern investigations in Norway is the presence in this country hitherto considered dolichocephalic, of regions where Mesaticephals and even a certain number of Brachycephals are far from being exceptions. Thus, in the southwest coast region, of which Stavanger is the capital, the percentage of inhabitants having sufficiently round heads to yield an index of 82 and over rises to 48. I hasten to add that this is an exceptional figure, and that directly we turn southeast and east the proportion of these relatively brachycephalic types diminishes. The two coast districts of Lister-and-Mandal and Nedenaes have only 24 per cent. and 16 per cent., and in the district of Bratsberg, further to the northeast, this drops to 12 per cent.

The general datum—let us carefully record it—yielded by all these researches is that there exist in Norway, particularly at certain points of the coast, people who do not belong to the main ethnic group peopling the country (the tall blond Dolichocephals). These men, whose heads tend more or less to brachycephaly, are tall men also. It has been thought, from this association of characters, that it might be possible to link these people to the representatives of the Adriatic race among the living populations of Europe.

Are we, perhaps, to take only the Norwegian past, dealing here with descendants of the brachycephalic people who, during the bronze age, peopled a part of the northern countries? We have seen that in Denmark and Sweden this ethnic group really seems to have appeared at this date. Their descendants are mainly scattered along the southern coasts of Scandinavia.

These tall Brachycephals would also appear to have been intrepid navigators. Far afield from Norway, to the north of Scotland on the route to Iceland we find groups of them in the Faroe Islands. It is certain that there are descendants of this race among the fisher folk of this little archipelago and among those who collect the Eider down.

It is chiefly in the south island that they are to be met with. Noted long ago by Arbo, these Brachycephals (and Mesocephals) have been recognized, with the detail necessary, by Jorgensson. He has shown that nearly one half of the indices examined express these two head-forms. Annendale, investigating in the middle island, found there a large proportion of mesocephalic types.

These islands were discovered in the ninth century by the Norwegians. It is thus certain that those who peopled them —perhaps also those who discovered them—belonged to the southwest group of this country which we have already noted and to which we need not return. Was it perhaps a group of navigators such as these who discovered the north coast of America?

Any observer surveying the region that stretches north of 57° and seeking to find out what kind of people inhabit it, would become aware of a fact whose interest can escape no one. Recent investigations have shown that the two territories facing each other across the northern portion of the North Sea —the southwest coast of Norway and the northeast coast of Scotland—appear to be peopled by men of the same race. Their numbers in relation to the rest of the population have not been exactly defined. But it is certain that these men represent an imposing percentage of the total mass of the people. The same ethnic physiognomy is revealed, north of 60°, by the Shetlands and the Faroes.[1]

These men, whom Gray considers to belong to the Dinaric race, are a strange exception to the great dolichocephalic agglomeration which almost completely encircles the North Sea. If they really belong to this fine human group whose principal home to-day is the east coast of the Adriatic, we ought to find out how this present-day division between them came about. And at once the question arises as to what was the original habitat of this race. Had it already its representatives among the Brachycephals whom we find appearing in such numbers during the polished stone age?

We still know too little about the anthropological character of the earliest population of the Balkan peninsular to

[1] **LXXXVI**; **LIII**, p. 61.

attempt to say where and when those tall Brachycephals first appeared. Even if we must one day consider them to be really autochthonous in their present homes, we shall still not have completed our task. We have yet to find out how they came to be in Northwest Europe.

It would seem that our modern researches do permit of our tracing the trail of these Dinarics from Venetia to Central Europe. And we have called attention several times to this infiltration. Have we perhaps lighted upon the way by which in the bronze age they came across Germany and Schleswig and penetrated to Sweden and Norway?

And did another lot of them at the same time cross the Straits of Dover and people the British Isles? Gradually advancing they would have reached the northeast of Scotland. Or was this region colonized by very early navigators coming from the Norwegian coast?

We touch here on one of the mysterious chapters of European History. Only twenty years ago it was filled with dense shadows. Thanks to Anthropology we are making headway through them—feeling our way, and halting at every step, it is true, but advancing nevertheless.

One last point which appears to me to be of importance: what kind of people, ethnically and morphologically, made up the population of the northwest of Scotland in the bronze age?

CHAPTER XI

The Slavs of Former Russia

THE Russia of other days has shrunk considerably since the great war. Finland, the Baltic countries, and Poland are to-day so many autonomous states; the Ukraine, the Crimea and the Republics of the Caucacus have likewise separated themselves. And if their autonomy in fact has ceased to exist since the Soviet régime, doubtless it is only temporarily suppressed.

During the last few centuries Russian policy, with its wide-spread tentacles—Russia was one of the most active agencies in setting European wars in motion—successively grasped and drew within the ancient empire of the Czars a considerable extent of country in which there are thickly populated lands of prodigious fertility, sterile steppes, some of the highest mountains in Europe, and depressions to-day lying below sea-level. To this diversity of physical conditions there corresponds an ethnic diversity no less great. Asiatics and Europeans rub shoulders in the territories of former Russia in an anthropological fraternity which naturally we see nowhere else save in certain parts of the Balkan peninsular. And among the civilized peoples of Europe where sedentaryism normally holds sway, Russia remains the land in which the ancient unfettered nomadic existence of prehistoric times—or very nearly so—is still possible. Great herds wander over the southern steppes in charge of herdsmen of Mongolian race, while in the north, Lapps (special race) and Samoyeds (Ugrians ?) range back and forth over the tundra with their reindeer in rhythm with the seasons.

Up till the revolution and the establishment of the new States, these varied and different peoples—Russians, Poles, Lithuanians, divers Finns, Turks, Tatars, Kirghiz, Lapps, Samoyeds and the rest—the map of the Caucacus is as piebald as could be—were all considered Russians. But only a few elements—numerically important, it is true—of this ethnic mosaic are " Slavs ".

As most of these peoples, under the name of Russians, had a share in History, any discrimination of their individual influence over the political movements of Eur-Asia would appear to be singularly difficult, perhaps even impossible. Who, for instance, can say that this or that decisive happening in Muscovite history was exclusively due to this race or that? Thus at first we are bound to consider ancient Russia as a whole. Having done so we shall then give a brief anthropological description of some among these new States.

Geographers having but the single end of convenience in view classed the Slavonic peoples in three groups—west, south and east. These it must be understood were simply linguistic groups. The group of Western Slavs comprised principally the Poles—of the three former Polands—the Bohemian Czechs and the Slovaks of Moravia and of some parts of Hungary.

The southern group is anthropologically the most heterogeneous. It is made up, going from the west eastwards, of Slovenes (Carniola, Istria), Serbo-Croats of Dalmatia, Bosnia and Herzegovina, and Serbia, and among the latest to be Slavonized, of Bulgarians.

The eastern group consists of the large group of Russians properly so-called. To it belong the White Russians or Bielorusses (dwelling in the upper Dwina, Vistula and Dnieper basins); the Little Russians or Malorusses (inhabiting the former Ukrainian Marches; those of the west are Ruthenians); and finally the Great Russians or Velikorusses.

*
* *

Since the immense quaternary ice sheet covered the greater portion of Russia, we are unlikely to find any traces of importance of the earliest prehistoric peoples in the territory occupied by the continental ice.

Nevertheless, men of the chipped flint period did advance to the southern edge of the ice sheet where the last moraines petered out. On this unstable land they hunted the mammoth and the reindeer. Discoveries have been announced from the year 1871, and all from the same region extending from the upper Vistula to the Dnieper, about the latitude of Kiev, that is to say, on the boundary of the great ice expansion. A Moustierian station has been found beneath a Magdalenian layer, at Wierzebow in former Russian Poland. Settlements ranging from the Acheulean to the Magdalenian have also been discovered in what was Russian Poland, and in the Ukraine, such as the Dupice cavern in the district of Olkusz[1]; the caves of the region of Oicow near Kracow; the Mashyka cavern near the village of Mashyce; Kiev, etc. It is difficult to synchronize these stations with those of Western Europe in a way which would enable us to date the various civilizations exactly, since the elements of the Western Magdalenian phase are absent in these stations of old Russia. The stations, however, enable us to assert the existence of Palæolithic man on the confines of the ice-free territory. But although remains of the art and industries have been found, unfortunately we know nothing of the physical type of these ancient inhabitants of South Russia and Poland; not a single skeleton was found with the remains of the industry.

The Neolithic folk are much better known. Among the numerous tumuli which are dotted all along the southern territories of the early Muscovite empire quite a number have been thoroughly excavated, and a number of caves—notably in the upper Vistula region—have been studied, so that we possess precious data bearing on the prehistoric life of these regions in those times.

It would appear that an identical civilization evolved at the same moment in the lowlands of former Russia, and all around the Black Sea and the Ægean—its similarities being characterized, among other things, by owl-headed statuettes. Still, it would seem to be no more possible, as yet, to synchronize the Russian Neolithic with the Neolithic of Western Europe than to establish synchronism in the Magdalenian. The polished stone age probably lasted longer in Russia.[2] Moreover, this is not the place for the discussion of such questions. It is necessary, however, to emphasize the interest they hold for History, and the same is true as regards the bronze age.

These eastern Neolithic folk—those, at all events, of the Russian kurgans—would appear to have been tall Dolichocephals. But they would not have been a pure race.

Zaborowski on more than one occasion has published in French the results of the anthropological observations made by our Slav colleagues. It is principally owing to him that we

[1] **CXXIX**, vol. i. No. 6.
[2] **LI**, p. 197; **CCL**; **CII**; **CCLXXI**, p. 478; **CCLXXI** *bis*.

know the details of the researches of Talko-Hryncewicz on the prehistoric and proto-historic craniology of the area watered by the lower Dnieper. This area, almost in the centre of former South Russia, will probably give us a sufficiently faithful picture of what the general aspect of the anthropological physiognomy of this part of the country must have seen.

These ancient Russian people must have been tall (61 per cent. of the kurgan people were 1 metre 70 in height and over). This by itself differentiates them from the present population. The crania showed 30 per cent. of Brachycephals. The remainder of the indices range from 64 to 75. Zaborowski considers that the Dolichocephals represent the earliest population, that of the stone age. The existence of Brachycephals coincides with the introduction of metals and objects of a foreign industry. To sum up, the Neolithic folk of former South Russia would have been, in the majority, tall Dolichcephals.

We must call attention to the interest of this finding, when we remember that in Western Europe (see the chapter on France) we met with tall Dolichocephals (the " Neolithic Dolichocephals of northern origin " of Hamy, G. Hervé, etc.) likewise in the Neolithic period. Our idea is not at once to imagine that both were derived from the same ethnic stock; we have not got sufficiently detailed nor sufficiently certain elements of comparison for any such hypothesis. But we certainly must not lose sight of this eastern population when we seek to discover the origin and relationships of the dolichocephalic Neolithic folk of Western Europe.

Talko-Hryncewicz studied, side by side with the human remains from the neolithic kurgans the skeletons found in the Scythian tumuli. These for the most part are distinguished from the earlier mounds by their greater size (7 to 8 metres in height) and by their architectural character—they were erected over chambers built of wood, and, occasionally, catacombs—and also by the appearance of the skeletons in them, which are never covered with coloured powder and are never in the flexed position like those of the earlier kurgans. These tumuli are also distinguished by the wealth, sometimes very imposing, of their funerary furniture. They frequently contain the products of the superior Greek civilization side by side with those of the native barbaric industry.

The skulls from these Scythian kurgans seem to be of every shape from those of Dolichocephals with a very low index up to hyper-Brachycephals.

*

* *

The most contradictory ideas have been put forward as to the origin of the Slavs. Some, who prefer the glamour of the Orient to facts, naturally consider that these people came out of Asia. Others contend that the real Slavs are tall, blond and dolichocephalic and thus that they belong to the "Germanic race". Others again have sought to establish some relationship between the Slavs and the anthropological Celts, and with insufficient approximations have created a Celto-Slav group. Some make them come from east of the Caspian, and others from the lower Danube. And this is the right place to call to mind the considerations put forward by Niederle according to whom[1] the ancestors of the greater portion of the present day Aryan peoples inhabited the country lying between the Baltic and the former Aralo-Caspian Sea during the Neolithic period. According to this writer they spoke the same language and their main concentration constituted a homogeneous anthropological whole. And at the close of the Neolithic, these Aryan tribes, already differentiated from one another, separated under the pressure of Ugro-Finnish invaders. Some remained where they were, in "the centre of dolichocephaly" and lack of pigmentation, which was somewhere not far distant from the Baltic. In this centre were congregated the Aryans who appeared later under the name of Gauls, Germans, etc. Towards the end of the first millenium before our era these groups became dislocated; the Germans departed in the direction of the Elbe. After them, the Slavs, who had hitherto remained between the Carpathians and the upper Don, "set themselves in motion, in the direction of Central Europe, southwards and finally eastwards."

Niederle sought first for the elements of these conclusions in philology and then in morphological characters. As regards the last point he found that the Slavs do not constitute an anthropological unit and that they often differ among themselves much more than they differ from their neighbours. In

[1] **CLXXV.** Report by Volkow in *Bull. Soc. D'Anthrop.*, Paris, 1897, p. 142.

Niederle's eyes brachycephaly was the feature common to all existing Slavs, but, he says, this brachycephaly, so very pronounced among Western and Southern Slavs, is less clearly marked in Poland, in White Russia and in Great Russia. And, on the other hand, these countries—the two first, especially—represent the maximum of blond coloration.

According to Niederle the true Slavs are no longer *in situ*, and the series of crania studied in Bohemia and Moravia go a long way to prove it in the view of the Czech authority. In the early burials the Brachycephals only represent some 25 per cent. This is more marked still in Poland where in the Slaboszewo necropolis, dating from the twelfth century, there is not a single brachycephalic individual. In the country of the old Slavs of Laba (Elbe) Lissauer met with only 13 per cent. of brachycephalic skeletons. And in spite of the fact that several Russian writers (Bogdanov, Ikov, etc.) found a large proportion of round-headed individuals in the old cemeteries of Kiev, Chernigov, etc., Niederle still draws the conclusion that in Slav countries the head-forms of ancient times were quite different from what they are to-day. It can be seen what political arguments extremists may find in such statements.

Niederle's general conclusions may be summed up thus: in the Neolithic period "the ancestors of the present-day Aryan peoples for the most part inhabited the vast stretch of country between the Baltic and the former Aralo-Caspian Sea, to the north of the Brachycephals of Central Europe. They spoke the same tongue and presented, in their nucleus at least, a homogeneous anthropological whole. Later, the Aryan tribes which, at the close of the Neolithic, were already distinguished from one another by their idiom, began to separate under the pressure of Ugro-Finnish invaders; the western tribes penetrated as far as France and Spain, the central tribes went south towards the Balkans and Italy and even Asia Minor, whence they penetrated into Iran and the Punjab."[1]

Is not this a purely theoretical view? Does it not amount to assuming the presence of influences about which we have little information, without any proofs? Niederle's theories may be seductive for those who have not got to look for the origin of a people in their physical make-up. To

[1] CCLXIII.

picture the Scandinavian and Germanic races on the one hand, and the Slav races (brachycephalic) on the other, as having once upon a time constituted a single anthropological whole—Aralo-Baltic Aryan peoples—is unacceptable in the judgment of an ethnologist. And, let us note, in such an hypothesis no account is taken of the pre-neolithic population occupying all these southern territories of the present-day Slavs! Can we accept the brachycephalization of the Ukrainian Slavs by contact with a Turki population as Niederle would have us do? And—if we are to believe in this morphological modification—should we not say Tatar rather than Turki?

Doubtless the problem of the origin of the Slavs is an extraordinarily complex one to solve. And the vast extent of the territory within which the problem is contained is not a factor calculated to facilitate the task. Numerous investigations have already been attempted in regard to ancient skeletons, and the morphological characters of the living populations, but these are mere crumbs scattered here and there over the scientific table of the ancient empire. A fine spirit of emulation reigned among the Russian experts who appeared to have every desire to become acquainted with the ethnic elements of their country, both spatially and in time, and we were full of anticipation. The great war put a stop to everything. Only when we have accurate knowledge of each of the human strata laid down in the course of the centuries in the present Slav countries shall we be able to dream of establishing their history on an anthropological basis and of attempting to work out filiations.

Slavists in general teach that the primitive Slav people must have had its cradle between the Oder and the Dnieper in that river and marsh region which extends north of the Carpathians as far as the Duna and the Baltic. This ethnic nucleus is supposed, by a succession of disaggregations, to have sent forth contingents, principally north and east, which split up again into the sub-divisions we recognize to-day. The twelfth century chronicle of Nestor mentions this variety of tribes of which the Russian (*Rous*) entity was composed.

This primitive geographical localization, accepted by various writers, is considered by Haddon to be a proven fact. In his map of the historic European migrations[1] we see the

[1] A. C. Haddon, *The Wandering of Peoples*, 1919, Map ii, Europe.

Slavs going forth from the region above indicated and spreading far afield. We follow their progress by means of arrows; but we are not told how the Slavs first came to be collected in this corner of Central Europe.[1] Did they always dwell there, or did they come from Asia? In a word, what is their origin? However this may be, this first group of Slavs, come one knows not whence, did not remain stationary in their western territory. They sent forth colonies in all directions—to the north towards the Baltic gulfs and the neighbourhood of Lake Ilmen; to the east in the region of the Oka and the Volga. On one side they came into collision with the Finns, and on the other with Asiatics of various ethnic physiognomies, on which matters, unfortunately, we are particularly ill-informed.

At the time of the foundation of the Gothic empire we hear chiefly of the Samatians in South Russia. Historically there was much talk of them and yet—what do we know of their ethnic origin? Nor do we know more of the anthropological character of the Huns who, in the fourth century, overthrew the Gothic power; nor of those of the Bulgars who, a hundred years later, succeeded them.[2]

During these invasions the Russians (we give this generic term to the Western Slavs) appear to have pushed up on the southeast towards the lower course of the Dneiper and the Don. It is even admitted that in the seventh century the Khazars swept along with them a certain number of these Slavs who crossed the Pruth and the Danube. There they found on the other side of the Balkans the descendants of emigrants of the same origin as their own, who had set forth several generations earlier.

Russian colonization to the south during the epoch of the Khazar domination appears all the more plausible in that the empire lasted two centuries and that it had very intimate

[1] In the 1919 edition, p. 47, Haddon says: "The Slavs who belong to the Alpine race seem to have had their area of characterization in Poland and the country between the Carpatians and the Dnieper; they may be identified with the Venedi". In Map i, Asia, he shows the movement of a portion of the Alpine race to this "area of characterization" of the Slavs, from a point somewhere north of Kabul and south of Samarkand, going south of the Caspian and the Black Sea, up towards the Danube, and thence to "the country between the Carpatians and the Dnieper". (Translator's Note.)

[2] These Bulgars were not the Slavonized people inhabiting the Balkan peninsular to-day, but the political precursors of those who were led by the Khan Isperikh (or Asparoukh).

political relations with the Greek empire which itself sheltered other Slavs.

*
* *

Was the Ukrainian group really such a great colonizer? Quite recently Dr. Velytchko and the "Prosvita" Society of Lemberg published ethnological maps of the Ruthenian-Ukrainian region[1] which gave to the latter a huge geographical domain and upwards of 20 million inhabitants. This wide zone thus attributed to the Ukrainians the authors consider as having been theirs from the ninth century at least. Even earlier than that they consider that Kiev was already the ethnographic and political centre of a federation of tribes known under the name of Russia.

Russia as she was at the time of the great war gradually took the place of this primitive Russia, and the Ukrainian explanation of the matter is as follows:—

Towards the thirteenth century Slav colonization of the basins of the Oka and Volga—peopled at that period by different groups, notably Finnish tribes—gave birth to a new "race" which, being subordinate to Russian princes, likewise took the name of Russian. But its ethnic and ethnographic characters were quite different from those which were to be found in Ukrainian Russia.

The label did not correspond to the goods. This new "race," having enlarged its territory, constituted, towards the middle of the thirteenth century, a State under the sovereignity of the Khan of the Tatars. This State, which called itself Russia, but which was known to Western Europe under the name of Muscovy, later transformed itself into a Russian empire. But South Russia did not form a part of this empire before 1654. This country, which had already begun to bear the name of the Ukraine (Ukraïnia), and had been annexed to the Duchy of Lithuania after the downfall of the Tatar domination, became a more or less autonomous province of the kingdom of Poland at the end of the fourteenth century, and thus remained within the sphere of European civilization. But the consistent tendency of the Poles to convert the Ukraine to Catholicism and to keep the mass of its people in subjection caused a series of agitations, and finally a revolution which

[1] CCLXIII.

deprived Poland of this huge area. Thus freed, the Ukraine placed itself in 1654 under the protectorate of the Muscovite Czars on condition that its autonomy should be fully respected. But very soon the Ukraine found itself stripped of all its political independence and annexed to the Russian empire under the name of Little Russia. One portion, however, of the old Kiefite Russia, East Galicia, remained apart, and was attached to the Austro-Hungarian empire.

Thus the Ukrainians deny that other Russians have any right to be considered as belonging to the " Slav race ". It is unnecessary to examine deeply the races of former Russia to see that their anthropological study—which ought to be absolutely objective—has been continually disturbed by political interventions. Coming from all sides these have warped understanding and travestied facts. Each of the Ukraine's neighbours claims the people of this country as their's. The Hungarians count the Carpathian Ruthenians among the Magyars in their statistics;[1] the Poles assert that the Ukrainians were merely a portion of the Polish group; and ethnography is invoked in proof thereof without a qualm. As for Russian officialdom it never recognized the ethnic existence of the Ukraine. In the ethnographic maps of the former empire one flat tint united in its aggressive simplicity every possible ethnic element. Certain of these stick-at-nothing Slavophils, capable of thus calmly doing violence to anthropological characters, must be feeling their position somewhat acutely to-day. For did they not help, with this interested policy and its deliberately ethnic colouring to let loose upon Europe the greatest misfortunes it has ever known! Most of the Balkan wars, preludes to greater ones, began with this hypocritical pretext of bringing together the " scattered brethren ".

Chancellories have even made use of incredible ruses to confuse issues and render them incapable of being understood by the vulgar. Volkow tells how the Ukrainian language does not figure in the official list of languages accepted for international telegraphic communication because Russia refused to recognize it. Yet it appears, nevertheless, under two other names—Little Russian (from a Russian source), and

[1] Still, I have before me statistical tables taken from the census of 1910 in which the minorities then inhabiting former Hungary—Roumanians, *Ruthenians*, Serbs, etc.—figure under their own names, despite Volkow's statement.

Ruthenian (from an Austrian source). It was just another device to make the world, thanks to such disguises, forget the existence of the Ukraine.

Ukrainian patriots have always protested against such ethnic assimilations. They have shown that their linguistic, ethnographic and morphological characters invest them, in the locality in which they dwell, with a " real presence " impossible to be denied.

It would certainly seem from the point of view of anthropological characters—which, alone, should be taken into account here—that the Ukrainian writers were justified in claiming that their country is peopled by a race both different from and more homogeneous than that of their conquering neighbours. Hamy, who was politically disinterested, had already distinguished the Ukrainians, with the Serbo-Croats, Slovenes, Slovaks and Czechs from the other Northeast Slavs—Wends, Poles, Great Russians and White Russians. In every work that has so far appeared Ukrainian Slavs are credited with a greater stature, a more pronounced brachycephaly, and a higher percentage of dark-haired individuals. But it is impossible to go all the way with Hamy in the " Slav association " which he establishes. It is certain, for instance, that the Serbo-Croats, in particular, are taller than the other " Slavs " beside whom he ranges them. Moreover, we shall meet these Serbo-Croats again presently.

Those tables in which we find the cephalic indices of the different groups of Ruthenians and Ukrainians figuring show a moderate degree of brachycephaly in these peoples. It is rare to find an index exceeding 84 (measured on the living). But it is certain that the short, broad heads are well in the majority. Failing the exact seriation, it is sufficient to see the percentage of indices exceeding 80. It is nearly always more than 70, and sometimes as high as 87 per cent. The Poltava district yields the lowest proportion of brachycephalic types, and the Ukrainians of Kharkov and the Huzul Ruthenians (Ruthenians of the Carpathian mountains) show the highest. The Podolians of the south of Podolia are Mesaticephals (index of 80.6). It is the mountainous regions which everywhere seem to have preserved brachycephaly best.

We shall come again upon these morphological differences between the people of the hills and the plains when we go into the question of stature.

The Galician Ruthenians are generally small (about 1 metre 64). But the work of Kopernicki and of Volkow has shown that in the hilly parts of this country height is nearly 2 cms. above the mean (1 metre 658). The Huzuls are even tall men ; those of Galicia (1 metre 689) equally with those of Bukovina (1 metre 695) and Hungary (1 metre 699). Readers who are still tempted to believe that a mountain life diminishes stature will here find evidence against their belief.

The Ukrainians, as a whole, are above the European mean in height. It would be somewhere in the neighbourhood of 1 metre 66 with slight geographical variations. And Deniker accepts this figure as the general average for Little Russians in his analysis of stature in Russia.

Hair and eye colour has not been so fully investigated as height. But it would seem that brown hair is predominant among the Ukrainian and Ruthenian peoples. Velytchko's results indicate low percentages of fair hair (the maximum for the series I have before me is 19 per cent.) The Huzuls of Galicia and Bukovina yielded the following characteristics to Volkow :—85 per cent. of brown hair, 58 per cent. of dark eyes. The largest number of light hair and eyes, respectively, were 16.7 per cent. and 13.3 per cent.

If, as some would have it, we are to admit that the Ukrainians and the Ruthenians represent the true "Slavs", then the anthropological diagnosis of the Slav would consist in a moderate degree of brachycephaly, a height probably above the mean, and deep pigmentation.[1]

*

* *

The Western Slav group consists mainly of the Poles.[2]

Long before the great war Polish intellect, with a view of a Polish renaissance, was concentrated on something more than history and literature. Like the rest, Polish men of science (those who were able to do so owing to the very nature of their investigations) gave their work a national orientation. They sought to discover from ancient sepultures what civilizations had successively been displayed on Polish soil, and what sort of men had initiated and carried them on.

[1] Without too greatly insisting on it, let us recall that the morphological characters of the prehistoric skeletons showed a predominance of tall dolichocephalic types.

[2] **CCLXXII**, p. 289 ; **CCXLIII** ; **LIII**, p. 101 ; **L**, p. 48.

They had to link the two together in order to assure to the Polish nation an ethnic continuity whose first link began in the most distant possible past in prehistoric times. The Poles know that theirs' is an ancient land and their race a very ancient race.

At the same time a fine spirit of emulation animated Polish anthropologists and archæologists, and their discoveries followed one another in quick succession.[1]

If we go back across the centuries, leaving aside the prehistoric people whose ethnological analysis would take too long, and turn to the Chronicle of Nestor, we shall find the names of several Polish tribes established in what is now Poland and in Pomerania, and who were soon to be dominated by the Poliani. By the close of the tenth century political unification appears to have been complete. This combination, born of the necessity to fight against the Germans in the West, was not pushed so far as to constitute a victorious power. The German pressure became ever greater, while on the other flank the threatening Tatar invasion, to Poland's great misfortune, took up all their energy.

The Polish nation seemed to be at the point of going under. Its western territories lost to the Germans, it concentrated again in rear of Pripet, and seeking an outlet, poured northwards and to the southeast. The experts on Polish matters assert that this Polish colonization was genuinely successful and that there was even a time when it just failed to swallow up a part of Russia, being absorbed into Muscovy instead.

There are quite a large number of anthropological works dealing with the Poles. The groups which have received most attention are those which inhabited the areas belonging to former Russia and former Austria-Hungary up till the great war. We have very little data about the Poles of Prussia. The few Kashub skulls examined long ago by Lissauer were, in general, mesocephalic. The Danzig district which provided these skulls thus belonged to that great ethnic area with no very strongly marked characters which lies between old Russia and Germany.

[1] The archæological review *Wiadomosci Archeologiczne* (Polish Archæological Bulletin) published in Warsaw, is extremely energetic.

The better known Poles of former Russia have everywhere yielded means showing mesaticephaly and sub-brachycephaly. It would seem that the first of these cranial forms may be considered as the " Polish form " since brachycephaly appears to become more and more frequent and more and more pronounced in the districts of the eastern periphery. The northern part of ancient Poland which lies between the Niemen and the Vistula is peopled by less round-headed men than the other parts of the Polish country. The Masurs and Podlasians have a mean cephalic index of which the lowest shows mesticephaly (81.8 in the provinces of Suwalki and Grodno), and the highest, sub-brachycephaly (82.2 in the Czczuczyn district in the north of the province of Lomza). Polish skulls come nearest to dolichocephaly to the west of the Vistula. Several hundred workmen, chiefly from Warsaw province, who were measured by Elkind, showed a cranial form on the boundary of sub-dolichocephaly (80.9). Is this due to German influence? Maybe a certain number of individuals of the Germanic race gave some of their blood to these neighbours of theirs.

A recent study by Stanislas Lencewicz[1] on the Kielce region sent the cephalic index of these Poles of the upper Vistula up to 82.4 (84.4 in the female series). The highest percentages of indices for both sexes is between 80 and 84. Talko-Hryncewicz formerly gave a much lower mean index. Lencewicz finds that the character of brachycephaly diminishes as one goes from south northwards, going from 84 in the district of Stopnica, to 81.6 in that of Opoczno. The greater part of these Kielce Poles have a short, broad face, especially the women. The proportion of leptoprosopes reaches 46 per cent. in the men. And the nasal index shows that leptorrhinian and mesorrhinian individuals are about equal in number. The Polish author draws attention, for the first time, he says, to the presence in this area of brunet brachycephals similar to *Homo alpinus*. They are present in a proportion of about 10 per cent. In this corner of Poland individuals with dark hair are numerous, somewhere about 85 per cent.; but dark eyes are relatively rare, only amounting to 11.7 per cent. To sum up, the Poles dealt with in this bit of work are mainly sub-Brachycephals with light eyes and dark hair.

[1] **CXLI**, p. 565 and 603.

There is one observation in connection with the Poles of former Russia—as has been mentioned elsewhere—which may have an historical bearing and from which the doctrine of social selection may draw some support. The Polish nobility appears to possess a higher degree of brachycephaly than the peasants, and, in general, than any of the other inhabitants.

Olechnowicz noted this[1] in his studies on the Poles of Lublin " government " and on the Masurs. And the difference between the mean indices is sufficiently clear cut for the observation to be worthy of closer examination. It must not be concluded, *a priori*, that the nobility represent greater purity of race than the peasants. It is generally the reverse.

The Poles of Galicia are better known than those of former Russian Poland. Long ago Retzius, and then Weisbach, published studies on Polish crania from former Austria. But these were restricted researches. The work of Majer and Kopernicki, which was carried out over large numbers, will best permit of our orienting ourselves. The roundest heads were those of the highlanders of the Tátra (index of 85.3). Further, in a general fashion the Polish highlanders of Galicia are more brachycephalic than their compatriots of the foothills and especially than those of the plains. If we make two groups following the principal geographical environments we find the following averages :—84.2 for the highlanders, and 82.5 for the plainsfolk.

This more accentuated brachycephaly of the hill folk is especially manifest in the case of the Podhalanians of the highest massif. As far back as 1881 Lebon drew attention to it in his journey to the Tátra mountains. He even accentuated it since he attributed an index of 85.8 to these Highland Poles.[2]

Thus, as a whole, the Poles are slightly brachycephalic, or rather mesaticephalic, individually.

Will the study of their stature help us to delineate this human type more clearly ?

Although the Poles within the Prussian kingdom prior to 1918 are very little known, it is quite a different matter as

[1] The work of W. Olechnowicz appeared between 1896 and 1897 in the *Recueil des documents pour l'Anthropologie* published by the Krakow Academy of Sciences, vols. xvii. and xviii. They were analysed by Deniker in **CLXXX**.

[2] Lebon. " De Moscou aux monts Tátra ; étude sur la formation actuelle d'une race," *Bull. de la Soc. Géogr.*, Paris, 1881, p. 97.

regards the Poles of former Russia and Galicia. Those "incorporated" in the Russian and Austrian armies furnish us with plenty of data.

The first ethnic characterization which appears is the very low stature of Polish recruits in general. Some 200,000 men yielded a mean height scarcely exceeding 1 metre 62. Anuchin, in a work of the front rank on the distribution of height in Russia, published in 1889, pointed out that, in the variation from one province to another, the minimum height (1 metre 62) for the then Russian empire was to be found in the province of Piotrokôw (Poland). And if, in the course of this geographical distribution, we find that stature is higher in the eastern than in the western part of the Polish area, demographic statistics will at once give us the reason why, namely that these eastern areas only contain 20 to 60 per cent. of real Poles, whereas the western area contributed 75 to 95 per cent. to the military forces.

I shall borrow from Deniker,[1] who made a careful analysis of Anuchin's work, a few general observations. If, after having noted that the Poles, as a whole, are men of low stature, we examine a few of their principal groups, we shall find it possible to grasp, on the one hand, this Polish racial characteristic of small stature, and, on the other, the clearly marked influence of neighbours of this ethnic group in increasing its stature. Height decreases as we go from east to west, that is to say, in proportion as we get further away from the Russians. But it is not a regular decrease ; it proceeds, here and there, by jerks. It is the south of ancient Russian Poland which contains the lowest statures.

In the loop formed by the Vistula to the north of the former Russo-Austrian frontier in the neighbourhood of the hills which culminate in Łysa Gôra, we meet with the lowest stature (1 metre 61) of all Poland. In the north the Masurs yield another very low figure (1 metre 61 to 1 metre 62). These small statures, measured on conscripts, are not the result of an accumulation of sub-normal statures due to the subjects not having arrived at full growth. The adult population of the same district likewise exhibits them. Thus in the district of Opatôw, to the east of Łysa Gôra, Olechnowicz found a height of 1 metre 61 after having measured a whole series of the adult inhabitants (their mean age was 32 years).

[1] II ; LIII, p. 99.

In noting the difference in height existing between the small nobility and the peasants, some writers believed that they had come upon persisting traces of two races, one a conquering (the taller) and the other a vanquished race. But what was the conquering race ? The Gobinists would probably have had something to say on the subject !

The northwest provinces watered by the Niemen, the territory dominated by the towns of Grodno, Vilna, and Kovno, show a greater stature than that of Poles eleswhere, and very markedly greater because it exceeds it by 2 cms This phenomenon without doubt is due to the presence on the frontier of representatives of the Lithuanian race. We know that as we go north from this region we shall come upon the zone of tall stature lying along both sides of the Baltic, especially the western shore. Thus it is probable that the (Polish) provinces now under consideration are peopled by a certain proportion of individuals of this race. Possibly there may also have been intermixture, due to mixed marriages such as happen in all political boundary regions, which would have raised the mean height. This one small fact may serve to demonstrate once again that the ancient localization of races—it is difficult to give it a date—has not yet been submitted to such profound dislocation that we are unable to retrace its boundaries in many places.

The Galician Poles seem to have a greater stature than the Poles of former Russia. But this does not apply, as we shall see, to the whole of the former Austrian province. In the first place we must make one observation which may be of great importance : the rhythm of growth is somewhat slow, it would seem, among Galician Poles.[1] The following figures represent the mean height at different ages : 1 metre 609 at 20 years of age ; 1 metre 612 at 21 ; 1 metre 625 at 22 ; 1 metre 643 at 25. This last figure should represent the height of Galician Poles, since it is the same as that worked out by Majer on the adult civil population.

When we examine the height of the Polish population of Galicia, the first thing we notice is that the smallest men inhabit the eastern areas. This is not merely a datum drawn from means. The number of tall statures is less in the old eastern military districts than in those of the west. And

[1] CXXVIII.

confirmation from another quarter lies in the fact that the number of temporary rejections due to insufficient height is greater among the men of the east.

Another interesting datum is that the Polish highlanders of Galicia—like the Ukrainian hill folk—are taller than their compatriots of the plains.

Thus anthropological investigation reveals a double phenomenon which may have a bearing on History: decrease of height as one goes from east to west, and as one goes from south to north. The Podhalanians of the Tátra have a height of 1 metre 65 and so also have the inhabitants of the West Beskiden; those of the Ost Beskiden are slightly smaller (1 metre 648).

But directly we advance from this massif towards the Vistula and the region around Kraków—except in the foothills —height decreases to 1 metre 625. Nevertheless stricter local investigations in these areas are required. In a general way the Polish mountain folk are the tallest Poles.

Now let us recall what the investigations into the cephalic indices showed us. These same hill folk are the most brachycephalic of all the Poles: the cephalic index decreases directly we get into the plains. Thus a medium height, equal to the European mean, and brachycephaly are the general morphological characteristics of the Poles of Upper Galicia.

The rest of Poland is made up of small men, and even very small men, whose heads are generally mesaticephalic. The Polish people does not, then, constitute a pure race. It is an ethnic complex—we do not speak of the Poland that was once under the dominion of Germany—in which elements supplied by the Germanic race do not appear to have played an effective rôle.[1]

Deniker, in his essays at classification, placed the larger part of the Poles in the secondary Vistulan race and a few among them in the Eastern race. Let us accept this classification for the time being. Nevertheless, I do not believe that these compartments will be called upon to last for ever.

*

* *

The White Russians (Bielorusses) occupy a part of the old so-called Polish territory of Pripet. One readily admits that in the west they have been strongly influenced, ethnically,

[1] L, p. 48.

by the Poles, whereas in the north the Lithuanians have contributed certain characters to their make-up. Linguists assert that this is the least pure of the Russian groups; statistically it is also the weakest of them.

Most of the mean cephalic indices so far indicated show them to be a sub-brachycephalic and sometimes mesaticephalic people. In the mid-Niemen area there even exists a high proportion of Dolichocephals. Whereas in the south, in the forest area of the Pripet marshes, the population is of a different type with mean cephalic indices of 84 and 85 instead of the mean of about 82, and the proportion of longheads at once becomes less.

For the rest, these southern Bielorusses are taller than their congeners of White Russia who are themselves slightly taller than their neighbours on the west, the Poles. They are also more frequently fair. Dark individuals are far fewer among them than among any of the other Russians.

Which of the types here localized should be considered as the "true" type? The Brachycephals or the others?

Investigations into the cephalic index, though not numerous, still permit us to get a general idea of the cranial shape prevalent in the locality. Certain facts interesting in their geographical distribution are revealed.

First of all, the series of White Russians all show, except for the southern Bielorusses, the mean character of sub-Brachycephaly. All the figures I have before me, and I am consulting those of several writers, lie within 81.1 and 82.9. If, then, we are to consider all the White Russians as a single group, their ethnic physiognomy will be easy to define. But we know how effectually averages can hide the most important facts. If we dissect these investigations we at once find that among the sub-Brachycephals of the western Bielorusses there are a large number of dolichocephalic individuals—as many as 36 per cent. according to Talko-Hryncewicz, and 43 per cent. according to Yantshuk. Yet the mean of these western Bielorusses (provinces of Vilna, Grodno, and Suwalki) is 82—and a little less in the female series.

The eastern Bielorusses (provinces of Vitebsk and Mogilev, the northeast of the province of Chernigov; northwest of the province of Smolensk), who are believed to be mixed with Velikorusses, as a whole keep within the general Slav physiognomy.

As for the southern Bielorusses or Poliechtshuki, distributed in the south of the province of Minsk and in the north of Volhynia, those marshy areas drained by the affluents of the Pripet, they show a sufficiently sudden difference from their compatriots both by a great increase of the mean cephalic index indicating distinct brachycephaly—principally among the men—and by a great decrease of the percentage of dolichocephalic types.

These findings have greatly struck anthropologists. And two arguments have been put forward in an endeavour to discern the modifying causes, namely the ethnic influences of neighbouring peoples and the influence of physical environment.

It would appear that linguists establish some relationship between these Poliechtshuki of the Pinsk Marshes and the Ukrainians. But the Little Russians who are geographically nearest to them do not present, as we have seen, the same morphological characteristics as these Bielorusses; they are less brachycephalic.

Is this because the lowlands, much encroached upon by marsh and forest, are to be envisaged as the laboratory in which the skulls of the inhabitants, thanks to these particular physical influences, became fashioned in such manner as to tend towards dolichocephaly? There are certain to be some writers ready to maintain a hypothesis of this kind.

I think the first of these two suggestions is more likely to be on the right path. So far as we can see, we have to deal with a group initially more brachycephalic which has been mixed, owing to the events of History, with a human group of different stock and which, along with this second group, has been localized in this particular environment.

The stature of the Bielorusses (probably 1 metre 64) is, for a mean, low. But it seems that it varies within somewhat wide limits according to the regions examined. The provinces of Minsk and Mogilev, where the Bielorusses represent 50 per cent. and even 90 per cent. of the population, in the one case belonging to the western and in the other to the eastern White Russians, show about the same statures. And we shall get the same figure if we add together all the districts containing these two kinds of Russians.

But the southern Bielorusses are certainly taller. In the region of the upper Düna, the district of Tsna exhibits 1 metre 669, about 4 cms. more than the mean for the other White

Russians. The eastern districts, east of Mogilev, show very much the same height. Thus it is certain that many groups of Bielorusses belong to the category of tall men. In regard to the northern districts there has naturally been talk of mixture with the Lithuanians, men whose mean height exceeds that of Europe in general—but is this by modifications due to intermarriage or to immigration of whole groups of taller people ? Our authors pronounce no decision on these delicate points. As regards any influence by Great Russians on the eastern districts of White Russia, this could not be manifested in an increase in stature because the Great Russians themselves are not sufficiently tall for that.

It is interesting to put some of the above facts side by side with those revealed by the cephalic index. I am quite ready to believe—though it is merely a guess—that a more careful differentiation of these two associated characters would lead to a demonstration of the infiltration of human elements from the Baltic. Is not the dolichocephaly we have noted, occasionally with disturbing frequency, likewise due to these taller people ? The result of investigations made here and there do not permit of certainty in this matter. Deniker attributes the White Russians to his small fair, sub-brachycephalic Eastern race. We know that a number of people belonging to the ethnic groups now under review would find considerable difficulty in accommodating one another within the confines of the race. Let us wait a little before we place them in it.

*

* *

The Malorusses and the White Russians have suffered less from Asiatic aggression than their neighbours of the north and east, the Velikorusses, whom we must now study in order to complete our review of the " Slavs " of former Russia. These Velikorusses are sometimes called Khazars by the Ukranians. This is a perjorative epithet recalling the long sojourn these Asiatics made on Russian soil. Are the Velikorusses partly descended from these Turanians ?

It must be said at once that our information as to the vast territory occupied by the Velikorusses is even more scanty, as yet, than that regarding the other two groups already studied. Moreover they are widely scattered. Seven writers, whose series I have before me, have examined a fairly large number of skulls from the different parts of Great Russia. The mean indices of these series vary but little—from 80.6 to 82. These two figures represent a sub-brachycephalic character. The most highly brachycephalic mean is that given by Landzert and is yielded by male skulls from the provinces of Moskva, Yaroslavl, Tver and Novgorod. In these different series the dolichocephalic skulls are rare ; several of the series do not contain a single one. Those which contain the most only number some 5 per cent. of them. Thus these skulls must have belonged to a race whose first morphological origin was brachycephalic. With regard to the 5 per cent. of dolichocephals, there are 60 per cent. of skulls whose indices exceed 80. Deniker drew attention to the constancy of the indices between 81.1 and 82.9 as "remarkable for Russian heads."[1] It has been thought that a more highly brachycephalic index must once have characterized the Velikorusses, and, to sustain this hypothesis, its supporters have taken their stand on the observations made by Talko-Hryncewicz[2] on the Starubriadtsı, schismatic Great Russians exiled in Transbaikalia since 1733, who have remained free from any mixture thanks to their isolation. The index of the schismatics was 83.1. But this religious group went out from an ethnic group whose morphological characteristics have been fixed for far longer than these 200 years. Further, their isolation was only relative. Proselytism can introduce into a sect men of no matter what ethnic group, provided they are ready to accept its dogmas—we demonstrated this as regards the Skoptzy eunuchs.

Anthropological investigations into the Velikorusses have not been carried out in all the districts of former Russia, and those of which we have the findings collected insufficient data. Still we have to be content with them. We shall try to make up one of two geographical areas by putting together several governments which can thus be placed together.

In the first place we will take the area of the north of Great Russia roughly comprising (a few districts are left out) the governments of Archangel, Olonets and Vologda—the vast territories across whose central portion runs the Dwina and whose northern portion shades into tundra. Its inhabitants,

[1] LV, p. 76.
[2] CXIV.

measured by Tarenetsky, are few and far between. The cephalic indices following the above geographical order, are respectively 81.7, 83.3, 83.3—that is to say, one is mesaticephalic and the other two are brachycephalic.

To the southwest of this wide region we will group together the four governments of Petrograd, Novgorod, Tver and Pskov. Their cephalic indices lie between 83.1 and 84.2. It is interesting to observe that that part of the government of Petrograd containing the city of that name is no exception to the rule. Nevertheless, a series of fifty women, measured in the district of Tsarskoye Selo by Madame Tarnowsky, furnished the relatively very low index of 79.5. The explanation of this sub-dolichocephaly presenting itself under such conditions may not be very hard to find.

In the centre of the old empire the governments of Kostroma, Yaroslavl and Vladimir yielded to Zograf and Tarenetsky mean indices running from 81.5 to 84 2. The more brachycephalic indices were met with in the district of Galich, on the upper course of the Kostroma, and in that of Kineshma situated further south, on the banks of the Volga (85.2).

The governments of Moskva and Ryazan, which are intermediate, are less brachycephalic. In the first of them Anuchin obtained an index of 82.7 and Vorobief obtained 81.5 in the second. The governments of Vyatka and Kazan, between the Urals and the Volga, are both sub-brachycephalic.

To sum up, this distribution according to governments yields a sufficiently remarkable homogeneity of cranial form for the Velikorusses. It is true that it is an affair of mean indices; nevertheless, since these are always of much the same value we may admit that counting by heads would not greatly alter the general aspect thus revealed. Still we must make one reservation—the score series, or thereabouts, from which this information is borrowed, are all of them insufficient in regard to numbers.

Putting all these researches together we may say that the great majority of Velikorusses are sub-Brachycephals; but the vast territories of Great Russia still remain anthropologically unexplored.

Is this relative unity of the cranial morphology in the Velikorusses maintained when we come to study their stature? One might believe it to judge from the published maps, with the exception, however, of a slantwise penetration by another ethnic group running from the Gulf of Finland to the most westerly loop of the Ural river.

In a general way the stature of the great Russians is small. It would seem to be fairly accurately represented by 1 metre 64. But in those provinces in which a sufficiently large number of ethnic groups live side by side, it is difficult to give a figure that has any real value. In fact, the Permiaks, Votiaks and other Ugrians of small stature on one hand, and the tall Western Finns on the other, are likely to modify the mean stature in both senses. Anuchin's series fluctuate round the figure we have given. The 30,000 workmen of the central provinces of Russia measured by Erismann have a stature of 1 metre 651. It is the same for those examined in Moscow by Kolubakin (1 metre 655). And this time, it is worth while remarking, the height of the factory workers in a large city like Moscow is greater than that of the population outside. This finding, which will disturb certain *a priori* arguments, should be noted by those who concern themselves with social selection.

In order to get information that has more real stability we must go to the provinces in which the highest proportion of the population consists of Great Russians, say round about 90 per cent. Still, even here we shall get contradictory figures. In the central provinces the men appear to be small. All the same, certain islands of greater stature would seem to indicate the presence, side by side with the Great Russians, of representatives of other races. In the province of Pskov, which is on the confines of the Baltic peoples, height goes up suddenly till it reaches even 1 metre 67. And the province of Novgorod, north of Pskov, likewise presents a zone of tall stature in the basin of Lake Ilmen, whereas the rest of its area lies within the domain of low stature.

The history of the invasions from the West informs us as to the tall statures we have just noted. We may recall that in the ninth century the Varangians, led by Rurik, established themselves to the south of Lake Ladoga and founded the Russian empire. These Varangians were Scandinavians who dwelt on the eastern shores of the Baltic. Their ancestors had aforetime crossed this sea, coming from the peninsular peopled by the tall adventurous warriors who went as far afield from the primitive home as England and France, propagating their ethnic influence in those lands.

The Novgorodian colonists, scattering over different regions of Russia, created these islands of tall stature which we find on the maps. They sowed with a different colour this almost uniformly tinted field representing Russian stature. We see these islands of tall stature constituted by the Novgorodian colonists in the northern provinces such as Archangel, where the people are small. We shall find them again in Vologda. In the sixteenth and seventeenth centuries these Novgorodian colonists, established on the shores of the White Sea and in the basin of the northern Dwina, pushed southeastwards. The memory of this exodus explains the tall stature we find in the province of Perm, where in many localities it exceeds 1 metre 67.

An explanation of the same nature must be sought for the islands of tall stature which we find in Siberia on the other side of the Urals. The basic stock of the earliest colonisation of Siberia was drawn from the governments of the east, notably from Perm, and we know why the men of this region are taller, in general, than other Great Russians.

Thus, by little facts such as these, justificatory of great events, Anthropology is able to confirm History.

NOTE.—Our knowledge of the anthropology of the Slavs of former Russia makes continual progress thanks to the continued efforts of Russian and Polish savants.

For Russia see the *Russian Journal of Anthropology* published at Moscow (articles in various languages). For Poland see *Archiwum nauk Antropologicznych*, Warsaw (with translations of memoirs in several languages).

CHAPTER XII

Slavs Outside the Former Russian Empire

INSERTED between the great mass of " Northern Slavs " and the relatively modest contingents of Southern " Slavs " there is the solid Roumano-Austro-Hungarian wedge which for ever separates these two linguistic groups. Before knowing anything at all of the history of the Slav migrations or building up hypotheses with the data thus obtained, which is a matter for the historian, the first question that presents itself is whether the Yugo-Slavs are related, otherwise than by the language they speak, to the Northern Slavs. Do these Northern and Southern Slavs belong to the same race ?

Before touching on Yugo-Slavia we must first examine the characters of the Slavs of Bohemia and Moravia and such Slovenes as form, as it were, the extreme western advance guard of the European Slavs. We shall also find " Slav " groups in the Balkans—Serbs, Bosnians and Herzegovinians, Montenegrins, and Bulgars, but these we shall see later on, when we come to deal with the Balkan peninsular. Imperialist Russia was lucky on many an occasion to find them on the road to Constantinople, since they could be made to subserve her designs for conquest. Did she not, to the great misfortune of Europe, exploit them fully and over a long period of time ?

The topographical plan of Bohemia would seem to offer perfect security to a people settling there for the first time, especially on the west and north, on account of the Bohemian forest, the Erz Gebirge and the Sudetes forming a rampart on three sides. The fourth side of the lozenge looking towards Moravia and Lower Austria is far from presenting any such obstacle.

Yet, despite these geographical advantages, Bohemia never knew ethnic unity. Few natural frontiers, seemingly designed especially to provide complete protection, have been more completely violated. Nevertheless, this was not because the defile through which the Elbe flows was not a favourable route for invasion—for we may repeat what we have already had occasion to remark in the case of Switzerland, that mountain passes, even the highest, have frequently been chosen as highways rather than river valleys. In Bohemia the Slavs were invaded again and again by the Germans established on the other side of the mountains.

The Slav country of former Austria had its palæolithic civilization, at any rate after the expansion of the Riesen glaciers. The Schipka station in Moravia on the upper course of the Oder, in that narrow corridor bounded on the south by the Beskiden; the Podbaba station, in the loess in the immediate neighbourhood of Prague to the northwest, in the elbow of the Moldau (Vltava); and that of Brüx (Brix), in the foothills of the eastern Erz Gebirge, have all three furnished not only implements, but human relics considered to be Moustierian. Only a few years ago the Ochos cavern in Moravia yielded to Rzchak a piece of jawbone of the same epoch.

For less early periods Brünn (Brno), the capital of the country, and Predmost, near the town of Prerau (on the course of the Beczwa, an affluent of the Mohra) are all Moravian stations of the Reindeer age quoted in every textbook. Predmost is the famous "field of mammoths" which Steenstrup formerly considered to be an ancient natural accumulation of bodies, a kind of elephants' cemetery, the ivory from which was used by Quaternary man. Few stations can be compared with Predmost from the point of view of wealth in fauna and implements. Several excavators have dug out human remains there.[1] Maska discovered a burial with four complete skeletons and the débris of six others. The human race of which specimens are buried in this loess-formation hillside were tall and dolichocephalic. And there can be no doubt about the exact age of these skeletons, because this collective burial was found beneath an undisturbed archæological stratum.

Makowsky found a very richly decked out skeleton in the Brünn (Brno) loess; there were more than six hundred pieces

[1] **CLXXIX** *bis*.

of *Dentalium badense* with it. The skull was dolichocephalic to a high degree. These bones, coloured red, were the subject of various controversies. On account of this very coloration Virchow would assign the burial to the neolithic period.

This region continued to be inhabited in the periods that followed. And although Bohemia and Moravia may not appear to have been thickly populated in neolithic times, the reverse was the case in the bronze and iron ages. They have yielded numerous sepultures of the bronze age with skeletons in the flexed position; and did not Pic,[1] the Curator of the Prague Museum, call the North Bohemian people of the early bronze age the crouched-skeleton folk?

Were there in Bohemia in the early bronze age two peoples differing morphologically as they differed in their funerary rites and their industries? Does the Bohemia of that distant period already present an ethnic picture resembling that of to-day in which two peoples in the main share her territory, the Czechs and the Germans?

This prehistory of Bohemia has been the subject of some lively discussions, to which we may give a concrete character by mentioning the names of Pic and Buchtela. Even as regards the Neolithic, Pic postulates a kind of hiatus between the end of the Magdalenian and the beginning of the bronze age, to which Buchtela[2] is in lively opposition, contending that Bohemia has an unadulterated Neolithic period, and a period of transition between the Neolithic and Bronze during which the passage from one to the other was effected smoothly by a natural progression, thus excluding any hypothesis of a violent invasion from the north. The bronze civilization, which arose in the fortified camps serving in those days as places of refuge for traders and workers, spread in several directions, towards Moravia, Lower Austria and Silesia; the valley of the Elbe

[1] **CLXXXIX**, p. 413. For the history of the bronze period, based especially on the study of funerary furniture and on technological comparisons, see the works of Schránil, the keeper of the National Museum at Prague (Dr. Joseph Schránil, *Studie o vzniku Kultury bronzové v Céchach*, with French summary, Prague, 1921). For the anthropology and prehistory of Bohemia and Moravia see the two reviews started since the Czecho-Slovakian régime and the revival of research, *Anthropology*, published by the Institute of Anthropology of the Charles University, Prague (Professor Matiegka); and *Obzor praehistoricky* (Professor Niederle), in which appear all the data relating to the origin of the peoples of this country.

[2] **XXIX.**

served as a commercial vehicle to carry it towards the Baltic.[1]

A Silesian invasion, probably commercial in character, manifested itself from the time of the 2nd bronze age. It would have penetrated to that angle which Silesia projects into Bohemia to the east of the course of the Elbe consisting of the Lausitz country, and since then Silesian influences have continued without intermission.

The la Tène civilization would have been introduced by the Boi about 50 B.C. It lasted till about 100 A.D.

Niederle in his second volume is almost silent[2] about these periods whose sociological elements are sufficiently obscure. He admits, but without going into any detail, that the cradle of the Czechs and Slovaks was further to the north than the area they now inhabit. Is this to recognize the ethnic influence of the Silesian region?

The date given for the establishment of the eponymous tribes, the Boi, is not the same with all writers; some of them talk of 400 B.C. These Bojnii were reinforced by "the arrival of Volcae-Tectosages who, according to Cæsar, decamped from the south of Gaul for the Hercynian forest, moving in a direction contrary to all other migrations, the cause of which is inexplicable." Was it merely that Cæsar was misinformed? At the beginning of the Christian era the Celtic Boi[3] would have evacuated Bohemia,[4] perhaps yielding before the pressure of

[1] The certainty that commercial relations were maintained by the Bohemians of those days is provided by the presence of marine shells and pieces of amber or of beads of this substance, in the bronze age burials. But although there was in Bohemia during the bronze age a movement of peoples inwards from the periphery, the points of departure for these movements are still ill defined. The belief in such a penetration is based on the variation noticed in the funeral customs. Thus, for instance, although incineration is sporadic during the earliest part of the bronze age, it became frequent later on. Buchtela attributes the change to a foreign people. But is it necessary always to drag in influences such as these to account for such changes? Why should it not have been that certain groups, which for a long while had not burned their dead, started at a given moment to copy their neighbours who did follow this custom? Do we not do very much the same to-day? Do there not exist, side by side in many parts of Europe, the two rites of inhumation and incineration, with merely quantitative variations according to the country? The resemblance and contemporaneousness of certain customs do not necessarily imply derivation.

[2] **CLXXVI**, p. 99.

[3] The author is here using 'Celtic' in the ordinary English sense. (Translator's Note.)

[4] See p. 109 *ibid.* The memoirs of both Niederle and Matiegka usually appeared in Czech, with a summary, in the Bulletins of the Viennese Society of Anthropology. **CLII**. The same Vienna Anthropological Review of 1892 contained a paper by L. Niederle on craniological studies.

Germanic bands? These indications are all dreadfully vague.

After having been overrun—or so it is said—on many occasions by bands of Slavs who thus preluded the great invasions, Bohemia was finally occupied by this people in the sixth century. The most celebrated of the Slav tribes, the Czechs, eclipsed the rest.

As for the Moravian "Slavs," their country is less well protected by nature than Bohemia; they seem to have had more trouble in establishing themselves. And their independence would not seem to have been secured before the ninth century.

A general anthropological study of Bohemia and Moravia has already been done in outline. The researches of Gregr, Zuckerkandl and Weisbach in Bohemia, and of Obolensky in Moravia have shown that the head-form in these countries is generally brachycephalic. Then there have been more extensive studies of the living population, and on more than 300 crania chiefly from the ossuaries of eastern Bohemia, undertaken by Niederle and by Matiegka, which have confirmed the brachycephaly indicated by the earlier writers. Eastern Bohemia appears to be particularly brachycephalic. Several hundred school-children measured in various localities of this area have even furnished mean indices showing hyper-brachycephaly.

The same finding holds good for the head-form in Moravia, where brachycephaly appears to be equally well represented in east and west, the mean indices ranging from 85.3 to 86.

None the less it must not be thought that all the inhabitants of Bohemia and Moravia without exception exhibit this morphological character. In certain localities we find a considerable diminution in brachycephaly, and we know, too, from various investigations—Niederle's in particular—that there are also great modifications in eye and hair colour.

Can the Germanic influence, which history shows has been considerable both in ancient Bohemia and in Moravia, be approximately calculated by means of the percentages of blue eyes associated with fair hair? These blond types are 18.3 per cent. of the population in Bohemia and 15.9 per cent. in Moravia. Still, to get an accurate notion of what has taken place it would be necessary to have carefully made local analyses of the central areas of Bohemia and the southern parts of Moravia, which have remained more homogeneous; and also of the Germanized belt which girdles these countries on three sides inside the encircling mountain chains. With analyses such as these we could find out whether this Germanic belt consists of people whose language alone entitles them to relationship with the great Germanic group, or whether the relationship consists in a genuine anthropological link with that race.

What we should require to know, in order to make valid comparisons, would be the morphological characters of the populations which one after the other contributed the polished stone, bronze, and proto-historic civilizations. Was the Silesian influence in Bohemia from the bronze age onwards, to which some archæologists have drawn attention, introduced by men who belonged anthropologically to the Germanic group?

The height of the Bohemian and Moravian Czechs is still little known. Niederle, in his book, makes use of the figures furnished by the small series studied years ago by Weisbach (1 metre 67).[1] Maybe this height really is right for the Czechs? We have reasons for thinking so. And maybe that in Moravia the people are not quite so tall (1 metre 66)? It would seem—we cannot be more dogmatic—that this proportion of tall men marks those districts containing the purest groups. But we must still find out whether this characteristic of greater height is accompanied by the brachycephaly and deep pigmentation which are the signs of the Dinaric race. Here again we come up against the inadequacy of anthropological research made with a view of a single character only—head-form, height, or coloration.

However that may be, and despite the penury of our documentation, it would appear to be impossible to place the Bohemian and Moravian Czechs on the same plane as those other Slavs we have already studied. Thus the "Slav" group appears more and more to be extremely disparate.

The Slavs of the Mark of Lusatia (Lausitz), surrounded on all sides by the German ethnic sea, and subjected throughout the centuries to the ever-recurring linguistic, social, and ethnic

1 **CCLXXVII**, preceded by another memoir on the Serbo-Croats.

action of the German tide which day by day flowed over and penetrated them—these Slavs to-day are no more than an anthropological relic.[1] Semnoni, Venedæ, and Sorabs, primitive tribes settled of old on these comparatively barren lands, what now remains of them ? Who, indeed, were they ? And how strong in numbers up to the time when Henry the Bird-Catcher created the Sorab Marches ? " Of the powerful nation of Slavs (it really does seem to have been very strong) which dwelt for centuries on the lower and middle Elbe, there remains but a few insignificant remnants," says Niederle.[2] But in what exactly did the puissance of this nation consist ? Was it due to the dominating and warlike valour of a few or of the mass—the " Slav " mass—of which it was composed ?

The history of the Lusatians is made up of struggles against the Germanic empire, struggles against the Roman Church, struggles amongst themselves. And it is admitted that between the twelfth and fourteenth centuries the Germans gradually got the upper hand, the Slavs " only presenting a few rare specimens of the race by the fourteenth century." In fact the Slavs appear gradually to have retreated, and it is sad for those who desire the liberty of all races to have to recognise the fact. The little island of Wends in the Lüneburger area, in that sparsely peopled country watered by the Elbe—that great Slav highway—and traversed by the Jeetze, is no more than a memory of a great period. Even the Slav tongue there is dead, as the mission sent by the Krakow Academy of Sciences discovered.

To-day, however, laudable efforts are making for the maintenance of this little ethnic unit[3] and the International Institute of Anthropology, anxious to obtain knowledge of and to preserve the smallest human groups (are they so well protected as the plant and animal " reserves "?) recently gave expression to the desire that an anthropological study of this island—to which the Germans of Saxony have accorded permission to retain the Slav speech—should be made with all necessary care.[4]

[1] Slavophils readily attribute to the ancient Polabs rather than to the Germans the burials by incineration to be met with in Lusatia. Still, some writers recognize that this is simply hypothetical.

[2] **CLXXVI**, p. 91.

[3] **CCLXII**, p. 283, 4.

[4] *C. R. Institut international d'anthropologie*, 1920, p. 248.

The Lusatians are apparently regularly diminishing in numbers—owing to Germanization and emigration. "Muka, travelling from village to village in 1880-84, fixed the Serb total at 175,966, finding 72,000 in Lower and 103,000 in Upper Lusatia. The official statistics for 1900 only give 93,032 Serbs speaking only Serbian."[1]

When we have before us the anthropological data about these islands of Western Slavs, we can understand the desire of the International Institute to obtain a knowledge of the morphological characters of these remnants. From the two or three scanty series of crania so far studied (de Quatrefages and Hamy were able to use for their *Crania ethnica* but a single specimen belonging to the Muséum de Paris) it would appear that the Lusatian Slavs—the Wends—are Brachycephals. The few crania measured by Virchow, near Kottbus, are clearly so; the rest, examined by Brœsike (crania from Saxony, in the Halle neighbourhood) and Spengel (Hanover) show sub-brachycephalic means. Deniker considers that he can give 84.6 as representing the cephalic index of this people in the living subject.

This little group of Slavs are far removed by their cranial characters from those members of their "race" who live nearest to them, that is to say, the Poles, on their east; but they closely approximate to the Czechs. Are they, perhaps, to be envisaged as an advance guard of these last who made their way north along the course of the Elbe? Or as a rear-guard which remained behind on the middle course of this river when the main body continued their southwesterly march, crossing the Erz Gebirge?

* * *

On the east of the Bohemian and Moravian Slav territory lies the chief homeland of the Slovaks, a region of tumbled primitive mountains whose melting snows are carried by innumerable streams into the Danube—the region dominated on the north by the Tátra and generally known as the Hungarian Highlands.

If we are to believe Slavists like Niederle, this people did not always inhabit this inner Carpathian zone. The Slovaks formed with the Czechs "at the beginning, an ethnic and

[1] **CLXXVI**, p. 96.

linguistic unit with occasional differences in dialect, which occupied the region situated to the south of the Sudetes and Carpathians. But this common domain was divided in two by the Carpathians, one part having its centre to the west and the other to the east. These geographical conditions gave birth to two political organisms. The Danube, which was the natural link between them, fell into German hands. In 1631 the Slovakian lands were detached from Bohemia and Moravia. The religious and literary links existing between the two groups never resulted in a re-knitting of the broken bond."[1]

Even within their own homeland the Slovaks were dissociated or grouped together according to the nature of the country that supported them, and tribes were formed. "The most venerable or the most authentic of these—because it has preserved the most completely the idiom and customs of the old Slavs—is the tribe of the Hornyaks or Highlanders in the hills threaded by the young waters of the Waag and the Nyitra. These, so far as can be conjectured from toponymy and bronze and iron age discoveries are, if not autochthonous, at least the earliest colonists in the central Carpathians. Their speech approximates to primitive Czech."[2]

Slovakia, the ethnic province, consists of some 1,700,000 souls.[3] The number of those amenable to its jurisdiction bear witness to a genuine vitality. In fact, the Slovaks have both assimilated a portion of their immediate neighbours the Germans—although of a higher civilization—and have sent colonists into many places.

If we leave aside the large cities, such as Vienna and Budapest, where they have large colonies, we shall find Slovaks constituting more or less strong islands in Hungary, not only in the comitats of Gran and Budapest, which lie at the very door of their own valleys, but in the great Theiss plain in Slavonia and Syrmia; near Semlin, and even in Bulgaria at Mitropolia, near Plevna. Unfortunately, anthropological data concerning these scattered members are of an altogether exiguous and insufficient nature, especially having regard to the size of these emigrant bodies. This is a great pity,

[1] **CLXXVI**, p. 131.
[2] **V**, p. 271.
[3] *Ibid*, p. 272.

because one sees at once how interesting it would be to know whether all these islands show the same morphological characters.

Niederle[1] has measured a few Slovakian crania, not only those from an ossuary of the eighteenth century at Ticha (Titschein) near Frankstadt, set aside for " Vlachs " (Wallachians), a group whose origin is " purely Slovakian and to whom was given the name of Roumanian Vlachs, who, in the eleventh and twelfth centuries went over into the Little Carpathians and became assimilated to the natives." These crania are brachycephalic (83.7). The same morphological conclusion results from a small series of Slovakian crania measured by the same writer (index of 84.9) at Altstadt near Koritschan Ung Hradisch to the west of the White Carpathians in the valley of the Morava.

This appears to be an ethnical characteristic of Slovaks in general, since another writer, Weisbach, also finds it in studying Slovakian crania from N.E. Hungary and Moravia (index of 83.5).

When we compare these figures with those yielded by other " Slavs " studied up to the present, we find that they differ widely from those furnished by their linguistic congeners the Poles, the Ukrainians, and various Russians. On the other hand they do approximate to the indices obtained from examination of series of Czechs and Lusatians. Do these figures alone establish the relationship of the Slovaks to Czechs and Lusatians ? A glance at the distribution of these groups on the map would lead one to think so. Lusatians, Czechs, Moravians and Slovaks represent under different names and with differences in their dialects, limbs of the same ethnic body. The Slovaks constitute, in the east, the last portion of that " Slav " cordon whose other end is to be found on the highway of the lower Elbe.

I have myself protested on too many occasions in the course of this work against the exaggerated value occasionally accorded to mean indices to utilize these without discrimination. All the same, it is impossible here not to be aware that it would be a strange concatenation of circumstances if, from Lusatia to the old Carpathian frontier of Hungary, these indices were never to represent anything but appearances.

[1] **CLXXVI**, p. 135.

Recall their values in geographical order, going from northwest to southeast—Lusatians, 84.6; Czechs, 85; Moravians, 85.6; Slovaks, 84.6. Then compare these figures with those of the Poles, their near neighbours. And would one not agree with the present writer that there is here an interesting comparative study to be undertaken? Until it convinces us to the contrary we may believe that Anthropology supports the historico-linguistic ideas which seek to show that the men of these four groups mentioned above are of the same race.

The small group of Slovenes who gave to the country lying between the Drave and Save the name which it bore up till the sixteenth century, represents the southwest portion of the Southern Slavs. It forms the last remnant of a once powerful contingent which at the beginning of the Middle Ages occupied the area contained within the bend of the Danube and the Adriatic highway and which penetrated deeply into the Alpine regions.[1]

We do not know when they first came to this territory. Niederle, who maintains a prudent reserve, thinks that from the beginning of the Christian era these Slavs "probably crossed the Danube and appeared in the neighbourhood of Lake Balaton and the Save." But, he adds, serious historical or archæological proof is lacking. What appears to be more certain is that we find these people in the country they occupy to-day at the close of the sixth century, and if Jordanes did not yet know of them in 551, that proves nothing. As early as 595 the Bavarians were struggling against the Slavs of Carinthia, who, in 600, menaced Italy.

Absorbed by the Slavs and then invaded by the Bavarians and Franks, the Slovenes were little by little Germanized by the Catholic Church. To-day their ethnic territory includes, according to Niederle, almost the whole of Carniola, "the north of Istria, Gorica, the Udine region in Friuli; the southeast portion of Carinthia, southern Styria and a small part of east Hungary (the two comitats of Vas and Zalad)".[2] It is considered that all the Slovenes put together (including the many who have emigrated to America) can be estimated at about 1,500,000. It is a group which increases but little.

[1] **CLXXVI**, p. 135; **V**, p. 298.
[2] **CLXXVI**, p. 139.

The anthropological data in regard to this island and its scattered members have been supplied by Weisbach and Zuckerkandl. The latter has published a study of 200 Slovene crania from Carniola. As a whole these crania are brachycephalic. Their mean index, 83.5, is not merely apparent, because there are no more than 0.8 per cent. of dolichocephalic individuals in the series, whereas the brachycephals number 80 per cent. Weisbach's series consists of far fewer individuals. His crania are also from Carniola and southern Stryia (Steiermark). They show 15 per cent. of dolichocephals ; I am at a loss to explain their origin. And these dolichocephalic crania, despite the presence of 75 per cent. of brachycephalic individuals, lower the mean cephalic index to 81.3.

This mountainous area dominating the extreme northern Adriatic does not appear to me to contain genuine "Slavs." That is to say, Slavs whose morphological and descriptive characters are like those of the majority of Russians. Such reserve is further imposed by an examination of stature. In fact, the height of these Slovenes is far greater than that of the other Slavs. It is probable that the mean is as high as and exceeds 1 metre 68, a figure which is far higher than that of the Poles or of Russians in general.

Do the inland territories inhabited by Slovenes perhaps contain the smallest men, while Istria and Küstenland (Litorale), on the contrary, shelter the tallest (1 metre 69) ? On the other side of the former Austrian frontier Italian Friuli shows tall stature to which Livi, moreover, has called attention ; so also has Tappeiner, in the area more to the northwest. It would seem evident that these coastal people, and those of the first belt of the hinterland, at least, belong to the tall brunet and brachycephalic Adriatic race.

The Slavonic speaking Slovenes are very likely only Slavonized. We have not yet sufficient information to warrant us in giving them a label en bloc. But it is highly probable that a large number of them, at all events, may be classified as of Adriatic race.

Both at Trieste and Venice one frequently comes across representatives of this handsome race. Travellers who are not entirely absorbed in their Baedeker or their Guides Joannes must have noticed them.

To bring this study of the "Slavs" to a close we have

still to examine several groups belonging, like the Slovenes, to the Yugo-Slav family—Croats and Serbs, and finally the Bulgars. Serbs and Bulgars we shall deal with when we come to the Balkan peninsular, but we must devote a few words to the Croats.

With the Serbs they once constituted a single group which the circumstances of history have split up into two nations. Difference of religion has added its profound imprint to accentuate the division between them. And I should imagine that the new State will need considerable subtlety and skill if it is to blend the various shades of dialect, the diverse tones of social life, the divergent religious conceptions and the memories of the past into that harmonious whole which a stable political State ought to be.

Constantine Porphyrogenetus tells how, according to tradition, it was in the reign of Heraclius (somewhere about 630-640) that the great migration of Serbs and Croats took place. Modern Slavists think otherwise, and make this movement of peoples at least a century earlier. Having set forth, we are told, as a single group, the different geographical nature of the lands they successively occupied made them in the end into two nations. Can we be quite certain of this geographical determinism ? It might equally well be invoked in the case of Croatia-Slavonia. But much less so for Bosnia, a large portion of whose territory turns its back to the sea and all of whose valleys run towards the Una and the Save, as the Serbian valleys run down to the Save and the Danube.

At first sight, and carrying a stage further what we know to be the case with Bosnians and Slovenes, the Croats—to whom we may add the Dalmatians—ought to belong to the Dinaric race, or at all events a large proportion among them. These Slavonized folk would thus be widely separated, anthropologically, from the Northern Slavs. Hence we can already see dawning a Yugo-Slavia whose ethnic characters are sufficiently distinct to admit of its being considered apart from the other Slav groups.

It must not be thought, however, that we base this appreciation on plentiful data, for these are still to seek. Nevertheless, investigations undertaken in various localities by the savants of former Austria-Hungary, some rapid travels in these regions and also some personal studies, lead us to believe in the existence of such a bloc—though not without its foreign elements. It forms a unit with that other bloc made up of scattered portions linguistically and politically diverse, which borders the eastern Adriatic and the Ionian sea as far as Cape Matapan.

The Croats of Croatia, Slavonia and Istria, and the Dalmatians in general, are round-headed. Their cephalic index must certainly exceed 85. Various maritime ports, however, would seem to lend to their immediate hinterland a less pure complexion—Ragusa and Zara, for instance, about which we have a certain amount of information, and where the inhabitants are less round-headed than elsewhere. This urban influence—exaggerated owing to the maritime character of the cities—is so real that even within its own district the index for the city itself is lower than that for the district as a whole.

The numerous islands strewn along the coast would seem also to have been populated by people of Dinaric race. The large islands of the Quarnaro—Veglia, Cherso and Lussin—have a highly-brachycephalic population. Maybe the other large islands to the south of the chaplet—Brazza and Lesina—dominated from afar by the mountains of Herzegovina, have a less unmixed population? Yet in Curzola, just beside them, the brachycephaly is accentuated. And the Cattaro district is one of the most highly brachycephalic areas that exists (index of 87.2)

The Dinaric race, as we have said! The head-form and the deep pigmentation have already justified this classification. Will the stature of the inhabitants support it?

Height is everywhere great, though principally in those areas facing seawards. Taking Slavonia-Croatia as a whole, it may be put at 1 metre 695, or even more, because the data utilized were chiefly measurements made on Army recruits who had not reached their full height. Maybe the inhabitants of Slavonia are slightly taller than the Croats?

Have the districts of Istria and Dalmatia likewise a smaller stature (1 metre 69)? In such a differentiation Fiume would be the locality having the lowest stature. The Dalmatians, on the contrary, would be the tallest. Their territory supplies several interesting facts of which we find it impossible not to make brief mention.

When we go through Dalmatia from north to south, leaving southern Croatia to go towards Montenegro, we find that whereas during one part of the journey the height of the people sensibly increases, in another it diminishes again.

Thus it is 1 metre 692 in the districts of Zara and Sebenico. In Sinj and Spalato it is 1 metre 707. At the foot of the Herzegovina, opposite the islands of Brazza and Lesina, the district of Makarska tops the scale of tall statures with 1 metre 737. It is probable that stature remains high all along this Herzegovinian frontier. The districts of Vrgorac and Narenta show 1 metre 727. This slight decrease may be merely an effect of the mean obtained from unequal or insufficient numbers. Then we find a fresh decrease in height in the districts of Ragusa (1 metre 691) and Cattaro (1 metre 698). In this area the influence of the very tall Montenegrins makes itself felt at once. The peasants—obviously of Montenegrin race—dwelling on the uplands show a stature of 1 metre 72 on the height scale. Travellers who have journeyed through Montenegro and Herzegovina will remember the very tall stature of the people ; it strikes the observer from the very first. It is certain that many of the inhabitants of these two countries left the mountains to come down to the seaboard, and that it is they who have sent up the height mean to this point in this last region.

Height likewise increases in the islands in a general way as we go from north to south.

These few complementary observations show us how very far Croats, Slavonians and Dalmations are from resembling the Slavs who live on the other side of the Hungarian bloc. And in these Yugo-Slavs we have a very good example of the anthropological mistakes to which a linguistic label may lead.

We cannot yet tell from what ethnic stock these Southern Slavs spring. But we can assert without possibility of error that it is not the stock whose representatives to-day are known under the name of Russians—of various nuances—and Poles. There is absolutely no community of origin between them.

How did these men of Adriatic race come to be Slavonized ? I have no idea, and it is not for me to find out. That comes within the province of History. I think, however, that the brief comparison just made between the Northern and Southern Slavs will convince anyone of the need for further research and more anthropological investigations if the truth is to be discovered.

Despite all the efforts of the Chancelleries it will be very difficult for the Northern Slavs, if it pleases them to begin anew wars which have an ethnic pretext, to invoke community of blood. In the eyes of those who know, the picture drawn of members of the same " racial brotherhood " who must be delivered from an alien yoke (the Turk knows something of this formula) will no longer glow with any but the colours manufactured from inaccurate statements. It will be worth about as much as a " scrap of paper." I am well aware that wars can be let loose by means of even less cogent arguments.

CHAPTER XIII

AUSTRIA

AUSTRIA, her former possessions on north and south amputated by the great war, occupies to-day, like Hungary, but a small place on the map. The plenipotentiaries cut her down more or less to her present linguistic frontiers—the Vorarlberg and the Tyrol (whose southern portion has been divided), the two Austrias, Styria, and Carinthia. This land of mountain and valley is not one that has been inhabited only from recent times. Palæolithic man roamed there in many localities, and beneath the thick layers of loess have been found numerous relics of his industry, and even of his art—for the Willendorf station has become famous as the site in which was found the "Willendorf Venus" made of oolitic limestone.

The German territory of Austria was inhabited more or less everywhere in the Neolithic period, and Lakes Constance, de Mond, and Atter[1] still contain thousands of sunken piles driven in by men of the polished stone age. As for the later periods, not a textbook but mentions the celebrated Hallstatt discoveries in the Salzkammergut, from which one of the iron age periods takes its name.

When the Barbarians drove out the Romans, who for a time dominated the country, they also, in the course of their onward march south and west across Austria to further and more brilliant conquests, drove before them into the highlands and valleys the descendants of many generations of prehistoric folk who had been established there for generations, Did the Barbarians in their turn mix with the former occupants? And if the answer is "yes," was this mixing slight or considerable? Did they influence the primitive race more than the Romans had done? It is difficult to give any certain answer to these questions at present.

[1] CLXVIII.

One ethnic group among the historic invaders, however, seems to have played an important part—the Slovenes—the rôle which, ethnically, devolves upon settled colonists. Towards the close of the sixth century, we are told, the Slovenes debouched by the corridors of the Lower Danube, pressed on by the Avars. They invaded the whole land as far as the Tyrol, by the Drave, the Mur, and the Enns. Then, strongly established in the Alps, these Slovenes freed themselves from the yoke of the Avars in 623, allying themselves with their trans-Danubian congeners. The German world, feeling itself menaced, was set in motion.[1] The Bavarians advanced, and soon Salzburg became the headquarters of Germanization. It was a tripartite organization which embraced Germanization, Christianization and colonization.

After Charlemagne had annexed to the Empire the entire territory of the Slovenes, German colonization became widespread through the agency of the Church and plantation by landed proprietors. They called in, it is said, German peasants, among whom Bavarians were naturally in the majority. For the accomplishment of this aim they had before them a large strip of accessible territory on the east, which was easy to cross.

It has been said that the German Austrians were transplanted and transformed Bavarians. Can anthropological investigation give us any information on this point ? We shall soon see. Anthropology has revealed one fact which we cannot pass over in silence, namely that the Germans—or rather, the German-speaking people—did not adventure far from the mountain massif. They did not penetrate into Hungary in compact masses any more than they did, in the south, into the Italian valleys of Venetia. They got across the Danube on to the left bank, but they were soon brought to a standstill by the Slav rampart.

The first anthropological investigations were undertaken in Austria in 1884, and eye and hair colour and head-form were investigated simultaneously. The first of these, of very wide extent as regards the numbers examined, and having school-children for its subjects,[2] must only be accepted with

[1] V, p. 42 ff.
[2] CCXXXIV.

caution, for we know how much the colour of the eyes and especially of the hair, is modified by years.

The second analysis was a craniological study by Zuckerkandl on German crania in different localities.[1] From that time forward useful research continued for many years, thanks, chiefly, to Weisbach.[2] They are being continued to this day[3]; and it is likely that soon we shall be able to draw up in accurate detail a map giving the Austrian ethnic character. For the time being, however, we are still restricted to generalities.

We must beware of certain early publications that are obviously inaccurate. It has been said, for instance, that one of the chief specific features in Austria was medium height among the Austrians properly so-called, and, by way of demonstration, statures of 1 metre 60 to 1 metre 69 were quoted. The mean, which would be slightly below 1 metre 65, would pretty well correspond to the European mean. But this conclusion is erroneous when put in this way, as we shall shortly see.

It was also said that the highlanders were smaller than the lowlanders, and this was pushed as far as finding 6 cms, a considerable difference, between them. The interpretation of this difference was naturally swayed by the doctrine of environmental influence—and we have already said what is to be thought of that.

Nevertheless, despite these errors of vision the geographers and publicists of those days brought out the interesting point that the German Austrians did not exhibit the same morphological and descriptive characteristics as the fair type of German from northern Europe, and this difference is capital. Its importance leaps to the eyes of the least informed.

In fact it was these anthropological studies undertaken in Austria which first began to disintegrate the ethnico-philological edifice of a Germanic race. Zuckerkandl, noting the obvious brachycephaly of the Austrians, came to the conclusion that this was a "shock to the dogma of German dolichocephaly". This shock developed into a complete crash. There were actually, then, Germans and Germans! In this case, as in

[1] CCXCIX.

[2] See LV, p. 58, for Weisbach.

[3] CXXXV.

that of Bavaria, for example, it is easily demonstratable that language does not make race.

Ethnic differences between the so-called Germanic groups are evident from neolithic times at least.

If we take the Alpine bloc within the jurisdiction of present-day Austria we shall see that, contrary to certain findings, its men are everywhere tall. We have proof thereof either in the means or in the percentages of tall individuals. And in this connection it is interesting to note that in the Tyrolese mountains the zone of tall stature stops short where the German language ceases to be spoken—we speak in a general way. The German Tyrol is inhabited by very tall men ; but stature drops directly we go into the Italian Tyrol. It would seem that in this area there is correspondence between language and race—the Italian-speaking Tyrolese morphologically approximating to the inhabitants of northeast Italy. Should not historians take advantage of this observation ? When the plenipotentiaries—they are usually the least well-informed of men—decided in 1918 on the new frontiers of Austria they were doubtless quite unaware of these facts or that a " nationality policy " based on race—a single example does not prove the rule—could have been envisaged.

In all the provinces of present-day Austria the mean stature of the inhabitants is above the European mean. Upper Austria has men of 1 metre 66 ; those in other regions all exceed 1 metre 67, and even 1 metre 68 in Carinthia. Nowhere do we find so low a mean as that (1 metre 60) formerly reported —we know not how—for Austria.

The interesting fact has been ascertained that height increases in German Austria as we go from west to east and from north to south. This is not a datum to be neglected. It may explain a great many things. If we link it up with what we have learned as to the routes of invasion we may be able to make some deductions which will not fail to throw light, to some extent at least, on the past. And I would at once remark that the Slovenes in the southeast are tall men whose height is equal to that of the German Austrians. Can these German Austrians, then, simply be Germanized Slovenes ?

Tall stature has been recorded in the heart of the Alpine massif in the upper valleys of the Enns and Mur in East Styria and in the southeast corner of Salzburg, an observation which runs counter to the theory of those who would make us believe that high altitude is unfavourable to the development of human stature. Perhaps we have here Slovene remnants who have been Germanized in speech. Austrian historians say that before the arrival of the Bayuvars all these lands were occupied by Slovenes. Does this morphological character demonstrate it ?

The cranial morphology of the German Austrians would seem to show the same homogeneity of character as does stature. Let us at once emphasise the following important fact. Deniker, in his memoir on the cephalic index, after having collated all the evidence placed at his disposal, said : " The Austrian Germans present a remarkable uniformity of head-form."[1] Present-day Austria forms a zone, sub-brachycephalic in its mean character, in which the indices lie between 82 and 83.

And if even at this stage we give a backward glance at the prehistoric periods we shall see that the picture presented by the Austrian population of to-day bears little resemblance to the ancient one. The neolithic folk of Austria were Dolichocephals. They very likely belonged to that same Germanic race which the Germans have met with in their early row-graves. In the iron age, at Hallstatt, among the salt workings which so greatly enriched the salt-lords of those days, the people were still dolichocephalic and dolichocephalic to a very high degree. Houzé suggested taking this physical type as representative of the long-headed race of the first iron age and calling it Hallstattian. Hence the changes in that part of Austria must have taken place at the very earliest at the close of prehistoric times.

We do not know if it is possible to say that what happened in the Dachstein mountains likewise happened throughout Austria, but it is probable that up till the iron age the majority of the Austrian people belonged to the long-headed type.

Provisionally admitting this extension of a local ethnic happening to the whole of Austria, we must conclude that the Austrians of to-day, instead of establishing by a natural genealogy their filiation with the prehistoric folk, will have to seek their origin among those migratory peoples who again and again appeared in the Alps. But which of them should be so envisaged ? We have to make good this Austrian

[1] LV, p. 58.

relationship claim by taking our stand on the results of anthropological investigation undertaken on a population which is both tall and brachycephalic—or sub-brachycephalic.

But let us first see how the cephalic indices so far ascertained are geographically distributed in German Austria.

The earliest work, that of Zuckerkandl on crania from Styria and Carinthia, yielded mean indices of 82.1 for Styria and 81.3 for Carinthia, that is to say, they showed brachycephaly. But when we examine the distribution of the different head-forms we see that the brachycephalic types are clearly in the majority. The relatively low indices are caused by the presence of a fairly large number of mesocephalic individuals and a few dolichocephals. These last, in the two regions mentioned, are respectively 4.2 per cent. and 5.7 per cent. These are but remnants and souvenirs—minorities of no importance. As for the brachycephalic forms they are respectively 76.4 per cent. and 65 per cent., Styria thus showing itself more brachycephalic than Carinthia. As we go from north to south, the head becomes rounder co-incidentally with an increase, as we have seem, in stature. Are we not getting nearer the domain of the Adriatic race?

Researches undertaken among the living population have revealed some highly interesting facts for those who would establish a link between Race and History; or for those who simply try to discover and isolate one ethnic group from among other human groups. We said that German Austria constituted a sub-brachycephalic zone. And we know from our previous studies that Austria is surrounded on all sides by round-headed people. What, then, does the distribution of the cephalic index show us on the Austrian periphery?

At the north of Lower Austria in the corner dominated on the west by the heights dividing Bohemia from Moravia, the Waidhofen and Zwettl districts have had their means raised owing to Czech influence. In Styria, in the neighbourhood of the brachycephalic Slovenes, we mark the same phenomenon.

Among observations of the same order we must also note this interesting fact that the district of Gmunden, in which lies the prehistoric station of Hallstatt, has the lowest cephalic index of all German Austria. Yet its geographical position places it in contact with sharply brachycephalic zones. It would seem difficult, then, to interpret this character in any other way than by the influence on the means of descendants of iron age Dolichocephals? A detailed analysis of the living population of this district would be particularly valuable. Moreover, such an investigation ought to be re-undertaken throughout the country and its results otherwise set out than by the artificial methods of distribution according to districts. When we examine eye and hair colour (this investigation also ought to be otherwise envisaged) we see that the brunet types (with dark eyes) and the blond types (with blue or grey eyes) are numerically fairly evenly distributed. Carinthia and Upper Austria appear to have more blonds than other regions, and, with Salsburg, to have the fewest brunets. Brunets are most numerous in Lower Austria, and then in Styria. As a whole the above provinces exhibit majorities of individuals belonging to what the Germans call *Mischtypen*, that is to say, types revealing mixed colouration.

If we put together all the data we possess and try to elucidate the origin of the present-day German Austrians, we must first of all conclude that the prehistoric folk, both those who fashioned in stone the statuette of the Willendorf Venus and those who so successfully exploited the salt-fields of Hallstatt, have left but few descendants. Their type, marked by dolichocephaly, barely survives in this corner of territory which, from its language and its history one would expect, at first sight, to show a different kind of people from those we actually find there. Still Philology and History must not impose upon us *a priori* ideas.

Thus, whereas in other parts of Europe we indubitably find in the same locality continuity of descent down to modern times—the descendants having kept through a succession of cultures their initial physical type—we do not find such filiation in Austria. In this country, as we have already said, new types intervened to make up the present population.

We know with some degree of certainty at what date we should place this influence, namely, after the iron age. Unless, indeed, we are to suppose that the salt-workers of Hallstatt themselves were foreigners in the land, miners and traders from the dolichocephalic areas of Northern Europe? Which, after all, is also quite possible! All the same, it is not very probable, since the burials containing the same physical type are too numerous. Among the groups which later invaded Austria and whose names history tells us, there is one which has preserved large contingents in the very regions we have been studying; we mean the Southern Slavs—Czechs and Moravians in the north, Slovenes in the south. And I am not far from thinking that which, indeed, our present knowledge would lead us to believe, that we can group together most of the people distributed over the country from the Sudetes to the Adriatic shore and give them a common label. This race has been disintegrated in the course of History since the early invasions. To-day one portion speaks a Slav and the other a German dialect.

But it is equally probable that to this race—because thus geographically delineated it would be a race—we should add a proportion, very likely a large proportion, of the Bavarians of the southeast.[1]

[1] The Magyar island—which we shall now study—is enclosed on almost every side by a human mass to which linguistic and social characteristics have given a heterogeneous appearance, and which bears a variety of names. A day will certainly come when we shall be able to define this mass as having had a common ethnic origin.

CHAPTER XIV

Hungary

PRIOR to 1914 Hungary was very much larger than it is to-day. Mutilated on all sides by the treaty of 1919, like its former associate Austria, Hungary looks a very small State to-day. It has lost all its mountain regions—the Tátra, the Beskiden and the Transylvanian Alps. It is now nothing but a plain, the Alföld. And even of this a big piece has been sliced off to the southeast to the advantage of Yugo-Slavia and Roumania.

Present-day statistics give Hungary a population of a little over eight million inhabitants.

During historic times and right up to the moment when the Magyars settled there, the flat alluvial lands traversed by the Danube and the Tisza had been the theatre of a considerable human ebb and flow, as had always been the case where these great plains, so favourable both for pasturage and agriculture, opened out.

Dacians, Yazigs, and Boi established themselves west of the Theiss (Tisza), then between this river and the Danube, continually pushing up into the west. Then they came into collision with the "Germanic" folk of Austria and Styria. To the south were Celts, Illyrians and Scordisks.

The Romans tried to bring order into this Pannonia ceaselessly undergoing invasions, but they never succeeded. On the other side of the Carpathians the Dacians were to accept the language of the conquerors and become Roumanians. But in the Alföld, though nearer Rome, the conquerors were not rewarded by the same success. The peoples of Hungary obstinately stood out against any such change.

Then came Goths, Vandals, Gepidæ and Huns. The Huns seem to have swept all before them, apparently becoming masters of the country. But did they annihilate the ethnic groups—many of whom may perhaps have been of the same origin—earlier settled on the same land? From the sixth to the ninth century the Avars dominated the country. The western portion of their empire, which was destroyed by the Franks in 803—the *Terra Avarorum* and the *Terra Hunnorum* —was thenceforward to hold a Christian people.

At the beginning of the tenth century the Magyars, come, it is said, from the Siberian steppes, pushed their incursions right into the heart of Germany and Italy. There they suffered reverses. Afterwards they re-formed their ranks and settled in present-day Hungary.

We know what arguments there have been about the primitive origin of the Magyars and how these discussions brought Vambéry and Hunfalvy into such violent opposition. Vambéry asserted that they were Turki-Tatars, Hunfalvy that they were Finno-Ugrians. The two champions sought their respective arguments the one in history (Vambéry) and the other in philology, and both found evidence, even in the armoury of the adversary, in support of their theses. It would have been interesting, no doubt, to have allowed the anthropologists to take part in this debate!

There is one certain fact and that is that the Magyars no more allowed themselves to become Slavonized like their neighbours than the earlier occupants of the land had allowed themselves to be Romanized. They put up an invincible defence against the transformation which at that time was going on all around them. They constituted the solid bloc familiar to us. And it must be recognized that a very high civilization led one to expect, before the war of 1914, that Hungary might be called to a great destiny in the empire of the Hapsburgs.

This Magyar resistance to absorption drew its strength from an extremely lively sense of race; this ethnic sentiment was perhaps somewhat muddled, but it translated itself into sharply defined national consciousness. This case merits the attention of politico-psychologists, who would do well to invite the co-operation of ethnologists in its elucidation.

The Magyars amplified this sentiment of an essential ethnic concentration, of whose value they were well aware, by inculcating a spirit of obstinate centralization to the detriment of their neighbours. All the aliens settled on the periphery of the Hungarian bloc were summoned by successive Acts, notably the Nationalities Law of 1868, to become integral elements of the Hungarian nation. Naturally the language of this nation was to be Magyar, made obligatory (save for the Croats) in all government publications, for University Chairs, and in the Diet, etc.[1] ; it must be recognized, as some excuse for the Magyars, that they were not alone in Europe in attempting such centralization despite differences of race and sociological ideas. It remains to be seen whether such-like aggregations, as heterogeneous as this was from the ethnic point of view, have any chance of lasting permanently.

The Magyars represent the most prolific element in former Hungary, and also one of the elements that was least given to emigration. These two tendencies explain why the statistics ever showed a steady increase of the Magyar group within the empire as a whole. A single example will indicate the comparative value of this group in Hungary alone, such as she was in 1914.

The statistics of 1880 to 1890, which may serve as typical, show that, whereas the Magyar increase was 14.88, the German increase was only 6.35, the Wallachian 7.64, the Ruthenian 7.52, and the Serbo-Croatian 7.40. And this should not be so surprising, for the ethnic prolificacy of the Magyars is not merely apparent. What we know of it is not just the result of a statistical operation, whereby different human elements geographically placed together in one bloc under the name of Magyars, might create an illusion. Dissecting these very statistics and isolating comitats with large Magyar, Slovak and Roumanian majorities, G. Thirring has shown the respective prolificacy of each. Taking a thousand inhabitants, the increase in births was as follows: Roumanian comitats, 4.69; Slovak, 6.22; Magyar, 9.40. Over a period of twenty years between 1870 and 1890 the increase works out (in the same order) at 9.10; 17.38; and 20.22.[2] Is not this sufficiently demonstrative?

The nationalist confidence of the Magyars—the glorification of a race conscious that it had occupied the land for a thousand years—was easy to see throughout Hungary before the war. A few hours in the country sufficed to make one aware of it. I have noticed it time and time again. This

[1] **V**, p. 241.
[2] **V**, p. 249.

sentiment of the grandeur of their lineage and of its relative unity will certainly prove a powerful lever for the present Hungarian leaders, for to-day it must be exacerbated. They will draw new energy from their misfortunes. For all who know the country it is perfectly certain that Hungary will rise up again from its economic ruin.

Before the dismemberment ordained by the treaties the Magyars in Hungary were divided into two groups of unequal size—the Székely in the Transylvanian mountains, and the Hungarians in the great alluvial plains. The first are now outside the political frontiers of Hungary. The second remain concentrated in the plains they have always occupied. They themselves are severally subdivided into Kumans, Yazigs, etc.[1] which for the most part appear to be merely reminiscent of the primitive tribes which settled in the Alföld.

Morphological differences dividing the inhabitants of Great Kumany (between the Maros and the Tisza) from those of Little Kumany (on the other side of the Tisza) and from the Yazigs (to the east of Buda-Pest, at the foot of the mountains) have been reported, the first being considered to be taller and pale-complexioned, and the second to exhibit Tatar characters (are these not mere literary fancies ?). The last—they are also of tall stature—were supposed to be famous for their physique and the beauty of their women. At what are we to value such information ? As the remarks of sentimental travellers, notes taken by people in a hurry, or as scientific certainties ?

The various anthropological investigations undertaken in Hungary at once brought out this general fact that the Magyars are small people. The figures for Army recruits published by the statistical Bureau of Pest, and in which the ethnic groups of Hungary are considered separately, already show this clearly. The Magyars are shorter than the Vlachs and Serbs, Slovaks and Germans who dwell side by side with them, and whom they at one time dominated. They are a little taller than the Ruthenians. I do not give the figures showing the

[1] In the region cut up by marshes, of which Debreczen is the centre, the Hajdu, settled in the marches which were granted them of old for services rendered, remember the ancient democratic republic founded by their ancestors. To the west and southwest of the Hajdu, the Yazigs and the Kumans also rejoiced in older times in almost complete autonomy. Up till the eighteenth century they kept themselves free from any responsibility towards the Hungarian State.

stature of these army recruits[1] because the stature of such youths, who have not finished growing, can only suggest incorrect ideas. But the figures can well be compared among themselves.

The mean height of the Magyars in general would not exceed 1 metre 64. Thus it is lower than the European mean. But we have seen that the Magyars by their policy of conquest have incorporated within their State a fairly large number of foreigners, and we have just noted that with the exception of the Ruthenians, all the alien people of Hungary are taller than the Magyars themselves. It arises from this, *a priori*, that the Magyar stature must be very low, at all events lower than the above mean. In order to get a correct idea of stature Hungarian anthropologists have more especially examined the districts in which Magyars are almost the only inhabitants; or those in which they are at least in a proportion of from 80 to 99 per cent. With majorities such as these the means may be considered ethnically stable.

In the basin of the Tisza the comitats thus almost exclusively peopled by Magyars everywhere show a low stature, inferior to the Hungarian mean. Hajdu and Yazigs figure in these comitats, the first, agriculturists, being very small (1 metre 61), and the second being a little taller (1 metre 63), but not reaching the country's mean.

To the west of Buda-Pest the Raab-Komorn (Györ-Komarom) district on both shores of the Danube, and in the south, the comitats of Stuhlweissenburg (Székesfehervár), Veszprem and Somogy—all to the west of this river—show a stature sometimes a little greater than that of the Hajdu, going from 1 metre 626 to 1 metre 639, and even in Raab (Györ)[2] to 1 metre 646. We can recognize in this increase in height to the west of the country the obvious sign of the "Germanic" or Slovene (see above) influence of Austria and Styria.

And the proof that this is a foreign manifestation due to the tall Magyarized settlers is to be found simply by noting the height of the Magyars living in the southeast corner of Transylvania. In the comitats of Csik (Cic), Udvarkely (Odorhei) and Heromszek (Treiscaune), populated by Székely,

[1] Published by the Statistical Bureau of Pest. Vol. v, p. 259.
[2] LIII, p. 117.

where the statistics indicate a proportion of from 84 to 90 per cent. of these folk and hence that it is in the heart of the domain of the Magyar race, the mean stature is 1 metre 62.

Thus wherever the Magyars have been able to preserve their ethnic purity we find small people. And if certain comitats, of relatively pure race, show an increase, though a feeble increase, in height, it is because they include large urban agglomerations. The urban influence in increasing stature is manifest in Hungary as elsewhere. It also modifies the means. In the urban regions of the comitat of Buda-Pest stature rises to from 1 metre 646 to 1 metre 656.

The Magyars are brachycephalic. All the series of the Alföld show round heads. To be convinced it needs only that one should look through the photograph albums published by Janko.[1] The mean indices would be round about 84. The Székely of Transylvania are brachycephalic like other Magyars. Possibly brachycephaly is even more accentuated in Kumany than elsewhere. This phenomenon can be explained by the geographical position of this central group protected on all hands against infiltration from the periphery by dense fringes of other Magyars which serve it as an ethnic rampart.

Present-day Hungary certainly represents a State in which homogeneity of race is associated with a linguistic character. Its present frontiers enclose—and this is rare in Europe—a relatively pure group.

What has become of the descendants of the many peoples whom the ancient historians put on record as having invaded the Hungarian plains a little before the Christian era, and also after it began? It is probable, given the morphological characters of the inhabitants of Hungary, that among the peoples who came from the east there were several which belonged to the same ethnic stock as the Magyars themselves. Otherwise we should have great difficulty in understanding the Maygar anthropological unity just noted. Or perhaps these peoples only passed across the Alföld! It is said that in 1239, 40,000 Kumans, under pressure from Mongol invaders, came and sought sanctuary of Bela IV, King of Hungary, who granted them the lands which their descendants occupy to-day.

[1] CXXI.

But these Kumans were probably but a portion of a larger group which in earlier times had already supplied Hungary with immigrants bearing different names.

It is also said that the Kumans were a Turki folk. I do not know what this assertion is worth envisaged from other points of view than that which we occupy here. Anthropologically it would seem worthless, especially if under the name of the Turki " race " the Osmanli are put forward as being the most representative of this ethnic group.[1]

It seems more and more evident to me that the Avar and Magyar invasions, which appear to be by far the most important, were but detachments of a single whole, or two outlets issuing from the same ethnic lake.

From the anthropological point of view the Hungary of to-day is a problem much simplified. In 1914 we could not have reached such a conclusion in speaking of Hungary. It would have been necessary to concern ourselves with the neighbours of the specifically Magyar area, and we should have had to unwind several of those wrappings of Magyarization with which the policy of " ethnic centralization " had in each generation enveloped them through the agency of the State, the Church, and especially of the Schools. In order to attain political ends—but once more the Magyars are far from being the only ones in Europe—a Magyar cloak was flung over the shoulders of a large number of non-Magyar people to whom it was then said—Behold! You are Hungarians! We know what protests followed each of these Acts. It is to be hoped that Hungary's neighbours, to whom the peace treaties have given the charge of Magyar groups, will not in their turn furnish occasion for similar protests.

Hungarian territory has been peopled from very early antiquity. It has furnished remains of palæolithic industry, especially in the low hills at the east of the great bend of the Danube, and the local museums such as that at Miskolcz, and the Geological Institute of Buda-Pest, etc., contain sets of implements going back to the Acheulean phase. But for the present we cannot picture to ourselves the physical type of the men who left these remains. Hungary has also furnished

[1] This possibility of a Turki origin may be envisaged somewhat differently.

numerous remains of the civilization of those periods which came after the flaked stone age.[1]

We have every reason to suppose that the pre-historic and proto-historic populations are not the ancestors of the Magyars. In Hungary the problem of filiation is singularly simplified, for the local genealogy is recorded in History.

[1] **CCXXIV**; **XCVIII**, p. 935, and the Congress of Geneva, p. 355; **CCXLI**, p. 28.

We know that on many occasions deformed skulls of macrocephalic type (Hippocrates' deformity) have been found in Hungary, see **CXXXIX** and **CXI**.

CHAPTER XV

THE BALKAN PENINSULAR

THE Balkan peninsular has played a considerable part in contemporary history. How many wars have drenched these lands in blood even since the great Turkish invasion! Russia, anxious, as she made out, to liberate these brethren of her race—but in reality hankering after the shores of the Black Sea and Constantinople—again and again, by bestowing upon them the borrowed name of Slav, stirred up the Orthodox of the Peninsular to revolt in the name of Slavism. Gradually the Roumanians, Serbs, Greeks and Bulgars, and finally the Albanians freed themselves from the suzerainty and then from the sovereignty of the Turk.

Austria-Hungary, whose greed went the length of wanting to annex Salonica, also did her best to dismantle the Ottoman empire in Europe. To-day Turkey possesses of her vast territories of olden days eastern Thrace only (officially she retained in Europe only the hinterland of Constantinople up till the Lausanne peace) and that is why we shall study the anthropology of the Osmanli Turks in the chapters dealing with Asia.

Owing to our penury of documentation I can give but little space to the Balkan States. Perhaps the day will come when in a new edition we can greatly extend the following chapter by making use of information which will since have been obtained.

*

* *

The anthropology of the Balkan peninsular is as interesting as it possibly could be. The historical events of these lands of themselves would justify a detailed study of this peninsular, traversed, as it has been, by so many European and Asiatic peoples.

The prehistory of the Balkan States is still more or less unknown. The existence of a somewhat vague palæolithic phase has barely been placed on record, and we are not even altogether sure about this determination. No pleistocene stratigraphy of any sort has yet been established. Nevertheless it is certain that the early folk of the Peninsular had their worked stone age just as the inhabitants of old Hungary and South Russia had theirs. We find the palæolithic fauna in the Balkans; we are still hoping to find traces of the hunters who pursued them.[1]

The neolithic period has come to light pretty well throughout the Peninsular—in Bosnia, Serbia, Moldavia, Greece, etc., and latterly in Albania. But although evidences of material life are quite plentiful even at that date, anthropological data, alas, are extremely rare. We shall not have to devote more than a few pages to them when we draw up the ethnical balance sheet for each State.

In any case it is impossible to dream of establishing any kind of permanent filiation between the present population and the prehistoric folk of the Peninsular.

Up till recent years the anthropological map of the Balkans showed wide spaces completely blank. And the parts shaded in were only extensions of local tints done by the aid of provisional data. To-day we are much better informed.[2] But wide investigation based on numerous local analyses are imperative everywhere.

Numerous peoples, or at least peoples who have different names, entered the Peninsular in every period, some coming from Asia and some from Europe. The Danube valley, a natural highway, accessible almost everywhere, established contact between the Asiatic and the European world. The neolithic Brachycephals followed this road, going up it as far as the Alps, which they both crossed and turned. Later on the Huns and Ottomans followed in their tracks to some extent, just as, in the bronze and iron ages, the traders who placed Scandinavia and the Archipelago in communication also took this route. The Barbarians were to come, some from the west, like the Gauls, and others from the Scythian plains. Many other names have been mentioned side by side with

[1] The Abbé Breuil ("Notes de Voyages paléolithiques en Europe centrale," *l'Anthropologie*, 1923, p. 333), after a tour of the museums of Central Europe, notes, not as a personal observation, but as an indication "furnished by Polish friends," Aurignacian discoveries in Bulgaria and Serbia. Aurignacian *pointes à base fendue* were found near Tirnova, and in the caves near Belgrade.

[2] **CXCV**, Introduction.

their's by the historians—Dorians, Thessalians, Pelasgians, Illyrians, Scythians, Thracians, Getæ, Dacians, etc. Many of these groups are already known to us. But we do not know either in their case or in that of the others which of them issued from a common stock or which of them were of different ethnic origin. Then there are the modern Asiatic peoples—Kurds, Armenians, Tatars, Czigany, etc. As we have already said, there is material in the Balkans to last the anthropologists for the rest of their natural lives.

I

THE ROUMANIANS

Since the great war the Roumanians have modified the axis of their geographical position, placing it further north. By the addition to their territory of Transylvania they have been removed further from the Balkans. They were already on the borders of the Peninsular. I think geographers might now agree not to count Roumania as one of the Balkan States.

Glacial phenomena were exceptional in Roumania. The highest summits of the Carpathians alone served as condensers of the eternal snows. The caves of this mountain chain ought to contain human relics of palæolithic times. A few attempts at excavation made long ago in the upper Jalomitza give me assurance of the fact. It would be highly desirable that the Roumanian savants should undertake researches in this direction.

Roumania was already peopled in the neolithic period. Skeletons of this period are still rare, but a few have been discovered at Cucuteni (Moldavia) which show that at that time the Roumanian race was already composite.

Beyond this meagre indication we know nothing, anthropologically, of the people who occupied Roumanian territory up to the present epoch. Thracians, Getæ, Peucini, Kumans, etc., who inhabited ancient Roumania—what were the ethnic characters which might enable us to relate them to one or other of the European races?

Present-day Roumania comprises approximately those areas considered by the Roumanians to be peopled by men of their race. The political results of the war have attached to the main body the Roumanians of the northern and eastern borders. There are naturally a fairly large number of folk of alien race in Transylvania, the Banat and Bessarabia. But there are also Roumanians rather far beyond the limits of the kingdom, notably the considerable groups of Koziani-Vlachs (Macedonian Roumanians, "one-legged" Vlachs, etc.), in the Rhodope and Pindus mountains, whom we also meet in other parts of the southwest Balkans, and the small group of Roumanians in Istria.

The Roumanian people is essentially a peasant folk. It is hardy, industrious and prolific. It holds in reserve the elements out of which a bourgeoisie—which Roumania does not yet possess—might be created. On many occasions homage has been done to the artistic sense of these peasants who are so skilled in the decorating of their domestic articles and their houses, and whose costume is so becoming, and, often, so magnificently embroidered.[1]

The first anthropological studies on Roumanians were made outside the kingdom: Weisbach studied the Roumanians politically subject to Hungary, and Bassanovitch those who had emigrated to northeast Bulgaria, early in the nineteenth century. The first of these investigations yielded a brachycephalic and the second a dolichocephalic index. In these contradictory conclusions there was matter for perplexity. Obédénare, himself a Roumanian, showed a few Roumanian crania at the Société d'anthropologie de Paris in 1874; two of them, considered to be pre-historic (?), were dolichocephalic.

Our knowledge was limited to these two or three obviously insufficient studies up till 1899, when I began my first anthropological investigations in Roumania.

I published a series of memoirs on the anthropological characteristics of this country in the *Bucarest Scientific Societies' Bulletin*. And I have also before me a considerable quantity of data with which to attempt, in particular, a geographical distribution of morphological elements according to districts. Unfortunately this evidence has not yet been published. However, we can form an approximate idea, from what is known, of the anthropology of the Latin kingdom of the Orient.

The mean stature of the Roumanians should be somewhere near what is considered to be the European mean, viz.: 1 metre 65. The Roumanians of Bukovina seem to be taller

[1] **CXXII**, *bis*.

and those of Hungary smaller. Sixty thousand Roumanians in the kingdom itself yield as their mean stature 1 metre 65.

Perhaps we should slightly raise this figure obtained from soldiers, and make it 1 metre 66, because these men might not have reached their full height.

The Roumanian head-form, like the Roumanian stature, is very much on a par with that of the European mean. I have before me a graph of the cephalic index taken from 326 crania. Brachycephalic and dolichocephalic types are almost equal in numbers, the former being slightly in the majority. The Roumanian mean cephalic index shows sub-brachycephaly.

When we classify them according to the hills and plains, the two main regions of the country, we find that the hill population is more brachycephalic than the lowland folk. Is this because the highland valleys of the Carpathians still hold a population that approaches nearer in ethnic type to what we may call the primitive Roumanian type? Nothing leads us to such a conclusion, unless it be the idea, *a priori*, that in hilly regions we shall find the least mixed population.

The Roumanians themselves readily confirm this supposition. When they talk of their history they agree with one accord in saying that at the time of the invasions their ancestors of those days, who had taken refuge in the high valleys and in the mountains, allowed the invaders to come into the country without themselves becoming incorporated with them or mixing with them.

From the results of a comparative study I have attempted in this direction—it is not yet adequate—it appears that the Roumanians of the Carpathians, both those in Transylvania and those in Roumania strictly so-called, are more brachycephalic than the others.

The mean cephalic index of the Roumanians in general is about 82.92. It indicates sub-brachycephaly. A series of nearly 200 Roumanians from Transylvania yielded me a higher figure—84.37—confirming what has been said above on the subject of the highlanders.

Taking the mean, Roumanians are leptorrhinians who come very near to being mesorrhinians. They have relatively short, broad faces. Maybe this chamæprosopy remains to this day more characteristic of the Roumanian highlanders than of the plainsfolk.

These people, whose stature is slightly above the average and who are in general sub-brachycephalic, practically never have fair hair. I found only 2.7 per cent. of fair-haired people. The hair is nearly always dark—either brown or chestnut, and often black.

Blue eyes are also rare (8.9 per cent.). Brown irides are far more frequent than those of any other shade.

The Roumanian nose is generally straight.

These few indications show us that we must not look to a people having the northern characters when we seek the earliest origin of the Roumanians; in spite of their migrations, the Goths and other Germanic folk cannot claim the Roumanian people as their descendants.

This finding in itself is of great importance. But it does not solve the problem with which we are faced. Obviously the original Roumanian stock must have been a race of medium height, brachycephalic and brunet in the majority.

What were the morphological characters of the Dacians and Getæ whom the Roumanians consider to be their ancestors—the men who so valiantly defended themselves against the Roman legions? Were their characters just those which we have reported above? We are absolutely without any knowledge on the matter. Maybe in the actual presentment of the present-day Roumanian we see the very image of those peoples.

In any case it is vain to seek an actual Roman origin for the present type of Roumanian. Though the Roman armies vanquished the ancient Roumanians, they have left nothing beyond their language to the conquered people.

To what race—or races—did those legions belong which invaded Dacia? To many, according to history. How many Latins, real Latins who were born in Latium, were there in the Roman armies at the period of the wars against Dacia which led to its conquest? What the conquerors gave to Roumania was the Latin tongue and a Latin administration. They did not give them much of their blood.

What fine anthropological work awaits the doing in Roumania! Having started it in the course of repeated travels I have not yet relinquished my intention of pursuing it. But why do our Roumanian friends not set their hands to this task?

They might well start by finding out the earliest filiation of their race—that which begins in palæolithic times.

There are a few neolithic skeletons, discovered at Cucuteni, at the University at Jassy. The people of that period, as we said, were already mixed. But what was the physiognomy of the people who certainly must have preceded them on Roumanian territory?

This youthful nation which places so many legitimate hopes in its future and which has so many intellectual resources, cannot leave on one side the study of its origins and the investigation of its "ethnic state."

II

THE SERBS

The Serbs are even less well-known, anthropologically, than the Roumanians.[1]

When Deniker's map of the cephalic indices of Europe was published Serbia was left blank. Nothing was known of the head-forms of this people. This indicates that all data relating to Serbia are from recent work.

Serbs and Croats primitively constituted a single ethnic group. Dwelling together "north of the Carpathians" they spoke the same language. The chances and fortune of migration quartered them in regions where certain existing differences became accentuated, and new ones developed. One group became Catholic, the other Orthodox. The Croats use the Latin alphabet for writing and the Serbs the Cyrillic.

Anyone who travels in the Near East very soon realizes the full social force of religion. On occasion "religious nationality" has been substituted for political nationality. And in the struggle with Turkey the Great Powers were well aware of the advantages to be reaped from such spiritual states of mind, Orthodox Russia on a large scale on the one hand, and Catholic Austria somewhat more modestly on the other.

Nothing could be more instructive, in this regard, than what happened in Bosnia before the war. Catholic Austria found no difficulty in attacking the Croats who were of the same communion as herself. All the resistance to a general rally came from the Orthodox Serbs. To obtain a majority the Viennese Government was obliged to associate the Croats with the "Turks"—geographically the Islamized Dinarics.

[1] CXCV, p. 99.

Constantine Porphyrogenetus tells us that the Serbo-Croat migration took place in the seventh century in the reign of Heraclius. Niederle puts it back considerably and places the march of the Serbian and Croatian tribes southeastwards in the fifth or sixth centuries.

The Serbs, a valiant nation whose future may be truly great, sent out colonies far and wide, especially to the lands lying north of Serbia. Groups even established themselves at different periods at a considerable distance—as far as the neighbourhood of Pest, and in the lower Dnieper area. Of the anthropological character of these we know absolutely nothing.

The neolithic period was probably a flourishing one in Serbia. Dr. Miloj Vassits described some years ago the discoveries made at Jablanica, where, at a depth of two metres, polished stone age remains, unmixed with any traces of metal, had accumulated. This station yielded clay statuettes known as " owl-faced," similar to those of Cucuteni, Butmir (Bosnia), etc.

We know nothing definite about the races which peopled Serbia in prehistoric and proto-historic times. In order to discuss them we shall be obliged to proceed by analogy with what took place in Roumania on one hand and in Bosnia on the other.

Are the present-day Serbs the ethnogenic product of the " Slav " invasions? By way of reply, let us examine their anthropological characters.

The stature of the Serbs is tall. It probably exceeds 1 metre 70. So far as our present knowledge goes it is one of the highest in the whole peninsular. And this character is not to be neglected in any research into the origin of this people. But the height graph shows that there are also, to the left of the mean, a large number of individuals who do not reach 1 metre 65. This first discrimination would seem to indicate that the Serbian people is composed of two main ethnic types.

The mean cephalic index of the Serbs (80.66) shows mesaticephaly. The distribution of the individual indices shows a predominence of Dolichocephals (39.2 per cent.) with a relatively large quantity of intermediate types (30.7 per cent.). The brachycephalic forms do not reach this percentage (29.8). This variation in cranial form complementing what has been said above with regard to stature, leads one to think that the Serbian population is an ethnic mixture.

On the other side of the Save the Serbo-Croats are much more brachycephalic (index of 86 according to Weisbach); so are the Serbs of Bosnia-Herzegovina (index of 85.7). In order to find dolichocephalic types in the neighbourhood of Serbia we must go southeast to Bulgaria, where they were reported in some early work. It is probable that a portion of the Serbs and of the Bulgars could be classed together as a special ethnic group.

The Serbians are leptorrhinian in mean character (but mesorrhinians are also plentifully represented); the irides are generally light (60 per cent.) and often blue even (about 20 per cent.). And if fair hair is rare (8 per cent.) among them, so also is black hair, which is even more infrequent (4 per cent.). The intermediate shades are the rule.

The Serbian nose is generally straight. But among this people we often meet with a turned-up nose that is depressed at the root.

To what race are we to link the Serbs? Are they really the descendants of the barbarian peoples who in the fourth and fifth centuries invaded the lands to the south of the Save and the Danube? Has there been unbroken continuity from the autochthonous people whom the Romans found there when they conquered the country? Up till the iron age the primitive peoples of the western Balkans—geographically the people of Bosnia-Herzegovina, which is the only region that has been studied from this point of view—were in the large majority long-headed. And the Serbs are very often dolichocephalic.

One can see how necessary it is that detailed research in the Kingdom of the Serbs, Croats and Slovenes should be undertaken before we can give any reply to such questions—and I do not say in the old Kingdom of Serbia alone. A better knowledge of the anthropological characters of the Croats and the Slovenes would certainly widen our horizon.

In any case I would wish to add this one further observation.

If we are to consider the Serbs as being the descendants of the Slav tribes which invaded the Eastern Empire, we then have a picture before us of what these hordes called in by

Heraclius really were, and this is an important bit of historical documentation for us to bring to the study of events in south-eastern Europe.

Did these Slav tribes of Serbs spring from the same ethnic stock as the Slavs who to-day people Russia and Poland —those areas supposed to be specifically Slav? In order to find out and to be convinced to the contrary we have only to turn to the chapters devoted to the Slav peoples. We can definitely assert that the Serbs are not their " racial brethren."

The full value of this conclusion can escape no-one. But it does not solve the problem of Serbian origins.

As for the Croats, although they may have been quartered " north of the Carpathians " along with the Serbs, and although they may have moved off at the same time that the Serbs did, they certainly do not belong to the same race. At least, what we know of their anthropology to date is demonstrative in this sense.

III

THE BOSNIAN-HERZEGOVINIANS

The Bosnian-Herzegovinians who now form part of the new kingdom of Serbia are among the best-known of the Balkan peoples. This is due to the creation by Austria-Hungary of a remarkable museum at Sarajevo, whose director and conservators constitute a scientific staff of the first order.

Three "religious peoples" shared Bosnia-Herzegovina before the war—the Catholic Croats, the Orthodox Serbs, and the Musulmen Turks. But these are mere labels which can form no sort of precedent for a judgment of the racial problem.

When the Roman legions advanced into Bosnia-Herzegovina (the first battle took place in 229 B.C.) they found the country occupied by the descendants of a very ancient people going back at least to the polished stone age. The neolithic civilization has left numerous remains in Bosnia. The neolithic folk were settled in the very faubourgs of Sarajevo. The bronze age has also left important remains. The largest known necropolis of these pre-Illyrians is at Glasinac, 26 kilometres northeast of Sarajevo.[1]

[1] CXCV, p. 127.

The people of prehistoric Bosnia seem to have been of quite another type from the present population. The necropolis at Glasinac chiefly yields Dolichocephals and Mesaticephals (about 76 per cent.). The Brachycephals represent only a fourth of the Bosnian folk of those days.

What a difference this is from what we see to-day! Bosnia-Herzegovina is inhabited by men of tall stature. They are one of the tallest peoples in Europe (1 metre 72). They are at the same time highly brachycephalic (index of 85.7) and brunet. They constitute one of the most representative elements of the handsome Dinaric (or Adriatic) race which we know to be distributed from Trieste, at least, to Cape Matapan.

The ancient Bosnian population morphologically approximated more nearly to the present-day Serbs than to the Bosnians of our times.

IV

THE MONTENEGRINS[1]

We know less about the Montenegrins than about any other people of the Peninsular. What can be said is that the inhabitants of Montenegro belong to the same race as the Bosnian-Herzegovinians. In the course of a hasty journey through Montenegro I was able to measure a few individuals. Very tall, highly brachycephalic, leptorrhine, brunet, with straight nose and very dark eyes, they possess all the characters of the Dinaric race.

V

THE BULGARS

Bulgaria holds men of diverse origin. One needs but a single glance at the maps giving stature and cephalic index to be convinced of it.

Like the Serbs, the Bulgars have played a premier part in the history of the European East. And when in the middle of the fifteenth century the death took place at Belgrade of Constantine, the son of Chichman, last Czar of the Bulgars, a shining orb had fallen from the firmament causing

[1] CXCV, p. 133.

night for more than four hundred years. Who were these Bulgars whose empire had been so flourishing ?

Certain authorities consider them to have been an important limb of the Turki tree, and this is held especially of those Bulgars of the Volga who, among other adventures, crossed the Danube in 679 under the leadership of Asparoukh, and penetrated into the Dobruja.

But before the arrival of Asparoukh the Balkan peninsular already held large contingents of Bulgars.

Between the third and sixth centuries, among the Barbarian hordes which crossed the Danube, there was one of " Finno-Uralian origin " which succeeded in founding a solid State. These Bulgars would at first have remained in Asiatic Sarmatia, " that is to say, according to de Guignes, in the plains to the west of the Volga, where, according to most writers, the name Bulgar originated."

But all this early history is extremely obscure, especially if it is separated from what is legendary. According to Kanitz[1] the first mention of the Bulgars by western writers dates from 485. The Bulgars soon achieved military success in the Peninsular. In 559 they menaced Constantinople. At various times they occupied a large portion of the Balkan States, occasionally allying themselves with the Serbs, or fighting them, and fighting against the Croats and Magyars. In the course of their sweeping movements they came right to the source of the Tisza.

What remained, at the end of a few centuries, of these hordes of primitive Bulgars ? More especially after the constitution of the great States like those created by the Simeon dynasty of Basils, or by Samuel who proclaimed himself " emperor of all the Slavs ", or by Joanice Asen II ? The incorporation of other Balkanic peoples certainly brought about ethnic mixture up till the time when the Tatars were to impose their dominion and perhaps their blood.

Does the anthropological analysis of Bulgaria show the character of unity, or, on the contrary, does it bring out the presence of such heterogeneous elements as might be explained by History ?

Up till the time when serious investigation was undertaken, descriptions of the physical characters of the Bulgars were

[1] *La Bulgarie danubienne et les Balkans*, Paris, 1882.

full of confusion. One has but to glance at the diagnosis given by Vivien de Saint-Martin in his *Nouveau Dictionnaire de géographie universelle* to be convinced! A little later, Obédénare recognized three Bulgarian types: (1) the Tatar Bulgars; (2) the long-headed Bulgars; (3) the Gaulish Celts, Bulgarized in language.

The Tatar Bulgars must have been Mongoloid in type. The long-headed Bulgars were regarded as pure Bulgars. While as for the Oriental Gaulish Celts, "they were considered to be the autochthones whom the Bulgarian invaders found in the Balkans".

Which of these three is the Slav race? asked Obédénare —the Tatar Bulgars? the long-headed Bulgars with low foreheads?—or those who resembled the Bretons and Roumanians at every point?

Obédénare, in asking himself these questions, was obeying historic and ethnographic suggestion, and it is better that all such guesses should be eliminated from our horizon.

In 1904 a fine piece of anthropological work was carried out in Bulgaria. Wateff, a Bulgarian savant, amassed, with the help of a certain number of colleagues, a large quantity of data bearing on the morphology of his compatriots. From these, together with material gathered by other writers, and what has since been collected, we can obtain a general idea of the anthropological characters of the Bulgars.

In height (1 metre 665) they are above the European mean, and the proportion of tall individuals is about 65 per cent.

The Bulgars are very frequently dolichocephalic. Brachycephalic types represent only a fourth of the population. Thus this human group can have received only a very little of the blood of its neighbours on the west, those Dinaric folk with short broad heads whom we have come to know in our examination of the Bosnian-Herzegovinians. Were we to take the head-form alone into account we should say that a certain number of Bulgars must be related to a certain number of Serbs. But we know that in order to establish relationship we need other characters besides this.

According to their nasal index the Bulgars are mesorrhinians. This should be remembered, because of all the Balkan groups the Serbs and Bulgars alone show this character.

The eyes and hair of the Bulgars are strongly pigmented in the large majority of cases. Grey eyes are common (about 25 per cent.), and blue eyes are not rare (12.5 per cent.). But it is a curious thing that these eyes with light irides do not belong to fair individuals. Such types are exceptional in Bulgaria.

What conclusion are we to draw from all these characteristics if not that the Bulgars do not represent a pure race? Do these people exhibit to-day the physiognomy of those who in olden times were led by Asparoukh? Are there among them descendants of the autochthones (let us call them Thracians in order to give them a name known in history and to fix one moment of it) or of the Tatars who, of all the invaders of the Peninsular, might have played a dominant part in the formation of the Bulgarian people? Maybe all these elements are present in the Bulgarian people, and others as well of which history never speaks—the long-headed folk revealed to us at Glasinac and who had been settled in this part of the world from neolithic times at least.

We must bring this note to a close by asking the same question about the Bulgars that we had to ask in regard to the Serbs—are these Slavs of the Balkan peninsular ethnically related to the Russian Slavs, and if so, in what degree? Here the question answers itself—and in the negative. Related they may be by religion and language, but no more. Naturally we are speaking not of individual Russian Slavs and individual Bulgars, but of these human groups as a whole. If a detailed examination were made we might find Bulgars who are Slavs. Groups of Bulgars dwelt for a long time in Russia before they came and settled in the Balkans, and they may well have brought "Slavs" with them in their migrations. And these Bulgar groups may also have left remnants in Russia.

Once more, I have the impression that it would not be difficult to isolate from among the Bulgarian nation and from among the Serbian nation a certain number of individuals having characters in common. We have noted on many occasions undeniable morphological relationships between certain portions of these two peoples. We should thus build up a relatively homogeneous group. And this group would be tall, with a tendency to dolichocephaly, leptorrhinian, and frequently light-eyed.

But what would be the origin of its members? Could they be related to the prehistoric people of South Russia, the folk who built the kurgans of the Black Sea shore? They, too, were tall dolichocephals, like the folk which in former times inhabited Bosnia, and their presence in southern Russia from the days of the polished stone age constitutes one of the most interesting anthropological problems of the day, and one from which we may expect much.

VI

The Albanians[1]

Post-war Albania is far from representing in their entirety those lands peopled by Albanians. Serbia and Greece both contain large numbers of Albanians—we speak especially of their frontiers—and many of these groups are only with difficulty made to accept "the foreign yoke". Such centres of irredentism, created by irresponsible plenipotentiaries, may one day become a danger for Europe.

Philologists have taken a lively interest in the Albanian tongue and sought to find for it a derivation from European and Asiatic languages. Anthropologists have not on their side so great an array of research. The earliest work on the subject dates from 1886, and is a study by Zampa on a few Albanian crania. But this information was a mere sample. To-day the data, without being abundant, already enable us to get a general view of this people whose history is so attractive and which in former times supplied so much energy to the Turkish empire. In the course of various sojourns in the Peninsular, and also during a tour of two months in Albania, I examined a fairly large number of Albanians of different regions.

The prehistory of Albania up to the age of metals was still completely unknown in 1921. During that year I had the good fortune to discover a neolithic station on the shores of Lake Presba; this is at the moment the one and only piece of documentation we possess on the stone age of the country. It is likely that future research will show that Albania was at least as much inhabited in the earliest times as her neighbour

[1] **CXCV**, p. 267.

on the north, Bosnia-Herzegovina. The metal age has left us necropoles in the environs of Scutari. They have not yet been adequately excavated.

Not a single Albanian skeletal relic of the prehistoric or proto-historic periods has found its way into ossuary or laboratory, and to find out anything about the anthropology of the country we must go to the living population.

The Albanians in general are tall men. I obtained a figure slightly exceeding 1 metre 67 from measurements on more than 100 men. The proportion of tall statures exceeds 66 per cent.

The majority of these tall men are brachycephals. The Albanians I studied exhibited a proportion of nearly 80 per cent. of individuals having short, broad heads. The dolichocephalic forms did not amount to 9 per cent. It is difficult to find a population whose cranial characters are more definite.

The majority of Albanians are leptorrhine according to their nasal index, but the mesorrhinians amount to 40 per cent. The hair and eyes of these people in general are deeply pigmented. Fair hair is exceptional (4 per cent.), but blue and grey eyes are not rare. And we emphasize this observation, the reader knows why.

The Shkumbi river separates the Albanians, by its grey stretch of water, into two groups, the Ghegs to the north and the Toshks to the south. There are differences in dialect between the two groups. Would anthropological analysis reveal ethnic differences? With a view of finding out I attempted some comparisons, chiefly making use of the characters of stature and cephalic index. I found that the Ghegs are a little taller and a little less brachycephalic than the Toshks. The tall stature of the North Albanians might be explained by the neighbourhood of the Montenegrins and Serbs of the southwest who are very tall. But I hasten to add that I do not consider these observations to be definitive—the series compared were not adequate for that.

I do not know whether linguists are now agreed as to the origin of the Albanian language. But I think anthropologists will agree without difficulty as to the place from which the race has come. Although research is not yet of an order to give us conclusive information it would appear that we can already place the Albanians in one of the compartments of our present classification of European races, under the Dinaric race—at all events a large number of them certainly belong to it.

One day in Scutari I had occasion to witness an assembly of clan chieftains from North Albania. The sight was of rare anthropological beauty. Costume apart, I might have thought myself in Montenegro, or in Bosnia, or in certain parts of Dalmatia. I had before my eyes magnificent specimens of that Dinaric race whose habitat extends southward, with certain attenuations in one or other of its characters, as far as southern Greece.

Not all Albanians belong exclusively to this race (the same may be said of Montenegrins, Bosnians, or Dalmatians). We find nothing in the history of this land to suggest that the people have preserved greater purity of race than their neighbours. The Dinaric race is composed of a majority of similar types—the proportion varies according to locality—but it has no more escaped intermixture than the other European races. It would be interesting to know to what period this intermixture dates and how it came about.

In the chapter devoted to Italy I said a few words about the Albanian colonies of the southeast of that peninsular. I do not think that the historical origin of these colonies is altogether clear. Certain traditions have it that they are constituted by Toshks who emigrated; others assert that these colonists are Ghegs who came to Italy at the time when Scutari belonged to the Republic of Venice.

The work of the Italian anthropologist, Livi, has shown that the people of these Albanian colonies of southeast Italy are small and that their head-form is generally sub-dolichocephalic. There is too great a difference between these indications and those given in this chapter about the Albanians to let us imagine that these colonists are pure Albanians, whether Ghegs or Toshks. Fresh investigations carried out on a different method from that of Livi as regards the kind of geographical division utilised might perhaps throw light on this problem.

It would be well worth the trouble to find out in Albania itself, by a broad analysis bearing on the whole country, what is the exact proportion of people of Dinaric race; I think it is a large one.

VII

THE GREEKS[1]

Would it not greatly interest historians, philosophers and artists—the whole world, in fact—to know to what race belonged the admirable sculptors, sages, orators, military chiefs, and great politicians of ancient Greece ?

Yet we are quite in the dark about it. We can only guess, and of what value are guesses ? We may well ask ourselves how it was possible that a question of such importance left those who went before us entirely indifferent. When we see what profit certain anthropo-sociologists would extract from ethnic characters, it cannot be unimportant to discover to what stock the Greeks of the great period may have belonged. We must not shrink from repeating that if such a discovery is now impossible, the blame lies at the door of classical archæologists. A part of their education needs beginning over again.

It has been said, though it is a purely theoretical statement, that the majority of Pelasgians were brachycephals, whereas the primitive Greeks were dolichocephals. We have not sufficient data to come to such a conclusion. And who were the Pelasgians ? The few existent crania of ancient Greeks, coming chiefly from Attica, show a majority of long skulls ; but there are among them, and by no means as exceptions, brachycephalic types (11 per cent.).

Moreover, the cranial series utilized for this indication is of minimum interest, because the individual skulls comprising it were not classified stratigraphically. What we want to know is what the anthropological physiognomy of Greece was like in each successive period.

If ancient Greece really was dolichocephalic, it has greatly changed to-day.

When we come to study the Balkan populations we find that the Greeks also are among the most imperfectly known. This is what Deniker wrote about them in 1913, in a communication to the Institut français d'anthropologie : " As for the Greeks, we have too few data on their anthropology. All that we can say is that apart from the two elements [West Balkan[2]

[1] CXCV. p. 233.
[2] Dinaric type.

and East Balkan[1]] that there must be among them a third—small, dolichocephalic, and very dark—related to the Ibero-Insular race distributed in the Iberian peninsular, in southern Italy and in the Mediterranean islands ". Since then I have contributed a certain quantity of fresh data and we shall see directly what we should think of the above statement.

When we come to examine, on the one hand, the territorial smallness of Greece, and on the other, the wide extent of the domains in which Greeks are established—in considerable numbers we are told—we ask ourselves from what locality all these Greeks *extra muros* can have come. No other group, except the Slavs, exhibits such wide settlement. The reason is that there are Greeks and Greeks, just as there are Slavs and Slavs! Many of the peoples around the Black Sea and the Ægean, and many of the peoples of Asia Minor and the middle Mediterranean were Hellenized without having ever had many Greeks among them, and without having had Greek blood in their veins. There were among the Greeks great colonizers as among the Phœnicians or the Romans.

The Greeks appear to be of middle height, perhaps a little above the European mean. Their cephalic index is sub-brachycephalic.

But the Greek population exhibits every kind of cranial form. Nevertheless, brachycephalic forms are the most numerous. I found among them nearly 49 per cent. as against scarcely 34 per cent. of dolichocephalic heads. When we examine the graph of individual statures and that of the cephalic index we are at once aware that a number of ethnic varieties are represented in Greece. These two characters alone suffice to show the heterogeneity of this group. It contains very small as well as very tall individuals, hyper-dolichocephalic and hyperbrachycephalic types.

The Hellenic peninsular is almost exactly cut in two by the 20th degree of longitude east of Paris. According to Deniker the people to the west of this line would belong in general to the Adriatic-Albanian type characterized by tall stature and a brachycephalic cephalic index, whereas to the

[1] Medium height—1 metre 65 to 1 metre 67, according to locality; less pronounced pigmentation than in the west; very low cephalic index. Deniker was not at that time aware of all the data that I have contributed towards the study of the Balkan peoples. His distribution, correct for the west of the Peninsular, is far too elementary in arrangement as regards the east.

east of 20 degrees longitude the Greeks of Thessaly "and perhaps a portion of those in Attica" would belong to quite a different type of stature and to a lower cephalic index.

But 20° long. E. of Paris passes notably to the east of the main Pindus range; and I think it would be better to use the mountain ridge as a dividing line, which would be of more use, too, as an eventual explanation of the phenomena observed. I recall that Deniker believed that the eastern Greeks were frequently dolichocephalic.

An attempt to classify the morphological characters by provinces gives chaotic results and nowhere permits of such an hyopthesis being accepted.

To the west of Greece the Ionian islands, according to Stephanos, appear to hold a brachycephalic or sub-brachycephalic population. It is the same for the large island Eubœa, to the east. Round heads in these two regions are very easily explained. Albania and the Epirus are quite close to the Ionian islands and we know that the people of both banks of the Aspro Potamo are brachycephalic. The brachycephaly of the inhabitants of Eubœa is likewise quite naturally explained. It suffices to call to mind the Albanian emigrations at the time of the struggle of Scanderbeg against the Turks. These colonists were probably true Dinarics. They have preserved their language and their race. It is a simple historic fact.

The Greek nose is usually straight; but the nasofrontal type which the sculptors represented does not exist as a normal morphological character; it is an esthetic creation. We find a fair number of Greeks having aquiline noses, or turned-up noses such as those we meet with so often among the Slavs. Is this a souvenir of some early ethnic influence from the North at the time of the invasions of the Byzantine empire? The intermixture of races is again confirmed by this highly special type of physiognomy.

The eyes of the Greeks are generally brown; but light eyes among them are not rare. Fair hair, on the other hand, is exceptional. Personally, I only noted about 1.5 per cent. The dominant shade of hair is dark brown and black. I am bound to say, in this regard, that this resumé of my personal observations does not square completely with the results given by various other writers. Thus Ornstein says that he frequently found individuals with blue or grey eyes, or with fair hair, in Greece. Stephanos says that fair-haired populations are known in modern Greece in the villages in the neighbourhood of the river Eurotas (Laconia), in the mountain villages of Mantinea, and in Eubœa on Mount Dirphys. Why do not the Greeks themselves inform us on this important point? Where could this fair-haired people with blue or grey eyes come from? Is it a remnant of the Barbarian hordes from the North, that "reservoir of light-eyed blonds"? The two writers neglect to indicate the characters concomitant with this weak pigmentation of hair and eyes. Were the men whom they examined tall or short? Dolichocephals or brachycephals? To know would greatly interest the history of the Balkan peninsular.

At the present time it is difficult to represent Greece otherwise than as a sort of anthropological cul-de-sac in which the invading groups of the Peninsular have been brought up short. The Greek population resembles a composite photograph of the Balkan peoples. But I recognize how thoroughly inadequate such a picture is. Maybe someday we shall succeed in sorting out the groups which make up the Greek population, and in putting each one into its proper place? But this work must be based on a knowledge of what the primitive population of Greece consisted in—first of all prehistoric, then classical Greece.

And that is why we urge on the Greeks themselves to tell us what were the morphological characters of their most distant ancestors.

If it were really to be demonstrated that the most primitive Greeks, let us say the Greeks of neolithic times in order not to be too difficile, belonged to the same ethnic type as that which, at the same period, built for its dead the kurgans of South Russia, that would already constitute a contribution of immense scientific value. I recall that Bosnia-Herzegovina holds, in its necropoles, human types which are probably related to this still enigmatic race. Gradually we should establish its geographical distribution, and we should perhaps discover its origin. Who knows, then, what affiliations we might not envisage with the prehistoric people of central and western Europe, in particular with those of palæolithic times?

Who can yet tell whether a less ancient derivation will not lead us from the Dolichocephals of the southeast of Europe to the tall Dolichocephals of western Europe of the dolmen period? And what problems would then be raised for History!

CHAPTER XVI

THE ÆGEAN PEOPLE

WHAT, we may ask, has been the ethnic destiny of the isles to the east and south of Greece that dot the Ægean, and one of which—Crete—had so magnificent a civilization? Did the men who first settled there come via the southern Sporades from Asia Minor or from Europe? Or were they navigators who had come from further afield, from the shores of Phœnicia or the ports of Egypt? In a word, what race first occupied these islands?

I believe that, to date, no remains of palæolithic civilization have been met with in Crete or in the archipelago to the north. These isolated territories are in this respect at one with the mainland shores surrounding the Ægean, where the earliest cultural traces yet discovered belong to the polished stone age. But does not the very fact that numerous remains of a neolithic civilization are to be found in these islands tempt us to think that the neighbouring continental regions must have known older civilizations—the upper Palæolithic, at least? The Neolithic, their successor by a natural continuity, would thus have passed over into the islands. It would be difficult to believe that these islands themselves spontaneously created this particular social phenomenon, complete, as it were, at the time of the polished stone age.

We are still far from being able to picture to ourselves with any certainty the course of human events in the Ægean. It is certain that all the islands d'd not at the same time possess exactly the same kind of civilization. There are even several of these scattered islets which appear to have remained outside the pale of neolithic influences.

One of the volumes of this series is devoted to the Ægean civilization[1] and readers anxious for documentation of this

[1] LXXXII *bis*.

kind have but to refer to that work, where they will find all the information they could possibly desire.

Crete alone of all these Ægean islands has provided us with noteworthy skeletal " documents ". We can but wish that they had been more numerous, more complete, and more representative of the events of which this island was the theatre. Crete having known different civilizations, we may well ask whether these were the fruit of a single or of several ethnical types. And in the last event, had each new social phenomenon its corollary in representatives of a new race?

Alas! the different stages of Cretan civilization have not each given us sufficient elements—leaving aside unutilizable iconographic data—to establish the ethnic physiognomy of each of these different periods. Nevertheless all is not gloom in the anthropological past of Crete. Thanks to the work of a number of English, German, American, and Italian anthropologists who have made a study of some fairly good series—particularly of crania[1]—we are enabled to construct certain hypotheses concerning the human events of the southern Ægean. We will outline them in brief.

These anthropological " documents " belong to the three Minoan periods in varying proportions. In addition, and by way of comparison, we have the results of research on the living population.

With a view of simplifying the task and keeping closely in touch with this series of the *Evolution of Humanity*, I will refer the reader to the chapter in which Glotz says a few words on the physical type of the successive inhabitants of Crete, and to begin with shall make use of the table of percentages of cranial forms—both sexes indiscriminately are included—which he draws up (it exhibits a few slight variations from mine) for the various Minoan periods (A) the Early; (B) the Middle; and (C) the Late Minoan.

	Dolichocephals.	Mesaticephals.	Brachycephals.
A.	55 %	35%	10%
B.	66.6%	25%	7·7%
C.	12.5%	50%	37·5%

Taking only the first and third column into consideration,

[1] See especially **CXLV** *bis*, which also contains important observations on the living population, posterior to and more complete than those of Hawes. They deserve detailed study, if we had the space to devote to it.

the fact that human events of very great importance came to pass in Crete between the Early Minoan and Late Minoan periods hits one in the eyes. Between the Early Minoan and the Middle Minoan the small differences to be seen in these percentages are due perhaps to the statistical phenomena, and it would appear, until we have more information, that a certain ethnic cohesion existed in Crete throughout the course of both these periods. In the Late Minoan this physiognomy suddenly changes. And as we cannot possibly admit that we are here witnessing a morphological transmutation of the hitherto existing population, we are bound to believe that there was some ethnic substitution at this date.

Nor was this any small historical adventure.

Looking no further than the Late Minoan we can try to picture to ourselves the human events which took place in Crete in the course of that island's early history.

As palæolithic civilization is unknown in Crete, we can put forward no continuity hypothesis as to the possibility of neighbouring human groups being considered as the ancestors of the neolithic Cretans. But we know that the polished stone age population which inaugurated (?) human life on the island was a dolichocephalic one. It was far from being purely dolichocephalic, as it included many intermediate types, but there are only a few brachycephals in it. The Neolithic in the Balkan peninsular provides us with a somewhat similar ethnic picture, but there the anthropological data are even more scanty. I recall that in central and western Europe the Brachycephals appear only—for the first time in the Ofnet station—in mesolithic times. It is a question of establishing the precise chronology of this period in central Europe in relation to the neolithic phase in the East.

The few long bones measured in Crete have enabled the stature of the prehistoric Cretans to be approximately arrived at. It was below the European mean. Maybe we should estimate it at 1 metre 62. Low stature and dolichocephaly characterize the primitive Cretan folk as they characterize the present-day population of part of the Mediterranean basin, notably of southern Italy. We may well believe that there they are in their early home, and that they are the natural descendants of those who occupied the country in prehistoric times. But Crete is rather far from Italy. How then, and by what means, could such peopling from the land of Italy be brought about before or at the beginning of the Neolithic? We must look even a little nearer than Italy.[1]

In continental Greece the people are very mixed, some being brachycephalic and others dolichocephalic. The cephalic index means take us from the hyperbrachycephally of the Epirotes to the dolichocephaly of the Thessalians. Nowhere in Greece do we find such low cephalic indices as in southern Italy.

Asia Minor is still imperfectly known, nevertheless we do know that the inhabitants are brachycephalic in the majority with a fairly high number of dolichocephalic types, notably in Lower Mesopotamia and Syria.

In Africa the present Egyptians (Copts and Fellahin) are almost all dolichocephals, but they are taller than the earliest Cretans seem to have been.

The substitution of population revealed in the Late Minoan invites us, if we are to understand it, to take into consideration for ethnic comparison only those remains of neighbouring populations which are of the same or very nearly the same period. But the data are largely lacking. We possess a few early Greek crania but these are meagre data. They reveal, as in Crete, a marked predominance of the dolichocephalic type with intermixture of a few brachycephals—about 11 per cent. But this figure is based on a very small number of observations.

The Phœnicians (see the chapter dealing with them) were also dolichocephals and their stature seems to have been low. We have to take these concomitant morphological characters into consideration. Ought we to try to establish a relationship between the inhabitants of Phœnicia and the early Cretans? It is possible that the Phœnicians and the primitive Cretans belonged to the same original group. There are even many reasons for believing that they did. Was Crete, then, the first stage on the way to the West accomplished by the Phœnicians?

We do not need, here, to go into the variations in the civilization of the two regions, nor into their respective periods. We simply note that the Phœnician population goes back much further than the Cretan in that it knew palæolithic civilizations, and that we are finding stations of those far-off periods in their

[1] It must be understood that we do not eliminate rapprochements with prehistoric Italy.

territory every day. At those early periods Crete appears to have been uninhabited. Why might not human groups from Phœnicia, land of an ancient stock, have discovered this large island at the beginning of the Neolithic, and there created the beginnings of that magnificent civilization we know? A meagre state of culture may suddenly blossom out when transplanted to another locality if it finds itself in a different atmosphere. Different environments may at the same period stimulate in like men ideas that are quite unlike. I only wish I had the space to develop and support my point of view. Nevertheless I recognize that in the case of Crete I am quite unable to bring any peremptory proof in support of my thesis. I merely put forward in a favourable chronological order—and that is always something—morphological concordances and a reasoned argument. The years will show what the argument is worth.

Whence came the brachycephalic people of prehistoric Crete? It is no easier to give a reply here. If we could have had at our disposal a large number of more or less complete skeletons of this human type it might have been possible to find a hereditary lineage somewhere in the different regions of the eastern Mediterranean. We know something of the brachycephals in northern Ægean lands, notably in that part of Asia Minor looking towards Greece, and we know them also in western Greece and all along the Adriatic shore opposite Italy. These last are the Dinaric people of whom we have spoken so often; they possess distinct morphological characteristics. As for the Asiatic Brachycephals we have not yet sufficient information about them to attempt any sort of approximation with the Dinaric people.

In regard to prehistoric times in areas in the neighbourhood of Crete, I recall that brachycephalic types are also met with in the neolithic stations of the Balkan peninsular. Troy also exhibits them. Are all these Mediterranean Brachycephals of the same family? It would be very interesting to group them together in order to study them as a whole with a view of placing then ethnologically.

A number of groups of brunet Brachycephals of tall or medium stature are to be met with further inland than the Asiatic shores, in the mountains drained by the Euphrates and Tigris, in the Caucasus, in Persia, and still further to the East. Do these people in their present habitat represent the stages of prehistoric migrations which moved West according to that " mirage " with which we are familiar ?

In Crete this ethnic replacement of the population by contingents of Brachycephals is seen late in the Minoan. If we are to admit some such hypothesis as has been outlined we must believe that the movement in Asia began in the Neolithic or at the beginning of the bronze age to end in Crete at its close, because it is at that moment that we see the Brachycephals settled in the island.

Glotz thinks that the revolution which was to put an end to the bronze age and to the Minoan civilization—this invasion by a round-headed warlike people—marked the arrival of Hellenes. Dussard is of the same opinion, because he speaks of invasions by the Achæans. It is possible. We know that even to-day there are on Greek territory numerous brachycephalic types and that it certainly sheltered them as early as the bronze age. But this does not prevent me from wanting very much to know what were the other ethnic characteristics of these invaders—who, if the Achæans came from Thessaly as is believed, might be representatives of the Dinaric race.

In connection with this radical change in the morphology of the inhabitants of Crete at the end of the bronze age, are we not justified in calling attention to the great importance anthropological research may assume for History ? Before Anthropology had disclosed human varieties no attention was paid to the " documents " of which we are making use in this book. The skeletons dug up in the course of excavations were simply skeletons and nothing more. They were left lying on the edge of the trenches, or they were broken up, or re-buried. Not an archæologist could have imagined that such bones would provide science with the means of interpretations, occasionally of wide bearing, or that they would throw light on obscure events.

To-day the majority of the inhabitants of the island of Minoa (Paros) are made up of Brachycephals, according to the observations of Hawes, who has studied several thousands of individuals.

To sum up, Cretan civilization was inaugurated by the Dolichocephals who brought with them the polished stone age, and these people were to be succeeded by their descendants almost up to the close of the bronze age. Then the Brachycephals, who, up till then had merely been " strays " among the rest, were to take their place. The round-heads became predominant and they have kept their numerical superiority up till the present day. We have put forward certain hypotheses relating to the origin of both. The final fate of these hypotheses will soon be indicated to us.[1]

[1] Must we call to mind, to refresh the memory, that steatopygous statuettes of women have been met with at various points of the Ægean, notably in neolithic Crete ? Must we bring in an ethnic interpretation to account for them ? Crete's relations with Africa are not to be denied. That would take us very far. I recall that during the Ægean copper age the steatopygous type disappeared. Was this a change in artistic fashions or a change in the population ? See the works of Sergi for the problems relating to the origin of the Mediterranean people.

PART III

THE RACES OF ASIA

CHAPTER I

General Remarks

PEOPLE of my generation have long been in the habit of looking frankly to the East when the origin of their race was in question, and many of them still do so. Their eyes turn to that great tumbled region in which the plateau of the Pamirs stands amidst the mountain massif, and whose snows feed, in four directions, the four rivers of Asia—a vision betokening uninterrupted communication, assurance of infinite fertility, and valleys providing natural highways down which mankind might flow, were it so disposed, as easily as the waters themselves.

An enchanting and most accommodating picture whose simplicity renders it particularly seductive !

By the Indus one can without difficulty reach the Punjab and the open sea—that ocean of infinite horizons whose shores provide sure guidance. By the Syr and the Amu Daria one can push forward towards the steppes of the Aral and the Caspian, where the Kirghiz nomads still show us to-day in miniature how migrations are accomplished.

This is the region of idyllic fancy, whence the hypothetical Indo-Europeans, driven away, it is said, by its increasing cold, scattered over the world they inhabit to this day. It is the hypothesis of monogenist anthropology, of human geography, and especially of philology.

This mental vision—scientifically it was no more—this armchair creation, this moral fable whose paternity goes back to Rhode[1], was given to the "cultivated world" like some gospel, chiefly by the Geneva savant, Adolphe Pictet[2], in a book

[1] CCXVIII.
[2] CXC.

that made a great stir. In his *Origines indo-européennes et les Aryas primitifs* he laid bare the beginnings of our European race and all the primitive life of our forbears! Pictet, coming of a family of naturalists and living in the midst of a brilliant scientific circle, gave his work a title that has an air of being strictly scientific, since he called it an "essay in linguistic palæontology"—as though the language of the most distant past could be represented to us with the same certainty as palæontological series!

This is not the place to recall the many discussions which followed, or to revive the memory of this great controversy which Salomon Reinach brought to a head in a work known to all specialists.[1] Neither am I qualified from the philological-historical view-point to take part in such a debate.

From the anthropological point of view, the only one which here concerns us, the problem should be stated, it seems to me, in the following manner: if, as is claimed, Indo-Europeans have a common origin, their descendants ought to exhibit similar anthropological characters wherever we may find them.

We should not argue otherwise were we dealing with the genus *Elephas* or any other mammalian genus.

If the Aryans represent a single human race it should be sufficient to study the Indians on the one hand and the European families on the other, and we should at once find absolute agreement when it came to comparing our observations. One sees how imperative is the necessity for a close anthropological study of southern and western Asia at least, and of nearly all the European peoples, were it only for the sake of solving, once for all, this dual problem. Asia has for long ages offered a home to Man and men have certainly dwelt there from very remote periods. It is even possible that one day we may find in Asia the cradle of mankind.

*
* *

This is the place in which, in chronological order, we should refer to the fortunate finds of remains of Pithecanthropus by Dr. Dubois at Trinil in Java.

This savant in 1890 was prosecuting palæontological researches in the central part of the island (province of Madiun) on the left bank of the Solo (or Bengawan). In this locality

[1] CCXIV.

lying between the villages of Trinil and Klitae there are a number of plant and animal fossils in the southern flanks of the Kendengs. They are embedded in the accumulations of volcanic tufa, of fluviatile origin, coming from the neighbouring volcanoes, principally from Lawu-Kukusan. Nearly all the species were different from those now existing and the general physiognomy of this fossil fauna recalls that of the Siwalik hills. These animals lived in Java when that island was still united to the Asiatic mainland.

Dubois' excavations were spread over several years. It was in 1891 and 1892 that the remains of *Pithecanthropus erectus* were discovered, first a third upper right molar (September, 1891), and then, in October of the same year, the celebrated calvaria. The femur was dug out in August, 1892; still other fragments were found later. Very few European anthropologists have had the good fortune to hold in their hands these venerable remains so impressive in the beauty of their fossilization, so stirring—especially when, after Dubois had freed the interior of the brain-case from the magma with which it was filled, the imprint of the cerebral convolutions became apparent.

Even to-day there are divided opinions as to the genealogical position of Pithecanthropus just as there are in regard to the chronological position to be assigned to the stratum in which he was found. The importance of the latter problem can be understood; if the fossiliferous bed in which the remains were found has to be brought nearer our own time and put forward from the Pliocene to the Quaternary, the place attributed to the Trinil fossil in human genealogy is likewise altered, and it can no longer figure in the direct ancestral line of Man, since Man was already in existence at that geological period.

The following are Dubois' conclusions in regard to the genealogical interpretation of the remains discovered: "After all the criticisms I still think that *Pithecanthropus erectus* belongs to the direct ancestral line of mankind, or at least cannot be far removed from it. In any case our ancestor could not have been very different, but must have been a near relative of *Pithecanthropus erectus*". Boule has made a very judicious remark in connection with this genealogy. He said: "But we must be exact, and this is a case in which it has to be repeated that resemblance does not always mean descent.

Because Pithecanthropus by all his known characters, which are but few, is actually morphologically intermediate between the large Apes and Man, it does not necessarily follow that he is to be considered as *genealogically* intermediate. And this distinction is not, as has been claimed, a verbal distinction only".

We know that the calvaria of Pithecanthropus in certain of its morphological characters and especially in its capacity is "really intermediate between that of an ape like the Chimpanzee and that of a man of an inferior order like Neanderthal man". The brain, whose morphological characters have been revealed by the intercranial cast, lead to the same conclusion.

The femur discovered is complete. It belongs to the left side. It is gracile, and in its main features represents the aspect of a female femur. The height reconstruction gives about 1 metre 65 (opinions vary between 1 metre 60 and 1 metre 70). It has often been said that had this femur alone been found it would have been attributed without hesitation to a man.

Confronted with all these morphological contradictions resulting from the discordant character of the skull, the femur and the teeth, several naturalists, Boule among them, have put forward the hypothesis that the remains of Pithecanthropus may have belonged to a form of giant ape related to the Gibbon group.[1] He would thus represent "an offshoot of the Gibbon branch more highly evolved, more specialized than the neighbouring offshoots, which withered early, perhaps on account of this very specialization. Pithecanthropus thus would not belong to the ancestral line of the genus *Homo*. The more or less 'human characters' of his calvaria and even his femur would be convergent and not derivative characters." This interpretation of the memorable Java discovery in no way subtracts from its interest. On the contrary I should be tempted to say that it augments it, because the human line, while retaining its independence, would thus appear to us less morphologically isolated than hitherto from its neighbouring

[1] See **XXI**, p. 109. Nevertheless, serious objections to this hypothesis may be advanced, based, in particular, on the relation between the growth of the encephalon and stature. It would be difficult to admit that a giant Gibbon, whose height would lie between 1 metre 60 and 1 metre 70, could be the possessor of a brain of 870 grammes! But this is not the place in which to discuss this point.

lines. It would be profitless to enter further into details in a book of this kind.

*

* *

If we are to accept the interpretation of their finds given by certain discoverers we should have to admit that continental Asia was already peopled in the Tertiary era. Theoretically, as we know, there is nothing against such a peopling. Noetling noted flints, which he believed to be intentionally chipped, in the pliocene conglomerate of Burma. Flaked stone implements accompanied by the remains of animals, many of which go back to the Pliocene, have been found in the alluvia of several of the Indian rivers.

The laterite deposits of the eastern Ghats which contain implements of Chellean form in quartzite and laterite are considered to go back at least to pleistocene times. Other palæolithic horizons have been notified in many parts of Asia, notably in Syria, where Chellean implements exactly resembling the European types have been found at the same time as more recent types—Moustierian, Aurignacian, and Magdalenian, and where Zumoffen has dug out human remains considered to be of Aurignacian age. In Ceylon Fritz and Paul Sarasin have brought to light in the course of their excavations implements having a palæolithic facies but of unknown age; and to the north of the Sayan mountains, in the terraces of the upper Yenisei, first Savenkow, then de Baye and Volkow, have discovered quartize implements of Moustierian and Chellean appearance in contact with a fauna analogous to that of our mammoth epoch. In 1896 Kuznetsof notified the discovery of palæolithic implements in a mammoth stratum of the loess near Tomsk.

For a very long time eastern Asia yielded no remains of Pleistocene man, and it was believed that the earliest civilizations of this region dated from the Neolithic. Matsumoto, however, has recently described a human sacrum discovered in the Chinese loess of Honan. Pleistocene man did, then, exist in China, which scarcely surprises us. And Japan, further, has yielded to several savants of that country traces of implements of palæolithic aspect. Thus daylight is gradually breaking over the prehistoric folk of Asia. This ancient continent out of which a portion of the European people came is gradually revealing herself to us. This, for many of us maternal, land whose most distant past is still hidden behind a veil, is being penetrated here and there by a ray of light. It is probable that when systematic excavation can be undertaken it will reveal to us the presence throughout the length and breadth of the continent of the same palæolithic industries as existed in Europe. Eur-Asia will then no longer be merely a geographical unity.

Will these industries present themselves in the same order of superposition in both continents? At this very time an American mission is undertaking excavation in Central Asia (we know what the American theories are relating to the peopling of their continent by Asiatics). Let us await results.[1] But if it is practically certain that the quaternary folk occupied

[1] [A telegraphic message to the American Museum of Natural History, as these proofs are being corrected, announces the discovery of extensive remains of late paleolithic culture, and two "pre-Mongol" human skeletons. Translator].

In addition to the Americans, French and Swedish expeditions are exploring the prehistoric ground in China. A note which appeared in *l'Anthropologie*, 1923, p. 630 (Père Teilhard de Chardin) announced the discovery by Fathers Teilhard and Licent of extremely important anthropological documents. In the loess, in a definitely stratified fossiliferous horizon, these excavators found floor levels exceptionally rich in stone implements of Moustierian type. The fauna included Horse, and somewhat less frequently Rhinoceros, Ox, Hyena, and Ostrich egg-shells, etc. Other floors have been discovered in a fluviatile formation of the same age as the loess, and also in the gravels at the base of the loess. Later, the same excavators laid bare human skeletal remains at a great depth in the alluvia of the Shara Osso Gol (S.W. angle of the Ordos). Detailed descriptions of these remains have not yet appeared, but the tremendous importance of this discovery as regards the primitive history of China can well be imagined.

Certain writers (Torii, the Japanese, for instance) think that large areas in Asia never knew palæolithic civilization.

For the Palæolithic in Asia, one may usefully consult the bibliography given by Deniker in the *Nouvelles géographiques*, Paris, 1892, and in *les Races et Peuples de la Terre*, Paris, 1900 (Eng. trans. *The Races of Man*, London, 1900). For the stone age in Asia see **XXXVI, CCC, CCLXXIII, CLXXI, CLXIX, CCLXVIII.** The earliest publication relating to the discovery of prehistoric implements in Asia is L. Lartet's "Note sur la découverte de silex taillés en Syrie", *Bull. Soc, géol. France*, 1865). Others are: Torii (R. & K.), **CCLVII**; P. & F. Sarasin, **CCXXVIII**; Mitra, **CLIX**, and especially Boule, who has summarized most of the discoveries, **XXI.**

American anthropologists, and many European savants with them, imagine that the prehistoric peoples of Asia—notably of central and northern Asia—migrated at different times into America. From the post-glacial epoch, at least, Asiatic groups would thus have crossed the Bering Strait and spread over North America. Northeast Siberia would have been, one might say, the temporary reservoir of these migrants for whom, having come from further afield, this region was merely a land of sojourn. This hypothesis does not lack substance; but it alone cannot be regarded as explaining the origin of the American races. The head of the American Anthropological Service, Hrdlicka, constituted himself the champion of this hypothesis at the Congress of Geneva in 1912.

Asiatic territory in almost every direction, we must recognize that we know nothing of the physical characters of these people.

Were they tall or small? Dolichocephals or brachycephals? It is impossible to attempt to connect them in any way genealogically with the human races of more recent times.

The Asiatic Neolithic is more common. It seems to be distributed pretty well everywhere, and the objects characterizing it are in general the same as our own. Mesopotamia revealed this civilization to J. de Morgan[1] as eastern Mongolia revealed it to Torii, and as the kitchen-middens of Japan and Manchuria have exhibited it to the Japanese investigators. We possess a few osteological remains of the neolithic period. But they are insufficient to authorize any sort of conclusions. What may be said is that at the polished stone age Asia as a whole, like Europe of the same period, already appeared to contain several anthropological types. The skeletons discovered at Tonking by Mansuy are of the dolichocephalic type (with a relatively short face) with indices of 73 and 77; the crania discovered much further north, in southern Siberia, are likewise dolichocephalic. This fact is of great import if we reflect that this morphological type is very far from being that of the living populations of Asia, save in the southwest (India, Persia, and Arabia). The bronze age is likewise richly represented almost everywhere. Its presence in certain localities in Asia sets us problems of very great importance. The history of the primitive peopling of Europe is deeply involved, as it is likewise concerned in comparisons of Eur-Asian Neolithic folk among themselves. Here Archæology has gone far in advance of Anthropology.[2] We anthropologists, alas, are still awaiting the most part of our data.

Let us now glance rapidly at the present Asiatic peoples.

If we are to judge by the few remains that have come down to us these people are not everywhere the anatomical heirs of those who occupied the same territory in prehistoric times. It is especially in the following pages that we must beware of deceiving ourselves. Our anthropological knowledge of the vast Asiatic continent is very slender and very fragile, and altogether inadequate to permit us to draw any serious conclusions, no matter what.

[1] CLXIII.
[2] LXVI.

Wide areas still remain virgin soil for anthropologists. And where they have laboured they have only studied quite small "series":—India, Japan, and parts of Western Asia are the best known. But if a few thousand inhabitants have been examined in India and China, for instance, this represents but a very slight percentage out of the hundreds of millions of men inhabiting these lands. And these huge continents are not made up of pure races—which renders the percentage even slighter. Hence, in going through these pages the reader must always make those mental reservations which are essential when confronted with work that is still in its inception.

When we reflect on the formidable civilizations which have been unfolded on the Asiatic continent a certain melancholy steals over us in that we are unable to recognize which of the groups now living can claim such ancestry. Maybe only a portion of the Kurds and Armenians, who are often racial brethren, and of whom one again became a nomad pastoral people, are to be regarded as the descendants of the great civilizations of Western Asia.

The rapid examination of the races of Asia which we shall make will leave on one side a large number of ethnic groups whose actions have never figured in history, at least in the history we know, such as the Samoyeds, Tunguses, Ostyaks, Chukchi and Kamchadales in northern regions, and in the south, many Indo-Chinese peoples, without counting Negritos, Andamanese, etc., who do not appear to have played a predominant rôle in the historical adventures of Asia. And, despite all the interest which these divers human groups may present, we shall not even draw the reader's attention to them.

The destinies of the peoples who were the leading participants in the History of Asia have been very different. Formidable empires whose dominion seemed to be everlasting, went down: young nations which seemed in no way predestined to such adventures broke with unheard of violence into the orbit of History. What has now become of the power of the Mongols who had such fantastic successes? To what causes are we to attribute first these advantages and then these reverses? Is this an example showing that each nation holds within itself the causes both of its glory and its decadence? Can the zoological value of human groups be invoked as an explanatory reason—as was so thoroughly believed during the last quarter of the nineteenth century?

When we try to make up an account of the morphological characters of the Asiatic populations we perceive that to-day, as in prehistoric times, Dolichocephals and Brachycephals confront one another in this huge continent, though in extremely varying proportions, and that these groupings are not limited within precise geographical bounds.

The dolichocephalic and sub-dolichocephalic types, if they are particularly frequent in the Indian peninsular (where they constitute almost a compact bloc, especially the genuine Dolichocephals) are to be met with elsewhere in Asia at a good distance from the south Himalayan country; among, for instance, the Ainu of Sakhalin and Yezo, the Japanese and Chinese, and even among the peoples of Western Asia (Tatars, Persians and Turkomans). But in many of these regions it would appear to be difficult to give the title of autochthones to these long-headed folk, because brachycephaly is there the rule.[1]

The Brachycephals occupy a large part of the west and centre of Asia.

To the north the Samoyeds and Tunguses belong to this type, and so do many of the Chinese of the centre, and the inhabitants of Turkestan.

We are in the habit of saying that Asia is the source of Brachycephaly. Modern research has shown that this "great reservoir" of Brachycephals includes also most imposing masses of Dolichocephals!

It is very difficult, in the eyes of anyone not a historian, to supply proofs based on universal History for isolated incidents. What reactions may the events of a distant land have had on the history of this or that other land, at this or that moment? At first sight, for instance, it would seem that no direct influence from the history of China on European events could be envisaged. And yet are we so sure? Do not the great excavations of Stein, Pelliot and von Lecoq, and the admirable discoveries to which they led, show us, on the contrary, these reactions extending gradually from China to Turkestan and from beyond the steppes of the Turkomans and the mountains of Persia towards Asia Minor and Arabia?

[1] We must note at once this interesting fact—the Indo-Chinese exhibit a very different cranial morphology from their neighbours the Indians: Annamese, Cambojans, Siamese, and Burmese appear from this morphological character alone to be of different race from that to which the Indians are related.

On the other hand, do not the Arabs, Tatars and Turks in the past, and the Japanese in the present, owe a part of their civilization to Asiatic peoples whose history has never passed beyond the confines of Asia ? I leave to those more competent than myself the task of coming to a decision. But it can be understood what difficulties confront anyone who is obliged, for opportune reasons, to make a deliberate choice. Such work is always lacking in fine distinctions because it demands too drastic a simplification, and because it ill accords with the scientific obligation to seek out the most remote causative agencies.

Having expressed these reservations, it would seem that in Asia attention may be especially directed to those races who made ancient history—the Persians, Medes, Assyrio-Chaldeans, Chinese and Indians.

And secondly to those who have made more recent history —the Arabs, Tatars and Turks, and finally the Japanese.

Let it not be imagined that we can supply much information about these races. Anthropology knows very little of the somatological characters of the living peoples of Asia. As for the peoples who made ancient history, we might as well say that we know practically nothing about them. It maddens one to think that those archæologists who excavated, in the thousands-of-years-old-soil of Western Asia, so many admirable monuments, could have cared so little about the human remains they came across ! One can never sufficiently protest against this scientific vandalism committed by men who claimed to be called " men of science ".

The question is always cropping up of the origin of the people who built Babylon and Niniveh. To what ethnic group did Sargon, Assurbanipal and Cyrus belong ? We might think that the present-day Persians, the Kurds and the Armenians, and some of the Turks, are the local descendants of the people of these ancient kingdoms. But who is to prove to us that their descendants have always remained in the regions in which their ancestors developed those astonishing civilizations ?

CHAPTER II

The Osmanli Turks

THE European domain of the Turks has been much reduced during the last fifty years. And the last war imposed upon them large sacrifices of territory in Asia.

Let us remember at the outset that not all the wide areas under Turkish rule bearing the generic name of Turkey in Europe or Turkey in Asia were peopled by Turks, and also, as has been instanced again and again in the course of this book, that many " Turks "—the Turks of Bosnia-Herzegovina, for example—were people sprung from different stocks who had been Islamized and given a common political label.

Who can tell the exact origin of the Turks !

It must be understood that here we speak especially of the Osmanli Turks, of those who, with the Turkomans of Persia and of Russian and Afghan Turkestan, and the Azerbaijani—those " Turkicized Iranians of the Caucasus and of Persia " (?)—constitute the Western Turkish group. And we shall leave on one side the other peoples—excepting the Tatars to whom we shall have to refer—speaking the different Turki dialects.[1]

We say especially the Osmanli Turks, because it is very difficult in the present condition of anthropological research to attribute predominance to this or that people contained within the Turkish dominions in regard to the successive phases of social dynamics which created Turkish history.

These men, originally of diverse race, who together made up the Western Turkish group, nearly all—Turkomans, Yuruks, etc.—remain nomads (the Osmanli form a marked exception). Travellers readily admit that these nomads represent the purer type of the race. But we must not allow ourselves to become the victims of suggestion in regard to the romantic idea that

[1] The Turki " race " has been the subject of a larger number of works than the Mongol " race ". Some idea of this may be obtained by comparing in *les Races de l'Europe : l'indice céphalique*, by J. Deniker, Paris, 1899, the number of memoirs quoted respectively with reference to Turks and Tatars.

the nomad never mixes his blood. The agricultural folk like the Sartes—and the Tatars—allowed themselves to be penetrated more easily by foreign elements—by Mongols and Tunguses in the eastern group, and by Indo-Afghans, Arabs, and Assyroids in the western group.

In reality, despite all the existing literature, we can state nothing with certainty as to the purity of race of the nomadic Turkish peoples.

Comparisons between the large social groups would not be lacking in interest. Has it not been stated that the Osmanli Turks were enabled to play their well-known part in History and to constitute a long-lived political organism because of their intermixture, whereas the ancient empires founded by other Turki groups—the Tatar empire, for example—rapidly came to grief ? What are we to think of such determinism as regards Turkish history ?

If we are to deduce the ethnic quality of the Turks from the events which led to the Osmanli invasions, it will appear beyond question that this people could not have been other than an anthropological amalgam. And this becomes certainty if we admit *a priori* that the victor was obliged to incorporate the vanquished in measure as he advanced into the conquered territories and in obedience to the facts of war.

It has been said that the European Turks were largely mixed with people of the Dinaric race because the Ottoman conquest politically incorporated a great number of the inhabitants of the western Balkan peninsular in the Empire. Nevertheless, we must not forget that the Osmanli is a Musulman, and that in those lands in which the conquered people did not accept the religion of the conqueror it was scarcely possible for these to marry into the Turkish group, because they were " rayas "—inferiors. I think this intermixture has been greatly exaggerated.

The " Turks " of Bosnia-Herzegovina who are no other, in the great majority, than Islamized people of Dinaric race, have not expanded and settled widely. They have participated to a very slight degree in ethnic intermixture. The larger part of these " Turkicized " people have taken the name of Osmanli and become Turks out of economic interest, especially many of the large landed proprietors. It was altogether to their advantage to take the religion of the conqueror in order to remain in possession of their domains ;

but, let us repeat it, these Turkicized people continued to marry among their own folk. Their race has been but little attenuated. They have constituted for us who look at them from a distance a particle in the great Turkish whole which has born the name of the entire group. This is not what is called, in chemical language, a combination. Rather is it a mixture, that is to say, an association of several ethnic bodies which had become indistinct thanks to political and religious apellations.

Many theories have already been published (I am not speaking of anthropological memoirs) with a view of proving the origin of the Turks. Philological and geographical "arguments" have been introduced, as well as others. It has been said that the Turks were Ural-Altaics—which did not require any great effort of imagination; and Ugro-Finns—which does not amount to much. People have even gone so far as to include them in an ethnic whole which bears the even more vague title of Ugro-Japanese! It would seem from the literature of the subject that the philologists on one hand and the historians on the other have long argued about the matter. Have they resolved the difficulty so far as it concerns themselves? Or have they only complicated it?

Many peoples established in Europe have been thus "Turkicized" in language, such as the Huns and the Volga Bulgars—but did these peoples ever belong to the great Turki branch? It has been said that the Scythians should be considered a Turki people. That is possible. But who has shown us the anthropological characters of the Scythians in a manner sufficiently precise and sufficiently scientific to enable us to attempt such an approximation? Many such filiations seem to us far too bold! Have we not been led too much to consider the Turks as a sort of *officina gentium* because they were the most warlike of the peoples coming from Asia and because their political order has been the most stable? This, too, is an oriental mirage.

From the anthropological point of view it is certain that many of these supposed relationships are inacceptable. We have just seen that the Huns have been thought to be Turks. But there is a wide gulf between Jordanes's description and any description that could be given of an Osmanli Turk. Nothing is less like a Turk than one of Attila's Huns.[1]

[1] It is thought that Atilla was a Tunguse.

Were the cohorts of the Turkish invasions really composed of that ethnic complex—a singularly piebald group so far as its physical characters are concerned—whose elements speak the different Turki dialects? Or was it composed of more particularly genuine Turki groups, that is to say, groups of Turki race (notably the group which bears that name), who successively invaded first the west of Asia, then Europe? Who will tell us the answer?

The Turks are certainly one of the handsome races of Eur-Asia. In the Balkan Peninsular, where one meets with many remarkable human types, the Turks are far from being relegated to the background. And we may say at once, having seen many Turks, that very few among them suggest that they and the Mongols could have had a similar origin.

We must not altogether lose sight of the fact that a small amount of foreign blood may have entered the veins of the Turkish people through their institution of the harem. Women of the non-Musulman Caucasus (the Georgians in particular), Greeks, Arabs, and even Negresses have often formed part of the Turkish gynæceum. But some of these mixtures also call for a little explanation. In the first place this introduction of foreign blood has only affected the wealthier portion of the population, which could afford the luxury of a more or less extensive polygamy. This, then, would be but a drop or two in a large vessel, and would not greatly change the nature of the liquid. We know that an aristocracy is always the most hybrid of social groupings. In no land is the nobility a racial nobility. Consequently a fairly large number of these Georgians, Greeks, and Arabs could certainly have been considered as belonging to the same race as the Turks, although bearing different names.

An attempt has been made to outline the physical type of the Turki race. Those individuals who have best preserved it, it is said, are those belonging to the central group (comprising especially the Kirghiz, Uzbegs, Sartes and Volga Tatars). A general diagnosis of them is as follows: stature above the average (1 metre 67 to 1 metre 68); head, hyperbrachycephalic (cephalic index of 86 to 87); elongated, oval face; non-Mongaloid eyes, but often with the external fold of eyelid; the pilous system moderately developed; broad cheekbones;

thick lips; straight, somewhat prominent nose; tendency to obesity.[1]

The Kirghiz Kazaks appear to be smaller than the Sartes and especially than the Uzbegs; these last seem to be much less brachycephalic than the Kara Kirghiz.

The people of the western Turki group have certainly been the best studied. And it is a curious thing that until recent years the Asiatic Turks have been the subject of more attentive research than the European Turks. The work of von Luschan, Elisiéf, and Chantre[2]—to mention the more important—represented series of greater demonstrative value as regards the Asiatic Turks than those of Weisbach and Ivanowsky as regards the Turks of Constantinople and eastern Roumelia, or of Bassanovitch as regards the Turks of northwest Bulgaria.

The published results give contradictory conclusions. Among other characteristics, so low a stature (1 metre 62) is assigned to the Turks that it was very difficult for those who know this people to accept such indications.

I took part in the debate in 1911, with a first study of 300 men whom I examined in the Balkan peninsular. And I do not think the future will greatly modify the ethnological considerations which follow.

Contrary to what has been said by some observers, the Turks are men of tall stature. Elisiéf and Chantre had already brought this out as regards the Asiatic Turks. I can confirm their conclusions on this point. The Osmanli Turks must be classified under the heading of tall men (1 metre 675-699).[3]

The mean cephalic indices obtained from measurements made in Asia and Europe also show contradictory results. The one shows quite distinct brachycephaly—Kizilbaches of Anatolia (Chantre) giving a cephalic index of 86.11, and Baktaches of Syria (von Luschan) 86.33; East Bulgarian

[1] **LVII**, p. 439 (Eng. trans., p. 377).

[2] **XLIV**; **CXLIV**. The work of Elisiéf (in Russian) appeared in the Journal of the Moscow Society of the Natural Sciences, vol. lxviii and lxxi; **LIV**, p. 68.

[3] None the less it remains true that there is a fairly high proportion of individuals of low stature. This one character already reveals a human aggregate in the Osmanli Turks.

Turks (Bassanovitch), 84.6; whereas the others yield mesaticephalic or even dolichocephalic characters, as, for instance, the series of Ivanowsky (index of 75.4).

The cephalic index, like stature, marks the heterogeneity of the Turki group. The series I personally studied showed a mean sub-brachycephalic character. One finds, on analysing the cases individually that the brachycephalic types are more numerous than the dolichocephalic, but one also finds that it is not these two extreme forms but those which are intermediate that give the best picture of the cephalic quality of the Turks. And it is probable that the anthropologists of the future will tell us that the craniological characteristic of the Osmanli—of those of Europe, at all events—is mesaticephaly.

How are we to interpret this lack of homogeneity?

The Asiatic Turks are certainly less hybrid than the European Turks. And these Asiatic Turks are distinctly brachycephalic. Is it legitimate to suppose that when they crossed the Strait for the first time their contingents were composed entirely of round-headed people? Or did they bring with them people belonging to other ethnic groups? Come from across the sea of Marmora and the Ægean, they met with a population which, under the generalized domination of Greeks, was nothing but an assemblage of different groups, particularly those who, for various reasons, had been attracted within the orbit of Byzantium. These masses, of varied ethnic characters, were partially incorporated into the group which conquered the Peninsular. They did not disappear from it. They intercalated themselves between the ranks of the newcomers. And to use chemical terminology once more, this was not fusion but an amalgam.

In support of what has been said we may call attention, by way of example, to the indication given by Ivanowsky which has already been mentioned. This writer, measuring Turki heads in eastern Roumelia, found that their mean cephalic index was 75.4. This is a dolichocephalic character. The provenance of this particular series was Slivno. Yet if we examine the ethnological map of Bulgaria we shall see that this locality is comprised within the dolichocephalic Bulgar zone. The Turki heads of Slivno were those of Turks in name only.

The Turki nose is generally straight and often has a tendency to be aquiline. Flat noses, like prominent cheekbones, reminiscent of Mongol relationships are very rare.

Here is a further observation whose importance will at once be grasped and noted by informed persons.

It has been said that Asia is a continent in which the pigmentation of eyes and hair is always pronounced. (For instance, I have never found blue eyes among the Kurds[1]; they are rare among the Lazes and the Armenians.) Yet the Osmanli Turks often have grey or blue eyes, and also fair hair. Chantre noted the presence of 20 per cent. of light-coloured eyes and 38 per cent. of fair hair among the men he examined in Western Asia. I have found among European Turks a relatively larger number of light eyes. Deniker notes that it is only among the blond European races (perhaps also among the Turki-Finnish races) that one finds light eyes, blue or grey.

As regards pigmentation the Turks, together with a certain number of Kurds, would then constitute a particular human group among the other Western Asiatic peoples.

In a Turkish tale which celebrated the merits of Sultan Orkhan Ghazi, successor to Othman, I find a very curious portrait of the conqueror: "His form corresponded to the greatness of his fame; his stature was majestic, his chest broad, his arms muscular. His fair hair and blue eyes, and his high forehead. . . ." Is this an authentic description? Or did the historiographer attribute to Orkhan the physical characters which at the time may have been considered the most highly remarkable, because they were the most rare? Certain impenitent pan-Germans assure us that Orkhan Ghazi could have been no other than a descendant of the Galatæ and that he represented the purest Germanic type—big, blond and blue-eyed; if we could only add long-headed, the portrait would be complete!

It is probable that there existed "somewhere" in Western Asia a human group in whom the iris instead of being dark, as it ordinarily is in this region, and as it is, moreover, throughout the rest of Asia, was grey or blue.

But what was the origin of this blue-eyed race? Are we to consider it as having originated in Asia itself? Has it sprung from prehistoric European migrants? Or from those

[1] von Luschan has found them.

who arrived in the first centuries of our era? There is here an important problem awaiting solution, and its solution would give to the present-day Turks a still greater anthropological interest. Who knows what approximations it might permit us to make?

I recall that in the Caucasus the Ossetes frequently show fair hair and light eyes. Ammianus Marcellinus, who saw them on the expedition to Persia of the emperor Julian, included them among the blond races—which is to exaggerate somewhat because blond hair among this people is only in the proportion of 10 per cent., and light eyes in a proportion of 25 to 30 per cent.

Thus, there certainly existed, in Western Asia at all events, and among many different political or ethnic groups (in a proportion varying according to locality) individuals having light eyes—generally blue—and fair hair.

This, perhaps, is the moment to recall the magnificent discoveries of von Lecoq in Chinese Turkestan. In the Museum für Völkerkunde of Berlin there exists (not shown to the public) an admirable collection of Buddhist frescoes brought before the war from Turfan by the German explorer. Among the individuals figuring in these frescoes there are, side by side with many others, men having light-coloured hair and blue eyes. I have protested too often against an unwarranted utilization for anthropological purposes of pictorial or plastic representations not to call attention to these curious paintings with all necessary reserve. But the interest of these paintings becomes the greater in that the philologists, I am told (I am quite incompetent in these matters), have recognized in many of the inscriptions traces of a Lithuanian origin. Thus we are brought back to the hypotheses of de Saussure. And the Lithuanians of the present day belong, in great part, to the Nordic race, one of whose characteristics is light hair and eyes. I will not press the matter further, on what, for me, is dangerous ground.

To sum up, the Turks, a tall sub-brachycephalic people, included among them numerous foreigners. Their presence in the European group may be explained by the actual history of the Balkan peninsular. Let us remember what assaults this region has had to suffer. And let us call to mind the number of different human groups which have precipitated themselves on to this corner of the earth, and have sojourned there for longer or shorter periods ! Then one can no longer be surprised to find a disparity of ethnic elements.

It would seem more than likely that at the moment of the Turkish conquest this heterogeneous mass was already constituted. Byzantium to some extent would have seen to that. Then, the invaders having conquered the whole Peninsular, many of its inhabitants accepted the economic facilities offered to those who would enter the conqueror's ranks. Little by little the political term of Turk replaced the native names wherever Islam took root. Gradually, without, of course, in any way changing their zoological characters, the conquered peoples became "Turki" peoples, to whom it was open to mingle their blood with that of the Osmanli. To-day, no longer remembering their origin, they call themselves "Turks" like those who subjugated them.

If we transport the problem to Asia Minor it presents itself under a somewhat different aspect. The Turki race is probably less mixed in Anatolian territory. I have elsewhere shown that a large number of Asiatic Greeks are no other than the descendants, Hellenized at different periods, of the autochthonous population. However active may have been the birthrate of the small Greek cities of antiquity, they could not possibly have built up the powerful agglomerations of the Asiatic "Greeks".

Future research in Asia Minor will perhaps show the presence of two races intermingled in very different proportions. The aspect which the curve of the cephalic index, for instance, will take, will yield us information on this point, always provided that the investigations are undertaken on a sufficiently large scale. It is to be hoped that the New Turkey which is now evolving will interest itself in making such an analysis of its ethnic elements.

To which of the Turki groups belongs the clan of the Emir Ertoghrul-ibn-Suleiman, father of Othman, to whom Ala-ed-din-Kaikobad II., sultan of the Seljuks (1245-1254) gave the small territory in which the famous empire originated ? Certain historians believe that Suleiman-Shah, the father of Ertoghrul, was one of Jenghiz Khan's generals and that he was no stranger to the great Oghuz Tatar family to which Jenghiz himself belonged. This clan, after having been in Khorassan, settled in the Erzerum region before it became possessed of the lands lying to the east of Olympus in Bithynia, the nucleus of the Ottoman power. Was this group led by Ertoghrul of Tatar origin ? Or was it of Turki origin ? Very likely we shall never know.

CHAPTER III

THE PHŒNICIANS

IT is quite certain that Carthage apart the Phœnicians took no share in bringing about the great modifications of history by warlike invasions. Nevertheless, it would be puerile to deny their very real influence on the development of European civilization—were they not skilled navigators? Are they not counted among the inventors of the alphabet? Thus it is impossible in a book like this to pass over in silence this people which impregnated a portion of ancient Europe with its own ideas and the ideas in which it trafficked.

What are we to think of the traditions, recorded by Herodotus, relating to the geographical origin of these people who, for several centuries, were the "Jews of the sea," thanks to their activity as religious and commercial agents? Did their primitive habitat extend, as has been thought, from either side of Arabia to the Persian Gulf and the Red Sea? Did the continual voyages of these navigators in any way modify their own ethnic characters or even those of the peoples among whom they came? Are their descendants lost to-day, as has been claimed, in the Arab ranks?

Despite the small credence we must place in the greater part of the accounts of the geographers and historians of antiquity, it would yet seem possible that the Phœnicians formed part of those Mesopotamian peoples which, known under different names but belonging to the same race, have evolved in different fashions.[1]

Legendary accounts (those collected by Justin) state that owing to earthquakes the Phœnicians of history migrated, first into the valley of the Jordan and the Dead Sea, and thence to the Mediterranean coasts where their extraordinary naval destiny awaited them.

[1] The most recent historical information about the Phœnicians will be found in Vols. vii, viii and ix of the English translations of *l'Evolution de l'Humanité*.

These historical questions are outside our province. The earliest geographical origin of the Phœnicians and their successive habitats only concern us here in so far as we can utilize them for ethnic interpretation. If the suppositions we have just recalled are founded on fact we ought to find in the Phœnicians the anthropological characters of the Mesopotamians or those of the Arabs or the Jews.

Confined within this narrow strip of territory, half mainland, half island, which has been so often described, the Phœnicians, owing to a perfectly explicable phenomenon of physical geography, never constituted a coherent political entity. But this lack of unity cannot seek its operative cause in ethnic diversity. In this case difference of race is not to be invoked as having been one of the possible disruptive factors.

The Phœnicians became great merchant navigators, voyaging all along the Mediterranean littoral. Has it not been said that Nîmes[1] owes its foundation to them (?), and that they settled in the Rhône valley ?[2] Has not the discovery of their graves[3] and their skeletons also been claimed many a time in the south of France ?

And has it not been thought that the key to the problem of the race to which the Phœnicians belonged has been discovered at the same time ?

We know to what a height of prosperity the Phœnicians brought this traffic between the three continents, but we have not yet grasped the full extent of the social influence these traders exercised. The Phœnicians were active missionaries who made Europe known to the East and the East to Europe, but who also, it would seem, developed industry and the exploitation of mines wherever they set foot.

Had Tyre and Sidon not been known, the Greeks would have remained Barbarians ; we should not have had Carthage, nor the counting houses in Italy, Gaul and Spain, whence the trading routes started which penetrated to the heart of Europe, carrying thither those reflected images of civilization which were to arouse the envy of our prehistoric ancestors.

[1] **CCXXXI**, p. 161 ; **CCLIII**, vol. i, p. 130.

[2] **CLXXXI**. See G. de Mortilet's contestation of this discovery in the *Bull. Soc. d'Anth. Paris*, 1870, p. 542.

[3] **CLXXIII**, p. 45.

For the Phœnicians were not only merchant seamen. Their land caravans, starting from the Syrian shores, went north, probably as far as Armenia and the Caucasus, and east to Babylon, and thence to India.

But in none of these directions did the Phœnicians contribute any anthropological influence. The Berbers of the Sahara caravans did not modify the physical characters of the people with whom they came in contact several times in the year for the purpose of trading. Maybe, even, the Phœnicians did not personally conduct the caravans of their period, but contented themselves with acting as the managers of the counting houses on the coast and as the sedentary administrators of the caravans? It has been claimed that groups of people preserving the Phœnician type have been discovered in Sicily, Sardinia, Corsica, Spain and the South of France. Another of those Oriental mirages!

Before the presence of such souvenirs and influences can be asserted it is essential first to be quite sure that we know what the somatological characters of the historical Phœnicians were, so that we can compare them with those of the people supposed to be the descendants of the Tyrians and Sidonians. But we are still without the means definitely to establish an anthropological diagnosis of the primitive Phœnicians, who go back to the furthest antiquity.

Phœnicia went through all the stages of lithic civilization. Chellean hand-axes ("coups de poing"), and implements of the Moustierian type have been found at Saida. Neolithic objects appear to be very numerous in this land. Modern excavators are in accord in finding that the Phœnician coast was thickly populated in prehistoric periods—we speak of the stone ages. Neophytus, one of these fortunate discoverers, says[1] that it must be conceded "that few localities could present to the same degree so many precious advantages as this coast offered to its inhabitants—marvellous and infinitely varied sites, high plateaux, delightful plains, steep mountains, deep valleys, a coastline indented and steep in some parts, and in others having sandy beaches where fishing was easy; thick forests full of game; and magnificent caves cut out in the cliffs on the banks of wild torrents. All the commodities of life were thus to be found in this little corner of the earth.

[1] **CLXXI**, p. 1.

Moreover, the coast is strewn with prehistoric stations from Akka to Tripolis." It remains to be seen if this idyllic description could be applied to Phœnicia of pleistocene times!

Louis Lartet, who, in 1864, explored the region of Nahr el Kelb, bear Bierut, recalled that it was in 1833 that Botta first called attention to the stone industries of Syria. Lartet himself undertook excavations in this ancient Phœnician territory.[1] Up till 1893 very few prehistorians followed in his tracks. Zumoffen[2] then began his researches, which are being continued to-day on a very big scale. There is no doubt that soon the most ancient parts of Phœnicia will be laid completely bare. But was this ancient past inscribed by those same Phœnicians of whom history tells? Because, if they are Mesopotamians, they would simply have superposed their civilization (at least from neolithic times) on that of the autochthonous people of the coast who had been there from the earliest times and whose ethnic relationships it is impossible for us to fathom to-day.

All specialists know the important excavations undertaken by L. Siret in the south of Spain where he has explored some 500 neolithic graves, dolmens, cupolas, etc., which have yielded thousands of objects of the late stone age. Among the exotic materials he recovered there are some, according to the discoverer, whose geographical origins betoken Phœnician trading.

The amber beads can only have come from Baltic beds, according to their chemical analysis and their succinic acid content (2 per cent.); the jet came from the British Isles; the callais (a mineral of the aluminous phosphates group accompanying tin) was obtained elsewhere than from workings of the staniferous beds of the Creuse or from Spain.

The Belgian authority considers that these different materials, as well as the beads of Ostrich eggshell and the objects of elephant and hippopotamus ivory, demonstrate "that during late neolithic times maritime routes linked the south of the Iberian peninsular on one hand with the Baltic, the British Isles, the Cassiterites, and on the other with Egypt and the East."[3]

1 **CXXXIV.**
2 **CCC.**
3 **CCXLII**, p. 142. Is this not where the Ægeans should come in?

Thus, in the polished stone age the Phœnicians had conquered a part of the Mediterranean and Atlantic world. But, let us repeat it, this was a purely commercial, moral, and religious conquest. Nowhere can they have modified the anthropological characters of the people among whom they voyaged. They were intermediaries who, once known, could no longer be done without, but nowhere did they settle in any numbers in the lands opened up to their exploitation—they never created what geographers call colonies of settlement.

"The Phœnicians were a mere handful of men lost in the immensity of the known world, incapable of raising an army and placing under subjection even the most primitive of nations. Without spilling a drop of their blood they conquered the West by the prestige of their own superiority, their skill in trading, their patience and cunning, by the lure of their wares and their perfumes, and by the effect of their unguents, drugs and magic."

The Israelites who had good reason to know the Phœnicians typified their commerce by likening it to that "of a courtesan prostituting herself to all the kingdoms of the world ".[1] We should only be deceiving ourselves were we to think we could easily find the ethnic features of the conquerors even in those places where they built flourishing cities or a metropolis such as Carthage. There, too, the Phœnicians themselves were but a handful of men. They could never have peopled these territories by their own unaided efforts. They occupied them and imposed on them their tongue and their customs. The trading centre, once created, was protected by a fortress. Then the native families, attracted by the trade, more or less quickly settled in groups in its neighbourhood, the more quickly as the benefits of all kinds to be had, material and moral, were the greater. First the village, then the town, was built up of inhabitants who were not Phœnicians. In the eyes of the world at large this town was Phœnician (and we to-day look upon it in exactly the same way): it has remained Phœnician for succeeding generations of historians. But it has this ethnic quality in appearance only.

When the Phœnicians landed for the first time on the shores of North Africa those shores were populated. Africa,

[1] **CCXLII**, p. 134.

like the other continents, but in different fashion, had already run through a portion of its evolutionary cycle. We know that at the time when Carthage was founded there had already developed on South African territory, as in Europe, a complete civilization beginning with the Palæolithic. And on the Tunisian shores the Tyrian folk met in particular with the people who built the megalithic monuments whose discovery a few generations since so greatly intrigued the first European observers.[1]

To obtain precise information as to the anthropological characters of the early Phœnicians we should need to possess the skeletons contained in the burials of the great Phœnician period on that same coast on which Tyre and Sidon developed their power as merchant cities. Unfortunately this important testimony has not yet been placed at the disposal of ethnologists. Some day, undoubtedly, it will be so placed, when such systematic research is undertaken as will conduce to the preservation of archæological objects and skeletons *at one and the same time.*

Up to the present day, anthropological data relating to the Phœnicians are scarce. At least I know of very few. The few crania which Nicolucci (1864) considered to be Phœnician were highly dolichocephalic (indices of 70 to 75). They had large orbits and prominent occipital bosses (*en chignon*). Pruner Bey published some notes relating to crania considered to be Phœnician. But their origin was very doubtful and we shall leave this anthropologist's communications on one side. As for the crania of Italia Nicastro[2], all we know about their morphology is contained in the following lines : " The crania examined were compressed in the temporal region and of almost rhomboid form ; the dental apparatus was very prominent, complete, and in good condition." One must admit that this does not amount to much. We might as well say that these few words teach us nothing at all. In the body of the memoir we find the following slightly more explicit phrase : " . . . and to the dolichocephalic and prognathous form characteristic of the crania of the buried race."

[1] The people who built the megalithic monuments were probably tall and dolichocephalic.

[2] **CXVIII,** p. 341 ; Acre, ruins on the Acremonte plateau dominated by Palazzolo-Acreide to the west of Syracuse. **CLXXXI.**

A few years later Nicolucci, Mantegazza and Zanetti notified the discovery of fresh crania, considered to be Phœnician, in Sardinia.[1]

In 1890 Dr. Bertholon, residing in Tunis, published the description of two Phœnician skulls[2], followed, two years later by a new memoir.[3] The gist of these morphological studies is as follows: rather small crania (these specimens must have been small people); straight, rather low forehead; "this dolichocephalic forehead is united to the median cranium of a brachycephal"; the *norma verticalis* of this skull is perceptibly rhomboid; the cephalic index is round about 77 to 78. The face was short and broad, the nose leptorrhine; the face of medium breadth. According to the author the Phœnicians would have been small and showing a tendency to dolichocephaly.

In 1884 Chantre studied a series of crania recovered from a necropolis in Sidon[4] by Hamdy Bey. Here the cranial form is quite different from that hitherto met with in the Mediterranean islands or in Africa. The mean cephalic index is 79.31. Yet it is lower than in the case of crania coming from Saida, which varied from 79.20 to 86.31.

De Quatrefages and Hamy[5] in their *Crania ethnica* indicate the characters of twelve crania brought from Utica by M. Herisson. The mean cephalic index of these skulls was most distinctly dolichocephalic, both in the case of men (74.86) and women (73.37). Bertholon, who had for a long time lived at Carthage, tried to identify the characters of the Phœnician skulls with those of the Basques. He gave the following portrait of men whom he considered to be the living descendants of the ancient Carthaginians: "These subjects had a very brown skin. This harmonizes with the Phœnician custom of colouring their statues a reddish brown with a view of representing the tint of the skin. The hair and beard are black. The hair is frequently wavy or even curly. . . . The eyes are very dark, almost black, so much so that one

[1] **CL**, p. 17.
[2] **XIII**, p. 314.
[3] **XIII** (1892), p. 179.
[4] **XXXIX**, p. 12.
[5] **CCV**, p. 502. The Carthaginians would have been tall people, well above the average height: 1 metre 678 according to the long bones found at Carthage. These data, however, are inadequate.

cannot distinguish the pupil from the iris. The eyelids are usually widely open. They have what are usually called large eyes. The nose is straight, occasionally slightly concave. It is generally fleshy and sometimes bulbous at the end. The mouth is medium, occasionally rather large. The lips are generally thick; the cheekbones are hardly at all prominent."[1]

Carthage itself, where systematic research has been undertaken, can provide us with testimony of a more demonstrative character. We owe it to Père Delattre that a fairly large number of human remains, met with in the course of his excavations, have been preserved. These remains were at first studied by Bertholon in a first memoir. Then Bertholon and Chantre, in their book on Barbary, brought together all our anthropological knowledge of the Carthaginians. We now definitely know that the Phœnician metropolis contained representatives of various ethnic groups. Is proof thereof, chosen from among the more demonstrative, desired?

Those who have visited the Lavigerie museum at Carthage during recent years will remember the magnificent sarcophagus of the priestess of Tanit discovered by Père Delattre. This sarcophagus, the most highly decorated and artistic of those found, and whose outer image probably represents the goddess herself, must have been the coffin of a very great ecclesiastical personage. And the woman it contained exhibited Negroid characters. She was an African by race!

It is certain that a great portion of the Carthaginian population was not Phœnician. It merely bore the Phœnician label.

In order to get a closer knowledge of the anthropological documents considered to be Phœnician and discovered in the old Punic metropolis, we will examine what Bertholon and Chantre, the latest writers to study them, have to say on the subject.

Their anthropological material was composed, first, of 117 crania (68 male, 49 female) from the ancient necropoles of Carthage, and collected by Père Delattre and Messrs. Gauckler and Merlin, the Chiefs of the Tunisian Antiquities Service. An examination of these specimens as a whole leads to the

[1] XIII, p. 663.

following conclusions: "The most usual features of the inhabitants of Carthage consist in a medium cranial capacity, marked dolichocephaly, mesoseme orbits, a leptorrhine nose and a very short face." These crania, placed in their chronological groups, show a cephalic index graduated as follows: sixth century, 74.44; fifth century, 74.18; fourth century, 74.90; third century, 68.79. This finding has a certain importance: the men buried in the Punic necropoles of the sixth to the third centuries would seem to have been remarkably dolichocephalic.[1] I said "would seem to have been". As a matter of fact, when we examine the individual measurements of these skulls (among which there are some Negroid specimens) we perceive that the series does not contain nothing but true dolichocephals. There are even three sub-brachycephalic crania (2.5 per cent. of the entire series); also 15.3 per cent. of mesaticephals, and 23.3 per cent. of sub-dolichocephals. Nevertheless it remains the case that of the people found in the Carthaginian necropoles a large majority (82 per cent). consisted of dolichocephalic types.

Other skeletal remains found in Punic Carthage and deposited in the Lavigerie Museum are of specimens discovered in private tombs that very likely belonged to the Carthaginian élite. The skulls are nearly all dolichocephalic. It is impossible for us to enter into the details noted by Bertholon and Chantre. Their general conclusion, in so far as concerns this special chapter, is as follows: the specimens that had received the honour of individual sepulture do not differ from the generality of the Carthaginian population. The Punic element would appear to be that which is marked by a cranium that is "mesaticephalic, rhomboid in *norma verticalis* owing to the high development of the parietal bosses, and with flattened vault. This type had large orbits, a leptorrhine nose, and a rather short face." It is a little different from that first defined by Bertholon. (See above.)

Is this the diagnosis of the true Phœnician type?[2]

[1] The mean cephalic index is 74.98. That of the women, a little higher, is 75.85. The nasal index is supplied by such a small number of individuals that it has seemed to me better to leave it out.

[2] The writers indicated above close their paragraph about the Africans of the Punic period with these words: "The Punic element, its character much changed by intermixture, was recognizable in at least a third of the Carthaginian population of the fourth century. These Libyan-Phœnicians

For the time being it is impossible to say one way or the other.

This rapid description shows us how little more advanced we are. All the same, maybe it is towards a dolichocephalic type of more than average stature that we must look, in spite of what Bertholon said ?—a type which would approximate to that of the classic Arab and perhaps to that of the classic Jew, but not to the people of Upper Mesopotamia.

Should the Phœnicians be included in the group we call Semitic ? It is possible. But it is not certain. We must await further information.

---

were lost amid a mass containing non-Phœnician elements in a proportion of 66 per cent."

These non-Phœnicians were thus composed :—

(i) Of a leptorrhine dolichocephalic type, ovoid in *norma verticalis*, with a nose frequently continuous with the forehead. Round orbits, and long face (modern Tunisian-Algerian leptorrhine dolichocephalic type).

(ii) Of a highly dolichocephalic type, pentagonal in *norma verticalis*, with a nasal index tending towards mesorrhiny (small dolichocephalic type).

The representatives of these two groups constituted, according to the authors, the main stock of the skeletons buried in the megalithic sepulchres of North Africa.

A third element lived side by side with the others in equal proportions with them. It is characterized by a mesaticephalic skull, vallate in *norma verticalis*, and by a highly leptorrhine nose. This people occupies to-day the least accessible regions of Barbary and the oases.

That is as far as we can get. It is not impertinent to hold that fresh studies are required.

CHAPTER IV

THE JEWS

THE descendants of two peoples whose destiny has not been without influence on the world's destiny inhabit the country to the northwest of Arabia which is watered by the Jordan and whose shores are bathed by the Mediterranean, though it is impossible either to number them or to outline their territorial boundaries with precision—and those peoples are the Jews and the Phœnicians.

I do not know what specialists think about the influence that may be attributed to the Jewish people in the general history of the Oriental peoples. It seems to me that if we take into consideration the two kingdoms of Judah and Israel only, that influence would appear to be a small one. Can we not say that it is thanks to their very dispersion that the Jews, in certain circumstances, have been more or less important factors in History as a whole? It has devolved upon individuals and groups and not on the nation to exercise a frequently decisive political influence. For anthropologists, though they may consider certain Jews to be inspired by the Israelitish racial idea, all Jews are very far from belonging to the "Jewish race." There is no such thing, said Renan, as a Jewish type—there are Jewish types. Nothing could be more true. We cannot consider the Jews of to-day—not even in Palestine, because the Sionist movement has imported all kinds and conditions of Israelites—as constituting a homogeneous ethnic group. The Jews belong to a religious and social community to which, in every period, individuals of different races have attached themselves. These Judaized people have come from every kind of ethnic stratum, such as the Falashas of Abyssinia and the Germans of Germanic type; or the Tamils—Black Jews—of India, and the Khazars, who are supposed to be of Turki race.

Which among the different morphological types exhibited by the Jews should be considered the authentic representative of the Jewish race?

I should say that, as regard European Jews—the best known—it is among the Jews known as Spaniols that we have the best chance of finding the original type of this "race" whose intellectual qualities are so remarkable. It is impossible to believe that the light-eyed, fair and chestnut-haired Jews whom one often meets in Central Europe can be zoologically related to the originally Israelitish people who in olden days inhabited the Jordan country.

But what are the "anthropological qualities" of the real Jews? Despite all the existing work, there is here a most important study to be undertaken. I have often suggested it to my students of Jewish "nationality."

I should think few peoples have been the subject of so many small local studies, but unfortunately there is nothing more definitive available. These studies have been undertaken in many parts of the world, in Europe, Asia and Africa, which, indeed, adds to their interest. They have led to different and occasionally definitely conflicting results, which well illustrates the heterogeneity of this social and religious group.

The cephalic index of the Jews ranges from dolichocephaly to hyperbrachycephaly. And whereas, for example, the stature of the Galician Jews of Poland is only from 1 metre 60 to 1 metre 62, which is quite low, one finds among the groups of Oriental Jews a stature exceeding 1 metre 66 and even 1 metre 699 (at Odessa), which is much above the European mean.[1]

This preamble shows how very necessary it is, if we are not to accept certain definitions blindly, to glance rapidly over what anthropological research can teach us on the subject of the Jewish race.[2]

It is estimated that there are 12 million Jews at the present day. They are spread almost all over the world, and abuse of this extensive distribution has many a time been made in order to claim that the Israelites are ubiquitous and possess unlimited possibilities of acclimatization.

[1] There is a considerable bibliography dealing with the anthropological characters of the Jews, which it is impossible for us to list here. We mention chiefly the works of Weissenberg because results obtained by the same writer using the same methods are the more useful for purposes of comparison.

[2] For a discussion in English see "Racial Origins of Jewish Types," Dr. R. N. Salaman, *Jewish Hist. Soc. of England*, Vol. **IX**, 1922, p. 163. (Translator's Note.)

One question arises at the outset. Has the relatively large number, indicated above, been built up by a natural excess of births over deaths during historic times ? Or must we explain it by the incorporation of other more or less large populations ? We have seen just now that on many occasions entire groups have become Judaized and thus contributed their numbers and their eugenic qualities to the Israelite contingent.

Jewish fecundity, noted everywhere as being of a superlative order, is observed to be very much on the wane to-day. In the period 1820-1866 a birthrate of 37.70 per 1,000 Jews was recorded ; comparative figures for 1902 show only 22.5. Fifteen years ago in Germany, where investigations of this kind are of interest since there are some 5 or 6 hundred thousand Jews in the country, it was found that there was a notable decrease in the number of Jewish births. A few years earlier another fact of great importance for the preservation of the "race" was observed, namely that mixed marriages were very much on the increase, and that not more than about a fourth of the number of Jewish children were being brought up in the Jewish faith.[1]

This is a very great step forward in the direction of "ethnic" incorporation by a neighbouring people. Such incorporation (it has existed everywhere and in all periods side by side with the contrary phenomenon) is particularly noticeable in certain large cities, notably in Berlin, where a large number of Jews have solemnly renounced their faith during recent decades.

An anthropologist, were he asked to outline the main features of the ethnic physiognomy of the Jews, would be greatly embarrassed.

Should we attribute to this type a dolichocephalic or brachycephalic head ?—a tall or small stature ?—blond or brown hair ?—blue or brown eyes ? Should we even bestow upon it the classic Jewish nose which draughtsmen have so often caricatured ?

To demonstrate this difficulty let us take those countries where Jews are numerous. Our documentation will thus be the more copious ; let us undertake a serious morphological and descriptive investigation, and ponder the results. It is certain that the composite picture we shall get will be meaningless.

Russian Jews show more mesaticephalic and less brachycephalic types than the rest of the country, says Weissenberg.

[1] See a note by Salomon Reinach in *Anthropologie,* Paris, 1903, p. 737.

But Ivanowsky[1] tells us that the Jews form a distinct and well defined group belonging chiefly to a brunet, brachycephalic, mesoprosopic type, having long arms and legs and poorly developed chest. In Germany Ammon finds a cephalic index of 83.5 for the Jews of the Grand Duchy of Baden; but Weissenberg[2], in Cologne and Frankfort-on-the-Main, found a mean index of 80.6, with variations ranging from extreme dolichocephaly (73.8) to extreme brachycephaly (88.6). And these few examples, taken at random, repeat themselves in all European lands. Are they also to be found in the other continents? The pages that follow will show.

We know to what an extent differences in rite divide the Jews into two main groups—the Sephardim and Askenazim. The Sephardi rite is followed by the Israelites—whom, rightly or wrongly, we imagine to be the more authentic members of the Jewish race.[3]

Hence it is worth while to study a series of those Jews who claim the aristocratic characters of the Jewish race.

In the lands of Eastern Europe—Turkey, Greece, Bosnia, Bulgaria, etc., there exist strong contingents of Spaniols who say that they are the descendants of the Jews driven out of Spain by the 1492 persecution; sometimes they call themselves Moriskos. Their number is estimated at a little over 300,000 persons. Weissenberg, who has published a whole series of interesting memoirs on Jewish anthropology, examined 175 Spaniols[4] of both sexes. He compared their morphological and descriptive characters with those of some Russian Jews whom he himself had studied. Here are some of his results.

The Spaniols were taller than the Russian Jews; their cephalic index is much lower (78.1 instead of 82.5). And whereas among the Russian Jews the proportion of dolichocephalic types was only 1 per cent., it was 14.6 per cent. among the Spaniols. On the other hand, whereas the Spaniols only numbered 25.4 per cent. of brachycephals among them, the figure for the Russian Jews was 81 per cent. Furthermore, the figures showed that among the Spaniols there were

[1] Ivanowsky, in the *Bulletin* of the Society of the Friends of the Natural Sciences, Moscow, 1904.

[2] **CCLXXX**, p. 269.

[3] Many Jews have told me that this is not correct.

[4] **CCLXXXI**.

79.2 per cent. of individuals with brown hair, while among the Russian Jews these only numbered 58 per cent.

Though we have no desire to take sides in this question of whether the Spaniols have a better right than the others to be considered as having authentically sprung from the primitive Israelites, it already appears from the above that the social and religious group known as Jewish is singularly heterogeneous. Weissenberg[1], pushing his analysis further still, examined Kohanim[2] and Levites, who claim to be the descendants of the great priests of Israel, and who, to preserve this privilege of caste, marry among themselves. Thus they represent the primitive Jewish type preserved in its pristine purity. Twelve Levites and thirty-four Kohanim were measured by Weissenberg.

First of all let us note that the people, in the midst of whom these so-called ethnic aristocrats dwell, yielded to the same writer individual cephalic indices ranging from 73.7 to 88.6. These, then, are the indices obtained from these two particular classes of Jews: in the Kohanim they range from 78 to 88; in the Levites from 78.2 to 89.1, both of them exhibiting, together with an equal brachycephaly, a lesser degree of dolichocephaly than the surrounding population. But, in a general census a fairly large number of Kohanim and Levites would melt into the ranks of their co-religionists. The number of fair individuals met with in these two Israelitish groups is the same as among their hosts.

If we pass on into Asia we shall find that the results are no less disturbing. And we shall again take our information from Weissenberg[3].

The Jews of Central Asia (Bokhara, Samarkand, Merv, and Herat) would seem to constitute a distinctly heterogeneous

[1] **CCLXXXII**, p. 961.

[2] The author uses the term "Aaronides", which is not in use among English-speaking Jews.

The Kohanim are the clergy or descendants of the clergy and boast their pure descent from Aaron, and are usually known as Cohen, Kun, Kühn, Cahane, Cane, etc., but occasionally as Aaronsohn or Aarons. Although according to Jewish law no Cohen may marry a proselyte, and custom outlawed a Cohen who married any but a strictly orthodox Jewess, there is no ban on marriage with the daughter of a proselyte. Though the "Aaronides" may not have preserved their blood as pure as the ban on mixed marriages would seem to suggest, the somewhat onerous disabilities of the priesthood are likely to have safeguarded the Kohanim from intermixture arising from other Jews claiming to be Kohanim without warrant. (Translator's Note.)

[3] **CCLXXXIII**, p. 103.

contingent if the small series of individuals from this region can represent a synthetic picture of the central Asian Jews as a whole. The distribution of cephalic types was as follows: mesaticephalic, 28 per cent.; brachycephalic, 39 per cent.; hyperbrachycephalic, 33 per cent.; that is to say that the brachycephalic element is dominant (72 per cent.) in the population. These results are a somewhat rude shock for those who believe in the dogma of Jewish dolichocephaly! Weissenberg did not find a single man having the ethnic character which is claimed to be the original one. On the other hand, we know that the geographical regions whence the Jews measured by Weissenberg came are peopled by brachycephalic groups. This fact alone might serve to explain matters.

Do the Jews of Persia, to west-southwest of Central Asia, show the morphological characters of their co-religionists of Central Asia? In the north of this country the Jews are brachycephalic (showing the influence, in particular, of the brachycephalic people of the Caucasus); in the southern portion they are dolichocephalic[1]. Weissenberg, also, noted the less brachycephalic character of the Persian Jews of southern Persia, who were also of lower stature (1 metre 63) than the Jews from the North and from the Caucasus (1 metre 64). The cephalic index of these Persian Jews was 79.8 (it was 82.5 for the Jews of Central Asia). And although not a single genuine dolichocephal was met with among the latter, there were 8.6 per cent. among the Persian Jews. Furthermore, the Persian Jews examined by Weissenberg all had brown hair, whereas in Central Asia only 89.9 per cent. were of this type.[2]

Further west still, in the Mesopotamian region, where the Jews have always been very numerous, four-fifths of the group had chestnut-coloured hair. These Mesopotamian Jews are smaller than the average (1 metre 64), and their cephalic index is not very high (78). Among them there is a proportion of 13.5 per cent. of dolichocephalic types.[3] They appear greatly to resemble their Persian congeners. Moreover, we must not forget that if Mesopotamia contains distinctly brachycephalic human groups, it also possesses dolichocephalic peoples, the Arabs in particular (they are taller). Has not Chantre found dolichocephalic Kurds in the same area?

[1] **CCLXXXIV**, p. 108.
[2] **CCLXXXV**.
[3] **CCLXXXVI**.

To the north of Persia and Mesopotamia the Jews of the Caucasus form little groups that differ somewhat from the ethnographic point of view[1]. In the governments of Kutais and Tiflis the Jews of the Gruze country have adopted the language and customs of the people among whom they live; so also have the so-called Mountain Jews in the Daghestan and Baku regions. These Jewish populations claim to have been in these localities since the beginning of the Christian era. And if this "race" had remained ethnically pure it would have been an interesting example of what different "environmental influences" can effect in the way of modifying human beings!

Weissenberg found that there was no perceptible difference between them. The mean height of both was 1 metre 64—fairly low. Kurdow found it a little more (1 metre 66). The mean cephalic index of the Gruzin Jews is 86; that of the Mountain Jews 84.7. These figures do not greatly differ from those found by Kurdow and Erckert (86.3). In this region the Jews are brachycephalic. They have the cephalic characteristics of the majority of the surrounding population.

Weissenberg did not meet with any fair-haired or blue-eyed people. He indicates that the physical type of these Caucasian Jews approximated to that of the Armenians. Yes! But we must also remember that the Armenians are taller. These Caucasian Jews—like the Spaniols in the Balkan peninsular—are quite ready to think themselves representative of the bluest-blooded Israelitish nobility. De Baye[2], who visited them, tells how they seem to despise the Western Jews, with whom they have the minimum of social relations. They claim to be the descendants of the Israelites sent there from Judæa by the Assyrian kings between the end of the eighth to the close of the seventh century B.C. What are our miserable titles of nobility, going back to the Crusades, beside this venerable antiquity?

Needless to say, the entire history of Transcaucasia was put together long after the event, and, moreover, that there is nothing to prevent anybody from declaring himself to be the direct descendant of *Eoanthropus dawsoni!* These Jews of the Caucasus have preserved—an interesting ethnographic

[1] **CCLXXXVII**, p. 237.
[2] **IX.**

quality—the language of the Tats from the Caspian shores. Chantre[1] measured a fairly large number of Jews in the course of his travels in Western Asia. He found them very markedly brachycephalic. Those of Akhaltsikh yielded a cephalic index of 85.19 and those of Urmia 86.34.

Finally, to bring this rapid outline of the anthropological character of the Asiatic Jews to a close we must add a few words about the Israelites of Arabia. And we must once more turn to Weissenberg.

This indefatigable Judeologist measured 64 Jews of the Yemen, men and women. This country, according to recent statistics, contains about 40,000 Jews of whom 3,000 live in Aden. The date of their first settlement is unknown.[2]

Those who have examined them[3] say they are poor and wretched. They speak Hebrew with the same pronunciation as the Askenazim. The Yemen Jews are much smaller (men 1 metre 594, women 1 metre 467) than other Asiatic Jews. There is scarcely a single example of brachycephaly among them. The cephalic index of the men is 74.3 and of the women 76.7. The so-called Jewish nose is exceptional among them. There are no fair-haired people among them ; all are black-haired. Their eyes are dark brown. It seems that the Arabs, their everyday neighbours, consider them to be people of their own ethnic group who have accepted Judaism. But, once more, the Arabs are much taller, and this impression, of a sociological order and without scientific basis, cannot satisfy us.

And now, what kind of ethnic picture will Syria and Palestine provide us with ? *A priori* a composite one, no doubt, because since the Sionist movement many Jews of various ethnic origins have gone to the ancient land of the Israelites. Had anthropological research been undertaken prior to our own period, might it perhaps have provided us with a more or less correct portrait of the Jewish type ? More or less correct, because probably intermixture had already taken place even in the homeland of the Jews from early, indeed, from prehistoric times.

[1] **XLI**, p. 246.

[2] It would appear that at the beginning of the sixth century there was an ephemeral Jewish kingdom in the Yemen.

[3] Weissenberg, " Die Yemenitischen Juden ", *Zeit. für Ethnol.*, Vol. XLI, 1909, p. 309.

The Syrian Jews examined at Damascus and Aleppo constituted two groups far from resembling one another. The Damascus Jews are taller (1 metre 66) than the others (1 metre 645), and have much less tendency to brachycephaly. While the cephalic index is 84 at Aleppo it is only 80 at Damascus. The Jews of Damascus, therefore, are mesaticephals. The nasal index in both cases shows leptorrhiny. An investigation undertaken at Dasmascus on hair-colour showed that out of 200 individuals 198 had black and only two light hair. The respective proportions of these two descriptive characters should be compared with those noted among European Jews to show the differences between them.

At the outset of his research Weissenberg published a paper on the anthropological characters of the autochthonous people of Palestine[1]. Therein he recalls the controversy between von Luschan and Auerbach on the origin of the Jews, whom von Luschan rightly considered to have been a hybrid race from a very distant period. This mixed race would have been constituted by brachycephalic Hittites, fair-haired Amorites, etc. Weissenberg considered that the autochthones of Palestine were dolichocephalic. In fact the Fellah stock, the modern population, is dolichocephalic and certainly represents the descendants of the primitive folk of the country. The same applies to the Samaritans. The native Jews, then, show at least a tendency to dolichocephaly. This conclusion of Weissenberg's supports the hypothesis of an original dolichocephalic type.

In Africa the Jews are numerous, particularly in the North along the Mediterranean, in Barbary. Their different groups in Tunisia, Algeria and Morocco have already been the subject of certain studies, but here, too, the "human material" is still inadequate. There has been more ethnographic than anthropological research. Certain groups appear to have been more resistant than others to ethnic invasion by their immediate neighbours. Enclosed in their religious nationalities as in an inaccessible fortress, the Jews of Morocco have not allowed themselves to be tainted by their Moroccan

[1] In 1911 the Jews who had emigrated to Palestine during the preceding thirty years were estimated at two millions. D. Trietsch, in "Die judische Palæstina", etc., *Zeitsch. für Demogr. und Statistik der Juden*, 1911. Since the Great War this immigration has been accentuated. **CCLXXXIX**, p. 80; **CCXC**, p. 129.

environment[1] as the Jews of Touat and Touggourt have done.

Tripolitania also contains a fairly large number of Jews. These colonies would be the remnants of those sent here, according to Josephus, by Ptolemy, king of Egypt, in 300 B.C. They prospered, and here, too, the destruction of the temples of Jerusalem reinforced their numbers. The Tripolitanian Jews, after having risen against the Roman power and been vanquished (215 B.C.) emigrated westwards. Their descendants to-day people, at all events in part, the Jewish quarters of Tunisia, Algeria and Morocco.[2]

Ethnographers have brought out the curious fact that many African Jews bear Berber names, such as Timsit, Fetussi, etc.; and others Spanish names such as Santillana, Medina, etc. These last are what are known as Livornians. They were driven out of Spain and came to Africa via the port of Livorno.[3]

Bertholon and Chantre studied a large series of Jews in Barbary. They give measurements on 551 individuals. They noticed great variation in their divers morphological characters. For example, low stature (less than 1 metre 62) is in a proportion of 23.5 per cent.; 29 per cent. lie between 1 metre 62 and 1 metre 65; the taller statures—upwards of 1 metre 65—account for 45.4 per cent. of this series. It would seem from this table that the origin of the Berber Jews might be sought in a group of medium height. But may not the tall stature found by these observers have been acquired through intermixture with neighbouring groups? The same query, moreover, might be made with reference to the small statures. And does this mean that research into their origin should be directed towards two initial groups, one tall—the Berber type?—and the other small?

The following are the variations in the cephalic index: dolichocephalic types (indices lower than and including 74), 21.9 per cent.; sub-dolichocephalic and mesaticephalic types, 67.8 per cent. As for the brachycephalic Jews, Barbary only

[1] The Moroccan Jews, like many others, consider their own group to be the most aristocratic. They claim to be the descendants of immigrants who left their own land after the destruction of Jerusalem.

[2] There is a fairly homogeneous and little known island of Jews in the Mzab consisting of some 900 individuals. **CXVI**, p. 559; **LXI**,

[3] **CLVIII**, Vol. I, p. 25.

contains 8.8 per cent. One sees how very different are the results yielded by this investigation from similar investigations undertaken with reference to the same ethnic group in Europe and in certain parts of Asia. Bertholon and Chantre[1] add that they found the familiar hooked nose was exceptional among Berber Jews.

Fishberg[2] also studied a large number of Jews in North Africa, especially children (606 boys of from 5 to 16 years of age). He first gives the following indications as to their hair colour: black and dark brown, 93.73 per cent.; and fair hair, 5.94 per cent. And he compares the proportion with that obtained from an examination of German Jews, as follows:—black and dark brown, 55.85 per cent.; and fair hair, 32.03 per cent. Fair hair is six times more frequent among German than among Moroccan Jews. Much the same applies to eye colour. Whereas North Africa contains only 17 per cent. of Jews showing light eyes, Eastern Europe has 40 to 50 per cent. An examination of the cephalic index was no less demonstrative for Fishberg in that the North African Jews were in the main dolichocephals. Brachycephalic types are rare there. Indices from 84 upwards are only 1.5 per cent. in Tunisia, and 5.6 per cent in Algeria; whereas the ranks of the brachycephalic Jews in Eastern Europe are swelled to 32.89 per cent.

Thus Fishberg's observations with regard to North African Jews amount to much the same as those of Bertholon and Chantre already indicated. The Moroccan Jews (adults) yielded to Fishberg a cephalic index of 75.92; those of Tunisia, 76.11. This writer adds that the Jews of Algiers and Constantinople have broader heads.

The shape and size of the nose among the North African Jews is also different from that of the Jews of Eastern Europe and Germany. The first have a longer and narrower nose: the aquiline type is rare.

In America the Jews are also very numerous. It is said that the city of New York alone contains 600,000, who have been driven across the Atlantic by the persecutions they have suffered in Eastern Europe. But they have not only gone to United States territory. Canada also has a large colony of Israelites, especially in the provinces of Quebec and Ontario.

[1] **XIV**, p. 360.
[2] **LXX**.

These Canadian Jews, recruited from among the Spanish and Portuguese as well as from the German and East European groups[1] have emigrated to Canada in large numbers since the years 1903-4. In 1908, 60,000 arrived. They have not yet been the subject of systematic anthropological study.

In the United States, on the contrary, the gigantic investigation undertaken by Boas[2] has made their zoological characteristics known. And we know that the American anthropologist made this the pretext for supporting his hypothesis as to the physical changes undergone by American immigrants—due to the influence of a new climate and a new mode of life.

In America the cephalic index of the Jews is notably lower (81) than in Europe (84). The brachycephalic Jews of Europe thus find that their skulls are modified when they get to America, becoming longer, and that their faces get shorter! This is not the occasion to indicate in detail my opinion on this thesis, which I think it would be difficult to prove.

À propos the American Jews, I will merely call to mind the work of Fishberg[3] who made 3,000 measurements on the living in New York, and who came to the conclusion that there is a complete lack of unity in the Jewish "race."

At the beginning of this chapter, with a view of providing the reader with some general ideas, I briefly referred to the anthropological research done in Europe on the Jews. But to give a view of the question as a whole in this continent would take up an entire volume. Since Beddoe wrote the first pages of this study in 1861, up to our day, how many statistics and memoirs there have been in Russia, Germany, Austria, Switzerland, Italy, France, England, etc.! Stature, cephalic index, eye and hair colour particularly have furnished the matter for these investigations. Before me I have the results of at least a hundred investigations; they fill six large tables. If I were to set out the bibliographical references they would certainly take up several pages.

We have noted, in a word or two, the variation in stature. For the different countries of Europe it presents a scale running

[1] **LXXXV.**

[2] Franz Boas, *Changes in bodily forms of descendants of immigrants.* The Immigration Commission, Washington Government Printing Office, 1910.

[3] **LXIX.**

from 1 metre 60 for the Polish and Russian Jews of Warsaw (Elkind, Zakrzevski) to 1 metre 70 for the Jews of the West End of London. The most frequently represented out of eighteen means in the table I am examining are statures of 1 metre 61, 1 metre 62, and 1 metre 63. The height of 1 metre 61 is that of the Jews of northwest Russia, of Poland, and Lithuania; that of 1 metre 62 is the height of the Jews of Bavaria, Galicia, Warsaw (a taller stature than that of the Polish townsfolk ?), the Ukraine, and Riga (for which the same observation applies). The Jews of Italy, Hungary, Austria, and Bosnia have yielded to Lombroso, to Weisbach, and to Schreiber a stature of 1 metre 63. Anuchin and Weissenberg found 1 metre 648 as the stature of the Jews of South Russia. They indicate 1 metre 654 for those of Bukovina; and Pantiukhof gives 1 metre 699 for a series of Jews measured at Odessa. I have found a height of 1 metre 656 among the Jews of the Dobruja[1]. And if a few of these means have been obtained from a small number of individuals, others represent series of several thousands of men.

Thus the stature of the European Jews alone will furnish us with a chaotic picture. The Russian Jews give us means of from 1 metre 60 to 1 metre 65, and even 1 metre 699 (Odessa). But this last figure may be explained in part by the influence of town life which, as has been noticed everywhere—or nearly everywhere—augments human stature. None the less does it remain that if large numbers represent something like accuracy, the mean height of the European Jews can be fixed somewhere in the neighbourhood of 1 metre 62. In fact, by eliminating the great urban centres, London and Odessa, I calculate the mean stature of the remaining sixteen series to be 1 metre 626.

Even as early as the *Thesaurus craniorum*, in *Crania ethnica*, and in other volumes of general information, we find a few indications relating to measurements of Jewish crania. But this cranial documentation, contained in a series of memoirs which have appeared in all sorts of places, is altogether minute in comparison with the documentation obtained from living subjects.

Several thousand Jews have been measured in Europe

[1] **CXCV**, p. 369.

notably in the central and east European lands. The figures of the mean indices do not vary much if we except the extremes —76 (for Turkey) and 87 (in the Caucasus). The most frequently represented indices are 80, 81, 82, and 83. But if we content ourselves with envisaging those mean indices alone we risk getting a very incorrect idea of the cephalic characters of the Jews. It is the percentage of the various forms that will give us most information.

I will not enter too much into detail; but I will consider simply two or three series which will furnish topical evidence. In London, 363 Askenazim studied by Jacob Spielmann included 28.3 per cent. of dolichocephals, 28.3 per cent. of mesaticephals, and 47.4 per cent. of brachycephals; 150 South Russian Jews (Weissenberg's series) included 1 per cent. of dolichocephals, 18 per cent. of mesaticephals, 81 per cent. of brachycephalic types. The first of these series yields a mean index of 80, the second, 82.4. One sees how risky it is blindly to trust to mean index figures! A group of 51 Sephardim, measured in London, show themselves to be less dolichocephalic (17 per cent.) and more mesaticephalic (34 per cent.) than the Askenazim group examined in the same city (see above). A large series of Galician and Lithuanian Jews give a proportion of 85 per cent. brachycephals and only 3.8 per cent. dolichocephals.

These examples suffice. They demonstrate how many different types there are in an Israelitish community. And this information furnished by the cephalic index confirms the variable character of the Jewish group brought out by the examination of their stature.

The pigmentation of eyes and hair will reveal the same variation. Whereas the Russian department of Mogilev only yields 4.9 per cent. of light-eyed Jews, the city of Vienna yields 30 per cent., and Galicia 23 per cent. While Constantinople furnishes demographic statistics with 69.9 per cent. of brown eyes among the Jews, we find only 45.9 per cent. in Austria. It is the same for hair: 230 Turkish Jews show 3 per cent. blond individuals; 100 Polish Jews show 4 per cent.; and 644 Ukrainian Jews show 15 per cent. And Bleichmann, in 1882, examining the hair colour of 700 Israelites in Riga, counted 36 per cent. of fair individuals.

But we need not go on. It seems to us that the least informed reader will come to the conclusion that no Jewish race, in the zoological sense of the word, exists. The Israelites constitute a religious and social community, certainly very strong and very coherent ; but its elements are heterogeneous in the extreme. In face of certain ethnic analyses, we may even ask ourselves to what extent this and that Jewish group includes any typical Jews—those who, in the neighbourhood of the Dead Sea, constituted that zealous people so familiar to us—the Chosen People.

And therefore we also see the poverty of the arguments at the disposal of that anti-semetism which would set up a Jewish race in opposition to the Christian races. There is no more a Christian race than a Musulman race. And neither is there any such thing as a Jewish race.

It is possible that, in all large Jewish communities there exist a certain number of individuals representing the genuine original Jew who is probably the Assyroid dolichocephalic type. But in the central and east European countries (Germany, Austria and Russia) this type appears to be in a minority. Maybe, as a group, the Spaniols represent it better than other groups ?

There are people who believe that the Jews, by a kind of exceptional adaptive quality, have acquired the morphological characters of the ethnic environment in which they live, because they sometimes appear to be dolichocephalic among a dolichocephalic people, and brachycephalic among a brachycephalic people.

It would be of the greatest interest for biology as a whole is such modifications could be proved. One is sensible of all the advantage that might be taken of such a transformative mechanism, confining it to the human domain alone, from the point of view of an easy moulding of individuals and groups ! It seems to me to be unnecessary to insist on the fanciful nature of such speculations for the moment.

CHAPTER V

THE ARABS

ARABIA to-day does not include within its natural boundaries, so well defined in almost every direction, the whole of the Arab race—such as it should really be represented—any more than it contains Arabs only. This race, whose chieftains dispersed it over many parts of Eur-Asia and Africa, has preserved more or less imposing contingents in many lands far from Arabia. On the other hand, many Arabs having filtered into the lands adjoining Arabia, thanks to their persistently nomadic habits, a certain number at least have remained in them. We shall even see that it is difficult, in many areas, to distinguish genuine Arabs from those who have merely been Arabized.

Whence came these Arabs that Scripture tells us are the children of Abraham through his son Ishmael, and that written history has almost always shown us to be independent? Is Arabia their true homeland?

During a certain period this people had a most brilliant destiny. We owe to the Arabs some of the best elements of our civilization. And we may ask ourselves what might have become of the Mediterranean world, contemporaneous with the great Arab civilization, if intestine dissensions had not rent this flourishing empire in pieces—maybe the Koran would to-day have been our Holy Book?

In the Arabian Peninsular, to which we naturally turn when we would endeavour to define their race, the Arabs constitute two groups whose social life is very different. On the one hand the cultivators of the soil and the sedentary folk of the cities, and on the other the nomads. It is admitted *a priori* that the latter have the more faithfully preserved the physical characters of the primitive Arabs. The chances are in favour of it, in any case.

Descendants of these intrepid conquerors certainly exist in the lands which they subjected and freely overran, as, for example, the Iberian peninsular. They no longer bear the names of their ancestors. They are disguised under different labels ; and it is for anthropologists to try to discover their ethnic origin.

On the other hand, in many areas of Africa and Asia, for example in Barbary, the collective name Arab is given to peoples who were embodied in the ranks of the invaders, without ever having ethnically belonged to the Arab group properly so-called.

The anthropological picture of the Arabs we habitually construct for ourselves is that of tall men with dolichocephalic heads, long faces, and black hair and eyes. Does this express the reality ?

It is thought that the purest Arab type is the inhabitant of the south of Arabia, of the Yemen and the Hadramaut. Outside these regions, which are considered as being least contaminated by "foreigners," Arabia has suffered considerable intermixture with the surrounding peoples, especially along her coasts. That is possible. Unfortunately, information about Arab anthropology appears to us to be especially scarce when we look for it under the heading of information bearing on the Arabian Arabs strictly so-called.

This scarcity of documentation and the certainty that at the time of the conquests different ethnic groups came within the Arab political orbit and thereby altered the real physiognomy of this people, explain the lack of agreement among writers who have studied "Arabs." Thus Giuffrida-Ruggeri[1], examining the skeletons of the necropolis of Abbasiya, near Cairo, which, we are assured, contains the remains of the Arab conquerors, notes a variety of human types in which brachycephals predominate. And the Italian anthropologist immediately thinks himself justified in writing: "The traditional dolichocephalic, leptoprosopic, leptorrhine Arab with high orbits (*hypsiconque*) is conspicuous by his absence."

I do not think it would be very difficult to reply that there is nothing to prove that the Abbasiya crania are those of veritable Arabs. At the time of the conquest the Arabs had long had their ranks swelled by different peoples who had come in of their own will or been drawn in by force, to march behind

[1] LXXXI.

the Arab standard. It has always been the same in enterprises of this kind.[1]

Bertholon and Chantre in an important work have studied among other North African peoples, different groups of Tunisian "Arabs" considered to be genuine Arabs by the surrounding populations, and settled north of the Mejerda—the Hedils, the Kroumir Arabs, the Chiahia, and the Djendouba[2]. The Chiahia are sub-dolichocephalic; the three other groups are most distinctly dolichocephalic. Two of these "Arab" contingents are leptorrhine, and two are slightly mesorrhine. Their stature varied from 1 metre 65 (Chiahia) to 1 metre 70, Djendouba (Hilalians). The Hedils (who came from Mecca) have a height of 1 metre 69, and so have the Kroumirs. If the Hedils "who came from Mecca" represent the descendants of the primitive Arabs we should find among them some of the morphological features considered to be the apanage of genuine Arabs, such as tall stature, dolichocephaly and a leptorrhine nasal type.

But there are still other data. Here are some of them: the Museum at Lyon possesses 25 crania brought from Aden by M. Buffard from a region where the original race is thought to have persisted. These crania have been studied by Chantre[3] The cephalic index of the men is 75.5; that of the women 73.18. They are thus, as a whole, dolichocephalic.

The Italian anthropologist, Mochi[4], examining 64 crania which had belonged to African and Asiatic Arabs, recognized the presence of two types in this series, in one of which the cephalic index oscillates round about 72-73, and in the other round about 82-83. The first type—dolichocephalic—is provided by the crania of Arabs from Africa and Palmyra,

[1] The Alemanni, as we have said, never were Germans by race. Yet who would risk separating them from the Germanic peoples in an outside definition of this group?

We might easily make the following supposition. We discover in Central Europe a necropolis of the period of Caracalla, whom history indicates as having been Germanic (the Romans were then fighting against the Germans). An anthropological examination of this necropolis brings us face to face with brachycephalic crania (the Alemanni were probably Brachycephals). To what conclusion should we come if not that the Germans belonged to the brachycephalic group because their anatomical remains showed the cranial form. Yet we know well that this is not the morphological type of the Germans. Suppositions of the same nature may be made as regards the necropolis studied by Giuffrida-Ruggeri.

[2] **XIV**, p. 347.

[3] **XIV**, p. 350.

[4] **CLX**.

and the sub-brachycephalic type by the Asiatic Arabs of Arabia and Syria. For my part I have measured 15 living Arabs who are descendants of colonists brought into the southern Dobruja in days gone by. Of this little series 80 per cent. was composed of dolichocephalic and sub-dolichocephalic individuals[1]. At first sight these findings seem to be disconcerting. But does not this contradictoriness spring, in part, from the fact that the observers have nearly always examined townsfolk? Everything permits us to suppose that the nomadic Arabs have retained with much greater fidelity than the others the ancestral characters. We are told, it is true, that among the wandering "Arabs" of North Africa there exist ancient autochthonous peoples (Berbers) sedentary in former times, and given to agriculture, who, after the conquest, had to accept this radical change in their mode of life and become nomads. Have we any proof of such modifications? Do we know of many peoples who, having once been sedentary, have become nomadic? I think, as regards the Berbers, these are somewhat gratuitous hypotheses, and we need something more than a simple supposition to convince us. Chantre, who has travelled a great deal in Asia and Africa in these very regions where the Arabs are dispersed, appears also to have been of this opinion. In 1881 he had already measured Beduin of the Anazeh tribe (19 men and 4 women) at Aleppo and Urfa[2]. The mean height of these people was 1 metre 71, and their cephalic index oscillated between 76.02 and 78.4. The same writer measured a fairly large number of wandering Beduin of various tribes in Lower and Middle Egypt during his anthropological researches in Egypt. For details relative to the eight tribes he studied[3] I will refer the reader to the book published by the Lyon anthropologist.

The mean height of 188 Beduin was 1 metre 68 (the mean stature of the groups oscillated between 1 metre 66 and 1 metre 73), indicating a stature classed in the category of "above the mean". And the author adds, with reference to one of these tribes: "The Aulâd 'Arab of the Fayyûm are thus the tallest Beduin we know outside Arabia."

These Beduin of Egypt as a whole have dolichocephalic heads. The mean index of the entire series is 73.96. When we

[1] CXCV, p. 521.
[2] XLII.
[3] XLIII, p. 194.

examine the details of Chantre's tables we see that there are wide differences between the value of the cephalic indices. The minimum index is that of the Aulâd 'Arab (72.82), and the maximum (75.39), that of the Aulâd 'Ali of Maryût. But it none the less remains that both are dolichocephalic. I calculate with the help of individual indices that the proportion of dolichocephalic types to the total number of individuals measured by Chantre is 90 per cent. This is a very high percentage.

All the Arab tribes examined by Chantre are mesorrhinians according to their nasal indices. This is a character to bear in mind. The individual indices show 19 per cent. of leptorrhinians and a still larger number of platyrrhinians. If we limit ourselves to the three characters above that have just been brought out, we shall have to conclude that these nomads manifest heterogeneity. And if we are to consider that these Beduin represent the ethnic physiognomy of the Arabs at the time of the conquest we must come to the conclusion that at that period the conquerors no longer represented a pure race. Moreover, did an exclusively Arab race ever exist ?[1]

The ethnic appearance taken on by the social, political, and linguistic picture of certain human groups is evident here also. The fifteenth century Arab chronicler Makrizi devoted a special treatise to the Beduin tribes of Egypt, and Chantre points out that among the list of tribal names mentioned by Makrizi only a few are to be found living in Egypt now.[2]

What became of the others ? Did they leave Egypt ? It is hardly likely. But do not their descendants who still people the banks of the Nile to-day bear other names ? Maybe a certain number of these nomads, when they became sedentary, simply took the name of the group into which they entered ? What, to-day, are the inhabitants of the Seine department if not a vast aggregate of diverse ethnic types which have very quickly forgotten their origin ? Do not the greater part call themselves Parisians ? But there are Arabs in Africa elsewhere than in Egypt. Historically the Arabs overran the whole of North Africa. What ethnical influence have they left behind ? Among the numerous tribes commonly known

[1] In our view this is merely a political, linguistic, etc., fraction of a large ethnic Asiatic group for which it is impossible, at the moment, to fix precise geographical boundaries, and to whom it is equally impossible to give a name.

[2] **XLIII**, p. 195.

as Arabs are there any authentic descendants of the conquerors of the name ? Or are all the so-called Arabs of Barbary simply Arabized Berbers ? Had the mass of the Arabs of the conquest been ethnically pure we should have had ample opportunity of finding a number of its elements to-day. But was it pure ? That is the question !

Bertholon and Chantre resolutely hold that the present-day Berbers are not Arabs[1]. After having noted great resemblances between the Aden crania (see above) and those of the ancient and modern peoples of North Africa, these writers ask themselves to which of the two geographical groupings they should turn to find out which has given its ethnic characters to the other. "Was it the Arab of the Aden type who emigrated to Africa, or was it African immigration which reached Arabia ?" "The salient characters of the Aden crania are those of the tall dolichocephalic race of Barbary crossed with some other ethnic element. This element has contributed its microseme orbit and its short face. The rather fine nose, the tall stature and the long head constitute the contribution of the leptorrhine dolichocephalic type." They go on : "We might ask whether the shortness of the face is not the consequence of the crossing of these tall dolichocephals with the short-faced brachycephalic Arabs, or perhaps with a dolichocephalic race having microseme orbits and disharmonic face. We are more inclined to credit this last influence."

"If these Arabs, so different from those described by Giuffrida-Ruggeri, are not autochthones, whence did they come ? We must seek their traces in the countries adjoining Arabia."

And the authors note that in India and Persia there are dolichocephalic peoples of tall stature. "The stature, head-form and shape of the nose are the same on both sides of the Persian Gulf."

These characters of tall stature, dolichocephaly and leptorrhiny were attributed by de Ujfalvy to the Aryan Indian element. Houssay has said that in Persia the Aryans are represented by the Parsis and the Luri.[2] These last often have light or blue eyes. Bertholon and Chantre then ask this question : do not the Arabs of the Aden type come of an early European migration, like the Persians and the Indians ?

In what direction was this emigration effected ? Perhaps

[1] **XIV**, p. 351.
[2] **CIV**, p. 101.

northwards? Has not Sayce indicated the presence in Palestine, nine centuries before our era, of non-Semitic peoples?[1] "It is remarkable that the heads surmounting the names of cities in Palestine taken by Shishak are those of Amorites and not of Jews. They reproduce the features of that white-skinned, fair-haired, blue-eyed, and long-headed race with which the earliest monuments of Egypt familiarize us."

European emigrants, clear-complexioned Dolichocephals, would thus have sent a fair-sized stream as far as Barbary. Their descendants would still be especially numerous in the province of Constantine. The inhabitants of the Tell would have gradually filtered right into the Sahara area, where various tribes "such as the Tuaregs, have been able to maintain, in a rather precarious fashion, a relative purity of race in the midst of a black population."[2]

Are these fair-skinned Dolichocephals the same folk whom the Egyptians knew from the earliest dynasties—the Tahenu or fair-skinned peoples? These Tahenu or Tamahu "in the fifteenth century before our era occupied numerous lands to the west of the Nile, like the contemporary Beduin." And, according to Sayce's view (explaining the origin of the Amorites) they migrated as far as southern Palestine. "Arabia, situated between these two streams—Aryan on the east, Berber on the west, and Amorite on the north—may have undergone an appreciable infiltration by these peoples. It would seem quite logical that a few tribes should have crossed either the Persian Gulf or the Red Sea and penetrated to Arabia. Such may have been the likely origin of the tall, long-headed 'Arabs'. They are not Arab, but Arabized peoples, like those of North Africa were later on. We know neither their numbers nor the proportion of them in Arabia."[3]

Thus the dolichocephalic "Arabs" we meet with in Arabia are not *in situ*. We must consider them to be foreigners, even in that land. They would be "Berber clans having immigrated into Arabia at various periods and having become Arabized by the inhabitants of that country". The true Arabs would be brachycephalic.

Another traveller in Western Asia, von Luschan, who, in

[1] An analysis by Sayce (Ethnography of Palestine) will be found in *Anthropologie*, 1894, p. 177.

[2] **XIV**, p. 353.

[3] *Ibid.*

the course of his many sojourns between the Black Sea and the Persian Gulf had occasion to study all the peoples of these lands, considers as we do that the genuine Arabs are those of dolichocephalic type. Three groups of "wirkliche Araber" examined by him have cephalic indices ranging from 68 to 81. Three other groups whom he calls "Pseudo-Araber" have indices running from 76 (exceptionally low) to 89. Von Luschan adds, and we are absolutely at one with him in his view, that, for such a large region as that over which the Arabs have spread, our knowledge is still extraordinarily fragmentary.[1]

If, to follow the conclusions of Bertholon and Chantre, the brachycephalic types are really to be considered the true Arabs, it remains to determine what their geographical origin was. Must we approximate them to the tall Brachycephals we meet with in Asia Minor, to certain Kurdish types in particular? And also to certain Armenians? Is this possible? I simply put the question.[2]

Historical documents dealing with North Africa would certainly seem to demonstrate that on many occasions the Arab invaders made use of considerable numbers of Berbers who had been converted to Islam. These came, we are told, from Tripolitania (?). The second century invasions, we are assured, numbered 400,000 persons (??). And this figure is taken, in part, as a basis for the statement that this immigration could not have come out of Arabia because that country could never have furnished so many warriors. I will admit that readily enough. But do the historians of Africa really believe that this invasion comprised so large a number of persons? How were they fed? Can we imagine this trek of 400,000 belligerents?

I think anyone will admit as a sane basis of appreciation that all the figures indicated by the chroniclers of antiquity and of the early centuries as representing invading armies were grossly exaggerated. It must have been the same in so far as concerns the warlike movements of the Arabs.

To sum up, the Arab problem—envisaged from the anthropological view-point—appears to us to be still very far indeed from solution.

[1] **CLXV**, p. 92.

[2] For a discussion in English of the affinities of the Arabs, see "The Physical Characters of the Arabs," Prof. C. G. Seligman, *Journal of the Roy. Anthr. Institute*, Vol. xlvii, 1917, p. 214. (Translator's Note).

CHAPTER VI

The Iranians (Kurds and Armenians)

TO the south of Eur-Asia there is a land linked to Europe by the Caucasus and to Asia by the Turan—a land almost surrounded by sea and bounded on the east by Hindustan, where are scattered those peoples whose names have so often appeared in history—Persians, Medes, Arabs and Turks. In these lands the ancient civilizations of the Assyrians, Babylonians and Phœnicians were developed. Three main races are to-day distributed over this wide area; to the east the Indo-Afghans; in the old Mesopotamian Turkish empire and in Persia, the Assyroids, side by side with men of Turki "race"; and, finally, the Arabs.

From the philological point of view these peoples are collected into the two dominant groups of Iranians and Semites.

Persia, Baluchistan and Afghanistan, as also the eastern portion of Asia Minor, are the domain of the Iranian "race," within which we recognize a fairly large number of peoples—in Persia, the Tajiks, Hajemies and Parsis; the Azerbaijani of the southern Caucasus, the Sartes of Russian Turkestan, and the Tats of the southwestern shores of the Caspian have been classed with them; to the east of the Persians, the Afghans and Baluchis; and in Asia Minor, in more or less imposing masses, or in islands, Kurds and Armenians.

After a first glance it is difficult to imagine that these Iranians of differing names could make up a single ethnological family. In reality, their cranial morphology alone would pronounce against it. Without counting the Pathans, dolichocephalic Afghans, we see on the one hand a large number of sub-dolichocephalic Persians contrasting with sub-brachycephalic Tajiks and Parsis: and sub-dolichocephalic Tats and Azerbaijani living side by side with definitely brachycephalic Armenians. Thus peoples of highly diverse origin sheltered themselves in former times under a single linguistic roof. The ethnic variety that we note in this corner of the world and which would certainly seem to be more than apparent may be explained by the very history of this region which has been ceaselessly subjected to invasion. Even to-day the south of Persia, for analogous reasons, is one of those Asiatic districts which is most pronouncedly piebald in an ethnic sense. Has not the Makran been signalized by all travellers as a very caravanserai of peoples ?

Among these peoples thus displaced and whose ranks occasionally run into one another, which should we envisage as the descendants of the great historic " races " ? Where are the Medes and Persians ?—Where the builders of the Babylonian empires and the founders of Assyria ?

Did the Medes and Persians in the period of their power constitute homogeneous anthropological units ? Or were they nothing but an assemblage of Persianized peoples ?

It must not be thought that these problems—whose historic importance is not to be denied—will always be insoluble, although they may be so to-day.

In Persia the peoples of to-day may be sub-divided into two principal groups. The western region of Persia, as it is to-day, is inhabited by the Hajemies (on the Caspian shores, by the Talyches and the Mazandarani ; between the Persian Gulf and the Ispahan region, by the Parsis). These, in the majority are dolichocephalic people (cephalic index, 77.9) of medium height (1 metre 65) who approximate in many of their characters to those other dolichocephals of Assyroid type, the Indo-Afghans.

To the east of these Hajemies, and to the east of the great Salt Lake, the Tajiks people a part of Baluchistan and Afghanistan. These folk, then, are sub-brachycephals (cephalic index of 84.9) of tall stature (1 metre 69). Thus they are very different from the first mentioned Iranians.

Persia still contains a notable number of Parsis. These Guebres, who came originally, it is said, from Farsistan, driven to emigrate by the Musulmans, asked a refuge of Hindustan. Their anthropological characters are still very little known. Are they, perhaps, similar to those of the Parsees who emigrated to India after the destruction of the Sassanide empire ? All that we know of them permits us to suppose that they are. Their religious caste is so close that it is difficult to admit that such a barrier would be thrown open for the benefit of foreigners. Ujfalvy, however, who measured some Bombay Parsees, notes that they are sub-brachycephals with a mean cephalic index of 82.

The Galchas, those Tajiks of the mountains, were formerly studied by Khanikoff[1], then by Ujfalvy. Tall stature (1 metre 69) is attributed to them, and a cephalic index showing brachycephaly (84 to 85). They would also be leptorrhinians. It is not beside the point to recall that the brachycephaly of the Galchas, put in evidence by Ujfalvy, and showing a higher degree of round-headedness in proportion as the degree of racial purity was higher, was the subject of a curious interpretation by Topinard. This anthropologist, having a Galcha skull in his hands, noticed that it presented "not mere resemblances, but complete identity with the most characteristic Savoyard crania." And he immediately established a genealogical link between these European Brachycephals and those of Asia. Another savant, de Quatrefages, countersigned this hypothesis. He said: "In the presence of these facts it is very difficult not to accept the conclusions of the author, and I think with him that the Tajik highlanders, the Savoyards, the Auvergnats and the Bretons are brethren. The first are a *witness*, having probably remained in the actual neighbourhood of the place of origin of the race, while the others are the descendants of emigrants who went out from it."[2]

Now that investigations have been multiplied and that comparative information is so much more abundant that our conclusions risk being seriously supported, we dare not go ahead so far or so fast in the domain of filiations!

None the less, we should dearly like to be able to prove the genealogical relation between the historic Persians and the present-day Persians by localizing our observations on Persian territory. The poverty of our documentation for any such attempt is extreme. What do the one or two "series" so far studied represent in face of the living population as a whole? Further, when it is a matter of grouping the comparative elements of the past our documentary poverty becomes still more evident—it is downright penury. When we think of the wide extent of the excavations undertaken in Persia, of the historic, esthetic, and linguistic riches that resulted, we must profoundly regret that the "anthropological material"

[1] **CXXIV.**

[2] **CCIX**, p. 489.

which would have thrown light on the ethnogeny of that ancient past did not have the luck to interest all the archæologists charged with these important researches.

The present peoples of Afghanistan and Baluchistan both appear to be tall folk in the great majority. We have a few figures representing the height of the Afghans ; it oscillates round about 1 metre 68. These same Afghans are dolichocephalic (index of about 76) and leptorrhine. The men of Baluchistan seem to be smaller than their northern neighbours (1 metre 66) ; and, although they are, like them, leptorrhinians, they appear to be less dolichocephalic. Rather does their index mark mesaticephaly. But this, it must be understood, is not conclusive.

Before leaving these Iranians of the east, we must touch on the Kurds and Armenians, those brother peoples whom ill-advised influences—Czarist, in the main—have rendered implacable enemies, but whom better shepherds may doubtless bring together again. Furthermore, it is these particular Iranians about whom we have the most anthropological documentation.

I

The Kurds

The Kurds " belong politically to two States ; to Turkey and Persia. But it is the former country which includes the largest portion of Kurdistan whose boundaries—of an ethnographic order—are sufficiently fluid. East and north of the middle and upper Tigris all the hill country is peopled by Kurds. And this geographical distribution, in an environment difficult of access, explains why this people has remained inviolate. Kurdistan corresponds to the most rugged portion of ancient Media, and to a large part of Assyria, and it encroaches also on Armenian territory "[1]. But the Kurds have on all sides overflowed the geographical domain which bears their name. From their hills they have flowed down on every hand, as they still do to-day, on to the restricted areas left to those herdsmen who pasture their flocks up in the hills in summer, and dwell in the valleys in winter,

[1] CCLXX.

and who constitute certain of the Kurdish pastoral groups.[1]

Early writers, like Rich[2] thought they recognized two physical types among the Kurds, namely the nomads, pastoral and warlike (the Assireta), and the sedentary agriculturists (Gurans)—the first having harsher and more rugged features, prominent forehead, etc. Are we not sensible of something rather romantic about such a description? A more interesting fact to the credit of these travellers of the last century is that they noted in the heart of this Kurdish population the common presence of light, even of blue eyes.

Since 1863, however, we have had a somewhat more accurate description of the Kurds. According to Colonel Duhousset, the Kurds "have a highly brachycephalic head. They are thick-set, robust and muscular. They have a brown complexion, black hair, thick eyebrows, large aquiline nose, square chin and prominent cheekbones; their type recalls that of the figures of the Sassanide coins."[3] Khanikoff states that "exteriorally they present a good deal of analogy with the Afghans. We find among them prominent noses, often aquiline and blunt. . . . Generally the eyes of the Kurds are black and larger than those of the Afghans; they are further apart than with the Western Persians, the Tajiks and the Pushtus. . . ."[4]

With the best will in the world one cannot help seeing how little is to be gleaned from such physical descriptions. Many an ethnic group could be recognized by these features. Nevertheless, there is one among these descriptions that must be quoted because it is not without the unexpected, and because it might serve as the point of departure for an important research. Solak[5] found that the complexion, the eye-colour and the shade of hair of the Kurds differed but little from that of the northern races, and, in particular, of the Germanic races, so much so that apart from their artificially dyed hair

[1] Statistics vary as to Kurdish numbers. In 1887, the *Nouvean Dictionnaire de géographie* indicated 1,828,000 persons, of whom 1,300,000 were in Asiatic Turkey. English statistics gave 2,250,000, of whom 1,500,000 were in Turkey.

[2] CCXIX.

[3] LXIV.

[4] CXXIV.

[5] CCXLV.

and their oriental costume, one might easily take them for Germans! One wonders where Solak got the elements of such a description, at least in such absolute form? I have myself[1] examined a fairly large number of Kurds, and I am obliged to avow that I cannot corroborate the existence of such characteristics.

There certainly are, in the Caucasus, fair individuals—among the Ossets, for example—and recently Zaborowski[2] has interpreted this type, and his interpretation is not far removed from that of Solak. According to him this human element "is the blond European, direct descendant of the old dolichocephalic neolithic race of southern Russian, with which have been intermingled, at various periods, other blonds, the Scythians and notably the Alans, very closely related by certain characters and by their admixture with the Goths of Germanic race."

In any case it would not be scientific to reject, *a priori*, Solak's observations. Maybe there exist among the Kurds varieties of type, of which one—that which is represented by lightly pigmented individuals—may have more especially come under the notice of this writer.

An expectant attitude of this kind is rendered all the more obligatory when we find that von Luschan, a professional anthropologist and a savant of great standing, has himself noted such characters.[3] He examined 221 Kurds, of whom 115 were from the environs of Karakush. He noted among them the presence of 53 per cent. of xanthochroid individuals. And the mean cephalic indices of the three groups, which, put together, constituted the above series, are respectively 72.9; 75.2; and 76.9.

In the view of the German author the Kurds were once all fair, and had blue eyes and long heads. And they became more and more brunet and brachycephalic as the result of being crossed with Turks, Armenians and Persians. Must we accept this conclusion? Where then is the original homeland of this dolichocephalic people with fair hair and light eyes?

If we add that the Kurds are tall men the concomitant

[1] **CXCV**, p. 463.
[2] **CCXCII**, p. 121. **XLV**, p. 165.
[3] **CXLV**, p. 92.

characters of the Nordic race would all be there ! ![1] What a fine chapter we should have reserved here for the historian !

Chantre, who lived long among the Kurds, indicates in his first study that out of 158 individuals examined he found 3 blonds[2]. All the others had black or chestnut hair. As for eye-colour, he mentions, further on, the presence of 8 individuals having light eyes out of 332 Kurds examined. We find here, nevertheless, a singular difference between these proportions and those of von Luschan. Is the explanation to be found in the variety of geographical localities, corresponding to tribes differently composed one from the others ?

Confronted thus with contradictory data, it will not be without value to study at somewhat closer range this people which has been considered to be the descendants of the Medes or early Chaldeans. Below will also be found summed up the respective studies of Ivanowsky and of Chantre, and also my own.

The Kurds are tall men (they certainly exceed 1 metre 68). Let us remember that this is the character we found among the Galcha Tajiks and the Afghans. In my series, 83 per cent. of the men were above the mean height. It may even be that certain Kurdish tribes greatly exceed this mean—the Radki, for example ; but, on the other hand, other tribes would be of rather low stature (Milanli and Yezdi, according to Chantre).

As for the cephalic index, the various writers are far from being in agreement. They furnish highly disparate cranial characteristics. Here are a few figures with reference to the cephalic index : Nassonof, 78.48 ; Chantre, 78.53 ; Pittard, 86.49[3] ; von Luschan, about 75. Chantre, who has studied

[1] Prichard indicates that Fraser (*Travels in the Himalaya*) saw a few Pathans or Afghan soldiers who had red hair and blue eyes. But it is probable that, if this observation is correct, these individuals were related, or had been at one time, to the " Nordics " ? indicated above ; it is not to Afghanistan then, that we should turn our regard when we seek the origin of this enigmatic " race ". **CCII**, p. 237. The " old neolithic dolichocephalic race of southern Russia " to which Zaborowski alluded (see above) is more and more coming to be considered by certain writers to be that which, later on, constituted the powerful ethnic group whose numberless and extraordinarily disturbing hordes were soon to spread over the Baltic and North Sea countries.

[2] **XLV**, p. 165.

[3] The highly accentuated brachycephaly we noted among the Kurds does not arise from cranial deformation. Many Kurds deform the heads of their children. But this modification does not necessarily carry with it an increase of brachycephaly. Chantre noted the custom of head deforming to be as prevalent in dolichocephalic as in brachycephalic groups.

a larger number of Kurds than any of us, mentions considerable variations in the cranial form of these people. The cephalic indices of his series run from 70.04 among the Yezdi to 86.48 among the Bilikani (further, as a whole, the Bilikani Kurds are sub-brachycephalic).

According to the nasal index the Kurds are leptorrhinians and, by their facial index, leptoprosopes.

The Kurds generally have dark eyes. Chantre made the same observation. I found grey eyes among them in a proportion of 9 per cent.; but not a single blue eye. In the same way I did not find a single man having fair hair (82 per cent. were black-haired; the rest chestnut and dark chestnut). These two observations do not at all agree with those of Rich and Solak, nor with those mentioned by von Luschan.

In the above series certain observations agree with those of von Luschan (dolichocephaly). Others are in flat opposition (eye and hair colour). One sees that there is room to start over again on a very large scale the anthropological study of the Kurds. I would wish to add, in concluding this paragraph, that I do not by any means deny the penetration into Asia of a European group of the Nordic race, nor its persistence, but that I do not yet see any proof of it.

II

THE ARMENIANS

The group of which the present-day Armenians are the descendants has played a considerable rôle under different names in the history of Asia. In their ancient genealogies—are not these, according to all specialists, of a somewhat adventurous character?—the Armenians are said to have long dwelt in Babylonia before they settled in the Ararat region. Few countries have been so often conquered as little Armenia. In the past the Armenians have been Assyrians, Persians, Greeks, Arabs and Mongols—to be divided to-day between Turkey, Russia and Persia.

It must not be concluded, however, that each time the conqueror took possession of their land the Armenians underwent an ethnic transformation. When they changed masters they simply changed the name of their nationality—nothing more.

It has been said that the Armenians primitively came from

Babylonia. But were they *in situ* in that region? If not whence did they come? Furthermore, at the time they seized the territory which has since become Armenia, it was certainly not empty. It is too favoured a land for settlement not to have sheltered some population; probably a large one. It has been thought that a part of this population became Kurds and a part Gruzins.

Administratively and politically all the inhabitants of the territories in which the Armenians settled naturally became known as Armenians. This fact alone would enable us to understand how it is that the Armenians—both of Armenia and elsewhere—can offer those different physical types which they present to our cameras and callipers.

Thus it is that Khanikoff, studying the Armenian colony in Astrakhan—which, according to the author, constitutes an ethnic island free from all admixture (they were fourteenth century immigrants)—finds them to be tall with a "decidedly Iranian and dolichocephalic head." He notes that the eyes are black, "more sunken within the orbit than among the Persians." The nose is very aquiline and long; the oval of the face is longer than with the Persians. Blumenbach, after having observed Armenian and Jewish traders in Amsterdam and London, approximated the general physiognomy of the Armenians to that of the Jews; which does not seem to me very odd if he is dealing with real Jews.[1]

Chantre has most thoroughly examined the Armenians in Asia Minor. He lived in their villages. He notes that the Armenian type varies from one locality to another. But these local variations need not disturb us. They could be obtained with a small number of "real types"—with two types alone, for example. These two types, mixed in varied proportions, could create a sufficiently large number of ethnic images if we look at it simply from the point of view of arithmetic.

Chantre notes that although the Armenians have been in contact with the Mongol Turki people in a number of different ways they never have narrow or oblique eyes; on the contrary, their eyes are large and widely open. This is simply because the Mongol conquest was not followed by colonization; and this is fresh proof in support of the opinion we have never ceased to maintain that the influence of conquerors on the conquered is usually small.

[1] XVII, p. 5.

The Armenians are above the mean height. Chantre found a stature of 1 metre 68 among the Armenians of the Caucasus; but other authors (Pantiukhof, Tvarianovitch, Ivanowsky) have published lower figures (from 1 metre 647 to 1 metre 666). The Armenians that I measured had a mean height of 1 metre 66. This figure, I should think, would represent fairly accurately the mean stature of this people.

The Armenians are brachycephalic as well as relatively tall. On this point those who have written on them are at one. The cephalic indices obtained by Chantre are as follow:—85.47 (Armenians of the Erivan province); 84.15 (Armenians of Yozgad). I personally measured 124 Armenians in the Balkan peninsular: they yielded a mean cephalic index of 85.69, similar to Chantre's of his first series, and I found 66 per cent. of individuals whose index was over 84. Chantre found 59 per cent. These results agree. The Armenians really are a distinctly brachycephalic people. In this character they approximate closely to a portion of their immediate neighbours, the Kurds, of whom we have just spoken, and to their other neighbours the Lazes. Thus we see constituted in this region of Asia Minor a large definite area peopled by Brachycephals—and I think it is likely to become considerably larger.

The Armenian nose is long and relatively it is not a broad nose. The Armenians are leptorrhinians according to their nasal index. I have never seen a platyrrhine Armenian. But a fairly large number of them are mesorrhinians. Besides being long the Armenian nose is straight, often with a tendency to become aquiline. It is often down-turned at the tip. I have many times noted this form of nose among the Kurds, and I believe Chantre has also remarked upon it.

The Armenians have dark eyes, generally brown (86 to 89 per cent.). Nevertheless, I have found among them a few blue-eyed individuals (4 per cent.). Chantre also mentions a certain proportion (11 per cent.) of light eyes.[1]

[1] One day anthropologists must group together all the peoples of Western Asia among whom blue eyes have been noted. It is necessary to approximate this character to other morphological and descriptive characters seen in such persons. Are they tall or short, dolichocephalic or brachycephalic? Are they leptorrhinians, and have they fair hair as well as blue eyes? We shall then see what is the real worth of the observation in regard to the Turks and Kurds, which we have mentioned, and which, to date, may seem to some more or less tendencious, or at least inadequate.

The Armenians nearly always have black hair, or at least dark chestnut. I have not seen any with fair hair. Chantre, on the contrary, indicates a few in his statistics.

From the above different observations it results that the Armenians issue from a highly brachycephalic human group, in the heart of which we might distinguish two main sections marked by a difference in height; a very tall section, approximating to 25 per cent; and a very short section (in a proportion of about 20 per cent ?). But should these two secondary groups, characterized by a difference in height, be considered to have been original groups ?

I have somewhere said that in my view the Kurds and Armenians were closely related and that a large number of them must have issued from the same ethnic group. I was led to this hypothesis by the similarity of certain measurements recorded en route in my anthropological registers, and by the external physical resemblances noted in the representatives of the two peoples. I remember, for example, at Constantinople and at Scutari in Asia, when we were examining the Kurdish and Armenian "Hammals" (porters), how frequently we found them alike. From my sojournings in the Near East I have brought back this impression that these two peoples were "ethnic brethren" and that it was the vicissitudes of History (this word sums up everything !) which made enemies of those who were brethren.

In order not to remain under a mere impression I compared among themselves the principal measurements and the descriptive characters yielded by both Kurds and Armenians, such as stature, height of chest, length of legs, cranial and facial diameters, cephalic index, and various relations. I will not go so far as to say that this comparison showed me the identity of these two groups, for that would be inaccurate, but it did show me various singularly demonstrative approximations.[1] Obviously there were certain dissemblances (notably in the proportion of different types of stature) alongside the resemblances. But these were not such as need surprize us.

In each of these two populations there is a strong contingent having the same characters. By putting these contingents together we should constitute a new anthropological

[1] CXCV, p. 510.

category, Armeno-Kurd, whose ethnic physiognomy would present no contrasts.

Would this new collective group, which might be thus characterized : tall stature ; brachycephaly ; deeply pigmented eyes and hair ; long, often big nose, straight or aquiline, and frequently hooked at the tip, etc.—would this give us the picture of the ancient historic peoples, the Medes in particular —not to go too far back ? For a demonstration we should require to have osteological data obtained from the latter source ; but a hypothesis of this kind is perfectly acceptable.

It is impossible for us to go back with any accuracy to the Armeno-Kurd prehistoric times, and we are absolutely ignorant of the human races of that period. The later iconographic documents, if we are not to reject them from the start, are altogether inadequate to throw any light on the matter. As for the historians, have they not attributed metallurgy and the invention of the cuneiform script to the "Turanian or Scythian race" ?

If I were to be asked to what ethnic group or groups I considered that the Assyrians, Chaldeans, Elamites, Arameans etc., belonged, I should reply, to begin with, that I do not know, because we have no precise anthropological indication about them. But were I to be pressed, I should say that in my opinion, according to the balance of probabilities, the Armeno-Kurds of to-day are probably existing descendants of these ancient peoples. Do not let us forget that the Empires of this part of Asia were nothing but early small kingdoms, populated by similar ethnic elements, on which Fortune had smiled, and which had grown into flourishing States. Obviously the ethnic characters of the population of these feudal domains, whether they were broken up into small groups or collected into powerful political communities, did not change with each succeeding event. Elam, which was wrecked by Assurbanipal in 640, included within its walls the descendants of the folk who created Susa ; and the successors of the people who were conquered by the Persians could still trace their descent back to their early forbears who were the actual founders of the Elamite power.

The untutored Kurdish herdsmen and the peasants and craftsmen of Armenia have had among their ancestors the founders of empires. These men were tall, brachycephalic and brunet, having that long nose of characteristic shape that the sculptors of antiquity have always taken care to represent.[1]

Undoubtedly political and economic facts, and perhaps invasion—though not in every case—may have brought different human elements, some of which may have been ethnically foreign, within the boundaries of these States. But the foundation of the population was as we have indicated it. For the rest, if these " foreigners " were at all numerous we should find some of their descendants to-day. Maybe, indeed, we do find them in the exceptional types of our series ?

From the Black Sea to the Persian Gulf, that is to say from the upper course of the Araxes and the sources of the Mesopotamian rivers, to the mountains of ancient Persia, there probably lived in the early days of the Asiatic world a population of nomadic hunters of a clearly defined type (it has been defined, above). Its great-great-great-grandchildren were later to bear divers names in the course of a very long historic period. They were to engage in cruel wars with one another. Sometimes, in order to justify their acts, they were to claim to be strangers one to the other. But they would only have to look a little more closely to see in the identity of their essential features the secret sign of their brotherhood.

Do not the Kurds and Armenians, so largely blood brothers, still, in these days in certain sad circumstances and under these two modern names, continue in the ways of the past !

[1] Prof. S. Langdon, lecturing at the School of Oriental Studies on " The Excavations at Kish, 1923-24 " reported in the *Times*, of June 27th, 1924, said : " We have now two actual skulls, one of a round-headed type and one of a long-headed type. These have been partially restored by Mr. Buxton, lecturer in Physical Anthropology at Oxford, who has proved that the Sumerian man had an oblique orbit of the eye-socket, entirely in accordance with the sculptured monuments of the earliest Sumerian period. He has shown from these two skulls that the Sumerian was an Armenoid type and highly civilized, possessing a head of great brain capacity ". He also said (*Times*, June 20th, 1924) : " Our excavations have proved that there were two races in the early period at Kish, Sumerian and Semite . . . Our excavations reveal [the Sumerian's] anthropological classification. He belongs to the pre-historic round-headed race which descended upon the fertile lands of the two rivers from Central Asia soon after the Glacial Period. The Sumerian racial characteristics as universally portrayed by sculptors of the early period entirely agree with the human remains which we have found at Kish ". (Translator's Note.)

CHAPTER VII

The Mongols or Tatar Mongols

HUXLEY gives to the Mongoloid race one of the five places he reserved for the main races of mankind,[1] and his secondary races are the Mongol, Polynesian, American, Eskimo and Malaysian. Topinard includes the Mongols in his group of mesorrhinian yellow races as Asiatic Yellows; Haeckel places them among the Euthykomoi (straight-haired people). In Deniker's *Essai d'une classification des races humaines*[2] the Mongols figure in group F, comprising straight-haired peoples, and having, besides, the following characteristics:—pale yellow skin, prominent cheekbones, Mongoloid eye, slight brachycephaly. Later on he adds these further details: "The Mongol race consists of two varieties or sub-races, the Tunguses or Northern Mongols, having an oval or round face and prominent cheekbones, distributed in Manchuria, Korea, North China and Mongolia; and the Southern Mongols with lozenge-shaped or square faces and wide cheekbones, to be seen more particularly in the extreme south of China and in Indo-China."

The geographical distribution of this race is thus considerable. But it appears that nothing is more vague than this same appellation of Mongol. And this results, among other reasons, from the fact that we have always been in the habit "both Europeans and Chinese, of giving the name of one of the Turki tribes, Ta-ta or Tatar, transformed to Tartar, to the Mongols and many of the Mongoloid peoples, like the Tunguses, for example." We will therefore examine what is known of the anthropological characters of the Mongol on one hand and of the Tatars on the other.

The Mongol group may be subdivided thus: Western Mongols (Eleuts), that is to say the Kalmuks; Eastern Mongols (Khalkhas, Shakars, etc.); and Buriats.

Nearly all Mongols have remained pastoral nomads.

[1] **CXVII.**
[2] **LVI**, p. 320; **LVII**, p. 440. (Engl. transln., p. 378.)

The area of dispersion of the Western Mongols in Central Asia is considerable. They are to be met with from Nan-shan to the north of the Caucasus. Large groups inhabit Dsungaria, and also the Astrakhan Caspian depression. This wide dispersion does not mean, however, that they are many in number. It is admitted that they do not exceed a million all put together.

The morphological characters of the Kalmuks do not constitute a type of beauty such as would be admired in Europe. The following is the description Chantre gives of the Kalmuks he and von Erckert studied in the northern Caucasus[1]:

" Physically the Kalmuk realizes the Mongol type in all its plainness—oblique and narrow eyes, nose much depressed at the root, prominent cheekbones, beard and eyebrows almost hairless, and bronzed skin " ; (the colour of light leather, Deniker was to say, later) " add to this thick lips, enormous stick-out ears and invariably black hair. They are also very small, but svelte and lissom, thanks to their custom of leaving the upbringing of their children entirely to nature. Hardly are they able to walk before they are on horseback and devoting themselves with ardour to the sports of wrestling and horsemanship," etc.

The Western Mongols in general are small men. The mean of a series of more than 300 Kalmuks of Dsungaria was 1 metre 629. This stature is very different from that found by measuring Astrakhan Kalmuks (1 metre 64). The latter figure, even, is below the European mean. The little we know of the cranial characters of the Kalmuks reveals a sub-brachycephalic people. And this indication would seem to express the actuality when we see that the Kalmuks of Western Dsungaria have a cephalic index of 84.5, and those of the lower Volga 82·1. We may endeavour to account for this difference by supposing inter-mixture with neighbouring peoples.

[1] **XL**, p. 243. Deniker in the article indicated above. See also **XCIII** and **LVIII**, p. 754. For the ethnographical characters of the Kalmuks, see **CLXXXIV** and **CCLX**, p. 715.

With regard to skin colour we may recall an observation made by Deniker in 1883 in the Jardin d'acclimatation in Paris when a Kalmuk baby was born. The new-born child during the first few days after birth had " a skin identical with that of our babies in their first days—white with rosy tints in it. But towards the tenth day its skin already showed a certain admixture of yellow. The other Kalmuk children had a lighter skin than their parents ".

If ethnic intermixture accounts for these different values in the cephalic index I think we must admit that the Volga Kalmuks are so far less mixed with their neighbours than the Central Asian Kalmuks, those of the Ili district in particular. As a matter of fact the Kalmuks of the Astrakhan region have on their borders populations more brachycephalic than themselves, the Kirghiz Kasaks to the north and the Nogai to the south. If the blood of these two peoples had penetrated into the veins of the Kalmuks[1] the brachycephaly of the latter, no doubt, would be increased. As for the Dsungarian Kalmuks they are surrounded by brachycephalic peoples whose cephalic index, so far as can be ascertained, is distinctly greater than that of the European Kalmuks.

The figure Chantre indicates for the Caucasus Kalmuks is still lower (81.7), than the mean of the Volga Kalmuks. It is the same with the figures given by Deniker (81.3).

According to their nasal index the Kalmuks appear to be mesorrhinians. In addition to these measurable characters there is one of a descriptive nature which strikes all observers—the Mongoloid eye.[2]

Eastern Mongolia has already been the subject of important researches. A few years ago two Japanese, Mr. and Mrs. Torii,[3] published the results of their observations in that country during a sojourn of more than ten years. Vast territories, to-day desert, had once a considerable population whose memory is kept green by numerous vestiges of all kinds, by ruins and the remains of enceintes and fortified places within which and under layers of earth, detritus and sand there are still to be found quantities of stone axes, flint arrow-heads and pottery. Such monuments, these authors say, are

[1] Has intermixture with the Kirghiz really taken place? These Kirghiz and Kalmuk peoples are separated by fierce enmity.

[2] The peculiarity consists, as we know, in that owing to the extremely high insertion of the outer palpebral ligament in the cranial bone the external angle of the eye is higher than the internal. Further, the upper eyelid is puffed out and the invisible ciliary border scarcely allows even the eye-lashes to show. The eyelid forms a fold at the internal angle which hides the caruncle.

In connection with the Mongoloid eye I will recall that observers have often noted its presence among the North American Indians in the children. We find here an argument in favour of the Asiatic origin of the North Americans.

[3] CCLVII.

to be met with at every step in the sandy plains and sand hills in the valleys and on the mountains. The Toriis did not discover any traces of palæolithic civilization in the course of their researches.

This area which seems to have been so well explored by our Japanese confrères was inhabited by the Tung-Hu, who must not be identified, as they were by Abel de Rémusat, thanks to a vague resemblance in the words, with the Tunguses.

We know nothing of the physical characters of these early possessors of the soil of Eastern Mongolia. And we cannot say whether the small people with a moderately brachycephalic head and leptorrhine nose who live there to-day on the site of this primitive civilization are their descendants. In regions such as those of Central Asia where displacement of a pastoral people is by no means a difficult matter, and occurred frequently, it would be risky with such a paucity of data at our disposal to infer anything whatsoever as to racial derivation.

The Buriats who, according to statistics, number some 250,000, are considered to be partly interbred with the Siberian natives (Yakuts, Tunguses, etc.). We again find in this people the main features of the Mongolian characters indicated above.

These characters are also recognized in the Tunguses whose 50,000 souls occupy the vast territories of the North Siberian lowlands. Their cephalic index seems to be somewhat lower than that of the Dsungarian Mongols ; and in the east, probably as the result of penetration by a Manchu element. taller than themselves, the stature is high (1 metre 67) and notably exceeds that of the other Mongols.

I think it is very difficult to find out what really were the Mongol ethnic elements which took part in the great historical movements of Jenghiz Khan and his successors. Were the Mongol hordes[1] exclusively composed of men of the type above described ? Did the Tunguses, for example, participate in them ?

There is no doubt whatever that there were genuine racial Mongols in the ranks of the invaders : the chroniclers' accounts, so uncertain on other points, are there to demonstrate the fact, for these writers could never have invented the

[1] For an excellent account in English of the organized military movements of Jenghiz Khan, based on modern research and discovery, see " Two Great Captains : Jenghiz Khan and Subutai " in *Blackwood's Magazine*, No. MCCCIII., May, 1924. (Translator's Note).

descriptive characters whose image they left to us and many of which certainly apply to the true Mongols. But it is equally certain that the Mongol invasions which struck such terror into European hearts[1] were not accomplished by bands that were ethnically pure. There were among them a considerable number of Tatars. That is the universal opinion to-day. I have held this opinion from my earliest encounters with the Tatars, and my later studies have only deepened my conviction. Moreover, I think that it is agreed that, even from the historic viewpoint, Jenghiz Khan set Tatar armies in movement.

There is no need to examine a large number of Tatars to perceive that this group is an ethnic complex. And one soon sees that the Tatars include among them far fewer Mongols or Mongoloids than one might have supposed *a priori*, under the influence, as one so often is, of historical accounts. It is practically certain, even, that many categories of Tatars have not got a drop of Mongol blood in their veins.

Nowhere do the Tatars constitute a State. After having been the masters of a vast empire they are now quite in the background. They are scattered in the southwest of Asia, in southern and eastern Russia, and in the Balkan peninsular. Sebastian Münster, who was a compiler, has left us a description of the Tatars in which, side by side with ethnographica characters, we find a few morphological indications.[2]

We may ask if he ever saw any Tatars. He lived at the beginning of the sixteenth century and it appears that he compiled his work, including the description of physical characters, from the works of early writers. I call to mind, however, that under Philippe le Bel, the relations of the French government with the Tatars were particularly cordial, so much so that the Frankish ambassadors to the Tatars were excused from " passing through the fire "—that is to say, from obligatory purification. Before preaching his crusade Clement V met Mongol envoys at Poitiers. If Münster had not himself seen any Tatars, the memory of their physiognomy must have been still fairly vivid among his contemporaries.

[1] See what Bergeron had to say on this subject: **XII.**
[2] **CLXIX.**

For a long period relations continued to be excellent between the kings of France and the Tatars. There was even question of creating a chair of the Tatar language at the University of Paris. Even to-day the geographical distribution of the Tatars is considerable. By way of simplifying the task of classification, certainly a very difficult one, many writers recognize four main groups of Tatars: (1) the Altai group; (2) the Siberian group; (3) the Caucasus group[1]; (4) the European group. Anthropologically speaking, however, even the elements belonging to many of these groups are very little known. For instance, the somatological data that I have before me concerning the Altai Tatars marks definite heterogeneity. The Caucasus group appears to be more homogeneous. Many of its subdivisions have been fairly thoroughly studied, notably by Chantre (the Azerbaijani, in particular).

In Europe (the Caucasus apart) the Tatars are especially numerous in the territory of former Russia from the Ural to Lithuania; and along the Volga from the province of Kazan to that of Astrakhan. Almost the whole of the Crimea may be considered a Tatar district.

The Tatars of Lithuania and Poland are to-day few. They first came to these regions in 1397 as prisoners. Three years later the Grand Duke Vitold called in a large contingent to fight the Teutonic knights. In 1631 it was estimated that there were 100,000 Tatars in Lithuania. Many migrated as the result of the persecutions of Sigismund III. They went to the Crimea and to former Turkey in Europe (the Dobruja and Bulgaria) and to Asia Minor.[2]

In the east of European Russia the Kazan Tatars con-constituted an imposing bloc, particularly in the neighbourhood of the lower Oka. They descended in part from the Kiptchak horde. They came to this district in the thirteenth century. It is admitted that there are among them a certain number of ancient Bulgars (sometimes called Bulgarliks). The Astrakhan Tatars must have come in large measure from the Golden Horde. The Crimean Tatars have provided in many periods large numbers of emigrants who went to the Balkan peninsular, particularly the Dobruja.

[1] **XL**, p. 238; **XLI**, p. 177.

[2] See **CCLXX** for general facts concerning the Tatars.

Ethnographers are in the habit of subdividing the Crimean Tatars into three Groups—the Tatars of the Steppes, Mountain Tatars, and Coast Tatars. They consider the first to be the true Tatars descended from the Nogai, whereas the others, the Tauridians or Krimtchaki constitute a mixture to which all the peoples who have inhabited the Black Sea shores have contributed their blood. I am bound to say that I am a little sceptical on the subject of these intermixtures.

The Tatars of the Steppes are smaller and have a lower cephalic index than the coast Tatars.

The somatological data collected about the Tatars are beginning to be quite plentiful, though still inadequate to give a faithful picture of the morphological characters of their various groups. They strike one at once by their heterogeneity.

The most plentiful of these data are in regard to stature, then come those giving the cephalic index. The means of this index range from 80.8 to 86.2. They indicate mesocephaly on the one hand and hyperbrachycephaly on the other. The presence of these two characters alone would show that there is considerable ethnic intermixture.

The variety of Tatar types had been observed long before our day. Pallas drew attention to it. Prichard[1], struck by the difference existing between the Tatar peoples, attributed it to a difference in diet and manner of living. All the Turkish races, he said, who had persisted in their early nomadic mode of life and wandered in the cold and barren deserts of Turkestan have what is known as the Mongol physiognomy, of which characters one still sees many traces among the Nogai of the Crimea. This was at a time when monogenism was a kind of intangible doctrine ; the influence of environment must serve to explain easily the variations presented by human races. And von Baer supported the *a priori* views of Prichard.[2]

[1] A certain number of Tatars still deform the heads of their children. This deformation tends to shorten the antero-posterior diameter. Thus there may be on this account some exaggeration of the brachycephaly that is the most common cephalic feature among the Tatars. **CCII**, p. 28; **CCIII**. Prichard says (p. 144, Fr. edition) that it has been noticed that the bodily form in different races appears to modify more under the influence of the manner of life and customs than under that of climate.

[2] " The Tatars provide a striking example of the great influence his manner of life and particularly his food exert on the outer form of man. The Kazan Tatars have by no means broad faces and prominent cheek-bones, but, quite to the contrary, they have narrow and very often long faces, with a very prominent nose often having the hooked shape of the beak of a bird of prey. Their skull is a medium form without dominant dimensions

Khanikoff[1], quoting the above opinions, remarks that if von Baer had pushed his excursions a little further to the east among the Bashkirs, and a little further south among the Azerbaijan Tartars, he would have met with nomadic Tartars having the same features as those of Kazan and the valley of the Kura, and he would have seen that Prichard's explanations lacked any foundation. He would have seen (so says Khanikoff) that wherever the Tartar is in contact with other peoples his type improves. (For example, the Volga and Orenburg Tartars with the Finnish races ; the Transcaucasus and the Azerbaijan Tartars with the Iranian race ; and the Tartars of Asia Minor with the Semitic race.)

One sees that Khanikoff is no dupe of the mesological explanations of Prichard and von Baer. Nevertheless, his own explanation is not more satisfactory. These intermixtures of Tatar blood with the blood of Semitic or Indo-European peoples appear to be somewhat problematical. The Tatars themselves would doubtless regard them with some repugnance. Do not let us forget that they are Musulmans and that the Musulman peoples do not readily intermarry with ethnic groups not professing the Musulman faith. Nor should we forget that wherever the Tatars dwell side by side with a people on a higher social scale than their own, they are generally regarded as inferiors. And in this domain a racial aristocracy is as strict as social aristocracy.

I have personally studied a large number of Tatars. For this very reason I find it difficult to attempt any description of their human type. A synthetic portrait which could claim to be accurate seems to me a chimerical task.

---

in either direction. I found the Tartars of the Kura Valley still more handsome. They no longer had the scoundrelly expression for which one has to reproach the face of the Volga Tartar. How is it, therefore, that other Tartars who inhabit the Volga and Ural steppes, neighbours of the Kazan Tartars and speaking the same language as they do, have broader faces, a less prominent and flatter nose, and that they wear, in general, an aspect of greater coarseness ? Like Prichard, I seek the cause in the difference of their manner of life, because I expressly observe that it is not here a question of different nationalities united by an ethnographer under a single name, but of a people which considers itself to be one and indivisible."

We see how greatly von Baer is still dominated by the importance that was attributed to language. Then, having drawn attention to the fact that the Kazan and Transcaucasian Tatars were agriculturists, whereas the others were nomads, von Baer thinks he can explain the difference in their outward appearance by their meat diet and their custom of living in tents !

[1] CXXIV.

Nevertheless, despite their obvious heterogeneity, the Tatars present a "something" in their characters taken as a whole which causes them to be recognizable from among the other Musulmans among whom they live, notably the Turks. They have very large ears; they are more hairless in the face than their co-religionists the Turks. Their face appears to be thicker and wrinkles plough deep furrows in it. Their cheek-bones are prominent. The nose is often depressed at the root. There is a wide space between their eyes and their eyes are heavy-lidded. Do we not find in this short and incomplete description some features at least of the Mongol face? The lips in some individuals, instead of being red are strongly violet—(I have made a note of this character again and again in my anthropological records).

Mongol face, did we say? Certainly. Then there are true Mongols among the Tatars? There is not a shadow of a doubt about it.

The Tatars in general are small men. Anuchin indicated 1 metre 609 as representing the height of 2,696 conscripts in the provinces of Kazan and Samara.[1] On the other hand, Deniker, in the series he quotes from Russian authors, mentions a height of 1 metre 628 for the Tatar provinces through which the Volga flows. The Tatars of other localities are often much taller. For example, the Astrakhan Tatars are 1 metre 680; and the Crimean Tatars 1 metre 664. These figures alone, different as they are, will demonstrate that the term Tatar is a label given to an agglomeration of human beings of diverse origin. The height of 215 men that I measured in the Dobruja (1 metre 657) approaches that of the Crimean Tatars.

It is necessary to point out at once that the mean stature of the Tatars is notably inferior to that of the Turks (about 1 metre 68) with whom certain writers have a tendency to group them.[2]

[1] One must remember that the height of conscripts can nowhere represent the real stature of a people. At the age when the men are militarily called up they are not yet full grown. And we do not know, for all the peoples, at what age full growth is attained.

[2] The following are a few figures for the height of Tatars additional to those already indicated: 6,567 conscripts of Kazan province, 1 metre 623; 678 Tatars of the same province, 1 metre 620; 349 Tatars of the province of Simbirsk, 1 metre 624; 110 conscripts of the province of Saratow, 1 metre 629; 33 Tatars of the province of Ryazan, 1 metre 642; 50 Tatars of the province of Tambov, 1 metre 639; 61 Tatars of the province of Ufa, 1 metre 620; 90 Tatars of Lithuania, 1 metre 628.

The studies relating to the cephalic index of the Tatars come especially from Russia. A series of 215 Tatars that I measured is sub-brachycephalic in mean. This observation, in fine, confirms those formerly made by Lygin, when he examined some Nogai Tatars of the Crimean steppes and mountains (index of 80.8); by Benzenger on the Tatars of the Ryazan government (82.8); and by Malief, de Quatrefages and Hamy, etc.

The Bulgarian Tatars measured by Bassanovitch (they came formerly from the Crimea) are brachycephalic. So were 82 Tatars of the steppes examined by Merejkowsky (index of 85 and 84.5). As one goes towards the south of the Crimea it would appear that the character of brachycephaly becomes accentuated. The southern Tauridians (Kharuzin, Ikof) are hyperbrachycephalic (mean index, 86.3).

In the west of former Russia, on the contrary, the cephalic index is lowered: 90 Tatars of Lithuania (Talko-Hryncewicz) had a mean of 81 to 82.[1]

From these results, whose number it would be vain to multiply, it would plainly appear that the Tatars as a whole lack anthropological unity. Taking the mean they are sub-brachycephals. But is this sub-brachycephaly simply a product of the averages or is it a morphological character possessed by the majority?

The series I studied, numerically the most important we have, shows that dolichocephals are scarce among the Tatars. Putting all forms of this cephalic type together we get 20 per cent.; whereas we find 61 per cent. of brachycephalic types. Thus it was brachycephalic individuals in the main who built up the Tatar group.

Very wide areas of Central and North Asia are characterized by sub-brachycephaly or brachycephaly. Thus it is to the Brachycephals of Asia—without our being able to particularize their derivation further—that the Tatars belonged: Brachycephals whose first origin, moreover, even in Asia, is absolutely unknown.

But whence came the Tatar dolichocephalic types? Did the Tatar invasion recruit Dolichocephals even at the period of its—or their—first setting forth? Or do these Dolichocephals

[1] This mean index is that which the Russians of this region habitually yield.

represent people who became politically Tatarized during the march ?

In their *Crania ethnica* de Quatrefages and Hamy also indicate the variety of anthropological characters among the Tatars.[1]

The eight skulls they studied and the three crania utilized by Blumenbach appear to us to-day to provide but slender data wherewith to characterize either the homogeneity or the heterogeneity of a human group ? All the same, it is interesting to note that these writers had already distinctly remarked that the ethnic type of the Tatar is not that of the Tatar Mongol only. But de Quatrefages and Hamy believed that there had been mixture of blood between Turks, Finns and Mongols in proportions which would yield on the one hand the Turko-Finnish type and on the other the Turko-Mongol. Had this mixture—if it exists—already taken place in Asia before the Tatar migration ? Or did it take place later, after their arrival in Europe ?

Before the anthropologists had begun to demonstrate by measurements and descriptions that the Tatars were far from representing a homogeneous human group, the notion that this people was made up of an ethnic complex had already been grasped and expressed by a few travellers. For instance, the Nogai were considered to be the genuine descendants of the Mongols. Thus Clarke wrote that the Nogays, a very different people from the Crimean Tatars, could be distinguished at the first glance by their small stature and their dark copper coloured and sometimes almost black complexion ; that they bore a striking resemblance to the Lapps, though their dress and customs appeared to be less civilized—probably the Lapps and Nogay Tatars sprang from the same stock ; and that it would indeed be difficult to give details at that date of the particular circumstances of their origin.

And then he recalls that Pallas particularly distinguished two races of Tatars—the Nogays and the Mountain Tatars. He adds that the latter had seemed to him to resemble in the outer appearance the Turks and the Tatars of Kostroma and Yaroslavl.[2]

I do not think that, following Clarke's example[3], one can

[1] **CCV**, p. 413.
[2] I suppress the references for want of space.
[3] **XLVII**, Vol. iii.

say that among the Tatars the Nogai represent in any exclusive manner the Mongol type. If the numerous Tatars I examined in the Balkan peninsular, notably in the Dobruja where I measured more than a thousand, have faithfully retained—I mean in a physical hereditary sense—a memory of the ancestral primitive hordes, one can merely say that the Nogai horde was composed of an ethnic element in which the proportion of Mongoloid Tatars appears to have been higher than among other Tatars.

In reality all the Tatar groups present, in varying degrees both Mongoloid and Turki types.[1]

Can we not explain[2] the diversity of the Tatar groups by going back to the great—not Mongol (it was that only in name) but Mongoloid invasion of the thirteenth century?

Admitting that the warrior bands led by Jenghiz Khan were exclusively composed of Mongols[3], their ethnic physiognomy must have rapidly changed. The gaps caused in the Mongol or Mongoloid ranks by the chances of war were continually being filled up by the invaded peoples. These had no choice but to follow their conquerors with a view of participating in their economic and political successes. The vanquished, or perhaps simply the "passed over" left their devastated lands to seek compensation in the conquest.[4] These "fill up" people, however, were mainly Turanians—Turki people. Therefore one can pretty well picture the ethnic physiognomy of the human hordes in question, once it was fixed—that of the Kiptchak horde, for example. It is the Turki type which is dominant, or rather, the Turki types. Side by side with these there were Mongol or Mongoloid elements, survivors of the original group (but gradually dwindled to a minority) and still other Turko-Mongol crossbred elements.

The present-day Tatars therefore are chiefly Turki and Tatarized peoples. Here and there among them the Mongol survives, either in the ancestral form more or less complete, and more or less pure, or represented only by one or more of

[1] Again—when was this admixture accomplished? Was it the result of cross-breeding between these two main types consummated in the course of the generations that have lived and died since the thirteenth century invasions? Or does it represent the physiognomy of the group as it has been from the beginning?

[2] **CXCIV**, p. 1.

[3] Élisée Reclus explains it very well: **CCXII**.

[4] See Translator's Note on p. 376.

his morphological characters transmitted to the Tatarized Turki peoples (prominent cheekbones, glabrousness, etc.).

A river which receives affluents from complex geographical regions naturally transports all kinds of alluvia—its own and those of its affluents as well. It mixes them together in its course and deposits them all together at its mouth. The original Tatar invasion presented this character.

At the beginning it may have been composed of Mongol—or Mongoloid—elements alone. In proportion as it proceeded westward it deposited its own elements and acquired others. Thanks to the continual contribution of the "fill up" peoples it maintained its numerical and warlike power. By the end of its course foreign elements predominated.

The Tatars generally have brown eyes. Light (grey or blue) irides, however, are in a proportion of about 20 per cent. And herein lies a problem which has often been attacked. The hair is always darkly or very darkly pigmented. Out of several hundred Tatars I examined from this point of view I did not find a single fair individual. On the other hand I did note, in the same series, the presence of nearly 60 per cent. of black hair; and I think, in a general way, that we may accept this proportion for Tatars as a whole.

The Tatar ordinarily has a straight nose. The Mongoloid nasal character only appears in a very small proportion (hardly 15 per cent.). Among their Mongol souvenirs the Tatars have not kept the nasal characteristics.

The conclusion to which one is led is that the Tatars are mainly of Turki "race." It is true that there are in their ranks a certain number of Mongols, even of morphologically characteristic Mongols with the nose, cheekbones and eyes which have so often been described. But this ethnic type is evidently in a minority.

One ought to be able to go further. It would be of great historic and philosophic interest to know with precision the ethnic facies of the men who participated in the great invasions.

If I were a historian I should want to picture to myself with the greatest possible precision the first assemblage of the Mongols, and to count their ranks and verify the "race" of those composing them. Was Jenghiz Khan the leader of an ethnically homogeneous horde—relatively homogeneous, of course—or was he the head, from the very first, of an " ethnic hotchpotch " ?

Doubtless we shall never solve this problem. But we can approach much nearer to a solution than we have done at present. For that we need to multiply our anthropological studies all along the route taken by these Tatar invasions, and to make them more detailed.

CHAPTER VIII

The Peoples of India

INDIA, said Ujfalvy, was neither the cradle of humanity nor the seat of primitive knowledge; but the part she has played in the history of the Asiatic peoples has been so important that it would be folly to try to ignore it.

This huge country has seemed to all who have studied it —anthropologists, philologists and historians—an inextricable jungle like some of its own districts. Endless social divisions, carried to a length unknown anywhere else, complicate the task of those who try to see their way through the tangle. It is true that studies destined to throw light on the origin of the Indian peoples have been many, ranging from iconography—what is the worth of such data from the strictly scientific point of view?—to pure imagination.

But these studies weigh little in the scales against this vast problem. We must not practice self-deception. Our great-great-grandchildren will perhaps know the truth; but to-day—basing ourselves, as we do, exclusively on historical evidence—we are still in the realm of conjecture. Indeed, it is impossible to study a land of 300 million inhabitants, many of whom are still almost un-get-atable, with the same simplicity that we examine a "series" in a laboratory!

Many things have been said about the origin of the Indian peoples which it is better, I think, that we should now forget. If our progress is to be cumbered by all the litter of utterly gratuitous guesses, we shall certainly have no chance of getting any further. We must not forget that the Indian problem is further complicated by the Aryan discussion.

India, without a shadow of doubt, is a land of very ancient civilization. Palæolithic implements mingled with the remains of extinct animals—some of these species being pliocene in southern Asia[1]—have been found in the alluvial deposits brought down from the Vindhya hills, and in the alluvium that forms the Deccan plateau.

[1] **XXI**, p. 360.

Seton Karr has found quartzies of palæolithic type in the laterites of Madras province, near Renigunta. These implements were undisturbed and are therefore of the same age as the argillaceous deposits to which the above writer assigns an amazing antiquity. Swynnerton has made similar finds in the State of Gwalior (Central India) ; and so have others (Rivett-Carnac, etc.). And this leaves out of account essays to establish a parallelism with the prehistoric periods in Europe such as were inspired by the wall paintings discovered at Raigarh (Central India), to which attention was drawn by Brown, and which, in the author's opinion, recall the Cogul paintings in Spain. There were implements of chipped agate in this cave.

Fritz and Paul Sarasin have made known the curious implements of rock crystal which they found in their excavations in Ceylon and which had come down from the former Veddas, the ancestors of the present-day people who are of such interest in connection with the phylogeny of the human races of Asia. If India passed through the same stages as Europe these implements might be attributed to the Magdalenian period.

The numerous dolmens of the Hindustan plateau, the arrow-heads and polished stone axes recall, in less distant times, our Neolithic. And, as with us, this period seems to have had as its natural successor a bronze age.

Thus from these observations India will appear as one of the most ancient of human territories ; on Indian soil primitive humanity must have evolved through the same stages as those represented by the European civilizations. This observation should be of some concern to the linguists[1] who try to establish ethnic relationships between the two countries.

The first point to emerge is that India was never a tenantless land whose first ethnic streamlet might have consisted of relatively recent civilizations, such, for example, as the Aryan. From the Quaternary onwards the soil of India has been trodden by the foot of Man.

But to what type or types did these men belong ? Up to the present we have no Indian human remains dating from the

[1] There is nevertheless need for great caution before we establish any synchronism between the peoples of India and those of Europe. In many regions of Asia certain monuments of neolithic type or of the bronze age appear to date from the historic period. Do not let us forget that in the seventeenth century many Siberian peoples were still in the stone age.

Palæolithic. And although the similarity of the objects found may permit us to attempt parallels in regard to industries, it is still quite impossible for us to say whether the palæolithic people who handled these like implements on the shores of European rivers and the banks of the Godavari and Kistna lived at the same period or belonged to the same race.

Nor do we know whether, in less distant times, the builders of the megalithic monuments were the descendants of the people of the flaked stone age or whether, as would appear to have been the case in Europe, the neolithic civilization properly so-called was the work of another race.

Many writers have thought that the Veddas of Ceylon represent the ethnic remnants of prehistoric India. This wretched population, studied especially by F. and P. Sarasin and by Seligman[1] would be a sort of living Indian fossil. It is quite possible. But the ethnic characteristics of the Veddas are not those of the larger part of the Indian peoples and this alone invalidates such a hypothesis[2].

In this connection it seems to me to be useless to enter into the controversy about the Aryans whom Grünwedel makes come two thousand years B.C. and whose presence is put back still another thousand years by Fergusson, whereas Ujfalvy adopts the fifteenth century B.C. as the approximate date of their appearance. Much ink has flowed from the pens of philologists and historians—and amateurs to boot—on this subject. It would appear that we still lack reliable information as to the region in which they were primitively grouped (the southwest shores of the Caspian ?) and on the period of their migration—we are here speaking of the Asiatic Aryans with regard to whom discussion has been less bitter than in regard to the so-called Aryans of Europe.

Maybe, in view of all these uncertainties regarding the first origin of the Indians, it will be more scientific simply to set forth what we know of the anthropological characters of the present-day peoples of India. Each one can then choose for himself in this rapid resumé.

Modern ethnologists, with a view of bringing some sort of order into the still very inadequate results—think what a

[1] *The Veddas,* C. G. and B. Z. Seligman, Camb. Univ. Press, 1911.

[2] If we are to consider the Veddas from the above point of view, must we not then give an explanation of the origin of those inhabitants of India who diverge from the primitive type ?

great mass of Indians there are, and how various they are in type, and then of the relatively small number of observers who have interested themselves in this question !—are willing to divide the peoples of India, provisionally, at least, into two big groups, the Aryans or Indo-Afghans, and the Melano-Indians or Dravidians.[1]

The Aryan peoples are concentrated in the thickly populated country watered by the Ganges and its affluents, in those lands bounded on the south by the Mahanadi to the east and the Nabada to the west. They speak various dialects—Hindi, Bengali, Punjabi, etc., and are probably composed of various ethnic groups. As a whole these Aryan groups possess morphological characters that differ from those of the Dravidians. In the border districts intermixture—despite caste endogamy—seems always to have gone on.

We saw magnificent specimens of these peoples—Brahmans, Rajputs, etc., bearing names familiar to us from our schooldays—in Europe during the world war in the British Armies, such as Sikhs and Ghurkas.[2]

When we glance over the multitude of peoples who inhabit India—not, however, as we must repeat, a multitude ethnically—we perceive that from the high Himalayan valleys to Cape Comorin and Ceylon there is a complete lack of morphological unity. As regards stature alone we find tall groups in the Punjab and very small people in the Nilgiri hills and in Ceylon.

The tallest people are to be found in the northwest among the mountains of Kashmir and the Himalaya foothills in the district between the upper courses of the Indus and Sutlej.

[1] This is the classification employed by Deniker, who bases his subdivisions solely on physical characters. Haeckel places the Aryans among his Euplokomoi. Deniker, in his *Essai d'une classification des races humaines* (**LVI**), places the Indo-Afghan race in group C among the wavy-haired people having brown or black hair and dark eyes, and the Dravidians in group B, among the curly and wavy-haired peoples. The other characteristics of these Dravidians he gives as dolichocephaly and a dark skin, and, in certain sub-races, a platyrrhinian and in others a leptorrhinian nose. The further Indo-Afghan characters are tall stature, dolichocephaly and a leptorrhinian nose.

[2] The Sikhs, looked upon as the purest type of this race, have a mean height of 1 metre 71. We must go to the Nordic—especially the Scots—or to the Dinaric race (Bosnians, Herzegovinians, Montenegrins etc.) to find taller men than this in Europe.

But there are also very small races in India : the Veddas of Ceylon, the Kurumbas of Wynaad, and the Irulas of the Nilgiri hills. Their stature is only 1 metre 56. It is thus about 10 cms. lower than the European mean.

They are also among the most highly dolichocephalic in all India (cephalic index of the Kashmiris, 72.2).

In proportion as we go southwards, first in Rajputana and then at the foot of the Vindhya hills and in Chota Nagpur, we find that stature gets lower. The stature of the inhabitants of the Punjab drops to 1 metre 68—which is still a very high mean. In Chota Nagpur the mean is much lower. And although the Oraons are 1 metre 62 in height, the Bhinya drop to 1 metre 57.

This synthetic picture which the analysis of human stature gives us is likewise provided by the cranial characters, though it is less clear cut. In general we may say that the whole of India is dolichocephalic. And when we know what a stronghold of brachycephaly is Asia north of the Himalaya, this finding takes on an importance that it is unnecessary to emphasise for all who concern themselves with Indian problems, even for all who are interested in Asiatic origins.

We do not know of a single brachycephalic group throughout the huge extent of India. If we consult the international lists giving the cephalic indices of India, we find here and there a few small islands of sub-brachycephaly. On the west coast the Parsees of Bombay; on the lower course of the Ganges, the Bengalis, who are also sub-brachycephalic.

When we examine the map published by Ripley of the world distribution of the cephalic index (which retains very nearly all its value as a general picture—we cannot ask more of it) we are struck by the brachycephalic mass, having a very high index, which dominates India from the north and seems to weigh down on it like a heavy burden. First of all the whole of trans-Himalaya, the Thibetan plateau, and Mongolia. Then, to the side, all northern Persia, the approaches to the Aral and Caspian, and Turkestan. Burma, too, shows high cephalic indices. Indeed, save on the west, a thick brachycephalic barrier encircles India. Even to the west the mean cephalic index is a good deal higher than that furnished by the Indians.

Thus India appears as an isolated anthropological province with her own particular characters in the great Asiatic ensemble. She is what we might call an autonomous anthropological province.

This in no way simplifies the question of origins, but it should be of considerable interest both to linguists who specialize in the study of Aryan languages and to historians who concern themselves with the beginnings of our own history.

From the ethnic point of view we may first of all ask whence came the peoples of India, and then—why was the country not penetrated more profoundly by the Brachycephals who surrounded it? But is not this rather the affair of the historian and the sociologist than ours?

We said that two large regions may be delimited in India. the North, largely peopled by Aryans or Indo-Afghans; then, from the Vindhya and Chota Nagpur hills, the centre and south of the country peopled by Dravidians. It is obvious that these are quite rough boundaries and that they have been overstepped on every frontier and in both directions by the representatives of these roughly synthesized groups.

Thus, in the southwest, the Nairs of the Malabar coast show morphological affinities with the Indo-Aryans, and so also do some of the Sinhalese. Further, the Lurka-Kols (or Ho) of Bengal have not the required qualities of physique to enable them to figure among the Dravidians.

Then there remain outside these large sub-divisions some special groups whose derivation is far from having been determined; the Nilgiri Todas, for instance, a little tribe of tall stature (1 metre 70), distinctly dolichocephalic (index of 73.1), mesorrhinian (index of 74.9), and light-complexioned. India still has a reserve of interesting tasks for the anthropologist.[1]

As another example of research yet to be undertaken we may instance that the Siahposh or Mamogis were considered by the early anthropologists—de Quatrefages, in particular—as bearing witness to the old "Aryan race" because in "all their physical characters" they "recall the most handsome white races." It has even been claimed that they were the descendants of the soldiers of Alexander! What are we to think about this race? To what ethnic stem must we attach it?

[1] The English have naturally supplied the most important contributions to our anthropological knowledge of the Indians. The information we require must be sought in the series of Thurston, Crook, Drake-Brock, Risley, etc. Naturally enough, too, the most numerous data relate to stature. Then come those giving cephalic and nasal indices. Many thousands of men have been examined and measured. But what are these in the face of the vast numbers of Indians and the complexity of the problem? For these series see **LVII**, p. 465 (p. 408-15 of English translation).

However that may be, the north of India appears to be the domain of the big race. As a whole there is not a notable difference between individuals the most widely separated geographically. In the most northerly regions of India the Chitralis, for instance, seem to have undergone some admixture of blood with the brachycephalic population living still further north. If these people have been indigenous for several thousands of years their reciprocal penetration of blood explains itself. Whereas the Kashmiris have a cephalic index of 72 like the Rajputs and the Sikhs of the Punjab, among the Chitralis it rises to 76.9, and to 77 among the Dards. And at the same time, as though to confirm the origin of a foreign element, stature drops.

Thus the increase of the cephalic index goes hand in hand with a decrease in stature on the northern border. It has been put down to the influence of the Mongol and Turki races. That is quite possible.

The Dravidian group would appear to be even more complicated. According to the idiom it uses it has been divided into two main groups—the Kolarians, and the Dravidians properly so-called. In general they are small people: the Mundas of Chota Nagpur (1 metre 58 to 1 metre 59); Bhumjis (1 metre 59); Kurmis of Chota Nagpur (1 metre 60); Santals (1 metre 61), all distinctly dolichocephalic: the Kolarians of the Northwest (index of 72.7); Bhumjis of Chota Nagpur (index of 75). The Santals have a relatively shorter head—76.1. Many among them are mesorrhinians, but entire tribes are platyrrhinian. Risley's measurements on the Bhumjis of Chota Nagpur (nasal index of 86.1), on the Santals (index, 88.8), and on the Munda Kols (index of 89) leave no doubt on that point.

As for the Dravidians properly so-called, they are divided, geographically, into two groups, the northern and southern.

It would seem that the northern Dravidians in general are smaller than the southern, with the exception, however, of the Nilgiri Irulas at least, whose stature is very low (1 metre 56). The Malis are only 1 metre 56. The Oraons of Chota Ngpaur are slightly taller—1 metre 62.

But these Dravidian tribes, among whom are some who have not got beyond a very primitive stage of civilization, represent a more genuine complex than the Aryans. This backward state of civilization has been the cause possibly of a fundamental error, dominated as we are by the doctrine of continual progress. Many anthropologists admit that the Dravidians represent the remnant of the most primitive population of India in an arrested and low stage of evolution. That might indeed be so. But then, were these the ancestors of the Dravidians who fashioned the Chellean hand-axes (" coups de poing ") so often found on Indian soil ?

And now—what relationship can these Indians, Aryans and Dravidians claim with the ancient Aryans of the philologists, geographers and historians ?

We know that it is near the source of the Syr Darya in present-day Turkestan that the hypothetical birthplace of this hypothetical race is placed.

De Quatrefages—in his day everyone believed in the existence of this " Aryana " and of the Aryans—taking as his basis the accounts of the Zend-Avesta and the geographical situation of the regions in question, indicates the routes that these migrations would have taken. But these are theoretical views, guided far more by imagination than by facts. They attempted to support the philological suppositions, then pretty generally admitted. They must have seemed natural enough to anyone looking at the map of the region, and at the same time thinking about the " migration of peoples."

Still we may regret that a man of de Quatrefage's worth—we mention him among many others because he is the most illustrious among them—supported with his great authority essays at demonstration such as this ! As a matter of fact, not a single morphological indication has ever been furnished in regard to these primitive Aryans the very colour of whose skin is not known to us with precision. In de Quatrefage's view the two chief cephalic types co-existed among the Aryans, which served as a simple explanation of these characters when we find them in the present-day population. But have we any proof that these two cephalic types co-existed ?

CHAPTER IX

The Chinese

THE Chinese alone account for about a third of the population of Asia.

Their history, at all events in modern times, has had no international echoes. The various wars China has carried on in the nineteenth century against European powers have not sensibly modified her territorial boundaries any more than they have transformed the general pacificism of the Chinese people. The wars against Japan were more disastrous for China.

If it were merely a question of these military contacts it might seem that we could pass by in silence this huge people, which, had it known different economic and moral conditions, might have become a factor of formidable importance in the world's history. Picture, for example, the influence of China as a great naval power—and the part she might then have played in the destinies both of the Far East and of the Pacific. China, with her illimitable possibilities of human expansion, might have conquered the world.

But if China has played no part outside her own continent, and if that part, despite numerous wars, has been a relatively modest one, she has nevertheless been a dominating figure in Asia, first under the Mongol dynasty and then under the Manchus.[1] She caused a large number of ethnically distinct peoples all around the geographical bounds of the present Republic to submit, as the historians say, to her laws. China enlarged her domain from the frontiers of India to northern Mongolia, and from Bukharya to Formosa. The Manchu emperors absorbed their neighbours for more than a hundred

[1] The results of recent research in this country are confirming this, especially researches based on the explorations of Sir Aurel Stein in Chinese Turkestan; the explorer foreshadowed some of these historical results in a paper read before the Roy. Anthr. Institute on 24th March, 1925, entitled: "Innermost Asia: its Geography as a factor in History," in which the early "military contacts" of the Chinese, from the Han dynasty onwards, were traced to Thibet and Russian Turkestan, by his personal archæological field-work on the track of their armies and frontier posts. (Translator's Note.)

years. During this period various races entered the Chinese political orbit. And to-day, in general, we call them all Chinamen.

What we have to do is to sort out from the anthropological complex of this huge territory, in parts so thickly populated and in many localities of which human movement would seem to have been relatively free—to sort out those people who may be considered to be the primitive human nucleus of China and the genuine Chinese. Even then, admitting that it is possible to find this primitive nucleus, who is to prove to us that it was these " genuine Chinamen " who played the effective rôle in the conquests ? (It would seem, indeed, that this was not so.) Might these conquests have been accomplished by folk who were Chinese in name, although belonging to another ethnic stock ? And would not the genuine Chinese merely have been the docile instruments in the hands of these dominating foreigners ?

Why has the rôle of the Chinese in the rest of the world been relatively so modest ? Are we to imagine some racial cause ? Is the oft-quoted pacifism of the Chinese really inherent in the race ? Does it spring from certain psycho-physiological contingencies ? Are certain morphologies incapable of developing those qualities which have turned the men of several other races, differently constituted, into chronic conquerors ? *A priori* we do not believe in such relations. That does not prevent the existence of an abyss between the, at least apparent, possibilities and the aptitudes and actions of the Chinese.[1] (We do not here envisage anything but events said to be historical.)

It is impossible in this chapter devoted to China to supply indications relative to the most distant past as have done for all the other regions. The prehistory of China is practically unknown. It offers wonderful perspectives to those who would interest themselves in the country. Up till now the Japanese alone have attempted research, and, recently, the Americans.

In their study of Eastern Mongolia Mr. and Mrs. Torii drew attention to the abundance of flint implements dating

[1] It has been said that the democratic education of the Chinese is at the bottom of this kind of political apathy. But why then did this people accept so completely the principles dictated to it ! A musician would say that the Chinese people is a piano only a part of whose keyboard had been used ; and that the pianist had played nothing but andantes.

from the neolithic age, which seems to have been followed by the metal periods. Like all other peoples the Chinese have evidently known a nomadic stage as hunters and fishers.[1]

In reality we know nothing of Chinese prehistory. It is only a few years ago that Cordier rightly indicated this. After having recorded all the suggested theories on the subject of the origin of the Chinese—and there are some very strange ones—this writer found that the problem still remained just where it had been. " If history, such as we know it, and archæology do not suffice to give us the key to it, this simply proves our ignorance of the past. Perhaps we should seek the link that binds China to the rest of humanity in an antiquity so remote that the present generation will never be able to reach it. We are entering the domain of prehistory, and in the case of China, that prehistory is for us still an unexplored country."[2] [3]

And because we know nothing, or practically nothing of the prehistory of China, we need hardly add that our ignorance is equally complete in so far as touches the skeletal remains of the earliest Chinese.

Naturally research has been undertaken along the line of History and Philology ; Chinese filiation with other ethnic groups has even been asserted. The Aryan theory has viewed the Chinese with sympathy. Do they not dwell close to the " centre of the human universe " ? Thibet touches the roof of the world. Is not such neighbourhood in itself sufficient to establish a bond of relationship ?

It is impossible for us to find out to-day what were the determining ethnic characters of Chinese history from the earliest times, because we do not know to what race they belonged. Central China has been considered to be the most ancient Chinese homeland ; still, no detailed anthropological investigation has been made in this region any more than in the regions situated much more to the west, beyond the

1 **CCLVII.**
2 **XLIX.**
3 Quite recent work in English includes " The Cave-Deposit at Sha Kuo T'un in Fengtien " in *Palæontologica Sinica*, Series D., vol. i., Fas. i ; " An Early Chinese Culture " in *Geological Survey of China Bulletin No.* 5, 1923, both by Dr. J. G. Andersson ; also " Early Man in China ", *Man.*, 10 February, 1925, by L. H. Dudley Buxton, describing the newly discovered culture in Honan and Fengtien. (Translator's Note.)

Kun-Lun, which are by other writers considered to be the cradle of the Chinese race.

When the great conquests of the seventeenth and eighteenth centuries took place was it contingents of the Manchu race, and therefore Mongol, or of the Chinese race, which constituted the armies that became the instruments of the political ambition of the Manchu emperors ?

It is certain that the ethnic term of Chinese has unfortunately been extended to peoples whose morphological characters are very different. To be convinced of this inaccurate generalization one has only to participate in quite a small reunion of Celestials. Who has not observed the distinct variety of the types present at a Chinese dinner which the guests, all in one plane, seem to offer to our anthropological examination ? We have then a sort of synthetic image of what we know of the nation—North Chinamen approximating to the Tatars ; South Chinamen in whom some degree of relationship with certain Indo-Chinese peoples stands confessed. The one has the narrow eye, so characteristic of the Mongol, the yellow skin, and the scarcity of hair on the face ; the other has the horizontal palpebral lids, and a skin approximating in colour to that of the Whites, and a thick beard—as have the Yuchis of North China, or the Miao-tse highlanders.

Although up to the present we have but meagre anthropological information, various investigations have nevertheless been made which authorize us to say a few words on Chinese morphology.

In North China the population seems to be taller (1 metre 67 for a type series from the districts of Chefoo and Kulja) than in the South. The skin, also, is generally lighter than with the southerners. The head of the North Chinamen appears to be shorter ; their cephalic index seems to be on the way to sub-brachycephaly ; and the face is less chamæprosopic than with the southern Chinese.

A large series of Chinese taken prisoner during the war of 1894-95 was examined by the Japanese anthropologist Koganei. The mean height of 942 adults was 1 metre 67, therefore relatively high, and their mean cephalic index was 80.2 (mesaticephaly). The proportion of cranial forms was as follows: dolichocephalic, 8.3 per cent. ; mesocephalic, 39.5 per cent. ; brachycephalic, 38.2 per cent ; hyperbrachycephalic, 12 per cent ; ultrabrachycephalic, 2 per cent. The brachycephalic types account for 52.2 per cent. of the series. The Chinese of relatively tall stature and relatively dominant brachycephaly came from the North, from that northern region where tall stature is a common character.

Since 70 per cent. of the individuals examined by Koganei exceeded 1 metre 65, the ethnic mixture must have been considerable. But where did the Chinese get the dolichocephalic individuals who figure in their ranks? There are no dolichocephalic people in Northern Asia other than the Ainu, and not even all of them have this character. A number of sub-dolichocephalic Japanese have also been measured. Koganei's series seems to prescribe pretty accurately the two principal cranial forms of Humanity required to make up, from this mixture, the anthropological image of the Chinese.

The same writer has studied a series of skulls from the northern provinces of Chih-li and Shan-tung. The cephalic index is a little less high (78.3) indicating mesocephaly, that is to say, another picture of intermixture. Similar characteristics were found by Gaupp in his work on Chinese examined at Peking—the same high stature (1 metre 67), and mesaticephalic index.

One notices the practical identity of the figures furnished by these two writers.

Three years ago Vaillant, living in Tonking, examined numerous Chinese Hakka established in the Tonkingese province of Moncay. These Chinese, natives of the northern provinces of Shan-tung and Shan-si, had got as far as Tonking by successive migrations which went on during several centuries. The French writer states that in the course of this exodus which gradually brought them south, generation by generation, the Chinese had received some blood from the different peoples among whom they had sojourned.[1] These Hakka are notably lower in stature than the North Chinese (1 metre 646); but their cephalic index has remained exactly the same as that indicated above (80.5). A small number of dolichocephalic types, large numbers of brachycephals, and, especially of mesaticephals—such is here the Chinese picture.

Thus, whether we turn to the Japanese, German, or French series, the greater part of the results remain identical. In Vaillant's series, although the mean stature is lower than in

[1] CCLXI, p. 83.

the preceding series, it still shows numerous tall and even very tall individuals. And this series confirms what we have learned of the morphology of the northern Chinaman (men above the mean height, generally brachycephalic).

Will South China provide us with the same ethnological spectacle ? In order to find out we have but very few data—Legendre's[1] observations in Sze-chwan for the mid-western area ; those of Girard[2] for a small group of Chinese from Kwang-si, a southern province ; and the sufficiently imposing observations of Duncan White[3] on the Chinese Hok-lo of the southwest in the province of Kwan-tung, etc. Without going into details these scanty observations bring out quite obviously that the southern Chinese are both smaller and less often brachycephalic than North Chinamen. Although the stature of the Hok-lo reaches 1 metre 64, that of the other South Chinese does not appear to exceed 1 metre 61. As for the mean cephalic index, it is almost everywhere about 79 to 80.

These few indications, although they are altogether inadequate to represent the anthropological image of China, will yet suffice to demonstrate the heterogeneity of this human group. We must repeat what we said at the beginning of this chapter : the vast republic is not peopled by a "Chinese race" in the zoological sense of the word race.

And thus the cardinal question presents itself—to which of these diverse ethnic groups peopling China are we to turn to see before us the veritable Chinese, the founders of the ancient empire ? Were they the North or the South Chinese ?

According to certain historians the first "Hundred Families" from whom the Chinese derive their origin[4] settled, after many peregrinations, in the provinces now known as Chih-li and Shan-si, in the country lying between the Hwang-ho on the south and the southern ranges of the northern Shan-si mountains, in that immense bend which the river makes before it flows into the sea.

The two or three indications we possess as to the anthropological characters of this area show that it is peopled by tall men, in the majority brachycephalic, with a small

[1] **CXXXVII**, p. 158.
[2] **LXXX**.
[3] **LXV**, p. 278.
[4] **CIXC**, p. 415.

cranial capacity and having a relatively high and narrow face with leptorrhinian nasal index.

It is said that the "Hundred Families," surrounded on all sides by uncivilized people, or at least people less civilized than themselves, little by little conquered these lower people and incorporated them in their pale.

To which of the two main groups revealed by our analyses are we to attach those legendary "Hundred Families"? To which of the principal Asiatic groups who shared the soil of China are we to attribute the important historic events which inaugurated the Celestial Empire?

It has been said that China was created by the centrifugal action of the primitive "Hundred Families." Is it not rather centripetal action which we should invoke?—The action, chiefly, of the Mongols, it would seem. The desire for an easier material existence may have drawn the peoples of the great mountain mass of the West towards the fertile lowlands of the East. In any case such action appears to have been more likely than that this country was peopled from the South—from the region of Burma and Tonking.

The diversity we notice in the Chinese stature from south to north might help us to discover the motherland from which this peopling was accomplished. The Indo-Chinese peoples are all much smaller than the Chinese themselves. In the North, on the contrary, the population is all taller. But we must frankly recognize that we are still very ill-informed. The hypotheses we put forward are very fragile. There is nothing to prove that someday they will become reality.

Considerable weight has been given to the share of the Lolos[1]—they number 3 million souls in the western provinces of Sze-chwan and Yun-nan, mountain countries difficult to penetrate—in the primitive formation of the Chinese people. Such a supposition would come somewhere midway between the two main hypotheses of a northern and southern origin.

To sum up, the Chinese anthropological problem remains unsolved by anything that has yet been published. Its solution will be a lengthy matter. New China may well find among her future young intellectuals men qualified to undertake this important work.

[1] **CCXLIX**, p. 211; **XLIX**, No. 5.

In any case it is certain that the strenuous endeavour to link up Chinese and Indians will lead to nothing. These peoples are very different one from the other. Just because certain legends have it that China was once conquered by refractory " Kshattryas tribes who, after having crossed the Ganges and wandered for some time in Bengal, crossed the eastern mountains and spread themselves in the south of the Celestial Empire "[1] there is no reason why we should acquiesce in such tales. Anthropology is somewhat more difficult to satisfy !

[1] **LXXXIV**, p. 466.

CHAPTER X

THE JAPANESE

WHEN the Flemish Franciscan Rubruquis (Guillaume de Rubrouéek) and the Venetian traveller Marco Polo made Japan known to Europe that country had been an organized empire, with its own laws and head, for nearly two thousand years—if we are to credit its history.

For a long time, up to the close of the nineteenth century, the history of Japan was to be unfolded entirely within its own domains, and it was the Japanese "race," without any intermixture with foreign elements, that during that period lived and recorded that history.

The knowledge of the West came to Japan principally through the Portuguese Jesuits, and later through the Dutch navigators and the Englishman, Will Adams, Pilot Major of the Dutch fleet which arrived at Nagasaki in 1600.[1] Thereafter the whole of Europe and the United States began to trade with the Empire of the Rising Sun, and it was then that we really began to know the " petits hommes jaunes aux yeux bridés."

During the last half century the Japanese have retraced, with incredible velocity, the main chapters of world History; and thinking men—who like neither wars nor conquest—are asking themselves to what terrestrial limits this extraordinary people will push their destinies, and how far this island folk, by seizure of Asiatic territory, will become the master of great continental regions.

Are these profound modern modifications in the social life of Japan associated with the arrival of foreign blood? We know very well that this is not so and that there is no particular ethnic reason to seek, no racial substitution to imagine, by way of an explanation of these formidable events.

[1] A portion of this fleet arrived at Nagasaki on April 19th, 1600. To Will Adams it was due that the foundations of English trade with Japan were laid, and also that the Dutch Settlement was founded.

The anthropological characters of the Japanese have been more fully studied than those of the Chinese. This is firstly because Europeans have been particularly interested, for quite diverse reasons, in the Japanese, owing to the incessant transformations of that country, and secondly because the Japanese themselves have " come into the movement " with enthusiasm since the creation of their Universities. They have become praiseworthy anthropologists and ethnographers, and the list both of their savants in these two disciplines of the natural sciences, and of their publications, is already a long one.[1]

The earliest writers to attempt morphological descriptions of the peoples of the empire believed they had discovered several types among the Japanese, among others what have been called—after Baelz, I think—the fine and the coarse type. By this rudimentary observation they had already marked the heterogeneity of this " race."

The first was an urban type, especially characterized among the upper classes of the nation. Its physical attributes were a greater stature than those of the other type, a relatively longer head and a leptoprosopic face. The obliquity of the eyes did not exist, one might almost say, in this section of the population save in a certain portion of the womenkind.

The second type was smaller : its head was shorter, and the palpebral lids slightly oblique (though less so than in the Chinese). Instead of the straight nose characteristic of the fine type the people of this group had a flat one.

But are these simply individual dimorphisms, such as are presented by all ethnic groups and of which certain temporary associations had struck the observers ? Or are we, on the contrary, really in the presence of descendants of human groups, primitively different, and who, having arrived together, created by their union the Japanese nation of to-day ?

Has the Empire of the Rising Sun succeeded to the ancient Ainu territory, as the anthropologist Koganei considers ?

Japanese writers are far from being in agreement on the subject of early origins in their ethnogenic home. And it is

[1] For an English book on the ancient Japanese, see *Prehistoric Japan*, by Dr. N. G. Munro, Yokohama and Edinburgh, 1911, with a chapter on the " Prehistoric Races ", illustrated by the author's own craniological material. A more recent summary of work done in Japan will be found in " Notes on the Stone Age People of Japan ", in *Am. Anthrop.* N. S., xxiii, 1921, pp. 50-76, by H. Matsumoto. (Translator's Note.)

difficult for anyone who has not first-hand knowledge of the prehistoric collections of the Japanese museums, and of the human skeletons recovered from the various horizons of the remote past history of Japan, to take sides on this question.

According to Tsuboi, the Japanese neolithic people consisted of two different races, one occupying the Riu-Kiu (Luchu) islands and Formosa, and, among other ethnographic characteristics, having no knowledge of stone arrow-heads.

In the island of Hondo (the main island) and in Yezo (the Hokkaido), on the contrary, the people did make arrow-heads of stone, worked bone and deer-horn, and made human figurines in clay. The stone axe-heads, also, are of different shape from those in the southern islands.

Taking only the large islands into consideration—central Japan—one finds that there is still no agreement among the Japanese savants as to the earliest ancestry of the people of Nippon. According to some it is the Ainu, whereas according to others the Ainu were preceded by an earlier folk.

Tsuboi, one of the leaders of the latter school, bases his opinion on the skeletal differences that exist between the oldest human remains he has studied, and the Ainu and the Japanese; on the fact that the most primitive figurines are never shown with any beard—so plentiful in the Ainu—and on various ethnographic characters, into which it is unnecessary to enter here, relating to diet, type of habitation, etc. This folk figures in the Ainu traditions—a very small folk whom they call the Koropok-guru.

Other writers do not credit this hypothesis. According to them the Koropok-guru, the creation of legend, are only an imaginary people. Koganei has shown that the stature of the neolithic people was no smaller than that of the present-day Ainu, and, for the rest, that their respective morphology is not sufficiently different to permit of any belief in the existence of two dissimilar races one of which was superposed on the other in the course of time.

The relative age of the kitchen-middens may bring support to the theory of an Ainu origin. These heaps, of various periods, are the less ancient as one goes further north. Thus these deposits mark the northward track which was taken by the Ainu migration.

Moreover those Ainu who have never come under Japanese influences do not know the legend of their hypothetical predecessors, the Koropok-guru; neither do those who came from the northern Kuriles to the southern islands. Furthermore, how would it be possible—if we are to credit the pre-Ainu hypothesis—that the Ainu themselves should leave no trace of their passage or their sojourn? The neolithic remains must belong to them.

This opinion would seem to be that of the great majority of Japanese authorities to-day (Torii, Koganei, etc.). But if the Japanese empire was really once Ainu territory, two questions still arise: what is the origin of the present Japanese population as a whole, so very different, morphologically, on the whole, from the Ainu? And what influences did the Ainu exert both on the composition of the present population and on its historical development?

Baelz, and with him many other savants, Japanese, American, and European, sum up the successive population of Japan in the following manner.

The Ainu constituted the substratum of the Japanese population.[1] They themselves belonged to an ensemble of peoples related to the Caucasic peoples, who were broken up by the arrival of the Turki-Mongols. A part of this people, thus broken up, moved west (thus a portion of the Russians would be their descendants); the other came to the Pacific shore, crossed the sea and peopled the Japanese archipelago. It is all quite simple!

But when we come to compare the anthropological characters of the Ainu with those of the Japanese, we cannot help feeling some doubt as to the ethnic influence of the former. As it is, their language and their ethnography removed them completely from the Japanese. Do not the anthropologists tell us that the Ainu differ from all the other peoples of Asia? And it is not easy to bring any confirmatory evidence of the relationship that is supposed to have been formed between them and the Caucasic peoples. We know that de Quatrefages approximated the Ainu to the Nilgiri Todas, whose complexion, however, is darker. Nevertheless, the illustrious

[1] Charency, **XLVI**, is of opinion that the Ainu were preceded by Negritos in the south of the archipelago. They were followed by the Pit-dwellers, related to the North American Indians, and then by the Koropok-guru indicated above; finally the Ainu arrived from Korea and also Malayo-Polynesians. According to this author, the Japanese, properly so-called, mixed with the Chinese elements in Korea, landed in Nippon in the early part of the Christian era. What questions this raises!

anthropologist did not go so far as to believe that there was any filiation between the two groups.[1] In his opinion both of them belong " to a common stock, possibly to the regular-featured, bearded race which some travellers have noted as existing in the north of China."

Japanese historians say that the Ainu inhabited the whole of Nippon many hundreds of years B.C., and up till the seventh century of our era they were still to be found in occupation of the northern quarter of the island. But who can say what ethnic influence these people left behind them (this influence is supposed to be traced in pilous characters) even in this region which is supposed to be the only one in which such a filiation research could be attempted ?

On top of this layer of descendants of Central Asiatics (??) the Manchu-Koreans are supposed to have arrived (but where did they, in their turn, come from ?). The tall stature of the latter—among other physical features—distinguished them from the descendants of the earlier occupants. They would first have peopled Hondo, then from the main island would have gradually spread to the others.

A third human layer was then formed by the Mongols or Malayo-Mongols.

To-day it is quite certain that these are gratuitous hypotheses : their bases are not sufficiently well-founded ; no serious work extending to all parts of Japan, and probing sufficiently deeply, has yet been recorded. No really pertinent data are forthcoming for any one region. It is certain that several of the morphological characters of the Japanese—stature for example—approximate them more closely to the Ainu than to the Chinese-Mongols. On the other hand the Ainu envisaged alone are an altogether inadequate factor to account for the peopling of Japan as we know it to-day. They cannot by themselves be considered as the ethnic forbears of the Japanese—far from it.

We must therefore seek elsewhere.

After having drawn attention to the " variety and multiplicity of races " contributing to the formation of the Japanese type, de Quatrefages turned his regard to India, that " reservoir of peoples." He finds, to begin with, that the Negrito element—both mainland and island—has completely fused

[1] **CCIX**, p. 469.

with the Japanese, among whom "there has not been found, so far as I know, a single representative comparable with certain Sakais or with certain Dravidians." But, he says, the presence of this element in a portion of the population is witnessed both by tradition and by the proverb recorded by Dr. Maget: "Half the blood in one's veins must be black to make a good Samurai." Then, like other anthropologists, he turned naturally to the Yellow peoples, the Chinese and Manchus from China and Korea, and to two different twigs of the same racial branch. I mention these suppositions merely to call them to mind.

Looked at from the viewpoint of their general characters the modern Japanese are small men (about 1 metre 58 to 1 metre 59 for the males, according to Koganei; 1 metre 47 for the females[1]. The mean cephalic index (present-day series) is 78.2, according to Deniker. This shows mesaticephaly. The fine type shows a higher proportion of dolichocephalic and the coarse type a larger proportion of brachycephalic heads.

It has been claimed that the Kuro-Siwo was the highway by which the Malayo-Polynesians found their way to Japan. It is quite possible. But is it not more credible that coastwise navigation, which keeps the mariner constantly in touch with the mainland and gives him that comforting feeling of always having land in sight (and this must have been of particular importance for the earliest seamen), would have gradually brought the islanders to Korea and even to Japan far more easily than the current itself? Or, at least, as far as Formosa? I am well aware that the Kuro-Siwo approaches both Formosa and the Riu-Kiu islands (the Luchus). The natives of the Riu-Kiu archipelago resemble the Japanese, it would seem. Their height is about the same (1 metre 58), but their skin is darker, and their facial hair more plentiful. Still, we shall not, on this account, imagine a relationship between the Riu-Kiu islanders and the Ainu!

As for the inhabitants of Formosa, they can only have the most distant relationship with the Japanese.

[1] Koreans are taller, about 1 metre 63. So are North-Chinamen. The Japanese height recalls that of the Ainu—1 metre 57 for men, and 1 metre 46 for women, according to Baelz. The cephalic index of the Ainu, according to the same author, has a somewhat lower mean than 78. The latest authority whom one can quote, Montandon, finds 1 metre 595 for the men and 1 metre 487 for the women. According to him the cephalic indices are 75.45 (men) and 76.39 (women). Those of Koganei are somewhat higher for both sexes. **CLXII**, p. 233.

We know very little of the physical features of the inhabitants of this island. Legend claims that it was first inhabited by Pygmies. The population, of a bronzed brown colour, seems to be taller than the Japanese (1 metre 60). Stature, however, presents great variation in both directions. It is interesting to note that the population appears to be most distinctly short-limbed, as are also the Chinese. The cephalic index, on the living, shows sub-dolichocephaly: but both genuine brachycephals and genuine dolichocephals[1] are to be found there.

In the discussion relating to the formation of the American peoples it has been suggested that various Asiatics arrived in both the Americas and as early as in prehistoric times. We shall return to this hypothesis. In this way the Japanese would have played their part in the constitution of several American groups. But naturally this would have been an involuntary rôle. Carried by ocean currents, Japanese junks would have reached the West coasts of America. From the extreme south of Alaska as far as southern Mexico traces of their landings would be found.

We know that the laws of ancient Japan forbade the construction of vessels capable of sailing the high seas. The authorities of those days did not desire that the Japanese should carry news of Japan too far afield. In the seventeenth century the law punished with death any Japanese who went too far from his native land. When this did happen, the shipwrecked people, blown by the winds, or carried by the currents, stayed where chance took them ashore. De Quatrefages has published, following C. W. Brooks in the main, a map showing the Japanese landings on the American coast.[2]

It is possible that these small Japanese groups, thus unexpectedly arrived on American soil, may have left a little of their blood in the veins of the natives of that great continent. These involuntary emigrants " were necessarily absorbed into the tribes which received them. But this infiltration, continued through centuries, none the less had a real influence on the local races." Still this infiltration has yet to be demonstrated by less doubtful observations.

Nevertheless, it is possible that there was an effective relationship between the Japanese and certain native Americans.

[1] **CCLVIII.**
[2] **CCIX**, p. 558, 559.

But it goes back further than the accidental landfall of Japanese junks on the American coasts. If that continent was really peopled from Asia, as it becomes more and more widely believed was the case, and if, on the other hand, the ancient peoples of Japan really came, in part at least, from the Korean mainland (and still further north, from Northern Siberia)[1], certain Americans and certain Japanese might be considered as the two branches of a common tree. In this connection the reader is asked to refer to the chapter in which the American peoples are dealt with.

The ethnogeny of Japan is one of the most interesting problems set to the sagacity of anthropologists. My impression is that, like the Chinese problem, it is still a long way from solution.

[1] V. Stefánsson has demonstrated in *Museum Bulletin No. 6.*, (*Anthrop. Series, No.* 3) published by the Canada Geological Survey, December 30th, 1914, dealing with "Prehistoric and Present Commerce among the Arctic Coast Eskimo" that regular trade communication between Alaska and Siberia was kept up by the Alaskan Eskimo, *over the ice, by sled*, the imports being chiefly reindeer skins (p. 2). He estimates that a Siberian trade article, such as a knife, would probably take five years to reach Hudson Bay from western Alaska. The paper throws a valuable sidelight on the question of intercourse between the two continents in prehistoric times. (Translator's Note.)

PART IV

THE RACES OF AFRICA

THE African races properly so-called, apart from the races of Egypt and a part of North Africa,[1] have not taken part in History as that word is intended by historians. Doubtless, as we have seen, prehistoric civilizations flourished on African soil. And the Africans of those days could rightfully take their place side by side with the Europeans who knew the same civilizations (we do not say at the same period).

If, as we may believe, an African contingent came to people Europe in the palæolithic period, it would not seem that we can find their descendants at any particular moment of written history. I do not shrink from the admission that we have in our veins a few drops of some African blood—the blood of a yellow-skinned African, likely enough—but we must admit that it is very difficult to find what is left of it.

Two human races alone, then, of those inhabiting Africa, have played an effective part in world History : first and foremost, and in no mean fashion, the Egyptians ; secondly the North African peoples.

[1] We hesitate to speak of the Abyssinians.

CHAPTER I

THE EGYPTIANS

After endless discussion the origin of the Egyptian race is to-day generally sought in Egypt itself and the Egyptians considered to be "autochthones" of the Nile valley. It should be added, however, that several savants, and not the least among them, still look upon Asia as the place of origin of the Egyptian people. Is this another instance of the persistent Oriental mirage? For example, in the opinion of men of the worth of de Morgan and Amelineau, Mesopotamia, whence came so many plant species, must be considered the cradle of the race which the Pharaohs led to such high destinies. So many ethnographic similarities permit of the supposition. Schweinfurth considers southern Arabia as one of the most important dispersal centres of mankind; and that it is to this region we must turn our regard when we seek the origin of the Nilotic peoples—thus the Egyptians would have issued from this radiating centre! He, however, speaks essentially as a botanist. His evidence for this anthropological filiation is to be found in the route taken by various plants, among others, *Persea*, a medicinal plant of the family Boraginaceæ (the present-day *Cordia myxa*), still widely employed in the East for the same purposes for which we use jujubes; and of *Ficus Sycomorus L.*, the wood of which was used by the ancient Egyptians for mummy coffins.

These writers, whatever their opinions, happily take us some way beyond the eighteenth century accounts, in which a Winkelmann, for instance, makes the Egyptians immigrants from China; or the translator of the younger Pliny, Poinsinet de Sivry, sees in them descendants of the Celts; or Denon, who, though he followed Bonaparte in Egypt, stated that the Egyptians belonged to the Caucasic race!

The idea that the Egyptians are indigenous was not born yesterday. The anthropologists who have maintained this opinion were only confirming what the Egyptians themselves believed, who, like many another people, felt that they were born of the soil on which they lived. But was their land of origin the middle and lower Nile valley only, or must we extend the field of our research to far more southerly regions[1], and pursue them westwards even, into those wide areas, so uncertain in their contour, of the Sudan? The Great Lakes region has been considered to be the cradle of the African races, probably with reason. A few years ago Henry S. Wellcome discovered in the southern Sudan, to the west of the Blue Nile, near Sennar, imposing souvenirs of a neolithic civilization on which had been superposed the remains of bronze and iron age civilizations. Among the Egyptologists who believed in the African origin of the Egyptian people we must quote Maspèro, Naville, and others besides. In their opinion the characters of the Egyptians are the same as those of the races of the Libyan mainland bordered by the Mediterranean: these Mediterranean peoples would have moved into Egypt.

Anthropological research in regard to the Nilotic peoples was at first undertaken chiefly by Americans—Nott and Gliddon[2], Morton[3], etc. Now that the number of works is considerable, is everything quite clear? Are all our problems solved? Most decidedly not.

Champollion has given the well-known picture of the human races of ancient Egypt after the paintings in the royal tombs of Bibân el Molûk (The Valley of the Kings). These men, led by the shepherd of the Horus peoples, belonged to four distinct families. The first, the nearest to the god, were of a dark red colour, well proportioned and with gentle physiognomy, slightly aquiline nose, long plaited hair, and clothed in white. Legend has given these folk the name of Rot-en-ne-rome, the human race, the men par excellence, that is to say—the Egyptians. There is no doubt whatever about him who comes next: he belongs to the Negro race known under the general name of *Nehasi*. The next one presents a very different aspect: his skin is fresh-coloured, verging on yellow; he is bronzed, with a strongly aquiline nose, and a thick black pointed beard, and he wears a short garment of many colours. This race bears the name of *Aamu*

[1] **CCXCI**, p. 328.
[2] **CLXXVIII**.
[3] **CLXVI**, *bis*.

(Asiatics). Finally, the last has the skin colour we call fresh-coloured or white-skinned in its most delicate tint, and a straight, slightly arched nose, blue eyes, fair or ruddy beard, and is very tall and slim ; he is clothed in an undressed bullock-hide, a veritable savage, tatooed on different parts of his body ; this race is called *Tamahu* (Europeans).[1]

Thus, if we can count on the accuracy of the paintings described by Champollion, and on the correctness of their interpretation, the Eygptian race would have had an aquiline nose and red-brown skin. These are not Negro characters. On the other hand, the skin-colour will not allow of our confounding this type with the clear-skinned Mediterranean peoples. The inscription at Bibân-el-Molûk shows no hesitation in differentiating the Egyptians from the Asiatics and Europeans. Therefore, it would seem, research should be directed in two directions—towards the analysis of skeletal remains—and mummies—throughout the entire country, especially of those dating from the earliest periods of Egyptian history, and then towards seeking whether there still exists in the Nile valley and the lands surrounding Egypt any peoples who might be recognized as those from whom the ancient Egyptians were derived.

Anthropological and historical research in Egypt has aroused so much interest among the savants of the whole world that thousands of crania and mummies have been extracted from graves and necropoles. Unfortunately a large portion of these data are of uncertain date. De Quatrefages and Hamy had already drawn attention to this : " In order to get a real knowledge of the ancient Egyptian type and the variations it has undergone throughout the centuries which separate the pyramid builders from the reign of Alexander it would be necessary to study separately and then to compare the large series of specimens taken from the necropoles whose date had been archæologically established with certainty ". Broca attempted such an analysis with human remains properly dated by Mariette. And others as well. Among the latest anthropologists to have attempted an ethnological synthesis

[1] *Tamahu* is translated " Libyans " by the authorities of the Egyptian Dept. of the British Museum. The word for " mankind " is *Romut*. (Translator's Note.)

of ancient Egypt Ernest Chantre and G. Eliot Smith[1] must be mentioned first and foremost.

Have the materials recovered always adequately differentiated the true Egyptians from the ancient subjects of the Pharaohs? Did the Egyptians, at the beginning of their history, constitute a pure race? And throughout all the subsequent periods, did they make any effort to prevent foreign blood from penetrating their veins?

A priori we may suppose that the cities of Egypt, thanks to their wide-spread renown, must have been cities whose tentacles drew to them all the surrounding peoples. The most apt among the foreigners—or the more favoured—would rank as Egyptians. And did not the historic invasions, at any rate the principal ones such as those of the Hyksos and the Assyrians, contribute new elements to the breed? It would be necessary to study the morphological characters of the conquering races side by side with the Egyptian race properly so-called.

Eur-Asiatic travellers of every period, struck by the grandeur of the Nilotic civilization, have left us descriptions of the Egyptian physique. Some of them date very far back. The year 484 B.C. saw the birth of a man at Halicarnassus in Caria whose travels were to revolutionize the mentality of his period in many ways. When Herodotus embarked he carried with him every prospect of success. He was wealthy, well educated, and took with him powerful credentials. But he had many preconceived ideas. He believed in the modifying influence of environment on mankind. Two thousand years before Montesquieu or Rousseau he wrote: "Since the Egyptians are born and bred under a climate that is different from all other climates and since the Nile is of very different nature from all other rivers, so do their customs and laws differ from those of most other nations". He sojourned a long while in Egypt. He it is who first made known the Pygmies. He tells how the Ethiopians maintained that Egypt was only a

[1] Elliot Smith has published a series of anthropological studies on the human remains excavated in the course of the Archæological Survey of Nubia. Unfortunately he did not establish all the comparisons that one might have hoped for from such a piece of work. Still, his contributions to the Report on this survey are a mine of invaluable information from which can be extracted just those comparative elements necessary to a synthesis.

Nevertheless, as I have already pointed out, there is a crying need to-day for an exhaustive craniometrical study which would bring together all the data already published, and others still lying in museums unpublished.

colony, its people coming from that great region of Meroe which extends east of Khartum between the Nile and the Atbara. Thus the Sudan would be the primitive homeland of the ancient Egyptians.

Those who refuse to admit the autochthony of the Egyptians declare that there are no monuments in Nubia earlier than the conquest of that country by the Pharaohs, imagining that in this absence of evidence lies the proof of their assertions. But monumental art was not born along with the Egyptians by a sort of accessory act of spontaneous generation. The most ancient uncoffined interments are much earlier than the sumptuous tombs. It is rather as though one were to say that there had never been any Frenchmen in places where there are no Gothic Cathedrals!

All the elements of one civilization cannot appear at the same moment. No people, however civilized, has begun in any other way than in a condition of "barbarism." The primitive Egyptians were probably a pastoral people who succeeded a hunting and fishing people. When they had finally settled in this geographical area which so generously assured them a living, a land so admirably bounded that one might search in vain on the map for a more precisely delimitated territory, the Egyptians proceeded to the agricultural stage. And on this soil whose fertility is still, after thousands of years, quoted as a marvel, and in this narrow valley which the desert protects against invasions, pacific or warlike, the Egyptian race has gradually created its own civilization.

How many centuries have flowed by between this supposed setting out from Meroe and the birth of that monumental art of which it is demanded that it should prove the existence of the Egyptian? We have absolutely no knowledge. But what we can state is that Egypt was peopled thousands of years before the "Egyptian monuments" were thought of. Like the rest of Africa, Egypt has its palæolithic and neolithic civilizations.[1]

Still, as we meet with traces of these civilizations well to the south of Egypt properly so-called, and, on the other side of the Great Lakes, right into southern Africa, we see no reason why the primitive peopling of the Nile valley should not have been effected from the south. We say, however, the primitive peopling, for Egypt, such as we understand it, was to be born

[1] See note at end of chapter (p. 432).

after some thousands of years' sojourn and after the passing of successive phases of civilization. But whereabouts in the southern Nilotic regions shall we find the precise area of this autochthony and of this departure ?

Edouard Naville gave an account to the International Congress of Anthropology and Prehistoric Archæology of 1912 (held in Geneva)[1] of his personal recollections of the discovery of the palæolithic Egyptian civilization by Lenormant and Hamy in 1869. The classical Egyptologists, led by the German, Lepsius, were for long to deny to the inhabitants of the Nile valley the honour of such a remote antiquity.

It happened when the Suez Canal was being opened. The boats with the invited guests were halted at Luxor. Lenormant and Hamy, with the rest, crossed the ridge separating the valley of Bibân el Molûk from the amphitheatre of rocks where the Dêr-el-Bahri temple stands, in order to visit the Valley of the Kings. "To do this they followed a narrow path much improved since then, as it is the one taken by Cook's tourists. At the top of the hill they stopped, dumb with astonishment. They had stumbled upon a work floor of flaked flints, still intact, such as one frequently saw then on the Theban hills. You can imagine that they returned triumphant, and on the boat they brought out of their pockets all the flints with which they had crammed them. The same evening we were invited to the Empress's boat, and I can still see Lenormant showing her Imperial Majesty these primitive implements, of which similar specimens, he said, were at the Musée de Saint-Germain. Probably I am the only witness who can tell of this scene. Those who were there, like the poet Ibsen, the painters Fromentin and Gérôme, the sculptor Guillaume, and many others, are no more. Hence I consider it to be my duty as an Egyptologist to testify to you that the first authentic discovery of a stone age in Egypt was due to two French savants, MM. Lenormant and Hamy.

And what, you will say, happened on the next day ? Lepsius went off immediately to this work floor, whose exact site had been indicated to him, and he too brought back a rich harvest—but to draw from it a conclusion diametrically opposed to that of the two French savants. He would not admit that these flints were other than natural productions. Mariette,

[1] **CLXX**, p. 102.

whom we saw shortly afterwards, was of the same opinion. For the rest, he published his views in several works. The following winter Lepsius wrote a long article in the German Journal of Egyptology, maintaining that the Theban flints differed so greatly from those which had been discovered in the graves that it was impossible for him to consider them as humanly worked. Lepsius died without changing his opinion; he never believed in an Egyptian stone age; and to-day, after long years, his disciple presides over the closing session of a Congress of prehistoric archæology."[1]

Mariette, wiser than Lepsius, or merely possessed of a more "scientific" conscience, was not slow to convince himself that he had been wrong. He frankly went back on his prejudices, and, feeling in some obscure way all that would issue from the study of African prehistory, he announced, in 1870, at the Institut Égyptien that "stepping aside from the known paths of Egyptian archæology, he was about to begin the study of worked flints at Thebes."

Typologically, the palæolithic Egyptian implements appear to be very similar to those of Europe. Unfortunately any chronological parallelism between the two regions is impossible for the moment. In Egypt flaked flints are found on the foothills of the two chains encircling the Nile, especially in the soil of the Libyan chain. A few finds have been made under stratigraphical conditions suggesting that a very great antiquity must be attributed to the objects discovered because they were found in alluvia dating from a period anterior to that of the drift deposited by the alluvial system of this valley. No human skeletal remains dating from the Pleistocene have been met with.

Those implements known as of neolithic period are very plentifully represented. There are numerous stations, and some of them occupy large areas.

The scattered material from work-floors is found over dozens of miles—arrow-heads, finely finished blades, knives, scrapers, awls, etc., and the hatchets in hard rock characteristic of this phase of industry. In the scrapheaps known as sebakh, which the Fellahin exploit as manure, are found neolithic

[1] Perhaps priority in this discovery should be accorded to Arcelin, the Mâcon geologist, who, in the winter of 1868-9, found at El Kab at Bibân el Molûk numerous flint objects such as blades, nuclei, hammer-stones, a scraper of Moustierian type, etc., on the borders of the desert and the cultivated ground. The historians must carefully verify and compare the dates.

implements mingled with objects in bone and a few copper articles.

It is probable that copper appeared at an earlier stage in Egypt than in Europe. In the earth burials Flinders Petrie has found crouched skeletons whose grave goods included copper and bronze needles side by side with flint tools and imperfectly baked pottery.[1]

The detailed study of these primitive burials is of great ethnographic interest. Funerary rites were not always identical. The body, which was not in those days subjected to the process of mummification, was placed just as it was on the ground, or in a jar, or on the skin of some animal. Why these variations in rite? Did this mean that the people were different, or that they were different classes of the same population?

The utilization of flint must have gone on long after the neolithic period. The metal ages had begun in Egypt many centuries before the use of flint implements was discontinued. Certain writers think that the use of such implements was maintained up till the 12th dynasty, although, from the fifth dynasty onwards one sees attempts at the use of iron mingled with the copper and bronze objects.

Before anthropological study had been systematized or had been given those exact foundations which we recognize to-day, it had often been sought to give a picture of the ancient Egyptians. The data at first employed were paintings and sculptures. These last, it was said, must have been faithful representations of the individual because of the religious belief in the double.

The earliest attempts at characterizing the human form gave men oval faces, lips that were very little prominent, and short hair.[2] Statues exist from the third dynasty onwards.

[1] This was written prior to Sir Flinders Petrie's discovery of the new Badarian civilization in 1924 which he characterizes as the "oldest culture known" (in the descriptive catalogue of the objects found), and which, after the further work in the season 1924-5, he now refers to a definite chronological period. Forty-eight skulls from a pre-Chellian level have also been found, and when the anthropological report on these is published there should emerge some definite proof of the provenance of the earliest palæolithic culture in ancient Egypt. Sir Flinders Petrie has stated that he considers the Badarian civilization to have come from Asia. The recent season's work has revealed, he stated in a lecture describing the recent discoveries, that the Badarians had boats, wove linen, ground corn, and used bone harpoons extensively. (Translator's Note.)

[2] CLXIV.

Can we consider them of any use as anthropological documents representing not only individuals (we must not forget that some names were substituted for others on certain statues) but as a synthesis of an ethnic type ? It has been said that various statues of the first dynasties, the celebrated wooden statue of Sheikh el Beled, for example, recall with precision the present-day Copt type.

Such representations may have been perfect ; but a naturalist may be forgiven for preferring—and very much preferring—the anatomical documents themselves to these paintings and sculptures.

From the Memphite period (which roughly extends from 4,400 to 3,200) onwards we possess a fair number of human remains collected from many places—Neqâda, El Amra, El Khosam, Saqqâra, etc. The crania recovered show themselves to be distinctly dolichocephalic (mean index about 74) and mesorrhinian (nasal index of the women, 51.06, slightly higher than for the men, 48). Dolichocephaly is a character pointing in the Negro direction, but mesorrhiny is not. And by means of these anthropological documents Verneau was able to reach the conclusion that " we must not go to the north for terms of comparison but well to the south and southwest, among the Ethiopians and the Fulani, among whom cross-breeding has not yet caused the ethnic characters of the two old prehistoric races of Egypt to disappear entirely."

This is the point at which we should remember a certain fact. We have already said that it has been sought to establish filiation between the ancient Egyptians and the Asiatic peoples with the aid of ethnographic similarities. And we must not lose sight of the fact that Asia, throughout a large portion of its territory, is a land of Brachycephals. If the Turki peoples are sub-Brachycephals, the Kurds, Armenians, Tajiks and Lurs are Brachycephals having high indices (Kurds 86,[1] Armenians 85, Tajiks 84.9, Lurs 84.5). These are far removed from the characters furnished by a study of the Egyptians. It is true that we should add that amidst this great brachycephalic mass of Asia we do meet with some dolichocephalic types, notably in the region of the eastern Mediterranean, where the Arabs show relatively very long heads[2].

[1] A certain number of Kurds are not brachycephalic.

[2] Moreover, all important as it is, cranial morphology must not alone be taken into account. To it must be added the other somatological and descriptive characteristics of which the sum serves to create the race.

To this period of civilization, of which Memphis was a kind of irradiating centre, the Theban period succeeded. It was then—perhaps from the twelfth dynasty onwards—that the Hyksos invasions took place. "It came to pass, I know not how, that God was averse to us, and there came, after a surprising manner, men of ignoble birth out of the eastern parts, and had boldness enough to make an expedition into our country, and with ease subdued it by force, yet without hazarding a battle with them."[1] Writers admit that during this domination, which lasted 500 years, there came to Egypt many Syrians and Israelites (what were their anthropological characters ?), and the primitive purity of the race was disturbed by these invaders. We may add that many of the Pharaohs who were great builders of monuments brought into the Nile valley large numbers of slaves taken in the neighbouring countries of Libya and Syria.

If we are to admit the arrival of these various foreigners as certain, we still have to find out what these contributions represented in numbers, and then what their ethnic influence may have been. Many times in the course of this work we have maintained the view that we nearly always get a false idea of the anthropological value of invasions. Warlike irruptions, especially in these remote epochs and in localities where communication with the rear could only be kept up with difficulty, could be accomplished only by small contingents. This numerical weakness itself assured their rapid movement, that is to say, their success. The seizure of a country must have been much more in the nature of an administrative conquest than of a complete ethnic occupation. The subjugated peoples remained where they were and accepted the laws of the victors ; and thus the anthropological characteristics of the conquered region could not have been greatly modified. As for slaves, it is not probable that they ever intermarried with the Egyptians of those days.

It would not seem that the ethnic groups which lived side by side in Egypt during the Theban period mingled their dead. The Ethiopians had their own hypogea, just as the Jews and Negroes had. This observation alone would show that ethnic intermixture must have been rare.

[1] This English version is from Whiston's translation, p. 789, of the *Works of Flavius Josephus*, Bk. i, Sec. 14, of "Flavius Josephus against Apion," in which he quotes from Bk. ii of Manetho's Egyptian History. Edinburgh, 1829. (Translator's Note.)

Excavators have found frequent disturbance of the Egyptian hypogea, and substitutions, which make anthropological research difficult. Chantre, studying crania of the 12th dynasty found that their cephalic index was highly dolichocephalic (73.65). A mesofacial face and mesorrhine nose were associated with this long skull. The mass of the people, however, appeared to be less pure. It has retained to a lesser degree the primitive dolichocephalic characters. A people's hypogeum of the 18th dynasty has provided a mean cephalic index of 76.37. And, which is interesting to note, if these crania of the masses of the people still associate the mesofacial character with dolichocephaly, the nasal characters no longer indicate mesorrhiny but leptorrhiny. Are we to conclude from this observation that a certain number of individuals with the long nose we so frequently meet in eastern Asia[1] (the Kurds and Armenians, for instance) have been intermixed with the Egyptian population ?

Do the Royal families of this period always belong to the primitive Egyptian race, as we might suppose at first sight ? The royal mummies of the 18th, 19th and 20th dynasties enable us to establish a general diagnosis of the ruling type. It is relatively tall (mean of 1 metre 67). Certain kings like Thutmosis II, Rameses II, and Rameses III, are very tall. The smallest of this series is Thutmosis I, whose height was 1 metre 55. We find further proof that the ruling families of the time belong to a tall race in that the estimated stature of the queen Nofritari, of the 18th dynasty, was 1 metre 64, which is relatively very tall for a woman. As to the cranial measurement relations, they always indicate long heads.

Numerous crania were exhumed from the Theban necropoles. Broca had already examined a large series dating from this period. The illustrious anthropologist found a mean cephalic index of about 74 from 40 crania from the necropolis at Dira' Abu'l-negga (11th dynasty), showing dolichocephaly (male skulls 74.20, female 74.62) and a leptorrhine nasal index (mean index of 46). The same writer, examining the skeletal contents of the people's hypogeum at Qūrneh, belonging to a much later epoch (18th dynasty), remarks that the cephalic index has not varied (mean, 74) ; which was later confirmed by Chantre with a series of 35 crania (mean index,

[1] But these long-nosed Asiatics ought also to be Dolichocephals !

73,62). But if, since the 11th dynasty, the cephalic index has remained very nearly the same, the nasal index, on the contrary, has somewhat changed. Primitively leptorrhine, it has become mesorrhine at Qūrneh.

The variety seen in the nasal index tables for this period seems to indicate that the Nile valley did not contain one human type only. The ethnic groups who lived side by side were dolichocephalic, but one of them had a nose relatively much broader than the other. Chantre thought that this last human type should be approximated to the present-day Barabra.[1]

That Egypt in the period of the New Empire showed a larger number of different groups than hitherto need not surprise us. Was this not one of the most disturbed periods of her history? Was it not at this time that Amosis I espoused an Ethiopian woman in order to increase his power in the southeast of Africa? And did he not make use of the strong arms of numerous Syrian and Israelitish immigrants to restore the Empire materially?

The Egyptians themselves were now to begin a series of conquests in all directions. The Egyptian legions, says Maspéro, "took the road to Asia that the remnants of the Hyksos had opened for them and had never forgotten. Henceforth, from the sources of the White Nile to the source of the Euphrates, and throughout Syria, it was continual victory and conquest." It would be somewhat surprising, despite all the reservations we may make on this point, if there did not result from these political and social movements some changes in the ethnic physiognomy of Egypt.

If the contributions of fresh blood came from those regions in which the birth of the Egyptian people may have taken place, that is to say, in the provinces of the Upper Nile peopled by non-Nigritic races (Nubians and Ethiopians), they would not lead to modifications in the physical aspect of the people. But if they came from Asia, especially from the northern regions, from upper Mesopotamia, then we ought to be able to make

[1] Sir Flinders Petrie, describing the results of the excavations of the British School of Archaeology in Egypt at Qau in 1924, at the exhibition, held at University College, of the antiquities found there, states in the Catalogue: "The second discovery is that the princes of Qua were of Galla origin, and were the ancestors of the 12th dynasty". (The Gallas represent the purest Ethiopian type, the Barabra a mixture of Ethiopians, Egyptians, Fellahin, and Arabs. Deniker, **LVII**, pp. 435 and 438, English translation.) (Translator's Note.)

them out, particularly by changes in the cephalic index which would cease to preserve its dolichocephalic character.

The Saite period seems to have been even more disturbed than the Theban. And we ought to be able the more easily to discover ethnic intermixture. There is a poverty in mummies of exalted Egyptian personages in the relevant anthropological documentation, which, however, is rich in material derived from the more popular levels of society. Of the two queens of the 21st dynasty measured by Chantre, Anhapu appears to have been a small woman (1 metre 47), and much less dolichocephalic (cephalic index of 78.33) than her royal predecessors, male or female, whereas with Henttoui we get back to the familiar type.

The general tall stature of the important personages of this, as of the preceding period, is remarkable. There are, however, exceptions. The Memphite noble, Hor Su, of the 26th dynasty, is only 1 metre 58, and the keeper of the lake of the Ammon Kaif-Zart temple is still smaller (1 metre 55). If such tall stature appears to have been the appanage of the greater part of the representatives of the royal families and higher functionaries, was it also characteristic of the other inhabitants of Egypt ?

It is difficult to claim that it was when we see that even the priests of Ammon, discovered at Dêr-el-Bahri by Grébaut in 1891, had only a mean stature of under 1 metre 62. We may say that the cranial morphology of these people appears in several instances to be exceptional, since it shows a highly accentuated brachycephalic character (index exceeding 86), hitherto unknown, and that the same group presents a mean cephalic index of much higher value (80.64) than any hitherto indicated. It is more than probable that these priests of Ammon did not belong to the Egyptian race. Maybe they represented a scheming policy which had placed men who were strangers in the land at the head of the Church ?

The hypogea at Qūrneh and Dêr-el-Bahri have provided numerous series of crania whose cephalic indices remain low and closely approximate to those furnished by the earlier dynasties. Still, the necropolis of Heliopolis, dating from the end of the Saite period, shows a considerable rise in the cephalic index. Were these different necropoles used as the repositories of the dead of different ethnic stocks ?

The wheel of time, however, never ceases turning. Once

again the history of the Nile valley records a transformation. In 330 Alexander conquered Egypt.

It would seem pretty certain that the Greek domination was merely a military and administrative seizure of the country. Greece had not at her disposal a sufficient number of inhabitants to transform her military conquests into genuine colonization. The conquered lands became, in the terminology of the geographers, colonies of exploitation. The Greeks, moreover, seemed to have admirably understood how to conduct themselves in Egypt. Instead of imposing their own civilization they accepted that of the vanquished. They developed the country without straining or altering its ethnographic character. The Ptolemies, in entering the current of Egyptian affairs, were content to take only the first places in the country. To some extent it is what we see happen to-day with the British in India—and also in Egypt.

Egyptian civilization, properly so-called, flourished exceedingly in this environment free from all ethnic compression, and it reached out afresh very far to the south. Just as in the most distant periods of their history, the Egyptians preserved their ethnic physiognomy. The Ptolemies ruled over men who had descended in direct line from the Theban people who themselves were the great-great-grandchildren of the earliest Memphite population. Despite its conquest, the Nile valley still contained between its two parallel mountain chains the same anthropological body with the addition of a few impurities.

There is a geographical doctrine which teaches that the Nile valley is immutable, that it quickly absorbs all the human contributions brought to it, no matter whence they come, and that it reduces them all to uniformity. Has anyone been able to show us this reducing mechanism? Is not such a doctrine merely an easy way of getting out of a difficulty? Would it not be more correct to say that Egypt only rarely received any human contributions whose characters were at variance with those of its own inhabitants?

When real "ethnic strangers" do come to Egypt they most decidedly preserve their own particular morphological characters; they remain more or less pure according to the social position these newcomers occupy. Such social position may either forbid or allow of ethnic intermixture, according to the laws of the groups concerned.

Do we see the twentieth century Egyptians mingling with their British administrative officials?

In the introduction to this chapter we said that the Asiatic origin of the Egyptians, once looked upon with high favour, has gradually lost many of its defenders. But although the great majority of writers to-day favour an African origin for the Egyptian race, they do not agree among themselves as to the locality of its birthplace. Flinders Petrie saw Libyans in the ancient Egyptians. That is possible. But before asserting it positively we must definitely find out what were the anthropological characters of these Libyans. We still know too little of the prehistoric civilizations of North Africa to be able to compare them with those that evolved parallel with them in ancient Egypt.

And then, and this is the main point, we do not yet know the anthropological characters of the Libyan people who were contemporaneous with the ancient Egyptians, the neolithic Egyptians in particular. We know nothing at all, even, of the anthropology of the Numidians of Masinissa. And so long as we are not in possession of this documentation it is better not to be too venturesome.

Further, is it really necessary to go to the Libyans? Did not palæolithic civilization flourish in southern and eastern Africa? And, by way of explaining the appearance of metals, are we not also aware of the frequency of copper in the Great Lakes region and of the extent of the knowledge of iron among the Blacks both now and formerly? Why always invoke Mediterranean influences when the upper Nile area itself can provide all the material elements of primitive civilization?[1]

Whatever knowledge the future may have in store, it seems to us that a sane logic would lead us to seek whether the people who inhabit the banks of the Nile to-day can be morphologically related to the peoples of ancient Egypt. Why may not the present-day Egyptians simply be the

[1] Professor Elliot Smith is also of opinion that the Libyans need not be invoked to explain the origin of the Egyptians. "Thus the new knowledge recently extracted from the graveyards of Nubia has made it abundantly clear that during the fourth millenium B.C. there must have been a series of kindred peoples, scattered along the Nile like beads upon a string, extending far away to the South of Egypt, even unto the land of the Negro. As Egypt's power became consolidated and she entered upon her career of abounding prosperity, these southern communities moved northward one by one, and so came within the ken of the student working on the southern portion of Egypt." G. Elliot Smith, *The Ancient Egyptians*, p. 76.

descendants of the Egyptians of former days, of the Egyptians from time everlasting, such as we have always pictured them?

Before passing on to this comparative examination, I would wish to place before the reader the morphological and descriptive diagnosis of the ancient Egyptians as established by the documentation furnished by art. Chantre, who has collected the data given by earlier writers such as Maspéro, Hamy, Virchow, etc., points out the presence of two synthetic types, of which one is refined and the other coarse, and whose respective physiognomy may be expressed by the following features:

The refined type "is tall and slim, with a proud and imperious deportment. His shoulders were broad, his chest full, his arms sinewy, his hands long and delicate, his hips slender and his limbs spare, the anatomy of his knees and the muscles of the calf standing out under the skin; his feet were long and slender, with a low instep, and they were flattened at the extremity by the habit of going bare-foot. The head is relatively short, the face oval, the forehead slightly retreating; the eyes are large, and the cheekbones not very prominent, the nose is substantial, and straight or slightly aquiline; the mouth is large with full, well defined lips; the teeth are small and even, well-set and in good condition; the ears are high. The skin, white at birth, tans more or less rapidly according to the exposure to the sun and hence according to locality. The men were generally represented as red in colour; the women, less exposed to the strong sun, were painted yellow in the pictures, the tint being lighter according as they belonged to a higher class and came from the south or from the delta. Their hair tended to wave or even curl in ringlets, especially in the south, without ever becoming the wool of the Negro. The hair on the face was scanty and was never thick except on the chin.

"The second, a more vulgar type, but less frequent, was thick-set, stumpy, and heavy. The chest and shoulders are broader in proportion to the loins, there was an ugly and obvious disproportion between the upper and lower part of the body. The loins are narrow and the legs slim. The head is long, slightly compressed in a backward direction and flattened at the top; the face is longer than in the refined type and frequently somewhat prognathous. The nose is straight, or slightly concave and short with wide, open nostrils; the eyes are small and sometimes a little narrow ; the cheeks are round, the chin square and the lips thick but not everted. The features of this type are in general coarse, as if they had been rough-hewn."

We must point out before we go any further that such descriptions must always be accepted with reserve. We do not know how far the artist himself is responsible for the typical character of these representations. We must always be extremely cautious in making use of artistic documents for scientific ends. It would be easy to cite large errors in certain representations—even modern ones—committed in all good faith.

This said, we may state that on certain points there exist sufficiently sharp divergencies between these descriptions and the morphological reality represented by mummies and skeletons. As regards the finer type, the relatively short head shown in the paintings does not correspond with the actuality. Remember the characteristic dolichocephaly of the Egyptians! And is not the white skin rather more white than is natural? Has its palor not a symbolic meaning, representative of aristocracy? As for the indicated difference in stature between the two types, the best thing we can do is to disregard it.

*

* *

We will now pass on to examine the people who still inhabit the Nile valley or its immediate neighbourhood to-day.[1] We shall naturally leave on one side the groups who belong neither to Africa nor Asia, and in whom it would be vain to seek the ancestors of the Egyptians.

The Egyptians have not left Egypt since the fall of the last Pharaohs. Where should we find any trace of such an exodus? But we must discriminate at once between the people of present-day Egypt. We know that the ancient Egyptians were dolichocephals and that they were of rather tall stature. Therefore it is to human groups possessing such characters that we must turn our regard.

If we first consider the Asiatics—we do not thereby follow the writers who sought the very origin of the Egyptians among these folk—we must resolutely eliminate several brachycephalic or sub-brachycephalic groups dwelling in the Nile

[1] XLIII, p. 147.

valley (moreover as relatively unimportant colonies) such as Turks, Armenians, etc. Remain, among those who are geographically nearest to the Egyptians, the Beduin Arabs, the Syrians, and the Jews. It is certain that the resemblance between such and such a Mesopotamian facies and this or that royal mummy is as close as that between two drops of water. But resemblance does not bespeak relationship. We shall return to this again directly. In the meantime let us see what are the characters of the present-day Egyptians, the Copts and the Fellahin.

The 650,000 Copts who inhabit Egypt, especially numerous in the upper Nile valley, and many of whose ethnographic features must go back to a very remote antiquity, are men slightly over the mean height (1 metre 66) among whom tall stature is far from being rare. They are dolichocephals (mean index, 75.40). They include among them a certain proportion of brachycephalic types (about 6.5 per cent.).[1]

The Copt face is relatively short ; the straight nose, with its rounded extremity, shows great variety in its size relations. The hair and eyes of the Copts are brown, the hair being frizzy or curly, the lips are full ; the colour of the skin ranges from dull white to brown, but the darker shades appear to correspond to latitude and to be due to climate, hence to a temporary influence.

As to the Fellahin, they represent the greater part of the Egyptian population—three-fourths of it. These peasants accepted Islam at the time of the Musulman conquest. In this connection it has been said that the Fellahin must have lost their ethnic characters on contact with the Arabs. But why ?

Travellers and savants have often described the Fellahin. At the time of Bonaparte's expedition to Egypt Jonard indicated the stature above the average, long body, broad shoulders and chest, and rather slender legs without much calf, etc., of this population. Are we not sensible in such a description of the influence of Egyptian painting and sculpture, and the desire to associate the characters of the living population with those of the earliest occupants of the soil as represented by their monuments ?

[1] To explain this intrusion we may at once recall that there have been, at given moments in ancient Egyptian history, after foreign intermixture, indices tending to brachycephaly, notably in periods of the later dynasties. Many of the Theban kings, even, had mesaticephalic indices.

A few series—generally small—of Fellahin crania (Morton, de Quatrefages and Hamy, Virchow, Schmidt, etc.) have been examined. The cephalic indices, always relatively low, varied according to the provenance of the crania. Sometimes the Fellahin (the poor are often less difficult in such matters than other folk) have allowed elements from Black Africa to penetrate among them. Schmidt notices Negroid specimens among the Fellahin crania he examined in Cairo. Extensive craniometrical study is still—we might say is especially—essential to-day.

Chantre, who measured numerous living Fellahin, gives them the mean height of 1 metre 68 (a little over that of the Copts); a mean cephalic index of 75.53, which represents a high degree of dolichocephaly (the hyperdolichocephaly of Deniker's classification). Of the individuals examined 87 per cent. are dolichocephalic and sub-dolichocephalic. About 10 per cent. have an index reaching and exceeding 80. The most frequent indices are those coming between 73 and 76. According to their nasal index the Fellahin are mesorrhinians (index of 77.77, the same as that of the Copts—77.59). Their hair, which is never either woolly or crisp, but often curly or frizzy, is a rather dark brown, like their eyes. The Fellahin nose is straight, sometimes aquiline.

Henceforward the Copts and Fellahin, two limbs of a single ethnological body, split up for religions and social reasons, appear to us to be capable of representing in these days the anthropological image of the ancient Egyptians.

But let us go a little further in our desire to find out exactly what this image was, and turn, not to the Sudanese Negroes who are numerous in the Nile valley and whose influence in the ethnological past of Egypt appears to have been practically nil, but to the Beduin Arabs, and to the peoples whom we may conceive to have influenced the ancient Egyptian race—the Bejas and the Bishari. The Arabs are numerous in Egypt. After their conquest (640) they were masters of the country for 600 years. And despite the fact that the usurpation of the Mamelukes and the Turkish conquest deprived them of political preponderance, "they have nevertheless continued to be the chief portion of the population in intelligence and ability. It has even been possible to say that the whole of Egypt is Arab."

What are the anthropological characters of these Arabs?

Their stature is generally above the mean. The height of six nomadic Arab tribes studied by Chantre was 1 metre 68. The cephalic index of these six tribes was dolichocephalic. The general mean was 73.96, indicating an even higher degree of dolichocephaly than that of the Copts and Fellahin. The nasal index everywhere showed mesorrhiny. The statement of these characters permitted Chantre to publish the following conclusions: The Egyptian Beduin (apart from the Aulâd 'Arab of the Fayyûm) present close affinities with the Fellahin and the Copts, as also with the Berbers of the Gabès and Kroumirie regions.

If the Beduin resemble the Fellahin and the Copts, these resemble the ancient Egyptians. Can we class these people of the past and the present together and consider that they represent two stages in the history of a large Afro-Asiatic ethnic group? Do the Beduin Arabs of Arabia and Syria still occupy the territory of their prehistoric ancestors as the Copts and Fellahin do in Egypt? In giving an affirmative answer we have to admit that there did at one time exist in the eastern angle of the Mediterranean and on either side of the Red Sea a tall dolichocephalic people of whom one contingent—that which occupied the Nile valley—created the great Egyptian civilization, whilst their racial brethren, for reasons unknown, retained their early traditions and even fought against them. And why can such an hypothesis not be envisaged? Do we not know of equally homogeneous groups of whom only one portion—sometimes a very small portion—created certain phases of civilization?

Among the human groups of a lower civilization belonging, *grosso modo*, to the same race, all did not evolve in the same manner. We have many examples of this among the Nigritic peoples without going outside Africa. And among the human groups of higher civilization we can certainly see the same thing happening. The various contingents of the Mediterranean race did not everywhere evolve in the same way at the same time; nor did those of the Celtic race, and many others along with them.

In the present state of our knowledge it is impossible to go beyond hypothesis. When the Arab burials of the most distant historic periods supply us with the skeletons of these old-time Arabs, we shall be able to put forward more positive conclusions.

To be complete, should we perhaps approximate to the above three ethnic groups considered as possible ancestors of the Egyptians, certain Nubians such as the Barabra ?

Until Chantre began his researches in the Nile valley the anthropometric and descriptive character of the Nubians were among the least known.[1] A few small series studied here and there in Paris, Berlin and Geneva had shown their dolichocephaly, and their relatively tall stature.

These Beja, Bishari and Barabra, indeed, are handsome races for whom the ancient Egyptians would have no cause to blush if we were to approximate one to the other with a view of proving filiation.

But is such a filiation legitimate ? If we are only to consider anthropometrical characters there is at first sight nothing against the ancient Egyptians and the Bishari or the Barabra of the same period being closely related. And we need not relinquish such a relationship merely because the Pharaohs fought against them.

These Nubians came of a noble race. And many Europeans might envy the refinement and distinction of their features, the smallness of their hands and feet, the beautiful colour of their skin, their slim height, and their straight noses. They have nothing of the Negro about them, neither prognathism, nor platyrrhiny, nor the Negro type of hair, save when they are intermixed with the Sudanese. Perhaps the Barabra are a little taller than the Bishari ?

Why is it that the various writers who have examined them have not dared, despite the finding of multiple resemblances, to relate them to the ancient Egyptians ? We find hesitation in their conclusions, after they have recalled the suppositions of filiation put forward by Champollion and some other Egyptologists. Is it because they are disturbed by the too wide difference between the civilizations ? Timidly they agree that " traces " of this people appeared at different times, notably in the Memphite period, and in different places, particularly in Upper Egypt.

But are not the nomadic Arabs of to-day the descendants of those who knew the great Arab civilization, the successors of the mathematicians and astronomers and of the builders of the Alhambra ?

[1] XLIII, p. 233.

PART V

THE RACES OF AMERICA

IS there any region on earth the first pages of whose history has been traversed by more unlikely guesses—guesses masquerading in scientific garb and guesses springing straight from the imagination—than the American continent! Has there ever been any human group whose ethnic origins have given rise to greater controversy, even in our own times, than the natives of America?

Hardly had the New World been discovered and the earliest indications relating to its native population reached Spain than the savants (?) set to work to draw up genealogical tables for the folk of whose existence they had just heard. With a total absence of any critical sense (although elements of comparison did exist in those days) the most unexpected filiations were established for these new-comers in the world's family.

At first, since scientific liberty did not exist and since death by burning at the stake of the Inquisition awaited anyone who had the audacity to claim that these Indians, so different from the European Whites, were of different stock, all were resolute monogenists. Had not St. Augustine said that "none of the faithful could ever doubt that all mankind, whatever their colour, stature, voice, proportions or other natural characters, had sprung from the same protoplasm"?

Need we be surprised at such an attitude? Was not the Church still all-powerful and all-knowing at the beginning of the sixteenth century? Did not a pope decree in 1512 that the natives discovered in America had descended, like other men, from Adam and Eve? I am aware that a few years later, in 1520, the Swiss Paracelsus made a vigorous protest with great courage. "We cannot admit," he said, "that the inhabitants of the recently discovered islands [America] are the sons of Adam, or that they are of the same flesh and blood as ourselves. Moses was a theologian, not a physician.

No physician of our days can admit the creation as described by Moses; he cannot accept it on faith and he can only put his trust in evidence and on the testimony of experience." But these were lone voices crying in the wilderness and they were immediately stifled. In 1574 a Spanish writer, Arius Montanus, seeking "scientific precision" in the Scriptures alone, explained how America was primitively peopled "by the sons of Joctan, great grandsons of Shem, of whom one, Seba, colonized China, and another, Ophir, went first to the northwest of the New World and then down as far as Peru, whilst the third, Jubal, went to Brazil."[1] Such guesses, extravagant as they are, have not yet, alas! been altogether banished from our horizon[2].

In a work which Vignaud considers "indispensable for a knowledge of the early views on the origin of the Indians," Gregorio Garcia, living in Peru in the sixteenth century, manifests a belief that the peopling of America was effected by the Jews. And I can retail arguments by the thousand as invoked by this immature ethnologist, such as that the Indians are cowards: so are the Jews; they—and this caps everything—are not grateful to the Spaniards for all that they have done for them—no more are the Jews! Grateful for the most abominable massacres ever placed on record and of which they were the victims? Dear, kind Gregorio Garcia!

The Phœnicians, likewise, had a great vogue in the tale of the primitive peopling of America. The fact that they were mariners, very doughty mariners, necessarily involved their circumnavigation of the globe. And it is not only the early writers (it must be said in excuse for them that they were very imperfectly informed) who uphold such extravagant hypotheses; many of our own contemporaries have gone back to this line of argument.

Among all these guesses that of a Syrio-Palestinian origin has been received with the greatest sympathy. We have already had the great-grandsons of Shem, the Jews in general, and the Phœnicians. Now we have to add to this list the Canaanites expelled by Joshua—the ten tribes of Israel.

Later on the search went a little further than the Biblical

[1] **CCLXIX**, p. 1.
[2] **CCXXV**, p. 190.

lands—though always in Asia. And it was imagined that it was the Carian-Turanians, expatriated en masse in the eighth century, who were carried by ocean currents first to the Antilles and then to the Amazon valleys.

Then in 1380 one of the naval squadrons of the great Tatar conqueror, Kubla Khan, which sailed to invade Japan, was wrecked on the western coast of South America. The shipwrecked mariners thereupon, through some unspecified turn of the wheel of fortune, founded the Empire of Peru!

It is not so long since Elliot Smith and his school, following up the geographical distribution of a large number of beliefs, customs and technical processes, concluded, by analogy, that the pre-Columbian American civilization was derived from the Nile valley.[1] There would be no purpose in adding to this list, whose contents are so fantastic, the hypothetical Atlantes which are so much in fashion to-day.

We see that Asia is almost alone in being invoked to explain the peopling of America. The greater part of Africa as we know it must naturally be eliminated because of the very colour of the majority of its inhabitants. Yet, St Augustine has said—! The American "Reds" had to have relationships sought for them—since the monogenist theory demanded it—if not among the Black, at least among the Yellows! The American natives had every chance of sharing their descent with the Asiatics!

This hypothesis of an Asiatic origin, stripped of all its old-time fantasies (need we recall the fact that the Maya calendar has been attributed to an Asiatic contact?) is taking shape again to-day; but based on different grounds. Those who seek to discover the ancestors of the Americans no longer turn their eyes to Syria and Palestine, but, as we shall shortly see, to Siberia.

We must first stress one point which is of importance; certain Americanists have maintained that there are resemblances—some have said identity—between all the natives of America. "Those who have had a close view of one Indian have seen them all; indeed, despite the slight difference sometimes to

[1] See *The Influence of Ancient Egyptian Civilization in the East and in America*, 1916, and *Elephants and Archæologists*, both by G. Elliot Smith, London, 1924; *The Children of the Sun*, W. J. Perry, London, 1923, and *The Growth of Civilization*, W. J. Perry, London, 1924, p. 99 ff, for an elaboration of this theory. (Translator's Note.)

be seen between them, they preserve a general resemblance which strikes the observer and which leaves no room for doubt that they belong to the same race. . . . It must be added that mentally, if one may so express it, they are all the same."[1] And such variety as, in spite of everything, one does observe and as one is forced to observe, among the natives of the different regions of America, is attributed to the influence of environment which fashions some after one manner and others after another. Is not this, after all, to reduce the problem to too great a simplicity? It is certain that the American natives do not resemble one another any more to-day than they did in the past.

If, then, the American natives have not all sprung from the same Asiatic stocks—as is asserted—we must necessarily fall back on the problem of autochthony which does not of itself solve the question. And here we come up against the controversial hypotheses for and against the existence of fossil Man in America.

We know what lively discussion the work of Ameghino stimulated everywhere. The Argentine palæontologist thought that in his native land were to be found the earliest human or prehuman remains in the whole world. But we also know that to-day most geologists and palæontologists—European and American alike—do not follow Ameghino's lead. What may be said is that the American Quaternary is far from having been fully studied, especially in South America, and that we must still be very reserved in regard to any conclusions on the subject of the autochthony of the American natives. Moreover, if Ameghino has given too great an antiquity to the origin of the South American Indians, he was not alone in holding that American fossil Man exists—a large number of writers give him an antiquity going back to the glacial periods. Boule himself, whose caution in this matter is extreme, has accepted American man as of pleistocene age.

This high antiquity, if it is finally established, in no way prevents us from believing in the Asiatic theory. Though it has to be demonstrated that the first men in Asia were earlier then the first men in America, or else to be conceded that the earliest inhabitants of the New World became extinct—as early as pleistocene times?—and were then replaced (but when?) by Asiatics. Any parallelism between the faunas

[1] **CCLXIX**, p. 17.

and industries of the two countries is far from being admissible in any of the pleistocene periods.[1]

The problem of the American races is nowhere near being solved. It is one of the most difficult there is. How, for example, are we to postulate links capable of uniting the present-day brachycephalic peoples of a great part of Central and South America with the long-headed prehistoric population which even the early excavations revealed to us? The Lagoa Santa race is highly dolichocephalic and the skull is high in the dome. It presents, moreover, a marked prognathism. According to Lund the race of men that lived in that part of the world was in general type the same from its oldest antiquity as that which inhabited it at the time of the European discovery of America.

Did there really exist in America from a very early epoch, difficult to specify with regard to its most distant date, two human groups characterized by the two extremes of cephalic type living side by side? That is what would appear to result from present-day research. Did these two races arrive together in the New World? If not, which is the earlier of the two? Up to date it is impossible to give any answer.

The data we possess concerning the contemporary native peoples of America show us different ethnic types—contrary to Vignaud's belief.

In South America the middle east seems to have preserved the ancient Lagoa Santa dolichocephalic cranial form.

As regards brachycephaly, it shows itself in the west when we leave the Atlantic coast, and increases in proportion to our westering. This is especially noticeable for the long wide strip of territory stretching from Pernambuco State to the mouth of the Rio de la Plata, and Ripley indicated it in his map.

The great belt of the Cordilleras is occupied as a whole, with considerable extensions in an easterly direction, by a mesaticephalic and brachycephalic population. These people appear to be distributed in Central America and Mexico, where they are in the majority, with the exception of the area surrounding the Californian gulf.

[1] This seeking for a relationship between American natives and certain peoples of Asia, no longer based, as we have seen above, on chimeras, but on scientific probabilities, was not a thing of yesterday. De Quatrefages firmly believed in such a relationship. He even admitted a very early derivation, since he thought that the Yellow People came into America from Quaternary times, and reached the Pampas. **CCIX**, p. 82.

North America presents less regularity as regards its cephalic distribution. If we except the stretches to the north of Hudson Bay and those which, more to the west, run along the Arctic borders of the northern continent—vast, ill-favoured expanses over which the long-headed Innuits wander—the remainder is inhabited by peoples whose cephalic characters tend towards if they do not clearly attain brachycephaly.

If we seek to associate other morphological points with head-form—stature, for example—we at once find that these ethnic groups which we were led to expect, merely from their cephalic characters, would be homogeneous, are, in fact, broken up. None but the Arctic aborigines, those furthest from the Bering Straits, keep their place in the ranks which physical conformation assigns to them.

The western portion of North America in which we should expect to find a solid brachycephalic block appears to associate its round heads with long bodies. But have investigations been pushed with sufficient completeness to enable us to assert this? If this morphological association of tall stature with brachycephaly is substantiated it will contradict the suppositions we put forward on the subject of an Asiatic peopling of North America. As a matter of fact, when we cross the waters of the Bering Straits and the Gulf of Okhotsk and land on the Siberian shore, we meet smaller people. The Chukchis, in whom it has long been sought to find a reproduction of the American natives, are not tall, nor are the Yukaghirs, who, however, do appear to be taller. The true Chukchis dwell to-day on the frozen lands which stretch from the Arctic shores to the Anadyr river. But it appears that in former times their habitat was much more to the west, in the districts north of Verkhoyansk. Long maintained pressure by the Lena Cossacks has driven them across the Yukaghir country to concentrate in the territory which forms a sort of cul-de-sac surrounded by the waters of the Bering Straits.

We know that in 1912 Hrdlička, head of the Anthropological Service of the United States, who wished to study this question of Asiatic and American relationships on the spot, went all over northern Siberia with a view of examining the autochthonous population there. He found, he said more than he expected. A partisan of the theories of Brinton, Holmes and others, he met in many parts of North Asia with confirmation of the congenetic suppositions of these anthropologists in regard to the ethnic groups of the two continents. He recognized along the course of the Yenisei, in particular, types among the survivors of the early aboriginal peoples that were identical with those of the American natives—the same skin colour, the same smooth black hair. He found mental identities even. This observation should be noted, coming from a savant like Hrdlička, accustomed to measure the physical characters of Man, and whose descriptions are not disturbed by other than scientific considerations.

It is quite possible that some of the American natives may be the descendants of some of the Asiatic natives of central and northern Siberia. But have we the right to extend this conclusion so as to embrace all the natives of America ?

I do not think we have, not by any manner of means, for the reasons given further back. Once again, the problem will not be solved until we can set identic discoveries in America and Asia side by side—identic as regards the data compared and identic with regard to the quaternary horizons from which these data are obtained.

To compare the present-day population is certainly interesting work. But in my opinion such work remains altogether inadequate in so far as it is not supplemented by an accurate knowledge of the primitive peoples. Let us bide our time till the question of American fossil Man—in both the Americas—has made further progress, and until physical anthropological studies in America and Asia are somewhat more numerous, before we venture to be positive about anything.

It is probable, moreover, even in these Americo-Asiatic regions whose physical conditions rendered them so unfavourable to human life that possession of them can hardly have been disputed, that ethnic intermixture occurred in former times. Not a single series so far studied is pure. All of them demonstrate complex agglomerations, whether in respect of stature, head and facial form, or colour of skin. Even the Hyperboreans—the best protected against cross-breeding—manifest dissimilar origins in both continents. And do not let us father these differences on to the different environments in which these peoples evolved. Here, too, such recourse to mesology would have little weight because it is altogether too facile.

Throughout the great extent of the two Americas the autochthonous Americans created no great civilizations, North America least of all.

A scientific philosopher might well inquire into the cause of these so different conditions of affairs. Those who are never at a loss for an answer to the most tantalizing questions will call to their aid differences in climate; they will assert that the wide stretches of the North American prairies and those of the Argentine pampas, where concentrations of population are alike more difficult to accomplish and less necessary, and where a nomadic life can continue uninterruptedly, are in themselves an explanation of the problem. They will also invoke many other reasons. But are they in the right? An examination of what has come to pass in other continents and in a similar environment might bring them cruel disillusionment.

The autochthonous American civilizations developed in the belt roughly contained within 25° N. and 25° S. lat., in regions mainly facing the Pacific. Must we, in order to explain this kind of geographical limitation, fall back on the centralizing influence of high plateaux? Or must we bring the "racial" factor on the stage? I do not know. It is beyond question that the civilization of these ancient peoples was far superior to that of the present-day Indians. "They were all in possession of the arts of weaving, building, and working in almost all the metals (save iron); they lived together in great cities, had powerful chiefs, regularly constituted armies, annual taxation, and a state organization, etc."[1]

These civilizations, which are painted in such brilliant colours by those Spanish chroniclers who were sympathetic to the Indians, succumbed in a few years beneath the blows rained on them with such blind brutality by the conquistadors. We know these civilizations only by their monuments—still, happily, numerous—and the often deliberately inaccurate accounts of historians.

In this area bounded by the frontiers of the present republics of Mexico and Chile several empires were constituted. Beuchat, who states how impossible it is to establish a comparative chronology—maybe the Maya-Quiché civilization is the older?.—indicates them, going from north to south, as follows: "1st, the Mexican or Aztec civilization, with the

[1] XVI, p. 253.

dependent civilizations of the Tarascos or Michoacans and that of the Miztecs and Zapotecs of Oajaca; 2nd, the Maya-Quiché civilization in Yucatan, Chiapas, and Guatemala and in a part of Honduras; 3rd, the civilization which may be called Central American, in Nicaragua and San Salvador, and which is perhaps the same as that of the ancient people of the Antilles; 4th, the Chibcha or Cundinamarca civilization of the pro-Columbian peoples of Costa Rica, the isthmus of Panama and the Bogota plateau (Republic of Colombia); 5th, the Peruvian civilization; 6th, the civilization of the Diaguites or Calchaquis who formerly occupied the Andean province of Catamarca (Argentine Republic)."[1]

It is not for us to set out here what is kow known of these civilizations. That is not our rôle, and several volumes of this series will be available to supply all needs in that direction. Let us try to set forth what the civilizers themselves must have been like.

The Mexican plateau known as the Anahuac (=situated by the water) has seen the civilizations of the Toltec, the Chichimec and the Aztec empires unfold.

Little, apparently, is known of the origin of the first of these. There existed on the Mexican plateau, maybe between the fourth (?) and eighth centuries, a highly civilized people who spread their sociological features throughout Central America. Did it likewise spread its own race? The historians of Mexico place a Chichimec "empire" between the close of this Toltec period and the foundation of Mexico.

It is important, first, to discover whether the human groups bearing these different labels had or had not a common ethnic origin. They are usually classed together under the name of the Nahua peoples or tribes. This, perhaps is a somewhat arbitrary procedure. At the first glance it would seem as though the Toltec, Chichimec and Aztec civilizations represent, in a manner, but the successive stages, with longer or shorter halts in the course of their wanderings, of the peoples who came from the northern regions, and of which we find considerable material manifestations further north than the present political boundary of Mexico among the Pueblos. Philology would seem to support this hypothesis.

[1] XVI, p. 254.

The story of these groups is chequered by incessant violence and fratricidal struggle even after the foundation of the Aztec confederation. This explains the relatively easy successes of the Spaniards at the time of the Conquest. They were only able to destroy the Aztec empire thanks to the collaboration of the Tlaxcaltecs, that aristocratic Republic which was then at enmity with those which Cortez invaded.

The material power of the Aztec confederation had reached a considerable height when the conquerors disembarked. And we may ask ourselves what the destiny of this State might have been, and what influence, proportionate to its development, it might have exercised on the general history of America if the 12th March, 1519[1] had not brought the Spanish forces to the Mexican coast.

In the pre-Columbian period the Maya-Quiché lived in the region which extends from the isthmus of Tehuantepec on the west approximately to the boundary of present-day Honduras and San Salvador on the east. It is said that they constituted one of the most homogeneous families of American ethnology. They consisted of three principal groups—the Huaxtecs, the Mayas, and the Quichés. Like the Mexicans they constructed great buildings, chiefly in Yucatan, where the first discoveries of these monuments so greatly surprised travellers. These early Americans were skilled sculptors, especially in the carving of complicated bas-reliefs in the living rock.

It would not seem that the people who occupied Yucatan at the period when the Spaniards arrived can be considered, if they were really the authors of their own civilization, as the descendants of the primitive Americans, the Pleistocene folk; because the explorations of N. Mercer, E. H. Thompson, and G. Byron-Gordon in the Yucatan caves have yielded nothing to throw light on the earliest origin (corresponding to our Palæolithic) of the occupants of the Maya country. The folk memories of this people hint at migrations from the south which finally peopled the Yucatan peninsular. It would seem that the Mexicans also invaded Yucatan.

Traditions appear to put the opening chapters of Maya history at the beginning of the Christian era. However, like

[1] Other writers give April 21st, 1519. See **CCXXXII.**

Mexico, Yucatan knew a far earlier phase of civilization than that of the Aztec period.[1]

*

* *

To what ethnic group are we to attach the pre-Columbian Mexican peoples? It is certain that the present occupants of Mexico are the descendants of those who were attacked by the conquistadors. American history records not a single migration in this area from the sixteenth century onwards. No event of physical geography has occurred such as might set peoples on the move. To study the existing human types is to become acquainted with the ethnic characters of the men who created the civilizations destroyed by the Spaniards.

An enumeration of the Aztecs shows that they now number about 150,000 souls. The census of 1896 indicated, in addition, 200,000 Tarascos, 265,000 Zapotecs, and a few thousand Miztecs.

Contrary to what has taken place in North America—where the nefarious work of the Whites has gone on too long—these Mexican and Central American peoples do not seem to be on the point of becoming extinct. Far from it. Is it not even stated that the natives are taking precedence to-day over the descendants of the former conquerors in all the multifarious phases of Central American social life? A just repayment of old scores!

The anthropological characters of these peoples have not yet been adequately investigated. The little we know of them reveals them as of small stature and brachycephalic. Their skin is dark brown, their cheekbones prominent. But the whole of Mexico does not seem to be populated by people of the same type; and if the existing tribes, as would appear, are *in situ*, it would be very difficult to find out what influence they may have exerted on one another, and what part those influences have had in the early history of this American region.

The Mexican Indians are divided into the two ethnographical groups of Sonorans and Aztecs. The northern groups, naturally enough, are linked up with the Indians of a large

[1] See, for example, **LXXVI.**

portion of the western United States, of whom they would appear to be but a southerly prolongation. They are thus unconnected with the central and south Mexican groups. Their civilization has been of the same nature as that of the Pueblos, and the physical type of the men themselves is generally identical with that of the cliff-dwellers of Arizona.[1]

These Sonorans of Mexico are tall men whose height reaches and exceeds 1 metre 70, and whose head is not round like that of a large portion of the natives of central and south Mexico. Like the Pimas of New Mexico and the Arizona Indians these Sonorans are sub-dolichocephals. The Yakis (Yaquis) and the Mayos, who are settled mainly on territories facing the Gulf of California (the two rivers bearing the same names as these two Indian tribes flow into it), are mesocephalic,[2] and ten Kate has called attention to their slender build and—a character which has a certain genealogical importance—their prominent noses.

If the ancient Mexican civilizations have come from the North, as has been claimed by some writers, the present peoples of central and south Mexico should still show individuals similar to these Sonorans[3]. So far as we know this is not the case. The absence of these descendants of northern Indians would of itself be an argument in favour of those who think that Mexican civilization was brought in by Inca groups from South America.

The name Aztec or Nahua is a collective one for a number of tribes which, two or three centuries before the arrival of the Spaniards, constituted a confederation of States on the Atlantic slope near Mexico, namely the Tezcuco (Alcolhuas), Tlacopans (Tepanecs) and Tenochtitlan (Aztecs) peoples. There were three other ethnic groups which we may include among the Mexicans properly so-called (Deniker). These are the Otomi inhabiting the Mexican plateau on the eastern borders of the State of Guanajuato (the Otomi language is pointed out as being unique, in America, as an almost mono-syllabic tongue); the Tarascos and the Totonacs. The

[1] An exception must be made of the tribes to which the Zuñis of New Mexico are attached, for they appear to belong to the same group as the early Aztecs. Excavation in the Pueblos has shown the presence, never-the-less, of brachycephalic individuals. These ancient habitats must have sheltered at least a portion of the peoples among whom the forbears of the Aztecs may be sought.

[2] **LVII**, p. 612 (p. 589 of Engl. trans.).

[3] Unless the civilizer himself did not bring his civilization with him.

Tarascos, of whom it is considered that a large portion is cross-bred, while another has kept its blood pure, are settled on the slopes of the Michoacan mountains on the slopes facing the Pacific. The localization of this people is modern. In former times they were scattered further to the north. But did they never go beyond central Mexico? They do not seem to be related in any way to the Sonorans. Do they perhaps represent the extreme advance guard of the northward migration of groups from the south at the period of the foundation of the early Mexican civilizations? The Totonacs belong to the Atlantic slopes and inhabit the province of Vera Cruz.

To the south of the Puebla plateau, in the mountainous region whose streams run in all directions, and in which the city of Oaxaca gives its name to a vast area comprising part of the isthmus of Tehuantepec, there are grouped numerous Central American tribes among whom are the Zapotecs, the Miztecs, the Zoques, Chapanecs, etc. The first are descended from a people, formerly powerful, whose civilization resembled that of the Aztecs. The physique of these South Mexicans is in its general lines that of the natives of the Anahuac plateau—small stature, brachycephaly, dark brown skin, prominent cheekbones—very different, as is seen, from that of the Sonorans. They certainly all belong to the same original ethnic group.

The Maya people inhabit the Yucatan peninsular (which is not merely the northern area bearing that name). It is considered to be the oldest in the Central American region. Many historians link the Mayas with the Toltecs; but their speech would completely separate them. This Maya people presents an important ethnogenical problem. It has been claimed, taking as a basis the philological resemblances to the language spoken by the aborigines of Cuba, Haiti and Jamaica, that the Mayas originally came from the Antilles. If we admit this approximation and also bear in mind that the Maya traditions place the arrival of that people in Yucatan about 800 years B.C., we shall have to admit that at that distant epoch there already existed sure means of communication between the greater Antilles and the American continent! I am aware that the more recent writers, such as Spinden, put forward by some centuries this supposed Maya migration and place it in the year 235 B.C. All the same I think that some reserve is called for.[1] These are but linguistic approximations and Indian traditions without any great consistency.

Many Americanists think that the Mayas, like the Mexicans, belong to the Nahuatlan branch. The great builders of the Maya monuments would thus have been Toltecs whom Aztec pressure drove into Yucatan. There is nothing very much against such an hypothesis from the anthropological point of view. There are certainly grounds for considering them both, that is to say—Mayas and Aztecs—as having derived from a common source.

From Yucatan the Mayas spread into Guatemala, Honduras and San Salvador. Their civilization was similar to that of the Mexicans, apart from the sanguinary cult which dishonoured the latter. To-day the Mayas are dispersed in a fairly large number of tribes in Mexico and Guatemala. Their physical characters as a whole are the same everywhere—small stature, thick-set body and brachycephalic head. The face shows a prominent nose and cheekbones. In all these characters they approximate to the other ancient Mexican peoples.

When at the beginning of the fifteenth century the Mayas abandoned the north of Yucatan they joined the Quichés in Guatemala. The union of these two groups constituted the Maya-Quiché ensemble. It is a curious thing that the Quichés are the people who hold the Yucatan traditions.

When we go further east we still find peoples whose physical characters remain similar to those we have just described. Their dispersion is not arrested by the isthmus of Panama. The traveller who climbs the most northerly slopes of the Andes chain will find them there ; and if his footsteps take him, still following this mountain range, as far as the high plateaux of Peru and Bolivia, he will rub shoulders with representatives of this ancient race all the way. That is what would seem to be indicated by the anthropological investigations—still extremely inadequate—which have been undertaken in the western portion of South America.

In Colombia the Chibchas (or Muyscas) appear to have belonged to the same civilization as their neighbours of the north. Unfortunately the Chibchas properly so-called have practically disappeared.

[1] CCXLVIII.

The Aymaras have left abundant megalithic remains in the region of Lake Titicaca. They have been considered by many writers to be the earliest of the civilizers of South America. The Quichuas inherited their culture. The Aymaras provided the Inca dynasties. At the time of the Spanish conquest the Indians who occupied the mountain belt facing the Pacific from 2° N. to 3° S. lat., were an Aymara or Quichua tribe. The origin of these Indians has occasioned as much discussion as that of the Mayas. Some, in accordance with Quichua traditions, hold that they came from the south from the neighbourhood of Cuzco, and, even further south still, from the region of Lake Titicaca. Others, on the contrary, think that they should be related to the peoples of northwest South America, and, consequently, to those of Central America and Mexico.

One of these tribes, becoming preponderant, dominated all the others and constituted the empire that the Spaniards first made known to us under the name of Peru, a name which the natives never used, as Rivet has shown. In the pre-Columbian epoch—the fact is stated by Garcilaso de la Vega who, an Indian himself, knew the Quichua language well, the word *Peru* was unknown in the region which to-day bears that name. This term, which was eventually to designate the Inca empire, designated, before the discovery of that empire, a river and a Colombian coast Cacique, and signified, in the local idiom, "water, or river."[1]

The Incas.—At the beginning of the sixteenth century the Inca empire had achieved its greatest power. It was then even larger than that of the Aztecs. But internal disturbances, and especially the arrival of Pizarro (1532) brought about its downfall. After having, with their customary violence, assassinated the last Inca, Atahuallpa, the conquistadors seized the country.

We may ask ourselves what this empire of the Incas might have become if it had continued to exist. It represented a form of government and a social state of enthralling interest, whose structure in some details at once suggests a certain approximation to the communist régime in present-day Russia.

[1] **CCXXII**, p. 289.

The Inca, a divine personage, was juridically the master of all the lands; but he delegated possession, by a temporary title, to heads of families. Each paterfamilias received from the State a certain superficies of inalienable land for the support of his household. As his household increased so was his holding proportionately enlarged. The remainder of the land belonged to the State; it was divided into two lots, one for the Inca and one for the Sun.[1]

All married men and women between the ages of 25 and 50 had to cultivate the State lands in addition to their own. The sick and old and the young were exempted from these duties. The produce was heaped up in storehouses, the property of the Inca. Each village had two, one in which the taxes in kind were collected for the Inca, and the other "consecrated to the Sun, served as a reserve in case of shortage." Stores were established throughout the empire for the upkeep of troops in the field.

The people were mulcted in other taxes in labour and kind, such as public works (irrigation canals, roads, etc.), and the equipment of the Army (tools, arms, clothing, footgear). The State provided the raw materials.

With a view of giving the greatest possible political cohesion to their empire the Incas forced all conquered peoples to speak Quichua, the official language. It is thought, also, that every able man had to do military service. And in order that the fields should be cultivated without interruption and that the State as a whole should suffer as little as might be from the conscription of the men, there were rotas for military duty. The network of roads was very extensive. They radiated from Cuzco in all directions. Each district was responsible for the construction and upkeep of the roads running through its territory.[2]

To what race belonged these builders of cities, palaces and temples—the most skilled architects of all America—these agricultural engineers from whom the most complicated irrigation held no secrets, these skilled potters from whose work our present-day decorators could draw unlimited inspiration, these organizers who like the Romans followed up conquest by opening up roads in all directions?

[1] It will be remembered that the Incas considered themselves to be Children of the Sun.

[2] **XVI**, p. 605 ff.

We have stated several times in the course of the foregoing pages how impossible it is to give a satisfactory reply to such a question. If we are to credit certain writers who are among the most documented, the peoples of Peru must very early have been influenced by the east. According to Rivet and Créqui-Montfort[1] the Aymaras were preceded, in the region of the high Andean plateaux, by the Urus or Oros, " a people of Amazonian origin who at one time were widely distributed and who are now reduced to about a thousand persons ".[2] Was this people descended from the early Dolichocephals of Lagoa Santa ?

Rivet, who lived for a long time in the country, and who conscientiously studied it, thinks that Peru transmitted its bronze technique to Mexico at a period which may not have been long anterior to the discovery of America, and that the technique of silver followed the same route.

But was this passage from south to north of the use of metals an isolated event ? Or should we look upon it as a stage in the ventures which, from the American palæolithic period onward, would always have been going forward—the earlier civilization of the two being first instituted in the Andean plateaux and then being propagated in a regular manner northwards ?

Or, should we, on the contrary, accept the hypothesis of a primitive civilization established in central Mexico and radiating outwards first to Yucatan (but it is said that the Mayas had an earlier civilization than that of the Mexicans) and then going thence across the isthmus, and, penetrating by the high valleys, getting even as far as Peru and Bolivia ?

From a perusal of the recent work of Americanists one perceives that the problem for them is far from having been solved ; both points of view have their supporters. Hence, with even greater reason it is still unsolved for us.

Has not a relationship been postulated between certain ethnographic characters of the Calchaquis—notably the stone buildings of a particular type—and the same characters seen, at an immense distance, among the Zuñis ?

A knowledge of the place in which the earliest civilization flourished would not be without value to anthropologists. On the contrary, we might find therein some useful information.

[1] CCXXIII.
[2] CCLXIX, p. 54.

Whence came these men, who, from Bolivia to Mexico—this geographical direction should not be accompanied in our minds by a corresponding chronology—created these flourishing empires and constituted these numerous tribes whose nominal varieties might have induced us to believe that they represented several races ?

It would seem that we must recognize in them, despite their various appellations, and despite their different idioms, a single ethnic group. And this group still occupies to-day the same area as its ancestors.

Let us recall what their ethnic characteristics are : small stature, brachycephaly, smooth black hair, prominent cheek-bones, prominent nose. We have found this type to exist everywhere that we have followed the tracks of the great indigenous civilizations.

Towards the north we can link these men with some of the southern Sonorans. But after that ?—And going further westwards ? Their area would seem to be limited to northern Mexico. Towards the extreme south we can establish their relationship with the Araucans. These geographical prolongations, even if they assure to us highly important fresh knowledge, in no way solve the problem as a whole.

The only conclusion an anthropologist may permit himself is to assert that at the period when Columbus discovered America there was, among the peoples of this huge continent, one large group of relatively pure race whose contingents were strung out from at least the extreme north of the Mexican plateau as far as present-day mid-Chili. Maybe several of these groups, in South America, had gone out and established settlements in the direction of the eastern fluvial plains ?

But what was the first origin of this race, differing as it does in its extreme southerly expansion from that of the Patagonians, differing from the dolichocephalic Brazilians who descend from the people of Lagoa Santa ; differing, again, to the north of present-day Mexico, from the greater part of the tall more or less long-headed Indians ?

We do not know in the very least. And it would seem that it is difficult to establish links between them and the Siberian aborigines, as present-day hypotheses would like to do.

Should we label these natives autochthonous ? This term does not mean very much to those who go deeper than mere words. Once again, we must wait till the discovery of fossil human bones allows us to speak with authority of an American origin for the American natives.

For those who would follow a certain school and seek to establish a relation between race and civilization, it is of great interest to remark that among the various American races a single ethnic group has presented such an imposing culture, a civilization of such grandiose aspect that in certain respects it has not been surpassed by any of the other celebrated ancient civilizations.

And if we find that a single ethnic group has created a civilization (under two very different aspects) we can also remark that two geographical regions alone, out of the huge extent of American territory, have been the theatres of these ventures. Is this simply because they were both inhabited by men belonging to the same race and that other conditions of development therefore had no influence either way ?[1]

The Spanish invasion, a profoundly sad event in the manner of its accomplishment owing to its cruelty, must also be regretted from the philosophical point of view because it brusquely suspended a social state which, in certain localities of America, had been brought to an extraordinary degree of development and whose natural destinies we should have liked to have followed up.

What might have been the present-day aspect of the Maya civilization—or the communist Inca State after 400 years of further experiment in the same laboratory and by experimenters of the same quality ? And if we twentieth century folk had suddenly discovered America, what might we have found ? Would these civilizations have spread ? Would they have been extended to other regions, hitherto of very different social aspect ? Or should we have had before our eyes, unchanged, the selfsame picture that the conquistadors saw when they landed ? Or, again, would these civilizations have collapsed of their own accord ?

We may imagine yet something else : might the Aztecs, Mayas and Incas, coming into contact with a European

[1] It is quite possible that this is the explanation. But even then the ethnic reason by itself does not give us the key to this dualism of culture created and maintained by the representatives of the same race.

civilization brought to them in peace, have modified their own customs by simply pooling both? Or would they have gone on "living their own lives" more or less completely as certain present-day African peoples do, although they are in permanent contact with White peoples?

These autochthonous civilizations having been violently broken up have nowhere and at no time revived in any of their characteristics. Do the natives, in these days, live happier lives than their ancestors lived under the despotic—and in Mexico, cruel—system of former times?

To-day a very happy resurgence of the primitive race is being reported on many hands. And bearing this revival in mind we may again ask ourselves this question—how much has cross-breeding got to do with the present energetic quality of the contemporary native? Is the Mexican renaissance—it is to be hoped that a similar state of affairs may come to pass elsewhere in America—an exclusively native fruit which is ripening afresh? Or are we to believe that a mixture of blood has re-endowed certain descendants of the ancient Indians with new vigour? This supposition, one may imagine, would at once bring to the fore all those hypotheses which ethnic mixtures of whatever kind give rise to; hypotheses relating, in particular, to the precise amount of mixed blood present and to the various reactions which may result therefrom.

What a fine study in social anthropology we may look forward to on the day when a sufficiently precise discrimination of the proportion of different strains present in a given generation can be made! In what proportion is a strain of foreign blood[1] the function of the actions of the present generation? And then shall we have to believe that relations between Race and History really do exist?

[1] In Central America three main races at least have contributed to the creation of the existing population—Indians, Spaniards, and Negroes. According as to whether they have in their veins a half, quarter or eighth part strain of foreign blood these crossbreds bear special names. Hamy long ago published the very complicated nomenclature of these crossings in Mexico according to Ignacio da Castro.

PART VI

THE RACES OF OCEANIA

OCEANIA is the geographers' description for Australia and the islands, great and small, scattered over the Great Ocean. The space thus included is immense (one-third of the planet), but the actual land above water only accounts for a part of it—8,960,000 square kilometres. Some 6,500,000 persons[1] inhabit these separated territories, and they are parcelled out among four human "races"—the Australian; Indonesian (Asiatic archipelago); Melanesian (natives of New Guinea and adjacent islands); and Polynesian, whose habitat is in the archipelagos of the eastern Pacific.

The origin of these races has always been considered to offer one of the most attractive, while at the same time one of the most thorny problems of general Anthropology.

A few ethnologists have been partisan to the autochthony of these races—which obviously does not necessitate much imagination on their part; the others have sought to explain the presence of these human groups, even in the most isolated archipelagoes, by migratory movements which have taken place at different periods. We know that de Quatrefages was the principal protagonist of this last opinion.[2]

The first point that has to be settled, and it is an important one, since a large part of our arguments depend on it, is the geological origin of this wide region.

Dumont d'Urville thought that Polynesia represented the remains of a great continent which was primitively joined to Asia, and that after sinking had taken place the highest summits alone emerged—as is the case with Corsica and Sardinia in Europe, both of which are the remains of a great quaternary pendant—thus constituting the present

[1] The peoples of the Malay archipelago are not included in this figure. They amount to 35,000,000 persons distributed over 2,444,000 square kilometres.

[2] CCVII.

archipelagoes. The Polynesians would be the descendants of the people who escaped from the catastrophe.

De Quatrefages, to combat this hypothesis, which, curiously enough, would appear to agree with the tradition of the great flood preserved by the Tahitians, and after having recalled the fact that zoological investigation contradicted it, adduces an argument drawn from Anthropology itself. He remarks that all Polynesians speak the same language with simple variations in dialect, and then he adds[1]: "The Polynesian area whose extreme bounds I have indicated, is of greater extent than the whole of Asia. Let us reflect on what an *Asiatic Polynesia* would have been if that continent had sunk, leaving only the summits of its mountains above the waters, on which a few of the present-day peoples might have taken refuge! Is it not obvious that each archipelago, and often each island in it, would have had its own race and language?" One might reply, nevertheless, that probably the linguistic multiplicity of Asia did not always exist—at the beginning of the Quaternary, for instance.

Geologists admit that the island world of the Pacific as a whole is of ancient origin.[2] In it we see a very ancient geography. Australia would not seem to have had continental communication with Asia after the close of the Cretaceous or the beginning of tertiary times. The large islands of Sumatra, Java and perhaps Borneo may have remained a part of Asia rather longer (up to the end of the tertiary era ?).

Thus, even if we can admit that a part at least of the Asiatic archipelago was peopled overland, this view becomes inadmissable as regards Australia on the one hand and the oceanic islands on the other. There is nothing left for it but that the migrations were by water as de Quatrefages, following Hale and a number of geographers, maintained.

But these migrants could only have started to people the Pacific ocean eastwards when navigation became possible, that is to say when man had invented seaworthy and navigable boats, since the chance factor of ocean currents, spatially important as these may be, must not be considered to the exclusion of all others.

It would thus seem that the primordial question is to

[1] CCVII, p. 140.

[2] Still, everyone knows that a large number of the Polynesian islands are of recent formation, notably the coral islands.

find out at what date these sinkings took place which created archipelagoes, and when navigation along the northern Pacific shores began. I am aware that those writers who most favour the foreign settlement hypothesis do not put the Polynesian migrations further back than historic times. The earliest navigators long antedated this epoch.

But if the Polynesians set forth from the eastern archipelagoes of Asia, how were those archipelagoes themselves peopled? It will be replied—by the self-same means employed later on by their own inhabitants when they went further east.

So it is all quite simple. In proportion as we trace these easterly migrations further west we must go further back in time! And thus the *appearance* of ethnic genealogy can be kept up. The eastern islands would only have been populated in relatively recent periods.

But if it was as easy as all this—reminding one of the "setting forth" of the Aryans—how are we to explain the considerable ethnic differences which separate the Malays, for instance, from the Australians, and both of these groups from the Polynesians?

Are we to admit that predestination was at work, some of the migrants being selected to populate Australia and others New Guinea, and so on?

Linguistic approximations are inadequate as reasons. The fact that the languages of the Pacific have a certain relationship with Malay speech might quite easily be explained without bringing in a movement of peoples, such as is suggested, to account for it.

And then, what would be said if it happened that traces of Man were discovered in the pleistocene strata of these separated lands? Such a discovery would by no means square with the above hypotheses. And from such a verdict there would be no appeal. Hence studies in human palæontology are much to be desired in Polynesia—that is, of course, where they are possible, namely in the islands that are geologically the oldest.

Up to the present, if we leave on one side the question of Pithecanthropus, Australia and Java have yielded the most interesting data.

Anthropologists have often approximated to certain types of fossil Man (*Homo neanderthalensis*, for example) the present-day Australians, who are considered to be the representatives of the most primitive type of humanity now living; but these, of course, are simply morphological approximations.

No-one can fail to realize that it would be of the very greatest interest to find out whether the present Australian race had quaternary ancestors living in Australia. Savants have long had this in view without result. But some recent observations begin to throw light on the matter.

Recently (in 1916) the find of a human tooth in a cave deposit at Wellington was notified. In 1905 a German palæontologist, Branco[1], published the result of his observation of the famous Warrambool (Victoria) imprints consisting of two feet and buttocks—discovered in 1896 by the head of the museum of this town, Archibald, and attributed to a human being who had evidently sat down on an early pliocene beach when the sand was still soft and so easily retained the impression made. To-day we are agreed in thinking, with Noetling, that these were the tracks of a kangaroo.[2]

But in 1914 a more interesting discovery was notified in Australia. It goes back to 1884, but had not hitherto been the subject of a scientific communication. This was the human skull found near Talgai, west of Brisbane, in the Darling Downs district (Queensland) at a depth of 2 metres 50 in a geological horizon containing the remains of extinct animals such as Nototherium and Diprotodon. This skull was that of a young man whose face was extraordinarily prognathous, much more so than that of present-day Australians. Boule[3] thinks that this skull represents a type of "proto-Australian, who had long acquired a human brain, but who retained in his face a more brutal souvenir of his origin." In the present condition of our knowledge this skull may be considered as dating from the Pleistocene.[4]

[1] Branco, "Die fraglichen fossilen menschlichen Fusspuren in Sandsteine von Warrambool, Victoria, und andere angebliche Spuren des fossilen Menschen in Australien". *Zeits f. Ethnol*, Berlin, 1905, p. 162. In this memoir (illustrated) there is a bibliography of Australian works relating to the question of fossil Man in that country.

[2] F. Noetling, "Bemerkungen über die angebliche Menschenspur", *Centr. f. Mineral.*, 1907). In 1906 Klaatsch stated that the size of the foot among the Australians was no more than 0 metre 08, as in the imprints in question. *Zeits. f. Ethnol.*, 1906, p. 764.

[3] **XXI**, p. 372; **CCXLIV**.

[4] For English accounts of this skull, first shown at a meeting of the British Association in Sydney, 21st August, 1914, see **CCXLIV** and **CXXIII** (1925 ed.), p. 448-457. (Translator's Note.)

If these human remains really belong to this stratigraphic horizon we must ask ourselves whence came these men who first peopled Australia in the Quaternary. And how did they get there? We may recall that Australia was separated from the Asiatic continent at the least at the beginning of the tertiary era. The problem is extremely difficult.

It is possible that other regions of Oceania will bring us face to face with identical problems. The discoveries made at Trinil, in Java (see the chapter on Asia) raise hopes in this regard; so do the same discoverer's find of the Wadjak crania, also in Java.[1]

Thus we see that the history of the peopling of Oceania is not so simple as it seemed at first sight, at all events to the anthropologists of a preceding generation. The Talgai skull and the remains of Pithecanthropus, unknown to our predecessors, invite us to maintain a cautious reserve.

Discoveries of flint and polished stone implements have been notified in the western islands of the Pacific. It would not seem that these finds have presented themselves with such stratigraphic testimony as would allow us to postulate a succession of palæolithic and neolithic periods like those of Europe and thus to establish any comparative chronology. It is possible that these implements are not very old.

The stone age, in some parts of Oceania, lasted almost to our own days. In this connection an interesting phenomenon has been observed—namely a complete lack of harmony between two social states. While Malaysia was incomparably further advanced in general culture—and gave its language to the Oceanians—many of these retained their primitive tools, notably their stone implements. The Malay languages went east very much faster than the material civilization. It is rather as though the Sudanese Negroes had allowed English to supplant their own tongue while they still retained intact their enthnographic characters. This, of course, is merely a simile.

In connection with this lack of ethnographical harmony in Oceania we must once more emphasise an observation

[1] For a consideration of Wadjak man's possible relationship to the Talgai man (his discoverer, Dr. Dubois regards him as a proto-Australian), in English, see **CXXIII** (1925 ed.) loc. cit. For Dr. Dubois's memoir (he was only induced to publish his skull after the publication of Dr. Stewart Smith's memoir on the Talgai man), *Konin. Akad. van Wetensch. te Amsterdam*, 1920, vol. xxiii, pt. 7. (Translator's Note).

alluded to by Deniker—namely that the Maoris of New Zealand knew nothing of pottery, despite their clay deposits, nor had they invented weaving, despite the presence on their island of Phormium and other textile plants.[1] This fact must be taken into account by geographers who concern themselves with human geography.

We will now glance rapidly at the races of Oceania—rapidly because these peoples have played no great part in History. And, as we travel eastwards we will abide by the four great divisions created by the geographers.

The Malaysians.—Anthropologists readily make a distinction between Malays and Indonesians among the peoples of Malaysia—about whom so many baseless guesses were formerly made.

The Malays properly so-called—we mean here the Malays in an ethnographic sense—inhabit Sumatra, Java, and the other islands of the Timor Sea as well as the greater part of the coasts of the northern islands. They represent, at first sight, a veritable ethnic jungle into which anthropologists have as yet not penetrated very far. Battas and Kubus, Ashinese and Rejangs—and still others in Sumatra; Nias islanders: Sundanese (on the west) and Javanese (on the east) of Java, to mention those only who, perhaps, are among the least unknown, claim a close examination.

Is there any essential difference between those peoples inhabiting the same regions known as Malay, and those known as Indonesians? It has been said that the Malays are related to the Mongols, and the Indonesians to the Polynesians. These are merely suppositions that a simple morphological examination quickly destroys. The Polynesians are among the tallest people in the world, whereas the Indonesians are to be classed among people of small stature. The Polynesians are brachycephalic, the Indonesians tend to be dolichocephalic. What morphologist could be induced to believe that these two kinds of people should be placed in the same ethnic division!

It is readily admitted that the Malays are a mixed nation, sprung from a mixture of Indonesians with various other elements—Burmese, Negrito, Indian, Chinese, Papuan, etc.[2]

[1] **LVII**, p. 548 (Eng. transl. p. 475, Note). Readers desiring further information will find it to a great extent in this work.

[2] **LVII**, p. 558 (Eng. trans., p. 486).

Intermixture with Chinese has taken place especially in Java, North Borneo, and the northern Philippines.

The Indian intermixture is most obvious in certain parts of Java, Sumatra, and southern Borneo, that is to say in those areas geographically nearest to this influence.

If the Malays represent the anthropological mixture they are said to do, we must single out from among them the original Malay stock. It is admitted that the Indonesians represent this pure element. And that is why they are sometimes called proto-Malays. Are we sure that the morphological characters of the Indonesians are those of the true Malays? On the average the Malays—the Javanese, for example—are taller (1 metre 61) and incomparably more brachycephalic than the proto-Malays.[1] If there is any one area in which a close anthropological study by regions and tribes is urgently needed, it is decidedly in this western portion of Oceania.

When we try to see our way through this ethnic jungle we are at once struck by the difficulties that face us. Not that we are altogether without anthropological data. But the series so far studied have nearly all been made up of a small number of individuals. And this is distinctly meagre documentation for so wide an extent of territory, so large a variety of tribes and so great an intermixture of every kind—or at any rate an intermixture believed to be so great. And then, to complicate the task still further, certain peoples deform the heads of their children.

I have endeavoured to find out, by the aid of data relating to stature and head-form, if it is possible to establish morphological localization in the area between Sumatra and New Guinea.

The Malays and Indonesians both show the general character of small stature. It appeared to me, at first, that the smallest men inhabited the eastern island group and that it was the Indonesians who most often showed this character. But I find that there are very small Malays to the west (Sundanese of Java, 1 metre 591) and, on the other hand, relatively tall Malays (1 metre 617) in Sumatra.

The cephalic index faces us with the same perplexities. The Papuans, it has been said, are highly dolichocephalic, and, on the other hand, that there has been a sensible Papuan

[1] CXXV.

influence on the Indonesians, and to a much less extent on the Malays. Thus it is the people in the east who, in the main, represent the least round-headed and the most distinctly long-headed elements (e.g. the people of Timor an index of 76.9; of Flores, 77.7; of Ceram, 76.3). But to the west the people of Nias are also sub-dolichocephalic (index of 77.6). And if I find Javanese with an index of 84.6, indicating sub-brachycephaly, and of 86.3, showing true brachycephaly, I also find Indonesians in Luzon, in the Philippines, with a still rounder head (index of 86.6). In any case the Mongolian influences of which so much has been heard appear to be imaginary.

There is a magnificent field for the anthropologist of the future to exploit in these areas[1]. In any case it is certain that the linguistic and ethnographic characters invoked to establish relationship between the Indonesians and the Malays, and between these peoples and the northern and eastern populations, are altogether inadequate to give us the information we require.

The Melanesians.—Even if the peoples of the wide Melanesian region appear to be somewhat less of an inextricable tangle than the Malaysian peoples, we are still far from being clear as to the precise characters which would enable us to classify this or that tribe in its proper ethnic group. For two great divisions of peoples are habitually classed under the denomination of Melanesians, namely the Papuans of New Guinea and the islands along its coast, to the west; and the Malanesians properly so-called in the island groups to the east. As a whole they appear to be different from the Malaysians and also from the Polynesians, and this has assured them some sort of unity.

In New Guinea the Papuans are divided up into a number of tribes. Perhaps those who dwell in old German New Guinea are the best known.

Anthropological literature can only show some score of "series" whose somatological characters have been studied relating to this population whose ethnic characters are so varied and of so high an interest, and whose dialects are so numerous. Maybe New Guinea is more brachycephalic than the islands situated to the east?

[1] Such discoveries as that of the Wadjak crania will now oblige us to investigate the descent of these peoples from the Pleistocene down to our own times.

Are we to hold the Malaysians responsible for this ethnic colouration? I hasten to add that those elements met with in New Guinea which show a brachycephalic tendency would seem to be exceptional.

Quite large series of crania have only shown it in meagre proportions (5 to 7 per cent.).

The New Hebrides[1], the Solomon Islands, and New Britain (Neu Pommern), though populated by people whose dolichocephaly is extreme (indices of 70.4, 70.7, 71.7, etc.) have no more than the others escaped from intermixture with foreign races, and with foreign races whose heads are not so long as those of the genuine natives. And even in New Mecklenburg (formerly New Ireland) some living individuals have shown a mesaticephalic index.

The New Caledonia islanders remain dolichocephalic (index of 76.5 on the living).

The stature of all these natives likewise shows extensive variation. Two series from the Bismarck archipelago only reach 1 metre 60 and 1 metre 62; and in the Solomon islands, 1 metre 61. Nevertheless we are bound to remark that whereas in general all these island peoples are below the mean height, including the Papuans of the north, there are at least two groups which exceed this limit and reach 1 metre 67, namely the Papuans of British New Guinea and the New Caledonia islanders. Still, 250 New Caledonia islanders, quite recently studied by Fritz Sarasin, are slightly—very slightly—smaller, 1 metre 667[2]. It would thus seem that stature increases as we go from north southwards and from the west eastwards[3]. Possibly a detailed study of the numerous peoples inhabiting the wide territory of New Guinea would explain this ethnological phenomenon.

Is there really any appreciable difference—other than that of their faces—any difference sufficiently sharp to enable us to divide the Papuans from the Melanesians properly so-called? It is quite possible that there is. One may even say, from the data so far collected, that it is quite probable. In order to effect such a separation we ought to have studies based on larger totals. Anthropology is already so greatly cumbered

[1] The most extensive anthropological investigation in the New Hebrides was that carried out by Felix Speiser, of Basel.

[2] **CCXXVII**, p. 83.

[3] **LVI**, p. 320.

by an extravagant creation of minor divisions ("petites espèces") that a tendency to reaction is manifest. But once again I recognize that at first sight, and especially after the examination of the nasal characters, one is tempted to separate the Papuans from the Melanesians.

The Australians.—We shall be equally brief about the Australians, because their part, too, in history is difficult to estimate. In this huge island the human race, like the fauna and flora, may be looked upon as a geological relic. It is quite possible that the present-day Australians are the descendants of those men of particularly brutal build whose existence as early as in the ancient Quaternary the Talgai skull would seem to have revealed to us.

In his *Essai d'une classification des races humaines* Deniker[1] placed the Australians in group B, having frizzy or wavy hair, and with the following diagnosis: dark chocolate-brown skin, wide nose, medium height, dolichocephalic.

Formerly Topinard thought it possible to establish a difference between the type of the coast, of smaller stature, and the tribes of the interior, of taller stature and with better formed features.[2] To-day we find considerable uniformity among the Australian tribes, the purest, however, being those which people the centre of the continent, well protected as they are by the bad habitable conditions of their country, and the tribes of the northern coast. It is in these regions, and studying these groups, the least spoiled by contact with Europeans—those incredible destroyers of all ethnography and of all so-called lower races—that the closest observers of the Australians, such as Horn, Spencer and Gillen, Roth, etc., have made known to us the interesting customs which, without there being any question of relationship, have done so much to explain our European prehistoric ethnography. Their works constitute an inexhaustible mine of information.[3]

The Australian tribes, of whom many, alas! are now disappearing completely—and the European colonists, we repeat, are alone responsible—consist of people whose height

[1] **LVI**; also **LVII**, p. 339 (Eng. trans., p. 285).

[2] **CCLVI**, p. 211.

[3] W. E. Roth, *Ethnol. Studies of the N. W. Queensland Aborigines*, Brisbane and London, 1897; the anthropological work on Horn's scientific expedition was done by Sterling, *Report . . . Horn Scientif. Exped. Centr. Austr.*, Part iv, "Anthropology", by E. Stirling, London and Melbourne 1896. Also **CCXLVII**, *a* and *b*.

appears to be above the mean. In central Australia, which contains certainly the purest specimens, anthropologists have noted a stature of 1 metre 67. This figure is also represented in other series. The smallest statures indicated at the present time are those of men from New South Wales (1 metre 63). The Australians are dolichocephalic as well as being relatively tall. They are even highly dolichocephalic; and up to the present they are so everywhere (the mean cephalic indices are nearly all represented by 71 and 72).

These morphological characters of the skull and face are reproduced with the greatest precision by Spencer and Gillen's photographs. The prominent eyebrow ridges—sometimes forming an extraordinary vault above the eyes—and flat nose depressed at the root with its extremely wide nostrils, lends a somewhat bestial aspect to the physiognomy even of the children. We have before us—without seeking any relationship between them—a living presentment of the people of the European Moustierian period.

Let us add that this nose, seen from the side, while sometimes slightly up-turned in the children, is often almost aquiline in appearance in adults. The lips are enormous, and projected forwards, thus giving an exaggerated prognathous aspect to the face. The colour of the skin is dark chocolate brown. The pilous system is highly developed, especially on the body, and some of the old men are even quite shaggy. The beard and hair are very thick, the hair being frizzy or wavy.

It is certain that in many of their morphological characters the Australians approximate to the Melanesians. I have before me some excellent photographs (given to me by my British confrère, Ramsay Smith, of Australia), among which there are several representatives of the New Hebrides, and it is obvious that various parallels might be drawn between these two races.

The Tasmanians, now quite extinct—exterminated by the Europeans who hunted them like partridges—do not appear to have differed much from the Australians. It is sufficient to see the pictures which have been preserved of this unfortunate people to recognize in them the greater part of the Australian characters. The hair of the Tasmanians seems to have been crisp (instead of frizzy or wavy) and therein would lie an important difference between them and the Australians. But have we sufficient data to discuss their relationship other than superficially?

The Polynesians.—The Polynesian ethnic problem has long proved a temptation for the theoricians of Anthropology. Has insular isolation in geographical regions, sometimes differing considerably from one another as regards their constituent elements, created particular ethnic types special to each region ? So it has been thought. And in so thinking, has it not merely been a matter of logically extending to Man what has been observed in the case of plants and animals ? And has it not thereby been forgotten that mankind is not dominated by his environment in the same way as are plants and animals ?

At the beginning of this chapter on the Oceanians I roughly outlined the autochthony and migration theories, and I endeavoured to show how complex was the problem owing to the insufficiency of our documentation. I also called to mind that the Polynesians are a very different type of people from those who live to westward of them. *A priori* one would expect to find a multiplicity of human types in these multiple islands because of the very variety of their conditions of existence in latitudes extending from 30° north of the equator to very nearly 50° south of it, and stretching, moreover, to vast distances in an easterly and westerly direction. One would picture each of them adapted to their numerous environments and having the concomitant modifications which theory demands. Nothing could be further from the reality, and " the Polynesian race shows almost the same traits from the Hawaii Islands to New Zealand."

But Deniker[1], from whom we borrow this sentence, explained the unity of type of the Polynesians by " constant migrations from island to island, and the active trading carried on among themselves, the effect of which is to efface, by process of intermixture, differences arising from insular isolation."

But why imagine at all costs that insular isolation must be accompanied by morphological modification ?

Looked at as a whole the Polynesians are tall men. Several series, whose characteristics I have before me, have all yielded a stature exceeding 1 metre 72, to reach, in the Marquesas, 1 metre 74. New Zealand alone shows smaller men (1 metre 68), but this Polynesian minimum height still exceeds—and it is a

[1] LVII, p. 574 (Eng. trans., p. 500).

characteristic to remember—that yielded by measurement of the Melanesians, the Indonesians, the Malays, and the Australians.

With this tall stature the Polynesian associates a generally dolichocephalic or sub-dolichocephalic head[1]. Curiously enough it is the western islands which appear to hold the most dolichocephalic men—Fiji, cranial index of 67.2; the Carolines, cephalic index of 69.4; Loyalty group, index both on the living and on the cranium, about 72. In New Zealand the Maoris are slightly less dolichocephalic, while still retaining relatively a very long head (index of 73.6). But this observation stops short at the natives of the Gilbert Islands, which, although so near, seem to have a sub-dolichocephalic head. The people of the Marquesas, likewise, are sub-dolichocephalic.

This dolichocephaly of the Polynesians and western Micronesians has always been invoked as an element of morphological relationship with the Melanesians, who are nearly all out and out dolichocephals. And the hypotheses of gradual migration dates from this morphological similarity. It is a pity that we cannot, within the limits of this book, speak more in detail of these hypotheses, in some ways so alluring; we should have certain arguments to advance against them.

I call to mind that among these hypotheses there is one, secondary if you will, but of an importance that will not be missed by anyone. In the course of their voyages, always to the east—whether deliberately, in search of adventure, or involuntarily at the bidding of storms—the Polynesians are supposed to have reached the shores of America. And the American natives would thus be, in part, the descendants of these Oceanic Vikings. We have seen whether the Americans properly so-called possess morphological characters which would authorize them to claim such an ancestry.

In any hypothesis of a peopling effected from the west

[1] I do not understand what made Deniker call the Polynesians sub-brachycephals! He himself indicates a mean cephalic index of 82.6, from 178 measurements on the living, and of 79 from 328 crania (p. 574). But I do not think I am making a mistake in saying that all writers have pointed out the dolichocephaly of the Polynesians. Moreover, in the appendices which accompany his work Deniker does not indicate a single figure in any way expressing anything other, as regards his least long-headed form, than sub-dolichocephaly. He must have made a slip of the pen. (In the English edition the Polynesians are included on p. 588 of *Races of Man* under sub-dolichocephalic peoples.) [Translator's Note.]

it must also be explained how the Polynesians managed to increase their stature as they changed countries, and how their straight or wavy hair was derived from the crisp—or at least frizzy—hair of the Melanesians; how their skin was emptied of its pigment and changed from the dark tint that characterized the Melanesian skin to the browny tint, or yellowy brown, which it shows to-day; and how their nose was transformed, and the prominence of their cheekbones, etc., etc. Faced with the difficulty of invoking mesological influences—in spite of the monogenist's strong predilections—a mixture of blood has had to be called in. This element of demonstration is not enough to satisfy us.

This handsome Polynesian race—the race of the amorous isles of the southern seas—has undergone, since the arrival of the Europeans, such outrage (was there ever in Antiquity any barbarous invasion which did more harm to Eur-Asia than the European invasions in the Pacific?) that soon it will only be but a shadow of its former self. As a race, it is no more than a memory.

It will not become entirely extinct, since certain morphological characters will be preserved by cross-breeding and reversion to type. But is it not sad to see the people which calls itself the most civilized and the most pacific (!) taking with it, wherever it goes as master, the practical certainty that the natives will become extinct? When the governments of the great European States have acquired a modicum of moral science they will have to try to imitate Denmark in her laws of protection for the Eskimo.

A CHAPTER OF CONCLUSIONS

SOME people, superficially reading various passages in this book may have supposed that, in so far as certain times and places are concerned, we are to believe that there is evidence of a relation between Race and History, one conditioning the other. Yet it will be found that I have refrained from being positive in any sense. Is it not, as a matter of fact, just as impossible to deny to-day the existence of such a relation as it is positively to assert it ?

None the less, when we see spread out before our eyes the anthropological map of Europe it gives us furiously to think.

It is beyond question that there have been and that there will be again certain races that are more pacific than others, or, if we will, certain races that are more enterprising, bold, or warlike than others.

But are we quite sure that such distinctions—though they can be traced very far back in time—can be drawn definitively ? Are we sure that these descriptions for these particular races are indelible labels and that they represent with precision and finality definite ethnic qualities of the same order, shall we say, as the colour of the skin ? Has not the same race, in the course of its history, sometimes been a pacific and sometimes a conquering race ? Are we quite sure that conquest and invasion and great social modifications can always be explained by a special morphology? Or must we, on the contrary, eliminate racial determinism and take account only of the factor of environment in seeking an explanation of the events of history ?

Was it, for instance, really the mediocre conditions of existence offered by the very situation of their homeland to the Nordic race, combined with their high birthrate, which alone explained the warlike movements of these peoples and their repeated invasions, undeniably more frequent, and, it would seem, more calculated to submerge the invaded, than those of other peoples ? Certain writers, eliminating such factors and taking their stand on the certainly impressive facts, invoke the " bellicose nature " of these northern peoples. But what is such an imperative as a " bellicose nature " if not a part of this ensemble of morpho-physio-psychological characters whose sum constitutes the race ?

I see that a new school in Germany is coming back to this " *gestalt* theory " and endeavouring to show that mental structure has its basis in the physical structure of the organism. But without seeking very far, do not certain examples in Europe suffice to invalidate such hypotheses ? Have not Scandinavia and Switzerland both passed through extremely bellicose stages to become distinctly pacific States ? It might be objected that the people of these two countries may not, outside the mould into which their policies are now cast, have lost their former psycho-physiological make-up. For example, did not thousands upon thousands of Swiss volunteers enter the French army during the great war to take part in that adventure ? It is a problem of extreme complexity.

In connection with conquering peoples must we not, before definitively implicating race, among other things liquidate a certain point of an historical order ? Has an attempt ever been made to define with adequate care the causes of certain great human events ? As, for instance, the real cause behind the invasions of Mongols and Huns, Slavs and Germanic peoples ?

It is repeated, parrot-fashion—" feeling the pressure of poverty in their own land " this or that Barbarian People were set in movement. Does this phrase mean that since the economic conditions of this or that region had become too unfavourable to permit of the normal life of the groups inhabiting it, they were bound at all costs to set forth and seek subsistence elsewhere ? It is possible ; but in that case are we to believe that the number of that country's inhabitants and the tale of its produce has been counted and balanced and that it was found that the economic deficit was serious enough to necessitate such a tremendous event, so potentially disastrous in its consequences, as a mass migration of the people ?

In complete opposition to such findings as these, have there not been known in the course of History, and do we not see in many parts of the world to this day, terrible famines

—endemic in many countries—which have never been the cause of real migrations ?

*
* *

The morphological characters of which we have made use in classifying the people of different States, and the ethnic discriminations we have made may appear to some altogether too "simplist." It could not be otherwise in a book of this kind. We are aware, for example, that Belgium, Holland or Italy are inhabited by representatives of other races than the two chief races and by numerous cross-breeds of these two. Following the plan we drew up we were obliged to keep to essentials, and to single out the primordial elements of which the people under consideration had been built up. Furthermore, it would have been difficult in the present state of anthropological investigation to go beyond the limit we set ourselves. Not a country in Europe has sufficient knowledge of the details of its ethnic composition to enable it to draw up an exact chart. Wherever local investigation has been carried sufficiently far to distinguish human elements sharply differentiated from the main body we have placed these on record and have endeavoured to interpret their physiognomy. In several countries—Scandinavia, Ireland, Italy, the Dutch-Belgian border country etc.—we have pointed out the presence of ethnic islands of the highest interest.

We are so imperfectly informed as to the human make-up of European countries—and from that it can be estimated how much we know of regions outside Europe !—that one of the first tasks assumed by the International Institute of Anthropology on its foundation was to seek information, with all the necessary details, about the ethnic composition of the countries belonging to the Institute, and to ask for the publication of monographs indicating what peoples or races had successively entered these various countries there to form the existing population.

Despite the above remark I wish the reader to carry away with him the clear impression that, contrary to what many people imagine, the domain of Ethnology is by no means a chaos. Our classifications are not final, far from it. Doubtless they will still undergo many modifications. But how far we have come during the last fifty years ! Where once there seemed to be nothing but disorder and lack of precision, order has gradually been established and we are approaching clarity. Every day more light penetrates to the obscurest depths of our knowledge. Here we are thinking, it is true, mainly of Europe ; but this order and precision will also come in their turn to the other continents.

Anthropology has already solved a certain number of problems in which History's interest is of the first order.

Thus our ideas on the subject of the routes taken by several migrations have become more precise ; the direction from which ethnic overlapping has taken place all over the world is becoming clearer to us : for example, China was not peopled from the South northwards, nor can the Polynesian races have issued from Malaysia, and so on. Certain ethnic influences considered *a priori* as highly important have been revealed as practically non-existant (e.g., Phœnician influence in Africa ; German influence in Iberia ; Roman influence in the countries which possess Latin languages). Our ethnogenic point of view, formerly guided alone by the accounts of ancient historians and the positive assertions of philologists, needs revising in almost every direction. On the other hand our researches have here and there brought out the influence of an almost forgotten ethnic group, as, for example, that of the Wends in Saxony. The peopling of a part of central Europe from the polished stone age onwards has been effected not only by way of the river highways but also, and mainly, perhaps, by way of the Alpine passes ; the very localization of certain ethnic groups is better known ; and more acceptable filiations, both spatially and in terms of time, may now be envisaged.

Our liveliest wish is that this volume may contribute to a demonstration of the great interest of anthropological research in quarters where such interest does not yet exist, and that it may give fresh impetus to it where it has begun to languish. So many problems are linked up with a more complete and more accurate knowledge of our ethnic elements : the biology of race to which some ardent minds, notably in Sweden, are at present devoting themselves, will prove of value only in so far as analytical investigations are pursued with sufficient activity to enable the divers constituent groups to be isolated from the whole.

* * *

Shall we indicate some of the important problems which still invite research?

First of all there is the origin of the blue-eyed peoples to be met with throughout a large part of central and especially western Asia. Are they a remnant of the German bands which moved into Asia Minor at a known date? Or must we go further back into the past for an explanation of their presence and bring in the neolithic peoples of southern Russia, the possible predecessors of the Germanic race? But what was the earliest origin of this race which it pleases us to consider European? Is it really European?

Then how are we to interpret a unique event in world history—namely, what happened in Attica between 500 and 300 B.C., when in a relatively short space of time there shone forth so brilliant a galaxy of illustrious men? By a concentration of the best breeds, is it suggested? Yes, but which breeds? Or was it environmental influences, and, if so, what were those influences?

And can the skeletons met with in the Portuguese Neolithic at Mugem be envisaged—at least the Brachycephals among them—as belonging to North Africa? And must we add the problem of this old Iberian race to those we raised in the first chapter of this book relating to a peopling of Europe during the Palæolithic by a population coming from East Africa?

Again, were the various palæolithic civilizations the handiwork of ethnically differing peoples, and did the disappearance in the pleistocene past of such and such a social facies correspond to the disappearance of a race? For instance, was the Moustierian civilization, as it would seem, an attribute of *Homo neanderthalensis?* Was the suddenness with which the Magdalenian civilization was extinguished due, as has been thought, to ethnic changes?

And how many more questions crowd together at the point of our pen!

* * *

Among the results from modern anthropological investigations there are many which radically modify the conceptions we had built up—somewhat theoretically by too facile extensions thought to be legitimate—with regard to certain human associations in certain parts of Europe.

We have indicated some of the more interesting among them, and we have occasionally reminded the historians how profitable an anthropological analysis might prove in such circumstances. In the chapter devoted to Scandinavia we pointed out large colonies of Brachycephals on that human background whose dolichocephalic unity appears to be so indisputable that it serves for an example in our classes and discussions. Nearly half the inhabitants of the territory of the southernmost coast of Norway, of which Stavanger is the chief town, have a cephalic index reaching and exceeding 82. This is a considerable breach in that citadel, apparently so homogeneously built up, of the Nordic race. Is this not where the historian should step in?

And, without quitting the North Sea, we may call to mind another very important ethnological finding. The Faroe Islands, far out from Norway in the open sea on the route to Iceland, contain a special population whose presence in such a spot is an enigma. Many of these fishermen are tall Brachycephals. Which of us could have expected to find such an ethnic presentment in such a spot?

Men belonging to the same group likewise people the Shetlands, and on the other side of the North Sea, the Scottish coast. There seems then to be no doubt at all about it —the northern part of the North Sea, on both its coasts and in its islands is inhabited by people belonging in the main to two races, the dolichocephalic Nordic race—as has always been taught—and this other race, characterized by its brachycephaly and its tall stature. And what is this other race?

Gray considers that these men are related to the Dinaric race. Then let us remind ourselves of the principal habitat of this race. The Adriatic and Ionian coasts, with a more or less extensive hinterland, constitutes the Dinaric realm. Did they, then, cross right over Europe? And when? In prehistoric times? Or in historic times? And if so, under what name? And how? What route did these Dinaric people follow in their journey across the continent? What was their first stage on the shores of the North Sea? It is of considerable import to us to find out! Was it Scotland or

Scandinavia? And when did they set sail from one of these points to go out and seek the other?

How many questions—and these are but the first of them—are raised by the results of an investigation which, at first sight, seemed merely to be a fresh scientific record!

Maybe this Dinaric migration—if we are to accept it—goes back a long way into the past? Maybe it was during the bronze age that these people passed into Scandinavia via the Tyrol—or Bavaria—North Germany and Schleswig?

Once again, whether it likes it or not, History can no longer do without Anthropology.

*

* *

Several chapters of this book have shown how extremely cautious one has to be in interpreting the morphological differences revealed in regions of varying geographical or economical types which seem by their very variety at once to give us the key to the phenomena observed. And as we looked through the literature we found explanations of this kind at every step to which we had to add a point of interrogation. Certain parts of Germany have been demonstrative in this regard. For instance, in Thuringia, where, in an apparently identical ethnic environment unfavourable economic conditions—if we follow the current theory—ought to have diminished human stature, we found statures much superior to those supplied by regions that are far more favoured economically. The explanation is that interpretations of this nature simply forget that the world is not peopled by representatives of a single race.

The same thing has happened as regards the influence of physical environment. We have seen in many countries how writers have strained every nerve to make certain morphologies square with certain natural boundaries. How much more simple it would have been to appeal to the only factor they forgot—namely the diversity of human races! It is because the great service Anthropology can render to Human Geography, Economics, and Sociology has been ignored that so many incorrect theories have been set up which we have now to demolish, and that so much good paper has been wasted which we shall discreetly leave to slumber in the peaceful shades of the libraries.

Unsuccessful experiments are often very useful. But it is necessary that the result of them should not be forgotten.

*

* *

There is one problem much talked of to-day in which Anthropology and History alike are intimately concerned—or perhaps we should say a problem which has once more become the subject of discussion, since the *Essai sur l'inégalité des races humaines* reposes on it in part—a problem which legitimately causes anxiety to many minds. I speak of ethnic intermixture, of cross-breeding and the results advantageous or disadvantageous which may flow from it for the White peoples.

A number of cases can be envisaged, and I will take two of these by way of example.

I.—Two considerable groups of American Indians—belonging, possibly, to the same race, which is not without import in the matter—have created the great civilizations of Mexico and the Andean plateaux. The arrival of the Spaniards completely destroyed this two-fold civilization. And we know what has become of the descendants of the Mexicans and the Incas—many of them, both in aspect and in culture are now no more than lamentable caricatures of Spanish-Americans.

In certain parts, however, and information from various points agrees as to this, we find that the natives—after a long servitude—are coming back to the front rank ; that they are becoming the mainspring of social life. Is not this page of history of the highest interest ? What has happened ? To what causes shall we attribute this coming back ? Is it entirely due to renewed environmental influence, and to the sole play of circumstances ? In other words, have the people themselves but a minimal and quite inert part in the matter ? Or, is this change due, on the contrary, to those mysterious elements which we call inherent racial possibilities ? And have we not enough examples of man's victory over the most unfavourable physical environment to justify us in postulating such a hypothesis ?

Let us admit that spatially the people alone are concerned since the environment itself has not changed for some centuries. If the new social group is of pure race we must admit that, over and above all other contingencies, race is capable of presenting the phenomenon of an extraordinary elasticity—in that sense in which the word is understood by physicists—

whose mechanism, at the moment, we do not quite understand. Such a finding would take us back to the old mystic conception of the good and ill luck of empires and their reverses followed again, one day, perhaps, by fresh good fortune ; this would be a genuine fatalism of history. If the social group in question is cross-bred we can then conceive of the intervention of those factors still too little known by historians, and also by anthropologists, which we call by that vague name of racial factors. Have not facts which might be extremely suggestive been recognized in this connection ? Hunt has shown that the brain of a Mulatto reverting to the White breed is notably heavier than that of a Mulatto reverting to the Black breed.

To take into consideration only this instance above, is it the introduction of White blood which, in the majority of cases, brings about this social regeneration of which we spoke ? If this is the cause, how much White blood is needed to bring about such a change—such rejuvenation—in a group apparently exhausted ? Will a fifty per cent. cross suffice ? Or must the hybridization be a quarter strain, or an eighth, or even less, up to the point when the European influence becomes so preponderant that the other is almost effaced ?

And what is the value, in the case of such a large proportion of European blood, of the small strain of native blood that remains ? Should it be considered, in lands where Europeans so easily grow soft, as the deflagrating agent of those latent European qualities which, without its admixture, would remain inert ? Chemistry shows us that in many cases it suffices to add but the minutest quantity of some particular substance to modify a combination completely. And we know, in physiology, what are the repercussions of intervention by the endocrine glands.

The structure, with all that word implies, having been modified, new possibilities result for the new race thus created. It almost amounts to physiological mysticism ! We questioned but just now whether such inter-relations are worthy of credence.

II.—Does the White race risk nothing by allowing itself to be penetrated by alien blood ?

Whether we like it or not, ethnic intermixture is going on all around us. But do not let us be misunderstood. When two peoples of different name and language but of the same ethnic origin fuse, such, for example, as Italians and French people of Mediterranean race, or Scandinavians and Germans of Nordic race, there is no risk to be run from heredity by either group. Both will retain their own qualities, their respective racial values. But when the amalgam is brought about as between two highly different races there is genuine danger for Eugenics.

The medical formula of " Cross the breeds " resulted from the fight considered necessary—but was it ?—against consanguineous marriages. It should not be stretched unduly —at all events not till we have more convincing information with regard to it.

We may believe that the influence of White blood will be the social salvation of certain races held to be inferior ; but has the influence on History of the opposite phenomenon been measured ?—of the introduction of alien blood penetrating into ours, imposing on it its own qualities, neutralizing ours, or causing them to deviate ?

There are in the United States, according to the American statistics I have before me, about 8 million pure-blooded Negroes and 2 million Mulattos. It is estimated that in the course of the last score of years the number of Mulattos has increased twice as fast as the number of Blacks. Then what, in a hundred and fifty years, will the ethnic physiognomy of certain American States be like ? What kind of chapter will these cross-bred people contribute to History at that period ? If, for instance, an adventure identical with that of the great war were to be set on foot, what would be the attitude of a country in which Negroes and Mulattos or other hybrids had reached such considerable proportions as to constitute a large part of the body politic ? Would History then repeat itself ?

The violent resistance many " Yankees " have made to the introduction of Blacks into no matter what department of American society has doubtless been inspired by a caste egoism, and many have blamed them for it. But has it not also been regarded as an urge of racial instinct which unconsciously is acutely aware of all the consequences of this too dissimilar human intermixture, diminishing, each time that it comes about, the " ethnic power " of the Whites ; aware of all the depreciation in value, all the defects which come to the top, and all the political surrenders—and of their repercussion on History ?

These problems of the mixture of races bear on the past as well as the future of Humanity in the most intimate manner.

*

* *

This book, though it might easily run to double the number of pages, must have a term set to it.

Is Anthropology capable of replying to-day with some degree of accuracy to the shoal of questions brought to it—as though it were some oracle charged with the task of solving every difficult problem ? Or capable at least of replying to some of the questions which have been raised in the first pages of this book ? We have seen that it is still far from having a knowledge of all that it would like to know.

As with other sciences it will never realize its ideal ; it will achieve but a part of its ambitions. Take the memoirs devoted to special researches, or, to state the matter in a still more elementary fashion, only those chapters treated of in this volume : study them, and it will be seen how little they contain in comparison with what we desire to know. Thanks to a thousand converging efforts we have learned two or three letters of a difficult alphabet or, if it is preferred, two or three pages of a very large volume. There our acquisitions end.

Yet they are not negligible. All the sciences appear to be discouraging in the beginning because of the multitude of problems they at once set before us. But Zoology and Botany, for instance, have mastered the abundance and complexity of the forms submitted to their examination. The multitude of stars which, at first, is veritably incredible, has not discouraged the astronomer. I am well aware that Anthropology presents, by reason of its very subject, difficulties which the other sciences have never known.

Anthropology has made sufficient progress and has lifted a sufficient number of veils since it was individualized to inspire the most complete confidence in its future. It is certain that a day will come when we shall have penetrated some of the mysteries which to-day are as forbidden ground to us. Thirty years ago the greater part of a book like this could not have been written. When Ripley published his book, *The Races of Europe*, and Deniker his maps, these savants had to use hatchings or colours to represent, by extension, the anthropological characters of considerable spaces about which we knew almost nothing.

It is not so very long since then, and already we can contribute, in many regions up till then ethnically unexplored, a whole mass of new data. Each generation thus accomplishes its task, contributing its bricks and mortar. To ours it belongs not to betray the legitimate hopes placed in it. Humanity, no matter what forms its activities may take (we have given proof of it) is in urgent need of the help of Anthropology.

It is only at the beginning of what it can do to help History, considerable though its aid has already been.

THE END.

BIBLIOGRAPHY

An asterisk indicates the more important works. Those that are essential are marked with two asterisks.

Ammon (O.) *Zur Anthropologie der Badener. Berichte über die von Anthr. Kommission..vorgenommenen Untersuchungen*, Jena, 1899, in-8°, 15 maps *I

Anoutchine, *De la distribution géographique de la taille de la population masculine en Russie* (in Russian), Mémoires de la Société russe de géographie, tome VII, fascicule I, 1889, with 10 maps *II

Apostolidès, *Quelques mesures sur le vivant prises en Grèce.* Bull. de la Soc. d'Anthropologie, Paris, 1883 III

Aragon y Escancena, *Breve estudio antropologico acerca del pueblo Maragato.* Annals of the Spanish Natural History Society, vol. XXX, 1902 IV

Auerbach, *Les races et les nationalités en Autriche-Hongrie*, Paris, 1898 *V

Aranzadi y Unamuno y L. Hoyos, *Un avance á la Antropologia de España.* Annals of the Spanish Natural History Society, Madrid, 1892 VI

Arbo, *Ya-t-il eu des immigrations successives dans la péninsule Scandinave?* In the Scand. review, Imer, Stockholm, 1900 VII

Bassanovitch, *Matériaux pour l'ethnographie sanitaire de la Bulgarie, district de Lom*, Sofia, 1891 (in Bulgarian, quoted by Deniker) *VIII

Baye (de), *Les Juifs des montagnes et les Juifs Géorgiens, souvenirs d'une mission*, Paris, 1902 IX

Beddoe, *Histoire de l'indice céphalique dans les îles Britanniques.* L'Anthropologie, Paris, 1894 X

Beldiceano, *Station préhistorique de Coucouteni (Moldavie).* Bull. Soc. anthrop. Paris, 1889.—*Nouvelles idoles de Coucouteni.* Ibid., Paris, 1890 XI

Bergeron, *Relations des voyages en Tartarie de Fr. Guillaume de Rubruquis, Fr. Jean du Plan Carpin, etc.*, Paris, 1634.—*Un traité des Tartares, etc.*, Paris, 1634 XII

Bertholon, *Deux crânes phéniciens trouvés, en Tunisie.* L'Anthropologie, Paris, 1890.—*Documents anthropologiques sur les Phéniciens.* Bull. Soc. anthrop. Lyon, 1892.—*Identité des caractères anthropologiques des Basques et des Phéniciens.* Bull. Soc. anthr. Paris, 1896 XIII

Bertholon et Chantre, *Recherches anthropologiques dans la Berbérie orientale*, Lyon, 1913 **XIV

Bertrand, *Nos origines, la Gaule avant les Gaulois, d'après les monuments et les textes*, Paris, 1891 XV

Beuchat, *Manuel d'archéologie américaine*, Paris, 1912 **XVI

Blumenbach, *Decades cranorium* XVII

Bolk, *Répartition dy type blond et du type brun dans les Pays-Bas.* Bull et Mém. Soc. d'anthropol. Paris, 1905 XVIII

Boué, *La Turquie d'Europe*, Paris, 1840 XX

Boule, *Les hommes fossiles*, Paris, 1921. (Eng. trans. by J. E. and J. Ritchie, London, 1923) **XXI
,, *L'homme fossile de la Chapelle-aux-Saints.* Annales de paléontologie, Paris, 1911-1913 **XXII
Breuil, *Peintures et gravures murales des cavernes paléolithiques. La caverne d' Altamira à Santillane près Santander (Espagne)* par Cartailhac et l'abbé Breuil, Monaco, 1906 XXIII
Broca, Bulletin de la Société d'anthropologie, 1886.—*Remarques sur les ossements des cavernes de Gibraltar.* Bull. de la Soc. d'anthropol. Paris, 1869 XXIV
,, *Sur les crânes des Grottes de Baye.* Bull. de la Soc. d'anthr. Paris, 1875 XXV
,, *Instructions générales pour les recherches anthropologiques sur le vivant*, Paris, 1879 *XXVI
,, *Instructions craniologiques et craniométriques*, Paris, 1875 *XXVII
Brunhes et Vallaux, *La géographie de l'historie*, Paris, 1921 XXVIII
Buchtela, *Vorgeschichte Böhmens. Nordböhmen, bis zur Zeit um Christi Geburt*, Prage, 1899; analysis by S. Reinach, l'Anthropologie, 1900 XXIX
Burckhard, *Untersuchungen über die erste Bevölkerung des Alpengebirges.* Arch. f. Schweiz, Gesch., t. IV XXX
Butureanu, *Rasele preistorice de la Cucuteni*, Assoc. rom. pent. înaintarea si respândirea sciintelor, Congresul de la Iasi, 1902 XXXI

Capitan, *Les Silex tertiaires d'Ipswich* (Angleterre). Revue anthropologique, Paris, 1922.—Capitan, Fourmariez, Fraipont, Hamal et Lohest, *Conclusions de l'enquête sur les silex d'Ipswich.* Revue anthropol., Paris, 1923 XXXII
Capus, *A travers la Bosnie et l'Herzégovine*, Paris, 1896.—*Sur la taille en Bosnie.* Bull. de la Société d'anthrop. Paris, 1895 XXXIII
Cartailhac, *Les Ages préhistoriques de l'Espagne et du Portugal*, Paris, 1886 **XXXIV
,, *La France préhistorique d'après les sépultures et les monuments*, Paris, 1889 XXXV
,, *L'âge de la pierre en Asie.* Cong. des Orientalistes, 1878 (see Breuil) XXXVI
Cerralbo, *Torralba, la plus ancienne station humaine de l'Europe.* C. R. Congrès de Genève, 1912 XXXVII
Chabas, *Étude sur l'antiquité historique*, quoted by Bertholon et Chantre XXXVIII
Chantre, *Crânes de la nécropole de Sidon.* Bull. Soc. anthrop. Lyon, 1894 XXXIX
,, *Recherches anthropologiques dans le Caucase*, t. I, Paris, 1885; t. IV, Paris-Lyon, 1887 **XL
,, *Recherches anthropologiques dans l'Asie occidentale.* Archiv. Museum Hist. nat. Lyon, 1895 **XLI
,, *Rapport sur une mission scientifique dans l'Asie occidentale, spécialement dans les régions de l'Ararat et du Caucase.* Arch. des Missions scientif., 1893 XLII
,, *Recherches anthropologiques en Égypte.* Lyon, 1904. **XLIII
,, *Mission scientifique en Transcaucasie, Asie Mineure, Syrie.* Arch. Mus. Hist. nat. Lyon, 1895 **XLIV
,, *Aperçu sur les caractères ethniques des Anshetriés o des Kurdes.* Bull. Soc. anthr. Lyon, 1882 XLV
Charencey, *Races et langues du Japon.* Ass. franç. pour l'avanc. des sciences, 1901 XLVI

Clarke (ed. Daniel), *Travels in Russia, Tartary and Turkey*, 1810-23 **XLVII**

Collignon, *Étude anthropométrique élémentaire des principales races de la France*. Bull. Soc. d'anthropol. Paris, 1883 ****XLVIII**

Cordier (H.), *Les Lolos*, T'oung-pao, vol. VIII, nº 5, Leide, 1907;—*L'origine des Chinois*, T'oung-pao, volume XVI, nº 5 **XLIX**

Czekanowsky (Y.), *Recherches anthropologiques de la Pologne*. Bull. et Mém. Soc. d'anthropol. Paris, 1920 **L**

Déchelette, *Manuel d'archéologie préhistorique, celtique et gallo-romaine*, Paris, 1908 ****LI**

" *Les tumuli de pierres du sud-ouest de la Bohême*, résumé. L'Anthropologie, Paris, 1901 **LII**

Deniker, *La taille en Europe*, 1908 ****LIII**

" *La taille en Europe, 2ᵉ supplément: les Turcs Tatars et les Caucasiens*. Bull. et Mém. Soc. d'anthropol. Paris, 1909 ****LIV**

" *L'indice céphalique en Europe*. Ass. fr. pour l'avanc. des sciences, Paris, 1889 ****LV**

" *Essai d'une classification des races humaines*. Bull. Soc. d'anthropol. Paris, 1889 **LVI**

" *Les races et peuples de la Terre*, Paris, 1900. (Eng. trans. Contemp. Sc. Series. London, 1900) ****LVII**

" *Sur les Kalmouks au Jardin d'acclimatation*. Bull. Soc. d'anthr. Paris, 1883 **LVIII**

" *Les peuples balkaniques (surtout les Serbes et les Bulgares) au point de vue anthropologique*. Inst. franç. d'anthropol. (séance du 16 avril 1913) **LIX**

Dottin, *Les anciens peuples de l'Europe*, Paris, 1916, p. XI **LX**

Doutté, *Les Marocains et la société marocaine*. Revue générale des sc., Paris, 1903 **LXI**

Drontschilow, *Beiträge zur Anthropologie der Bulgaren* (thesis), Braunschweig, 1914.—*Die Körpergrösse der bulgarischen Rekruten und ihre Verteilung in den einzelnen Distrikten*. Arch. für Anthropologie, Band XIII **LXII**

Dufréné, *Étude sur l'histoire de la production et du commerce de l'étain*, Paris, 1886 **LXIII**

Duhousset, *Etude sur les populations de la Perse*, Paris, 1863. **LXIV**

Duncan White, *Notes on the height and weight of the Hoklo people of the Kwantung province of South China*. Journal of the Royal Anthropological Inst., 1911 **LXV**

Dussaud (R.), *Les civilisations préhelléniques dans le bassin de la mer Égée*, Paris, 1914 ****LXVI**

Entente internationale pour l'unification des mesures anthropométriques sur le vivant (reporters: Duckworth, Rivet, Schlaginhaufen), compte rendu de la XIVᵉ session, Genève, 1912 (appeared in 1914) **LXVII**

Fiala, *Praehistorischen Wohnstäte in Sobunar bei Sarajevo*. Wiss. Mitth. aus Bosnien und der Herzegowina **LXVIII**

Fishberg, *The Jews, a Study of Race and Environment*. Contemporary Science series, London, 1911 **LXIX**

" *Beiträge zur physichen Anthropologie der Nord Afrikanischen Juden*. Zeitschr. für Demogr. und Statistik der Juden, 1905 **LXX**

Folmer, Nederlandsche Schedels, Nederl. Tijdschr. voor Geneeskunde, Amsterdam, 1892 **LXXI**

Fontes, *Note sur le Chelléen de Casal do Monte* (1915) in the Communicaçoes of the Portuguese Geological

Service.—*Station paléolithique de Mealhada. Instruments paléolithiques*, in the prehistoric Collection of Geological Service, Lisbon, 1915 LXXII
Fraipont, *Les Néolithiques de la Meuse*. Bull. Soc. d'anthr. Brussels, 1898 *LXXIII

Gaet, *Sur les Phéniciens d'Acre*. Bull. Soc. d'anthropol. de Paris, 1886 LXXIV
Galippe, *L'hérédité des stigmates de dégénérescence et les familles souveraines*, Paris, 1905 LXXV
Gamio, *Los excavaciones del Pedregal de Sad Angel y la cultura arcaica del Valle de Mexico*. American Anthropologist, 1920 LXXVI
Gaupp, *Vorläufiger Bericht über anthropologische Untersuchungen an Chinesen und Mandschuren in Peking*. Zeitsch. f. Ethn., 1909 vol. XLI, p. 730 LXXVII
Geikie (J.), *The Antiquity of Man in Europe* Edin., 1914 *LXXVIII
Geoffroy Saint-Hilaire, Mém. Soc. d'anthropologie Paris, 1861 LXXIX
Girard, *Les tribus sauvages du Haut-Tonkin*. Soc. de géogr., hist. et descript., 1903 LXXX
Giuffrida Ruggeri, *Crani egiziani antichi e arabo egiziani*. Atti della Soc. romana d'anthropol., vol. XV, fascicule II, 1910 LXXXI
,, *Contributo all' antropologia fisica delle regioni dinariche e danubiane e dell'Asia anteriore*. Archivo per l'Antropologia e l'Etnologia, 1908 *LXXXII
Glotz, *La civilisation égéenne*. N° 9 de l'Évolution de l'Humanité, Paris, 1923. (Eng. trans. *The Ægean Civilization*, 1925, in *History of Civilization*) *LXXXII *bis*
Gluck, *Zur physichen Anthropologie der Albanesen*. Wiss. Mitth. aus Bosnien und der Herzegowina, Vienna, 1897 LXXXIII
Gobineau, *Essai sur l'inégalité des races humaines*, Paris, 1884 *LXXXIV
Goldstein, *Die Jüdische Bevölkerung Kanadas*. Zeitschr. für Demogr. und Statist. der Juden, 1909 LXXXV
Gray (J.), *Physical Characteristics of the People of East Aberdeenshire*. Transact. of the Buchan Field Club, 1895 et 1897. Résumé *in* Proceed. Brit. Assoc. adv. Sc., 1895 (Ipswich) LXXXVI
Gumplovicz, *La lutte des races*, Paris, 1893 LXXXVII

Haeckel, *Essai d'une classification des races humaines*. Bull. Soc. anthropol. Paris, 1889 LXXXVIII
Hahn, *Albanesische Studien*, Jena, 1854 LXXXIX
Hamy, *Contribution à l'anthropologie de la Haute-Albanie*. Bull. Muséum d'hist. naturelle, Paris, 1900 XC
,, *Précis de Paléontologie humaine*, Paris, 1870 **XCI
Hecquart, *Histoire et description de la Haute-Albanie*, 1859 XCII
Hell, *Les steppes de la mer Caspienne*, Paris, 1845 XCIII
Hervé, *Populations mésolithiques et néolithiques de l'Espagne et du Portugal*. Revue mens. de l'École d'anthropologie, Paris, 1899 XCIV
,, *Les Germains*. Revue École d'anthropologie, Paris 1897 *XCV
,, *Les populations lacustres*. Revue École d'anthropologie, Paris, 1895 *XCVI
,, *Crânes néolithiques armoricains de type négroïde*. Bull. et mém. Soc. d'anthropol. Paris, 1902 XCVII
Hillebrand, *Ueber die neueren paläolitischen Höhlenfunde Ungarns*. Zeitsch. für Ethnol., 1913; XIV.

International Congress of Anthropology and Prehistoric Archæology, Geneva, 1912 XCVIII
Himmel, *Körpermessungen in der Bukowina.* Mitteil. der Anthropologie Gessellschaft, Vienna, 1888. See Revue d'anthropologie, 1889 XCIX
Hippocrates, *On Airs, Waters, and Places.* (Eng. trans. in Genuine Works of Hippocrates. 2 vols. London, Sydenham Society, 1849) C
His and Rutimeyer, *Crania Helvetica.* Sammlung Schweizerischer Schädelform, Basel and Geneva, 1864, 1 vol. in-4° with atlas **CI
Hoernes, *Der diluviale Mensch.* **CII
Hoppeler, *Untersuchungen über die erste Bevölkerung des Alpengebirges.* Arch. für Schweiz. Gesch., v. 33 CIII
Houssay, *Les peuples actuels de la Perse.* Bull. Soc. anthr. Lyon, 1887 CIV
Houzé (E.), *Rapport sur les crânes de la province de Namur* (*Wancennes, Franchemont, Bois des Sorcières près de Florennes*). Bull. Soc. anthropol. Brussels, 1883, t. II CV
,, *Comparaison des indices céphalométriques et craniométriques.* Bull. et Mém. Soc. d'anthropol. Brussels, 1887, t. V CVI
,, *Communication préliminaire sur quelques nouveaux caractères qui différencient les races en Belgique.* Bull. Soc. d'anthr. Brussels, 1888 CVII
,, *Les Francs des cimetières de Belgique, Étude anthropologique.* Bull. Soc. d'anthropol. Brussels, 1891, t. IX CVIII
,, *Les néolithiques de la province de Namur.* C. R. Congrès d'archéol. et d'histoire, 1903, Namur, 1904 **CIX
,, *L'indice nasal des Flamands et des Wallons.* Bull. de la Soc. d'anthr. Brussels, 1882 CX
,, *La taille et la circonférence thoracique, etc., des Flamands et des Wallons.* Bull. de la Soc. d'anthropol., Brussels, 1888 CXI
,, *L'indice céphalique de la Belgique.* Bull. Soc. anthr. Brussels, 1887 **CXII
Hoyos Sainz, *Caractères généraux de la Crania Hispanica.* C. R. du XIVe Congrès intern. d'anthropol. et d'archéol. préhistoriques, Genève, 1912, t. II CXIII
Hryncewicz, Talko, *The Aryans, Contribution to the anthropology of the Great Russians. The Seméiskié Schismatics* (*Staroobriadtsi*) *of Transbaikalia* (in Russian), Tomsk., 1898 CXIV
Hubert (H.), *La date de l'arrivée des premiers Bretons en Grande-Bretagne.* L'Anthropol., Paris, 1922 CXV
Huguet, *Les Juifs du Mzab.* Bull. et Mém. de la Soc. d'anthropol. Paris, 1902 CXVI
Huxley, Journ. Ethnol. Soc. London, 1870 CXVII

Italia-Nicastro, *Sur les Phéniciens d'Acre.* Bull. Soc. d'anthropol. Paris, 1886 CXVIII

Jacques (V.), *L'ethnologie préhistorique dans le Sud-Est de l'Espagne.* Bull. de la Soc. d'anthropol. Brussels, 1888, t. VI CXIX
,, *La Zélande, compte rendu du cinquième Congrès de la Fédération des sociétés d'histoire et d'archéologie de Belgique.* Bull. Soc. d'anthr. Brussels, t. VIII CXX

Janko (J.), *Magyarische Typen*, first series, *Die Umgebungen des Balaton ;* Ethnogr. Samml. des Ungar. National museums, II, 1900, in-4°, with 24 pl. CXXI
Johansen (avec la collaboration de Knut Jessen et de Herluf Winge), *Une station du plus ancien age de la pierre dans la tourbière de Svaerdborg*, Copenhagen, 1920 *CXXII
Jorga, *L'Art populaire en Roumanie*, 1923 CXXII *bis*

Keith, *The Antiquity of Man*, London, 1915. (Revized and enlarged ed. in 2 vols. London, 1925) **CXXIII
Khanikoff, *Mémoire sur l'ethnographie de la Perse.* Mém. Soc. de géogr. Paris, 1866 CXXIV
Kleiweg and Zwaan, Various works on the Anthropology of Malaysia, Amsterdam, 1908 CXXV
Koganei (Y.), *Kurze Mittheilung über Messungen an mannlichen Chinesen-Schädeln.* Intern. Zentral Blatt für Anthropol., 1901 CXXVI
„ *Messungen an Chinesen*, Report (in German) of the Medical Faculty of the University of Tokyo, 1903, vol. VI CXXVII
Kopernicki (Majer et), *Physical Characters of the Population of Galicia* (in Polish). Collection of Papers published by the Krakow Acad. of Sc., vol. I, 1877 ; vol. IX, 1885 **CXXVIII
Krukowsky, *Les fouilles des cavernes de la chaîne de Cracovie, Wielun.* Soc. des sc. de Varsovie, décembre 1920, Archiwum nank anthropologicznych, vol. I, n° 6 CXXIX

Lagneau, *Anthropologie de la France.* Extracted from Dict. encycl. des Sc. méd., Paris, 1879 **CXXX
Lalanne, *Bas-reliefs à figuration humaine de l'abri sous roche de Lausse (Dordogne).* L'Anthropologie, 1912 CXXXI
Lapouge, *Les sélections sociales*, Paris, 1896 **CXXXII
, (Vacher de Lapouge), *L'Aryen et son rôle social*, Paris, 1889 **CXXXIII
Lartet, *Note sur la découverte de silex taillés en Syrie, accompagnée de quelques remarques sur l'âge des terrains qui constituent la chaîne du Liban.* Bull. Soc. géol. de France, 19 June 1865 CXXXIV
Le Bon, *De Moscou aux monts Totras : étude sur la formation actuelle d'une race.* Bull. Soc. géogr. Paris, 1881 CXXXIV *bis*
Lebzelter, *Unsere Kenntnisse von der physichen Beschaffenheit der Völker Osterreichs.* Zeitschr. für österr. Volkskunde, Vienna, 1914 *CXXXV
Legendre, *Études anthropologiques sur les Chinois du Setchouen.* Bull. et mém. Soc. anthropol. Paris, 1910 CXXXVI
Lehmann-Nitche, *Ueber die langen Knochen der südbayerischen Reihengräber-Bevölkerung*, Munich, 1895 CXXXVII
Lejean, *Ethnographie de la Turquie d'Europe*, Gotha, 1861 CXXXVIII
Lenhossek, *Des déformations artificielles du crâne en général, etc.*, Budapest, 1880 CXXIX
„ *Die Ausgrabungen zu Szeged-Othalom, etc.*, Vienna, 1886 CXL
Lencevicz, *Population des montagnes de Kielce au point de vue anthropologique*, in the publications of the Warsaw Scientific Society, 1916, p. 565, résumé in French, p. 603 CXLI
Lissauer, *Crania prussica.* Zeitschrift für Ethnologie, 1874. —*Crania prussica.* Zeitschr. für Ethnol., 1878 *CXLII

Livi, *Antropometria militare : Risultati ottenuti dallo spoglio fogli sanitarii dei militari delle classi* 1859-63. Parte I, *Dati antropologici, Roma*, 1896. Parte II, *Dati demografici e biologici*, Roma, 1905 **CXLIII

Luschan (Petersen and), *Reisen in Lykien und Kibyratis*, Vienna, 1889 **CXLIV

,, *Voelker, Rassen, Sprachen*. Berlin, 1922. *CXLV

Mackeprang (Ed.), *La taille des conscrits en Danemark. Memoir on Danish Anthropology* (in Danish), vol. i. Copenhagen, 1907 (French résumé by J. Deniker) CXLVI

Man, *Bijdrage tot de Kennis van de Schedelworm in Walcheren*, in Nederlands Tijdschrift voor geneeskunde, 1885 CXLVII

Manouvrier, *Réponses aux objections contre le Pithecanthropus*. Bull. Soc. anthropol. Paris, 1896 CXLVIII

Mansuy, *Gisement préhistorique de la caverne de Pha-Binh-Gia* (Tonkin). L'Anthropologie, Paris, 1909 CXLIX

Mantegazza et Zanetti, *Note antropologische nelle Sardegna*. Arch. anthrop. et ethnol., 1876, vol. IV CL

Marett, *Pleistocene Man in Jersey*. Archæologia, LXII, 1911. (and LXIII ; also LXVII, 1916) CLI

Matiegka, *Contribution à la connaissance de la constitution physique des habitants du Nord-Ouest de la Bohême*, résumé in Mitth. Anth. Gessells. Vienna, vol. XXII, 1892.—*Origine et progrès des études anthropologiques des pays tchèques*, 1898 CLII

Mayet, *Note sur les sciences anthropologiques en Hollande et en Belgique*, Lyon, 1902 CLIII

Meillet, *Les langues dans l'Europe nouvelle*, Paris, 1918 CLIV

Meisner (Dr), *Zur Statistik der Körpergrösse der Schleswiger Wehrpflichtigen*. Arch. f. Anthr., vol. XIV, 1883. *Die Körpergrösse der Wehrpflichtigen im Gebiete der Unterelbe, insbesondere in Holstein*. Arch. für Anthropologie, vol. XVIII, 1889 CLV

,, *Die Körpergrösse der Wehrpflichtigen in Mecklenbourg*. Arch. für Anthropologie, vol. XIX, 1891 CLVI

Mendes Correa, *Origin of the Portuguese* (extract from the American Journ. of Physical Anthropology). See Archiv. suisses d'anthrop. générale, 1919 CLVII

Mercier, *Histoire de l'Afrique septentrionale*, t. I CLVIII

Mitra, *Prehistoric Cultures and Races of India*, Calcutta, 1920 CLIX

Mochi, *Sulla antropologia degli Arabi*. Archiv. p. l'Antropologia vol. XXXVI, 1907, fasc. 3 CLX

Moir, *The Occurrence of a Human Skeleton in a Glacial Deposit at Ipswich*. Proceedings of the Preh. Soc. of East Anglia, I, 1912. *Further Discoveries of Humanly-fashioned Flints in and beneath the Red Crag of Suffolk*. Ipswich, 1920-21 CLXI

Montandon, *Notice préliminaire sur les Aïnou*. Archiv. suisses d'anthr. gén., Geneva, 1911 CLXII

Morgan (J. de), *L'Humanité préhistorique, esquisse de préhistoire générale*, Paris, 1922. (Eng. trans. *Prehistoric Man*, in History of Civilization, London, 1924) **CLXIII

,, *Recherches sur les origines de l'Égypte, l'âge de la pierre et des métaux*, Paris, 1896 **CLXIV

Mortillet (G. de), *Formation de la nation française*, Paris, 1897 CLXV

Mortillet (G. et A. de), *Le Préhistorique*, Paris, 1900 **CLXVI

Morton (S. G.), *Crania œgyptiaca, etc.*, Philadeplhia and London, 1844 CLXVI *bis*

Muller (S.), *L'Europe préhistorique* (translated fr. the Danish by E. Philipot), Paris, 1907 *CLXVII

Munro, *Les stations lacustres d'Europe aux âges de la pierre et du bronze*, Paris, 1908 **CLXVIII

Munster, *La cosmographie universelle, etc.*, par Sébastien Monstere, édition de 1714 CLXIX

Naville (Édouard), *Discours au Congrès int. d'arch. et d'anthrop. préhist.*, Geneva, 1912 CLXX

Néophytos et Pallary, *La Phénicie préhistorique*. L'Anthr., Paris, 1914.—Néophytos, *La Préhistoire en Syrie, Palestine*. L'Anthropol., Paris, 1917 CLXXI

Néophytos, *Le district de Kerassunde au point de vue anthropologique et ethnographique*. L'Anthropologie, Paris, 1890.—*Le Grec du nord-est de l'Asie Mineure*. Ibid., Paris, 1891 CLXXII

Nicolas, *Inscription phénicienne gravée sur un calcaire schisteux*. Bull. Soc. d'Anthropol. Paris, 1898 CLXXIII

Nicolucci, *Sul l'Antropologia della Grecia*. Atti della R. Acad. delle scienze fisiche e matem, Naples, Vol. III, 1867 CLXXIV

Niederle, *Sur l'origine des peuples slaves*, Prage, 1896. Report by Volkow in the Bull. de la Soc. d'anthropol. Paris, 1897 CLXXV

„ *La race slave: statistique, démographie, anthropologie*, Paris, 1916 **CLXXVI

Nopcsa, *Beiträge zur Vorgeschichte und Ethnologie Nordalbaniens*. Wiss. Mitth. aus Bosnien u. Herzegowina, vol. XX CLXXVII

Nott (J. C.) and Gliddon (G. R.), *Types of Mankind; ethnological researches based upon . . . etc.*, Philadelphia, 1854 CLXXVIII

Obédénare, *Roumains*. Dictionnaire des sciences médicales. —*Présentation de quelques crânes roumains*. Bull. Soc. d'anthropol. Paris, 1874 CLXXIX

Obermaier (H.), *Der Mensch der Vorzeit*, 1912 *CLXXIX *bis*

Olechnowicz, *Les caractères anthropologiques de la petite noblesse de Grabowo (Pologne)*, 1895 CLXXX

Ollier de Marichard et Pruner bey, *Les Carthaginiens en France*. Bull. Soc. d'anthropol. Paris, 1870 CLXXXI

Oloriz, *Distribucion geografica del indice cefalico en España deducida del examen de 8268 varones ädultes*, Madrid, 1894 **CLXXXII

Ornstein, *Ueber Farbe der Augen, Haare und Haut der heutigen Bewohner Griechenlands*. Gessellsch. für Anthropologie, Berlin, 1879 CLXXXIII

Pallas, *Sammlungen historischer Nachrichten über die mongolischen Völkerschaften*, St. Petersburg, 1776-1801 CLXXXIV

Papillaut (G.), *Entente internationale pour l'unification des mesures craniométriques et céphalométriques*. Proceedings of the 13th session of the International Congress of Anthropology and Prehistoric Archæology, 1906, Monaco, 1907 CLXXXV

Paula e Oliveira (F. de), *Notes sur les ossements qui se trouvent dans le musée de la section géologique de Lisbonne*. Proceedings of the Congress of Archæology and Anthropology, Lisbon, 1880 CLXXXVI

Pereira da Costa, *Da existencia do homen em epochas remotas no valle do Tejo*, Primeiro opusculo : *Notícia sobre os squeletos humanos descobertos no Babeço da Arrudo* (with French trans.), Lisbon, 1865 CLXXXVII
R. de Saint-Périer, *Statuette de femme stéatopyge à Lespugue* (Haute-Garonne). L'Anthropologie, Paris, 1922 CLXXXVII
Pic Starozinosti, *Antiquité de la Bohême*, Part I : *La Bohême préhistorique ;* Part II : *Le peuple des tumuli de pierre*, Prage, 1900, 1 vol., résumé by Déchelette in l'Anthropologie, Paris, 1901 **CLXXXIX
Pictet, *Les origines indo-européennes, ou les Aryas primitifs*, 2e éd., Paris, 1878 CXC
Pichler, *Quellen und Forschungen zur alten Geschichte und Geographie*, herausgegeben von W. Sieglin, Leipzig, 1902. Heft 2, *Austria Romana*, I CXCI
Pittard (E.), *Un crâne présumé quaternaire trouvé en Espagne*. Revue de l'École d'Anth. de Paris CXCII
" *Crâne dolichocéphale trouvé dans le vieux Néolthique palafittique suisse*. Arch. sc. physiques et naturelles, Genève, 1922.—*Ethnologie des populations suisses*, L'Anthropologie, Paris, 1898. *Découverte de l'âge de la pierre en Albanie*. Arch. suisses d'anthrop. gén., Geneva, 1921 CXCIII
" *Ethnologie de la péninsule des Balkans* Mém. Soc. de géogr. Geneva, Le Globe, 1904 CXCIV
" *Les peuples des Balkans*, Geneva and Paris, 1920 **CXCV
" *Crania Helvetica :* I. *Les crânes valaisans de la vallée du Rhône*, Geneva and Paris, 1909-1910 **CXCVI
" *Influence de la taille sur l'indice céphalique dans un groupe ethnique relativement pur*. Bull. et Mém. Soc. d'anthropol. Paris, 1905 CXCVII
" *Ethnologie de la Savoie et de la Haute Savoie*. Bull. Soc. géog. Geneva, 1900, t. II CXCVIII
Pittard and Tchéraz, *Le développement de la mandibule et des dents en fonction de la capacité cranienne*. Ass. franç. pour l'avanc. des sc. 1906 CXCIX
Pittard and Karmin, *La taille humaine en Suisse :* I. *Le canton du Valais*. Journal de statistique suisse, 43e année, 1907 CC
Pouqueville, *Voyage dans la Grèce*, Paris, 1826 CCI
Prichard, *Natural History of Man*. London, 1843 CCII
" *Researches into the Physical History of Mankind*. London, 1837-1841 CCIII
Pruner Bey, Bull. Soc. d'anthropol. Paris, 1870 CCIV
Quatrefages and Hamy, *Crania ethnica :* Les crânes des races humaines, Paris, 1882 **CCV
" *Hommes fossiles et hommes sauvages*, Paris, 1884 **CCVI
" *Les Polynésiens et leurs migrations*, Paris, s.d. (1866 ?) **CCVII
" *L'espèce humaine*, Paris, 1878 **CCVIII
" *Introduction à l'étude des races humaines*, Paris, s.d. CCIX
Ranke (J.), *Die Schädel der Altbayerischen Landbevölkerung ;* Beiträge zur Anthr. u. Urgesch. Bayerns, vol. II, Munich, 1877 (1st divis., ch. I to IV) ; vol. III, 1880 (2nd div., ch. V) ; vol. IV, 1883 (ch. VI and VII) *CCX
" *Zur Statistik und Physiol. der Körpergrösse derbayerischen Militärspflichtigen in den 7 rechtsrheinischen Regierungsbez.* ; Beitr. z. Anthr. u. Urgesch. Bayerns, vol. IV, Munich, 1881, p. 1, 2 maps CCXI

Reclus (É.), *L'Asie russe*, Paris, 1882 CCXII

Reinach, *La station néolithique de Jablanica* (*Serbie*). L'Anthropologie, Paris, 1901 CCXIII

,, *L'origine des Aryens*, Paris, 1892 CCXIV

Retzius (G.), *Crania suecica antiqua, eine Darstellung der schwedischen Menschenschädel aus dem Steinzeitalter, dem Bronzezeitalter und dem Eisenzeitalter, etc.* Stockholm, 1900 **CCXV

Retzius (G.) and Fürst (C.), *Anthropologia suecica, Beiträge zur Anthropologie der Schweden*, Stockholm, 1902 **CCXVI

Reygasse (M.), *Observations sur les techniques paléolithiques du Nord Africain*, Constantine, 1920.—*Nouvelles études de palethnologie magrhébine*, Constantine, 1921.—*Etudes de palethnologie maghrébine* (*deuxième série*), Constantine, 1922 CCXVII

Rhode (J. C.), *Die heilige Sage des Zende Volkes*, Frankfurt am Main, 1820 CCXVIII

Rich (Claudius James), *Narrative of a Residence in Koordistan*, London, 1836 CCXIX

Ripley (N. Z.), *The Races of Europe*, London, 1900 **CCXX

Rivet (P.), *Recherches sur le prognathisme*, L'Anthropol. Paris, 1909 CCXXI

Rivet, *A propos de l'origine du mot Pérou.* L'Anthropologie, Paris, 1911 CCXXII

Rivet and Créqui-Montfort, *L'origine des Aborigènes du Pérou et de la Bolivie.* Acad. Inscript. et Belles-Lettres, 1914 CCXXIII

Romer, *Résultats généraux du mouvement archéologique en Hongrie*, Budapest, 1878 CCXXIV

Roo (P. de), *History of America before Columbus*, Philadelphia, 1900 CCXXV

Roth (W. E.), *Ethnol. Stud. of the N.W. Queensland Aborigines*, Brisbane and London, 1897 *CCXXVI

Sarasin (F.), *Étude anthropologique sur les Néo-Calédoniens et les Loyaltiens*, Archives suisses d'anthropol., 1916-1918 **CCXXVII

Sarasin (P. et F.), *Ergebnisse naturwissenschaftlicher Forschungen auf Ceylon, Die Steinzeit auf Ceylon*, Wiesbaden, 1908 *CCXXVIII

Sarauw (G. F. L.), *Ein Stenalders Boplads i Maglemose ved Mullerup Aarboger for Nordisk Oldkyndighed og Historye*, 1903, Prähistorische Zeitschrift 1911 to 1914 CCXXIX

Sasse, *Beitrag zur Kenntniss der Niederlandischen Schädel.* Archiv für Anthropol., 1873.—*Nederlandsch tijdschrift voor geneeskunde*, 1884 CCXXX

Saussaye (de la), *Numismatique de la Gaule narbonnaise*, Paris, 1842 CCXXXI

Saville, *The earliest notice concerning the conquest of Mexico by Cortes in 1519.* Indian notes and monographs, 1920 CCXXXII

Schenk, *Les sépultures et les populations préhistoriques de Chamblandes.* Bull. Soc. vaud. des sc. nat., 1902-1903 CCXXXIII

Schimmer, *Erhebungen über die Farbe der Augen, der Haare und der Haut bei den Schulkindern Oesterreichs.* Mitth. Anthr. Gesel., 1884 CCXXXIV

Schliz, *Die vorgeschichtlichen Schädeltypen der deutschen Länder in ihren Beziehungen zu den eizelnen Kulturkreisen der Urgeschichte.* Arch. f. Anthropol., Bd. IX, Braunschweig, 1910 CCXXXV

Schmidt (R. R.), *Die diluviale Vorzeit Deutschlands* (with the collaboration of E. Koken and A. Schliz), Stuttgart, 1912 **CCXXXVI
Schoentensack, *Der Unterkiefer des Homo Heidelbergensis, aus den Sanden von Mauer bei Heidelberg*. Leipzig, 1908 CCXXXVII
Schrader, *L'Asie*, Rev. École d'anthr. Paris, 1895 CCXXXVIII
Schuck, *Ueber die Istro-Rumänen*, Sonderabd. aus Band XLIII der Mitteil der Anthropolog. Gesellschaft, Vienna, 1913 CCXXXIX
Schwalbe (G.), *Ueber eine umfassende Untersuchung der physik. anthr. Beschaffenheit der jetzigen Bevölkerung des deutschen Reichs*. Correspondenz-Blatt d. Deutsch. anthropol. Gessellschaft, 1903, n° 9 CCXL
Schwerz, *Die paläolitischen Forschungen in Ungarn*. Arch. suisses d'anthropol. gén., Geneva, 1916-17 CCXLI
Siret, *Les Cassitérides et l'empire colonial des Phéniciens*. L'Anthropologie, Paris, 1909 CCXLII
,, *Les origines de la civilisation néolithique* (*Turdétans et Egéens*). XIIIe Congrès intern. d'arch. et d'anthr., Monaco, 1908, t. II CCXLIII
Smith (Dr Stewart A), *The Fossil Human Skull found at Talgai, Queensland*. Phil. Trans. (Ser. B.), 1918, vol. ccviii CCXLIV
Solak, *Persien, das Land une seine Bewohner*, Leipzig, 1845, quoted in the Nouveau Dictionnaire de géographie universelle CCXLV
Sollas (W. J.), *Paviland Cave*. Journ. of the Roy. Anthrop. Inst., 1913 CCXLVI
Spencer and Gillen, *The Northern Tribes of Central Australia*, London, 1904.—*Across Australia*, 2 vols., London, 1912 **CCXLVII
Spinden, *A Study of Maya Art*, Cambridge, 1913 (quoted by Vignaud, p. 44) CCXLVIII
Star (F.), *Lolo Objects in the Public Museum Milwaukee* Bull. of the Public Mus. of the City of Milwaukee, vol. I, 1911 CCXLIX
Stolyhwo, *Les fouilles préhistoriques dans la caverne Dziewicza à Lazy près Olkusz*. Warsaw Scientific Soc., Arch. Nank anthropologicznych, I, n° 4 CCL
Strabo, The Geography of Strabo, literally translated with notes, the first six books by H. C. Hamilton the remainder by W. Falconer, London. Bohn's Classical Library, 1848 CCLI

Tappeiner, *Die Abstammung der Tiroler und Raetier auf anthropologischer Grundlage*, Innsbruck, 1894 CCLII
Thierry, *Histoire des Gaulois*, Paris, 1898 CCLIII
Tocilesco, *Fouilles et recherches archéologiques en Roumanie*, Paris, 1899 CCLIV
Topinard (P.), *Éléments d'anthropologie générale*, Paris, 1885 CCLV
,, *Étude sur les races indigènes de l'Australie*. Bull. Soc. d'anthropol., Paris, 1872 CCLVI
Torii (R. and K.), *Archæological and Ethnological Studies on the Primitive Peoples of Eastern Mongolia*. Journ. of the College of Science, Imperial University of Tokyo, 1914 CCLVII
,, *The Formosan Aborigines*. Journ. of the College of Sc., Imperial University of Tokyo, 1910 CCLVIII
Trietsch (D.), *Die Juden in Palestina, etc.*, Zeitschrift für Demographie und Statistik der Juden, 1911 CCLIX

Ujfalvy, *Le Ferghana Kuldja, etc.* Iconographie et anthropologie irano-indeinne, Paris, 1879 CCLX

Vaillant, *Contribution à l'étude anthropologique des Chinois Hak-Ka de la province de Moncay (Tonkin).* L'Anthropologie, Paris, 1920 CCLXI

Vaux Phalipau (Mme de), *Les Wendes.* Revue anthropologique, Paris, 1920 et 1921 CXLXII

Velytchko, Carte ethnographique de la nation ruthéno-ukrainienne publiée par la Société de l'instruction "Provista" à Léopol, 1894. See C. R. par Volkow, Bull. Soc. d'anthropol. de Paris, 1897 CCLXIII

Vendryes (J.), *Le Langage, Introduction linguistique à l'Histoire,* Paris, 1921. (Eng. trans. *Language: A Linguistic Introduction to History,* in History of Civilization, London, 1925.) CCLXIV

Verneau, Revue anthropologique, 1886 CCLXV

„ *Les fouilles du Prince de Monaco aux Baoussé-Roussé. Un nouveau type humain.* L'Anthropologie, Paris, 1902.—*Les Grottes de Grimaldi,* t. I, fascicule I, Anthropologie, Monaco, 1906-1919 **CCLXVI

„ *Résultats anthropologiques de la Mission de M. de Gironcourt en Afrique occidentale.* L'Anthropol., Paris, 1917 CCLXVII

„ *Les crânes humains du gisement préhistorique de Pho-Bin-Gia (Tonkin).* L'Anthropologie, Paris, 1909 CCLXVIII

Vignaud (H.), *Le problème du peuplement initial de l'Amérique, etc.* Journal Soc. des Américanistes de Paris, 1922 CCLXIX

Vivien de Saint-Martin, *Nouveau dictionnaire de géographie universelle,* Paris, 1887 CCLXX

Volkow. Proceedings of the XVIth International Congress of Anthropology and Prehistoric Archæology. Geneva, 1912 CCLXXI

„ *Rapport sur les voyages en Galicie orientale, en Bukovine, etc.* Bull. et Mém. Soc. d'anthr. Paris, 1905 *CCLXXII

„ (with de Baye), *Le gisement paléolithique d'Aphontova-Goza.* L'Anthropologie, Paris, 1889 CCLXXIII

Vram, *Su alcuni carateri anthropologici dei Cicci.* Bollet. dell. Soc. adriatica di Sc. nat. in Trieste, vol. XXI, 1903 CCLXXIV

Wateff, *Contribution à l'étude anthropologique des Bulgares* (translated by Deniker). Bull. et Soc. d'anthropologie, Paris, 1904 **CCLXXV

Weisbach, *Die Schädelform der Rumänen,* Vienna, 1869 CCLXXVI

„ *Die Herzegowiner verglichen mit Tschechen und Deutschen aus Mähren, nach Major Himmel's Messungen.* Mitth. der Anthropolog. Gessellschaft, Vienna, 1889.—*Die Bosnier.* Mitth. der Anthropolog. Gessellschaft, Vienna, 1895 CCLXXVII

„ *Die Schädelform der Türken.* Mitth. der Anthropolog. Gesellsch., Vienna, 1873 CCLXXVIII

„ *Die Schädelform der Griechen.* Mitth. Anthropolog. Gessell., Vienna, t. XI, 1881 CCLXXIX

Weissenberg, *Zur Anthropologie der deutschen Juden.* Zeitschr. für Ethnol., Berlin, 1912 CCLXXX

„ *Die Spaniolen, eine anthropometrische Skizze.* Mitth. der Anthropol. Gesell., Vienna, 1909 CCLXXXI

Weissenberg, *Beiträge zur Anthropologie der Juden.* Zeitschr. für Ethnol., 1907 CCLXXXII
,, *Die zentralasiatischen Juden in anthropologischer Beziehung.* Zeitschr. für Demographie und Statistik der Juden, 1909 CCLXXXIII
,, *Zur Anthropologie der persischen Juden*, Zeitschr. für Ethnologie, Berlin, 1913 CCLXXXIV
,, *Die persischen Juden in anthropologischer Beziehung.* Zeitschr. für Demogr. und Statistik der Juden, 1911 CCLXXXV
,, *Die mesopotamischen Juden in anthropologischer Beziehung.* Arch. für Anthropol. Braunschweig, 1911 CCLXXXVI
,, *Die kaukasischen Juden*, Arch. für Anthrop. Braunschweig, 1909 CCLXXXVII
,, *Die yemenitischen Juden.* Zeitschr. für Ethnologie, LXI, 1909 CCLXXXVIII
,, *Die syrischen Juden, Anthropologische Betracht.* Zeitschr. für Ethnol., Berlin, 1911 CCLXXXIX
,, *Die Autochtonon Bevölkerung Palästinas in anthropologischer Beziehung* (Fellachen, Juden, Samaritaner). Zeitschr. für Demogr. und Statistik der Juden, 1909 CCX
Wellcome (H. S.), Prehistoric Discoveries in the Southern Soudan. Report of the XIVth Congress of Anthropology and Prehistoric Archæology, Geneva, 1912 CCXCI

Zaborowsky, *Le Caucase et les Caucasiens.* Revue anthropologique, Paris, 1914 CCXCII
,, *Crânes de Kourganes préhistoriques, scythiques drewlanes et polanes.* Bull. et Mém. Soc. d'anthropol., Paris, 1900 CCXCIII
,, *Les Hétéens, les Migrations de l'âge du bronze en Europe, le rite de l'incinération des cadavres.* Bull. et Mém. Soc. d'anthrop., Paris, 1920 CCXCIV
,, *Crânes anciens de la Russie méridionale et du Caucase.* Bull. et Mém. Soc. d'anthr., Paris, 1901 CCXCV
,, *Sur seize crânes d'un tombeau grec, etc.* Bull. de la Soc. d'anthropologie Paris, et nombreux autres mémoires CCXCVI
Zampa, *Anthropologie illyrienne.* Revue d'Anthropologie, Paris, 1886 CCXCVII
Zimmerle, *Die Deutsch-französische Sprachgrenze in der Schweiz*, Basel and Geneva, 1899 CCXCVIII
Zuckerkandl, *Craniologische Untersuchungen in Tirol und Innerösterreich.* Mitth. Anthr. Gesells., Vienna, 1884, t. XIV. CCXCIX
Zumoffen, *L'âge de la pierre en Phénicie.* L'Anthropologie, Paris, 1897.—*La Phénicie avant les Phéniciens*, Beyrout, 1900 CCC

INDEX